REDS

TED MORGAN

REDS

McCarthyism in
Twentieth-Century
America

RANDOM HOUSE

NEW YORK

Library of Congress Cataloging-in-Publication Data
Morgan, Ted.
Reds : McCarthyism in twentieth-century America / Ted Morgan.
p.   cm.
Includes index.
ISBN 0-679-44399-1
1. Anti-communist movements—United States—History—20th century.
2. Internal security—United States—History—20th century.   3. McCarthy, Joseph,
1908–1957—Influence.   4. United States—Politics and government—20th century.
5. United States—Foreign relations—20th century.   6. United States—
Foreign relations—Soviet Union.   7. Soviet Union—Foreign relations—United States.
8. Communism—United States—History—20th century.   I. Title.
E743.5.M578   2003   320.973'09'045—dc21   2003046509

Printed in the United States of America on acid-free paper
Random House website address: www.randomhouse.com
2 4 6 8 9 7 5 3 1
First Edition

Book design by J. K. Lambert

This book is for

EILEEN

ACKNOWLEDGMENTS

Special thanks to my editor, Joy de Menil, who has an uncanny ability to detect flaws in a text and elicit improvements; to Ileene Smith, who finished the job; and to Robin Rolewicz, who was always helpful.

To my wife, Eileen, for her superb and indispensable editorial work over a period of six months.

To my daughter, Amber, for her editorial help.

To Herbert Romerstein, known as "the eminence," for his unsurpassed knowledge of Soviet espionage and subversion, and for letting me use his collection of transcripts of congressional committee hearings.

To Robert Louis Benson of the National Security Agency, for supplying full transcripts of the Venona decrypts.

To Morris Weisz, for the material on Val Lorwin.

To M. Stanton Evans, for alerting me to the Stefan hearings and the Thayer loyalty report.

To David S. Foglesong for his landmark book, *America's Secret War Against Bolshevism*.

Special thanks also to the following librarians and archives:

Philip M. Runkel of the Marquette University Special Collections, for showing me the personal papers of Joseph McCarthy.

Thomas Branigar, archivist at the Dwight D. Eisenhower Library, for his help and guidance.

Rodney Ross, at the Center for Legislative Archives, National Archives, for his help and guidance.

The people at the Harry S. Truman Library in Independence, Missouri.

The people at the State Historical Society in Madison, Wisconsin.

CONTENTS

PREAMBLE

The premise of this book is that the Cold War began in 1917, with the Bolshevik Revolution. American attempts to subvert the revolution under President Woodrow Wilson followed almost at once, resulting in the landing of U.S. Army troops on Russian soil and pitched battles with Bolshevik soldiers. With the formation of two American Communist parties in 1919, the Soviets obtained a logistical base for their own subversion on American soil. Espionage activities started in 1924 under the cover of the trade association Amtorg and increased with the U.S. recognition of the Soviet Union in 1933. The World War II period, when Russia was our ally, saw the recruitment of government servants who were ideological sympathizers.

In this context, McCarthyism existed long before Senator Joseph McCarthy, in its dictionary definition: 1. The political practice of publicizing accusations of disloyalty or subversion with insufficient regard to evidence. 2. The use of dubious methods of investigation in order to suppress opposition.

McCarthy did not emerge in a vacuum, but as the most prominent in a long line of men who exploited the Communist issue for political advantage, recklessly smearing their opponents with false accusations. These McCarthyites used forged documents to make their case, or conducted raids of questionable legality to enhance their political reputations, or suborned perjury in the testimony of professional informants, or used the Communist issue to smear the New Deal.

The other side of the equation was that the American Communist Party served as a recruitment pool for Soviet agents. American Communists by the dozens penetrated the government, some at high levels, and stole scientific and political secrets, including information on the atomic bomb. This was confirmed by the release in 1995 of the Venona transcripts, the decoded cable traffic between the Moscow KGB and its American stations. But McCarthy and his predecessors knew nothing of Venona, and flayed about like blindfolded men in a room full of bats. The bats were there, but beyond their reach.

Now that we know the extent of Soviet espionage, it is possible to assess the impact of McCarthyism. The danger was real, but by the time McCarthy came on the scene it was all but spent, and the Communist Party was moribund, so that he was in fact whipping a dead horse. The apoplectic reaction he provoked in the nation was off in its timing. The threat was much reduced by the time he denounced it, but there had been one in the thirties and forties. McCarthy exploited something akin to the Cheshire cat's smile, which lingers after the cat is gone. Did he have a cleansing effect, or was he merely a demagogue playing on nativist fears? Was he the leader of what Dean Acheson called "the attack of the primitives," a populist revolt against the elite? Did he appeal to "status frustration"? Was he the champion of the dispossessed, or of Texas oil millionaires whose anti-Communism was a cover for their lobbying efforts against the regulation of wildcatters? Did he appeal to Southern racists who equated Communism with integration, or to Western conservatives who wanted a "get tough" foreign policy? Was he the stalking-horse for a party kept out of power since 1932? The Republicans got behind him because his success in dramatizing the Communist issue was also a way of discrediting the New Deal and the Truman administration.

McCarthy capitalized on the fears in American society—fear that the Russians had stolen the atomic bomb, fear of spies in government, fear due to the loss of China, and fear of the Korean War. His party was the party of fear. He mobilized the masses of the alarmed.

The brief McCarthy era, which lasted from his Wheeling speech in 1950 to his censure in 1954, had less to do with the object of his attack than with the paradoxical culture of fear that seized a nation at the height of its power. The recurring McCarthyite figure was a by-product of American anti-Communism, which became a fixed principle after the 1917 revolution. Over the years it kept reappearing through its various incarnations. It has recently reappeared in the methods Attorney General John Ashcroft has applied to counter terrorism, which are similar to those used by the government in its anti-Communist operations: deportation, detention without due process, the targeting of ethnic groups, and alarmist announcements about perils, real or imagined.

REDS

THE RUSSIAN
REVOLUTION THROUGH
AMERICAN EYES

On July 30, 1914, posters went up in Russian cities ordering reservists from the ages of nineteen to forty-three to report to their barracks. Czar Nicholas II had promised his French allies that he would attack Germany with 800,000 men if war broke out, drawing enemy divisions to an eastern front. The Czar presided over a population of 180 million that was 80 percent illiterate, in a nation four times the size of the United States, stretching five thousand miles from Europe and the Baltic Sea to Asia and the Pacific. He ran his domain like a private and gated estate.

To farms where no word came more distant than that of the nearest market town, the mail brought a summons for the peasant to appear "with his riding horse." The defense of the fatherland had a resonance that was instinctively obeyed, and hastily formed divisions trooped to the front from the eastern isolation of Siberia, from the banks of the Volga, from the steppes of Turkestan, the men wearing steel helmets and shouldering rifles with long bayonets. Russian commanders designated their units as so many bayonets.[1]

By October, more than four million men were under arms, but it was the nineteenth century fighting the twentieth, Cossack horses and outdated maps against mechanized armies with telegraph and telephone, rifles against machine guns—and when the ammunition ran out, bayonets against machine guns, the officers leading the charge with drawn swords, as they had against Napoleon in 1812.[2]

And yet, only Russia among the Allies fought the Central Powers on their own soil, invading East Prussia in August, and suffering severe losses. With a seemingly inexhaustible supply of reserves, the Russians were willing to mount offensives on demand, tying up German and Austrian troops and taking 2,700,000 prisoners. Marshal Ferdinand Foch later said: "If France was not wiped off the map of Europe, we owe it first to Russia."[3]

By March 1915, 200,000 new recruits a month were being mobilized, while fifty thousand rifles came off the production lines. The stories of unarmed Russian infantrymen waiting for the weapon of a fallen comrade were not German propaganda, but the demoralizing truth.

On September 1, 1915, after the Russians had retreated from Poland, the Czar himself took command, determined as a matter of personal pride not to lose face before the Allies. With 11 million men in the ranks, and four million more to be called up in 1916 and 1917, Russia could fight on. But Russia was bleeding, not only on the battlefield but on the home front. Those millions of men had to be fed, as did tens of thousands of horses using up tons of fodder. Priority for the army meant severe shortages of food and fuel on the home front.[4]

———

Every war has its profiteers, who nibble rodentlike around the edges of events and don't much care what side they are on so long as they get paid. Such a man was Alexander Helphand, a Russian-born adventurer who began his career as a Socialist journalist in Germany at the turn of the century, writing under the pen name "Parvus."

In 1900, Helphand was operating an illegal press in a suburb of Munich, one of the European centers for Russian revolutionaries in exile. A leading firebrand, the thirty-year-old lawyer Vladimir Ilich Ulyanov, had recently finished a three-year term of exile in Siberia, and had taken to calling himself Ilyin or Lenin. Helphand agreed to print Lenin's newspaper, Iskra (The Spark), which was distributed illegally in Russia.

Caught up in Lenin's cause, Helphand took part in the failed revolution of 1905, and was arrested and sent to Siberia. In exile, his revolutionary fervor dimmed. Escaping to Turkey, he went into the import-export business and made a fortune. His only interest now was self-interest, but he maintained his radical contacts in the hope that a new regime in Russia would bring him some advantage.[5]

On January 9, 1915, the German ambassador to Constantinople, H. Wangenheim, reported to Berlin that he had been approached by a Dr. Alexander Helphand, who was "definitely pro-German" and who advocated "the total destruction of czarism and the division of Russia into smaller states." Germany would be successful, said Helphand, if it "kindled a major revolution in

Russia. . . . The interests of the German government were therefore identical with those of the Russian revolutionaries." Helphand offered to organize the rising but would need considerable sums of money and wanted to present his plan to Berlin.[6]

The Germans were willing to consider any plan to destabilize Russia and take her out of the war. Helphand was summoned to Berlin on March 6. He saw Kurt Reizler, an aide of Chancellor Theobald Bethmann-Hollweg, to whom he gave an eighteen-page memorandum entitled "Preparations for Mass Political Strikes in Russia." Helphand proposed that the Germans subsidize a splinter group of the Social Democratic Worker's Party, who called themselves "The Majority" (*Bolsheviks*), and whose leader, Lenin, lived in Switzerland in exile. His plan was quickly approved: the next day Arthur Zimmerman, an undersecretary in the Foreign Ministry, asked the Treasury for 2 million marks to fund Russian revolutionary propaganda, half of which was turned over to Helphand.[7]

In May 1915, Helphand went to Bern to discuss with Lenin the prospects for a revolution in Russia. Lenin was at first receptive to the plan, for his own slogan at the time was "transform the imperialist war into a civil war." He blamed the war on giant banks and "surplus capitalism"; it was but a convulsion of the corrupt bourgeois state. When he saw his old friend, Lenin was dismayed by his appearance, for with his bloated face and heavy paunch over stumpy legs, Helphand seemed the very caricature of an imperialist banker. Lenin learned from those in Helphand's entourage that the man he had known as a revolutionary was now a shameless displayer of wealth, staying at the best hotel, drinking champagne for breakfast, and surrounded by a retinue of pretty young women. It seemed more than likely that he was getting his money from the Germans. Any connection with the Germans would be fatal for Lenin, who would be accused of being in their employ.[8]

Lenin decided to keep his distance from Helphand, who with his secret funds had launched a paper in Berlin called *Die Glocke* (The Bell), which followed the Foreign Ministry line. He wrote that *Die Glocke* was "an organ of renegades and dirty lackeys surrounding the cesspool of German chauvinism."[9]

In any event, Helphand's account of his meeting with Lenin must have sounded encouraging, for on July 6 the German Foreign Secretary, Gottlieb von Jagow, asked the Treasury for 5 million marks to promote propaganda in Russia. In August, Helphand moved to Copenhagen, where a branch of his firm was located and where he had his most devoted admirer, the German envoy, Count Ulrich Brockdorff-Rantzau. It was said that Helphand practically dictated the envoy's cables to Berlin. On August 14, 1915, Brockdorff-

Rantzau gave him a ringing endorsement, reporting that Helphand was "an extraordinarily important man whose unusual powers I feel we must employ for the duration of the war."[10]

Helphand was by no means the only German spy on the Bolshevik beat. The Germans were particularly active in neutral countries like Sweden and Switzerland. In Stockholm, their chief agent was an Estonian nationalist, Alexander Keskula, who hoped that with the breakup of the Russian empire his small Baltic country would gain its independence.

Among Keskula's multiple operations was an office at the Stockholm railroad station where he explained to Russians coming home from the United States and Canada how they could avoid mobilization in the Czar's army. He also recruited Russian revolutionaries living in Sweden to write defeatist pamphlets that were smuggled into Russia after being printed on his press. One of his efforts was a picture book describing the excellent treatment afforded by the Germans to Russian prisoners of war. It was intended for distribution in the Russian trenches and included photographs of grinning Cossacks eating sauerkraut and bratwurst.

Keskula was on friendly terms with Lenin, and sent him copies of the pamphlets he was preparing for Russian barracks, calling for mutinies. Lenin in turn sent Keskula the situation reports he was getting from his people in Russia, which Keskula passed on to his control on the German General Staff in Berlin, an intelligence officer named Steinwachs. All this activity took money, and Steinwachs paid Keskula 20,000 marks a month.[11]

On September 30, 1915, Keskula went to Bern to see Lenin, who listed the conditions under which he would be prepared to make a separate peace with Germany if his revolution succeeded. This fanciful manifesto included Russian troops liberating India from English imperialism, though he also announced his intention to confiscate large landholdings. Lenin's willingness to sign a separate peace was uppermost in the mind of the German envoy in Bern, Baron Gisbert von Romberg, when he sent a long and astonishing dispatch to Berlin, stating that "in Keskula's opinion, it is therefore essential that we should spring to the help of the revolutionaries of Lenin's movement at once. . . . He will report on this matter in person in Berlin. According to his informants, the present moment should be favorable for overthrowing [Russia's] government." Thus from two sources, Helphand and Keskula, Berlin was getting the same advice: back the Bolsheviks.

On December 26, 1915, the German Foreign Ministry authorized 1 million rubles for Helphand, to be paid by the legation cashier in Copenhagen. On January 23, Helphand reported that the rubles had been smuggled into Petrograd (St. Petersburg). The money would be used to launch a series of strikes, but he now preferred to delay the uprising, for there was talk of deposing the Czar. At this point, because of the delay, Foreign Secretary von Jagow lost patience with Helphand and concluded he was a fake, possibly pocketing Treasury funds; Helphand found himself out in the cold. An accidental alliance of opportunists, Baltic nationalists, and Leninists had coalesced around the idea of a Russian revolution. The German Treasury was funding them, so far with little to show for it, and Lenin was stranded in Switzerland, with no hope of return to Russia.[12]

———

In the fall of 1916, von Jagow resigned as Foreign Secretary in protest against the resumption of the unrestricted submarine warfare that would bring the United States into the war the following April. His successor was Arthur Zimmerman, a man given to bold policy initiatives. He was the author of the telegram that bears his name, inviting Mexico to enter into an alliance with Germany against the United States in exchange for which she would regain "her lost territory in Texas, New Mexico, and Arizona." Intercepted and decoded by the British, the Zimmerman telegram was published in March 1917 by President Woodrow Wilson and helped prepare American opinion for U.S. entry into the war. Zimmerman was also strongly in favor of the Bolshevik strategy to shut down the Eastern Front, which to some in the Foreign Ministry seemed as farfetched as the offer to Mexico.[13]

In the end, events in Russia had a momentum of their own. Rasputin, the Czarina's sinister adviser, who was suspected of plotting to make peace with Germany, was murdered in December 1916. Food shortages a month later in Petrograd brought thousands to the streets, demanding bread and breaking shop windows, in what became known as the February Revolution.

William Chapin Huntington, the commercial attaché at the American embassy, witnessed the riots without surprise. The food situation was so acute, he reported, that people were living on herring and apples and *vobla*, fish dried in the sun that stank to high heaven. *Vobla* used to be a swear word, but now it was lunch. One of the translators at the embassy had seen a woman sitting on the pavement quietly lie down and die, without a groan. The Cossacks were ordered out against the rioters. Formerly they would have drawn their weapons and fired but now they rode up and down the sidewalks in silence.[14]

Huntington was able to observe the decisive moment when the czarist regime fell. As the troops faced the crowd, there was a flicker of hesitation when a soldier had to decide whether to fire on his countrymen—and in that fraction of a second, the men in the barracks sided with the rioters and turned against their own ruler.

Out of the Petrograd riots came the Czar's abdication and the formation of a provisional government. Nicholas II was urged to withdraw so that he would not be an impediment to the pursuit of the war. A delegation of members of the Duma, the Russian parliament, went to see him in the city of Pskov, 150 miles south of Petrograd, on March 15, 1917. "My abdication is necessary," the Czar wrote in his diary in the early hours of the next morning, "for the sake of . . . maintaining calm in the army at the front. . . . All around is betrayal, cowardice and deceit." And though he could not know it then, fifteen months away, death in a cellar by firing squad, at age fifty, with his wife and children.[15]

In the chaotic days after the Czar's abdication, when the Provisional Government was formed, its outstanding figure was Alexander Kerensky, who was named Minister of War and Justice, and in July, Prime Minister. As a young Socialist lawyer, Kerensky had been the fiery defender of revolutionaries, but once elected to the Duma in 1912 he calmed down. He backed the policy of joining the Allies, but became disgusted with the regime's conduct of the war and urged its dissolution. In a time of extremes, Kerensky was caught in the classic dilemma of the moderate leader, the conductor whose only purpose is to keep the train on the tracks.[16]

He had to contend not only with factions inside the government, but with a countergovernment in the rise of the soviets, which started out as a kind of Russian town hall, an outlet of the disenfranchised for all the piled-up grievances of generations. The Petrograd Soviet of Workers and Soldiers elected one deputy per thousand workers and per military company, who supposedly expressed the popular will, with infusions of agitprop from the Bolshevik minority, which eventually took it over. The soviets thus became the vehicle through which the Bolsheviks overthrew the Provisional Government, which one historian described as "responsibility without power confronting power without responsibility."[17]

The Petrograd Soviet set up its own Military Section, which infiltrated the Petrograd garrison of 150,000 and drew up the infamous Order No. 1, broadcast to the troops at the front and designed to destabilize the army. The order abolished the death penalty for desertion, demoted all officers to the rank of soldiers, and called for the election of soldiers to committees, which then proceeded to elect their officers. Committee meetings took the place of military discipline.

Kerensky did what he could, purging the high command and bringing in the excellent general A. A. Brusilov, who had won some important battles in 1916, as commander in chief. He sent commissars to the front to whip up offensive spirit in units where Bolshevik agitators preached defeatism. Officers who refused to take up advance positions were court-martialed. The goal of the Provisional Government was clearly expressed—to keep fighting the Germans.[18]

———

David R. Francis, the American ambassador, was not a career diplomat but a Democratic wheelhorse who had served as mayor of St. Louis, governor of Missouri, and Secretary of the Interior under Grover Cleveland in the 1890s. At the age of sixty-five, he was white-thatched but still vigorous, a big man, thick in the chest, with the stern demeanor and upright carriage of a Western sheriff. One expected to see spurs at the cuffs of his striped pants. When he arrived in Russia in March 1916, Francis left behind his wife but brought with him some of the comforts of home—a black valet, a portable cuspidor (he astonished the Italian ambassador by hitting it from a distance of four feet), and a supply of chewing gum, which he masticated happily at diplomatic receptions. He was a man of strong opinion, though he knew precious little of Russia's history, culture, or language.[19]

Francis was overjoyed when Nicholas abdicated. He was tired of czarist rule and thought the Russian people were too. Suspicions abounded as to the loyalty of the German-born Czarina, and he was convinced that German spies lurked in every department of the Czar's government. From the window of his embassy office at 34 Pourstadtskaia Street, the ambassador had an excellent view of the February events. He saw a barricade go up at the corner of Serguisky and Litainy streets. He heard desultory firing. He was told that a regiment whose barracks were two blocks away had mutinied and killed their colonel.[20]

When the Provisional Government was formed, Francis presented his credentials to its Foreign Minister, Pavel Miliukov, who told him: "This government has come to stay." Francis sent a two-hundred-word cable to Washington recommending recognition and went up to the Mariinsky Palace for the swearing-in ceremony. "I have not lost faith," he wrote to his son, "in Russia coming out of this ordeal as a republic and with a government which will be founded on correct principles."[21]

Woodrow Wilson, reelected in 1916 on the promise of keeping America out of the war, was in the spring of 1917 inching toward the fray. But declaring war had to be presented in Wilsonian terms, as a crusade between democracy and an evil military empire. In this context, the despotic Czar's overthrow was providential, for Russia could now be shown in a democratic skin, ready to join an alliance of free nations. On March 22, Wilson announced that the American government would be the first to recognize the novice regime. He hailed the February Revolution as a major step toward building a desirable postwar world order. There was a hearty round of applause in the American press for what was too quickly seen as the advent of Russian democracy. Now, it was said, the Russian people would be fighting for themselves instead of for a corrupt and possibly pro-German monarchy.[22]

On April 2, in his message to Congress asking for a declaration of war against Germany, the President said that the United States now had in Russia "a fit partner for a league of honor." Carried away by his own rhetoric, he opined that Russia was "always in fact democratic at heart, in all the vital habits of her thought, in all the intimate relationships of her people that spoke their natural instinct, their habitual attitude towards life."[23] In fact, for the great mass of the Russian people, the habitual attitude toward life was despair, but Wilson's optimistic assessment helped to justify the need to go to war. "It is a fearful thing to lead this great peaceful people into war," Wilson concluded. On April 6, Congress complied, and America was at war.

———

By the time Lenin heard the news of the Czar's abdication, he had moved from Bern to Zurich, which had better libraries. In his ratty rooms at Spiegelgasse 14, which he shared with his dough-faced wife, Krupskaya, he tried to take it all in. One thing was clear: military failures had shaken czarism and created the conditions for a revolution. He had to get back to Russia at once. But how? By plane? Via Sweden? With a wig over his bald head? He would get no help from the French and the British. Germany was the only possible route. He would have to act with great care, so as not to be seen as an instrument of German scheming.

In Bern, the German envoy von Romberg reported on March 23, 1917, that "leading Russian revolutionaries" wished to return to Russia via Germany. From Copenhagen on April 12, Brockdorff-Rantzau appealed for the reinstatement of his friend Helphand. He knew only too well, he said, that Foreign Secretary von Jagow had been "especially fond of whetting his sharp tongue on him," but Helphand "now finds himself to be a German, not a Russian. . . . Give him a hearing . . . he could be extremely useful." Helphand was predicting that if Germany backed the extremist element, the Russian army would disintegrate in three months. After seeing Helphand in Berlin, Foreign Secretary Zimmerman advised the General Staff that "since it is in our interest that the radical wing of the Russian revolutionaries should prevail, it seems advisable to allow transit."[24]

The German plan was to help the Bolshevik leaders in Switzerland to get home and to secretly assist them in gaining the upper hand. They would wait for the military situation to deteriorate and would then try to negotiate a separate peace. On April 1, 1917, the Foreign Ministry asked for 5 million marks for secret work in Russia. Once the Bolsheviks returned to Petrograd, part of this money would be passed on to them via Helphand in Stockholm.

Von Romberg reported on April 4 that Lenin and the others wanted permission to travel by sealed train through Germany at once. As bait, they promised that once back in Russia they would secure the release of some German prisoners of war.[25]

Final approval from Berlin came on April 5, 1917. Two second-class carriages waited on the German side of the Swiss border, at Gottmadingen, thirty miles north of Zurich. On Monday, April 9, a group of thirty-three Bolsheviks assembled for the trip home, among them Lenin and his wife and daughter, and his Paris-born mistress, Inessa Armand; his sidekick Gregory Zinoviev with his wife and son; and Karl Radek, the Polish-born wanderer, who had attached himself to Lenin and made himself useful. Their carriages were connected to a larger Berlin-bound train. As they crossed Germany on April 12, Kaiser Wilhelm mockingly proposed that they be given his traditional Easter message to read. They proceeded from Berlin to Sassnitz, a German port on the Baltic, then by ferry to the southern tip of Sweden and up to Stockholm on April 13, where Helphand, who was waiting at the station, tried to see Lenin but was rebuffed. He did, however, later see Radek, who stayed in Stockholm to run the Bolshevik office there. The others went on to Finland and took the train to Petrograd, where they arrived on April 16.[26]

"Lenin received a splendid welcome from his followers," von Romberg reported to Chancellor Bethmann-Hollweg on April 30: "Three quarters of Petrograd workers are behind him. . . . It is not clear which course the revolution will take."

On June 3, Foreign Secretary Zimmerman noted the "growing disorganization and unwillingness to fight of the Russian army. Lenin's propaganda is growing stronger and his paper *Pravda* is printing 300,000 copies. Work in the armament factories is at a standstill. The transport crisis is acute." The German plan, astonishingly, seemed to be working.[27]

———

In Petrograd that July, Kerensky faced a Bolshevik coup. Trucks packed with mutinous soldiers and sailors suddenly appeared in the streets. A red flag flew from one of the trucks bearing the words: "The first bullet is for Kerensky." This time, enough loyal troops were found to put down the mutiny. Trotsky was arrested and Lenin fled to Finland.

William Chapin Huntington, the American commercial attaché, called it "a spurt of anarchy." He saw men driving around in trucks firing machine guns while others were shooting out the windows from the top floors of buildings. The only result so far as he could see was sixteen dead horses. He counted them himself on the Litainy Prospect.[28]

Meanwhile, conditions continued to deteriorate on the Eastern Front. Albert Rhys Williams, a Protestant minister and newspaper correspondent who was covering the war, succumbed to the syndrome of sympathizing with the side he was writing about. Won over by the suffering of the Russian people, he came to believe that only the Bolsheviks could lift them out of their misery and became their ardent apologist. At the front in a village in the Ukraine that July, about three hundred women and forty old men and boys crowded around Rhys Williams. He asked them how many had lost someone in the war and nearly every hand went up. An eerie collective moan spread among them, like a winter wind blowing through the trees; Rhys shivered from the sheer intensity of the suffering they communicated.[29]

Bolshevik propaganda was destroying the Russian army. Robert F. Leonard, one of the hundreds of Americans in Russia at the time, was at the front in August 1917, not far from Kiev, as part of a YMCA team, and saw the soldiers selling machine guns to the Germans for 5 rubles, and a six-inch gun for a bottle of brandy. Then they would start for home. Most of the weapons were American-made.[30]

By now, seven thousand copies of *Pravda* were arriving daily at the front, encouraging the men to vote instead of fight, and to dismiss their officers, who were beaten and horse-whipped. Utterly shamed, several officers committed suicide. At the end of July 1917, General Anton Denikin, who commanded the summer offensive, stated: "We no longer have an army."[31]

In August, Riga fell, under clouds of yellow cross gas, which ate into the clothes and body, rendering gas masks useless. The Germans now had an open road to Moscow, three hundred miles away. Kerensky replaced Brusilov with the disciplinarian general Lavr Kornilov, whom a month later he would imprison after an aborted coup attempt.[32]

———

In June 1917 there arrived in Washington an ambassador from the Russian Provisional Government. For thirty-seven-year-old Boris Bakhmeteff, a one-time physics professor at the Polytechnic Institute in Petrograd, this was the second tour of duty in the United States. He had come in 1915 as head of a purchasing commission, to buy weapons for the Czar's armies, and felt drawn to Wilsonian principles. As a member of the liberal Kadet (Constitutional Democratic) Party, he was named deputy minister of commerce and industry after the Czar's abdication. His sympathetic grasp of American political life made him a fitting choice for ambassador. He had a knack for saying what Americans liked to hear. His method could have been borrowed from the professional optimist Emile Coué, who wanted everyone to say, upon rising in the morning: "Every day, in every way, I am getting better and better."

Boris Bakhmeteff seemed to embody the democratic, pro-Ally resolve that President Wilson was looking for in the Russians. At a White House dinner on June 21 he eagerly expounded on the great Russian offensive. In his meetings at the State Department, he played down the demands for peace in the streets of Petrograd. He told the *New York Times* that all of Russia had agreed to fight the war.

When Bakhmeteff presented his credentials on July 5, he and Wilson got along like kindred spirits. In August in Boston, he told a receptive crowd that "Russia, the great democracy of the East, will stand hand in hand with you, her eldest sister, this great democracy of the West." Even after the summer offensive turned into a rout, he told the *New York Times* on September 4 that "only one or two per cent of the army" was unreliable and asserted that "the Russian army is not crushed and is not going to be crushed."

Bakhmeteff was such a salesman, it was said that he could have sold feathers to the Indians. Even Robert Lansing, the Secretary of State, who had little faith in Kerensky, liked him. Lansing was a deeply religious Presbyterian Elder and a "Bourbon Democrat," who believed in government by incorruptible elites. His distaste for big government and robber barons was exceeded only by that for the "virus" of Socialism.

Colonel Edward M. House, who had won the President's trust and affection, was his closest adviser and back-channel agent in foreign policy. More of a pragmatist and less of a moralist than either Wilson or Lansing, House saw the Czar's overthrow as beneficial, if only his successors could act more like American liberals. "Bakhmeteff and I speak the same language," House wrote in his diary that August. Wilson was so taken with the Russian envoy that he granted him a $100 million credit to cover the costs of the military contracts he was taking out. In October, the Treasury Department gave him another $50 million.[33]

Bakhmeteff was sketching a distorted picture of events in Russia. Wilson's dilemma was that he was not receiving an accurate and detailed counterversion from his ambassador, who was under a cloud—a cloud no bigger than a lady's hand. On the boat over from New York in 1916, Francis had made the acquaintance of the captivating, cosmopolitan Matilda de Cram, who could charm men in four languages. She was married to a Russian with whom she had emigrated to the United States when the war broke out because he was too closely involved with the Germans in business deals. Having left two sons behind, she went back to visit them (though certain reports said she had taken the same boat as Francis purposely in order to meet him).[34]

In Petrograd, the fortyish but still enticing Matilda was a frequent guest at the American embassy, supposedly to give the ambassador French lessons. Sometimes she spent the night. Embassy personnel were concerned, for the ambassador's living quarters adjoined the file and code room. In the diplomatic community, tongues wagged about the elderly ambassador with the roving eye who had left his wife in Missouri.

Intelligence officers at Allied embassies warned General William V. Judson, the American military attaché, that Russian counterintelligence listed Madame de Cram as a German agent, but to no avail. They stopped sharing with Judson sensitive information that might be revealed to Madame de Cram as pillow talk.[35]

Judson was a brigadier general who combined the jobs of military attaché and chief of the U.S. military mission. Pugnacious and opinionated, he was also an astute analyst and a beaver for facts, who viewed Ambassador Francis with disdain as an "indoor man," while he was the "outdoor man," on his rounds gathering information. Nor did he have much regard for the Russians, whom he described in a letter to the War College as "mostly ignorant as plantation negroes." His greatest fear was that Russia would stop fighting and "become practically a German colony . . . to render vitally needed assistance to the Central Powers, which will more than likely enable them to win the war."

After his recall to Washington, Judson wrote an eight-page report to the Secretary of War, Newton D. Baker, in which he mentioned the ambassador's private life: "I personally appealed to the ambassador to see Madame de C. no more and I showed him the dossier relative to her which Captain [E. Francis] Riggs [assistant military attaché] borrowed from the Interallied Passport Bureau. Thus I was the only one who personally approached the ambassador on the subject of Madame de C." But Francis held Judson's advice against him.[36]

Since Francis was out of his depth and romantically entangled with a possible German spy, President Wilson and the State Department were to some extent cut off from the undercurrents and intricacies of the swiftly evolving Russian drama. In an attempt to remedy the situation, a number of special envoys were dispatched to Russia in 1917.

—

When President Wilson performed his about-face from neutrality to war in April 1917, he felt the need to whip up anti-German ardor in pacifist-minded pockets of the country and in ethnic enclaves where the melting pot had failed to melt. Wilson created the Committee on Public Information, the propaganda arm of the war effort, and the granddaddy of all the Voices of America and information agencies yet to come. It was a peculiarly American attempt to sway people abroad through direct appeal, rather than through government-to-government diplomatic channels.

To run what was essentially a gargantuan advertising agency, Wilson picked his old friend George Creel, the hard-driving, Missouri-born newspaper editor who had won his spurs as editor of Colorado's *Rocky Mountain News*. Creel's volatile mind threw out ideas the way a parade scatters confetti, with the aim of channeling the nation's energies into constructive patriotism. His committee churned out features and films, pamphlets and cartoons. He papered the country with fifty thousand billboards, such as "Halt the Hun" and "Loose Lips Sink Ships." He sent out eighteen thousand "Four-Minute Men" to give short speeches from coast to coast. No proposal was ignored, though Creel balked when he was urged to bring to the United States for display some of the Belgian children whose hands had been chopped off by the Germans.[37]

Creel launched an international department to counter German lies and sent emissaries to the major European capitals. In June he dispatched a journalist of good reputation, Arthur Bullard, to Russia, to promote a gung ho, stay-in-the-war publicity campaign.

Bullard was not only Creel's envoy, but the unofficial emissary of his friend Colonel House. The Bullard mission was one of several that left for Russia in the summer of 1917. What they had in common was a muted intelligence function. When a Red Cross mission left in June, its key figure, Raymond Robins, was destined to play a pivotal role in the first months of the Bolshevik Revolution.[38]

———

Robins was born in 1873 into a deeply dysfunctional family. His mother, Hannah, was diagnosed as a schizophrenic and institutionalized when he was twelve; his father, Charles, was a business failure, always trying to recoup his losses; his brother, Saxton, committed suicide. But Raymond was a survivor, strong-willed and hardworking, whose inordinate drive to succeed was tempered by do-gooder instincts. At the age of seventeen he worked in a Tennessee coal mine, earning credentials as a friend of labor. In his twenties, he caught the gold fever and headed for the Klondike. Instead of gold, he found religion, and went to Nome, Alaska, in 1899 to run a church called the Hospice of Saint Bernard. Nome was a lawless, anything-goes, shoreline tent city in its wastrel boom period. Minister Robins preached the gospel, tended the sick, and buried the dead. He fought typhoid and corruption and made his mark as a muscular reformer who carried a six-gun.[39]

In 1900 Robins left Alaska for Chicago, where he plunged into settlement work, parks and playgrounds, housing and soup kitchens: all the areas of social improvement then handled by private agencies. Robins became an important figure in the municipal landscape, went on speaking tours, joined a dozen organizations, and liked to call himself a "Fighter, Slum Dweller, and Preacher of a new social gospel." These periods of whirling activity alternated with bouts of depression that required hospitalization. In 1905 he married Margaret Dreier, a beautiful German-American suffragette and social activist of the Major Barbara type. Margaret was five years older than Raymond and about a million dollars richer. To deflect rumors that he was after her money, Robins invented a gold strike in Alaska that had made him rich. Theirs was a highly compatible and happy match that lasted forty years—the willowy Margaret, with her perfect oval face and long chestnut hair in a bun, and the short, stocky Raymond, like an overgrown barrow boy, with a forelock dangling over a high brow and a look of stubborn resolve in his dark eyes.[40]

Robins got into Chicago politics as a labor organizer. He joined the Progressive movement and backed Theodore Roosevelt, who broke away from the Republican Party and ran in 1912 as a Progressive or Bull Mooser. Roosevelt split the Republican Party down the middle and Wilson won. In 1914 Robins ran for the U.S. Senate on the Progressive ticket from Illinois, but lost.

In June 1917, Robins was spinning his wheels when he heard from Teddy Roosevelt. His old friend had recommended him for the Red Cross Commission, the brainchild of copper magnate William Boyce Thompson, which was being formed to go to Russia. Thompson was fixated on maintaining the Eastern Front and hoped, under cover of the Red Cross, to shore up the Provisional Government. Another motive for the rotund Wall Street pirate was his determination to match or to outdo his mogul friends in winning the war.

Thompson's Red Cross outfit consisted of a team of thirty, including doctors and sanitary engineers. They had uniforms and military ranks, and were in the service of the International Division of the U.S. Army, reporting to Secretary of War Newton Baker. Thompson planned to do the regular Red Cross relief work, but also to prop up the Kerensky regime. Wilson was not overjoyed to see Robins, who had backed Teddy Roosevelt in 1912, on the commission, but Newton Baker liked him and told Wilson that his "old friend Robins [would] do what he could to break up the contraband ring headed by pro German Russians."[41]

Behind Thompson, there was the hidden presence of the President, who had given the copper millionaire a secret letter of instructions. For Wilson, Bolshevism meant not only the end of the Russian war effort, but a threat to the stability of any postwar global order.

When Robins first learned that Thompson would be his boss, he asked, "What's that Wall Street reactionary doing on this mission?" Thompson was no happier about Robins, whom he called "That uplifter, that trouble-maker, that Roosevelt shouter. What's he doing on this mission?" But once in Russia, both men revised their opinion.[42]

On arrival in Petrograd in early August 1917, the mission took rooms at the Hotel Europe. "All here is chaos!" Robins wrote his wife, whom he addressed as "Blessed One," on August 7. "The government will last no one knows how long . . . the outlook is stormy in the extreme." On the front, the Russians were in retreat, "and about 18,000 Russian troops have been shot by their own brothers." Robins visited the Czar's residence, Tsarskoe Selo, fifteen miles from Petrograd. The children's playthings were scattered in the nursery, amid notes scratched by young hands. One of them said: "Our French lesson was very hard today."[43]

In Petrograd, Robins saw long lines for bread, milk, meat, and sugar. Old women sat on the sidewalk and knitted while they waited. Robins thought the government would go the way of the lines: if they got shorter it would live, if they grew longer it would die.

To Robins, the Kerensky regime seemed little more than a paper affair. When he traveled about and showed local officials his Kerensky credentials, they laughed and told him to see the chairman of the soviet. This was, he discovered, the only way to get things done. If he wanted six wagons to carry grain from the village to the station, he asked the soviets and got six wagons. Orders did not come from the Winter Palace, where Kerensky was entrenched, or from the Duma, but from Smolny, the headquarters of the Petrograd Soviet.[44]

Once the Red Cross supplies had been unloaded and stored, Thompson and Robins concentrated on the political work. Thompson was eager to launch a pro-war, anti-Bolshevik propaganda campaign. He offered to subsidize the two liberal non-Marxist parties, the Social Revolutionaries and the Kadets or Constitutional Democrats. He formed the Russian Committee to hire speakers, produce pamphlets, and buy newspapers and presses. In the initial capital outlay for this campaign he spent $1 million of his own money.[45]

Back in Washington, President Wilson applauded Thompson's "helpful interest in Russia's fight for freedom" and the "finely practical" form it was taking.[46] Thompson and Creel were doing much the same kind of work that the German Foreign Ministry had previously undertaken, but the momentum that fall was all on the side of the Bolsheviks, whose Red Guards patrolled the streets of Petrograd.

On September 29, 1917, the German Foreign Ministry indulged in a bit of self-congratulation. Disgraced after the publication of his telegram to Mexico, Zimmerman had been replaced as Foreign Secretary by Baron Richard von Kuhlmann, who reported that "German military operations . . . were seconded by intensive undermining activities inside Russia . . . to further separatist endeavors . . . and give strong support to the revolutionary elements." The secret German policy of arranging for Lenin's return and funding the Bolsheviks was paying off. As von Kuhlmann put it, "The Bolshevik movement could never have attained the scale or the influence which it has today without our continued support."[47]

September had seen a right-wing coup by General Kornilov; the coup had failed but it succeeded in dividing the army into commissars and czarists. "Kerensky has acted with vigor and real courage," Robins wrote his "darling blessed one" on September 13. But by September 24 it was no longer clear if the government would last or if the Bolsheviks would establish the Commune (as in the Paris Commune of 1871). Would the Germans take Petrograd? Would the food supply last? It was the wildest and most uncertain time.[48]

The growing influence of the Bolsheviks was all too apparent. Judson, the military attaché, reported back to Washington that the Germans were spending $10 million a month to pay their expenses. Thompson asked Washington for $3 million a month to keep his campaign going, but Wilson exploded that he had "gone crazy." Creel, who acted as a liaison between the President and the Red Cross mission, told Thompson on October 24 that Wilson's refusal was not "due to any lack of willingness, but to the iron limitations imposed by our law and our public opinion." At his wit's end, Thompson on Friday, November 2, called an extraordinary meeting of the Allied military missions to figure out a way to shore up the collapsing Eastern Front.

The French and the British came, and of course Judson and Robins, as well as a Russian general and Kerensky's private secretary. Major General Alfred Knox, the British military attaché, who had served in India and Egypt, thought of the Russians as colonial natives "who have got to have a whip over them." He launched into such a vicious attack on Kerensky's incompetence that the two Russians present left in protest. Only Robins stood up to him. Knox turned on him and said, "You are wasting Colonel Thompson's money."

"If I was," Robins said, "Colonel Thompson knows all about it."

"I am not interested in stabilizing Kerensky," Knox said. "The only thing worthwhile in Russia is to establish Kaledin [the Cossack leader] and a Cossack military dictatorship."

Robins replied that unless he was mistaken there would be a very different kind of dictatorship.

"You mean Lenin, Trotsky, and this Bolshevik soapbox stuff," Knox said.

"That is what I mean," Robins said.

"Colonel Robins, you are not a military man," Knox said. "You don't know anything about military affairs. We military men know what to do with that kind of agitation and agitators. We shoot them."

"Yes," Robins replied, "if you catch them you shoot them."[49]

It was a dialogue of the deaf, between a British general who refused to acknowledge the growing mass support behind the Bolsheviks, and the American social worker with his ear close to the ground, who saw a Bolshevik victory as inevitable.

—

John Reed, the hyperactive former captain of the Harvard water polo team and cheerleader for the football team, arrived in Petrograd in September 1917 on assignment from the Socialist newspaper the *Call*. If we think of cheerleading as a form of propaganda, he found his calling early. Upton Sinclair called him "the playboy of the revolution," but he was more than that; he was a chaser of stories all over the map, whether it was Pancho Villa, the Paterson silk strike, or the Bolshevik Revolution, with a penchant for getting a little too involved in what he was covering.

Autumn in Petrograd meant a chill fog, dull gray skies, and damp winds from Finland. Reed patrolled the streets and heard ladies in tea shops wishing that the Czar would return. A woman on a streetcar threw a fit because the conductor called her *comrade*. At a café on Tverskaya, the waiter refused a tip. At the Alexandrinsky Theater, the Imperial Box was empty and the statue of Catherine the Great had a little red flag in its hand. In the Smolny Institute, the former finishing school where the daughters of the rich learned how to curtsy and a hundred doors were still marked "ladies' classrooms," the unladylike banging of boots echoed in the vaulted corridors, and Lenin drew up his plans. Reed had arrived during that peculiar interval when the two regimes co-existed side by side.[50]

On Tuesday, November 6, Smolny was humming as the noon cannon boomed from Peter and Paul Fortress. The streetcars were running on the Nevsky and shops were open. The bustle of the capital seemed normal, but during the night, the Bolsheviks had captured the Telephone Exchange, the Baltic railroad station, and the Telegraph Agency, and Kerensky had fled. Reed saw squads of soldiers with fixed bayonets, but could not tell whether they belonged to Kerensky or the Red Guards.

The next day Reed managed to get inside the Winter Palace, where the same old ushers in their brass-buttoned blue uniforms were still on duty. He walked through the long halls and paneled rooms, under crystal chandeliers and gilded cornices. The Provisional Government was abolished that day and those of its members still in their offices were arrested.[51]

That evening, Robins was walking along the bank of the Neva when he saw gunboats coming up from Kronstadt, the naval base on Kotlin Island under the command of sailors who had murdered their officers. He watched the shells explode on the walls of the Winter Palace, and wrote his wife that the scene belonged to the Dark Ages. There had been nothing like it since the birth of Christ.[52]

On the morning of November 8, after the final taking of the Winter Palace, Rogers Smith of the National City Bank saw prisoners being led out by sailors from Kronstadt. He saw factory workers outside military barracks converting soldiers to the new platform—bread, peace with Germany, and land for everybody. Smith was arrested in December, when the Bolsheviks took over the bank. They sent a squad of men over and the squad leader told them they were all arrested and the bank was arrested. National City had deposits of 300 million rubles, which the state confiscated. The jewels and gold and silver in the safe deposit boxes were also confiscated.[53]

Oliver Saylor, the theater editor for the *Indianapolis News,* happened to be in Moscow that November, where the fighting was much heavier. He personally saw five hundred red-draped coffins buried in a long, trenchlike grave. But within a week life had settled into a kind of desultory disorder. On the Arbat, Saylor saw an endless procession of soldiers in olive drab marching between railroad stations on their way home. Nine out of ten carried rifles that they were taking to their farms.[54]

For Frank Keddie, who was doing relief work for the Quakers, it had all evolved in a natural, almost inevitable way. First the Czar abdicated. Then the soviets came to life. Then Kerensky cried "one more offensive." Then the soldiers deserted. Then a little Russian gunboat came up the Neva and the soviets became the government. It had all evolved out of the war weariness of the people. Then the soldiers came home in a mad rush, in carts, on horseback, on top of trains. When their money ran out they knocked at large landowners' castles for food, and if the watchmen fired on them, they fired back. They arrived in their village and found their cottage in a wretched state. The government had failed to pay the family allowance and the wife had sold a horse or a cow. And here they were, back after three years in the trenches, minus an arm or a leg, to find this mess.[55]

So far as the clergyman–war correspondent Albert Rhys Williams could see, the only ones who rallied to the Kerensky government were a few Cossacks and the Woman's Battalion inside the Winter Palace. The Bolshevik Revolution, he estimated, was accomplished in Petrograd with only about eighteen people killed, most of them Bolsheviks standing outside the Winter Palace, who were shot from bunkers on the inside. Even Lenin commented on how easy it was, like "lifting a feather."[56]

———

Raymond Robins did not know what to make of this strange upheaval and the crackdown that followed. "Think of it," he wrote his wife in November, "the most extreme semi-anarchist government in all the world, maintaining its control by the bayonet, proscribing all publications . . . arresting persons without warrants and holding them for weeks without trial. . . . It is a wild and stormy ride."[57]

Frederick H. Hatzel, who ran the condensed milk operation for the Red Cross mission, could testify to the general lawlessness that followed the revolution. He had 500,000 cans of condensed milk in a warehouse and had to put a new label over the Bordens label on each one, saying it was from the Red Cross and was not to be sold. He also had three thousand barrels of salted beef intended for Romania, but the Bolsheviks broke into the warehouse and stole it. They left the milk alone, more interested in raiding wine cellars. Later they opened stores to sell the stolen goods to the public.

Life was not safe. If you carried a package, the Red Guards took it. People were shot at night in the streets for no reason. Hatzel himself had crawled into a doorway on his knees three times, right on Nevski Prospect, their Broadway. One day, walking past the canal on his way to the warehouse, he saw a crowd of men and women yelling like fiends. They had a long pole that they were pushing up and down in the water and Hatzel asked one of them what was going on and he said they were just killing a thief. They threw him into the canal and pushed him down with the pole.[58]

Robins saw quite clearly from the beginning that the Bolsheviks were there to stay. In his comings and goings, he could tell that the people were for the revolution. Lenin and Trotsky were in the saddle. He knew nothing about Marxism, but judged events as he would have in Chicago, in terms of power politics, and these fellows couldn't be worse than some of the ward-heelers he'd dealt with back home.

On November 8 he told Thompson: "Chief, we've got to move pretty fast. Kerensky is as dead as yesterday's 7000 years. We either have to work with Lenin and Trotsky or pack our grips and go home." Thompson, who had so wholeheartedly (and expensively) backed Kerensky, was now persona non grata, vilified in *Pravda* as a Wall Street shark trying to get his hands on the Russian economy. He could no longer be of any use. But both men agreed that the mission should soldier on and lobby the new regime to stay in the war at a time when America's soldiers were dying on the Western Front. Thompson put Robins in charge and left at the end of November.[59]

Trotsky, the Commissar of Foreign Affairs, was the Bolshevik leader who could give the green light for the Red Cross mission to continue its work. Although he had described Trotsky as a "dangerous leader of the extreme left" in a letter to his wife, Robins was prepared to sup with the devil. In Chicago, he had worked with bigger crooks.

On November 10, three days after the Bolshevik coup, Robins and his interpreter, Alexander Gumberg, went to see Trotsky at Smolny, a great stone building with an iron fence around it. Lions' heads on the keystones looked down on them as they climbed the twelve steps to the twenty-foot-high arches at the entrance, where guards positioned behind heavy machine guns inspected their documents. Inside, the ornate anterooms and corridors were now barracks and arsenal, smelling of gunpowder and tobacco. In the gilded dining room, with its French doors and parquet floors, Red Guards and People's Commissars sat at long tables, sharing bread and cabbage.

In front of Trotsky's office, a young captain stood guard. "Say to the commissioner that I know a corpse when I see one," Robins told him. "I believe the Kerensky government is dead and I regard the commissioner as holding the effective power in Russia. Does he want the American Red Cross to remain? If not, we will get out." Trotsky, a short, brisk man with a small goatee, thick curly hair, and beady eyes behind a pince-nez, beckoned them in. The apostle of social justice and Christian charity came face-to-face with the Jewish atheist revolutionary, but Robins wanted to discuss practical problems rather than ideology or religion. "I want guards around my supplies, to protect the supplies from being stolen," he told Trotsky. "Will you give me the guards, and will they take my orders?" Taken aback by this peremptory American, but seeing the advantage of Red Cross supplies in a time of food riots, Trotsky promised to provide the guards. The Red Cross warehouses, so tempting to looters with their stocks of food, clothing, and medical supplies, were kept under armed Bolshevik guard.[60]

In acting on his own to establish contact with the Bolshevik leadership, Robins was going against the instructions of Secretary of State Lansing to avoid all contacts that might be construed as recognition. Ambassador Francis obeyed the letter of the law, writing Lansing: "I live in the embassy and since the beginning of the revolution have not left it except to attend a meeting of the diplomatic corps and to take an occasional walk after dark."[61]

"Our diplomacy is past speaking about," Robins wrote to his wife. "I, a Red

Cross man, am the only person in any authority that is permitted by our government to have any direct intercourse with the de facto government that has complete control of over three fourths of Russian territory."[62]

———

The Soviets declared a unilateral cessation of hostilities on November 26, 1917. An armistice was signed with the Central Powers on December 15, and peace negotiations opened on December 22 in the German-held city of Brest-Litovsk, but quickly bogged down.

The Allies were stunned by the Bolshevik defection, which might prolong the war by several years, and struggled to formulate a suitable policy. One plan, favored by the French, was to back anti-Bolshevik forces in the south of Russia. In London, the War Cabinet was split, with Prime Minister David Lloyd George fearing that backing dissidents would throw the Bolsheviks into the arms of the Germans, while Lord Robert Cecil, the undersecretary of state for foreign affairs, saw a chance to dethrone Lenin.[63]

It was in the midst of this conundrum that William Boyce Thompson left Moscow for London on November 26. Under the influence of Robins, Thompson was now a convert to cooperation with the Bolsheviks and hoped to bring about a change in British policy. At lunch with Lloyd George at 10 Downing Street, Thompson made his case. "At present they are nobody's Bolsheviks," he said. "Don't let us let Germany make them her Bolsheviks. Let's make them our Bolsheviks." Lloyd George seemed to like the idea and repeated: "Let's make them our Bolsheviks."[64]

For the moment, the British decided on a two-track policy, one track maintaining unofficial relations with the Bolsheviks, and the other funding the Cossacks in the south.

In Washington, President Wilson, under the influence of the rigidly anti-Bolshevik Lansing, adopted a policy of no contacts and no recognition. Thompson briefly saw Lansing, who called him "a crank." Wilson would not see him, saying that he did not want Thompson plugging recognition at him. Thompson tried to spread the word around the State Department that good relations with the Bolsheviks might keep them in the war, but got nowhere.[65] The irony was that in Russia he was viewed as a Wall Street pirate, while in Washington he was seen as an apologist for the Bolsheviks.

The Bolshevik leadership, while friendly to Robins, seemed to be deliberately trying to antagonize the United States. Here was a regime about to sign a separate peace, abandoning its allies, repudiating hundreds of millions of dollars' worth of debt owed by the Kerensky government, and calling for a worldwide proletarian revolution.

Ambassador Francis thought the Bolsheviks were demented. They violated diplomatic immunity by seizing the Italian ambassador, Diamandi, on January 13, 1918, and ordered that all telegrams from American consulates in Russia be sent in clear instead of cipher. The Red Guards were given license to steal and kill. They broke into homes and stuck bayonets through works of art. Francis could do nothing to protect the American colony.[66]

The Reverend George A. Simons, pastor of the Methodist Episcopal church in Petrograd, now had to dress in a workman's old Russian shirt that hung down to his knees and a beat-up slouch hat so that he looked like a Bolshevik and could move freely among the people. He found that the average man had not the slightest clue as to what the revolution was about. In January 1918, Simons was in his office talking to the head deaconess when, out the window, he saw some Red Guards shoot two Russian soldiers right in front of the church. From then on, Simons kept a little friend in his back pocket by the name of Browning. When the Red Guards came around to extort money, he had two fox terriers doing police duty and was taxed 50 rubles per dog. If you had a piano or a bathtub it had to be registered. Then he was fined 500 rubles for not shoveling the snow on his sidewalk and had to appear before a workmen's court. The three judges said, "We do not want to hear your testimony. You are a bourgeois. We want to hear what your *dvornki* [servant] says."[67]

Roger E. Simmons, a Department of Commerce trade commissioner, was stationed in Russia from July 1917 to November 1918, studying the timber industry. Very soon after the revolution it became impossible to satisfy labor demands in the lumber mills. Men who floated logs up to the skidder in the millpond demanded the same wages as the skilled laborer who handled the saw. If there were no class distinctions, everyone had to be paid the same. In Moscow the orderlies in the hospitals wanted to be paid as much as the doctors. The mill that Simmons was studying had to be shut down.

In July 1918 Simmons was in the forest district outside Vologda, some three hundred miles east of Petrograd, when he was arrested for no apparent reason and sent to Moscow for trial before the Special Council to Combat Counter-Revolution, Sabotage, and Speculation. Taken to Lubyanka Prison, he was thrown into a holding cell with eighty other men, most of whom did not know why they were there either. One was a peasant who had refused to give up the grain he had grown. Another was a mechanic on marine engines who had worked for the Czar's navy. Also, five British sailors who had been on reconnaissance on the White Sea in a gunboat when they were overtaken by a Red cruiser and sent to Moscow. But the one Simmons would never forget was Valenkin, the lawyer for the British consulate, who had been sentenced to the firing squad. He woke Simmons up at two in the morning and said, "Will you talk to me? I die at six. Tell me about America. . . . Tell me anything to occupy my mind." At six, the soldiers came and led him out in the usual formation. Not a day passed without someone being taken out.

The American diplomats had left Moscow, but Simmons wrote a letter to the Swedish consul and gave it to a guard with a 100 ruble note. The guard pushed it into his boot. Thirty-six hours later a package came with a loaf of bread and some toilet articles and a note that said: "Hold your nerve. We will have you out soon." Four hours later the consul arrived and obtained his release.[68]

———

When the Russian Revolution erupted in November 1917, Boris Bakhmeteff, the ambassador to the United States for the Provisional Government, was in Memphis on a speaking tour to sell Americans on the Russian war effort. He hurried back to Washington in the hope that Kerensky would rally and return to power, but that hope was short-lived. The Wilson administration immediately suspended credits and contracts to Russia, which now might go to the Bolsheviks. The aid to Kerensky had been conditional on his staying in the war. Between March and November, the United States had promised Bakhmeteff $325 million in credits, of which $188 million had been delivered. Much of that money he had spent on military matériel, but he still had between $60 and $70 million on deposit at the National City Bank in New York.[69]

What could Bakhmeteff do now? He was in the odd position of being an ambassador without a government. It all hinged on President Wilson, whose mind seemed to contain two airtight compartments, one for the expression of lofty sentiments and the other for carrying out covert maneuvers. There was Wilson the high-minded Big D Democrat, and Wilson the cunning back-channel schemer. "Everything great and small must be referred to the President," one official in the State Department observed, "who receives no one, listens to no one, seems to take no one's advice."[70]

For all his secretive ways, however, Wilson did listen to the information arriving from his envoys in Russia. On November 9, 1917, a dispatch arrived from Felix Willoughby Smith, the U.S. consul in Tbilisi, the principal city south of the Caucasus Mountains. Smith reported that the population in trans-Caucasian Russia was anti-Bolshevik. The Cossack general Ataman Kaledin was rallying troops, but needed funds. This information reinforced Lansing's belief that the Bolshevik regime could not survive, and he began to consider the possibility of an anti-Bolshevik trans-Caucasian government. But how could they get funds to Kaledin without alerting Congress and the press and without antagonizing the new regime? Thus, the stirrings of an anti-Bolshevik covert policy dawned only a few days after the revolution. At the State Department, Assistant Secretary of State William Phillips noted in his diary on November 20: "A feeling of misrule is arising among the people, and a military dictatorship is expected soon." The next day the *New York Times* proclaimed Kaledin "Russia's New Man of the Hour."[71]

In the meantime, Bakhmeteff, eager to clarify his situation, went to see George Creel on November 24. He argued that the Bolsheviks did not represent the whole of Russia and that he did not intend to recognize their authority. He hoped, he told Creel, that President Wilson would distinguish between this upstart regime and the great Russian people. As a result of this meeting with Creel, an arrangement was made whereby Bakhmeteff would stay in the embassy and continue to operate as though nothing had happened. There was no official announcement, but the information was leaked to the *Times*, which reported on November 25 that "the administration does not recognize the Bolsheviks but does recognize the ambassador." Bakhmeteff could continue to make payments from the funds at his disposal, so long as he had State Department approval. The details of this arrangement were worked out with the State Department counselor, Frank Polk, who told Boris he could pay for supplies for which he had already contracted if he submitted a weekly list. One reason for this unusual agreement was to protect U.S. firms from losses on contracts. Another was that the funds could be used to assist anti-Bolshevik forces in Russia, circumventing Congress and the press. Boris Bakhmeteff thus became a disbursing agent for President Wilson's private slush fund and the Russian embassy became a dummy corporation to secretly finance and assist anti-Bolshevik armies.

A first withdrawal was made in November 1917—£3 million to cover the cost of rifles previously ordered in London for the Provisional Government. Further payments were made in December—$325,000 to the Remington Company for rifles and $2,075,000 to J. P. Morgan in connection with a Westinghouse arms contract. The goods not already dispatched to the Kerensky government would now end up in the hands of anti-Bolshevik forces. A memo explaining this hidden policy was later written by two assistant secretaries of the treasury, Nicholas Kelley and Van Mark-Smith, on August 6, 1920: "Our understanding of the fiction of the Russian Embassy was that it represented the 'Russian people' at present submerged under a despotic minority . . . we felt convinced of the wisdom of asking the continued existence and functioning of the embassy."[72]

At the same time, it was evident from Wilson's remarks at cabinet meetings that he was souring on the Bolshevik regime. On November 26, he told the cabinet that he thought the "actions of Lenin and Trotsky sounded like opéra bouffe." On November 27, he read aloud a speech by Trotsky charging that America had intervened in the war when "the finance capitalists sent an ultimatum to Wilson." This was an insult to the image of an unselfish America making the world safe for democracy—but any response would imply recognition. On November 30, Wilson felt the situation in Russia was "too chaotic to act yet," but he added that he was paying "sympathetic attention" to the efforts of Kaledin, while he found the Bolsheviks "insulting and naive."[73]

By this time, any dissenting opinion was dismissed. On December 4 Wilson heard from the astute military attaché General William Judson. In a cable to the War Department, Judson said that "any plan to form fronts with . . . Kaledins et cetera, appears most chimerical," and of no benefit to the Allies, since Russia was "past carrying on the war" against Germany. Judson held the view, shared by Robins and Thompson, that the Bolsheviks were in control and that the Wilson administration was uninformed as a result of the no-contact policy. He believed, as he wrote Ambassador Francis on December 26, that the United States should "enter into helpful, sympathetic and friendly relations" with the regime. This was not what Wilson wanted to hear. Moreover, Judson had broken the no-contact policy by meeting with Trotsky on December 1. Lansing had him recalled in January 1918 and reemphasized to Ambassador Francis on December 6 that "the President desires American representatives [to] withhold all direct communications with the Bolsheviks."[74]

The U.S. consul in Moscow, Maddin Summers, also on the Kaledin bandwagon, cabled on December 9, 1917, that Kaledin and another Cossack general, M. V. Alekseyev, "had formed a well equipped army of 50,000 cavalry and a trusted infantry force." This was wishful thinking at best, but on the basis of Summers's information, Lansing sent Wilson a memo on December 10 presenting the case for aiding the Cossacks in south Russia. Lansing still believed that overturning the Bolsheviks could keep Russia in the war, which would mean "the saving to this country of hundreds of thousands of men and billions of dollars." He worked on Wilson all week, seeing him daily to press his case and comparing Kaledin to Ulysses S. Grant, who had restored the Union. Wilson came around, appalled by the reports he was getting of lawlessness in Petrograd. He had been told that Ambassador Francis had faced down a mob at the door of the U.S. embassy with a pistol in his hand and his loyal valet at his side. At a cabinet meeting, Wilson read a cable from Francis saying that "in Petrograd people broke into the Winter Palace and took all the wine and got drunk and went around shooting up the town." This was indeed the Wild East.[75]

Lansing felt that his mission in life was to prevent a populist rabble from taking power in his own country, and was now applying his principles to a distant land. He was explicit in his opinion that only a military dictatorship could save Russia. But what of Wilson, the champion of self-determination? At a cabinet meeting on December 11, 1917, he said he "hated to do nothing about Russia but was puzzled how to take hold."[76]

He was dissembling, for he had by now almost made up his mind to secretly back a dissident general against the established government of Russia. Lansing returned to the White House that night and convinced the President to intervene. The following day, Lansing drafted a telegram to Oscar Crosby, the Treasury Department representative at the U.S. embassy in London. The Kaledin movement, he explained, offered "the greatest hope for the re-establishment of a stable government and the continuance of a military force on the German and Austrian front" and "should be encouraged, but secretly." It would be unwise to support Kaledin openly, because "this government cannot under the law loan money to him . . . the only practicable course seems to be for the British and French government to loan them the money to do so." This plan for covert financing of an anti-Bolshevik army was so sensitive that Wilson and Lansing did not tell their closest aides. No one at the State Department saw the cable to Crosby. But Wilson wrote on Lansing's draft, "This has my entire approval."[77]

On December 11, 1917, Boris Bakhmeteff withdrew $500,000 from his account to buy 3,688,652 ounces of silver, which were handed over to British officials in San Francisco to pay Kaledin's troops in the Caucasus. Basil Miles, the head of the Russian desk at the State Department, which approved the transaction, wondered about this use of funds "for purposes which may well be regarded as inimical by the Russian people." He argued that it was "a grave responsibility to direct the City Bank to pay $500,000 for silver to be sent through the British to Kaledin. That involves a question of state."[78]

On December 15, Kaledin's Cossacks and Alekseyev's troops captured the important city of Rostov-on-Don, four hundred miles northwest of Tbilisi. This seemed like quite a victory, and Maddin Summers, the consul in Moscow, sent his assistant, DeWitt Poole, to Rostov to size up the situation. Poole met with Kaledin, who told him that some of the younger Cossacks were "infected with Bolshevism." Kaledin wanted to fight, but he had no artillery and practically no infantry—the Cossacks were mounted troops. Poole reported that "the position of the Kaledin government is lamentably weak," but nonetheless recommended funding it.

On December 17, doubtless cheered by the Rostov victory, Wilson formally approved Lansing's proposal to help Kaledin. The following day Lansing sent a wire to Sir William Wiseman, the head of British intelligence in the United States, who was then in London. "President believes it is essential to give whatever aid is possible to the Polish, Cossacks and others that are willing to fight Germany," he cabled, "and while he has no power to lend money directly to such unorganized movements, he is willing to let France and England have funds to transmit to them."

The time-honored Wilson method was to act through surrogates, in this case by using Bakhmeteff in Washington and his British and French allies. In this way, America would appear to be uninvolved and Wilson could continue to take the ideological high ground in public, as he did on January 8, 1918, when he addressed a joint session of Congress and listed in fourteen points America's terms of peace. He had already violated the sixth point, "evacuation of Russian territory and Russian self-determination."

As President Wilson presented his Fourteen Points, the Kaledin forces seemed to be doing well in the Caucasus, with the help of American funds. By December 31, 1917, 1 million rubles had been paid, plus 3 million rubles to buy arms in Teheran. The French had promised Alekseyev 100 million rubles, but had delivered only 300,000. This was a fraction of what was needed, and Poole warned in mid-January that Kaledin had an "urgent need of cash." The American money pipeline via Oscar Crosby in London did not begin to function regularly until February 1918.

But by that time, Kaledin had suffered serious reversals. At first he lorded it over the Don region north of the Black Sea, where refugees from Bolshevism gathered. But in the homeland of the Cossacks, these bourgeois from the north were seen as intruders, and in an industrial city like Rostov, Kaledin had the workers against him. In late December, the Bolsheviks sent an army to destroy him. The advances of the Red Army, coupled with an uprising in Taganrog, west of Rostov, led Kaledin to withdraw from the Don. In despair, he shot himself in the heart on February 11, 1918. Red forces retook Rostov-on-Don twelve days later.[79] President Wilson's first attempt at a covert operation to overthrow the Reds had turned into a complete fiasco. It could hardly be taken as a good omen, but it would not be his last.

II

THE FIRST
AMERICAN ATTEMPT
AT REGIME CHANGE

In October 1917, when Kerensky was still in power, George Creel sent reinforcements to Russia in the person of Edgar Sisson, who was the head of the Russian section of his propaganda committee. Sisson was one of Creel's newsmen cronies—he'd served as city editor of the *Chicago Tribune*, managing editor of *Collier's* magazine, and editor of *Cosmopolitan*. Short and wiry, his hair parted in the middle, his alert eyes taking in all he saw through rimless glasses, Sisson exuded nervous energy. His job was to back up Bullard and the Red Cross mission with a campaign of education and propaganda to keep Russia in the war. Creel told him to "drive ahead full speed regardless of expense."

Sisson set sail on October 27, but by the time he arrived in Petrograd on November 25, the Bolsheviks were in power. "The city is quiet," a British officer told him at the Finland station. "The Bolsheviks have control. We may hear shots but they will mean nothing. Patrols fire into the air to keep their fingers warm."[1]

Sisson paid his respects to Ambassador Francis, who showed an angry disdain for the new regime, saying, "I never would talk to a damned Bolshevik." Francis left all contacts to Robins, who saw the Bolshevik leaders with such regularity that he was given a pass to the Smolny Institute. At first, Sisson worked with Robins to try to keep the Bolsheviks from signing a separate peace. Robins welcomed him as a colleague, and introduced Sisson to Trotsky.

Sisson soon turned against the regime and began to see Robins as the willing accomplice of its leaders. He dismissed the Bolsheviks as a gang of trained demagogues who had come to power armed with slogans for the war-weary. On December 14, he wrote Creel: "Russia is out of the war. She cannot be counted on as a fighting factor. . . . The Bolsheviks played the peace card. . . . I found Ambassador Francis without policy except anger at the Bolsheviks."[2]

The more Sisson saw of the regime, the more upset he became. On December 11 came the arrest of the Kadet (Constitutional Democrat) leaders. The opposition press was suppressed. Law courts were replaced by people's tribunals. Sisson attended one of these and saw a woman of the wealthy class brought in and charged with firing her maid without notice. The jury verdict was that she pay the maid a month's wages.[3]

On January 11, 1918, Robins took Sisson to meet the forty-seven-year-old Lenin in his small corner office on the third floor of Smolny, so that Sisson could present him with a copy of Wilson's Fourteen Points speech. Lenin offered to distribute thousands of copies of Wilson's speech to the soldiers at the front, in Russian and German. They discussed the peace negotiations at Brest-Litovsk, and German demands for the annexation of Russian lands. The question was whether Lenin would pay the price of peace with land or raise a new army. There seemed to be a ray of hope that Russia would stay in the war.

During the course of the conversation, Lenin volunteered the information that he had been called a German spy. Robins saw the remark as candor; Sisson as an admission. Robins admired Lenin as a great statesman, committed, steady, and incorruptible. Sisson sensed something malleable in Robins that he was certain Lenin had also discerned. General Knox, the British military attaché, would later describe Robins as "a fanatic with the temperament of a hero-worshiping schoolgirl."[4]

———

Two weeks after the Bolsheviks seized power in November, elections were held throughout Russia for delegates to an assembly that would draft a constitution and set up a government. This assembly was the first elected body chosen by universal suffrage and secret ballot in a thousand years of Russian history, the keystone for Russia's future. The results were not favorable to the Bolsheviks, who won only 175 out of 707 delegates while the Social Revolutionary Party, which was popular among the peasants, won 410. As the date set for the opening of parliament on December 11 approached, the question arose as to who would prevail—the millions of Russian voters, or Bolshevik rifles. "The Bolshevik government does not control this body," Robins wrote to his wife, "and it may have to be dissolved by force."

Lenin delayed the December 11 opening on the grounds that too few delegates had arrived. On January 18, 1918, as the delegates filed into the Tauride Palace, martial law was declared and Red Guards surrounded the palace. Crowds outside with banners that said "All Power to the Constituent Assembly" were scattered, and in the melee the Red Guards began firing, leaving six dead and thirty-four wounded. Inside the meeting hall, the Bolsheviks withdrew, charging that a counterrevolutionary majority had been elected and that the party lists were outdated. The doors of the Tauride Palace were locked. A wave of arrests followed. Two of the ministers in Kerensky's government, Andrei Shingarev and F. Kokoshkin, who had been arrested in November, were now transferred to a special ward in Marinskaya Hospital. On January 20 a squad of Red soldiers and sailors broke into their room and stabbed them repeatedly with bayonets until their sheets were drenched in blood.[5]

Ambassador Francis could not believe the news and sent the American attaché, William Chapin Huntington, to the morgue, where he went from marble slab to marble slab until he found Shingarev's corpse. He was a little doctor from south Russia, completely inoffensive, thought Huntington, and eleven armed men had slipped by the guards in the hospital and murdered him in his bed. And now orders streamed out daily from Smolny. No shoulder straps for officers. Equal pay for all ranks. The people's tribunals punished previously unknown crimes, such as "abuse of one's position," "sowing discord," and "belonging to a hostile class."[6]

In the wake of the dissolution of the Assembly, Sisson observed the disintegration of the Russian army. Portions of the front in January 1918 were bare of troops. Elsewhere, barbed wire was removed to facilitate fraternization. On the unpaved roads of Russia deserters trod by the thousands. Sisson began to take more seriously the charges that Lenin and Trotsky were German agents. In Washington, Creel agreed that it was worth looking into.[7]

On February 4, 1918, Ambassador Francis received a visit from Evgeni Semenov, a Petrograd journalist who had been writing for an anti-Bolshevik and anti-German evening newspaper. He had made himself useful to the Kerensky government in its efforts to discredit the Bolsheviks as German agents, but after the November coup his paper was shut down. In January 1918, Semenov was lobbying the Allied embassies for a loan for the Kaledin forces in Cossack territory. To bolster his case, he showed Allied diplomats, including Francis, documents that purported to establish Lenin's German connection. Francis put Semenov in touch with Sisson, who was extremely interested.

Semenov brought Sisson copies of documents that appeared to show incontrovertibly that Lenin and Trotsky were abjectly obeying orders emanating from a secret office of the German General Staff in Petrograd. In one such order, the German agents told Lenin whom to place on the Bolshevik Executive Committee. In another, German agents summed up the terms under which Germany would control Russian industries. A third described how Bolsheviks and German officers had arranged for the assassination of nationalist leaders. Sisson paid Semenov handsomely for the documents (Creel had told him to spare no expense) and asked for more, which Semenov provided.[8]

A big, self-assured man with a heavy black beard, Semenov told Sisson that he had agents inside Smolny from whom he had secured the documents. In addition, he said, he was in touch with a military and naval group that was intercepting the telegraph messages between the Soviet delegation at the Brest-Litovsk negotiations and Smolny. The Bolsheviks, Semenov said, were "slothful and incompetent."

Sisson became convinced that the Bolshevik leaders were taking orders from the German high command. He showed the documents to Robins, who said he had already seen them and that they were fakes.

When Sisson asked Semenov for the originals to take back to Washington, Semenov told him he would have to wait: the Bolsheviks were about to move their headquarters from Petrograd to Moscow, fearing a German attack if the talks collapsed. When the government made its move and boxed its archives for shipment to Moscow, Semenov said, his agents inside Smolny would have a chance to raid the files.

The move took place on the night of March 2, 1918. Sisson went over to Smolny the next morning and saw pine boxes, their sides broken, lying in the snow in the courtyard. It was a little accident, he was told: some guards had dropped the boxes. That night, Sisson and Bullard met with Semenov and about seven of his colleagues. They gave him fourteen original documents, and he gave "each man enough rubles to get out of the country." One of them toasted "a historic occasion."[9]

Semenov explained that his agents at Smolny had helped pack the files and knew exactly in which case the documents from the German General Staff Bureau in Petrograd were located. His agents led the sailors on guard to believe that the cases contained gold. The sailors broke into them but, finding no gold, left them open and unguarded in the yard. Semenov said his agents recovered as many documents as they could before the broken cases were discovered. This was fantastically implausible, but Sisson bought it. He thought he was sitting on the scoop of the century and would be hailed as a hero in Washington.[10]

Sisson left Petrograd at once, crossing Finland by sled over ice and snow and finally reaching Norway, where he cabled Creel on April 8, 1918. "I have in my possession documents proving completely and conclusively that the

German government not only created the government of Bolshevik commissars," he wrote, "but that during the whole farcical negotiations for peace this government was operated by the German General Staff."[11]

When Sisson arrived in New York on May 6, he could already see the headlines: "Soviet Leaders Revealed as German Spies." In Washington, he showed the documents to Creel, who wrote to Wilson on May 9: "They are absolutely conclusive and contribute the most amazing record of double dealing and corruption." Wilson saw them that evening and was impressed. On May 23, Ambassador Francis corroborated Sisson with a dispatch that said he was "almost convinced that Lenin and possibly Trotsky are pliable tools if not responsive German agents." A chorus of voices informed the President that the Bolshevik leaders were not patriotic Russians but treacherous schemers.[12] For the moment, however, Wilson delayed the release of the Sisson documents on advice from the State Department, which feared reprisals against American envoys. The disappointed Sisson lobbied influential Democrats. He showed the documents to State Department counselor Frank Polk, who recalled that Sisson's "attitude was rather one of a newspaper man who had secured what he thought was the greatest scoop in history and which was not being made use of by his superiors." Sisson became the most vocal proponent of American intervention in Russian affairs.[13]

—

In Brest-Litovsk, a German-occupied Polish fortress town, sixty miles east of Warsaw, that had been part of the Russian empire before the war, the peace negotiations begun on December 22 were stuck over German territorial demands—the Ukraine, Finland, the Baltic states, and the Soviet part of Poland. The Soviet position was "no annexations or indemnities."

When Trotsky walked out in February, the Germans renewed their offensive, threatening Petrograd. Francis and the embassy staff left the capital in a private train on February 27 for Vologda. Famous for its cathedrals and lace, and its twice-churned butter, Vologda had the advantage of being a railroad hub, at the juncture of the Trans-Siberian and the line from Moscow to the White Sea port of Archangel.[14]

In Moscow, where he had gone with the Bolshevik leadership, Robins followed the drama of the Brest-Litovsk negotiations minute by minute. Slowly, he was changing from an impartial go-between to a believer in the Bolshevik cause. Francis complained that when Robins wrote about the Bolsheviks in his dispatches to Vologda, he said "we." He had come to identify with the leaders he so admired, Trotsky and particularly Lenin.

With the Germans at the gates of Petrograd, the Bolsheviks signed the

Treaty of Brest-Litovsk on March 3, ceding the western tier of the non-Russian nations accumulated by the defunct czarist empire, an area three times the size of Germany. Later in 1918, Lenin repudiated all foreign loans obtained under the czars and Kerensky.

The treaty, opposed by the left wing of the Bolshevik party, which clamored for guerrilla war against the Germans, still had to be ratified by the Fourth All Russian Congress of Soviets, scheduled to open on March 14. If Robins could block ratification, there was an outside chance that Russia would stay in the war. What he needed was a swift offer of U.S. economic and military aid.

On March 5, he saw Trotsky, who according to Robins told him, "give us military support and economic support . . . if you will do that we can defeat the ratification of the Brest peace." Trotsky said he spoke also for Lenin. Robins asked for a request in writing that he could send by cable to Francis in Vologda, who would transmit it to Washington. That afternoon he wired the request to Francis in cipher. But in the move to Vologda, Francis had mislaid the cipher books and was unable to decode Robins's wire. As a result of this mix-up, the message did not reach Washington until seventeen days later, by which time it was too late.[15]

Robins attended the opening of the congress on March 14, hoping that a reply from Washington would arrive in time to create a bandwagon effect against ratification. A message came from President Wilson that dashed his hopes. The President cabled that "the government of the United States is unhappily not now in a position to render the direct and effective aid it would like to render." During the debate, many of the 1,164 delegates spoke of the Brest-Litovsk treaty as a shameful peace, a robber peace, a peace at the point of a bayonet. Then Lenin summoned Robins to the platform and asked if he had heard from his government. Robins said he had not. Lenin told him, "The peace will be ratified." And it was, on March 16, 1918, by a three-to-one vote. Robins was heartbroken; he had been in a position to change the course of the war and modern history, but was foiled by a bureaucratic snafu.[16]

In Moscow, Maddin Summers, the anti-Bolshevik U.S. consul, was incensed that Robins was acting like an official envoy. He cabled Washington in early April that "there can be no cooperation between Robins and myself." If truth be told, Robins had begun to think of himself as the de facto ambassador. On April 3 he told his Red Cross assistant, Allen Wardwell, that "between the Ambassador and myself there is perfect good will and no little cooperation. . . . I am still being used by him for all relations between the two governments. . . . Still I know that if he held me over a cliff and could afford to let go he would do so with a sign of genuine relief."[17]

From Moscow, Summers kept up his anti-Robins campaign until Francis was forced to act. Not wanting to lose Summers, he wired Robins on April 20 that he did not feel "justified in asking you to remain any longer in Moscow." Lansing asked him to come home on April 26: the heady Russian days were coming to an end. Robins saw the machinations of Sisson behind his recall. "Sisson is pledged to destroy me publicly and politically," he wrote his wife, "and will use a genuine ability and cunning." On May 13, the day before his departure, Robins received a note from Trotsky expressing gratitude for the great services he had rendered. In closing, Trotsky added, "you are one of the few who realized the immeasurable difficulties under which the Soviet government had to labor."[18]

Back in the States in June, Robins received a cool reception in Washington. He saw Lansing and Newton Baker, but not President Wilson. He thought the President would welcome his firsthand knowledge of Trotsky and Lenin; instead he was placed under surveillance and forbidden to speak in public. His old boss, William Boyce Thompson, told him, "You've got something to learn. There isn't much difference between hero and zero."[19]

For the next thirty-six years, until his death in 1954 at the age of eighty-one, Robins was an unrelenting apologist and propagandist for the Soviet Union. He was the prototypical fellow traveler, who extolled the regime while remaining blind to its crimes. He saw the Soviet leaders, including Stalin, as brilliant innovators rather than tyrants. The Bolshevik Revolution was so intimately tied up with his personal history that he instinctively overlooked its drawbacks.

Robins never wavered in his admiration for the Soviet regime. He was blind to the ruined economy and the tens of millions of victims. He described the purge trials of the thirties as a "master stroke of Stalin's policy and statesmanship," even though a number of his old friends ended up facing a firing squad. Russia was like a lost love too fondly remembered—he blocked out all negative thoughts, for he knew in his heart that it was a land of miraculous accomplishments.

———

Before the war, the only Russian port connected to Petrograd by rail was Archangel, on the southern shore of the White Sea, which was frozen six months a year. In 1915, the Russians built another port, Murmansk, three hundred miles north of Archangel and seventy-five miles east of the Finnish border, on the Kola Peninsula. Although Murmansk was north of the Arctic Circle, on the Barents Sea, it was ice-free thanks to the Gulf Stream. A new rail line was built from Murmansk to the capital. While Russia was in the war, the Allies shipped large quantities of war matériel to Murmansk and Archangel. Murmansk looked like a logging camp, with unpaved roads and cabins, while Archangel was a city of fifty thousand, with docks and warehouses, and a cathedral with six onion-shaped spires.[20]

By the time of the revolution, 160 tons of supplies had accumulated in the depots of Archangel, thanks to Russian inefficiency. The payment for those supplies was covered by credits that the new regime announced it would not honor. In February 1918, when the port was frozen, the Bolsheviks started moving war stores to the interior. The Allies were indignant. Then the Bolsheviks took control of Murmansk, murdering the Russian admiral who commanded the naval base.

In late February and early March, with the Germans advancing on Petrograd, there appeared to be a threat to the railroad line with Murmansk. On March 14, Trotsky sent a message to the Murmansk Soviet: "You must accept any and all assistance from the Allied missions and use every means to obstruct the advance of the plunderers." Upon Trotsky's invitation, several hundred British Marines landed to defend the port. Thus did the Allies gain a foothold on Russian soil.[21]

The British wanted to draw their American allies into the Russian adventure, though President Wilson was at first reluctant. But pressures to intervene were coming at him from all sides. At the time of the initial British landing, Foreign Secretary Arthur Balfour told Wilson that "since Russia cannot help herself, she must be helped by her friends." What he had in mind was an Allied occupation of her two northern ports. In Washington, Boris Bakhmeteff also pushed for intervention. On May 8, Ambassador Francis wired from Vologda that "allied intervention should not be delayed." The next day Wilson saw the Sisson documents and told Colonel House that he thought they were authentic. Under the influence of the documents, he became more receptive to the idea of an American military expedition in north Russia. Perhaps the Russian people would welcome an American force. Two weeks later he told the British ambassador, Lord Reading, that Trotsky was "absolutely untrustworthy" and that the "only certainty in dealing with such a man is that he would deceive you."[22]

On May 26, 1918, General Tasker Bliss, the American delegate to the Supreme War Council in Paris, informed Washington that an occupation of the ports of Murmansk and Archangel was about to be approved by the British. Bliss said that he intended to vote for it since there was "a pressing danger to these ports." After the signing of the Brest-Litovsk peace treaty, it was feared that the Germans would seize the ports and turn them into submarine bases.[23]

Wilson quickly approved military action in north Russia to protect the stockpiles and to ward off the Germans. Bliss was told on May 28 that the President was "heartily in sympathy with any practical military effort, which can be made at and from Murmansk and Archangel." The Supreme War Council approved a plan on June 3 that would also involve defending the railroad lines leading to the ports. The plan, known as SWC Joint Note 31 and signed by Tasker Bliss, made it clear that Allied troops might have to "penetrate into the heart of Russia." This went much further than Wilson had ever intended. Nonetheless, on July 22, 1918, the President approved sending three battalions of U.S. troops to north Russia. A few days earlier he had received a cable from Felix Cole, the U.S. consul at Archangel, that warned: "Intervention cannot reckon on active support from Russians."[24]

With all its facets and geographically remote danger zones, as well as the differing interests of the Allies, the Russian puzzle was logarithmic in its complexity. Wilson complained to Colonel House that his "overburdened mind" was "becoming leaky." William Judson, who was back at the War College, urged the President to send fifty thousand U.S. troops to Siberia to rally anti-German Russians. But it was not feasible to move U.S. troops from France halfway around the world. Wilson was now considering two separate American military interventions on Russian soil, one in European Russia in the ports north of Petrograd, and one in Asian Russia in Vladivostok and Siberia.[25]

In late May, Wilson was alerted to a development in Russia that was tailor-made to satisfy both his chivalric aspirations and his pragmatic bent. This was the plight of the Czechoslovak Legion, one of the truly bizarre episodes of the war. A large number of Czechs and Slovaks, submerged in the Austro-Hungarian Empire with no country of their own, had been drafted into the armies of the Central Powers. About 65,000 of them either avoided the draft or deserted, and formed a corps that fought on the side of the Allies. They fought not only to win the war, but in the hope of obtaining an independent Czechoslovakia after the peace. Tomas Masaryk, the head of the underground Czech liberation movement, who helped to organize the legion, would be elected the first President of Czechoslovakia in November 1918. The Czech Legion fought in the Ukraine as a special unit of the Russian army. But when the Russians pulled out of the war in March 1918, the Czechs were stranded. They wanted to continue to fight, but could not go south through German lines to join the Allies. They were placed under French command and a plan was formed to take them on the Trans-Siberian railroad to Vladivostok and then ship them to Europe. Because they had fought side by side with the Red Army in the Ukraine, and because he did not want a well-armed foreign army on Russian soil, Trotsky gave them the right of transit and placed sixty-five trains at their disposal.

In March 1918, they started off from Kursk, about three hundred miles south of Moscow, on their four-thousand-mile trek eastward across the entire expanse of Russia. Their progress was slow: at every station they were stopped by gaping-eyed Red Guards who wondered at these well-disciplined troops and the open cars they had devised with six machine guns on each side. The long trains kept moving, from Kursk to Penza, then crossing the bridge over the Volga to Samara, then puffing across the Ural Mountains into the Siberian steppe. By April 4, the first Czech troops had reached Vladivostok and waited for the others, strung out along the Trans-Siberian from the Volga to the Sea of Japan. But in Vladivostok there were no Allied ships to carry them to France.[26]

At the same time as the Czechs were heading east, other trains were heading west, filled with German and Austrian prisoners of war who were being released from their camps in Siberia as a provision of the Brest-Litovsk treaty. On May 14, as a contingent of Czechs loaded supplies at Chelyabinsk, just east of the Urals, a train full of Hungarian POWs who had served in the Austrian army also stopped at the station, coming from the opposite direction. The Czechs despised the Hungarians, who had fought for their Austrian masters, and when they saw them a few feet away on the tracks, jammed into their 40 and 8s (forty men or eight horses), clanking and bobbing at a snail's pace, hoots and catcalls were exchanged. An iron bar was thrown at a Czech, who was hurt. Czech soldiers grabbed the Hungarian culprit and hanged him from the nearest lamppost. The Czechs then seized the arms in the Chelyabinsk arsenal and pulled out.[27]

On May 25, Trotsky ordered the Czechs to disarm: those found armed were to be shot. Their actions were seen as an infringement on Soviet sovereignty, and it was feared that as they crossed Russia, they might become a magnet for anti-Bolshevik elements. But the Czechs refused to disarm. They decided to fight their way to Vladivostok, seizing stations and towns as they went. They held thousands of miles of railroad track, the lifeline of Siberia. With boxcars for homes, they formed a mobile infantry that cleared the way across the steppe, detraining whenever they met resistance to battle their way through. By mid-June, they held the entire line from the Urals to the Pacific, except for a Bolshevik stronghold at Irkutsk on Lake Baikal. Resistance was weak, and when they took a town they encouraged the formation of an anti-Bolshevik government. Their aims were changing en route, from an evacuation to France to an anti-Bolshevik holding action in Siberia.[28]

On June 3, 1918, when Masaryk met with Secretary of State Lansing in

Washington, he asked for ships to carry his men to France. But Lansing, who saw in the Czechs a way to launch a new anti-Bolshevik drive, said the Allies were short of ships, but that if the Czechs could rally other anti-Bolshevik troops in the area some might be found for their eventual return. On June 17, Wilson began to glimpse "the shadow of a plan." "Is it not possible," Lansing asked Wilson, "that in this body of capable and loyal troops may be found a nucleus for military occupation of the Siberian railway?" Masaryk kept insisting that he did not want his men to fight the Red Army, but Lansing and the State Department were already making plans to help the Czechs do just that. The intervention was presented to Wilson as a mission to rescue the gallant Czechs, which appealed to his humanitarian instincts.[29]

On July 4, 1918, Lansing reported to Wilson that the fifteen thousand Czechs in Vladivostok had overturned the Bolshevik regime there. This gave Wilson an added reason to come to their support, and on July 6 he agreed to send them weapons so that they could link up with their compatriots strung out along the railway line. By now, Wilson was thinking of sending seven thousand Americans to help guard the railroad. The U.S. troops would come from the Philippines, a mere two thousand miles south of Vladivostok. This small force could bail out the forty thousand stranded Czechs, an operation at once limited and altruistic. On July 8, the President told Colonel House that he was "sweating blood over the question of what is right and feasible . . . it goes to pieces like quicksilver under my touch." He finally decided on a course of action in mid-September, approving $1.5 million to be paid out of the Bakhmeteff account for provisions and winter clothing for the Czechs, which suggested that they would not be leaving any time soon. In addition, 200,000 rifles were sent to Vladivostok, as well as machine guns and sidearms.[30]

Thus, in the summer of 1918, the architect of national self-determination approved two military operations designed to invade Russian territory—one aimed at protecting the ports north of Petrograd, Murmansk and Archangel, the other on the Pacific side of Russia at Vladivostok, to help the Czechs. Both operations ran the risk of pitched battles with Bolshevik troops.

———

In Murmansk, the pugnacious British general F. C. Poole had three thousand men, but wanted more. Poole planned extensive operations in the Russian interior, where, he grandly proclaimed, he could rally 100,000 friendly Russians. An invasion of the hinterland went far beyond what Wilson and Lansing intended. Ambassador Francis, who had arrived in Archangel on July 26, joined the chorus for more action. The infantry battalions were on their way, and Francis, as he wrote Lansing, planned to encourage them to take part in General Poole's sweeping deployment.

On August 2, anti-Bolshevik forces in Archangel overthrew the local soviet by prearrangement with Allied warships waiting to sail into the harbor. Two days later, fifty U.S. sailors from the USS *Olympia* landed and joined British troops that were chasing the Bolsheviks down the railroad line to Vologda.[31]

On September 4, 1918, three troopships steamed into Archangel harbor carrying the 339th Infantry Regiment, then stationed in England. Known as "Michigan's Own," the regiment consisted of 4,487 men and officers who wore the regimental insignia of a polar bear atop an iceberg, fitting for their destination. The commander, Colonel George Evan Stewart, knew only that he was supposed to render assistance to General Poole. For any clarification, he had been told to consult Ambassador Francis.

The men were draftees, some with only a few days' training, while the officers were ninety-day wonders, just out of Officers Training Camp. As their ships anchored in the wide Dvina River, they got their first sight of the docks and warehouses on the ten-mile-long riverfront, and, further back, the onion-shaped cathedral spires of the White City.[32]

Influenza had claimed the first casualties on the trip over from England, but now the flags were run up and the Navy band played "The Star-Spangled Banner." As they stood at attention waiting to land in their sheepskin coats and fur-lined caps, many of the men wondered why they were there. Was it to secure the stores? To restore the Eastern Front? What good could they do when they were practically at the North Pole, arriving just as the Arctic winter was about to settle in, with no sun for three months, temperatures reaching fifty below, and the harbor frozen over?[33]

The American troops were placed under the command of General Poole, who lost no time sending them out on operations. Some went straight from the ships to the mosquito-ridden swamps of north Russia. One battalion was assigned to guard duty in Archangel, one joined British troops on the rail line to Vologda, and the third was sent up the Dvina River, where the Bolsheviks were entrenched 350 miles south in the town of Kotlas.

On September 16, the Bolsheviks counterattacked and the first American was killed. Ambassador Francis reported that three British sailors had also been killed on the railroad and that the barbarous Reds had cut their arms off. But even the ardently anti-Bolshevik Francis noted that General Poole's "general mistrust of Russians will handicap American policy." The 100,000 Russians Poole expected to rally to the cause were nowhere to be seen.[34]

———

Back in the United States, Major General William S. Graves, who had been serving as secretary to the General Staff and was generally considered a self-reliant, honest, and thoughtful officer, was placed in command of the 8th Infantry Division, based at Camp Fremont in Palo Alto, California. On August 1, General Graves received a cryptic order to proceed by train to Kansas City, where the Secretary of War, Newton Baker, would meet him in the station. The next day, Baker told the general that he was being sent to Siberia with about eight thousand men to help deal with "this peripheral spasm in the world's nervous system." He gave General Graves a sealed envelope and had time only to say, "Watch your step; you will be walking on eggs loaded in dynamite," before boarding an eastbound train. The envelope contained unsigned instructions dated July 17, which clearly came from the President, telling Graves that the only reason for military intervention in Russia was to help the Czechs, which explained the urgency of his mission.[35]

Siberia, where one's breath froze on contact with the air, so that icicles hung from one's nostrils, and where eyebrows and mustaches looked like the lace on granny caps, would be quite a change for the two Philippine-based infantry regiments shipped off from Manila on order of the War Department. They arrived in Vladivostok in mid-August—fifty-three officers and 1,537 men from the 27th infantry regiment and forty-six officers and 1,375 men from the 31st. General Graves arrived on September 1 with five thousand "strong, hardy men" from Camp Fremont.[36]

Vladivostok was in such confusion that there was not even a customs post or a quarantine station to register Graves's arrival. The Czechs were in charge, with the connivance of the Allied commanders and their troops. The Japanese by then had fifty thousand men in the area, but they conducted their own operations north of Vladivostok and along the 3,400 miles of the Chinese Eastern Railroad in Manchuria. Each nation had its own agenda. The Czechs supposedly wanted to leave for Europe, but in the meantime they occupied the Trans-Siberian from Vladivostok to the Urals. The French and British wanted to mount a counterforce to the Bolsheviks to keep them from handing Vladivostok over to the Germans. The Japanese intended to take over the Chinese Eastern Railroad and set up a buffer state in eastern Siberia by fostering a pan-Mongol movement.[37]

The streets of the city were crowded with the uniforms of many nations. Czarist officers in brilliant epaulets and sabers paraded down Svetlanskaya, the main drag. The post office, the railroad station, the utilities: all were under their control.

General Graves knew that President Wilson was intensely interested in the fate of the Czechs, and sent his men along the railroad tracks to supply them and to guard culverts and bridges. He wanted nothing to do with the French and British efforts to restore the Eastern Front and, consequently, was seen by their officers as uncooperative.[38]

———

On September 15, 1918, to prepare public opinion for the dispatch of American troops to Russia, President Wilson authorized the publication of the Sisson documents. He told Colonel House on September 24 that their release meant "a virtual declaration of war on the Bolshevik government."

The documents were given to the press in installments and made the headlines that Sisson had been hoping for, such as "Lenin Exposed as German Spy." The next day Henry Alsberg, an editor of the *New York Evening Post*, claimed they were forgeries. Alsberg's source was a Finn named Santeri Nuorteva, who was soon unmasked as a Bolshevik agent and went back to Russia. The mainstream press accepted the documents as genuine.[39]

George Creel and his Committee on Public Information had gone to great lengths to check the ink, the paper, and the typefaces of the Sisson documents and pronounced them incontrovertibly genuine. In addition, prior to publishing them in October as No. 20 of his War Information pamphlets under the title *The German Bolshevik Conspiracy*, Creel had the documents examined by two eminent historians on the National Board for Historical Service: J. Franklin Jameson, the longtime editor of the *American Historical Review*, and Samuel N. Harper, a professor of Russian language and institutions at the University of Chicago. Although Jameson did not know Russian and could not read the documents, it took the professors only a week to come up with a 2,300-word report. The fifty-four documents dated after November, they had "no hesitation in declaring genuine." In the other documents, dated prior to the revolution, they saw "little that was doubtful."[40]

On September 19, 1918, a dispatch to the State Department from the U.S. ambassador in London, Walter Hines Page, related that the British War Office had received the same documents from one of its agents. The War Office, the Admiralty, and the Foreign Office had examined them and came to the conclusion that some were of a "doubtful character." The British postal censor found that the same typewriter had been used to type documents that ostensibly came from different sources. "The inference," Page concluded, "is that all or most of his [Sisson's] alleged output are forgeries."[41]

By this time, 137,000 copies of Creel's pamphlet had been distributed by his Committee on Public Information. Creel continued to vouch for the documents' authenticity. It would have been embarrassing for him to change his mind, since he had instructed Sisson to buy them.

President Wilson also believed they were genuine. After he had seen them in May, he hardened his stance toward the Bolsheviks and became more receptive to intervention in Russia. Since Wilson kept Sisson's original documents until his death in 1924, when they disappeared, the question of authenticity could not be resolved. It was not until 1955 that they turned up in the National Archives and that, in a June 1956 article in *The Journal of Modern History*, George Kennan was able to demonstrate that they were forgeries.

It was inconceivable, Kennan pointed out, that German officers would give away the names of their agents as they did in the documents—it was contrary to tradecraft. More damningly still, in the letters supposedly from German officers, written in excellent Russian, they inexplicably signed their names in Cyrillic characters.

A secret office of the German General Staff, Kennan went on, could not possibly have existed in wartime Petrograd, and in any case the seals on its purported letters were crude and obviously homemade. Finally, the signatures of well-known figures such as Trotsky bore no resemblance to their usual signatures. All the signatures were by the same hand.

Kennan's research showed that Semenov, the journalist who sold the documents to Sisson after being rebuffed by the Allied embassies, was a go-between for a more shadowy figure, Martynovich Ossendowsky, a professional purveyor of anti-German material and paid propagandist for Russian business circles. Kennan compared samples of Ossendowsky's handwriting with the signatures and the marginal notes in the documents and concluded that the similarity was "ubiquitous and convincing." He concluded that the Sisson documents "were unquestionably forgeries from beginning to end."[42]

Edgar Sisson could be said to be the first McCarthyite, just as Raymond Robins was the first fellow traveler. Caught up in the drama of the revolution and his anti-Bolshevik convictions, Sisson was gulled by clever conmen. He badly wanted to believe that the documents were genuine, so that he could come home with a sensational scoop that would discredit a regime he had come to detest. There was plenty of accurate information he could have used to denounce the Bolsheviks, but he did not stay in Russia long enough to collect it.[43]

By convincing Creel, who helped to convince Wilson, Sisson was able to have the documents published by a government agency, with the imprimatur of two distinguished historians, one of whom, Harper, later admitted that he was only trying to help the war effort. Sisson helped shape the President's Russian policy, which led to intervention and the first rollback operation to be conducted against the Soviet Union.

The nature of McCarthyism from Sisson onward was to make unsubstantiated charges, which ultimately invalidated the case of the person making them.

———

On November 11, 1918, the long agony of Europe ended when French and German delegations met in a railway carriage in the forest of Compiègne and signed an armistice. Kaiser Wilhelm abdicated and took refuge in Holland. Those soldiers who survived emerged from their trenches, and the others remained in their graves, marked and unmarked. Battlefields were turned into cemeteries, and Grave Registration became a military department.

The war was over and the doughboys went home—all, that is, but the stranded soldiers fighting a pocket war in Russia. In Archangel, four thousand Americans patrolled a sector three times the size of France with a population of 500,000. In the winter, it was so cold that the peasants had to build fires around the cows before they could milk them. Poole sent the men of the 339th hundreds of miles up the Dvina River in cattle barges. They crossed tundra, forests, and swamps waist-deep in mud, looking for Bolsheviks. In October, forty-eight American casualties left Archangel for London aboard the battle cruiser *Olympia,* before the harbor froze over. Also on board was Ambassador Francis, who departed from Russia to have his inflamed prostate operated on.[44]

On November 5, General Edmund Ironside, a six-foot-four, 270-pound behemoth known as "Tiny," replaced General Poole. This future chief of the Imperial General Staff was also the model for John Buchan's character Richard Hannay, an upper-class Englishman caught in a conspiracy in the classic thriller *The 39 Steps,* which became an equally classic Hitchcock movie.

Ironside established a fan-shaped defensive perimeter whose point was Archangel and whose crescent was two hundred miles south, with blockhouses at strategic spots. He did not, like his predecessor, yearn to advance deep into the Russian interior, which he said was like "pushing one's hand into a great sticky pudding."[45]

On November 11, a day of rejoicing on the Western Front, the men of the 339th, scattered along Ironside's perimeter, had nothing to celebrate. They knew that their fellow shavetails were going home, while their transports were frozen fast in the harbor and they were mired in the tundra. On that very day, three hundred Americans and a company of Royal Scots fought for their lives on the Dvina River at a hamlet called Tulgas, two hundred miles from Archangel. The Americans, stationed in trenches and log blockhouses, saw five hundred "Bolos," as they called the Reds, pour out of the woods. Their tactics were rudimentary—charge the enemy—but they learned more with each battle. Sergeant Silver Parrish recalled that "we licked the Bolo good and hard, but lost 7 killed and 14 wounded . . . the Bolo lost about 475 men."[46]

Archangel had been transformed into a boomtown teeming with British and American troops and anti-Bolshevik refugees, enlivened by a garrison-fueled black market economy. Sleigh taxis pulled by reindeer slid down the snow-covered streets, and recreation ranged from concerts and ballets to the more carnal pleasures of bathhouses and institutions like the Café de Paris, where the waitresses doubled as whores, ensuring a high rate of venereal disease among the men. Harold Weimeister of Ambulance Company 337 recalled that "the price of a piece of tail was a Hershey bar for all night."[47]

When the streetcar personnel went on strike, the men of Michigan's Own, some of whom were motormen and conductors in Detroit, manned the trolleys without collecting fares. The men in Archangel had it pretty good compared to those on the perimeter, who were harassed by marauding Reds—not to mention trench foot, rheumatism, scurvy, and frostbite. When Harold Weimeister took his ambulance sled to the blockhouses to pick up the sick and wounded, he was sent a note by one of the platoon leaders, Lieutenant Jeffers: "Private Okowski had his penis frozen during the attack on Kotlas. Will you please look him over?"[48]

While these young draftees were subjected to combat and Arctic indignities, peace negotiations were being conducted in tapestried halls and paneled rooms, interrupted by six-course champagne lunches. Among the dignitaries who gathered at the Paris conference in December 1918 was Boris Bakhmeteff, who had been given permission by his State Department handlers to attend and lobby the anti-Bolshevik cause. He was the only Russian represented.[49]

The Germans, who had surrendered, had no say in framing the peace. Nor did the Russians, mired in civil war, which made the survival of the Bolshevik regime uncertain. The absence of these two belligerents would come back to haunt the men of Versailles. Wilson and Lloyd George had both hoped that there would be a Russian representative. As Lloyd George wrote in *The Truth About the Peace Treaties:* "Personally I would have dealt with the Soviets as the de facto government of Russia. So would President Wilson. But we both agreed that we could not carry to that extent our colleagues at the Congress"—by whom he meant French Premier Georges Clemenceau, who felt that Russia had betrayed France by signing a separate peace and was not a fit partner in the talks.[50]

In January 1919, Winston Churchill, the implacable foe of Bolshevism, was named Secretary of State for War in Lloyd George's cabinet. In February,

Churchill came to Paris to persuade Wilson that the withdrawal of Allied troops "would be the destruction of all the non-Bolshevik armies in Russia." According to the minutes of the meeting of the Council of Ten on February 14, Wilson replied that "he himself felt guilty in that the United States had in Russia insufficient forces, but it was not possible to increase them. It was certainly a cruel dilemma. At present our soldiers were being killed in Russia, if they were removed many Russians might lose their lives. But some day or other the Allied troops would be withdrawn."

Wilson had lost his appetite for American intervention in Russia, and in the War Cabinet Churchill also found determined opposition to his views. Nonetheless, he continued to wage what became known as "Mr. Churchill's private war."[51]

On the Archangel defense perimeter, there were no champagne lunches, though the men had plenty of dry leaves and moss to roll cigarettes. In January 1919, the perimeter began to shrink as the Americans lost several positions. The Red forces were much improved in armament and tactics. On January 19, Lieutenant Mead and the forty-five men of the 4th platoon were at a forward position near the town of Shenkursk, on the Vaga River, two hundred miles south of Archangel, in one of those insignificant villages that would become place names in the regimental history. In their log blockhouse it was forty-five below zero. If you lost a mitten, your hand froze. If you touched your bayonet, the skin came off your fingers. Across the frozen Vaga, Lieutenant Mead saw puffs of smoke in the fir forest and realized they were coming from artillery emplacements hidden in the snow.

Hundreds of dark-clad Bolos waded through the snow under cover of the artillery barrage, holding their rifles chest-high. Three sides of the bunker were under fire. On one side a second wave of Bolos in white camouflage was only about two hundred yards away—they must have sneaked up in the night. One of his men, though shot through the jaw, fired his machine gun into the advancing Bolos, and, hit twice more, died as he fired. The Bolos charged with fixed bayonets as Lieutenant Mead tried to exit the bunker. A Bolo lunged at him and the bayonet missed him by an inch. Lieutenant Mead emptied his automatic into the white-clad figure and found a cluster of his men. He ordered a retreat through waist-deep snow to fortified positions eight hundred yards away. In the few minutes it took to cross the valley, twenty-five of his men were killed. Of his forty-five-man unit only seven survived.[52]

Now, as Sergeant Gordon Smith put it, "we are no longer fighting for the Russian people. We are fighting to save our own hides." Weeks went by without a shot being fired, and then suddenly there was an attack—the Bolsheviks were using ski troops and cavalry. American morale was sagging. It was the dead of winter, with complete darkness from noon until 9:00 A.M. the next day. The Bolos dropped leaflets designed to appeal to the union men in the 339th, taunting them with the "Shame of being a Scab." Sergeant Silver Parrish, a veteran of Tulgas, protested so often about being there that he was dubbed the Bolo platoon leader. In March there was a rash of self-inflicted wounds and one suicide; a number of men died of exposure. Finally, there was a state of near-mutiny when four men from Company B sent an ultimatum to Colonel Stewart, the regimental commander, saying that after March 15 they would refuse to advance on the Bolo lines since "the interests and honor of the United States of America are not at stake and we have no quarrel with the Russian people." Normally they would have been court-martialed, but the affair was forgotten as the ice in the harbor began breaking up and everyone sensed that it was time to go home.[53]

Protests in Michigan and Wisconsin had stepped up and Senator Charles E. Townsend of Michigan was getting a lot of mail. In the House of Representatives, a young member from New York, Fiorello La Guardia, called for the return of the troops. On June 1, 1919, the American consul in Archangel, Felix Cole, warned Lansing that "every foreign invasion that has gone deep into Russia has been swallowed up."

President Wilson finally realized that the intervention in Archangel had accomplished nothing except arouse the hostility of the Soviet regime and fuel isolationism at home. He decided to withdraw the troops, who had by then been there ten months. They sailed home at last in June and July.

The total American casualties for this futile expedition were about four hundred dead, but only eighty-six bodies were recovered and shipped back to the States in caskets. In Detroit's White Chapel Memorial Park, there is a plot with eighty-six markers where the fallen men of the 339th lie in close formation. Above them hovers a Polar Bear monument with an inscription quoting the naval officer Stephen Decatur: "Our country, right or wrong in her intercourse with foreign nations."[54] For the British, who by then had eighteen-thousand troops there, the evacuation of Murmansk and Archangel was a major undertaking, covered by rear-guard actions. The withdrawal took place from August until mid-October 1919.[55]

———

In Siberia, unlike Archangel, where American troops were placed under British command, General Graves kept the command of his men and refused to let them be used for any mission other than the one specified in his instructions: to help the Czechs. This did nothing to improve his relations with his more aggressive British counterparts, especially the obnoxious General Knox. Graves had his men occupy strategic points along the railroad as far as 125 miles from Vladivostok. They lived in boxcars and improved their rations by catching salmon in the rivers. After the November 11 armistice he pulled them back for garrison duty.[56]

Admiral Alexander Kolchak, commander of the Russian fleet in the Black Sea under the Czar, refused to serve under the Bolsheviks and fled to Omsk, a major city on the Trans-Siberian, poised almost midway between Moscow and Vladivostok. He was named War Minister in the anti-Bolshevik government that had formed there with the help of the Czechs. On November 18, 1918, he staged a coup and modestly proclaimed himself Supreme Ruler of All Russia. General Knox was a moving spirit of the coup and his two British battalions marched around Omsk as if they were at Buckingham Palace. Kolchak surrounded himself with czarist officers who vowed to restore the monarchy. Churchill saw Kolchak as the savior of Russia and sent him rifles and munitions. He also wanted the Prime Minister to recognize the Kolchak government, but Lloyd George and others in the cabinet thought that was extremely unwise.[57] In early December 1918, Ernest L. Harris, the American consul in Irkutsk, also on the Trans-Siberian, about 1,200 miles west of Vladivostok, recommended that the Wilson administration back Kolchak. Lansing, still on the lookout for a Russian strong man, was receptive. He wanted to send Kolchak a wide range of supplies, from boots and rifles to locomotives. On March 22, 1919, while Wilson and his Secretary of State were at the peace conference in Paris, the State Department asked the Paris embassy to buy $150,000 worth of spare parts for forty thousand rifles.

On June 27, Frank Polk told the House Committee on Expenditures in the State Department that "between $25 and $30 million worth of supplies had been shipped to Russia during recent months." On that same day in the Senate a resolution was voted to ask the President to give reasons why U.S. troops should remain in Siberia. They were told the troops were there to maintain the Trans-Siberian as "an artery of trade."[58]

In Vladivostok, General Graves did not share his government's enthusiasm for Kolchak, whom he saw as a petty tyrant. Kolchak's officers wore epaulets, the symbol of a reviled regime, and when farmers fled their homes to escape forced conscription, his men set fire to the villages and beat the women. Graves refused to back any faction: they were all, other than the Czechs, equally abhorrent.[59]

The War Department and Newton Baker backed Graves's policy of restraint, but the State Department complained about his "rigid and aloof neutrality," and said he was lacking in "large experience in affairs."[60]

Traveling up and down the Trans-Siberian, Graves often came through

Omsk in the summer of 1919, and saw that Kolchak's boast of victories was a sham. On August 7, Graves cabled the War Department that Kolchak's demoralized troops had pulled back to the Ishim River, only 225 miles west of Omsk. In September, Graves saw Kolchak's army actually melt away as its men deserted, taking with them the carts and horses they had stolen from peasants. On September 16, Graves received a shipment of rifles for Kolchak, but refused to turn them over, following an incident where his Cossacks had arrested and whipped an American corporal. Washington insisted and Kolchak got his rifles. A State Department man said the incident "ought to cost the general his head."[61]

———

When Wilson returned from Paris in July 1919, he presented his plan for the League of Nations to the Senate, asking: "Dare we reject it and break the heart of the world?" To which the Republican majority responded with a hearty "Yes!" In September, Wilson set forth on a crusade on behalf of the treaty and the League, traveling by train across the country. To underline the need for collective security, he hardened his position toward the Bolsheviks. In Des Moines on September 6 he told his audience that the "poison had spread" and some "of that poison has got inside the veins of a free people. . . . That sort of revolution means government by terror, government by force, not government by vote. It is the negation of everything that is American."[62] Wilson was concerned about the inroads of Bolshevism on American soil.

Another speaker in Des Moines that September, the Republican senator from California, Hiram Johnson, got an ovation when he rebutted Wilson, saying that "Bolshevism is born in the bosoms of the women whose sons were drafted for a war with Germany and who were sent across the water to be shot in Siberia." Wilson's incursions in Russia worked against him in the postwar climate of isolationism. The League of Nations, which Wilson had succeeded in making a part of the Paris peace treaties, was seen as committing the United States to continued meddling in the affairs of Europe. As Johnson put it: "I am opposed to American boys policing Europe and quelling riots in every new nation's back yard."[63]

Besides Johnson, Progressive leaders Robert La Follette of Wisconsin and William E. Borah of Idaho castigated Wilson for conducting an undeclared war against Russia. In the House, Speaker Champ Clark of Missouri and Ernest Lundeen of Minnesota called for the return of the troops. The Kansas newsman William Allen White spoke for the Midwest when he wrote in October 1919: "Let the thing fry in its own grease . . . the trouble with Russia is Russia."[64]

The strain of his cross-country train trip was too much for Wilson. After giving thirty-four major speeches, he collapsed in Colorado on September 25. On October 2, he suffered a stroke that paralyzed the left side of his face and body and that may have affected his mind. In the near-helpless limbo of his seizure, Wilson was isolated from day-to-day affairs, which were conducted by a bedside cabinet consisting of his wife, Edith Bolling Galt Wilson, a headstrong Southerner with no grounding in foreign policy, assisted by the President's doctor, Cary Grayson, and his devoted aide, Joseph Tumulty. Some said that Edith had become the first woman President, scripting a flurry of edicts and deciding what was worthy of bringing to the President's attention.[65]

Wilson was unable to lead the fight for ratification of the treaty and the League, except to denounce all compromise. He told the Senate Democrats to vote against a watered-down treaty, and when the final vote came on March 19, 1920, forty-nine senators voted for ratification, falling short of the required two thirds. Of the thirty-five senators who voted against, twenty-three were Wilson Democrats. Thus the United States was kept out of the League of Nations by its principal sponsor. Wilson died in 1924, at the age of sixty-eight.[66]

———

In Siberia, General Graves could have told Hiram Johnson that it wasn't the Reds he was worried about, but the Whites and the warlords. In October 1919, he had to deliver fifty thousand rifles to Kolchak via the Trans-Siberian, but the Cossack chieftain Grigori Semenov would not let the Americans through unless he was given fifteen thousand rifles as the price of transit. Graves told his officer at the scene, Colonel Morrow, to shoot his way through if necessary, and Semenov let the men pass after a tense standoff. Graves informed the War Department that he would turn over no more weapons to "the worst criminals in Siberia." But the incident with Semenov led to repeated skirmishes. On January 9, 1920, the warlord's armored car fired at an American boxcar, killing one of Graves's men and wounding another. Colonel Morrow was astonished to find an American officer with Semenov, detached to him by Ernest Harris, the consul at Irkutsk. An angry Colonel Morrow told the officer: "Do you know what a murderer is? Do you know he has killed some of my men?" The officer replied: "Semenov is the only thing between civilization and Bolshevism." General Graves had the officer brought back to Vladivostok and shipped home.[67]

Omsk finally fell to the Bolsheviks in mid-November 1919, and Kolchak fled eastward to Irkutsk. By this time he had few friends. Even the Czechs were disenchanted by the brutality and corruption of his officers. On January 4,

1920, Kolchak was forced to leave Irkutsk and was captured by the Czechs. They turned him over to the Irkutsk authorities, who handed him over to the Bolsheviks, who shot him on February 6, 1920. His body was thrown into the Angara River.[68]

With Kolchak's demise and Wilson's paralysis, the American intervention in Siberia ended. Graves and his men left in March and April 1920. As they boarded their ships, a Japanese military band played "Hard Times Come Again No More." American casualties were 170 dead and fifty wounded. In his memoirs, Graves described the operation as a disaster, illegal and useless.

The Czechs sailed for home between May and September 1920, ten thousand a month on American troopships, via the Pacific Ocean and the Panama Canal. It can be said for the Czechs that throughout their three-year odyssey, they maintained their discipline and military effectiveness. They contributed to the overthrow of Soviet authority in a large portion of western Siberia. Theirs was a long voyage home, but at least they now had a country to call their own. The French and the British left too, and only the Japanese remained, until 1922, having failed to establish a buffer state.[69]

In the Soviet Union, these futile American operations continued to fester long after the last troops returned home. The Americans were accused of trying to smother the infant regime. They had invaded Russian soil and fought Russian troops. There was no doubt in Soviet minds that they would try again. That such a vast nation, overlapping Europe and Asia, would fear encirclement was a peculiar form of Russian paranoia, passed on down the generations from Lenin to Stalin.

On the fortieth anniversary of the November Revolution, in 1957, *Pravda* wrote: "For over three years the Soviet Republic was obliged to fight off the mad armed attack of the combined forces of the imperialist beasts of prey." When Nikita Khrushchev visited Hollywood in September 1959, he recalled that "America's armed intervention in Russia was the most unpleasant thing that had ever occurred in the relations between our two countries . . . our troops have never set foot on American soil, while your troops have set foot on Soviet soil."

The American incursions under Wilson were followed by a long period of nonrecognition, so that after 1920 there were no diplomats in Russia to collect data and it was difficult to obtain a dependable appraisal of the regime.

The truth did not come out regarding the regime's callous indifference to human suffering, and its brutalized and inflexible apparatchiks bred in revolution and civil war. *Liquidation* was a term much in use, *surveillance* another. As one historian put it, you need a great ideal to commit great crimes. It was only with the Khrushchev speech in 1956 that some of Stalin's crimes were revealed. And only in the last ten years, with the opening of the Soviet archives, have we had a fully documented account of the vast apparatus of repression.

As for American policy toward the Soviet Union, Wilson established the paradoxical precedent that in a democracy, the President must act covertly to escape the scrutiny of Congress and the press. It was a precedent that would be repeated with a vengeance under post–World War II Presidents, even as the McCarthyites clamored that they were soft on Communism.

III

RED SCARE
AND SCARY REDS

The Bureau of Investigation was formed as a separate unit of the Justice Department in 1908, to investigate federal crimes, such as antitrust cases, crimes on government land, and bankruptcy fraud. Until 1908, the Justice Department had no detectives of its own and had to borrow them, when needed, from the Treasury Department's Secret Service. Charles Joseph Bonaparte, who was Attorney General under President Theodore Roosevelt, went before the House Appropriations Committee on April 2, 1908, to ask for a small investigative force for the bureau. But his request was denied by a Congress that considered a federal detective service a form of Big Brotherism, contrary to democratic principles. George E. Waldo of New York was one of many congressmen who denounced the idea, saying it would be "a great central secret-service bureau such as there is in Russia," which was then still under the czars.[1]

With the blessing of President Roosevelt, and with Congress in recess, Bonaparte in July hired a small force of full-time investigators in spite of congressional opposition. In February 1909, a month before a new administration came in under William Howard Taft, Bonaparte once again faced a hostile House Appropriations Committee. Michael Driscoll of New York feared that "a man who is a detective . . . cannot be a man of high moral ideals. . . . Of necessity they must and do live lives of deception."

Bonaparte promised to keep tight control over his detectives. In any case, Taft was inaugurated in March and named a new Attorney General, George W. Wickersham. The Bureau of Investigation was now in business and its scope was extended as Congress passed new laws such as the Mann Act in 1910, which prohibited the transportation of women across state lines for immoral purposes.[2]

The war brought another boost to the bureau's activities, to which were added antiwar agitation among radicals and rounding up draft dodgers, who were shipped to Army camps. The great wave of immigration in the 1880s from Eastern Europe and Italy had made the labor movement more militant, and aliens were regarded as incipient subversives.

Sweeping wartime measures, such as the Espionage and Sedition Acts, laid the basis for the prosecution of antiwar elements like anarchists and Wobblies (Industrial Workers of the World). By 1916, the bureau had expanded from one hundred to three hundred agents. President Woodrow Wilson warned in April 1917 that there was not only a war in Europe but one at home against "a lawless and malignant few." Wilson called the Wobblies "a menace to organized society."[3]

Founded in Chicago in 1905, the Wobblies recruited unskilled immigrants, outcasts shunned by the American Federation of Labor, and vowed to seize the factories and abolish capitalism. They took hold in the rural West among loggers, construction workers, and agricultural laborers, the "harvest stiffs." The question was how to prosecute them: there were no laws on the books to deal with a legitimate labor union. The Bureau of Investigation took over the assignment and sent an agent to the West Coast in 1915, who found that in the states of California and Washington they numbered around four thousand, mostly "panhandlers without homes, mostly foreigners, the discontented and unemployed, who are not anxious to work."[4]

President Wilson declared war on April 6, 1917, and the April 14 issue of the *Industrial Worker* ran the following:

> *I love my flag, I do, I do,*
> *Which floats upon the breeze,*
> *I also love my arms and legs,*
> *And neck, and nose, and knees.*
> *One little shell might spoil them all*
> *Or give them such a twist,*
> *They would be of no use to me,*
> *I guess I won't enlist.*

In the summer of 1917, as George Creel was beating the drum for 200 percent Americanism, the Wobblies peaked at sixty thousand members and staged wildcat strikes in the copper mines of Arizona, in the lumber mills of

Washington, in the mines of Montana, and in the iron range of Minnesota. These were crucial war industries; the strikes threatened to cripple shipbuilding and airplane production—not to mention that a shortage of wooden boxes could tie up the Pacific Northwest fruit harvest. The Wobblies were seen as public enemies hampering the war effort.

Attorney General Thomas W. Gregory ordered an all-out campaign to break the strikes. On September 5, 1917, Bureau of Investigation agents raided sixty-four Wobbly headquarters, seizing their files and arresting hundreds in Chicago, Sacramento, Wichita, and Omaha, of whom 166 were indicted for violating the Espionage Act. This was the first Justice Department experiment in a massive, multicity raid, designed to cripple an organization by subjecting its leaders to costly and protracted court proceedings.

With the Wobbly raid, the Bureau of Investigation was transformed from an agency that looked into antitrust cases into one that was responsible for the internal security of the nation.[5] In 1935, it added the prefix "Federal" to its name, as the symbol of a greater autonomy.

—

In the final quarter of the nineteenth century, the anarchist movement, founded on the belief that government is both harmful and unnecessary, spread to half a dozen European countries. The Italian branch of the movement developed the theory of "the insurrectionary deed," advocating the assassination of heads of state, in the futile hope of weakening the structure of authority. These Italian anarchists tallied up quite a score between 1894 and 1900: President Sadi Carnot of France, murdered in Lyons in 1894 while attending a trade fair; Prime Minister Antonio Cánovas del Castillo of Spain in 1897; the beautiful Empress Elizabeth of Austria, on a visit to Switzerland in 1898; and King Umberto I of Italy in 1900.

In America, the anarchists took advantage of the open-door policy and arrived in droves with the intention of creating havoc. In a land where free speech was protected, they were allowed to advocate murder and publish their bomb-making manuals.[6]

On September 6, 1901, President William McKinley was inaugurating the Pan-American Exposition in Buffalo on the theme of a century of progress in the New World. He gave his speech in the fair's Temple of Music, and was standing around shaking hands when he was approached by the twenty-eight-year-old Polish-born Leon Czolgosz, who shot him in the chest and stomach at point-blank range with a gun covered by a handkerchief. Among the military guards near the President, one acted swiftly, diving at Czolgosz and bringing him to the floor. As the guards beat the assassin with rifles and clubs, the mortally wounded, semiconscious President said: "Go easy on him, boys." McKinley died on September 15. Czolgosz went on trial on September 23, was sentenced to die on September 26, and was electrocuted on October 29. When Presidents were murdered, justice was swift. There were no last-minute stays of execution.[7]

Congress, however, was another matter. A year and a half later, on March 3, 1903, the lawmakers enacted an immigration law that excluded "anarchists or persons who believe in or advocate the overthrow by force of the government of the United States, or the assassination of public officials." This was the first time that much debated phrase, "advocating the overthrow of the government by force," was used. Congress was not acting arbitrarily, but in direct response to the planned violence of a lawless sect.[8]

An anarchist diaspora, ejected from Italy and mingling with the flood of new immigrants of the period, arrived in America and took root in cities like New York, Chicago, Boston, Philadelphia, Pittsburgh, and Cleveland. They constituted an anti-clerical, anti-government, and anti-capitalist subculture, and displayed a fondness bordering on vanity for proclaiming their convictions in small Italian language newspapers with dramatic titles such as *Il Grido Degli Opressi* (The Cry of the Oppressed).

The most prominent anarchist in America was Luigi Galleani, who looked like a turn-of-the-century opera singer, with his Borsalino, his cane, his drooping mustache, and his habit of posturing, Napoleon-like, with his hand inside his jacket. For Galleani, America was truly the land of opportunity, where an open and lenient society had welcomed an army of immigrant workers looking for a fair shake.

On the prowl for disruptions that he could aggravate, Galleani in 1902 fastened on the Paterson, New Jersey, silk workers strike. When he took to the podium to tell the strikers that they must free themselves from capitalist oppression, he was indicted for inciting a riot. He fled to Barre, Vermont, which had a cell of anarchist stonecutters from Carrara working in the quarries. It was there that in 1903 he launched *Cronaca Sovversiva,* which became the most widely read anarchist journal. Galleani was a natural leader, a gifted speaker who could make the outrageous seem reasonable.

Where else in the world but America could he have preached bomb throwing and assassination with impunity? In 1905 he published a forty-six-page manual on how to make bombs, priced at 25 cents, which knowledgeable anarchists refrained from using: it contained incorrect instructions that could prove fatal. By the time he moved to Lynn, Massachusetts, in 1912, Galleani had thousands of followers—quarry workers in Barre, silk workers in Paterson, shoe workers in Lynn (among them Nicola Sacco), fishermen on Cape

Cod (among them Bartolomeo Vanzetti), cigar workers in Tampa, coal miners in Pennsylvania, machinists in Detroit. *Cronaca* had a circulation of five thousand. Galleani was revered by his disciples, who called themselves Galleanists.[9]

In New York City, the bombs started exploding in 1914. On July 4, an explosion in a tenement on Lexington Avenue between 103rd and 104th streets killed three anarchists who were making a bomb (perhaps with Galleani's manual). It was intended to blow up John D. Rockefeller's Tarrytown estate, in the vicinity of which a fourth member of the group was arrested. On October 13, a bomb exploded inside St. Patrick's Cathedral (minor damage). A third was found and defused on November 14 at the Tombs prison police court, under the seat of Judge A. L. Campbell, who had sentenced some anarchists to prison terms.[10]

And New York was not alone. On September 25, 1916, three anarchist leaders were arrested in Boston during an antiwar demonstration. Animated by a tit-for-tat spirit of vendetta, the anarchists exploded a bomb on December 17 at the Salutation Street station of the Boston harbor police.

One year later, on September 9, the pastor of an Italian church in Milwaukee held an open-air loyalty rally in a park. The crowd was singing "America" when a band of anarchists rushed the dais and tore down the flag. The police charged in and after an exchange of gunfire, eleven anarchists were arrested.

Mario Buda, the Boston-based apostle of "direct action" known as Nasone (Big Nose), vowed revenge. In Chicago, the anarchist hub in the Midwest, he picked a team led by his fellow Galleanist Carlo Valdinoci to carry out the reprisal. On November 24, a foot-long pipe bomb was placed in the basement of the Italian pastor's church. It was found by the cleaning woman's eleven-year-old daughter and removed to police headquarters. Detectives were handling the bomb when it went off, killing ten of them, as well as a woman who was filing a robbery complaint.

The eleven anarchists arrested at the open-air meeting went on trial the day after the burial of the ten detectives. Some observers felt that they were on trial as much for the explosion as for the gunfight at the rally. The jury deliberated for seventeen minutes before bringing in a verdict of guilty for all eleven. Judge A. C. Backus sentenced them to twenty-five years in the Waupin state penitentiary. "You have said that the American flag is a rag," he observed, "the president ready to be killed, America a jail, the church to be destroyed. . . . All of you are aliens, in this country but a few years. . . . You are not a creative or a constructive force. Your purposes are destructive and ruinous."[11]

The cycle of revenge continued. Valdinoci, the publisher of *Cronaca*, decided to plant a bomb in the Milwaukee home of the prosecutor. He knew an eighteen-year-old girl from New Britain, Connecticut, Gabriella Antolini, known as Ella, who at the age of sixteen had married an anarchist factory hand, August Segata. Both were devoted Galleanists. He summoned her to Youngstown, Ohio, and she agreed to take a black leather grip packed with dynamite to Chicago. At eighteen, Ella still looked like a child, small and slim and fair-skinned, with blue-green eyes and bangs. She was about as far from the stereotype of the wild-eyed anarchist as you could get. But when Valdinoci saw her off on the train, on January 17, 1918, they both seemed nervous and the porter became suspicious. When Ella left her compartment, he examined the contents of her grip—thirty-six sticks of dynamite wrapped in paper and a .32 caliber Colt automatic. The porter alerted the conductor, who telegraphed ahead to Chicago. On arrival, Gabriella Segata was arrested and turned over to federal authorities. She went on trial on October 21, 1918, pleaded guilty to illegal possession of dynamite, and was sentenced to eighteen months and a $2,000 fine. The case was then turned over to an agent for the Bureau of Investigation, Rayme W. Finch.[12]

Tall and stocky, with dark hair combed back and a mustache, Finch was a resourceful gumshoe. He went to Youngstown on January 22, 1918, to work the leads provided by landladies. He was told about an Italian bricklayer, Giovanni Scussel, who lived in one boarding house but picked up his mail at another. Finch went to Scussel's Woodland Avenue address in the evening when he would be home from work. Surprised to find a bureau agent at his door, Scussel allowed him to search the room. Finch found a copy of Galleani's handbook on dynamite, as well as a brand-new .38-caliber Smith & Wesson revolver, with a cartridge belt and a holster. It was clear that Scussel was connected to Galleani. Finch went to New York to urge Bruce Bielaski, the bureau chief, to launch another inquiry into the *Cronaca Sovversiva*.

In Boston, Finch learned that although *Cronaca* was banned from the mails, it was being distributed across the country by American Express. He also learned that the paper's publisher was the same Valdinoci who had been in Youngstown. On February 22, 1918, Finch led a second raid on *Cronaca* in Lynn, Massachusetts, with a team of BI agents and local police. As luck would have it, the latest issue was in the office, bundled and ready for shipping. Finch obtained from the labels the names and addresses of three thousand subscribers. Anthony Caminetti, the Commissioner General of Immigration in Washington, noted that they now knew "the activities and whereabouts of a large number of leading anarchists in the country, whom it is desired to take into custody."[13]

After the raid, the Bureau of Immigration issued about one hundred warrants for deportation under the February 1917 immigration law. The law specified that any alien teaching anarchy, the overthrow of the government by force, the destruction of property, or the assassination of public officials could be deported. Aimed at Wobblies and anarchists, it created a class of deportable aliens.

Finch led the roundup on May 15, 1918, when some eighty *Cronaca* activists were arrested. On May 16, Galleani himself was arrested. An order of deportation had already been recommended, but in August, Caminetti ruled that the evidence against him did not justify such a severe measure. Galleani had five children living in America and his distinguished bearing impressed the immigration inspectors.[14]

Cronaca was outlawed on July 18. Galleani secretly shipped the presses to Providence and put out two more issues in March and May 1919. That June, he was rearrested with eight of his disciples, whom the Immigration Bureau considered "among the most dangerous aliens yet found within this country." All nine were transferred to Ellis Island and on June 24 they were deported to Italy. The fifty-eight-year-old Galleani, who had lived in America for eighteen years, left behind his wife and children, and never returned.[15] Although he never committed a murder, Galleani was the instigator and chief terrorist, much as Osama bin Laden is today, but he was never sentenced to a prison term in the United States.

Until June 1940, the Bureau of Immigration was a branch of the Department of Labor, since immigrants were mostly workingmen. Thus, a warrant to arrest an alien liable for deportation had to be signed by the Secretary of Labor, but the arrest itself was carried out by the Justice Department's Bureau of Investigation, which detained and questioned the alien to obtain a confession and gather evidence. The matter of whether or not the alien should be allowed to have an attorney present was determined by the Department of Labor. The deportation hearing was conducted by immigration inspectors and the actual deportation came only after an order signed by the Secretary of Labor.[16]

In spite of this bifurcated procedure, deportation became the instrument of choice for getting rid of undesirable aliens. It was preferable by far to criminal indictments and long trials with longer appeals. The alien was given a hearing, and if found deportable, the Secretary of Labor's decision was final. According to a bill passed in 1919, it didn't matter whether the alien had an American wife and ten American children, or whether he'd lived in America for forty years. To civil libertarians, deportation was a veiled and unjust punishment. Zechariah Chafee of the Harvard Law School said it conjured up an *Alice in Wonderland* situation: "I'll be the judge, I'll be the jury, I'll try the whole case and condemn you to death." But the Department of Justice saw it as the best way to avoid the snail's pace of the courts, a simple and effective method of getting rid of violent agitators.[17]

———

In mid-January 1919, Captain Harry S. Truman of the 129th Field Artillery wrote his sweetheart Bess Wallace from "a dirty little old French village": "It's my opinion we'll stay here until Woodie gets his pet peace plans refused or okayed. For my part, and I'm sure every AEF [Allied Expeditionary Force] man feels the same way, I don't give a whoop (to put it mildly) whether there's a League of Nations or whether Russia has a Red government or a Purple one, and if the president of the Czecho-Slovaks wants to pry the throne out from under the King of Bohemia, let him pry but send us home. . . . For my part I've had enough vin rouge and frogeater victuals to last me a lifetime." The future President's homesickness was tinged with a palpable urge to escape the troubles of Europe and return to a tranquil and uncomplicated America.[18]

But postwar America was not quite the same. Along with the relief that came with peace and the lifting of wartime constraints there was a sense of unease, a fear that something malignant and foreign was contaminating the nation. It derived not only from the doctrinaire violence of the anarchists and the disruptive tactics of the Wobblies, but from the Bolshevik example in Russia, where a tiny party had seized power, overthrown the government, and instituted a reign of terror. Bolshevism had spread to Germany and Hungary. Could the same thing happen in America? There was a transfer of repugnance from the war-mongering Germans, who had raped nuns and butchered Belgian children, to the atheistic Bolsheviks, who murdered priests.

The first evidence of this mutation came in January 1919 in Seattle, which the *New York Times* called "the hot-bed of IWW insurrection on the Pacific coast." The war had made Seattle an industrial city, employing 35,000 workers in its shipyards, who turned out one in four ships built in the United States from 1914 to 1918. Once the war was over, the state legislature passed antiunion laws. Radical leaders were jailed and police broke up demonstrations that cheered the Russian Revolution. On January 21, 25,000 shipyard workers walked off the job. In a test of labor's postwar power, the Seattle workforce planned a general strike, which to some seemed comparable to the Bolshevik insurrections in Germany and Hungary, spawned by events in Russia.[19]

On February 6, 1919, all the unions went along, shutting down the city in the nation's first general strike. More than 100,000 men and women struck or were idled. The house painters stopped painting, the barbers stopped barbering, the teachers stopped teaching, truck drivers stopped trucking, waitresses stopped waitressing, and newspapers stopped publishing. Their slogan—"Together We Win for Better Economic Conditions"—was pretty tame, but public officials waved the red shirt. Mayor Ole Hanson saw a repetition of the Ten Days That Shook the World and said that "the sympathetic revolution was called in the exact manner as was the revolution in Petrograd." Washington Congressman Royal Johnson said the strike leaders included "a great array of Sloviniskis and Ivan Kerenskys and names of that sort." The normally thoughtful *Baltimore Sun* called the strike "an attempted Bolshevik revolution." Mayor Hanson called out the Army and Newton Baker sent eight hundred troops into downtown Seattle, posting some in front of police stations with machine guns. The strike only lasted four days, but it was an effective display of worker solidarity. Hanson became a national hero and went on a lecture tour.[20]

———

In January 1919, Ludwig Christian Alexander Karlovich Martens arrived in New York as the Soviet representative to the United States and set up shop in Manhattan's World Tower Building at 110 West 40th Street. A short man with a high-pitched voice, close-cropped blond hair, and a toothbrush mustache, Martens was born in Russia of German parents. Educated as an engineer under the Czar, he became a revolutionary and was deported in 1902. He moved to England, where he learned the language.

His instructions from the Soviet Foreign Commissariat were to act "for the defense of the interests of the Soviet Republic and above all for the struggle against intervention and for commercial goals." The Wilson administration ignored him and continued to recognize Boris Bakhmeteff and his ghostly embassy. The purposeful Martens launched operations on several fronts: to convince American firms to trade with the Soviets, to promote anti-intervention propaganda, and to discredit Boris Bakhmeteff.[21]

Martens lost no time in obtaining some of Bakhmeteff's correspondence. "As you probably already know," he reported to Moscow on January 29, 1919, "the Bakhmeteff embassy with the permission of the American government" is printing Russian rubles and sending them "to Siberia and probably to European Russia for the financing of counter-revolution." Thanks to Martens's snooping, the Soviet government was alerted to President Wilson's covert use of the Bakhmeteff embassy to fund intervention in Russia. Martens told Moscow he had exposed this activity by distributing a press release that was picked up by American magazines such as *The Nation* and *The New Republic*.[22]

Martens obtained bills of shipping for munitions sent to Siberia, which showed that the U.S. government was behind Bakhmeteff's spending. In January 1920 he sent out another press release saying that "a large part of Russia's debt to the United States," particularly "the 187 million dollars which were given to Mr. Bakhmeteff, have been used by this man for purposes utterly hostile to Russia and in deliberate efforts to besmirch and to overthrow the Soviet government." Martens generated enough press attention to expose American funding of anti-Bolshevik elements in Russia.[23]

When members of Congress started asking questions about the status of his embassy, Bakhmeteff asked Frank Polk at the State Department on March 6, 1920, whether he should shut down operations. Polk assured him that the administration "was not embarrassed by his presence." Only in June 1922 did another congressional inquiry cause Bakhmeteff to close his embassy and return to private life. By this time, Warren Harding was President, the civil war in Russia was over, and Martens was gone.[24]

When Martens presented his credentials to the State Department in March 1919, saying that the Soviet Union wanted to buy large amounts of finished products, such as tractors and machine tools, he received no reply. Despite his cool reception, Martens reported to Moscow in April that he was besieged by offers from big American firms like Ford and Swift. On April 5 he wrote that "I am doing everything possible here in order to bring the necessary pressure to bear on Washington through industrial and banking circles" in order to improve relations. Martens claimed to have signed $20 million worth of deals with U.S. firms.[25]

On the propaganda front, Martens funneled accounts of Soviet achievements to radical publications such as *Class Struggle* and *Liberator*. He also published his own weekly, *Soviet Russia*, which refuted anti-Bolshevik tales like the one about free love and the recruitment of women for immoral purposes. As a wave of strikes spread across the nation, his appeals to workers were more successful, Martens said. He reported that dockworkers in Seattle and Baltimore had refused to load shipments of weapons to White forces.[26]

———

As Americans became aware that Bolshevism had migrated to their shores, the press took up the cry with its usual vigor. On November 1, 1919, *The Saturday Evening Post* said that the "Russo-German movement" was trying to "dominate America." The *Los Angeles Times* said that "Bolshevism is a right-here-now American menace and the sooner the American people wake up the quicker the problem will be solved." A clergyman called for the deportation of Bolsheviks "in ships of stone with sails of lead, with the wrath of God for a breeze and with hell for their first port."[27] Bolshevism was a word, a thing, as unfamiliar and as alarming as a new species of toxic mushrooms.

It took a pro-Soviet rally in the nation's capital in February 1919 to wake up Congress to this new threat. Poli's Theater in downtown Washington was showing a vaudeville revue starring Fred and Adele Astaire and a chorus of "100 Winter Garden Beauties." No matinee had been scheduled for Sunday February 2, when the League to Enforce Peace and Democracy rented the hall. By 2:00 P.M. the theater was packed with people who had come to hear "The Truth About the Soviet Union" from Albert Rhys Williams and Louise Bryant, both of whom had lived through the revolution. Ushers hawked the pamphlet *Six Months in Russia,* by the onetime minister turned Red. Louise Bryant, whose delicately lovely, vibrant-eyed face was shaded by a wide-brimmed hat, was married to John Reed. She had accompanied him to Russia and shared his uncritical admiration for the revolution. "America sooner or later is going to accept the Soviet government," Rhys Williams said. The audience erupted in shouts of "Hurrah for the Bolsheviki!" When Bryant condemned the United States for intervening in Soviet affairs she was met with a storm of applause, although a reporter said she expressed "a string of platitudes." The *New York Times* wrote that she was "a partisan of the fiercest sort."[28]

The next morning, having read the papers, members of Congress were up in arms. The Red rally was a topic of intense discussions. Many were the expressions of "grave concern." Senator Charles Thomas, a Colorado Democrat, told his colleagues that the speakers had advocated "virtual treason."[29] Senator Thomas J. Walsh of Montana urged that the subcommittee of the Judiciary Committee that was investigating German propaganda should look into the Bolsheviks as well. The subcommittee had been sitting since September 1918 to investigate pro-German brewery interests. Most senators, including the subcommittee chairman, Lee S. Overman, a sixty-five-year-old North Carolina Democrat, agreed with Walsh and his resolution to extend its scope to cover Bolshevik efforts "to incite the overthrow of the government . . . by force, or by destruction of life or property, or the general cessation of industry."[30]

Overman, who had been in the Senate since 1903, was a rural Southern conservative who wanted to restrict immigration to Anglo-Saxons and who did not look favorably upon "foreigners" advocating violent revolution. Sitting with him were fellow Democrats William King of Utah and Josiah O. Wolcott of Delaware, and Republicans Knute Nelson of Minnesota and Thomas Sterling of South Dakota.[31]

This was the first of many congressional investigations of Communism, which in 1919 was a brand-new topic. The senators reacted to what they heard sometimes naively and sometimes with consternation. They saw Bolshevism as obviously incompatible with American democracy and they earnestly sought to inform themselves. Over the years, congressional committees looking into Communism would be vilified for witch-hunting, and the Overman hearings were the first in which the term was used in that sense. Some of the members did not know what it meant, such was the degree of innocence at the time.

The Overman subcommittee hearing on Bolshevism opened on February 11, 1919, but prior to that, in a closed session, the senators heard Archibald Stevenson, a New York lawyer and former special agent in the Bureau of Investigation. As one of the few American experts in Bolshevik propaganda, he was said to be the only man in the country the radicals feared.

Stevenson said the Bolsheviks had already organized soviets in U.S. industrial centers and listed a number of Bolshevik publications: *Novy Mir* (in Russian), *The Workman, The Peasant.*

This was all new to the senators. "The idea, then," Overman asked, "is to form a government within this government and overthrow this government?"

Indeed it was, Stevenson assented. Overman also inquired about Soviet morals: "Do they have as many wives as they want?"

Stevenson: "In rotation."

Senator Nelson: "A man can marry and then get a divorce when he gets tired, and get another wife?"

Stevenson: "Precisely."

Major Edwin Lowry Humes, a member of the subcommittee research team: "They can renounce the marital bond at will?"

Stevenson: "Precisely."

Overman: "You think this movement is growing constantly in this country?"

Stevenson: "I think it is growing rather rapidly, if we can gauge it by the amount of literature that is distributed and the number of meetings held. . . . I conceive this to be the gravest menace today."[32]

Stevenson confirmed the senators in their belief that Bolshevism was immoral and already a threat to America. But the bulk of the testimony had nothing to do with Bolshevism in the United States, for Senator Overman in the open hearings decided to hear only from witnesses who had been present during the Russian Revolution. One of these was the commercial attaché at the American embassy, William Chapin Huntington, who told the senators what he had seen and heard on his travels from Petrograd to Irkutsk. "I have seen the complete overturn of all we know in our present life," he said, "and absolute chaos in all human relations . . . maintained by terror . . . the total lack of freedom. . . . Everyone was under orders. . . . Under the czars, the bargain was observed and the grease was standardized, while at present people take the money and turn on the donor."[33]

Then came Catherine Breshkovsky, the beloved "Grandmother of the Russian Revolution," who had been exiled for thirty-two years in Siberia under the Czars and returned to join the Kerensky government in 1917. It was to her that the copper magnate William Boyce Thompson had given $1 million to keep Russia in the war. When Kerensky fell, she became a sworn enemy of the Bolsheviks. And now this stooped woman with the wrinkled face who had spent half her life in exile told the senators: "We have simply gone from one form of despotism to another. It is not easy to change ancient forms. . . . So we came under [the rule of] two gendarmes, Lenin and Trotsky. . . . We are like mendicants now. . . . We need paper, we need scissors, we need matches, we need leather for boots. . . . Everywhere where the Bolsheviks are, there is not intelligence . . . they destroyed all the intelligent people, the best professors, the professional men, the best men we had. . . . A government now springs up controlled by brigands, like bubbles out of water."[34]

The senators were impressed by this aged woman who had defied both the Czar and the Bolsheviks. John Reed and Louise Bryant were not subpoenaed, but they asked to testify—they were eager to tell their side of the story. In addition, they both had books coming out, and may have thought the hearings would give them exposure. On February 20, when the husband and wife star witnesses took the stand, the hearing room was packed, half-partisan, half-patriot. The audience was so spirited, breaking out with cheers and hisses, that Overman had to clear the room.

Here at last were the bohemian revolutionaries, back from their appointment with history, the radical playboy, initiated into the class struggle by way of Mabel Dodge's Fifth Avenue Salon, and the willowy beauty who had been Eugene O'Neill's muse. There was almost too much colliding charisma between them. Reed, the big-boned, florid-faced man of action, and Bryant, headstrong and impulsive, doggedly unconventional, who had deserted her husband, an Oregon dentist, for a more exciting life.

Bryant testified first, and there was some question as to whether she could take the oath, since she insisted that she did not believe in Christ.

Senator Wolcott: "Do you believe in punishment hereafter and a reward for duty?"

Bryant: "It seems to me as if I were being tried for witchcraft."

Senator King interjected that to her an oath would be meaningless.

Bryant: "Very well, I will concede—I concede there is a hell . . ."

It was when the audience applauded her reply that Senator Overman had the room cleared.

". . . You see," she began, "I am the only witness who wants to bring about amicable relations between Russia and America." She explained that Bolshevism was "in a transitory state that is always necessary in establishing new governments. We had to do it. We had to disarm the Tories and we even shot some of our Tories." She insisted that "I have always spoken against the scare word we have made of Bolshevism. The Bolsheviks are Social Democrats."

This would have been news to Lenin, and it led Senator Nelson to observe that she was deluded. "Do you believe," he asked, "that the government should own all the land and that the tillers of the land should be nothing but tenants?"

Bryant: "You have just discovered Socialism."

The day ended with Bryant deploring that the *Washington Post* had called her "a female Trotsky," and that the senators' questions had "a rather cutting tone, a certain rough manner."

On February 21, Louise Bryant resumed her testimony and admitted to being a propagandist for the Bolsheviks.

Senator Overman said she seemed to want to make a martyr of herself. She sparred with the committee, saying it was one-sided and that Senator King had given her the third degree. "I do not think the Russians are such beasts and fanatics as many have tried to make out," she said.

Senator Josiah Wolcott noted an announcement by the Commissioner of the Interior, Litovsky, that not more than 13,700 had been shot on orders of the commission set up on January 1, 1918.

Bryant: "They do that in the south when they lynch people."[35]

For once, Senator Wolcott had no repartee.

Then it was Reed's turn. In Petrograd in 1917, he became an actor in the spectacle he had been sent to observe. The journalist turned evangelist, working in the Soviet Bureau of International Revolutionary Propaganda. After six months in Russia, Reed was back with his notes and his memories, working on *Ten Days That Shook the World*, which would be published in New York later that year.

Major Humes of the committee's research team asked him if he had said at a meeting in Yonkers the previous Sunday that in Russia three million workmen had three million rifles and that shortly there would be three million rifles in the hands of three million American workmen to be used in the same manner they had been used in Russia.

Reed: "I never said such a thing in my life. How foolish! How could you get three million rifles in the hands of three million American workmen?"

Wolcott: "You say that over there a man cannot employ anybody to work for him?"

Reed: "Not on the farms."

Wolcott: "The American farmer would like that."

Reed: "If a man does not work in Soviet Russia . . . he does not eat."

Wolcott: "That puts me in mind of where we had a communist system over here at Jamestown. Two or three did all the work, and the rest of the bunch were loafers, and Captain John Smith had to get a gun and go after them."

Reed pointed out that to spread out the workforce, the Russians had passed decrees for the forced migration of populations.

Major Humes: "The state requires them to emigrate to some new locality?"

Wolcott: "I live in Dover, Delaware, and suppose it got to be such a state of affairs that the community would say, 'Here Wolcott, you will have to get out. It is up to you to move.'"

Reed: "Well?"

Wolcott: "Well, there would be trouble. They would have to carry me out."

Here were five American senators face-to-face with Bolshevism, which they found incomprehensible. Nothing in their own upbringing, in a country where personal freedom was an article of faith, had prepared them for a system where the work a man did and the place where he lived were governed by the state. Russia was as strange to them as another planet, where the atmosphere is too thin to breathe.

On March 6, it was Raymond Robins's turn to testify. He introduced himself as a major in the Red Cross, stationed in Russia from July 1917 to June 1918 and assigned to food supply and refugees. He failed to mention that he had been the only American official after the revolution who maintained contact with Trotsky and Lenin, and that he had become an apologist for the regime. But his sympathies were revealed when he recounted a conversation with Lenin. "The Soviet will one day be in command in Berlin," Lenin told him. "Do you think America is immune? Your government is entirely corrupt. You elected men to your Congress on expansive ideas while in fact they are elected on hidden economic interests. Instead of having a lawyer for Mr. Gary or Mr. Schwab, you ought to have Mr. Gary and Mr. Schwab, the producers of steel, not the parasites. That is what we are doing. The Donetz coal basin will be represented by the producers of coal."

The senators, after listening to Lenin's attack on the institution to which they belonged, began proposing new laws to stop Bolshevism in America. Senator Overman called for a law to prevent the carrying of the red flag, while

Senator Nelson said that stopping the distribution of Red propaganda was a priority.

Robins told his audience that the way to get rid of Bolshevism was not by a witch-hunt but by educating the people of America. Senator Overman was not familiar with the term and asked what it meant.

Robins: "When people get frightened at things and see bogies, they then get out with proclamations and mob action and all kinds of hysteria takes place."

Overman observed that by Robins's definition, their committee had been called a witch-hunt in the left-wing press.

Begun on February 11, the hearings concluded on March 10, 1919, after the appearance of about twenty-five witnesses, most of whom had been present during the revolution. In their report, released in July, the senators revealed that they had been shocked by the horror stories they had heard. The Bolshevik government, said the report, had inaugurated a "reign of terror unparalleled in the history of modern civilization." In America, said the report, "parlor Bolsheviks" were still few, though some radicals were "fanning the flames of discontent." All this, however, meant little to the average American.

Congress took no immediate action: the events described by the subcommittee in faraway Russia seemed remote. There was so little interest in the report that the print run was cut from ten thousand to twenty-five hundred. Few then cared whether and how Bolshevism was spreading in the United States.[36]

———

Following the deportation law of October 1917, which had been used against Galleani, a leaflet was distributed in New England in February 1919 with the headline "Go-Head!" and the message: "Deport us! We will dynamite you." This was no bluff, but an announcement of coming events.

On the morning of April 28, 1919, a small package arrived in the mail for the mayor of Seattle, Ole Hanson, neatly wrapped in brown paper and postmarked New York City. The return address was Gimbel Brothers, at Broadway and 32nd Street. Stamped on the package in red letters were the words *sample* and *novelty*. Hanson was in Colorado giving a speech and the package was opened by a member of his staff, William Langer. Inside was a seven-inch-long cardboard box wrapped in green paper and inside the box was a homemade bomb consisting of a wooden cylinder fastened to a small bottle of acid. A coiled spring was positioned so that when the package was opened at the top end the spring would be released and break the bottle. The acid would ignite three fulminate of mercury caps (an explosive salt) resting on a stick of dynamite inside the cylinder. The dynamite was surrounded by metal slugs. Langer opened the box at the wrong end and the bottle of acid fell out. The bomb failed to go off and he called the police.

The next day, an identical package arrived at the Atlanta apartment of former Senator Thomas Hardwick, who, as chairman of the Committee on Immigration, had been co-sponsor of the 1917 deportation bill. Hardwick was not home, but his wife thought the package was a box of pencils and asked her black maid, Ethel Williams, to open it. Ethel dutifully unwrapped the package and it blew off her hands. Mrs. Hardwick was burned on the face and neck, and a metal slug cut her upper lip and loosened her front teeth.

Reading about the Hardwick bomb in the morning paper, Charles Kaplan, a clerk in the parcel post division of the New York General Post Office, remembered that he had set aside sixteen packages from Gimbel's for insufficient postage. He turned them over to the police—they were all bombs. Alarms to other city post offices found three more, addressed to senators Overman and King and to a special assistant in the Attorney General's office.[37]

About thirty bombs in all were sent out in that last week of April 1919, and not a single one harmed its intended victim.

Newspapers called the explosive mail "the most widespread assassination conspiracy in the history of the country." The boldness of the synchronized bombs, and the eminence of the targeted victims, who included Supreme Court Justice Oliver Wendell Holmes and John D. Rockefeller, sent waves of alarm through the public. One of the recipients, the outspoken Mayor Hanson, scathingly denounced federal policy toward radicals as "skim milk, weak and vacillating." He wanted Washington to "buck up and hang" all the anarchists. Faced with mounting criticism, the authorities marshaled a task force of investigators.[38]

In Washington on June 2, Attorney General A. Mitchell Palmer, who lived at 2132 R Street, was in his pajamas at 11:15, preparing for bed, when he heard something fall on the lawn below. Seconds later, the porch was ripped off his house, the windows were shattered, and Palmer was showered with broken glass. Uninjured, he walked down the stairs through the wreckage. Franklin Delano Roosevelt, then assistant secretary of the Navy, who lived across the street, went over to help and recalled that the Attorney General had lapsed into his childhood Quaker. "He was theeing me and thouing me all over the place—thank thee Franklin and all that."[39]

The bomber, probably mistaking the timing of the fuse, had blown himself up. Body parts were scattered all over the neighborhood. What seemed at first to be a finger in the street that could be used for prints turned out to be a toe. On the roof of a house on S Street was a piece of scalp with dark curly hair.

The police took the scalp to a French hairdresser, who boasted: "Show me a man's hair and I will tell you his nationality." The hairdresser proudly proclaimed that the scalp belonged to an Italian in his twenties. Also recovered were two handguns, remnants of a black imitation leather grip, an Italian-English dictionary, shreds of a black pinstripe suit, and a blue polka dot tie. In addition, fifty copies of the leaflet *Plain Words*, printed on pink paper and signed "The Anarchist Fighters," were found scattered around the neighborhood.[40]

The Bureau of Investigation agent assigned to the case, William J. West, eventually discovered that Carlo Valdinoci had purchased the Colt automatic recovered at the site. Valdinoci was a legend in anarchist circles for the number of actions he had carried out. Already indicted for his role in the Youngstown conspiracy, he was also sought on a deportation warrant, but escaped capture by hiding out in safe houses provided by the movement in the Boston area. Three years later, West located Valdinoci's sister Assunta in Millis, Massachusetts. Assunta said her brother usually stayed in touch, but that no one had heard from him in several years. She thought he might have gone to South America. Asked to describe him, she said he was "a tall young man, 27 or 28 years of age, clean shaven, with very black, curly hair." On November 9, 1922, West reported to the bureau that "the person killed in Washington D.C. on June 2, 1919, was Carlo Valdinoci." Although a piece of scalp could hardly be called conclusive evidence, nothing was heard from Valdinoci again.[41]

———

Archie Stevenson, the Bolshevik expert, was disappointed that the Overman Committee had called only witnesses who had been in Russia, and did not examine the extent of Bolshevik propaganda in the United States. He put together a report for the Union League Club, a conservative Republican outfit, which he showed to a fellow member, State Senator Clayton Lusk, another dedicated anti-Bolshevik who would later belong to a patriotic organization called the Paul Reveres.

Lusk decided to conduct hearings, which opened on June 12, 1919, at City Hall in Manhattan, and named Stevenson as assistant counsel. On that day, against the backdrop of the spring bombings, the committee asked federal agents and the state police to raid the office of the Soviet emissary, Martens. His files were collected, as well as two tons of propaganda leaflets. Martens's staff had by then grown to a total of thirty-five, including Arthur Adams, later identified as a Soviet spy specializing in technology theft, and Kenneth Durant, later head of the Soviet press agency TASS in America.[42] When he testified before the Lusk Committee, Martens admitted receiving $50,000 from the Soviet Union between March and June 1919. He also received donations from sympathetic Americans, he said. The raid dampened his hopes of success, and he reported on July 2 to G. V. Chicherin, of the People's Commission for Foreign Affairs, that the press was now conducting a "dirty campaign" against him. The vilification of the Soviet Union had taken on "unbelievable dimensions." New York State Attorney General Charles D. Newton, the chief counsel for the Lusk Committee, charged that the Martens bureau was the "clearing house" for all radical activity in the United States.[43]

―――

There is nothing like an assassination attempt to focus a man's thoughts, and on June 3, 1919, Attorney General Palmer invited a group of congressmen on a guided tour of his partly destroyed home. "The outrages of last night," he declared, "indicate nothing but the lawless attempt of an anarchist element to terrorize the country and stay the hand of government. . . . These attacks will only increase the activities of our crime-detecting forces." Palmer vowed to hunt down the bomb-throwing radicals who were slipping through the American sieve like minnows.[44]

A forty-seven-year-old Quaker pacifist and Democratic stalwart born in Moosehead, Pennsylvania, A. Mitchell Palmer had been on the job only since February, having been named by President Wilson as a reward for his faithful service. First elected to Congress in 1908, he had served three terms and built up an impressive record as a Wilson-directed legislative whip. By 1912, he was vice chairman of the Democratic National Committee. Because he was hardworking and as loyal as a basset hound, Wilson made him floor leader at the 1912 convention. Palmer helped Wilson win the nomination by swinging the Pennsylvania delegation over. His critics called him a party hack, but to Palmer that was a compliment. He was a classic machine politician who professed Quaker virtues while making backroom deals, an important-looking man, beefy-faced, homburg-wearing, cane-carrying and insufferably bombastic.[45]

In October 1917, when Wilson created the Office of the Alien Property Custodian, Palmer received his first recompense. In his new position, he had custody of some forty thousand firms and trusts, mainly German, worth a little under $1 billion. A year into his tenure, he had three hundred employees and a New York office. Francis P. Garvan, who disliked foreigners even though he was the son of a first-generation Irish contractor, was hired away from the

New York District Attorney's office to head an investigative branch responsible for hunting down German assets.

A great believer in the spoils system, Palmer used his office as a patronage hub, steering influential Democrats to lucrative jobs as lawyers for German companies. His mandate was to Americanize enemy assets, which he sold at private sales rather than at auctions, to prevent enemy agents from bidding. Not surprisingly, much of the enemy property was sold at bargain prices to Palmer's cronies.[46]

Palmer managed to sell six thousand German dye patents to the Chemical Foundation, a private company formed expressly to buy them. The president of the company was Francis Garvan, who had been Palmer's chief investigator and a member of the advisory committee that recommended the deal. By 1922, the Chemical Foundation had made $1 million on these patents. Harlan Fiske Stone, who was named Attorney General in 1924, only to begin a long and distinguished tenure on the Supreme Court a year later, sued the Chemical Foundation for a return of the patents. "Nothing in any oil transaction," he wrote a friend, "not even the acts of Albert B. Fall* has any more sinister aspect. You would hardly believe that such things could happen in our government." Palmer turned the Alien Property Custodian Office into a gigantic cookie jar that his cronies dipped into until the war ended and the office was abolished.[47]

After his house was bombed, with Congress clamoring that the radicals be hunted down, Palmer overhauled his department. On June 4, he brought in his pal Garvan as assistant attorney general in charge of the radical problem. William J. Flynn, formerly head of the Secret Service, was named the new head of the Bureau of Investigation. Though the bureau did not catch any bomb-throwers, it put out reassuring releases. June 6: "We are making progress." June 29: "Making slow but sure progress."[48]

On June 13, 1919, Palmer appeared before the House Appropriations Committee to ask for a $500,000 increase in his budget. He told the committee that Flynn, the new Bureau of Investigation chief, was "the great anarchist expert in the United States. He knows all the men of that class. He can pretty nearly call them by name." When Garvan went before the Senate Appropriations Committee a few days later, he encountered some skepticism. Senator Reed Smoot of Utah asked: "Do you think if we increased this to $2,000,000 you could discover one bomb-thrower—get just one? I do not mean in the papers. I mean actually get him."

---

* President Warren G. Harding's Secretary of the Interior, who went to prison for leasing government oil fields to cronies.

Garvan: "I can try. That is all I can say."

The half-million-dollar increase was granted.[49]

On June 17, 1919, Palmer held an all-day meeting with Garvan and Flynn to devise a new strategy of mass deportations. The following day, Palmer told the press that the recent bombings were part of a plot by "alien anarchists" to overthrow the government. "Those who cannot or will not live the life of Americans under our institutions," he added, ". . . should go back to the countries from which they came."[50]

———

On July 1, 1919, an up-and-coming twenty-four-year-old Justice Department lawyer was promoted special assistant to the Attorney General, reporting to Garvan. The name of this dumpy, pug-faced little fellow was John Edgar Hoover, and Palmer was the first of nineteen Attorneys General he would serve under in the course of his fifty-year career in the FBI.

Hoover was born in 1895 into that tribe of Washingtonians who are federal bureaucrats down the generations. He grew up in a society of civil servants as closed and regulated as a Hindu caste, where belonging conferred inside knowledge in the methods and maneuvers of gaining and keeping a government job, which separated the chosen from the untouchables. His father and grandfather both worked in the print shop of the U.S. Coast and Geodetic Survey, and his brother Dick worked for the Steamboat Inspection Service.[51] The practice then, which Hoover followed, was to get an entry-level job that would launch him in the civil service seniority chain, while taking law courses at night at George Washington University. At the age of eighteen, Hoover modestly began as a junior messenger in the Library of Congress, and soon moved up to the catalogue division, where he learned how to set up an index file. He passed his bar exam in 1917, and went to the Justice Department, which was then expanding due to the war, and where he would spend the rest of his life. He had an intuitive grasp of the stratagems and specifications required to rise in a large and sensitive government department.

In 1917, Hoover was assigned to the Alien Enemy Bureau, where he handled the case files of German aliens, writing reports on which ones to intern. He quickly became known as a young man willing to take responsibility, as he sent men and women twice his age behind barbed wire with a stroke of the pen. When an eighteen-year-old German was arrested in El Paso as he tried to enter the country, he said under questioning that he would help the Kaiser if he could. Hoover recommended detention for the duration. When another German, Otto Mueller, called President Wilson "a cock-sucker and a thief," Hoover again recommended internment, but Charles M. Storey, head of the Alien Enemy Bureau, ruled that "his offense is no more than a failure to keep his mouth shut, and I feel that internment for the war for mere talk is rather severe. Three or four months in jail will be equally effective."[52]

At the age of twenty-two, Hoover came across as a stern and finicky young fogey, who was already developing the fixed routine of an elderly bachelor, living at home with his widowed mother, and devoting himself to his work to the exclusion of a social life. After the Armistice, when Palmer was focusing on radicals, the Alien Enemy Bureau was shut down, and one third of Bureau of Investigation agents were assigned to anti-radical work. On August 1, 1919, Hoover was made the head of the anti-radical division, which he renamed the General Intelligence Division. This soon became the largest section of the bureau. He had been chosen because of his experience in tracking down undesirable Germans. Despite his youth, his zeal and moral certainty inspired trust.[53]

A *New York Times* editorial on October 17, 1919, chided Palmer for leniency "when all over the country, alien or foreign-born agitators are carrying on in many languages, in 500 or more papers and magazines, the Bolshevist and IWW propaganda for the overthrow of the government." Ultimatums came from both houses of Congress and public opinion demanded retribution. The Attorney General was expected to act forcefully. Indeed, he wanted to act, for he believed that 90 percent of the Reds were aliens. At the same time he had one eye on the presidency in 1920, now that Wilson had suffered a stroke. He could build up political capital with a vigorous anti-alien sweep.[54]

It was in the summer of 1919 that the shrewdly ambitious Hoover sniffed the direction of the wind and positioned himself as an intransigent anti-Communist. He began looking for radical organizations to raid, but he was ahead of his quarry. There was no Communist Party as yet, and the anarchists did not keep membership lists. He had to settle for the Union of Russian Workers, which had about four thousand members in some dozen industrial cities. The group did have a genuine subversive component, though in practice it was used by many Russian-speaking immigrants as a club where they could take English lessons, drink tea, play cards, and sing songs.[55]

The Labor Department had determined that membership in the Union of Russian Workers was a deportable offense. This was good enough for Hoover, who needed only a membership card or a name in a membership book to build a deportation case, which could then be turned over to the immigration inspectors at the Department of Labor. A raid on the URW would be the first step in Palmer's goal "to rid the country of Red agitators." Hoover's agents collected six hundred names of URW members, which he sent to the Labor Department for warrants.

On November 7, 1919, helped by local police, the BI agents raided URW headquarters in twelve cities and executed 452 of the six hundred warrants. Many more people were arrested without warrants for being on the premises, but most of them were released. Of the two hundred suspects arrested in New York City, only thirty-nine were held. In a report on the raid, Hoover said that when a lecturer was arrested in Philadelphia, "certain influences were brought to work on his behalf, it being claimed that he had tuberculosis and that he had but one lung. . . . I do know that even though he had but one lung it was sufficiently strong enough for him to deliver to a group of Russians, non-citizens of the United States, a lecture upon anarchy."[56]

Public response to the raid was overwhelmingly favorable. Palmer received hundreds of letters of congratulations, and followed Ole Hanson and Woodrow Wilson into the triumvirate of anti-Red heroes. With Wilson stricken in the White House and absent from cabinet meetings, Palmer was seen as the strong leader who could take his place in 1920.

It took about a month and a half to process the 452 cases; deportation orders were signed for a little over half, 246. Hoover added to the mix two notorious Reds, Emma Goldman and Alexander Berkman, both Russian-born, both veteran anarchists, both imprisoned during the war for anti-conscription activities, and both deportable. At Emma Goldman's deportation hearing on October 27, Hoover presented the government's case, quoting from the interrogation of Leon Czolgosz to prove that she had inspired him to kill President McKinley. Czolgosz admitted that he had met Emma at a club in Cleveland and that he had read her articles and been influenced by her ideas. On November 29, her deportation order was signed.

Hoover borrowed a troopship from the War Department, the *Buford*, dubbed the "Soviet Ark," to send his quarry home. On December 21, 249 aliens boarded the ship, 184 of them from the URW raids, fifty-one anarchists, and fourteen rounded up for deportable crimes such as pauperism. Hoover was on hand for the departure. "Haven't I given you a square deal, Miss Goldman?" he asked Emma, whom the press had dubbed "the Red Queen." Staring bemusedly at this roly-poly, moon-faced youth of twenty-four, she replied: "Oh, I suppose. . . . We should not expect from any person something beyond his capacity."[57]

It was Hoover's first time in the limelight and he was feeling rather pleased with himself. He had a distinct feeling of accomplishment, as well as something to celebrate at his upcoming birthday on New Year's Day 1920.

———

Hoover's dilemma, the absence of an organized Communist Party to go after, was solved in September 1919, when two competing parties came into existence. One, the Communist Party, was made up mainly of foreign language federations under the leadership of the Ohio Socialist-turned-Communist Charles E. Ruthenberg. The other, the Communist Labor Party, had as its leading lights John Reed and the young New York Communists Jay Lovestone, Ben Gitlow, and Bert Wolfe.

Both parties, which would eventually receive orders from the Kremlin to unite, were openly dedicated to the violent overthrow of the American government. The American Communist Party was not a conventional political party, busily fielding candidates for state and national office. Candidates were a marginal pursuit, and when the Communists did run a presidential hopeful, he was liable to spend more time in Moscow receiving instructions than on the campaign trail. One of the party's principal activities from the start was to recruit spies and agents for the Communist International, or Comintern.

———

Back in New York City, the Lusk Committee was rolling along on its own momentum. Heartened by his publicity, State Senator Clayton Lusk announced after the June raid of Martens's offices that New York could boast at least fifty radical publications, that Martens was "the American Lenin," and that vast sums had been placed at his disposal.[58]

In its headline hunting, the Lusk Committee had a tendency to leapfrog from one topic to the next. They dropped Martens to go after fresh game—the Wobblies, the Communists, and the Rand School, which had Socialist leanings and an enrollment of five thousand. The Lusk Committee's ace in the hole was that it could order up raids like a *plat du jour*.

On November 8, 1919, the day after the Hoover raids on the Union of Russian Workers, Lusk provided an encore. Seven hundred police raided seventy-three radical centers, including the offices of the newly formed Communist parties. Five hundred were arrested. The aliens considered deportable were turned over to federal agents, while thirty-five American citizens were held on state criminal anarchy charges. Once again, Lusk made sensational claims. The *New York Times* reported that "proof that Lenin himself had dictated Bolshevist operations in this city is said to be in the hands of agents of the Lusk committee."[59]

After that raid, the Lusk Committee wound down, producing, on April 14, 1920, a four-volume, 4,428-page report of which only 400 pages dealt with its investigation. The rest was filler from books and articles. One historian called the committee "erratic, sensational, and completely haphazard."[60] In its headline grabbing, its irresponsible extrapolations, its slipshod and rambling style, and its lack of results, the Lusk Committee was a precursor of the McCarthy hearings to come.

The Lusk material was so inconclusive that in January 1920 the Senate Foreign Relations Committee took another stab at Martens, naming a subcommittee of five under Senator George H. Moses of New Hampshire to investigate the unrecognized ambassador. Martens's lawyer, surprisingly, was former Georgia Senator Thomas Hardwick, the target of an anarchist bomb. Moses, who did most of the questioning (the others rarely bothered to attend the meetings), was fairer and more probing than Lusk. The Moses report, filed in April 1920, recommended deportation and turned the case over to Attorney General Palmer. The State Department approved the recommendation, and so did President Wilson, calling Martens "pestiferous." Finally, on December 16, 1920, a deportation order was signed, but Martens was allowed to leave the country voluntarily before he was thrown out. Back in Russia he was named head of the Soviet Metallurgical Trust.[61]

That this renegade ambassador of an inimical state, acting as an agent to undermine and vilify the government of which he was a guest, was able to remain in the United States for two years is proof that in the midst of the so-called Red Scare, there was a surprising laxity toward Bolshevik agitators. That he was smoked out at all was due to the labor of two congressional committees.

———

Following the success of his November 1919 raids against the Union of Russian Workers, Hoover secretly planned more massive raids in January 1920. He acted in the context of continued anarchist violence and nationwide strikes. His aim was to round up a large number of radical aliens in cities across the country and to have them deported by the Labor Department under the 1917 immigration law that made membership in a subversive organization a deportable offense.

This was a huge undertaking, requiring extensive preparation. As Attorney General Palmer put it, it was "a Herculean task because they [the foreign-born] live in sections which are not often visited by ordinary Americans." To find evidence of membership, Hoover planted informants in the Communist parties, which, having formed in September, were eagerly seeking recruits. The informants could supply the names of members, but their identities had to be kept secret: they could not be confronted with those they named. Hoover's tactical response was to obtain a confession right after arrest. To do this, there would have to be no lawyers present. As Hoover told Anthony Caminetti, the Immigration Commissioner, lawyers would only bog down the hearings unnecessarily and "defeat the ends of justice." With lawyers around, there would be no self-incriminating confessions.[62]

There was only one problem: the regulation stipulating that aliens could be questioned without a lawyer present had been amended in March 1919 by the fair-minded Secretary of Labor, William Wilson. The lawyers of arrested aliens could now take part in hearings from the beginning. After trying out the amended rule for three months, Caminetti reported that it "interferes materially with the prompt and efficient handling of cases." As it happened, Wilson was out sick in December 1919 and the Acting Secretary of Labor, John Abercrombie, agreed to change the rule on December 27, a few days before the raids. The new rule read that the alien should be told he could have a lawyer present "preferably at the beginning of the hearing . . . or at any rate as soon as such hearing has proceeded sufficiently in the development of the facts *to protect the government's interest.*"[63]

For Hoover, who said grace before meals, and who immersed himself in the writings of Marx and Lenin in order to quantify their malevolence, the raid was not a job, but a mission. He churned out memos with the passionate energy of the true believer, pestering the Immigration Bureau to raise the bail of radicals, urging that visitors of aliens detained at Ellis Island be searched and that their lawyers should not be present without supervision, and arguing that photographs could serve as affidavits of identification. At the age of twenty-four, Hoover was already an unrelenting overseer whose mastery of detail would ensure the success of a dramatic, attention-getting, nationwide operation.

On December 22, Hoover sent Caminetti the names of 2,280 members of the Communist parties, culled by informants, and asked for a total of 2,768 warrants; the remainder were for anarchists and other assorted radicals. The warrants were signed on December 27 and sent by wire to the cities where the raids would take place. The informants were told that they should endeavor to arrange meetings of the local Communist branches on the evening of Friday, January 2, 1920, so that Hoover's men could make mass arrests and avoid house-to-house searches.

At 7:00 P.M. on January 2, 1920, 579 Bureau of Investigation agents, assisted by local police, raided radical clubhouses and meeting halls in thirty-three cities and twenty-three states from Maine to California and arrested about ten thousand suspects, 3,500 of whom were detained as deportable aliens. They raided restaurants, cafés, bowling alleys, pool parlors, choral societies, schools (where they picked up both teachers and students), and small shops. Impatient agents in Chicago would not let a barber finish shaving his customer. In Detroit, they raided merrymakers at a ball and also arrested the orchestra.[64]

Hoover told the chief clerk at the Justice Department to keep the bureau offices open all night, as he was planning "arrests totaling over three thousand persons charged with being communists, who will be held for deportation." Hoover himself manned the phones in the bureau offices.

Across the country, it soon became apparent that so many aliens had been arrested that the BI agents had no place to put them. In Detroit, where twenty-six halls and meeting places were raided, eight hundred aliens were taken to the Federal Building and herded into a fifth-floor hallway for up to five days, with newspapers and coats for bedding, one toilet, and no windows. A prominent Detroit citizen said it was like the Black Hole of Calcutta. The BI chief in Detroit, Arthur L. Barbey, observed that "the public should bear in mind that this is not a picnic, and the Department of Justice is not providing settees for criminals." The Labor Department could not handle the mass of deportation cases, and high bail kept the aliens locked up for months while waiting their turn, although they had not been charged with any crime. They could not support their families, which seemed harsh and unfair.

The Palmer raids, which sought to rid the country of a genuine radical danger, triggered the first great McCarthyite debate over whether Hoover's methods were permissible and legal under the American system. The debate would continue down the years, over President Truman's loyalty investigations, the Smith Act trials, and McCarthy's Red hunting, but it was after the Palmer raids that the lines were drawn in stubbornly partisan terms: on one side "protect our civil liberties" and on the other, "save the country from treacherous radicals."

At first the newspapers hailed the sweeping roundup in headlines such as: "All Aboard for the Next Soviet Ark." On January 5, 1920, the *New York Times* declared that "if any or some of us impatient for the swift confusion of the reds have ever doubted the alacrity, resolute will, and fruitful intelligent vigor of the Department of Justice in hunting down the enemies of the United States, the questioners and doubters now have cause to approve and applaud." Hoover was so pleased with his notices that he kept an exhibit of trophies in his office, including Red banners and life-sized pictures of Trotsky and Lenin seized in Newark.[65]

But the praise soured in mid-January, when William Wilson returned to the Department of Labor. He had deep misgivings about the raids and changed back the rule on lawyers right away.[66] He found the Immigration Bureau swamped as thousands of detained aliens awaited hearings. Still ailing and seldom in the office, he named Assistant Secretary Louis F. Post to expedite the deportation cases, which made Post de facto Secretary of Labor. Given Post's opinion of the January raids and their mastermind, this was like naming the head of the Anti-Conscription League to rule on draft dodgers. Post called the raids "a cruel hoax" and compared Hoover's agents to the labor spies of private detective agencies.[67]

Post, whom President Wilson had named assistant secretary of labor in 1913, became known as a champion of labor while serving on the Chicago school board and fighting for the right of teachers to organize. In 1920, at the age of seventy-one, he looked a little like Trotsky, short but erect in stature, narrow-shouldered, with a wild mop of gray hair, a Vandyke beard, and wire-rim glasses. On March 6, he "plunged into the clutter" of the thousands of deportation cases, with the conviction that the Palmer raids "stood revealed as a stupendous and cruel fake." Post was shocked that a portrait of Karl Marx, kept as a trophy in BI headquarters in New York City, on Park Row, had been "mutilated." One of the detectives had drawn a red clown's nose on Marx's face and slashed a hole through his mouth, then placed it in front of his own face like a mask and smoked a cigar through it. "The founder of Socialism smoked gaily," observed Post, "to the delight of the office force."[68]

Post directed the immigration inspectors to bring him one hundred cases a day to "clear up the clutter." Preferring bail to prolonged detention, he declared that "there is no purpose in imprisoning aliens in expulsion proceedings unnecessarily." Accordingly, he reduced high bail from $10,000 and $5,000 to $1,000 and $500. Many aliens were unable to meet even the lower bail.[69]

As the deportation warrants landed on his desk, Post canceled more than he signed. He rejected confessions obtained by Hoover's agents as invalid. He ignored the provision of the 1917 immigration law that party membership was sufficient cause for deportation. The scratch of a pen on a card or a membership list were not enough, he ruled. When Post broke the cases down one by one he saw that one man was arrested for joining a choral society, while another had wanted to attend a dance. Some had been tricked into joining a group whose leaders did not disclose their true purpose. By insisting on evidence of personal guilt, Post cut deeply into Hoover's catch. By mid-April he had decided 1,600 cases, out of which he canceled 1,100 warrants.[70]

Consternation gripped the Justice Department. Hoover noted in his General Intelligence Bulletin that the "cancellation of warrants by Mr. Post continued as usual." Attorney General Palmer told Secretary of State Lansing that Post was "a Bolshevik himself." Palmer, who was being hailed as "Uncle Sam's Policeman" and "The Rooter Out of Reds," kept fanning the flames in preparation for his run at the Democratic convention in June. In a magazine article in February, he warned that revolution was "licking at the altars of the churches, leaping into the belfry of the school bell, crawling into the sacred corners of American homes, seeking to replace marriage vows with libertine laws, and burning up the foundation of society."[71]

On April 12, 1920, Washington state's Albert Johnson, the chairman of the House Immigration Committee, called Post "a friend of the aliens." Headlines trumpeted: "Labor Department Bored from Within" and "Post Charged with Being Easy on Reds." But Post was not without allies: on April 23 another member of the committee, the Alabama Democrat George Huddleston, reported that he had been told by "a well-informed gentleman from New York City that most of those arrested did not know the difference between Bolshevism and rheumatism."[72]

Prodded by the Attorney General, on April 27 the House Rules Committee launched an impeachment hearing against Post on charges of obstruction of justice. When Post appeared before the committee on May 7, 1920, he did not receive a friendly reception. There was, among congressmen from the heartland, an inbred revulsion against foreign and domestic radicals who disrupted American society. The tone was set by Representative Philip P. Campbell of Kansas when he asked: "Don't you think that these high-brow anarchists, these college professors, these Harvard and Yale anarchists, these fellows who weep in articles about the laboring man but never labored a day in their lives . . . are more dangerous than the poor ignorant fellow who is willing to take his hatchet and go out and break up the government. . . . Don't you think that the high-brow philosophical anarchist is the more dangerous of the two?"

Post: "Tolstoi was not a dangerous man, and Tolstoi is the very type of the philosophical anarchist."

Representative Albert Johnson of Washington: "It must be apparent to all that under the guise of Tolstoian philosophical anarchists, a lot of dirty devils are in the United States doing their work to urge these United States into one grand world conglomerate."[73]

To many of the congressmen, the Red threat was real: the aliens were real, the bombs were real, the strikes were real.

When he was asked why he had reversed so many deportation verdicts, Post explained that he wanted to recognize the rights of the individual to a fair trial. Even an alien had rights: the right to counsel, the right to cross-examine witnesses, and the right to bail that was not excessive.

Asked point-blank by Representative Edward W. Pou of North Carolina if he was a Red, Post said: "I am colorblind. . . . I can remember my grandfather telling me how . . . Thomas Jefferson was denounced as a 'Red Republican.' . . . Then in my own day . . . the color scheme changed from red to black and Abraham Lincoln . . . was in my time a 'Black Republican.'"[74] Pou was won over. "I believe you have followed your sense of duty absolutely," he said, even though "I am probably not in sympathy with some of your views." Pou then rose from his seat and walked out of the hearing room. Post knew at that moment that he would not be impeached.[75]

Palmer appeared before the committee on June 1 and made a speech that lasted two days. Hoover, who helped him prepare it, told him not to mince words. Once again, across the political divide, two men, Palmer and Post, were locking horns, each one trapped in his own intransigence. Palmer had gone too far in the size and inequities of the raids, and Post in his blanket dismissal of cases.

Palmer's thirty-thousand-word statement fell flat. The *New York World* called it "a smoke screen." *The New Republic* said that Post had turned the tables against his accusers, having first been cast in the role of Unpatriotic Worm or Inexperienced Theorist, but soon becoming the Curator of Facts.[76]

On June 23, a respected federal judge, George W. Anderson, ruled in Boston, where a number of radicals were interned on Deer Island, that in neither of the two Communist parties could membership lead to deportation. The provisions of the 1917 immigration law, he argued, were too broad. Guilt had to be proven by acts such as advocating violence, and not merely by membership in a subversive organization. Anderson denounced the Justice Department for its use of undercover agents, arrests without warrants, and excessive bail. He concluded that "a mob is a mob, whether made up of government officials . . . or vicious classes." As a result, three hundred Communists were released, along with seventeen Deer Island radicals.[77]

———

The Palmer raids, which were meant to launch the Attorney General as a national figure, turned out to be a liability. Palmer announced his candidacy on March 1, campaigning on his record as the nation's protector. On June 2, the *Indianapolis News* called him "something of an alarmist." The "Fighting Quaker" became the "Quaking Fighter." He did poorly in the primaries and arrived at the Democratic convention in San Francisco that June as an also-ran. James Cox, the governor of Ohio, won the nomination and picked Franklin D. Roosevelt as his running mate, but lost in November to another Ohioan, Warren G. Harding.

Palmer, once the hero of our fickle press, was now its villain. H. L. Mencken wrote in the *Baltimore Sun* in September 1920 that he was "perhaps the most eminent living exponent of cruelty, dishonesty, and injustice."[78]

When Congress reconvened, a subcommittee of the Senate Judiciary Committee conducted a postmortem on the Palmer raids from January 19 to March 2, 1921, called "Charges of Illegal Practices of the Department of Justice."[79] Once again, the legislators were divided between those who felt that Palmer had responded appropriately to a genuine danger and those who thought he had trampled legality.

Palmer, who was through as a politician, was on the defensive when he appeared before the subcommittee. In the fall of 1919, he said, he had been denounced for inactivity. He was, he recalled, "shouted at from every editorial sanctum in America from sea to sea . . . to do something." Under the pressure of public opinion, he planned the raids. Some arrests, he conceded, were made without warrants. Undercover informants, while unpalatable, were necessary to ferret out radical units. The raids would have been more successful had it not been for Louis Post and others, with their "tender solicitude for social revolution and perverted sympathy for the criminal anarchists of the country."[80]

"I saw the evidence," Palmer proclaimed, certain that he had acted in the national interest. "I have personally read and examined hundreds and hundreds—possibly thousands—of the pamphlets and literature. . . . There was a well-defined propaganda . . . which was found, if left unchecked . . . to result in serious violence and disturbance through the country."[81]

Senator Thomas J. Walsh of Montana was skeptical. There was nothing, he said, "in the nature of preparation for a military uprising. No guns, no munitions of war . . . no drilling of soldiers or anything of that kind. . . . For myself, I find it difficult to conceive of a course more powerfully calculated to excite widespread hatred of our government. . . . Justice 'for a season bade the world farewell.'"[82]

One by one, the subcommittee dealt with the major issues. The first was guilt by membership, which would bedevil the courts for years to come.

Senator Walsh: "How is a name on a roll evidence that the man is a member of that party? That alone would not establish the fact of his membership at all, to my mind."[83]

Struggling with issues that were new to them, the senators fell back on their own experience. Senator William King of Utah said: "I differ from you. . . . Take church members. They have a roll of members with the names of the children and everybody and that is kept in the church, and I think that membership on that roll would be prima facie evidence of membership in the church."

Walsh: "That is quite a different thing. . . . You could not establish a crime in any such way as that . . . because you find a paper in which his name appeared."

King: "Assuming that it was the habit to call the roll at the beginning of the meetings, and members would answer 'present,' and assuming that he was participating at the meetings . . ."

Walsh: "You can assume a whole lot of things, you know. . . . Suppose that we are going to get up a Democratic club. Somebody says, 'Here is Joe Smith down here; he will be glad to be a member.' Down goes Smith's name and he is a member of the club. You could not convict that man of a crime on such proof."

King: "Of course you could not."[84]

Palmer and Hoover were seated side by side facing the subcommittee members, like Tweedledum and Tweedledee, and the hearings seemed to turn into a vaudeville act where they passed the hot potatoes back and forth.

When Walsh asked how many search warrants had been issued, Palmer replied: "I cannot tell you. . . . If you would like to ask Mr. Hoover, who was in charge of this matter, he can tell you."

But Hoover passed the buck to the agents in the field: "The search warrants were entirely a matter which the agents in charge of local officers handled."

And so it went, with Palmer placed in the position of pleading ignorance. When questioned about the change in the rule to have lawyers present, he said: "I know nothing at all about it. I never heard of it until long afterwards." The civil libertarian Zechariah Chafee, when asked about the same matter, said: "I cannot think of any dirtier piece of business than that."[85]

Palmer concluded his testimony by insisting that he had acted properly. "I apologize for nothing that the Department of Justice has done in this matter," he said. "I glory in it. I point with pride and enthusiasm at the results of that work. . . . If some of my agents in the field . . . were a little rough and unkind, or short and curt, with these alien agitators . . . I think it might well be overlooked in the general good to the country."[86]

But Palmer's protestations could not change the vivid impression that the raids had been conducted at the expense of due process. Commenting on Hoover's December 27 letter of instructions, Senator Walsh said, "It is difficult to conceive how one bred in the law could ever have promulgated such an order."[87]

The raids that bore his name were a public relations disaster, and Palmer returned to private life, while Hoover in later years modestly refrained from taking any credit, insisting that he had only carried out Palmer's orders.[88]

The lesson for Hoover was that subsequent operations would have to be handled with greater care. Massive raids had too many built-in dangers for the bureau. In the future he would leave arrests and prosecution to local and state authorities, while he continued to gather information and build up his files. But how could anyone say there was no radical threat when his files told him that the toll from anarchist bombs in 1919 and 1920 was thirty-five killed and two hundred injured? The Communist Party of America had 24,000 dues-paying members, of whom roughly 22,000 were aliens who did not speak English, while the Communist Labor Party had 10,000. That made a total of 34,000 Communists, all of whom were bent on overthrowing the government by force. A Communist party leaflet in February 1920 called on railroad strikers to launch an armed insurrection. To Hoover, those who criticized the raids did not know the facts.[89]

For the Communists, the raids were a setback from which it took several years to recover. Hundreds of members had been deported, and a number of leaders were in jail. In the party correspondence can be found many letters testifying to the disruption. In Cleveland on March 23, 1920, James E. Wood reported that eight members had been arrested in the raid and "everything was upset." In Detroit, the party was in such a chaotic state that no one could be found to distribute May Day leaflets. From Nucla, Colorado, W. F. Leibenberg wrote: "I have tried to get contributions for the Communist cause but it is hard to find men and women here in this bourgeois community that are not afraid of jeopardizing themselves to the American tsar. . . . We have failed so far now that the persecution is on . . . as the headquarters was raided we have been without our address. . . . Under our next president there will probably be death penalties added."[90]

A few found their resolve strengthened by the raids. From Chicago, Ed Fisher wrote in disgust on April 11, 1920: "The Communist party was mostly a fake organization, that is the rock bottom truth. . . . Essentially, it was a hip-hurrah society for the celebration of good news from Russia. . . . Do you think I would remain were it not for the government assault which alone gives it significance?"[91]

One after-effect of the Palmer raids was to demonstrate the glaring need for a body of law to deal with the emerging threat of anarchist violence and Communist subversion. No two courts agreed on how to rule in these unprecedented cases. One court said the bail set for detained aliens was too high, another said it was not excessive. One court ruled that membership in a Communist organization was not deportable, while another said it was. The rules of evidence also needed to be spelled out. What was to be done when the evidence consisted of tickets to meetings, contributions to milk funds for children, and postcards signed "Yours for Communism"? The purpose of congressional hearings was to determine the need for new legislation. Senator Walsh drafted a bill to exclude the Bureau of Investigation from the administration of the immigration laws, but it died in committee. Congress was far more eager to curtail the admission of undesirable ethnic groups and enacted the Emergency Quota of 1921, which limited the number of foreign-born immigrants according to nationality. Admissions were sharply reduced—from 805,228 immigrants in 1921 to 309,556 in 1922.[92]

IV

THE POLITICS OF FAMINE

Long before he was elected President in 1928, at the age of fifty-four, Herbert Hoover's life had been eventful enough to fill two thick volumes of memoirs. The son of an austere Quaker blacksmith, born in a two-room frame house in West Branch, Iowa, he retained from his upbringing the art of friendly (or at times unfriendly) persuasion. Departing from Quaker rules, he smoked and drank and fished on Sunday and swore like a longshoreman. Orphaned at ten, he was raised by an aunt in Oregon. Hoover attended a newly opened college called Stanford, then tuition-free, and graduated in its first class, in 1895, as a mining engineer.

His life resembled a series of vignettes in a boy's adventure book: Hoover the globe-trotter, caught in China's Boxer Rebellion or trekking through the Burmese jungle. Hoover the London-based financier who raised money for promising mining ventures in distant lands. Hoover the mogul in czarist Russia, investing in oil fields in the Caucasus, gold mines in Kazakhstan, and the million-and-a-half-acre Kyshtin estate in the Urals, which had its own mines and ironworks. Hoover the wire-puller and market manipulator, whom his rivals called a conniver, buying an interest here, promoting a stock there, and always selling out at a profit.[1]

In 1911 he went to Kyshtin and found a modern refinery in a semifeudal environment, "a microcosm of all of Russia," as he recalled. "At the top a Russian noble family and at the bottom 100,000 peasants and workers. . . . Peasants devastated by famine . . . a hideous social background. . . . Always there was the feeling among us that some day the country would blow up." At a railroad station, he saw a long line of men and women chained together and marched aboard a freight car bound for Siberia. Despair was in their faces. The scene so shook the normally impassive Hoover it gave him nightmares.[2]

Although the Kyshtin mines became the biggest copper producer in Russia, turning out 25 million pounds a year, Hoover had premonitions and got out in 1916, a year before the Bolsheviks seized foreign-owned mining companies. He lost an estimated $15 million, but not his shirt. World War I found him living the good life in London, as director of eighteen companies with business interests on five continents, from zinc in Australia to silver in Burma. He was a millionaire several times over, though resented as "a pushful American."[3]

In 1914, looking for an area of the war where his organizing abilities could be of use, Hoover focused on the plight of the eight million Belgians, occupied by Germans who refused to feed the civilian population, and cut off by the British naval blockade from the ships that could have brought food.

Mass starvation loomed. Hoover stepped in and founded the Commission for Relief in Belgium. He thought it would be a short war; it was just a matter of tiding the Belgians over until the next harvest. He went to Berlin to obtain an agreement for the passage of his ships and the distribution of food. When he discussed the issue of instructions to U-boat commanders with Chancellor Bethmann-Hollweg, Hoover told him a joke about a man who asked his neighbor to keep his bulldog tied up. "Oh, he won't bite," the neighbor said. "You may know he won't bite," the man said, "I may know he won't bite, but does the dog know it?" It was the only time he got a laugh from a German.[4]

In the next two and a half years, Hoover bought, carried, and distributed 2.5 million tons of food for Belgium and German-occupied northern France. The British and the French paid for about 90 percent, or $226 million, with donations making up the rest. Raised to prominence by his good works, Hoover dealt with chiefs of state and cabinet ministers, negotiating treaties with belligerents on both sides, and enforcing compliance by threatening to cancel the mission. He obtained the right-of-way for his ships to clear the British blockade and the U-boats, and proceed through a mine-free channel to Rotterdam. In the unlimited submarine war of 1917, three of his ships were sunk, even though they carried big signs from stem to stern that heralded: BELGIAN RELIEF COMMISSION. The Belgians sold empty flour sacks to the Germans, who used them as sandbags in the trenches; the British were furious when they took trenches after weeks of battle and found sandbags stamped BELGIAN COMMISSION.[5]

Famine fighting was like running a corporation: strict accounting, tight administration, one CEO. Hoover got the job done, and when he came home in

May 1917 he was famous, the great humanitarian who had single-handedly saved millions from starvation. All over the country, mothers told their kids to eat their spinach and think of the starving Belgian children. One of his admirers, President Wilson, named him to the post of Food Administrator, responsible for regulating prices, assuring supply, and eliminating speculation, but he also continued as chairman of the Commission for Relief in Belgium, or CRB. Now the United States paid the bills, which rose to $75 million over the next six months.[6]

When the Russian Revolution came in November 1917, Hoover followed events at the Kyshtin estate he had once owned. Upon learning that the technical staff had been driven out as bourgeois idlers, he cursed the Bolsheviks' "enthroned ignorance." Here was a copper refinery that he had helped build, with highly complicated chemical and metallurgical operations. Its machinery required expert mechanics to keep it in good order. And what did these Bolsheviks do? They threw out the people who knew how to run the plant. "A thunderclap guided by blind stupidity shattered this tuned intelligence in an instant," he recalled. "In a week the works were shut down. The very furies of ignorance were in the saddle."[7]

In 1917, as Hoover continued his Belgian program, he clashed with his own government, for the priority of the U.S. Army was shipping men to France, not food to Belgium. And yet the appeals kept coming. Malnutrition and tuberculosis were taking their toll. Belgians were fainting in soup lines, children were dying, but Hoover could not obtain the ships to meet his quota. General Peyton C. March, the Army Chief of Staff, a man as willful as Hoover, told him bluntly, "If we do not get the men to France, there will be no Belgian Relief problem."

Two years of infighting in London had turned Hoover into a shrewd negotiator. He devised an argument that turned food into a weapon scarcely less important than military victories. The Belgian population was divided between French-speaking Walloons and Germanic Flemish. The risk of jeopardizing relief, Hoover told President Wilson, was that the Flemish half might secede and form a pro-German state. The French would suffer a terrible blow to their morale if the Flemish were to defect. Thus, curtailing relief could damage the war effort. Out of necessity, recognizing that only military imperatives would sway the men in charge of the war, Hoover invented the politics of famine.[8]

Scrambling for ships, he diverted freighters from the Cuban sugar trade and rationed American candy makers. He urged King Albert of Belgium, in exile in France, to intervene with the King of Sweden. America's envoy to the Belgian King, Brand Whitlock, found Hoover brusque and peremptory. "What a bully!" Whitlock exclaimed. "He would even bully a poor exiled king!" Hoover got his Swedish ships, as well as a handful of British ships after a direct appeal to the Prime Minister, Lloyd George.

On November 11, 1918, the fighting was over, but not the help to destroyed nations. In Hoover's words, the Horsemen of War and Death had passed by, only to be replaced by the Horsemen of Famine and Pestilence. He was now internationally famous, the subject of poems and songs, such as:

> *Who kept the Belgians' black bread buttered?*
> *Who fed the world when millions muttered?*
> *. . . Hoover—that's all!*[9]

Hoover lobbied the President and his cabinet with his plans to use food as an instrument of postwar policy. In the starving inhabitants of defeated nations, he saw the specter of revolution. Among his converts was Secretary of State Lansing, who agreed that hunger bred social upheaval. "Empty stomachs mean Bolsheviks," he wrote on October 28, 1918. "Full stomachs mean no Bolsheviks."[10] The President too was won over, and said in his remarks to the state food administrators on November 12, the day after the Armistice, that "the world has to be revictualed." Hoover would continue to lead "the fight against famine," for "famine is the mother of anarchy." Wilson asked Hoover to transform his Food Administration into an agency for the reconstruction of Europe, the American Relief Administration. In January 1919, Wilson asked Congress for $100 million. There was considerable opposition from isolationist Republicans like Representative Henry F. Ashurst of Arizona, who exclaimed on January 20: "I do not propose feeding anything but hot lead to murderous Bolshevists." But Democrats who backed the plan sold it on the grounds that food shipments would "stem the wave of Bolshevism," so that "our boys" would not have to "fight another war." The funds were approved at the end of January.[11]

By that time, Hoover was in Paris. He had left New York on November 16 aboard the SS *Olympia*, to invade the Old World with his armada of food, which he would command and navigate. Frank Polk, the State Department counselor, cabled Colonel House in Paris: "Confidentially, I think you will have to calm Hoover down a little as his plans may be resented by the allies."[12]

The press now dubbed Hoover "Food Administrator to the World." He remained in Paris while the peace negotiations dragged on from January to July 1919. His secret purpose, approved by Lansing, was to feed the anti-Bolshevik elements in Russia, as well as in other countries where the Bolsheviks were active. As such, he became the key figure in America's policy of containment, under the cover of food.

Hoover loathed "the plague" of Bolshevism and believed that "no greater

relief of human misery could be undertaken than" the suppression of the Soviet regime. His feelings were founded on his experience in the Russian copper
mine, which he had made efficient and productive, only to see it ruined by the
Bolsheviks.[13]

Hoover's policy was aimed at preventing the Bolsheviks from spreading
beyond their borders to the Baltic states and Finland, or to Germany and Hungary, where they were already agitating. Under the guise of his American Relief Administration, he became deeply involved in foreign policy and military
affairs. Ostensibly, he was in the business of sending food. But covertly, he was
supporting anti-Bolshevik regimes and sending both food and military equipment to anti-Bolshevik armies. Once again, Hoover was conducting a war
within a war.[14]

Vanquished Germany was a case in point. In the months after the Armistice, Germany was a wasteland mired in revolution and civil war. Famine
and lawlessness gripped the nation and pitched battles were being fought in
the streets of Berlin. The Kaiser had fled, and the Social Democrat Friedrich
Ebert had formed an interim government, but if it was to succeed, he would
have to put down the uprising of the Bolshevik-inspired Spartacist League,
who intended to bring about a Socialist revolution.

Ebert was elected the first German President in January 1919, but the civil
war dragged on. By March, the Bolsheviks were in control of Munich and
Hamburg. Hoover thought food was the answer. The German people were
starving, penalized by defeat, not even allowed to fish in their own waters.
Hoover organized a conference in Brussels with the British and the Germans
on March 13, 1919. Admiral Sir Rosslyn Wemyss, who had handled transport operations in the Dardanelles, went up to Hoover and said: "Young man,
I don't see why you Americans want to feed these Germans." Hoover replied:
"Old man, I don't understand why you want to starve women and children
after they are licked." Hoover started moving food to Germany in April and
propped up the Ebert government, which adopted the motto, "without order,
no bread." The uprisings subsided and Germany was saved from a Bolshevik
government. Hoover was confirmed in the belief that "whoever controlled the
food controlled the state. . . . It was nip and tuck keeping ahead of the Communist movement."[15]

More deadly than the medieval plague, the dismemberment of the Hapsburg empire removed every semblance of orderly rule. In those ruined lands,
the broad belt of submerged races, tossed between hunger and reawakened
dreams of nationhood, were cast adrift. A lordless and exhausted people
drained of hope and energy were easily manipulated. The scourge swept
away the stores of food and seed, most of the domestic animals, and the ac-

cumulated capital of housing and tools that represented the labor of many generations. And here were these newly formed nations, naked as Adam, which had to start over, with nothing to implement their needs, while diplomats in Paris discussed the terms of peace. Here was Hungary, which had once taken pride in the pompous name of empire, now rejoicing in its separation from Austria.

In Hungary, where Hoover saw "a sort of unending procession of tragedies," Count Michael Karolyi had been named President of the liberal government. Two thirds of the newly minted republic were occupied by Romanian and Czech troops. Hoover sent trainloads of food for starving Hungarians, but his supplies could not keep Karolyi in power. On March 22, 1919, Bela Kun, a Hungarian soldier captured by the Russians and converted to Communism, set up a Soviet republic and launched a Red Terror. Hoover had a train of twenty-five carloads of food en route to Budapest even as Bela Kun arrested and executed some of his Hungarian relief council members. On Hoover's initiative, the Allies declared on June 26 that food would only be sent to a government that represented the Hungarian people. Just one month later, Kun was overthrown by trade union leaders and the army, and fled to Russia. Food shipments rapidly resumed. Hoover was strengthened in his conviction that food was the best way to topple Bolshevik regimes. Food was restorative and altruistic and did not require mayhem or sordid compromises. It was an inspired way of meddling in the affairs of other countries.[16]

In ill-fated Austria, the cat's-paw of German expansion, the Hapsburg bubble burst. Entire divisions of subject troops refused to advance to the front. Soldiers shot their officers. Sailors drowned their captains. Mobs roamed the countryside, stealing and plundering. Austria was reduced to a small republic, and the people of Vienna, now the capital of a diminished and bankrupt state, appealed to the world for food.

When Hoover learned that the Bolsheviks would try to take power on May Day 1919, he had posters put up all over Vienna that said: "Any disturbances of the public order will render the food shipments impossible and bring Vienna face to face with absolute famine." There was no May Day takeover and Hoover wrote in his memoirs that "fear of starvation held the Austrian people from revolution."[17]

Vanquished Germany and Austro-Hungary were not the only countries that risked sliding into Bolshevism. Those countries that had been part of the Russian empire before the war, such as Finland and the Baltic states, did not escape the postwar turmoil.

Finland, the pawn of Scandinavia, was a land of nomadic hunters and fishermen conquered by Sweden in the thirteenth century, then lost after the war with Russia in 1809. As subjects of the Czar's empire, spending Russian coin, licking Russian stamps, obeying Russian laws, and serving in Russian regiments, the Finns developed a fierce desire for self-rule as an armor against "Russianization."

Finally, in December 1917, they took advantage of the Bolshevik Revolution to declare their independence, but the country soon lapsed into civil war. A strong man arose, the former Russian general Carl Gustaf Mannerheim, whose White army defeated the Soviet-backed Red Guards in a bloody four-month campaign. Mannerheim named himself Regent and at the start of 1919 he expressed a desire to carry on the anti-Bolshevik struggle to nearby Petrograd. In February he told a U.S. naval attaché that his army was "capable of defeating the Bolsheviki in northern Russia" and that he was ready "to commence hostilities immediately" if "assured that the United States would hasten sending food supplies to Finland."[18]

In exchange for taking Petrograd, Mannerheim demanded the Kola Peninsula, an area the size of England bordering on Finland. Robert Imbrie, the U.S. vice consul in the Finnish border town of Vyborg, reported to the State Department on March 2, 1919, that the Finns had "perfected a military organization numbering, they state, 10,000 men." Their objective was "the capture of Petrograd and afterward Moscow and the overthrow of the Bolsheviks." Having already committed American troops in Archangel and Vladivostok, the State Department took a cautious approach. Counselor Frank Polk replied on March 8 that as Washington did not have "adequate information regarding Russian Whites," it was "not in a position to offer any support or assistance."[19]

Hoover, however, was eager to help. He told President Wilson in April that he was impressed by the Finns and their "sturdy fight" for democracy. He arranged to ship them food on credit, and persuaded the President to grant Finland diplomatic recognition so that the Finns could open accounts with New York–based banks to pay for the food.[20]

On June 19, 1919, Mannerheim signed an agreement with Nikolai Iudenich, a czarist general who had fled to Finland after the Bolsheviks took power, for a joint attack on Petrograd. With his army of six thousand, top-heavy with fifteen hundred ex-czarist officers, Iudenich was keen to enter the fray. His was one of the half-dozen White armies then engaging the Bolsheviks on as many fronts. In Paris, Secretary of State Lansing and other heads of delegations gave Mannerheim the green light on July 7, telling him they had "no objections" to his attack on Petrograd. Hoover said that "no greater relief of human misery could be undertaken than the occupation of Petrograd" and the suppression of the Bolshevik regime. But by then it was too late: in July Mannerheim lost the election for President, which brought to power in Finland a center-left coalition opposed to intervention.[21]

Hoover redirected his energies toward Latvia, Lithuania, and Estonia. During the war, these three small Baltic states had been occupied by the Germans, but after the Armistice, nationalists and Bolsheviks fought for control. As Hoover put it, the Soviets were "spreading Communism by infection."[22]

In Lithuania, the Bolsheviks swept into the power vacuum created by the departed Germans and formed a Soviet Socialist Republic in the capital of Vilnius in January 1919, backed by Red Army units. This unpopular regime lasted only three months and was deposed by Lithuanian nationalists in April. Hoover's American Relief Administration quickly moved in with food for the fledgling regime. On June 22, Captain Russell of the Red Cross reported on the struggle of "the little army of Lithuania . . . to free the country from Bolshevism." He noted that "Mr. Hoover's men . . . are following every military advance here as quickly as the railroad bridges can be repaired."[23]

In Latvia, a republic was proclaimed after the German collapse, in November 1918, under the nationalist leader Karlis Ulmanis, who had spent eight years in exile teaching at the University of Nebraska. In January, the Red Army captured the Latvian capital of Riga and ousted Ulmanis, who moved his government to the port city of Libau, where it was protected by a British naval squadron. The Allies had asked the Germans to remain in Latvia as a buffer against the Red Army. It was an odd arrangement to be using the enemy as a border police against former allies. "Paradoxical as it might seem," Lansing noted, "the Allied governments were, by the Armistice, allies of Germany in the Baltic provinces."[24]

In May 1919, Hoover wrote a memo to the Council of Four at the Paris conference outlining the situation in the Baltic states. He warned that the Bolshevik government in Riga, "being unable to provide foodstuffs, was mobbed by the populace and has withdrawn its army from the city, which was given over to complete anarchy of wholesale massacre and murder." The news from Riga horrified him. The Communists had set up a Latvian Soviet Republic, opened the prisons and let loose the convicts, who were plundering and looting the city. Hundreds were killed in summary executions, their bodies dumped into trenches. Hoover asked for military protection to safeguard food deliveries to Riga. In a letter to Wilson on May 9, he urged "definite action" in the Baltic, where "the population in none of these states is Bolshevik. . . . In many places they are putting up a good fight to try and establish their independence from the Moscow tyranny." Hoover wanted to send "military supplies to the established governments."[25]

When Wilson stalled, Hoover decided to take action. Waiting was "slower than I could bear," he recalled in his memoir. "In desperation, I sent a telegram to General von der Goltz [the German commander in Latvia] asking him to occupy Riga." Here was an American official, without any authorization, ordering a German general to occupy the capital of a Baltic country. Von der Goltz moved on Riga on May 22. Fortunately for Hoover, on May 23, the Council of Foreign Ministers approved his proposal to send arms and munitions, as well as food and clothing to the Baltic states. Hoover dispatched a forty-wagon train of food to Riga with a few soldiers under an army lieutenant named Harrington. When they reached the outskirts of the city, men were still fighting in the corpse-littered streets. The railroad tracks were damaged, so Harrington took the food in by handcart. By May 24, he was providing one meal a day to 200,000 Latvians.[26]

The Red Terror in Riga lasted from January to May 1919. According to Hoover, the Bolshevik revolutionaries killed as many as one thousand a day, mowing them down with machine guns, and singling out clergymen, teachers, and doctors. A White Terror of vengeance followed once von der Goltz occupied the city, and another round of executions. When Hoover protested, he was told the executions would be limited to proven criminals.[27]

Directly to the north of Latvia was Estonia, whose border with Russia was a scant eighty miles from Petrograd. After the Armistice, the Estonians proclaimed their independence. The Red Seventh Army invaded and established a puppet government in the border town of Narva. With the help of Allied war matériel, a British naval squadron, and three thousand Finnish volunteers, the Estonians fought back, and by February 1919, Estonia was free.[28]

By this time, the British and the French were calling for an aggressive campaign for the defeat of Bolshevism. "We shall not be far behind the mine sweepers that the British Navy are sending into the Gulf of Finland to clear the channel," Hoover promised, "if Petrograd is captured by the Russian army now operating against the Bolsheviks southwest of the city."[29]

Following Mannerheim's defection, General Iudenich had found a haven in Estonia and formed an army of fifteen thousand men, which he called, rather grandly, the Northwest Army. Iudenich himself was slack and uninspiring, but he had an able aide in General A. P. Rodzianko.[30] On June 11, the American Relief Administration agreed to deliver directly to the Northwest Army their entire ration. "It looked," Hoover said, "as if this was a military adventure offering genuine assurance of definitely re-establishing order and freeing the territory . . . from Bolshevik control." Some food had arrived by July 7, when Hoover wired, "Glad our food is winning in the cause of law and order."[31]

Soon afterward, the USS Democracy and six other American ships steamed into the Gulf of Finland with eighteen thousand tons of flour, 1,500 tons of bacon, and other rations. On July 26, General Rodzianko conveyed his thanks to Hoover that "the Northwest Russian army, which is fighting against Bolshevism in the direction of Petrograd for the restoration of the lawful order of things in Russia, is now existing practically upon American flour and bacon." Hoover wired Lansing on August 30, 1919, that "Iudenich could at an early date take Petrograd."[32]

Poised that September with his army in the Estonian border town of Narva, Iudenich felt that he had to act. His restive troops had begun to desert. His plan was to march on Petrograd in a swift and decisive thrust and capture the city. The British, though they had little faith in this enterprise, gave him six tanks manned by English-speaking "volunteers,"[33] three thousand rifles, and plenty of ammunition. He knew he could count on the Americans for the four thousand tons of food a week to feed the population of Petrograd. His strategy was to reach a point on the Petrograd–Moscow railway, which he would seize, isolating the old capital before taking it.[34]

The offensive opened on September 28, 1919, as Iudenich's army started off from Narva and headed southeast toward the town of Luga, which was on the railway, about sixty miles south of Petrograd. The British tanks demoralized the enemy, and from Luga the Northwest Army advanced due north toward the old capital in the delta of the Neva River.

On October 16, Iudenich's advance guard entered the deserted town of Gatchina, twenty-five miles south of Petrograd, where Catherine the Great had built her six-hundred-room summer palace. Here was the imperial Russia the Northwest Army hoped to restore, and the statue of Czar Paul in front of the palace seemed to be welcoming them with outstretched arm. They bivouacked in the deer park, the deer having long since been butchered to feed the two million citizens of Petrograd. Down a long avenue strewn with yellow leaves, a pair of half-starved dogs tore at the carcass of a horse, and a dead soldier lay face down in the decaying foliage.[35]

By October 20, Iudenich had captured Pulkovo Heights, overlooking the old capital; his troops could see Petrograd spread out before them—the golden dome of St. Isaac's Cathedral, the gilt spire of the Admiralty, and the Nevski Prospect. Officers through their field glasses could see the trains pulling out of the Nikolai Station and heading toward Moscow. Their puffs of steam trailing across the autumn sky spelled defeat for Iudenich, for he did not have enough troops to hold the railway line, and the trains would be bringing back reinforcements.[36]

There was considerable excitement in Washington when the first reports came in claiming that the Northwest Army had occupied Petrograd. In reality, Trotsky, the Commissar for War, had taken command. Petrograd was the cradle of the revolution; its workers had stormed the Winter Palace and placed Lenin in power. Trotsky mobilized and armed these workers, until his Seventh Army outnumbered the Northwest Army three to one. Riding his horse from sector to sector, he made sure that roadblocks and barricades went up at key intersections. He improvised some armored cars to face the tanks. He manned an out-of-commission battleship, the *Sevastopol*, berthed in the Neva River, whose guns served as his artillery.[37]

On October 21, when Iudenich attacked with his cavalry exposed in the floodplain, Trotsky's naval guns sent them galloping in all directions. Outgunned, and outmanned by workers' battalions charging with fixed bayonets, the Whites fell back toward Gatchina. The attack, which depended for its success on a speedy capture of the city, was broken. With the Red Fifteenth Army coming at him from the east, the exhausted czarist general was caught in a pincers movement.

Iudenich was pushed back to his starting point, the town of Narva in Estonia. An epidemic of typhoid spread through his ranks, killing many of those who had survived the battle. The Estonians, fearing Soviet retaliation, disarmed and interned what was left of the Northwest Army. Iudenich fled to France, where he died in exile in 1933.[38]

American efforts to topple the Bolsheviks failed on all fronts: in Siberia and Archangel, and in the Baltic provinces. Later, it was argued that American meddling had helped keep the Bolshevik regime afloat. Commander John Gade, the naval attaché with the U.S. Baltic mission, observed near the end of 1919 that "allied intervention and the blockade have been important weapons in the hands of the Soviet leaders . . . for purposes of propaganda. The result has been that a patriotic wave has swept through Soviet Russia, resulting in the present strong Soviet army. . . . The Petrograd population supported the Soviet government wholeheartedly when Iudenich advanced."[39] These were the first secret rollback operations—halfhearted, intermittent, piecemeal ventures that ended disastrously. They would not be the last.

———

By the end of 1920, the civil war was over. Exhausted by the convulsions of revolution and isolated from the rest of the world, Russia was about to sink into famine. The economy lay in ruins and the peasants were up in arms over a new government policy of requisitions. They had been given the land in 1917 with the slogans "pillage that which has been got by pillage" and "peace to the cottages, war to the palaces." What this meant, they believed, was no more taxes, rents, or debts. But now they were being made to turn over their entire harvest, setting aside a meager portion for their own needs, at a fixed price, in exchange for which they were promised basic supplies such as oil, salt, and cloth. When these supplies failed to arrive, most peasants refused to hand over their harvest surplus. In comments collected by the party investigator J. Yakovlev in 1920, one peasant said: "You receive an order on Feb. 20 stating that if you don't pay a tax by February 15 you will be fined. Whether you want to or not you begin to pay not only the tax but the fine. . . . The peasant is like a sheep. Whoever needs wool, fleeces it. He was fleeced by the Czar and the landlords and now the Comrades."[40]

As will so often be the case in a system run by bureaucrats trying to impress their bosses, the provincial committees of the People's Commissariat for Food routinely inflated their estimates for the harvest. Armed detachments known as the Food Army came in to seize the hoarded surplus by force and fought pitched battles, destroying entire villages. In some areas, the Food Army took even the seeds for the new harvest, and a decline in the cultivated acreage ensued.

In entire regions, fertile but overtaxed, such as the lower Volga and western Siberia, famine now threatened and peasant revolts broke out. The commander of the military district in Samara Province reported on February 12, 1921, that "crowds of thousands of starving peasants are besieging the barns where . . . the grain has been requisitioned for urban areas and the army. . . . The army has been forced to open fire repeatedly on the enraged crowd."[41]

Lenin had to appease the peasants, on whom the regime depended for survival in a country that was 85 percent rural. At the Tenth Party Congress in March 1921, he admitted that the policy of forced requisition had been a mistake.[42] The requisitions were abolished as part of the New Economic Policy, a strategic retreat from the extremism of wartime Communism. The peasants, after paying a tax in kind, would be allowed to dispose of their surplus. A modified market economy would be sanctioned in small industries, with profit-and-loss accounting. The currency was stabilized, and wages were now scaled according to responsibility.[43]

The New Economic Policy introduced a temporary loosening up of state control, but there were some things the state could not control, and one of these was the weather. In the spring of 1921, when the fertile Volga plain should have been soaked with rain, hot dry winds blew out of the steppes of western Siberia and the fields remained cracked and parched. The grain burned as it came up from the ground. No one in the government dared to utter the dreaded words "drought" and "famine."

On June 28, 1921, *Pravda* reported that people were "in mass flight" in the provinces of Samara and Saratov, and that peasants were eating grass and bark. On July 12, Mikhail Kalinin, the president of the Central Executive Committee of Soviets, admitted at last in *Pravda* that "in numerous districts, the drought this year has destroyed the harvest."[44]

Maxim Gorky, world-famous author of *The Lower Depths* and the founder of socialist realism in literature, issued an appeal to the press: "I ask all honest European and American people for prompt aid to the Russian people. Give Bread and Medicine."

One of those who responded to Gorky's plea was none other than President Warren Harding's Secretary of Commerce, Herbert Hoover. The famine-fighter and anti-Bolshevik (who insisted that he did not mix relief and politics) could now fulfill his frustrated dream of sending a relief mission to the Soviet heartland. Since Harding had maintained Wilson's policy of non-recognition, there were no contacts between the two countries. Here was a chance to observe what was going on inside Russia and to make direct contact with Soviet officials. Hoover might be able to show the Russian people, by his example of efficient aid, that Bolshevism did not work. It was even within the realm of possibility that the relief mission could hasten the end of the Bolshevik regime.[45]

Hoover wired Gorky on July 23, 1921, that the American Relief Administration would distribute food in the famine areas under the following conditions:

- The release of Americans held prisoner in Russia.
- An official request from Soviet authorities.
- The ARA must move freely in Russia, without government interference.[46]

On July 28, 1921, Lev Kamenev, the chairman of Pomgol, the government commission hastily set up to try to help the famine-stricken population, accepted Hoover's offer. Hoover's envoy, Walter Lyman Brown, left for Riga to hammer out the details with Maxim Litvinov, the deputy chairman of the Commission for Foreign Affairs. As negotiations proceeded in neutral Latvia, the principal stumbling block was Hoover's desire to organize local relief committees. This sent Lenin into a fury—he denounced it as interference in Soviet internal matters and called Hoover "an insolent liar." On the American side, Secretary of State Charles Evans Hughes asked Hoover to talk to Litvinov about taking back seventy-five Russians arrested in the Palmer raids, even though they had no passports. Hoover declined to present a demand that might jeopardize the overall negotiations. Already the Soviet press was suggesting that he was planning political activities.[47]

Hoover finally had to consent to some measure of Soviet control and an agreement was signed on August 21. "They were afraid we were trying to set up a state within a state," Walter Lyman Brown wrote to Hoover from Riga, "to influence the Russian people toward counter-revolution by use of 'food as a weapon.'"[48] The Russians kept their promises on at least one item in the agreement: seven Americans were let out of Soviet jails.[49]

The way was now open for Hoover's team to do its work. It would remain in Russia for nearly two years, feeding up to 10 million Russians a day in a population of 120 million. Aside from the soldiers who had fought in Siberia and Archangel in 1919, and the diplomats who had long since left, Hoover's people were the only Americans to get a close look at the Soviet system. The Hoover mission was a formative event in the gestation of American anti-Communism: the first time Americans and Russians had worked together for a common goal.

Hoover himself, busy in Washington with his duties as Secretary of Commerce, didn't set foot in Russia. The leader of the ARA team was Colonel William N. Haskell, a West Pointer who had commanded the "Fighting 69th" in World War I, and who had run the American Relief Administration program in Armenia and Romania. Hoover figured a military man would carry more weight with the Russians than a civilian. On August 27, 1921, the first seven ARA men rolled into Moscow's Windau station.[50]

Five days later, the SS *Phoenix* steamed into Petrograd with two hundred tons of rations. When it was unloaded, the ARA supervisor, D. L. Noyes, noticed that the stevedores were using their hooks to rip open bags of rice and sugar and fill their pockets. Another ARA man, Donald Lowrie, asked a Soviet guard to arrest a stevedore with bulging pockets. A Soviet official explained that it was a long-standing custom to take one day's pay in pilferage. When the incident was brought to Lenin's attention he saw the ARA protest as an affront to the Soviet state and swore to curb the overzealous Hooverites.[51]

Not all Russians were quite as combative. Lev Kamenev, the chairman of the Soviet famine agency Pomgol, a stocky man with a trim beard and a pince-nez, was courteous and friendly, and would become the ARA's friend at court. It was typical of the Soviet way of doing things that the liaison man with the ARA, Alexander Eiduk, was a member of the Secret Police. Two years earlier he had been assigned to the organization of gulags. The Americans knew him as a heavy-handed and interfering flatfoot.[52]

On September 7, the first ARA kitchen opened in Petrograd. On that first night, it fed fifteen thousand children. In Moscow, the kitchen that opened on September 11 was housed in a former luxury restaurant called the Hermitage. The Americans—there were by now two hundred of them—wanted to move into the famine areas as quickly as possible, but difficulties arose over small things such as locks for storerooms, scales, and paper and pens for keeping accounts. They had not realized they would have to bring everything with them. The Americans were appalled by Russian apathy. The general attitude was "Why hurry? There will be hungry people for a long time."

At first only children were fed: the rule at the feeding stations was that the meal must be eaten on the premises, which angered parents. Moving eastward to the Urals, the ARA men reached a town near Samara where the streets were covered with a layer of garbage six inches thick.[53]

Despite the obstacles, the Americans and their thousands of Russian employees had by December 1 set up feeding stations in 191 towns and villages and were feeding 568,000 children a day. Hoover needed more money, and President Harding backed him in a request to Congress for $20 million. His argument was that the program would ultimately benefit American farmers and shippers. The relief bill passed the House, but protests arose in the Senate. One senator said it was time for "Uncle Sam to stop being Santa Claus to the whole world." But the bill eventually passed the Senate and Harding signed it into law on December 24, 1921. Now that Hoover's funding increased, a new agreement was signed on December 30 to feed adults as well.[54]

The Russians also agreed, after more deliberation, to provide transportation from the border to the food warehouses. In a document recently released by the Soviet archives, we have the reactions of Lenin, Trotsky, and Stalin on October 18, 1921, to Kamenev's proposal for this free transportation:

Lenin: "We *should* do this, for they are giving us pure profit for the hungry and monitoring rights. . . . Therefore, we ought *not* to take payment for shipment to the warehouses . . . on condition that all be monitored."

Trotsky simply said, "Agreed."

Stalin opposed free transportation: "The issue," he wrote, "is obviously trade and not charity." He wanted to exempt the food from customs and taxes, and charge the donors for transportation and warehouse facilities.[55]

In the early months of 1922, the difficulties multiplied. When the food was moved from ship to rail, they found the switching yards useless, the railroad ties broken, the locomotives in need of repair. The confiscation of food by the Soviets to feed the Red Army, and the arrest of Russian ARA workers were more serious obstacles.

Pressed for time, the ARA had hired local volunteers regardless of their class background. Complaints began to come in from Eiduk, their friendly policeman. What about Madame Depould, who had appeared in an ARA kitchen "in diamond rings and bracelets and décolleté and by her external appearance alone evoked the protest and indignation of the hungry crowd of children and their mothers." Eiduk had her arrested and found that her husband was a baron who had fought with Kolchak.[56]

A flurry of other arrests followed. On November 4, the ARA's top Russian agent in Samara was jailed; on November 11, two in Kazan; and so on. The ARA suspended the feeding in places where their employees were being detained. The Soviets backed off, but only for a while. The arrests soon resumed, on such vague charges as "offenses against the proletariat." The ARA saw the arrests as part of a pattern of obstruction, a way for the Soviets to control food distribution through the intimidation of its Russian employees. American protests intensified, and then the Russians removed an overzealous official who was responsible for some of the arrests. The Bolsheviks were baffling in their randomness: You never knew which way the cat would jump.

When Lenin suffered a stroke in May 1922, Stalin solidified his hold on the party. The most suspicious of the Soviet leaders, he was convinced that the ARA was a front for espionage. "Trading and other missions are at the same time the most efficient spy agencies of the world bourgeoisie," Stalin said, "which now knows Soviet Russia, knows her weak and strong sides." This need for secrecy, this poisonous suspicion, was to be the hallmark of a regime that had much to hide. Trotsky told the American Communist journalist Anna Louise Strong that the ARA was "a highly-qualified feeler, sent forth by the American government into the very heart of Russia."[57]

There was, of course, a kernel of truth to this, for the ARA went beyond its mission and sent reports on economic and political conditions to the State Department and the Department of Commerce. "My work after we remove the camouflage is certainly to a considerable measure semi-official," Walter Lyman Brown wrote to the State Department. Colonel Haskell reported to Hoover on October 20, 1921: "The Soviet government has a stranglehold on Russia but lacks the support and confidence of the people." Haskell also contributed data on Soviet leaders, with whom he was in daily contact, and spiced it with Moscow rumors. Thus did a private relief agency assume the information-gathering functions of a consulate or embassy.

As part of the distribution program, officers serving on U.S. destroyers were allowed to go ashore at Black Sea ports on ARA business. Occasionally they indulged in a bit of snooping. In September 1921, Lieutenant Dunn of the USS *Gilmer* visited Novorossik and reported to his fleet commander, Admiral Bristol, the number and locations of the gun emplacements and minefields he had seen.[58]

Now that the ARA was feeding adults as well as children, the amount of food being distributed doubled. The trouble was, the Russian transport system could not cope with the increase. Thousands of tons were stranded in freight cars at railroad stations and sidings. The railroad workers, also on short rations, refused to work unless they were fed. Colonel Haskell turned over to them 4,500 tons of corn. Even then, the ARA could not move its food to the feeding stations. The relief program was in a state of crisis. On April 10, 1922, Colonel Haskell sent Hoover an uncoded message: "Attitude of Soviets has grown steadily more indifferent and disagreeable," he cabled. "Seizure of American relief supplies, especially corn in transit, has begun. . . . Abuses continue and promises are made only to be broken."[59]

Suddenly Kamenev, who had been too busy, agreed to see the ARA director. Haskell accused him of seizing ARA supplies to feed the Red Army. "There is no use in bringing supplies to Russia," he said, "if they don't reach the starving." The confiscations ended. On April 12, Kamenev arranged a meeting with Felix Dzerzhinsky, the much-feared head of the Cheka (secret police), who was also Commissioner for Transport. Dzerzhinsky gave orders that ARA seals must never be broken and that the trains must stick to schedule. Hoover's food trains now had a high priority. From then on, Colonel Haskell dealt directly with Dzerzhinsky, and they established what the Russians called *poriadok*—an orderly way.[60]

When the ice broke that spring, river transport became available to places where trains did not go. In the villages, the arrival of food slowed down the movement of refugees. Seeds were planted and the death count was reduced, although five million of the estimated 29 million in the famine zones died in 1921 and 1922.[61] By August, 1922, 10.5 million Russians were getting daily meals in 18,073 ARA feeding stations in twenty-five provinces. The famine operation was now running smoothly.

Gorky, who had turned against Lenin and gone into exile in Italy, sent a letter to Hoover on July 30, 1922, from Sorrento: "In all the history of human suffering," he wrote, "I know of no accomplishment which in magnitude and generosity can be compared to the relief that you actually accomplished."[62]

Even Trotsky had a change of heart. In a speech on March 12, 1922, at the Bolshoi Theater to a plenary session of the Moscow soviets, he praised the selflessness of the American effort while deploring past policies to help Whites:

> We have been getting help from that American quasi-government agency known as the ARA. This help is growing day by day and it is obviously playing a gigantic role in our lives. . . . Of the 117 [American] employees of the ARA, 15 have caught typhus. . . . When you think of these sacrifices, you want to remind yourself that there are still people . . . who are motivated exclusively by feelings of humanity and inner

nobility regardless of their class affiliation. . . . I read the obituary of Violet Kilara, the Anglo-Saxon woman. She was a young, weak, fragile creature, and came to Buzaluk in very harsh, backward, and barbaric conditions. She died doing her duty and was buried there. Here tonight we have counted six such graves—there most likely will be more. . . . The Great Republic across the ocean has shown ten times more generosity than all of Europe. . . . But for the sake of honesty we should admit that we have mixed emotions. . . . We often hear the names of the leaders of the ARA associated with statements that are hostile to us. . . . The day when the men in Washington firmly and clearly state that they have had enough of Wilson's experience with Kolchak . . . that the United States will not provide any support for new candidates for the role of executioner of the Russian workers and peasants. . . . We will see the role of the ARA in its true light. . . . The ambiguity that exists in our attitude towards the ARA arises from an entire situation that is telling us to be careful.[63]

Such was the reaction of the fierce Commissar of War, a mixture of genuine admiration and lingering suspicion, America as savior, and America as enemy, conspiring to overthrow the Bolshevik regime.

—

In the summer of 1922, the Soviets announced that the famine was over and Russia was on its feet. The harvest looked promising and Hoover thought it was time to get out: the ARA was a rescue team, not a welfare agency. By mid-September, adults were no longer fed and meals for children were down to a million a day. Hoover realized that the Russians wanted to use the ARA as a springboard for recognition. But he agreed with the Secretary of State that recognition would be a mistake. As Hughes put it: "The fundamental doctrine of the men who govern Russia is . . . to overthrow and destroy the government of the United States, of England, of France, of all the civilized nations of the Western world."[64]

With a bountiful harvest, sufficient to meet Russia's food requirements, the Soviet leadership in the fall of 1922 hit upon a scheme that would give a boost to the New Economic Policy. They could export grain and buy machinery if the ARA remained in Russia and took up the slack. Kamenev told Colonel Haskell on November 6 that Russia would be able to ship $50 million worth of grain if the ARA stayed on. But Hoover was not prepared to provide charity so that the Russians could sell their surplus. He wrote to Colonel Haskell on November 18: "The ARA . . . must protest against the inhumanity of . . . exporting food from starving peoples in order to secure machinery and raw materials for the economic improvement of the country." Nonetheless, Hoover authorized on December 19 the feeding of three million children, who he did not think should suffer from the cynical policies of their leaders.

When Hoover reduced the aid, the Soviets retaliated with various pinpricks and restrictions. The ARA staff had to pay cash for telegrams. The number of railroad cars at their disposal was reduced. They were asked to move to more modest offices in Moscow. The Soviets seemed to have countless ways of making life unpleasant. The kitchens and food stations fell under their control, the mail was held up, and in December the privilege of sealed pouches was suspended. Five ARA staff were deported when they tried to take articles of value such as icons and furs out in the pouch to avoid the export tax. An exposé in *Izvestia* under the headline "How They Are Helping" said the articles were valued at several trillion rubles. It took time to close the stations, so that despite the harassment, the ARA stayed on until July 1923.[65]

Hoover had hoped that the ARA mission would introduce a sliver of democracy into the Bolshevik system, and that it might take hold like a grafted shoot on a growing plant. The result was just the opposite. The ARA contributed to Russia's economic recovery and helped shore up the regime. It gave Lenin breathing space to implement the New Economic Policy and averted local rebellions. Instead of stemming the tide of Bolshevism, as Hoover had hoped, the ARA secured the regime more firmly in power.

At best, by its efficient handling of the task at hand, the ARA was a living contradiction to the dogma of class warfare. Here were the emissaries of the richest country in the world rescuing the workers and peasants of a Bolshevik state. Yet if Hoover had stayed out of Russia in 1921, the Bolshevik regime, like any regime that cannot feed its own people, would have been in serious trouble.

Over the years, as Soviet history was rewritten according to the policy needs of the moment, the Hoover mission became a convenient target. The thread of hostility could be traced back to the ARA's arrival in August 1921, when *Pravda* wrote: "Hoover's messengers carry themselves with a splendid disdain, like a duke visiting the hut of a charcoal burner."[66]

The bad aftertaste lingered, rather than the memory of good deeds. On April 2, 1924, a Moscow paper reported that Soviet citizens had been arrested in Kiev and charged with accepting ARA food in exchange for conducting espionage. On May 18, two men were tried for this post facto crime: One was sentenced to ten years, the other to five. Hoover, from Washington, said the convictions were "an impossible barrier against the renewal of official relations."[67]

The campaign of disparagement spread to official tomes. In 1928, the *Great Soviet Encyclopedia* said that "under the guise of charity," the ARA had relieved a crisis of agricultural overproduction in America. In 1949, the historian A. N. Kogan wrote an article entitled "Anti-Soviet Acts of the ARA in Soviet Russia," on the theme of intervention by other than military means. In 1950, the *Great Soviet Encyclopedia* promoted the ARA to "an apparatus for spying and wrecking activities." In 1960, a Soviet history textbook said that the ARA was "expected . . . to secretly organize an insurrectionary force."

For millions of ordinary Russians, however, their only firsthand knowledge of the United States came from Hoover's people, who had arrived in towns and villages where the wheat cellars were empty and the livestock was bleached bones, and who had fed them when their own government could not and asked nothing in return. One of these Russians was the writer Viktor Nekrasov, who wrote in *Novy Mir* in December 1962 that as a boy he had known of America from postage stamps and Fenimore Cooper and "through ARA condensed milk. . . . We collected the labels from the cans, with their pictures of Indians and bisons. . . . I remember the milk and snow-white bread, soft as cotton."[68]

V

THE ROAD

TO RECOGNITION

A fter the affable clubhouse Republican Warren G. Harding was inaugurated in March 1921, he brought in as Attorney General an old Ohio
crony who had managed his campaign for the nomination, the thick-necked,
bowler-hatted, diamond-stickpinned Harry Daugherty. Harding's poker pal
was even less suitable than Palmer to run the Justice Department, which became known under his tenure as the "Department of Easy Virtue." In August,
Daugherty named his friend of thirty years, William J. Burns, to head the Bureau of Investigation. The twenty-six-year-old John Edgar Hoover was named
assistant director because of his familiarity with bureau routine. To ensure
favorable publicity, Daugherty made the owner of the *Washington Post*, Ned
McLean, an honorary "dollar-a-day" special agent, and gave a badge to his
alcoholic son Draper, who wrote bum checks when he was sober.[1]

Stately, plump, cigar-chomping William J. Burns was one of the best-
known private detectives in the country. According to the popular dime novels of the period, the great detective was born, not made, part actor, part
preacher, with a knack for making people talk, and the canny persistence to
track down leads. He lived up to the adage that it takes a liar to catch a liar and
a thief to catch a thief. Burns had all these qualifications, which he first employed in the Secret Service, where he handled counterfeiting cases. In 1909,
Burns opened the International Detective Agency and made headlines in
high-profile cases such as the bombing of the *Los Angeles Times*. Twenty
workers were killed when the printing plant exploded in 1910 as part of a
campaign to organize the typesetters. Burns uncovered the culprits, the labor

leaders and brothers James and John McNamara, whose denials made them symbols of labor's struggle against capital. Just before the trial opened in October 1911, the brothers reversed themselves and pleaded guilty. John was sentenced to life and James to fifteen years.

The case established the Burns agency as one of the top union-busters in the country, sending its spies into factories to report on worker unrest. In an age when detectives were celebrities, Burns burnished his image with a series of popular books on his greatest cases.

There was a seamy side to the profession, and Burns was accused of jury tampering, office break-ins, and wiretapping. He brought into the Bureau of Investigation some of his former employees, one or two of whom had criminal records, and continued to use the methods that had served him so well, such as bugging and black bag jobs (breaking and entering).[2]

It was under Burns that a central fingerprint registry was established. President Harding did his bit by posing for the cameras while having his prints taken. With the hearty approval of Burns's assistant, the bureau's drive against radicals continued unabated. In his three years as assistant director, Hoover began taking more of an interest in life outside the office, though he still lived at home with his parents. He joined the University Club and the National Geographic Society. He took up golf at a suburban club. He became a Mason, submitting to the arcane initiation rite, blindfolded with a noose around his neck, and swearing at the point of a dagger never to reveal Masonic secrets. With regard to his fellow humans, he remained standoffish. The framed photograph on his office desk displayed his beloved Airedale, Spee De Bozo, whom he took for walks each morning when he bought his paper.[3]

Anti-radical nativism remained a powerful political force in twenties America, giving Hoover's General Intelligence Division a mandate to expand its surveillance of suspect organizations. In June 1921, the Boston field office reported that Harvard was employing the British economist Harold Laski, known for his "radical utterances," and that Wellesley College "offered a course in anarchism" in which the theories of Marx and Lenin were discussed.[4]

Burns stayed on the good side of influential congressmen by hiring their constituents. In a memo on May 5, 1922, he informed Hoover that "Mr. Holland . . . is the man that Mr. Husted has been after us to put on." (James William Husted of New York was a member of the House Appropriations Committee.) . . . "He is a very high-class man and we want to start him at $8.00 a day. . . . Senator [Frank] Gooding of Idaho has two men. . . . The Attorney General says to put one of them on."[5]

Unfriendly congressmen, of whom there were quite a few, were targeted for surveillance. When Senator Joseph France of Maryland, a critic of the deportation raids and a partisan of recognition, toured Russia in 1921, every scrap of information concerning his visit was collected in Hoover's files, including a telegram from London saying that he had arrived safely after his trip. Field agents in the United States continued to cover France's activities. The Chicago field office reported in July that he had spoken to a group of unemployed workers.[6]

In September 1922, the Minnesota Republican congressman Oscar E. Keller called for the impeachment of Attorney General Daugherty after his brazenly anti-labor conduct in the strike of railway shopmen. These repair and maintenance workers were striking to block a $12^1/2$ percent wage cut. Declaring that "the government lays its hand on rich and poor alike when they do not obey the law," Daugherty obtained an injunction from a federal judge barring the workers from any word or deed that would hamper railroad operations.[7]

Twelve hundred strikers were prosecuted for contempt of court and convicted. The strike was broken, thanks to the flagrantly partisan tactics of Daugherty, Burns, and Hoover.[8]

When Congressman Keller made his charges, which got nowhere, BI agents broke into his Washington office and went through his papers. Under Daugherty's leadership, the bureau confirmed its critics' worst fears. As one newsman put it, the BI became "a private hole in the corner goon squad for the Attorney General. Its arts were the arts of snooping, bribery, and blackmail."[9]

A former BI agent later explained the agents' methods to a Senate committee: "Oh, search this—find out all the mail that comes, all the papers. . . . Find out in his home. . . . There is a servant working in the house. If she is a colored servant, go and get a colored detective woman . . . to entertain her, find out the exact plan of the house, everything they discuss at the table. . . . Find out what he has up in his office. . . . Have people go to his office and go through it."[10]

Protesting the bureau's zeal, J. Thomas Heflin of Alabama said on the floor of the Senate in 1923 that "these detectives went through the office of the senator from Arkansas [Thaddeus H. Caraway] and they read his correspondence; they went through the office of the senator from Wisconsin [Robert La Follette] and God only knows how many other offices. . . . That was a 'general fishing expedition'; it was fishing in the night when senators were at home asleep . . . and alert detectives were quietly going through their offices."[11]

In spite of the raids on congressmen's offices, when Burns appeared before the House Appropriations Committee to discuss his budget, he usually received a sympathetic hearing. In the spring of 1922, he described the scope of the bureau's activities:

Representative George H. Tinkham of Massachusetts: "Do you do prohibition work?"

Burns: "Some . . . very often a great deal of it."

Tinkham: "What investigations are now the principal ones?"

Burns: "The anti-trust work; we are doing a tremendous lot of work of that now. Army and Navy frauds; we are doing a great deal of that. . . . Automobile thefts. . . . Bank frauds. . . . Crimes on Indian reservations. . . . False impersonation of federal officers. You would be surprised at the great amount of work we have, and the trouble it is causing us. . . . Passport and visa applications. We have a great deal of that."

Tinkham: "Have your bankrupt investigations increased in numbers?"

Burns: "They have very perceptibly, and the radical activities have increased wonderfully."

Representative James W. Husted of New York: "Would you say that those radical activities are particularly dangerous or of a violent character at the present time?"

Burns: "Very. I cannot impress upon you too much how dangerous they are at the present moment."[12]

Two years later, in his annual appearance before the Appropriations Committee, Burns said: "Radicalism is becoming stronger every day in this country. . . . The proof is very conclusive. In fact, it is overwhelming."

Representative William B. Oliver of Alabama asked, "Could you give us the general nature of the propaganda that they are distributing, and which you say is dangerous?"

Burns: "Their propaganda principally consists of urging the working men to strike, with the ultimate purpose of bringing about a revolution in this country."[13]

In his annual appearances, Burns stressed the growing number of radical publications, which were being circulated in churches, schools, and colleges. In the summer of 1923, he told the committee that the Communists "have schools all over the country, where they are teaching children from four to five years old." For children from the age of six on, he said, they had athletic clubs.[14]

Although the bureau's annual budget depended on conveying the impression that pernicious forces were at work to undermine the most sacred sanctuaries of American life, Burns's remarks had a foundation in fact. The party did have a children's section, called the Young Pioneers, founded in 1922 and modeled on the Boy Scouts. The children of Communist parents were enrolled as newborn babes and given aliases "to replace bourgeois christenings," as the *Daily Worker* put it. At the first national Young Pioneer convention in Philadelphia in May 1926, the children all wore red mufflers and heard a fifteen-year-old speaker tell them: "The children who attend school must be taught class hatred and it is the purpose of the Young Pioneers to do this."[15]

A Young Pioneer pamphlet instructed that Lincoln and Washington should be unfavorably compared to Lenin and Marx, and recommended that the children act out little dramas at meetings. "Say Lincoln is worried about the military situation during the war," advised the pamphlet. "He walks up and down, talking to his cabinet. 'How can we weaken the southern armies? Ah! We'll free the slaves behind their lines. . . . We have to do it. Anything to destroy the enemy!'" The author of the pamphlet observed: "This method drives insight right home."

On Washington, the pamphlet said: "He was the richest slave holder in America and spilled the blood of artisans and poor farmers in order that his own class should rule."

A tableau on Negroes was also proposed: "A town in the south: Big Sign: 'Nigger, don't let the sun set on you in this town.' Negros and Whites organize and compel the removal of the sign."[16]

———

In the summer of 1923, fifty-eight-year-old President Harding went on a transcontinental tour that took him to distant Alaska. On the way home to Washington on August 2, he stopped at a San Francisco hotel, where he suffered a fatal stroke. Harding's death was like the lancing of a boil. All the pus secreted by his administration began to leak out, from the President's extramarital affairs to the malfeasance in the departments of Interior and Justice. The Secretary of the Interior, Albert B. Fall, had secretly sold the lease to a naval oil reserve at Teapot Dome, Wyoming, to an oil company. The Attorney General, Harry Daugherty, tried to block a Senate investigation of the swindle.

Harding has gone down as the worst President in the nation's history up to the year 2000, unfit for the office and manipulated by corrupt cronies. Another way of looking at his uncompleted term might be to see him as a transitional figure who steered his country back to normalcy in the first years of peace after a cataclysmic world war, with normalcy meaning, among other things, a sprinkling of skulduggery and hanky-panky in high government circles.

Vice President Calvin Coolidge served out Harding's term as the Senate inquiry into the oil leases got underway. Feeling insecure in the new administration, Daugherty tried to convince the cautious Coolidge that he was a valuable cabinet member. But with Coolidge running for President in the 1924 election, and with Daugherty mixed up in Teapot Dome, he became a political liability and walked the plank in March.[17]

In April, Coolidge appointed Harlan Fiske Stone, a New Hampshire Yankee of granite integrity, with whom he had gone to Amherst, to replace Daugherty. Stone, the dean of Columbia Law School, was named as the antidote to his predecessor, having been a vocal critic of the Palmer raids.

After three years of Daugherty and Burns, Stone was just the man to clean up the Bureau of Investigation, which he thought was in "exceedingly bad odor." Burns embodied, to his mind, all of its undesirable aspects, and Stone fired him in May. The new Attorney General, who had been brought up in the Puritan tradition of probity in word and deed, wanted the bureau to cease its political investigations and restrict itself to violations of federal laws. On May 15, he issued this statement to the press: "There is always the possibility that a secret police may become a menace to free government and free institutions, because it carries with it the possibility of abuses of power. . . . The Bureau of Investigation is not concerned with political or other opinions. . . . It is only concerned with such conduct as is forbidden by the laws of the United States."[18]

To replace Burns, Stone wanted "just the right man for the job." But who was the right man? Stone was new; he didn't know the personnel. He asked Mabel Willebrandt, the assistant attorney general in charge of Prohibition enforcement. Willebrandt told him that J. Edgar Hoover was "honest and informed and one who operated like an electric wire, with almost trigger response." Hoover was not yet thirty, and Stone observed that "everyone says he's too young, but maybe that's an asset."[19]

And so it was that on May 10, 1924, the Attorney General invited Hoover to his office and offered him the job of Acting Director. The man responsible for the planning and execution of the deportation raids, the man who had run the anti-radical operations of the Harding years, now presented himself in the guise of a reformer.

"I'll take the job, Mr. Stone, on certain conditions," he said.

"What are they?" Stone asked.

"The Bureau must be divorced from politics and not be a catch-all for political hacks. Appointments must be based on merit. Second, promotions will be made on proved ability and the Bureau will be responsible only to the Attorney General."

"I wouldn't give it to you under any other condition," Stone said. "That's all. Good day."[20]

On the surface, Hoover scrupulously followed Stone's efforts to end the spying, bugging, and undercover work, and to cut the personnel and field offices. "Are you not contemplating contracting the work of the bureau?" he was asked on May 15, when he appeared before the Brookhart committee investigating Daugherty. "Most certainly," he replied. "Instructions have been sent to offices in the field to limit their investigations to violations of the statutes." By the end of the decade his staff would be down to 339 agents from a high of 570 in 1920, and field offices had been cut from fifty-three to twenty-two.[21]

In the brief tenure of Attorney General Stone, Hoover's Red-hunting General Intelligence Division was dissolved and wiretapping was banned. The bureau was told not to investigate political activities. Hoover continued, cautiously, to use informants and agents to keep abreast of developments in the Communist Party. He was practicing what he thought of as preventive medicine. It was ludicrous to think that a federal investigative agency should not keep files. There was no awareness in any other government agency of what the party was actually doing.[22]

———

We now know, thanks to the Soviet archives, that the American Communist Party, though small in numbers and isolated from the mainstream, was busily establishing a subculture that acted in hidden ways, attracting not only a loyal membership, but a number of agents assigned to special tasks.

The routine use of espionage as an instrument of the state was foreign to the American experience. Although most other countries had their spies, the United States did not have an intelligence agency. As Herbert Hoover's Secretary of State Henry Stimson famously said, "Gentlemen do not read other people's mail." In the Soviet system, however, with its inbred fear of domestic and foreign enemies, and its oppressive mania for control, espionage permeated every agency of government. Behind every village mayor, behind every railroad stationmaster, there was an all-powerful Secret Police keeping tabs, whether it was called the Cheka, the OGPU, the NKVD, or the KGB. This secret police, operating at home and abroad, was the very heart of the Soviet system.[23]

In the United States, where the Soviets did not have the convenience of installing their spies in consulates, they had to devise other means. One was mail drops for letters to the American party (then based in Chicago) from the Comintern. On November 25, 1925, the Workers' Party complained to the Comintern that sloppy handling had exposed some mail drops: "In place of individual letters being sent, we have received ten to fifteen letters in one envelope, which made the package so bulky that it was sent to the customs authorities and the letter was opened. . . . This practice must be stopped."[24] Habits of secrecy and clandestine work had to be formed, such as aliases, the use of ciphers, and ways to escape surveillance.

Moscow gold continued to keep the American party afloat, financing publications and front groups, paying the salaries of the several hundred permanent staff, as well as the core of activists who could turn out the troops to man a picket line, beef up a demonstration, or stuff envelopes. In 1921 and 1922, the party received a total of $80,379, equal to $650,000 today. In 1923, the party leader Charles Ruthenberg complained that the $37,500 he received was "far from sufficient."[25]

In 1924, the Soviet trade agency Amtorg opened an office at 261 Fifth Avenue. Its commercial activities were a cloak for illegal work. Among the Amtorg staff were members of the OGPU. While engaged in a substantial amount of legitimate trade, including deals with Ford and General Electric, Amtorg was also a front for espionage activities.

In addition to using official agencies allowed to operate in the United States, such as the Red Cross and Amtorg, as a cover for espionage, Soviet intelligence began in the twenties to plant spies who either came from Russia or were recruited from the American party. These spies were called "illegals," distinguishing them from agents under legal cover. By 1927, the Fourth Department of the Red Army (the GRU, or espionage branch) had an illegal, Alfred Tilton, living in Edgemere, Long Island. Tilton and his wife, Maria, had entered the country with Canadian passports in the names of Mr. and Mrs. Joseph Paquette.[26] Tilton was a Latvian, and he scouted the American party for a fellow Latvian who could be recruited for underground work. The man he found was Nicholas Dozenberg, a fair-haired, sallow-skinned little man, born in Riga, who had come to the United States in 1904 at the age of twenty-two. He rose in party ranks until he was named "head of the literature department" for the *Daily Worker*. Dozenberg did not shrink from any task. In 1922, he had taken part in a wildcat strike of Lithuanian mineworkers in Herrin, Illinois. When the mining company brought in scabs, the Lithuanians captured a number of them, put them up against a wall, and shot them. Dozenberg was then the business manager of the Communist publication *Voice of Labor*, which called for a "Gunmen Defense Fund" to provide each striker with a high-powered rifle and five hundred rounds of ammunition.[27]

In 1927, Dozenberg was instructed to go to a restaurant in New York on Lenox Avenue, where he met Tilton, who told him to drop out of the party and work for Soviet Military Intelligence. For thirteen years, Dozenberg served the GRU in America, Europe, and Asia, living the life of a traveling spy, which, by his account, was one of stultifying drudgery. When Dozenberg testified before the House Un-American Activities Committee in 1940, he was asked if he had ever obtained any military information. "Never," he replied. "You can show me a blueprint of a watch and tell me it is a battleship and I wouldn't know the difference." By his account, Soviet espionage was a haphazard, ineffective, and muddled enterprise.[28]

Having become a skilled photographer under Tilton, who was able to obtain and photograph a complete set of plans of the British warship *Royal Oak,* Dozenberg was sent to Bucharest in 1931 to set up a newsreel company. Then, inexplicably, he was transferred to Tientsin in northern China, where he ran a store selling film and cameras. "My activities," he later testified, "were absolutely nothing else but to attend to my business."

Life in Tientsin was drab but stressful. For months at a time he received no word from Moscow, and no money. By then he was married, and his wife was depressed; she didn't think they would ever leave China. Her condition worsened and she died on January 1, 1936. "The difficult life," Dozenberg told HUAC, "that's what killed my first wife. She took too much to heart that condition." From China he was sent to Corregidor in the Philippines, a good spot to spy on American bases, though all Dozenberg had time for was selling Bell & Howell cameras at the Fort Mills post exchange. Later, when he was arrested, he was found to have quite a few suspicious calling cards from officers at Fort Mills; he explained they were only business contacts. What he was proudest of was that over the years "I have sold no less than half a million dollars worth of American goods."[29]

Dozenberg returned to the United States at the end of 1938 and was arrested a year later on a false passport charge. He served his year and a day in the federal prison in Lewisburg, Pennsylvania. Once released, like so many retired Americans, he moved to Florida. When he was asked why he had gone into the GRU, he said, "partly conviction, and partly once you run into a game of that sort, well, it becomes so regular that you don't pay attention to it." It was like any other boring and underpaid job, with neither a promotion nor a pension.[30]

In their humble beginnings, hampered by nonrecognition, Soviet spies in the United States stumbled along, improvising. One of Dozenberg's cutouts complained that it was hard to find good people. But still they came, thanks to America's lenient policies of entry, these unwanted emissaries, arriving on our shores under false pretenses to carry out illegal missions on behalf of a foreign government. Trained in underground work, they exercised a minimal caution in security-lax America and went about their business. From time to time, one of them might come to the notice of the government to provide a fleeting image, like the blurred snapshot of a careless photographer, only to vanish and resurface ten years later, on another continent, with a different name.

One such agent, who replaced Tilton in 1929 for the GRU, was Mark Zilbert, whose real name was Moishe Stern. A graduate of the Red Army's prestigious Frunze Academy, he recruited William M. Disch, a draftsman for the Arma Engineering Company, which did classified work for the Navy on instruments such as gyro-compasses. Stern offered Disch $2,000 for the compass blueprints in $100 bills, which he turned over to the FBI. Stern was followed to the Amtorg offices, where he took the blueprints to be photographed, which proved that the trading agency was involved in espionage.

An FBI agent told Disch: "Gee, Bill, you did open up a hornet's nest." Stern then vanished, and the FBI man said, "He must have flown the coop." Seven years later, in 1938, the agent showed up with a photograph and asked Disch, "Do you know who this fellow is, Bill?" "Yes, that's my old pal," Disch said. "He is supposed to have been killed in the Spanish civil war," the agent said. "That is a trick of theirs. He will pop up again under an assumed name." But Stern/Zilbert did not pop up again. In Spain he had become a legendary figure in the International Brigades, General Kleber. Upon returning to Russia in 1939, Stern fell victim to the purges, and died in the gulag.[31]

———

During the Depression years, when Herbert Hoover was President, the Communist subculture flourished and gained the self-sufficiency of a state within a state, with its own unions, housing projects, insurance company, legal defense system, and youth organizations. There were so many Young Pioneers in New York that they had to rent Madison Square Garden for the 1930 Christmas celebration. On the stage, a "revolutionary" Christmas tree was decorated with a cartoon of the President, whose head was an apple, and placards lampooning war and the police. Then came a boxing match between science and religion with the left-leaning columnist Heywood Broun as referee. In the seventh round, religion won by KO. Then "God" in a business suit danced around the tree with an entourage of priests and rabbis carrying signs that said "Dope Peddlers." The *Daily Worker* reported that "the children's animated faces and readiness to sing their revolutionary songs and yells was as big a treat as the circus itself."[32]

In 1930, Hazel Chatfield, a district superintendent of public schools in the Bronx, where the party owned housing projects, noticed that the absentee rate for twenty-two schools in the district rose by 20 percent on May Day, the day of the Communist parade, but not a legal holiday. She was informed that at PS 89, stickers on the glass transoms over the door, on desks and on walls, urged the children to stay out of school on May 1. In another violation of school rules, one youngster in an eighth-grade class declined to salute the flag and pledge allegiance. The principal told the student that her graduation to high school was in jeopardy and still she refused and was suspended. When the time came for a hearing, instead of her parents a lawyer for the Communist-controlled International Labor Defense showed up. He was told this was a school matter and he had no business there. Finally the mother and her fourteen-year-old daughter appeared, and the mother said she was not aware that her daughter was setting a bad example. The girl promised to salute the flag in the future and was admitted to high school. In another case, the eighth-grade student Leo Shapiro refused to stop distributing circulars that said, "The only flag the Pioneer salutes is the Red flag." Hazel Chatfield was aware that in PS 89, a school of sixteen hundred, there were three hundred "of that type." Most of them lived in the housing cooperative at 2700 to 2800 Bronx Park East.[33]

Dr. William J. O'Shea, the New York City superintendent of schools, knew that a small number of children were imbued with a fanatical spirit. It had started in 1928 in PS 61, which was made up mostly of the children of Russian and Polish immigrants. The Young Pioneers went around the classrooms asking, "Are you in favor of taking care of miners' children in Pennsylvania?" Of course any child would say yes. He felt, however, that this sort of fanaticism existed in only a handful of the city's seven hundred schools. He had the problem under control. Anyone teaching Communism would be under suspension in twenty minutes.[34]

———

Obedience to the party line was paramount, for the line zigged and zagged like a polygraph needle, on the whim of Moscow, and it was pointless for the American Communist leaders to maintain convictions based on their own experience. William Z. Foster, the American party's trade union boss, found this out the hard way, for he had been carrying out the strategy of "burrowing from within" with some success. He was convinced that any attempt on the part of the Communists to establish unions of their own, tagged with the party label, and in competition with the dominant AFL, was doomed to failure.

But in 1928, Stalin changed the line. In the so-called Third Period, the workers were told to take the offensive and form their own unions. Foster, who had always rejected separate Communist unions, known as "dual unions," calling them "a malignant disease," meekly obeyed. All alliances with the AFL were broken. Under the slogan "class against class," Foster threw himself into forming dual unions such as the National Miners Union and the National Textile Workers Union.[35]

In March 1929, Foster sent Fred Beal to organize workers who were walking out in wildcat strikes in mill towns in North and South Carolina. He told Beal, who had started working in textile mills at age fourteen as a bobbin boy, "You're a real American, you'll fit in better than those who look like foreigners."[36]

Beal went to Gastonia, North Carolina, to recruit for Foster's new Communist textile union. On March 29, the Loray Mills, who paid $9 to $12 a week, fired twenty workers who had signed his membership cards. Beal called a strike, selecting mill hands to lead it. "They had that look, you know," he recalled, "able to get people excited."[37]

Beal wanted to stick to bread-and-butter issues, but once he had done the groundwork, the Communists sent in trained agitators. "They all flooded in and colonized the strike," Beal recalled. "They took the reins and told us what the policy was." Communist militants passed out the *Daily Worker*. "This strike," its editorial trumpeted, "is the first shot in a battle which will be heard around the world." The party sent down an agitprop specialist, Edith Miller, who schooled the strikers' children by showing them scenes of the Paris Commune of 1871.[38]

The Gastonia police chief, O. F. Aderholt, personally led a raid on a tent colony of strikers on June 7, which exploded into a firefight. Aderholt and two other police officers were killed, as well as seven strikers. At that point, the strike actually did become a shot heard 'round the world. Beal and six others were arrested and tried for murder. The International Labor Defense, the Communist-controlled legal aid agency, rented office space in Charlotte and sent its lawyers down to defend the Gastonia seven. But as Beal soon discovered, their purpose was not to get him off but to make him into a martyr.[39]

When Edith Miller took the stand in the packed Charlotte courthouse, she was shown an illustration from her book on the Paris Commune. "And it purports to show a child firing a cannon and a lot of dead people in soldiers' uniforms?" the ILD lawyer asked. "Yes," Edith Miller said, "it shows a child taking part." As he listened, Fred Beal took one look at the jury and knew that her testimony wasn't going to do him any good. He knew right then and there that he would be found guilty.

The *Daily Worker* published a cartoon of Judge Barnhill, his hands dripping with blood, which was circulated around the courtroom. Maybe, thought Beal, the jury got a look at it. Then the Communists elected a mock "labor jury," half Negro and half white, and brought them into the courtroom, knowing full well that the blacks would be stopped and told to go upstairs. The white jurors went upstairs with them, and someone in the courtroom said, "Oh God, they are convicted now." The mock jury brought in a verdict, published in the *Daily Worker*, that the judge was guilty.[40]

Fred Beal and the other defendants were out on bail, paid for by the ILD. Their lawyers persuaded them that they could not get a fair trial and that they should jump bail and flee to the Soviet Union. The ILD made the travel arrangements, obtained the false passports, and saw them off. In Russia, Fred Beal was sent to Uzbekistan to pick cotton and later worked in a tractor plant in Kharkov. He finally managed to get back to the United States, thoroughly disenchanted. In 1938 he was arrested and extradited to North Carolina to serve out his prison term.[41]

———

Between 1925 and 1930, as radicalism surged in the Depression years, the Bureau of Investigation was in hibernation, due to Harlan Fiske Stone's instructions not to investigate anyone for their political activities. The vacuum was soon filled by private organizations, for which anti-Communism was identical with patriotism.

Ralph Easley's National Civic Federation was originally formed to bring together business and labor leaders. After the First World War, Easley steered the NCF away from mediating labor disputes and into anti-Communist work, conducting his own investigations, with his own informants, and setting up a Department of Revolutionary Movements.[42] For Easley, the Bolshevik menace was the urgent issue of the day.

Aside from monitoring Communist activities, the former Kansas City newspaperman was one of the leading figures in opposing the diplomatic recognition of the Soviet Union. The clash over recognition lasted from 1919 to 1933, under five Presidents, pitting the anti-radicals against a coalition of fellow travelers such as Raymond Robins and Lincoln Steffens and a handful of isolationist senators. Both sides pressured successive Presidents, with Easley and Robins as the chief lobbyists for their respective camps.

William Borah of Idaho, a maverick Republican who served in the Senate for thirty-three years, thought it was foolish not to recognize the government of such a vast and populated nation. They had as much of a right to their form of government as we did to ours, he said. No sane people, he argued, should allow questions of trade to hinge on likes and dislikes. We traded with the ruthless Turks, after all. The Soviets had bought $16 million worth of wheat from Canada, and Borah wondered, why not from the United States?[43]

Borah was chairman of the Senate Foreign Relations Committee, and with the prompting of his friend Robins, he named a subcommittee in January 1924 to hold hearings on Soviet recognition.[44]

Prior to the hearings, Borah asked Robins for help in framing a rebuttal to the charge that "the Soviet government was responsible for any propaganda in this country during the last three years. . . . I am convinced there is nothing to the charge." Borah was expecting a barrage of anti-Soviet testimony from the State Department, which was presenting the government's side. To document his case, Secretary of State Charles Evans Hughes asked J. Edgar Hoover for a memo on radical activities. Hoover responded with a report of more than four hundred pages, which he later described as "setting forth in detail what has been carried on in this country by the Communist groups among the children, among the churches, among the labor organizations, and in practically all walks of life."[45]

At the hearings, from January 21 to 24, each side marshaled a phalanx of witnesses. Robert F. Kelley, the learned chief of the State Department's Eastern European Division, carried the day with testimony based on the Hoover memo that the Soviets wanted world revolution and should be treated like an outlaw state. Borah's resolution in favor of recognition got nowhere. Why open the door to a country intent on subverting the government that received it? It was like inviting rattlesnakes into your home.

———

Among the members of Easley's National Civic Federation were a couple by the name of Roosevelt. In 1927, forty-five-year-old Franklin was about to return to public life after having been stricken with polio. The popular governor of New York, Al Smith, was planning a run for the presidency in 1928 against Herbert Hoover, and picked Franklin as his anointed successor. Although polio confined him to a wheelchair, Franklin's magnetic personality and political acumen more than made up for his limited mobility. Forty-three-year-old Eleanor, mother of five children, was finally emerging from her husband's shadow and the dictates of her overbearing mother-in-law. She often went to Albany to lobby for reformist legislation like the forty-eight-hour week and a minimum wage. She wrote magazine articles on women and politics, such as "Women Must Learn to Play the Game as Men Do." She was on the lecture circuit, and sometimes spoke at NCF meetings.[46]

As a strong advocate of women's rights (then known as the suffrage movement), Eleanor was sympathetic to any group she thought was being unfairly treated. In June 1927, responding to one of Easley's frequent warnings about the radical danger, Mrs. Roosevelt wrote him about "the fool organizations which are constantly sending out propaganda and letters of warning as to the Bolshevik who is to be found around the corner and under every bed. I think we are in much more danger in this country of hysteria on this subject than we are of lack of information."[47]

In early March 1928, Matthew Woll, the head of the photoengravers union and the most prominent labor leader active in the NCF, sent out a mailing of postcards to NCF members, which they were asked to sign. The cards would then go out to members of Congress and news outlets. The statement said: "I approve of the NCF endeavor to bringing an end to Communist propaganda in the United States." On her card, Mrs. Roosevelt wrote: "I disapprove of the constant propaganda and fear which the NCF is spreading and think it does more harm than good."

Easley invited Mrs. Roosevelt to meet Woll on March 8, hoping to win her over with an array of facts and figures, but she stuck to her guns. She made fun of reports she had heard of Bolsheviks buried in backyards, ready to rise for the revolution. She told Woll that the AFL was using the Communist scare to gain sympathy. Easley finally lost his temper and ended the meeting abruptly.[48]

The next day, an apologetic Easley wrote to Mrs. Roosevelt: "I hope you will overlook my little outburst during our conversation yesterday. It was caused by the fact that you used so many of the—may I say—stock criticisms of the NCF made by radicals of all degrees."[49] Easley followed his apology with a lecture: there were now two thousand American factories with Communist cells. The FBI was no longer able to stay informed, there was no federal antiradical law. "In other words," he said, "there is not now in Washington any bureau that can spend one cent to keep itself informed about those forces which are working day and night to undermine our institutions. . . . I can well understand that with all the important activities in which you are engaged you have not had time to make a comprehensive study of the extent and menace of Communism in this country."[50]

———

Although Easley was usually well informed in his arguments, there was one instance where he faltered badly, either out of unscrupulousness or wishful thinking. He was so intent on finding documentary evidence of Soviet malfeasance that he eagerly seized on forgeries to prove his case. In his lack of caution, his rush to judgment, and his willingness to use tainted evidence, it was Sisson all over again.

Since the government refused to take the lead, Easley hired a former investigator for the Treasury Department, James F. La Salle, who had some Russian contacts in New York, one of whom worked for Amtorg. In January 1930, La Salle told Easley that his informant wanted to sell documents from the Amtorg code room for $6,000. "Go through with it," Easley urged him. "Get the stuff!" La Salle bought several letters for $3,000, which seemed to reveal plans for a revolutionary uprising in New York and other cities on or before May Day.[51]

Convinced that he was on to something big, Easley decided to push for a congressional investigation and contacted Representative Hamilton Fish of New York, a longtime anti-Communist whose great-grandfather had been an officer in Washington's army, and his grandfather the Secretary of State under Ulysses S. Grant. [52]

A big man, six foot four and 250 pounds, he was an all-American tackle at Harvard and a classmate of John Reed's, whom he picked as team cheerleader. In World War I, he commanded a black regiment, the 369th Infantry, known as the Harlem Hell-fighters, internationally celebrated for its outstanding band. The regiment fought well in the July 1918 offensive and Fish won the Silver Star in September. In 1920 he was elected to Congress and made the study of Communist subversion one of his fields of expertise.[53]

In 1928, Jimmy Walker, the lovable playboy mayor who spent more time in speakeasies than City Hall, made the affable Grover Whalen, whose previous job had been general manager of Wanamaker's department store, police commissioner of New York on the strength of his performance as official greeter for the city. Whalen recalled in his memoirs that he took the police job because "New York was becoming a hotbed of Communism. The crash of 1929 created great opportunities. . . . When in 1930 the unemployed reached the 10 million mark the Communists began feverishly to organize them."[54]

In 1929, Whalen assigned fifty young policemen to infiltrate the party. They reported that the Communists were training a Workers Defense Corps in cells of eight to battle the police in demonstrations. Then came the cafeteria strike in January 1930, when the Defense Corps threw stink bombs into cafeterias throughout midtown Manhattan. On January 16, an armed Communist militant who had wounded a police officer was killed in a shootout. As he lay in state at Communist Party headquarters, with a coin box at each end of the casket, four of the sixteen men in the Guard of Honor were Whalen's agents.

In early March 1930, the agents informed Whalen that the party had sent out 100,000 postcards for a rally on March 6 at Union Square. When a crowd of thirty thousand gathered there on the appointed day, Whalen was ready for them with a thousand police and firemen behind every hydrant with a wrench and a hose. Young women stood in the front ranks and spat in the faces of the police or used the hatpins in their berets to stick into horses.[55]

Certain that the Communists were the number one threat to public order, Whalen was receptive to any scrap of information that could lead to arrests. James La Salle had by now bought six letters from his Amtorg source. After the riot, he showed them to Whalen. Five of the letters, dated December 1929 and January 1930, came from a Comintern official in Moscow, who gave various instructions to Amtorg officials in New York, such as "turn over funds to comrade Liza" for the support of strikers. Gregory Grafpen, the secretary treasurer of Amtorg, was instructed to organize a May Day riot in Seattle. The sixth letter was from Amtorg to Moscow, listing the Soviet agents who had arrived in the United States. Whalen was convinced that he now had proof that Amtorg was conducting subversive activities masterminded in Russia. On April 30, he told the New York Chamber of Commerce that strikes in the city were staged under Comintern instruction.[56]

Meanwhile, back in Washington, Hamilton Fish was pressing the House to conduct an investigation of Amtorg and Communism. In mid-April, Fish took his cause to the Rules Committee, arguing that Congress, "through its do-nothing policy," was giving the Communists a free hand.[57]

On the day after the usual May Day parades, Whalen convened the press and released the six Amtorg letters. He explained that the letters had been "secured by the undercover agents of the police department." Inspector John Lyons, head of the Radical Squad, reported that in his opinion they were authentic. Whalen released copies of the letters in Russian, with English translations, and said the letters came from the secret files of Amtorg and showed that Amtorg was the channel through which Moscow supplied funds and instructions to the Communist Party. The next day, the New York Times ran the story under the headline: "Whalen Discloses Secret Orders—Amtorg Implicated."[58]

Howard Swain, the managing editor of the Evening Graphic, asked John L. Spivak, one of his star investigative reporters, to look into the story. The Amtorg people claimed that the letters were crude forgeries, with improper forms of address, incorrect names, and words misspelled. Spivak called local foundries to get the names of printers who cast Russian Cyrillic type. Hoffman Foundry cast the kind of type used in the letterheads; it had seven buyers in Manhattan for that typeface.[59]

Spivak's investigation took him to a small print shop at 104 East 10th Street, a shabby five-story brick building. He walked into a narrow room fifty feet deep. At the dark, cluttered back of the alcove, a stooped and wizened little man was setting type by a soot-covered window. Spivak asked the printer, Max Wagner, if he had type to match the letterheads. Wagner said he did. Four months earlier, in January, a man named Yasora with some connection to a Russian-language paper had asked him to print one thousand copies each of three letterheads in Russian. The man explained the style of type he wanted and the next day he came in for proofs and left a small deposit, but he never came back to pick up his order. Wagner went looking for him and was told he had left the country.[60]

Spivak asked the printer if he had any proofs left. Wagner dug through his drawers, came up with two of the letterheads, and gave Spivak one. Spivak asked him to write a brief affidavit on the back of the letterhead. "I printed this about four months ago and submitted two copies as proof," Wagner wrote, "but the man did not come back for the order."

On the evening of May 6, when Howard Swain returned to the *Graphic* after dinner, he found Wagner's proofs and affidavit on his desk. The next morning, Swain called Whalen to warn him, but Whalen wouldn't discuss it: he was on his way to Washington to testify before the House Committee on Immigration and Naturalization. Swain sent Spivak to Washington to show Wagner's note to Fiorello La Guardia, then a liberal congressman from New York City. On May 9, Spivak briefed La Guardia, who promised to denounce the Whalen letters as forgeries before the entire House.[61]

On May 10, Whalen testified in closed session before the House Immigration Committee. He said that Amtorg was the major channel for Soviet funds to the American Communist Party, and that the money was being used to organize strikes and rallies. He said he had six letters to prove it.

Two days later, La Guardia spoke for eight minutes on the floor of the House. "I think I am safe in saying that our Department of State had an opportunity of knowing about these records and has given no credence to them at all," he said. He concluded that "someone has sold the police department of New York a gold brick."[62]

The next day, Spivak's article ran in the *Graphic* under the headline, "Red Plot Forgery Confirmed."

La Guardia's warning fell on deaf ears. In the second week of May, the House Rules Committee authorized a special investigation into Communist propaganda. Bertrand H. Snell, the chairman, recommended a committee of five, even though, as he explained, he was normally against investigations. The problem to his mind was that "there is no one connected with the government at the present time who knows the exact situation in regard to what Communists may or may not be doing in the United States."[63]

The committee, chaired by Hamilton Fish, was approved by a vote of 210 to 19. Congress was now committed to the first investigation of Communism since the Overman Committee of 1919. In June, the House voted to give the committee $25,000, despite La Guardia's objection that he did not think the country was in danger just because "some Communist furrier in New York is going to take a needle and stick it into the fleshy part of Grover Whalen's anatomy."[64]

The committee left for hearings in New York that opened on July 15, 1930, on the fourteenth floor of the Justice Department building on Lexington Avenue. Detectives from the Bomb Squad lined the walls of Room 1401 as the five congressmen began their questioning of Amtorg employees. Hamilton Fish dominated the hearings, directing the choice of witnesses and determining the strategy of interrogation. Edmund Wilson, who covered the New York hearings for *The New Republic*, described him as "Hannibal turned tailor's dummy," while granting him that "he never bullies or insults the witness."[65] Another committee member, Carl Bachman of West Virginia, recalled that Fish "admitted no wrong—he was always right." The committee's aim, as Bachman put it, was to obtain proof "that the Communist Party in America is controlled and financed by Russia."[66]

Amtorg, which had continued to operate after Martens's expulsion, had a sizable presence in the United States. It was installed in five floors of a building at 261 Fifth Avenue. Its chairman, Peter A. Bogdanov, refused to take the oath when he testified on July 22, saying he did not believe in God. With his blue eyes, trim mustache, and beard, Bogdanov looked like a portly version of Czar Nicholas II. He stalled and mumbled and was exasperatingly evasive, but he did admit that the Soviet Union owned Amtorg and that there were 489 employees, of whom 105 were Russian. In 1929, he said, 552 Russians had come to the United States on Amtorg business, visiting factories and negotiating contracts.

Far more forthcoming was an Amtorg defector, Basil Delgass, who had resigned as vice president a few weeks before, after learning of the Fish Committee investigation, because, he said, he did not want to commit perjury. Recalled to Moscow, he sensibly declined to go, and was sentenced to death in absentia. Delgass testified in a closed session for his own protection, providing the first glimpse of the inner workings of a Soviet trade office that operated as a front for illegal espionage activities. He revealed that the Comrade Liza mentioned in the Amtorg letters was the office political commissar, who collected contributions for causes such as the Passaic strike and supervised the conduct of employees.[67]

Delgass said that as many as thirty-nine Amtorg employees had obtained visas under false pretenses. Upon applying at the U.S. consulate in Berlin, one employee said she was being sent by the tractor construction bureau, while in fact she was Bogdanov's secretary and knew nothing about tractors. Another said he represented the Donetz Basin Coal trust, when he was actually a buyer for the Aviation Department, sent to place illegal orders for war matériel. A third said he worked for Gostorg, the state trading company, when he was in charge of the Amtorg code room.[68]

"I have some information . . . about the military espionage conducted by employees of Amtorg," Delgass announced in the closed session. He had been asked in 1927 to "undertake the supervision of the automotive and aviation departments of Amtorg . . . and the buying of Liberty engines, which were at that time prohibited to be exported." He set up a dummy American company to buy the plane engines from the War Department.[69]

Harry A. Heeney, who was in charge of the factory in Detroit that rebuilt the engines, testified that they were sent in parts by steamer to Russia. He said he had bought about four hundred Liberty engines, released as surplus in Navy yards. One of the Amtorg men who came to Detroit told him that in Russia he had seen 250 planes flying those engines—the sky was just black with them.[70]

The hearing revealed conclusively that Amtorg served as a cover for Soviet spies. Boris Skvirsky, an Amtorg official who would later become a key figure in the recognition negotiations, was an OGPU agent. George Djamaroff, a Russian monarchist and naturalized American, testified that he had known the general manager of Amtorg, Fiodor M. Ziavkin, as head of the Cheka in Rostov in 1920. Djamaroff, then an officer in the White army, recalled that Ziavkin had questioned him and "he slapped me to my face so I remember him pretty well."[71]

The New York hearings also grappled with the mystery of the Amtorg letters. Grover Whalen appeared with a white gardenia in his buttonhole and vouched for their authenticity. He offered to produce the agent who had brought him the letters, who was none other than James La Salle, Easley's investigator. La Salle was so pleased with his testimony that he wrote Whalen on July 22 that the committee was "convinced that the photostats were not forgeries."

In *his* testimony, however, the Amtorg chairman Bogdanov had insisted that the letters were forgeries, but that whoever produced them "apparently knew something about Amtorg, particularly the names." This was a view that Spivak endorsed when he testified on July 22. He was followed by the printer, Max Wagner, who said that Spivak had come to see him on May 3, the day after Whalen's release of the letters. Wagner knew it was May 3, for on that day he had seen the documents reprinted in the Jewish *Daily Forward*. "In ten minutes," Wagner said, "Mr. Spivak was in my store and he said, 'have you any of those documents or copies?'"[72]

We now know that Spivak was a secret Communist, who aside from writing for the *Graphic* wrote for the *Daily Worker* without a byline. He was also the author of pamphlets published by the party-owned International Publishers, such as *Georgia Nigger* and *On the Chain Gang*. He was, in short, on the party payroll. Aside from his work as a journalist, he carried out a number of underground assignments, such as the burglary of the renegade Communist Jay Lovestone's papers from his New York apartment in 1928. Described by the head of the party's illegal apparatus, Rudy Baker, as a "highly qualified specialist in phone tapping and party secrecy," Spivak was assigned to weed out suspect Communists. A valuable agent in the secret apparatus of the party, known as "Comrade John," Spivak at one time held the important position of head of security.[73]

Spivak, a veteran dirty tricks expert, was at the heart of the Amtorg letters episode. He knew exactly where to go to find the letterheads and he exposed the letters as forgeries with the help of a gullible congressman. The Amtorg letters had all the earmarks of a sting operation to discredit Grover Whalen, who was aggressively pursuing Communists in New York. The operation succeeded, for Whalen soon resigned as police commissioner and went back to his old job at Wanamaker's. Easley was also discredited, as was to some extent the credibility of the Fish Committee, which had been formed thanks to the release of the letters.

In October 1930, as the Fish hearings were winding down, Easley asked Basil Delgass, the Amtorg defector, to analyze the letters. Delgass told him that the letter from Amtorg to Moscow was an obvious forgery, as "all secret documents are written on onion-skin paper." Easley found it difficult to accept that in his enthusiasm he had been duped.[74]

The conflicting testimony made Fish retreat from his earlier conviction that the Amtorg letters were authentic, and the committee pointedly avoided any further examination of the issue. From New York, in late July, the committee went on the road in its private Pullman car to more than a dozen cities to learn what the Communists were up to around the country. Its travels were also a way of stirring up public interest and headlines.

The hearings ended in November 1930, with mixed reviews. *The New Republic* wrote that its discoveries were only "a melange of the commonplace, the dubious, and the absurd." *Commonweal*, however, struck a more judicious note when it wrote that "no more powerful searchlight has ever been directed against Communist operations in this country." Communism "is a real menace," said the liberal Catholic magazine, "even if its seriousness may be easily exaggerated."[75]

In January 1931, the Fish Committee issued a sixty-six-page report. It had heard 275 witnesses in fourteen cities. It had subpoenaed three thousand cablegrams between Amtorg and Moscow and turned them over to the Code and Signal Section of the Navy Department, which tried in vain for five months to decode them. The Navy at that time had only two code experts, who excused their failure by saying the cipher was the most complicated they had ever seen. But why, the committee wondered, did a trading company need to encipher its telegrams?

The report repudiated the Amtorg letters, saying that "measured by the rules of evidence and the burden of proof resting on the proponents of the documents, we find that the testimony failed to establish the genuineness of the so-called 'Whalen documents'." This was a slap in the face for Easley, who in retaliation called Fish a "hot air artist" and a "brainless nincompoop."[76]

———

From the moment of his return to the United States in 1918, Raymond Robins became the chief proponent of recognition of the Soviet Union, just as Easley was its leading opponent. Indeed, the ardent Sovietophile and admirer of Lenin and Stalin hoped to become the first American ambassador to Moscow. To this end, he lobbied four Presidents, gave hundreds of public addresses, and did missionary work in all the branches of government. His worst enemy was Secretary of State Charles Evans Hughes, who demanded that the Russians meet three conditions: payment of debt; restoration of American property, such as banks and factories; and an end to revolutionary propaganda in the United States. Robins complained that Hughes "would like to have all the Bolsheviks join the Baptist church."[77]

When Coolidge won the 1924 election and told Robins that Hughes would be keeping his place in the cabinet, Robins replied, "The only place I care to see Mr. Secretary Hughes is in a box with a lily in his hand." Robins knew that he would have to bide his time for at least another four years.[78]

Robins faced another setback in 1928, when Herbert Hoover won the Republican nomination. Hardened by his experiences with the Soviets as head of famine relief, Hoover was fiercely anti-recognition. But Robins managed to find common ground with the Republican candidate, for they were both ardent prohibitionists. In July 1928, Hoover invited Robins to his Washington home, as a leader of the dry coalition, to help him prepare his nomination acceptance speech. Running against the Catholic and wet governor of New York, Al Smith, Hoover swept into office in a landslide in November.[79]

After Hoover's victory, Robins often dined at the White House and sometimes spent the night, sleeping in Teddy Roosevelt's room. But then the Depression came, casting its pall over the nation, and Robins lost faith in Hoover. By 1931, he decided that the President was "a complete washout as political leader . . . he has failed completely in the worst economic crisis I have ever known this country to suffer." And yet Robins concealed his feelings and continued to support Hoover in the 1932 campaign, helping him write his speeches.[80]

Robins was a man at odds with himself, overworked and overstressed, campaigning for a President he felt had led the country to ruin. His mental health was fragile, for he had a long history of depression and seizures. On September 3, 1932, he was in New York's Grand Central Station, on his way to Washington, where he had an appointment with Hoover. But he never got to Washington. All he could remember later was a jumbled sense of pain, danger, and darkness, a little town, two rivers, mountain trails, a house, kindly folks and shelter, and the silence of the forest.[81]

Robins was found ten weeks later in a boarding house in the North Carolina hill country, suffering from amnesia and using a different name. He said he was a Kentucky miner and seemed perfectly lucid. He had become a familiar figure in the small community of Whittier, giving speeches for Hoover's reelection. On that point he was not amnesic. His wife, Margaret, had him admitted to a sanatorium in Asheville, where he had to be kept in isolation until he regained his lost identity. For eleven weeks, he had not known who he was, and now he worried that he would be seen as a quitter.[82]

———

With Hoover incapable of coping with the Depression, a Democratic victory seemed likely in 1932. One of the jokes going around was that if Hoover won, Mahatma Gandhi would make the best-dressed list.[83]

After declaring for the presidency in January 1932, Franklin Roosevelt urgently needed to gather around him a group of advisers, who became known as the brain trust. The first of these was Raymond Moley, a professor of public law at Columbia University, who had written a speech on prison reform when Roosevelt ran for governor in 1928. It was said Moley put the "organ music" in Roosevelt's speeches. But Moley, a reform-minded Ohio progressive, hostile to Wall Street bankers and sympathetic to the little man, did much more than that.[84]

In preparation for the convention that June in Chicago, FDR laid out his program for the New Deal at a Jefferson Day speech in St. Paul on April 18. Moley worked on ten "Articles of Faith," which added up to a commitment to economic planning, including large-scale public works, federal regulation of utilities, and farm relief. One of the ten articles was directed at a specific foreign country, and that was the one calling for recognition of the Soviet Union.[85]

Thus was the idea of recognition planted in FDR's head. Moley expanded on the policy in an influential memo on May 19, which would become the blueprint for the New Deal. Recognition, he argued, would act as a stimulus for American commerce and industry. The conditions he stated were that Russian agents should not conduct propaganda in the United States and that the debt question should be settled. "The old shibboleths as to whether Russia is a democratic government or not," Moley wrote, "should not weigh in the discussion. . . . We should recognize a de facto government without attempting to force it into the form of our conception of what a government should be."[86]

When Roosevelt was nominated and elected, recognition became for the first time a possibility. Recovering in Florida, and encouraged by signs that FDR was open to the idea, Robins dreamed of returning to the land of Lenin and Trotsky, where he had an open invitation. On April 9, 1933, prodded by the favorable environment at home, Robins sailed for Russia, arriving in time for the May Day celebrations.

All seemed wonderful in the Workers' Republic, from the bayonets to the banners, from the tanks to the factory workers, and he was swept up in the revelry, which he saw as "the apotheosis of Stalinism." Robins visited Lenin's tomb and found his embalmed face "utterly lifelike . . . as I saw him in the Great Hours of the Revolution." On May 13, he spent an hour with Stalin in the Kremlin, "an able man at the helm, direct, quiet, unassuming, a master of detail." Convinced that he had seen the real Russia, Robins found it all splendid, "youth in the saddle, a new order of things."[87]

Had he looked behind the facade, he would have seen a Russia in convulsion, in the midst of a terrible famine, a Russia carrying out a campaign of terrorism against the kulaks (property-owning farmers). The Five Year Plan, decreed in 1929, which some American intellectuals so admired, was based on the forced relocation of the kulaks, who were opposed to collective farms. In December 1929, the "quiet and unassuming" Stalin ordered "the elimination of kulaks as a class." In 1930 and 1931, the OGPU rounded up 1.8 million kulaks, of whom half a million escaped or died. The remaining 1.3 million were resettled in work camps. Kulak labor was sent to the Dnieper to work in stone quarries and help build the 150-mile-long canal from the Baltic to the White Sea.[88]

In 1932, famine broke out in the Ukraine, the Don, the northern Caucasus and Kazakhstan, affecting 40 million people, of whom six million died. Unlike the 1922 famine, when the Soviets pleaded for help, the 1932 famine was covered up. Stalin called it "a fable about famine."[89]

In a top secret report on March 25, 1932, recently released by the Soviet archives, the health inspector Dr. A. J. Kiselev described the situation in a village in the Pokrovka region of the Ukraine to the regional board of health. Dr. Kiselev visited the Sidelnikov family, where the mother had given birth five days earlier: "Four small children pale as wax with swollen cheeks sat at the filthy table like marmots and ate with spoons from a common cup that contained a mixture of hot water and a white liquid of questionable taste and sour smell, which turned out to be skim milk." The father, Konstantin, had traded his wife's clothes for bread. In another home, Filipp Borodin, with three small children, "cries like a babe and asks for death for his children. . . . In the Borodin home there is unbelievable filth, dampness, and stench. . . . Borodin swears at the children, 'why the devil don't you die, I wish I didn't have to look at you.' . . . He is slipping into psychosis due to starvation, which can lead to eating his own children." There had already been reports of cannibalism in the famine regions, where the population was living on food substitutes such as sunflower stems, hemp seeds, goosefoot, and dried potato peels. "The homes are polluted by human waste," Dr. Kiselev said, "diarrhea caused by these substitutes." He described in minute detail what Stalin called "a fable."

Stalin knew of course what the real situation was. In April 1933, he received a letter from Mikhail Sholokhov, who would go on to win the Nobel Prize in literature in 1965. Sholokhov, the author of *And Quiet Flows the Don* and *Virgin Soil Upturned,* a book about the collectivization of agriculture, sought to inform Stalin of conditions in his home district of Veshenski in the Don region, which had "failed to fulfill its grain quota this year not because of 'kulak sabotage' but because of bad leadership at the local party headquarters." In December 1932, Sholokhov said, an official arrived and requisitioned all the grain, including the seed grain for the 1933 harvest. He divided the quota due the state by family. The result was that the peasants hid their grain. Some of the methods used to recover the buried grain were:

- The worker was stripped and left naked out in the cold.
- The feet of female workers were doused with gasoline and set afire.
- One official named Plotkin forced the kolkhoz (collective farm) workers to stretch out on a white-hot stove.
- In the Lebyazhenski kolkhoz, the workers were lined up against a wall for a mock execution.

"These are not abuses of the system," Sholokhov wrote. "This is the present system for collecting grain."[90]

Stalin replied on May 3, thanking Sholokhov for revealing "the open sores in party work," in that "our officials . . . sometimes . . . sink to the point of sadism." But "the other side is that the esteemed grain-growers of your region have conducted a sit-down strike (sabotage!), and were not against leaving workers and the Red Army without bread. . . . The esteemed grain growers actually carried on a 'quiet' war against Soviet authority. . . . The officials guilty of these terrible acts should be punished accordingly. But it is as clear as day that these esteemed grain growers are not as innocent as they appear." For Stalin, anyone who defied state policies, however arbitrary and unjust, was guilty.[91]

Ukrainian historians today call the famine a genocide, in that the regime deliberately let millions die, mainly kulaks and Ukrainians. Famine was a weapon to force subservience in the final battle between the Bolshevik state and the peasantry.[92] This was the Russian version of the politics of famine.

Robins returned to America with his fairy-tale version of a barbarous regime. Before a nationwide radio audience on July 26, 1933, he stated: "The penal system of the Soviets has abolished all punitive elements." He was by now a craven propagandist for Stalin.[93]

—

After his inauguration in March 1933, the President looked for the right person to initiate talks with the Russians. The State Department was packed with anti-Bolsheviks from the days of Charles Evans Hughes. FDR turned to his friend and Hyde Park neighbor, Henry Morgenthau Jr., whom he had named Secretary of the Treasury, and told him that the Russians could absorb some of America's surpluses in raw materials and industrial products. Hitler had recently come to power in Germany, and Japan had invaded Manchuria. Russia was a potential ally against the Germans in Europe and the Japanese in Asia. Like his brain truster Moley, FDR felt that nonrecognition was pointless. Whether we liked it or not, they had their government and we had ours, and theirs was recognized by Britain and France and other major powers. Roosevelt the internationalist believed that alliances could prevent wars, but first there had to be recognition.[94]

Morgenthau complained that no Russian he spoke to was willing to assume the necessary authority. "Gosh," said the President, "if I could only, myself, talk to some one man representing the Russians, I could straighten out the whole question." This was a familiar refrain. There was no policy matter, FDR believed, that he could not solve instantly by going one-on-one with the right intermediary. He proposed that Morgenthau tell the Russians that "the President would like to send some person to Moscow . . . in order to break the ice," but nothing happened.[95]

In late September, FDR asked Morgenthau, "What do you think of bringing this whole Russian question into our front parlor instead of back in the kitchen?" The next day, Bill Bullitt turned up at Morgenthau's office for lunch.[96]

William Christian Bullitt was born into an affluent and socially registered Philadelphia family. At Yale, he was Phi Beta Kappa, editor of the *Daily News,* and Scroll and Key. The class of 1912 voted him "most brilliant." As the Washington bureau chief for the Philadelphia *Public Ledger*, he met and became close friends with President Wilson's éminence grise, Colonel House, who urged him to join the Foreign Service, which he did. Bullitt, by then twenty-seven years old, was part of the American delegation to the Paris peace conference in 1919. In March, he was sent on a secret mission to Russia to investigate the stability of the Bolshevik government. He returned with a recommendation that the United States recognize the new regime. Colonel House backed Bullitt, but Wilson and Lansing felt that he had gone beyond his instructions, and he was repudiated.[97]

Bill Bullitt was not accustomed to dealing with setbacks. He left the Foreign Service and went to Europe to lick his wounds, after divorcing his first wife and marrying John Reed's widow, Louise Bryant, in 1926; they later divorced. After a decade in voluntary exile, Bullitt returned to the American political arena in 1932 to support FDR and contributed $1,000 to his campaign. Colonel House, now a seventy-five-year-old elder statesman, arranged an introduction for Bullitt to the presidential candidate in September. As men of similar backgrounds with similar worldviews, they hit it off, and FDR asked Bullitt to join the campaign as a foreign policy adviser. In November 1932 and January 1933, he traveled to Europe on information-gathering missions. The London press called him "Roosevelt's secret agent." Thirteen years after having been dismissed by Wilson, Bullitt found a presidential hopeful who recognized his abilities and was eager to use them.[98]

FDR was pleased with Bullitt's work and found him highly compatible. After the inauguration, he named Bullitt special assistant to Secretary of State Cordell Hull. With his oversize ego, Bullitt may have thought he could become FDR's Colonel House.[99]

The President asked Bullitt to focus on the formulation of a recognition policy and to work with Morgenthau. This was FDR's first venture into personal diplomacy, a style of unpublicized negotiation that would run through his four terms. Bullitt began walking Morgenthau to work in the morning to brief him on the benefits of recognition, one of which would be American aid, "the means by which the Soviet Union could break away from its dependence on Germany and could become a bulwark against the aggressive tendencies . . . developing in Japan."[100]

With Morgenthau, Bullitt was preaching to the converted, but he also had to convince Hull, who objected to the lack of religious freedom in Russia. Americans in Russia, Hull insisted, should be allowed to worship as they please. Hull was also concerned about the war debt that went back to the Kerensky government, and interference in American affairs by Moscow-directed American Communists. Bullitt sent Hull a memo on October 4, laying out the conditions for recognition, which addressed his concerns:

- No Communist propaganda in the United States.
- Protection of civil and religious rights for Americans in Russia.
- Agreement on the repayment of debt.
- A waiver on Russian counterclaims regarding the Archangel and Murmansk expeditions.[101]

Hull was apparently appeased, for he later wrote in his memoirs: "In some respects, we stood to gain more than Russia by a restoration of diplomatic relations," since they knew so much more about us than we knew about them. Recognition, he hoped, would level the playing field.[102]

On the home front, a dozen pro-recognition committees sprang up. The issue of debt was now less combustible. Russia was not the only country to default on war loans. What about England and France? World peace was a more urgent issue. The United States, which had failed to join the League of Nations (while Russia had joined), was isolated. A rapprochement with Russia might restrain the expansionist governments of Germany and Japan. The American Women's Committee for the Recognition of the Soviet Union presented a petition to the White House. The Russian-American Chamber of Commerce asked for a meeting with the President.

So many groups were pleading for recognition that the President said at his September 22 press conference that "over the last three months there have been all sorts of people . . . running around to various people in the administration" about it. FDR did not want the hubbub, feeling that success depended on quiet diplomacy.[103]

On October 11, 1933, Morgenthau put Bullitt in touch with one of his Amtorg contacts, Boris Skvirsky, who was also an officer in the OGPU, identified in the Fish hearings. The plan was that Bullitt would give Skvirsky a letter from the President to Michael Kalinin, president of the Central Executive Committee of Soviets and the titular head of government, proposing an exchange of diplomats. In a game of cat-and-mouse, Bullitt told Skvirsky, "I have a piece of paper in my hand. It is unsigned. It can be made into an invitation for you to send representatives here to discuss diplomatic relations. We wish you to telegraph it by your most confidential code and learn if it is acceptable." On October 17, Skvirsky came back with a draft of Kalinin's reply. Bullitt then took from his pocket the letter signed by FDR, which said that he was contemplating an end to the "abnormal relations" between 125 million Americans and 160 million Russians.[104]

———

Since his return from Russia, Robins had been hoping for a meeting with the President. He saw FDR finally on October 13 for forty-five minutes. Recognition was on both of their minds, and the President said he had read a book called *First to Go Back: An Aristocrat in Soviet Russia,* by Irina Skariatina, which gave a sympathetic account of the regime. FDR asked Robins what he thought of it. Not wanting to sound too pro-Soviet, Robins said it was "a little too favorable, i.e. not enough on the cost in hunger, death and bitterness." FDR said he was troubled by two concerns—freedom of worship and Soviet subversion in the United States.

Robins went straight from the White House to Union Station and took the first train to New York, where he conferred with Peter Bogdanov, the head of Amtorg, who cabled Stalin for advice. On October 14, Robins wrote a letter to the President, in which he enclosed a statement of Stalin's on noninterference in the affairs of other countries and France's formal statement of recognition in 1924.[105]

Robins felt that his meeting with Roosevelt "spelled VICTORY for the fifteen years' struggle." But the truth was, he had little to do with the President's decision. With the exchange of letters, negotiations were already underway. Kalinin's reply to the President had been that the "abnormal relations" had an "unfavorable effect" not only on Russia and America but "also on the international situation, increasing the element of disquiet . . . and encouraging forces tending to disturb the peace." It was clear from the letter that Stalin too was worried about the unrest in Europe and Asia and appreciated the benefits that would accrue from recognition, such as American loans and American aid.[106]

On October 24, Skvirsky told Bullitt that Foreign Affairs Commissar Maxim Litvinov would come himself to Washington in November to handle the negotiations. He wanted to be taken off the liner at the quarantine station to avoid demonstrations by White Russians.

Litvinov arrived in the United States on November 6. A Russian Jew, with a round, pudding-like face, and shrewd eyes behind rimless glasses, he had been named Foreign Commissar in 1930. He spoke fluent English, having escaped arrest by the Czar's police in 1901 and fled to England. His jovial manner masked a steely determination to do Stalin's bidding. The talks began on November 7, when Litvinov met with Hull and Bullitt. It soon became apparent that Litvinov's purpose was to obtain recognition without any conditions. His negotiating position was that it should be granted outright.[107]

Litvinov stalled for a week, apparently thinking that by not giving in he could wear the Americans down. On November 15, Bullitt and Litvinov argued for two hours on the debt issue. Bullitt told him that the Johnson bill, which barred loans to nations in default, was sure to be passed in January (which it was), meaning that the Soviets could not get one penny of credit from the United States unless they agreed on a plan to pay back the debt.

"What sum would you consider might be acceptable to Congress?" Litvinov asked. "You of course will say $150 million."

"I will say nothing," Bullitt replied. "I cannot predict what Congress will do, but the president can predict very exactly what Congress will do, and you should address that question to him."

Litvinov said that he had complete confidence in FDR's fair-mindedness, and that when he found out that most of the loan to the Kerensky government had been spent by Bakhmeteff to buy supplies for Kolchak's army, he would agree that the Soviet government should not have to pay back money used by its enemies. The Soviet envoy was due to meet with the President at 2:00 P.M. that day. Prior to the meeting, Bullitt advised FDR: "I think you should endeavor forcibly to get him to fix at least $100 million as the lower limit."[108]

At his meeting with Litvinov, FDR turned on the charm. In one of those avuncular asides that the President used to break the ice, he said: "Now, you know, Max, your good old father and mother, pious Jewish people, always said their prayers. I know they must have taught you to say prayers. You must know all the good Jewish prayers." Catching Litvinov's startled look, FDR went on in his cordial way: "Now you may think you're an atheist. You may think you don't have any religion, but I tell you, Max, when you come to die do you know what you're going to do? You're going to be thinking about what your father and mother taught you . . . that's what you'll be thinking of when you're dying."[109]

Probably realizing that this meeting with the President was his last chance to obtain recognition, Litvinov began to make concessions. He made a "gentleman's agreement" to pay $75 million on account on the Kerensky debt. The next day he wrote FDR a letter promising that the Soviet Union would refrain from conducting any agitation or propaganda in the United States. In this final stage of the negotiations, the letters were flying. FDR wrote Litvinov on November 16 to ask about religious freedom, and on the same day Litvinov replied that Americans in Russia would be given the right to practice their religion. On that day, notes of agreement were exchanged initiating diplomatic relations, and the White House made an announcement to the press, for recognition was a decision the President could make on his own without going to Congress.

Editorial approval was widespread, for a variety of reasons. The *Dallas News* saw recognition as a boost for the sale of Texas cotton. The Catholic magazine *Commonweal* praised the protection of religious minorities and saw recognition as a way to moderate the atheism and tyranny of the regime. The *St. Louis Post-Dispatch* expressed vague Utopian hopes in an editorial on November 19: "There is a destiny of nations which transcends all such immediacies as those which have estranged the United States from Russia. We bear a prophetic relation to the rest of the world, and so does Russia."[110]

Litvinov remained in the United States until November 25, and in New York he saw D. H. Dubrowsky, a Soviet agent who ran the Russian Red Cross. "He came in all smiles," Dubrowsky recalled, "and said, 'Well, it's in the bag. We have it. They wanted us to recognize the debts that we owed them and I promised we were going to negotiate, but they do not know we are going to negotiate till doomsday. . . . The next one was a corker; they wanted me to give them freedom of religion. And I gave it to them. . . . I was very much prompted to offer that I will collect all the Bibles and ship them out.'" For Litvinov, Dubrowsky said, "The general motive is that any promise given to a bourgeois state is not worth the paper it is written on."[111]

On November 24, 1933, the Russian-American Chamber of Commerce held a banquet in the Grand Ballroom of the Waldorf-Astoria in honor of Litvinov, who was going home the next day. Among the 1,700 who attended were leaders of the American establishment: On the dais were Paul Cravath of the eminent law firm; James Goodrich, ex-governor of Indiana; Alfred Sloan, president of General Motors; Gerald Swope, president of General Electric; and Thomas Watson, president of IBM. In the background the Stars and Stripes hung next to the Hammer and Sickle. The American leaders rose when the band played "The Internationale." It was Raymond Robins's finest moment.[112]

After recognition, Soviet-American relations deteriorated. Despite their promises, the Soviets never paid a penny on the debt. Those businessmen who expected an increase in trade were disappointed, for the Johnson Act barred the Soviets from receiving U.S. loans, and they found new trading partners in Europe. The attendance of American Communists at the 1935 meeting of the Comintern in Moscow was a violation of the pledge on propaganda and agitation. As for the advantages of having Russia as an ally on the international scene, Cordell Hull observed in his memoirs: "The beneficial influence I had expected Russo-American cooperation to have on the political situation in Europe and Asia did not materialize. I argued again and again with Soviet ambassadors that it was disastrous to let the comparatively small sum of Soviet indebtedness and other modest differences stand in the way of our thorough-going political relations. I pleaded with them again and again . . .

for a common moral front to the aggressor nations. . . . But a common front did not come until long after war had begun."[113]

Recognition did not stop Stalin from signing a pact with Hitler in 1939, which gave the Führer a free hand in the west to attack Belgium and France.

Perhaps the most disappointed partisan of recognition was Bullitt, who went to Moscow as the first American ambassador, full of high hopes that he would be the architect of a lasting friendship. Ignored by Stalin, he got nowhere on debt collection or any other issue. He left in 1939 thoroughly disillusioned and convinced that the government was "a conspiracy to commit murder and nothing else."[114]

The drawbacks to recognition were many. It gave the Communist Party a kind of legitimacy that ushered in the Red Decade. With the opening of an embassy and several consulates, the espionage hives were soon buzzing and spy rings in Washington penetrated government agencies.

"The ink was hardly dry," Dubrowsky recalled, "when an active member of the foreign department of the OGPU was sent here as my assistant—Jacob Sterngluss. He was sent from Afghanistan, where he was the OGPU chief. He had nothing to do with Red Cross activities. . . . The special work of Dr. Sterngluss . . . consisted of organizing the theft of United States mail from the mail boxes of private individuals. . . . Dr. Sterngluss was also developing contacts among minor employees of Western Union, Commercial Cable, and Radio Corporation of America, with the view of intercepting telegrams." Dubrowsky sent a memo to Skvirsky, who was now counselor at the embassy in Washington, saying this was a violation of the recognition understanding. Skvirsky replied: "Understanding be damned, I cannot do anything. The OGPU is supreme."[115]

VI

WELCOME
SOVIET SPIES!

Recognition opened the door for Soviet spies. Both networks, the NKVD and the GRU, could now operate under the cover of the Soviet embassy in Washington and the consulates in New York and San Francisco. This system of "legal" spies, protected under diplomatic cover (sometimes the ambassador himself, sometimes a lowly clerk), long since established in every other Soviet embassy, was now adopted in the United States. In tandem with the legals, the Soviets expanded the illegal networks of agents who came on false passports as immigrants and acted under the cover of various occupations.

An open society such as the United States, where snooping is frowned upon, and where congressmen in the early days of the FBI had compared its tactics to those of the czarist Secret Police, was unprepared to deal with the widespread and determined efforts of a horde of Soviet agents who were now allowed to enter the country. After the negative publicity that followed the Palmer raids, and after the reforms of Harlan Stone, the FBI had gone into a period of hibernation. By statute, the bureau was limited to "the detection and prosecution of crimes," and since no federal laws were on the books to punish Communist activities there was no crime to investigate. By 1930 Hoover's staff was down to 581, from 1,127 in 1920.[1]

There were times when Hoover, under orders from the White House, was obliged to act in violation of departmental policy. Late in May 1932, small groups of unemployed veterans began to gather in Washington, arriving from near and far, on foot or by hopping freight trains. They were called Bonus Marchers. In 1924, Congress had promised them a bonus, not payable until 1945. But they needed the money right away. Soon their number grew to fifteen thousand. They squatted in an open space called the Anacostia Flats, creating sanitation and food problems and becoming an embarrassment to President Hoover, a seething, daily reminder of his inability to cope with the Depression. Their aim was to pressure Congress to pass a bill for immediate payment of the bonus, but in mid-June, the bill was narrowly defeated. The disappointed Bonus Marchers lingered on, until late July when they were ordered to evacuate. Most of them left, but about two thousand diehards remained. On July 28, the President ordered the Army to have the veterans removed. General Douglas MacArthur, who was in command, ignored the President's directive to use unarmed soldiers and stormed in with tanks, cavalry, tear gas, and a bayonet charge, leaving four dead and hundreds wounded.[2]

An appalled President Hoover, who was about to launch his campaign for reelection, summoned J. Edgar Hoover to the White House on August 1. The bureau could help him discredit the marchers by obtaining evidence that they were Communist-driven. Sensing that the President could not win in November, Hoover did as little as he could. Why help an administration on the way out? Hoover agreed to search his fingerprint files to see if any of the arrested Bonus Marchers had records. He also sent agents to railroad yards, where they monitored the movement of the marchers as they rode the freights back home. But the bureau did not obtain any hard evidence that the Bonus March was a Red plot.[3]

As expected, Herbert Hoover lost the election, ushering in FDR and the New Deal. At first, Roosevelt's victory posed a serious threat to Hoover's tenure as FBI Director, for the President chose as Attorney General Thomas Walsh, the senator from Montana who had vowed to get rid of him. The seventy-four-year-old Walsh had just married the widow of a Cuban sugar planter, but the honeymoon exhausted him and he died of a heart attack on March 2, 1933. Hoover was saved, and FDR hurriedly found a replacement for Walsh in Homer Cummings, a Connecticut lawyer who had been chairman of the Democratic National Committee in 1919.[4]

FDR brought to the presidency a broad view of the use of federal powers and a predilection for making the FBI his private detective agency. He came to office at a time when the threat of war in Europe and Asia increased the danger of espionage at home and made it necessary to expand Hoover's jurisdiction. As a result of both the world situation and the President's fondness for undercover shenanigans, Hoover flourished during the twelve years FDR was in office, under four Attorneys General. Indeed, it seemed that one of the requirements for the post was that the occupant be on good terms with Hoover.

The President dealt directly with Hoover, instead of making his requests through the Attorney General. Thus the FBI became a service organization for the White House. It was under FDR that the myth of Hoover as the indispensable man emerged. FDR was thankful that Hoover managed to sidestep legal niceties that might have hampered some investigations, while Hoover soon realized that this President had "a natural affinity for the intelligence process," as one historian put it, "a gossipy and voyeuristic delight in the insider's role, and a callousness to the claims alike of privacy and free expression."[5]

It was FDR's concern regarding pro-Nazi groups in America that overturned Harlan Stone's 1924 ban on investigating political activities. Suspecting that these groups had ties to the German government, FDR called a meeting at the White House on May 8, 1934, attended by Hoover, Attorney General Homer Cummings, Secretary of the Treasury Morgenthau, Secretary of Labor Frances Perkins, and W. H. Moran, head of the Secret Service, a bureau of the Treasury Department assigned to the protection of the President, among other duties. FDR asked Hoover to collect information on homegrown fascists, who were calling the New Deal a tool of the Communist conspiracy, and to determine whether the German embassy had any connection with them, which would of course require the use of wiretaps. Two days later, Hoover instructed his field offices "to initiate an intensive investigation of activities of the Nazi group." On May 18, Hoover's bailiwick was further expanded when FDR signed a series of bills giving the FBI the authority to investigate cases involving extortion, kidnapping, fugitives, and the murder of federal officers. In a time of threats to national security and notorious crimes such as the kidnapping of the Lindbergh baby, it seemed not only natural, but imperative, to rely on the FBI.[6]

In a climactic meeting in the summer of 1936, FDR secretly gave Hoover the authority to investigate all subversives, not just the pro-Nazis. FDR summoned Hoover to the White House on August 24 to discuss the dangers of foreign espionage. According to Hoover's memo of the meeting, he briefed the President on right-wing as well as Communist intrigues, while providing more detail on the latter. Harry Bridges's West Coast longshoremen's union, he said, "was practically controlled by the Communists," who also "had very definite plans" to seize control of the United Mine Workers and who had considerable influence in the Newspaper Guild. "I told him," Hoover's memo went on, "that my information was that the Communists planned to get control of these three groups and by doing so they would be able to paralyze the country in that they could stop all shipping in and out through the Bridges organization; stop the operation of industry through the mining union of

[John L.] Lewis; and stop publication of any newspapers of the country through the Newspaper Guild."[7] He also mentioned Communist infiltration of government agencies, such as the National Labor Relations Board. Although Hoover's information was well founded, his conclusion was hyperbolic.

Impressed by Hoover's alarming scenario, FDR asked him to investigate "subversive activities in the United States."

Hoover said the FBI had no authority to conduct such investigations.

FDR asked him if he had any ideas.

Hoover mentioned a 1916 statute that allowed the Secretary of State to authorize FBI investigations, which was broad enough to include political activities. FDR liked the confidential aspect of the arrangement, for it did not require congressional approval, and it would protect him against attacks from civil liberties groups. He arranged a meeting with Hoover and Secretary of State Cordell Hull the next day.

At the meeting, FDR told Hull that Communist and fascist activities were "international in scope and that Communists in particular were directed from Moscow." FDR said he wanted the FBI to investigate subversive activities, which required a request from the State Department. Hull, who came from the Tennessee hill country where feuds were commonplace, reportedly replied: "Go ahead and investigate the cock-suckers."[8]

With this secret verbal instruction, FDR gave the FBI a clear mandate to gather political intelligence, which it continued to do for forty years. Bureau surveillance was quickly expanded to labor organizers, university professors, journalists, and radical political leaders. The effort to recruit informers was stepped up.

While FDR unshackled Hoover in the pursuit of Communists, the climate of the New Deal was in some ways favorable for Soviet espionage. Since some sixty new federal agencies had to be staffed, hundreds of lawyers, many of them friendly to the Soviet Union and some of them already Communists, came to Washington and became the mandarins of the regulatory state. George Peek of the Agricultural Adjustment Administration (known as the Triple A) called them "the boys with their hair ablaze."[9] Among them were recruited a sizable number of Soviet spies. They were hired without any sort of loyalty check, in the frenetic urgency of the New Deal.

———

The first "legal" NKVD *Resident* was installed as the Soviet consul in New York in early 1934, a few months after the recognition agreement. Peter Gutzeit was a rather slight, fine-featured young man with wavy brown hair, who was so eager to recruit agents that he had to be restrained by his Moscow superiors. He was told to proceed cautiously, so as not to "complicate our relations with the masters of your country. . . . The slightest trouble in this direction can cause serious consequences of an international character."[10]

As Gutzeit noted in an April 1934 memo to Moscow, his dilemma was that "at present we don't have any agents. It is necessary to start this work with a blank slate." This is where the American Communist Party performed a crucial function, pointing out to Soviet agents party members with interesting government jobs, and recruiting other members directly into the espionage underground. The American Communist Party always maintained a liaison officer with the Soviet espionage apparat. For years, Earl Browder, the General Secretary of the party from 1932 to 1945, filled the job of talent-spotter.[11]

Cresting the waves of young men who tumbled into Washington in 1933 to join the administration were romantic anti-fascists, college liberals, party members, and their friends. Lawrence Duggan was almost all of the above, for he was not a party member. His parents, who lived in White Plains, an affluent suburb of New York City, were New Deal liberals. His father, Stephen, had taught political science at City College before being named director of the esteemed Institute of International Education. His mother was active in social causes, such as the Negro Welfare League. At Harvard, Duggan was a friend of Henry Collins's, who would be recruited as a Soviet agent while working for the Department of Agriculture. Two years after graduation, in 1929, Duggan's father named him director of the Institute of International Education for Latin America. He spent much of his time roaming around the hemisphere to set up student exchange programs, and learned to speak fluent Spanish and some Portuguese.[12]

The IIE was a launching pad for the State Department, which Duggan joined in 1930, continuing to specialize in Latin American affairs. In 1932, he married a Vassar graduate, Helen Boyd. Two of his friends at State, Noel Field and Alger Hiss, were Soviet agents. Tall and athletic-looking, with a broad face and pug nose, Duggan was like a camp counselor, fun to be with, but trustworthy. He was popular at State, and came under the wing of Assistant Secretary of State Sumner Welles, a confidant of FDR's who was sometimes thought of as the de facto Secretary of State, in light of Cordell Hull's poor health and other limitations. Duggan was so well thought of that he was promoted three times in 1935. The career diplomat Joseph Green observed in his diary that "His career has certainly been meteoric. . . . I fear he has created some jealousies."[13] But since he was under Welles's protection, the envy was muted.

Duggan was a garden-variety liberal dedicated to the principles of the New Deal. In the anti-fascist climate of the times, he was sympathetic to the Soviet

Union, which he saw as a forward-looking, peace-loving nation. His willingness to spy for the Soviets came out of a gullible desire to please rather than any doctrinaire Communist convictions.

When his agents approached Duggan in October 1934, Gutzeit was far more impressed with Helen, whom he described as "an extraordinarily beautiful woman, a typical American, tall, blonde, reserved, well read, goes in for sports, independent." Duggan was depicted less thrillingly as "a very soft guy . . . under his wife's influence . . . cultured and reserved." What Gutzeit mistook for softness was Duggan's penchant for self-examination. Once he agreed to spy for the Soviets, he constantly fretted—had he done the right thing, was he putting his family at risk, would he get caught, was the Soviet Union sincere in wanting to avoid war?[14]

In 1935, Gutzeit passed Duggan on to the German-born, Washington-based agent who had recruited him, the wily and seductive Hede Massing. In the Soviet underground since 1929, she had been married briefly to German Comintern agent Gerhart Eisler—until he went off with her younger sister. Her second husband, Paul Massing, an anti-fascist publisher and writer, was sent to a detention camp when Hitler came to power in 1933. Hede fled to Washington, where Paul joined her in 1934 after being released.

Her first coup as a recruiter was the State Department man Noel Field, whose wife, Herta, was German. Looking rather severe with her blond braids pinned up in a circle, Massing gave them the obvious pitch: "We must fight fascism." Field, a close friend of Alger Hiss's, was willing. He was about to join the open party, but Massing convinced him that underground work was more important. Despite his qualms, Noel Field provided classified State Department reports until he left State in 1936 to work for the League of Nations in Geneva.[15]

—

Along with the Soviet embassy and consulates, the trading agency Amtorg continued to provide cover for Soviet spies. Gaik Ovakimian, whom the FBI called "the wily Armenian," operated under Amtorg cover from 1933 to 1939. He is something of a celebrity in Soviet espionage circles, not only for the number of spies he recruited, but also for his nimble avoidance of the purges.[16]

Ovakimian had such a high forehead that his features seemed compressed beneath the dark and bushy demarcation line of a single eyebrow. He had a doctorate from the Moscow Higher Technical School and worked at Amtorg as an engineer, which gave him the credentials to gather scientific intelligence.

Ovakimian's prize catch was the only member of the United States Congress known to have spied for the Soviets. Samuel Dickstein was one of the four sons of a Russian rabbi who brought his family to America in 1887, when Sam was two. Sam said he didn't want to follow in his father's footsteps because he didn't like beards. Instead, he studied for a law degree and went into politics in his Lower East Side tenement neighborhood. In 1917, he was elected alderman and got the firemen a raise. He went on to the New York State Assembly in 1919 and opened a law office, defending tenants against landlords. When he ran for Congress in 1922, all the tenants he'd helped voted for him. He stayed in the House for twenty-two years and continued to serve the interests of his immigrant constituents.[17]

Samuel Dickstein's political career was founded on his posture as a super-patriot. He said he loathed the philosophy of Socialism, which he described as "borderline Communism." When he was elected to Congress, he boasted that he had defeated the only Socialist in the House, Meyer London.

In the New York law office he shared with his brother, Dickstein specialized in immigration issues. People came asking, "How can I get my sister to America?" He told them to go to Montreal and see his friend the American consul, who would provide a visa. For a fee, he would draw up a guarantee that the immigrant would not be a public burden. Always a protector of the underdog, as long as he got paid for it, Dickstein ran a visa racket in cahoots with the U.S. consul.[18]

When Hitler came to power in 1933, Dickstein turned his attention to the Nazi issue. Fascist groups like the Silver Shirts and Friends of New Germany sprang up. Heil-Hitlering Bundists goose-stepped down Manhattan's 86th Street and sang the "Horst Wessel" in swastika-draped beer halls. Dickstein sounded the alarm against the "Brown Menace." As chairman of the House Immigration and Naturalization Committee, he convinced Congress in March 1934 to sponsor a special committee to investigate Nazi propaganda, offering himself as chairman. But the speaker of the House, Henry T. Rainey, turned to the tall, dour Boston Democrat John W. McCormack instead. McCormack expanded the committee's mandate to include Communist propaganda as well. After a few perfunctory hearings, the McCormack Committee closed down at the end of 1934, having accomplished next to nothing.[19]

On July 8, 1937, an Austrian illegal working for the Soviets and code-named *Buby* came to Dickstein's law office for help in obtaining citizenship. Dickstein told him that the 1937 Austrian quota of 1,413 had already been filled and proposed the Montreal solution. He had settled dozens of similar cases, he told Buby. It would cost $3,000. After clearing the deal with his station chief, Ovakimian, Buby paid Dickstein $1,000. Dickstein protested that "others take huge money for these things . . . and I, Samuel Dickstein, am a poor man."[20]

Ovakimian reported to Moscow that Dickstein headed "a criminal gang involved in shady businesses, selling passports, illegal smuggling of people . . . getting the citizenship."

Perhaps Buby let slip a clue as to his real occupation, for Dickstein sensed a more lucrative opportunity than selling visas. As a member of the House, he had entrée to embassies, and paid a visit in December to the Russian ambassador, Alexander Troyanovsky, who sent a report to Moscow, explaining that Dickstein had served on the McCormack Committee and investigated Nazi propaganda. Dickstein claimed to have found a connection between Nazi agents and White Russians in the United States, but lamented that Congress had not provided funds to investigate the Russian fascists. He offered to give Troyanovsky the information he hoped to develop, if the ambassador would let him have $5,000 or $6,000 to pay his investigators.

Troyanovsky soon received instructions from his NKVD boss in Moscow, Nikolay Yezhov, to recruit Dickstein. The Russian ambassador saw Dickstein again on April 20, 1938, and introduced him to his contact, code-named *Igor*. Dickstein was given the code name *Crook*. He wanted a retainer of $2,500 a month, but *Igor* offered $500. They compromised on $1,250. On May 25, 1938, Peter Gutzeit, who handled Dickstein with Ovakimian, endorsed the arrangement, saying that Dickstein had access to useful information regarding American fascists. He added, however, that "we are fully aware of whom we are dealing with. . . . This is an unscrupulous type, greedy for money . . . a very cunning swindler."[21]

When Dickstein failed to get named to the 1938 House Un-American Activities Committee chaired by Martin Dies, his stock plummeted. Gutzeit was hoping to obtain grand jury interrogations of suspected German agents. Dickstein was told that he wasn't giving the Russians their money's worth. *Igor* reported that "He blazed up very much . . . that he is employing people and . . . demands nothing for himself." Dickstein told his handler on June 23 that when he had worked for Poland he had been paid without question. And when he had worked for the English he was paid good money. Only with the Russians did he have any trouble. Once Dickstein had revealed that he was a congressman for hire, *Igor* pointed out that while his other involvements had been for money, this time he should be guided by ideological consideration in the struggle against fascism.

Gutzeit was summoned back to Moscow during the 1938 purges and shot as a suspected Trotskyite. Such was the reward for many a Soviet operative in the thirties, when Stalin's security apparatus devoured its own. The NKVD soured on Dickstein and warned that any further dealings were dangerous because he was "not simply a crook but a mercenary of many intelligence services."[22]

———

By 1940, Ovakimian had so many agents under his supervision that he was overworked to the point of exhaustion. He saw as many as ten a day and his bosses in Moscow noted that his workload had "blunted his vigilance." The purges had thinned the ranks of Soviet agents operating in America. One NKVD memo noted "an acute crisis in operatives."[23]

Ovakimian was recalled in 1941. The FBI got wind in April that he was leaving the country. His car and other belongings had been crated and loaded onto the SS *Annie Johnson,* a ship chartered by Amtorg and scheduled to leave New York in May for Vladivostok via the Panama Canal. A warrant for his arrest was issued on April 26. On May 5, as Ovakimian sat in a taxi with an agent code-named *Octane,* who was passing him documents, the cab was surrounded by FBI agents. Ovakimian jumped out and tried to break free. *Octane,* who has never been identified, fled out the other side. Ovakimian was taken in handcuffs to the federal courthouse, where he was charged with violating the Foreign Agents Registration Act. A Soviet consular official soon appeared, claiming that Ovakimian had immunity as an Amtorg official. He was charged and released on $25,000 cash bail, which was paid by Amtorg.[24]

The Soviet embassy eventually struck a deal with the State Department to exchange Ovakimian for six Americans who were being detained in Russia and Russian-occupied Poland, charged with illegal possession of firearms and being "bourgeois capitalists." Ovakimian left in July aboard a Soviet ship, but only three of the six detained Americans were returned. Once again, the Soviets broke their word. [25]

———

In June 1939, with Europe on the cusp of war, Attorney General Frank Murphy, Homer Cummings's successor, proposed to FDR that all "espionage, counter-espionage, and sabotage matters" be handled by the FBI and military intelligence, who had "perfected their methods of investigation."[26] FDR approved in a memo that amounted to a formal charter for the FBI: "It is my desire that the investigation of all espionage, counter-espionage, and sabotage matters be controlled and handled by the FBI, the Military Intelligence Division of the War Department, and the Office of Naval Intelligence. . . . No investigations should be conducted . . . except by the three agencies mentioned above." By then, a number of laws had been passed that facilitated the FBI in making arrests. The Foreign Agents Registration Act of 1938 allowed the FBI to arrest spies who had not registered. The Hatch Act of 1939 barred federal employees from membership in any political party that advocated the overthrow of government.[27]

In September 1939, when Germany invaded Poland, FDR declared a national emergency and ordered Attorney General Murphy to hire at once 150 more FBI agents. Hoover instructed his field offices to compile a list of "German, Italian, and Communist sympathizers." On that list, a number of names were flagged to be arrested in case of a national emergency. As the President's policy evolved from neutrality to assisting England, he asked Hoover to investigate those who sent telegrams to the White House calling him a warmonger and opposing national defense measures. In the name of national security, when fifteen Negro mess attendants aboard Navy ships protested racial discrimination, Hoover launched an investigation of the National Association for the Advancement of Colored People, which went on for thirty years.[28]

———

Aside from its "legal" agents, that is, those who had diplomatic immunity as embassy or consular officials, the Soviets ran a network of "illegals" out of New York, who settled in the city as private citizens, working at jobs or small businesses. Alexander Ulanovsky, a veteran revolutionary, arrived in New York in 1931 with his wife, Nadia. They had previously served in China and found Manhattan more congenial. As Nadia put it, "If you wore a sign saying 'I Am A Spy,' you might still not get arrested." There was no place like New York for an illegal Soviet agent. Where else could a man who spoke broken English pass unnoticed among millions of other immigrants? The teeming, polyglot metropolis was a protective habitat for the illegals, who were at a greater risk, since they did not wear the cloak of diplomatic immunity. If they were caught, no deals could be made with the State Department.

In and out of a dozen czarist jails, Ulanovsky had been imprisoned with Stalin in a Siberian camp, from which he made a sensational escape. One of his agents, Whittaker Chambers, recalled that "there was something monkeylike in his loose posture, in the droop of his arms and roll of his walk . . . [and] about his features, which were small, lined and alert. . . . It was his brown eyes that were most monkeylike, alternately mischievous and wistful. . . . They had looked out on life . . . from top to bottom, from stinking prison cells to diplomatic dinners."[29]

The Ulanovskys lived in a sumptuous apartment, in a brownstone off Fifth Avenue, at 7 West 51st Street. It belonged to a wealthy Communist, Paula Levine, who was doing espionage work in France and was later arrested there. They also kept a workshop on Gay Street, a short, curving block in Greenwich Village, in a house owned by a Negro schoolteacher who rented the second floor to the apparat.

Prior to recognition, communications with Moscow depended on microfilm and messages in invisible ink. German Communists working as stewards or seamen on the Hamburg-American Line smuggled letters into New York. The tiny frames of microfilm were concealed between the glass and the backing of Woolworth dime mirrors. The Ulanovskys' workshop was set up to enlarge the microfilm and develop the invisible ink. Letters typed triple space would be soaked in a bath of potassium permanganate until the reddish brown Russian script appeared between the typed lines.[30]

With the ascent of Hitler in 1933, the courier system collapsed. It was in any case made redundant by recognition, for the Soviets could from 1934 on use coded cables to and from the embassy and consulates.

Aside from the time-consuming labor of deciphering instructions from Moscow, the Ulanovskys collected tons of technical and scientific documents that were freely available in America's open society. From the U.S. Patent Office they obtained hundreds of patents, which they mailed to Moscow by the box. From the Government Printing Office, they ordered technical manuals. From an explosives manufacturer they bought a sample of flashless powder. Coming from a country where even a telephone directory was considered a confidential document, they were amazed at what was up for grabs in America.

Beyond obtaining what was openly available, however, the Ulanovskys were abject failures. Several attempts to steal submarine blueprints came to nothing. Alex tried to recruit the muckraking, pro-Soviet author Lincoln Steffens, who wasn't interested.[31]

In the spring of 1934, Alexander and Nadia were recalled to Moscow. They left New York with genuine regret, having come to appreciate the features that made Manhattan life agreeable, from Woolworth's and the Automat to Central Park at sundown. Nadia had given birth to a daughter, who, being born on American soil, had the right to U.S. citizenship.[32]

In its formative years, Soviet espionage in America was a scattershot affair, tentative and mismanaged. The illegals often spoke no English and seemed ill-suited to their task. They landed in New York and stayed at the garrison-like Hotel Taft. A note would arrive with "greetings from Fanny" for the newcomer, who was given his instructions.

Valentin Markin operated concurrently with Ulanovsky, but lasted less than a year. The son of a Petrograd janitor, Markin was so short that he wore elevated shoes. His hair stood up, like the hair of cartoon characters struck by electricity, adding another inch, and his arrogance compensated for his bantam size. Since he did not speak a word of English, he communicated with other agents in German. He turned up drunk at meetings and was given to tantrums. Told to focus on Washington and develop agents in the State Department, his only achievement was to recruit a conman code-named *Leo*, who invented two State Department sources, sending Markin their fictitious reports, which included transcripts of recorded conversations between Cordell Hull and foreign ambassadors. For these fabrications Markin paid a total of $900 a month. Eventually, he came to his senses, and a cable to Moscow on November 27, 1934, said: "We assume there is no *Daniel* or *Albert* and that [they] were created fictitiously by *Leo* to increase his remuneration."[33]

At the end of the year, Markin came to a violent end. Emerging from a bar in midtown where he had flashed a roll of bills, he was mugged and left to die in a gutter with a fractured skull. The official account in his Moscow file states that he was killed in a car accident.[34]

———

These inept illegals would have been lost without the American Communist Party, which provided from its ranks assistants who acted as guides, couriers, handlers, and all-around gofers. For, upon being dropped into New York, the illegals knew nothing about such vital matters as the geography of the subway system or how to order breakfast at a diner. If they got lost, they did not know enough English to ask for directions. The maps and mores of the country they had been sent to spy on were an enigma, and it was here that their helpful American accomplices could be as indispensable as a seeing-eye dog. They had to be reliable Communists who spoke German, the lingua franca of the GRU (since Germany was then the main enemy), with a pliant personality that would not be offended by their gruff and overbearing charges.

The liaison between the GRU and the American party was a Swiss barber, Max Bedacht, whose day job was to run the party's insurance company, the International Workers' Order. In June 1932, Bedacht was looking for the right person to work with the newly arrived Ulanovsky. On a sweltering summer day, he summoned to his office on 13th Street a thirty-one-year-old Communist who was then editor of *New Masses*, Whittaker Chambers. An overweight, placid man, Chambers wondered why Bedacht, whom he knew only as the self-effacing father of five, wanted to see him.

Looking disapprovingly at Chambers, who always appeared somewhat rumpled, Bedacht asked him, "What are you doing now, Comrade Chambers?" When Chambers told him, Bedacht said, "For some reason, they want you to go into one of the party's 'special institutions.'" Chambers looked blank, so Bedacht added: "They want you to do underground work." He would have to give up his party membership and leave the editorship of *New Masses*, for which he had a particular affinity. He would have to discard his friends and his pleasant daily routine. Chambers had been in the party seven years, mainly as a writer for the *Daily Worker;* he knew nothing about underground work. His wife pleaded with him not to accept such a risky job. But Chambers was elated at having been chosen. Someone, he thought, must have seen in him the ability to handle a difficult assignment.[35]

Actually, the principal point that recommended Chambers for his new job was that he spoke German. His acceptance, however, had much to do with the ingrained party discipline. If you were given a job, you obeyed, even when you had no idea what that entailed. It was a tribute to blind obedience that a talented intellectual such as Chambers would give up an important editorship to become a courier, a glorified messenger boy.

Chambers soon grew weary of waiting for hours under streetlights, taking roundabout ways to get to a contact, meeting ships at dockside to collect a pocket mirror concealing microfilm. It was wearing him down and wrecking his home life, for he rarely saw his wife and baby daughter.

———

In early 1934, the Hungarian Communist Josef Peters took over the underground section from Max Bedacht, becoming one of the two or three most powerful men in the American party. Short and energetic, looking somewhat like a mustached and bushy-eyebrowed chow dog strutting on its hind legs, Peters had first been sent to America in 1924 to organize unions in the Midwest. He became the man in charge of spies just as the mushrooming bureaucracy of the New Deal began to hire a scattering of Communists. Peters proposed to develop them as agents, who would be organized into cells, and to move them from alphabet agencies such as WPA and Triple A into old-line agencies like the State Department, where they would have access to classified information.[36]

Chambers was assigned to work with Peters and help carry out the new line. In the spring, Peters took him to Washington to introduce him to the man who was running the main cell of Communists in government, Hal Ware. The son of Mother Bloor, the party's grande dame, Hal was an unlikely spy, having spent his entire adult life on farm problems. With his rimless glasses and plain, down-to-earth, reassuring manner, he looked like an associate professor at a Midwestern agricultural college, who could tell you a great deal about soil grades and average rainfall. In 1922, during the famine, he'd taken twenty-two tractors to Russia to teach the peasants mechanized agriculture and ended up staying there eight years and being decorated by Lenin. When he came back to America, he carried $25,000 in a money belt, which the Comintern had given him to organize American farmers.[37]

Ware had excellent contacts in the Department of Agriculture and was assigned in 1933 to recruit agents in the Agricultural Adjustment Administration, which drafted the codes to limit agricultural production, in order to raise farm prices. With its staff of five thousand, it was dubbed "the greatest law firm in the country." Jerome Frank, the general counsel, had sixty lawyers working on marketing agreements, from Oregon apples to Florida strawberries. His closest advisers were the two Harvard Law School classmates Lee Pressman and Alger Hiss. Pressman, the son of Lower East Side immigrants, knew nothing about agriculture and was said to have asked, during discussions with macaroni producers, "I want to know what this code will do for the macaroni growers." Pressman headed the licensing section and Hiss headed the benefit payments section. Pressman said of Hiss: "If he was standing at the bar with the British ambassador and you were told to give a package to the valet, you would give it to the ambassador before you gave it to Alger."[38]

Hiss, then twenty-nine years old, helped draft the cotton contract in late 1933. Cotton, grown on large Southern plantations, was picked by tenant farmers and sharecroppers, most of whom were black. Under the contract, every third row of cotton had to be plowed under all over the South, from Texas to Virginia. This one-third crop reduction program threatened to displace an equal percentage of sharecroppers, who were slated to share Triple A subsidies with the owners. Feeling sympathy for the dispossessed sharecroppers, Hiss drafted a provision in the contract to limit the rights of landlords to evict tenants. He also wanted Triple A checks to be made out separately to owners and tenants, who were being "robbed blind with a fountain pen," as he put it. To his astonishment, Hiss received a visit from the powerful Southern senator Ellison "Cotton Ed" Smith of South Carolina, a plantation owner himself. "Young fella," he said, "you can't do this to my niggers, pay checks to them. They don't know what to do with the money. The money should come to me."[39] In the summer of 1934, Hiss took a leave from Triple A to serve as counsel on the Nye Senate committee that was investigating munitions makers, the "merchants of death" who had reaped colossal profits during World War I, but he continued to work on the sharecropper problem in his spare time. A memo initialed by Hiss landed on the desk of Chester Davis, the head of Triple A, in February 1935, arguing that landlords should be made to keep all their sharecroppers. This was anathema to influential Southern senators, whom the Department of Agriculture had to appease if they wanted to maintain Triple A appropriations.

"Alger, this is a dishonest opinion," Davis said when he called Hiss in. "It isn't true, it can't be." The ultimate result of the landlord-sharecropper dispute was the purge of Triple A: Jerome Frank and Lee Pressman were fired and Hiss resigned to continue his work with the Nye Committee.[40]

When Whittaker Chambers accompanied Josef Peters to Washington in the spring of 1934, he was surprised at how easily the espionage network fell into place. Ware, he recalled, "was like a man who had bought a farm, sight unseen, only to discover that the crops are all in and ready to harvest. All he had to do was hustle them into the barn. The barn in his case was the Communist Party." At a cafeteria on Pennsylvania Avenue, the two men met Hal Ware and Alger Hiss. The meeting was brief, but Chambers became a close friend of Hiss's after that, and of his family. He sensed a strange dichotomy in the courtly, personable lawyer, who was a model of rectitude, yet seemed almost to be acting a part. Chambers felt that there were layers to Hiss, like geological strata. Beneath the surface formality, contempt for the establishment. Beneath the external sweetness of manner, a capacity for cruelty. In conversation, he could be unnecessarily vehement, as he was when he unleashed his contempt for FDR, seeing the crippled President as a symbol of America's breakdown. Hiss seemed to take pleasure in challenging the accepted wisdom. At one point, he told Chambers, "I'm sorry, I just don't like Shakespeare. Platitudes in blank verse."[41]

After the meeting with Hiss, Hal Ware took Chambers to his sister Helen's studio near Du Pont Circle, where she taught the violin over a florist shop. She had one large, bare, loftlike room, where Chambers spent the night. The next day, he met the eight members of what he called Apparatus A, better known as the Ware group, a directorate made up of the leaders of the seven or eight cells that Ware controlled. Six of the eight worked in Triple A, while the two others worked for the National Recovery Administration, which drew up fair competition codes for business.

The meeting was held at the home of one of its members, Henry Collins, a converted coach house in a mews off Connecticut Avenue, in a large, book-lined living room with a cathedral ceiling, and brightly colored Ethiopian tapestries, which Collins had collected on trips to Africa. When he stepped into Collins's living room, Chambers entered a new world, far removed from the gruff and primitive Soviet illegals. The Ware group was confined to young men with a promising future in government service, men from Ivy League universities with Phi Beta Kappa keys. Some were the high-achieving sons of Jewish immigrants, while others came from old American families. A graduate of the Harvard Business School, Collins was born into a Philadelphia family that had arrived from England in 1640. He worked in the Soil Conservation Service of the Department of Agriculture. Chambers recalled that he "served voluntarily and in fact irrepressibly as a recruiting agent for the Soviet apparatus."[42]

Nathaniel Weyl, another Ivy Leaguer, also came from a family whose roots in America went back to the seventeenth century. Weyl joined the party in 1922 while attending Columbia University. Later he would explain that in the early days of the New Deal there was a benign tolerance of Communism, which was viewed as the inoffensive left wing of the Progressive movement. He did not, however, feel suited to underground work and quit the Ware group just after Chambers arrived to run the School on Wheels, which toured farm areas with party-approved textbooks.[43]

Hiss, as a lawyer for the Nye Committee, was able to subpoena classified documents from the State Department, which he gave to Chambers to photograph. His friend Lee Pressman, who was also in the Ware group until he was fired from Triple A, had joined the party out of a sense of hopelessness when faced with the Depression at home and the rise of Hitler abroad.

Of the four remaining members, John Abt, Nathan Witt (born Witowsky), Charles Kramer (born Krivisky), and Victor Perlo, all but Perlo were in Triple A. Kramer had a cell of his own, which met at his home on Euclid Street, in a room stacked with *Daily Workers* and Communist agitprop pamphlets. Nathan Witt, gaunt and mustached, the warm and outgoing son of a tailor, worked his way through Harvard Law School by driving a taxi. In Witt, a strong indignation factor was always ready to surface—runaway profits while millions were reduced to misery, the money changers pushed out the front door and coming back through the side door, and so on.

A second-generation Polish immigrant, Perlo was a mathematical prodigy at City College, hired at the age of twenty-one as a statistician for the National Recovery Administration. Arrogantly doctrinaire, he castigated New Deal reforms and spoke of private charity as alms. When FDR named Joseph Kennedy to head the Securities and Exchange Commission, Perlo was incensed, saying that Kennedy had made his millions as a bootlegger and that FDR was capitulating to "the most vicious political elements."

The Ware group lasted just over a year. On August 13, 1935, its leader, known for driving at breakneck speeds, was on a trip to visit Pennsylvania miners when he crashed his car into a coal truck. Hal Ware died the next day in a Harrisburg hospital, at the age of forty-five, leaving behind his wife, the beautiful Jessica Smith, a Quaker he had met in Russia in 1922 known as the "Golden Goddess." She later married John Abt, who became the lawyer for the Communist Party.[44]

In its year under Ware's direction, the group's principal activity was not the collection of classified information, but the placing of its people in positions of influence. In 1934, Nathan Witt joined the National Labor Relations Board, which had the crucial responsibility of organizing and certifying union elections, and rose to the position of secretary in 1937. Lee Pressman became general counsel of the CIO, the Congress of Industrial Organizations, in 1936. John Abt in 1935 was assistant general counsel in the Works Progress Administration under Harry Hopkins, and by 1937 he was chief of the Trial Section in the Justice Department's Antitrust Division, with the title of special assistant to the Attorney General. Shuttling between Washington and New York, Chambers acted as the liaison between the Ware group and Josef Peters, reporting on their progress in infiltrating the government.[45]

Chambers moved away from the Ware group and began to recruit new agents for a "sleeper apparatus," a new group that would be ready to start operating as soon as it was called upon to act. When a new Soviet agent arrived in 1936, the overburdened Peters passed Chambers on to him. On a rainy autumn afternoon during rush hour, Chambers was walking up Fifth Avenue with Peters when, looking across the traffic to the steps of St. Patrick's Cathedral, Peters said, "There's our man." He pointed to a short fellow with red hair and reddish eyelashes, dapper in a tailored worsted suit. Chambers was introduced to Boris Bykov, a colonel in the GRU, with whom he spoke German. Chambers worked with Bykov until his defection in 1938, and came to see him as a man warped by underground work, "a pathological coward," nervous and high-strung, afraid of his own shadow, bad-tempered and vituperative.[46]

Bykov wanted to push Chambers's sleeper apparatus directly into espionage and went to Washington to make his pitch. This was the united front period when the American Communist Party sought allies on the liberal left, backed FDR in the 1936 election, and infiltrated the newly born CIO. American anti-fascists saw the Soviet Union not as a threat, but as an ally against Hitler. The party was able to assume a hidden role in the New Deal and the labor movement. Thus, Bykov told Chambers's agents that the Soviet Union needed the help of comrades abroad. It needed information concerning fascist plans, actual documents relating to Germany and the Far East, for the fatherland was threatened with encirclement. As Chambers put it, "The water was in the pipes. Bykov's function was simply to turn on the faucets."[47]

Chambers took as much pride in his apparatus as a baseball coach would in a World Series team. His four stars were led by Harry Dexter White, perhaps the most valuable American spy the Soviets ever recruited, who was Secretary of the Treasury Henry Morgenthau's right-hand man.

Next came Alger Hiss, who after serving on the Nye Committee had moved on to work for Solicitor General Stanley Reed. Chambers suggested that he transfer to State, where one of his many mentors, Assistant Secretary Francis Sayre, had beckoned. At State, Hiss began to furnish documents almost at once. Transmissions were made at weekly or ten-day intervals. Hiss would bring documents home in a briefcase and Chambers would pick them up and photograph them, bringing them back the same night, so that Hiss could return them the next morning.[48]

Julian Wadleigh, Chambers's third star, a young graduate of Oxford, was also in the State Department, in the Trade Agreements Division. Although not a party member, Wadleigh had agreed, at the party's request, to move from Agriculture to State. His thick-lensed glasses and feathery uncombed hair gave him a brooding, owlish appearance, which was offset by a puckish sense of humor—he sometimes used the alias Jasper Q. Sprigg.

Last and least of the four was Abraham George Silverman, director of research at the Railroad Retirement Board, whose main utility was that he was a close friend of Harry Dexter White's and helped him resolve his ambivalence about espionage. Silverman, slight and wiry, combined a childlike spontaneity with a permanently worried look.[49]

Chambers moved to Baltimore, where he kept an apartment to photograph the documents his agents produced, handing over the undeveloped film to Bykov in New York. There was so much material that at one point he had three photographers processing it. Pleased with his sources, and with Christmas coming up, Bykov wanted to reward them with cash gifts. Chambers thought it was a crude gesture, which sullied the selfless ideological motives of his agents. But Bykov insisted: "Who pays is boss, and who takes money must give something back," he said.

"You will lose every one of them," Chambers warned.

"Then we must give them some costly present," Bykov replied.

He gave Chambers $600 to buy four Bokhara rugs, hand-woven by the tribeswomen of Turkistan. All four were sent to Silverman, who kept one and delivered the other three, taking elaborate precautions. The rug for Hiss changed hands near a restaurant shaped like a boat off the Baltimore Turnpike. Silverman drove up beyond the restaurant with the rug in the back of his car and Hiss and Chambers arrived in Hiss's Plymouth. With the headlights turned off in both cars, Chambers carried the rug, a loud red with an intricate design, about nine by twelve feet, from Silverman's car to Hiss's car. As Chambers learned over the years, espionage was mostly schlepping.[50]

———

In 1936 and 1937, Stalin's purges and show trials created a crisis in the American party. In the absence of any succession mechanism, Stalin had a simple and direct way of eliminating his rivals—he murdered them. The sordid spectacle of Bolshevik leaders confessing to absurd charges before facing the firing squad tested the faithful. Were all these men who had been in charge of building Socialism—men favored by Lenin, such as Bukharin and Zinoviev, as well as the General Staff of the army, 80 percent of the party secretaries, the bulk of the OGPU, two heads of the Five Year Plan—were all these men traitors?

In the fall of 1937, the purges were giving Chambers serious doubts, for they had begun to reach beyond Soviet borders. On September 3, the Swiss police found the body of Ignace Reiss, the Paris-based head of NKVD operations in Europe, on a road outside Lausanne, riddled with twelve bullets from a machine gun. The murder of Reiss, who had defected after writing Stalin, "I cannot continue any longer," moved Chambers deeply, for he too was about to defect, having come to the conclusion that Communism under Stalin was a malignant force.[51]

Although badly shaken by Reiss's murder, Chambers told himself that it had taken place in Europe, and that such a thing could not happen in America. But less than six months later, he learned that his old friend Juliet Poyntz had disappeared. Chambers had known Poyntz, a tall blunt woman from Omaha, Nebraska, since the twenties, when she ran for Congress on the party ticket. Caught up in party factions, she had the distinction of giving her name to an "ism," when the *Daily Worker* called for the liquidation of "Poyntzism." As her *mea culpa*, she served in China for the Comintern in 1935. Returning to the United States in 1936 via Moscow, she was horrified by the first show trials and quietly dropped out of the party. In June 1937, she vanished. One of the last of her friends to see her was the Italian anarchist Carlo Tresca, who later told the police that "she confided in me that she could no longer approve of things under the Stalin regime."

On February 8, 1938, the *New York Times* ran a story, quoting Tresca, that she had been "lured or kidnapped to Soviet Russia by a prominent Communist . . . connected with the secret police in Moscow, sent to this country for that purpose." Tresca said Poyntz was "a marked person, similar to other disillusioned Bolsheviks. . . . I need only recall the case of Ignace Reiss."[52]

Chambers learned from his own sources that Poyntz had gone to Central Park to meet an old lover who was now an NKVD agent. She left the light on and an unfinished letter on the table in her room in a hotel for women on 57th Street. In the park, she was pushed into a car by two men who probably murdered her. The thought of this brilliant, stubbornly independent woman ending up as fishbait made Chambers physically ill, though her fate remained a question mark.

The fate of his fellow agent Arnold Ikal was far more disturbing. Ikal, an affable, easygoing Latvian, had arrived in New York in May 1932, with the mission of obtaining passports for Comintern agents. He had a team of assistants who combed the death records in the Genealogical Division of the New York Public Library, looking for native New Yorkers who had died as children. They copied the information in the records, names of father and mother, date of birth, and so on. Then, Ikal would apply by mail for a birth certificate with the New York City Department of Health, enclosing a fee and a cover address. Armed with the birth certificate, one of Ikal's assistants would go down to the Passport Bureau with a witness ready to swear he or she had known that person more than five years, and presto, a passport. Once he got going, Ikal was sending as many as one hundred passports a month to Moscow, which meant that about one thousand Soviet agents a year were using good, safe, American boots (as the Russians called passports).

Ikal liked life in New York, and began to think of himself as a small businessman, turning out piece goods. In 1933 he met Ruth, an attractive young American divorcée, whom he married in 1935. Soon he and his new wife had a summer place on Jamaica Bay and a motor launch, which they moored at the Oyster Bay Yacht Club. Life was good.

In September 1937, Ikal was summoned home. This was the time of the purges, but he decided to go when he got a personal message from his mentor and fellow Latvian, General Eduard Berzin, the head of the GRU Fourth Department (military intelligence). Berzin could not have sent it because he had been executed in August. Ikal took his American wife along for insurance, since the recognition agreement specified that U.S. citizens could not be detained. They left in October on the Italian liner *Rex* with two sets of passports, one set made out to Donald L. Robinson (born in Queens in 1905 and died in 1909) and Norma Birkland (born in 1906 and died in 1916). The other set was made out to Mr. and Mrs. Arnold Rubens, the name under which Ikal had applied for naturalization papers.[53]

On November 5, they checked into Moscow's Hotel National as Mr. and Mrs. Rubens. The next day, Ikal vanished. The hotel staff told his distraught wife that he was in a hospital. Loy Henderson, the number two at the American embassy, got wind that an American couple was in trouble and came looking for Ruth at the hotel. By then, she too was gone. According to the recognition treaty, embassy officials had to be notified within seventy-two hours of the arrest of an American in Russia. This was a clear violation of the treaty. Cordell Hull sent Litvinov, the Foreign Minister, a cable to remind him that Mr. and Mrs. Rubens were American citizens. Litvinov finally admitted in December that the couple was in custody, but concocted a story that they had visited Trotsky in Mexico on their way to Russia. This attempt to brand Rubens/Ikal as a Trotskyite was denounced as a fabrication on December 21 by the philosopher John Dewey, who at the age of seventy-eight had gone to Mexico City, as the head of the Committee for the Defense of Trotsky, to hear Trotsky's rebuttal of the charges brought against him in the Moscow trials.

The Rubens/Ikal story made front-page news in the American press and eroded Soviet-American relations. In Washington, Ambassador Troyanovsky asked the State Department to drop its inquiry. When the State Department refused, Litvinov capitulated and on February 10, 1938, Henderson was allowed to visit Ruth in Butyrka Prison in the presence of a Red Army officer. Visibly intimidated, Ruth said she did not need help. In April 1939, the U.S. embassy was promised that Ruth would stand trial. In June, after eighteen months in jail, she appeared at her trial, which lasted forty-five minutes. She was found guilty of entering the Soviet Union with false documents and was sentenced to eighteen months retroactive and released from jail the next day. Ruth declined to return to the United States, where she faced possible prosecution for violating passport laws, became a Soviet citizen, and moved to Kiev. In December 1939, Ikal confessed to being an agent of the Berzin fascist organization. He was sent to a gulag and died there.[54]

After the show trials, the murder of Reiss, the disappearance of Juliet Poyntz, and the imprisonment of Arnold Ikal, Chambers was determined to quit the underground. "If you have ever clubbed rats to death in a closed room," he later wrote, "you will have an exact picture of the state of affairs in the Soviet secret services in 1936, 1937, and 1938." He did not intend to be one of the rats. In April 1938 he made his getaway. After finding work translating *Bambi*, the huge best-seller by the Austrian novelist Felix Salten, he fled to Florida with his wife and daughter. This would be the start of an odyssey that would bring him, ten years later, before the House Un-American Activities Committee as a witness. In the fallout that resulted from his flight, Josef Peters was demoted and Boris Bykov was recalled to Moscow.[55]

———

The loss of Chambers was not seen as particularly serious, since he was a lowly courier, not an agent of influence. The Soviets still had three valuable agents in the State Department: Lawrence Duggan, Noel Field, and Alger Hiss. With the turnover in Soviet handlers, they were now under the control of the NKVD station chief in New York, Boris Bazarov, a dour man with thinning brown hair combed straight back from a high forehead, and glasses that rested on his beakish nose. Bazarov had arrived in December 1934, following the murder of Valentin Markin. In Washington, Hede Massing continued to supervise Noel Field, and worried over his indiscretions. He liked to pull stunts like standing on the steps of the Lincoln Memorial and singing "The Internationale" at the top of his lungs. He left copies of the *Daily Worker* lying around at home.[56]

The problem was solved when Field quit the State Department in 1936 and took a job with the League of Nations in Geneva. In September 1940, George Dimitrov, the head of the Comintern, instructed Communist Party boss Earl Browder to recruit agents who could infiltrate the relief committees then forming in Europe. This would give them the freedom of movement to act as Soviet couriers in the warring nations.[57] A month later, Field resigned from the League of Nations and joined the Unitarian Service Committee as head of its Marseilles office. He spent the war years acting as a courier among the underground Communist parties in occupied Europe. One of his colleagues on the Unitarian Committee recalled that "the whole world is wrong but not Noel Field. He did not brook disagreement."[58]

When Hede Massing was transferred to Paris in June 1936, Bazarov reported to Moscow that Duggan wanted to work directly with Soviet illegals rather than with intermediaries. Duggan had told Massing, according to Bazarov, that "the only thing that kept him at his hateful job in the State Department, where he did not get out of his tuxedo for two weeks, every night attending receptions, was the idea of being useful to our cause." Duggan set out the rules under which he would cooperate. He agreed to one meeting a month with someone who knew stenography. He refused to turn over documents.

Bazarov assigned Norman Borodin, a young illegal who had already been stationed in Norway, Germany, and France, to handle Duggan. At their first meeting, Duggan was wary. His wife was pregnant, he had to think of his family, he'd be found out, fired from State, and even blacklisted. But by midsummer, he had thawed, and was turning over documents and coming to meetings every two weeks. Duggan gave Borodin a recent State Department handbook and personnel list, which Bazarov forwarded to Moscow, commenting that he had noted Alger Hiss's name on the registry, "but the neighbors [GRU] stole him. . . . Having Hiss one does not need others."[59]

In May 1937, at the age of thirty-two, Duggan was promoted to head of the Latin American division, which meant that he was cleared to receive all the classified cables coming into the State Department. The job was such a plum that Moscow cabled, "We cannot lose him for any reasons."[60]

When a grateful Moscow Center (NKVD headquarters) proposed paying Duggan in the spring of 1937, Bazarov objected that Duggan would surely reject cash, as he had rejected a monogrammed alligator skin toiletries case. Duggan was an idealist and paying him would only serve to alienate him.

The trouble was that Duggan's idealism worked both ways, and he expressed a growing concern over Stalin's purges. On July 2, 1937, he raised the question with Borodin: Why had senior Bolsheviks he had learned to respect turned out to be traitors? He was so worried he could not sleep and wanted to break off.[61]

In August, Bazarov passed Duggan on to a more senior illegal, Iskhak Akhmerov, a Tartar of peasant background who had arrived in New York in 1934 by way of China and the NKVD. Akhmerov was six feet tall, with downward-turning eyes, full lips, and thick, wavy chestnut hair. In New York, he found it so easy to fit in that he married Earl Browder's niece, Helen Lowry.

Duggan went on vacation to Mexico in October and when he returned his doubts had doubled. At a meeting with Akhmerov on January 3, 1938, he was still harping on the purges. How could the traitors include diplomats whose devotion to the U.S.S.R. he knew to be unquestionable?

Duggan was now under State Department scrutiny, as he learned when he was summoned by his mentor, Sumner Welles, in March and told to be "exceptionally careful in your contacts." With the new powers conferred upon it by FDR in 1936, the FBI was on the job. Welles added: "It does not fit a person of your status to have Marxist books," a sign that the FBI had done a black bag job on his house. In April 1939, Duggan told Akhmerov that he was no longer receiving cables from other departments, which meant that he had lost his security clearance.[62]

———

On August 24, 1939, Hitler and Stalin signed a nonaggression pact; they would soon be allies in a war against Poland. In September, the politics of revolution became the politics of war. Chambers, who after his defection from the underground had joined the staff of *Time* magazine, received a visit from the anti-Communist author Isaac Don Levine, who told him it was time to tell what he knew. Chambers reluctantly agreed, recalling the words of another defector: "In our time, informing is a duty." The shock of the Berlin-Moscow agreement prodded him into action.[63]

Levine arranged a meeting with Assistant Secretary of State Adolf A. Berle Jr., who was in charge of intelligence matters at the State Department. On September 1, Nazi tanks invaded Poland, their rumbling drumroll announcing a world war. The next day, Chambers and Levine went to Woodley Hall, the nineteenth-century mansion Berle had rented from Henry Stimson, soon to be Secretary of War. They found an agitated Berle, who told them "we may be in this war within 48 hours and we cannot go into it without clean services" (meaning a government that was not penetrated by spies). After dinner, they sat outside in lawn chairs, as the smell of honeysuckle drifted on the muggy September air. Fortified by whiskey, Chambers began to tell the story of his espionage ring. As Berle listened in astonishment, Chambers named men who were his State Department colleagues, such as Hiss, Duggan, and Field, as well as many others.

After more than two hours on the lawn, they went back into the house. Berle sat down at a little desk just inside the front door and began to make quick notes, abbreviating as he went along, and Chambers filled in the details. It was after midnight when Chambers and Levine left. In great excitement, Berle was on the telephone dialing a number, which Chambers assumed to be the White House, as they went out the door.[64]

"Saturday night," Berle wrote in his diary entry for September 4, "I had, to me, a singularly unpleasant job. Isaac Don Levine . . . had opened up another idea of the Russian espionage. He brought a Mr. X around to my house on Saturday evening, after a rather unhappy croquet game had been played between Secretary Hull and some of the rest of us at Woodley. Through a long evening, I slowly manipulated Mr. X to a point where he told me some of the ramifications hereabout; and it becomes necessary to take a few simple measures. A good deal of the Russian espionage was carried on by Jews; we now know that they are exchanging information with Berlin; and the Jewish units are furious to find that they are, in substance, working for the Gestapo."[65]

An alarmed Berle called Assistant Secretary Dean Acheson about Hiss and his brother, Donald, whom Chambers had also named. Acheson told Berle that he had "known the family and these two boys since childhood and he could vouch for them absolutely." Berle confided to his diary, "You had a chain of endorsements . . . and this seemed to negate any immediate danger."

Thus, Berle did not notify the FBI of his talk with Chambers until March 1941, one year and five months later, and he didn't provide his notes until June 1943, so that the high-level spy ring that might have been shut down continued to function.

Chambers, however, had a different explanation for Berle's inaction. "I was told," he later wrote, "that Mr. Berle had carried my story to a higher authority . . . and he had been told to go and jump in the lake, only in somewhat coarser language. . . . I was given to understand that the president told this to Mr. Berle."[66]

In the case of Duggan, however, who was already under suspicion, Berle seems to have acted. On October 2, 1939, a month after the meeting with Chambers, a shaken Duggan told Akhmerov that he had been approached by a State Department security officer who told him he was known to have given secret material to Soviet intelligence and should start looking for another job. Duggan insisted on breaking, suspecting that there was a leak from the Soviet end. He was demoted to the position of personal adviser to Cordell Hull in Latin America, in the hope that he would resign.[67]

———

In late 1939, following the outbreak of World War II, a swarm of Soviet agents were recalled to Moscow, among them Akhmerov and Borodin. Akhmerov, newly married, took his American bride back with him. When he said goodbye to Duggan, with whom he had spent so many hours, he felt he was leaving a friend. For want of an agent in charge, the New York *Rezindentura* was closed down (in NKVD parlance, "the point was put in storage") and the agents became inactive.

When Hitler invaded Russia in June 1941, there was an urgent need for intelligence from the United States. Akhmerov was sent back in August to reestablish the illegal *Rezidentura*, traveling with his wife, Helen, on Canadian passports in the name of Reed. Since most of his agents were in Washington, Akhmerov settled in Baltimore. His cover was a small business that made fur hats and jackets, of which he was co-owner.[68]

Akhmerov tried to reactivate Duggan, who was still at the State Department. When they met in February 1942, Duggan said that he had recently seen Adolf Berle, who warned him about maintaining links with left-wing elements. Akhmerov realized that Duggan was burned out, and told Moscow the situation was "unsatisfactory." Moscow replied on November 26 that Akhmerov should be firm, although there was no thought of blackmail. Akhmerov tried again, and Duggan supplied some information in March and June of 1944. In July, he resigned from the State Department and replaced his father as director of the Institute of International Education.[69]

In August 1948, Chambers made his stunning allegations about Alger Hiss before HUAC. In December, Chambers testified before a federal grand jury. On December 10, Larry Duggan was at home in Scarsdale, recovering from a spinal disk injury. Two FBI agents came to call and repeated the names given to Berle by Chambers, of which his was one. Duggan denied being a Communist or a spy, but told the agents he had been approached twice in the thirties, once by Henry Collins and once by his Harvard classmate, Fred Field, heir to the Vanderbilt fortune and an open Communist.[70]

On December 20, Duggan received a subpoena to testify before a federal grand jury investigating Soviet espionage in Washington. That evening, shortly after six, he jumped from the sixteenth-floor window of his New York office on West 45th Street. He was forty-three years old. There was no note. His body was found with one shoe on. The other shoe was in his office. At midnight Representative Karl Mundt of HUAC summoned reporters to announce that Duggan had been named by Isaac Don Levine on December 8 in executive session. A reporter asked if there were any other names. Mundt said, "We'll give them out as they jump out of windows."

In a sympathetic editorial on December 23, the *New York Times* said that Duggan "fell, leaped, or was pushed to his death." Mr. Mundt had made "charges of treason" against a man "who was dead . . . and could not answer them." And who was this man, asked the *Times?* He was a man whose colleagues in the State Department "vouch for his honesty and his loyalty. Other close friends say he was a brilliant man, loyal to his bones to those principles of democracy in which must lie the hope of our world."[71]

VII

THE PINK DECADE

In the thirties, as Soviet spies proliferated, the American Communist Party streamed ahead. Favorable winds filled its sails. At home, the Depression allowed the party to transform itself into a champion of the unemployed. With the rise of Hitler and Mussolini, the party wrapped itself in the politically acceptable cloak of anti-fascism. In the 1932 election, the Communist Party ticket of William Z. Foster and James W. Ford (the first black nominated for national office) won 102,785 votes. This was seen as a great success, though it badly trailed the 884,000 votes won by the Socialist candidate, Norman Thomas, and Roosevelt's 22.8 million. The party noted in explanation that many of its members were aliens who could not vote.[1]

Between 1929 and 1931, some fifteen thousand Americans visited the Soviet Union. It seemed as if most of them upon their return wrote a book or went on a lecture tour. Going to Russia became a fad, akin to the Hula Hoop or quiz shows. Two New York debutantes who made their pilgrimage in 1930 wrote an article in *Good Housekeeping* entitled "Prisoners of the *Cheka* in Red Russia"; they had been briefly detained after taking photographs of a railroad station.

Most of the visitors liked what they saw, though there were a few dissonant voices. Upon his return from the Soviet Union in 1930, Thomas Edison said: "The Reds have done pretty well but they are cruel. And they are bucking human nature." The former heavyweight boxing champion Gene Tunney lost his sympathy for the regime when he saw church bells being melted down for use in factories.[2]

Countless others brought back, shimmering like a mirage, the image of the perfect society. Stirred by the heroism and sacrifices it took to create a new system, they praised its humane spirit of fraternity. Others had made up their minds before reaching Moscow, and looked only for evidence that would support their convictions.

One of the boosters was Dr. Frankwood Williams, who in 1930 was Harry Hopkins's psychiatrist. Hopkins, who would soon be running the massive make-work programs of the New Deal, was seeing Dr. Williams because he was in love with a younger woman and was trying to decide whether to divorce his wife, which he eventually did.[3]

Dr. Williams belonged to a number of Communist fronts, such as the National Committee for the Defense of Political Prisoners. He was the advisory editor of *The Champion,* the magazine of the Young Communist League. In 1934, after visiting Russia twice within ten months, Dr. Williams published a book, *Russia, Youth, and the Present-Day World,* which served as a prototype for the myth of the perfect society.[4]

He found a country where mental illness, prostitution, and juvenile delinquency had all but vanished. The eminent director of the Neuro-Psychiatric Institute in Moscow told him that he had searched the hospitals for a manic-depressive to show his students, but could not find one. As for prostitutes, four out of the five *Prophylactoria* where they were rehabilitated had been closed. The stocking-making machines used to train them in socially acceptable employment were sent back to the factory.

"Neither juvenile nor adult delinquency is a grave problem in Russia," Dr. Williams went on. "Even political crime . . . gives less concern, although the government remains alert." The divorce rate was "said to be falling, although a divorce may be obtained in ten minutes by either party." In the relations between parents and children there was a "lack of neurotic tensions of the kind one saw in American families."

In America, by comparison, said Dr. Williams, "the incidence of mental disease continues yearly to rise. The rate of delinquency increases . . . the rate of divorce increases." In Russia you could see "the building of a new civilization. . . . The Russians are still in the process of building a Communistic state and are far from their goal. . . . [But] it would appear that Russia is a place where all problems of human relationships have been solved, where there exists no nervous or mental disease, no delinquency, no marital difficulties, no child-parent difficulties, no adolescent problems, no maladjusted schoolchildren." The Soviets had accomplished the impossible.[5]

———

In September 1934, the Soviet Union joined the League of Nations. The Commissar for Foreign Affairs, Maxim Litvinov, helped by his British-born wife, went to Geneva to portray the U.S.S.R. as the champion of resistance to Hitler.

Stalin's intention was to use the League to form an effective anti-Axis alliance.[6] In July and August 1935, the Seventh Comintern Congress in Moscow adopted a new line that went hand in hand with Stalin's need to bring the Soviet Union out of its isolation. The foreign parties were instructed to form alliances with the non-Communist left.

This meant that the American party could now work with labor, with the unemployed, and with anti-fascist liberal groups. It could applaud democracy and the New Deal. FDR was no longer a fascist tool of Wall Street, but the protector of the working man. The new slogan was "Communism is Americanism." The Communists suddenly seemed housebroken and socially acceptable. They were invited to parties. This was Communism with a smile, benign and neighborly.

Gone was the "Crazy Red." Here was the "Lincoln Club," celebrating Mother's Day. Instead of "read Engels on housing," it was "we're just folks." The Young Communist League celebrated Paul Revere's ride more noisily than it did the birth of Lenin.

Spearheading the new line was Earl Browder, with his pinched gray face, his drooping mustache and red-rimmed eyes, known in party circles as "the bookkeeper." The *Daily Worker* stressed his ancestry, which went back to Littleberry Browder, sworn in as a soldier in the Continental Army of George Washington in the spring of 1776.[7]

In a democratic society, where people were encouraged to take part in the political process and support worthy causes, and where a large portion of the liberal left had grown sympathetic to the Soviet Union, the new Communist combine spilled its seeds on fertile ground. The invention of front groups, which posed as socially uplifting non-Communist associations with innocent-sounding names, enabled the party to create mass organizations controlled by a small number of Communists, promoting honorable goals. "Useful idiots" were enlisted to front for the party.

Since its birth, the party had targeted the Negro minority with disappointing results, but all that changed with the new line. When Mussolini invaded Ethiopia in 1935, the black Communist organizer Louis Rosser was asked to start a "Friends of Ethiopia" front group in San Francisco's black community. At a meeting to discuss the picketing of the Italian consulate in Los Angeles, a non-Communist black read from a *New York Times* clipping that said the Soviets were selling war matériel to Italy to use against the Ethiopians. Rosser's credibility in portraying Russia as a friend of the dark races suffered a serious blow. Despite the Ethiopian setback, however, in 1938 the party launched a successful nationwide front, the National Negro Congress, and finally reached a broad black audience.[8]

Thanks to the fronts, from 1935 to 1939 the American Communist Party luxuriated in a popularity it would never regain. Known to the Communists as "Innocents' Clubs," they had inoffensive names such as Foster Parents for Children in Spain, or the West Side Mothers for Peace Committee. Their purpose was to win the support of non-Communists for Communist policies, and to create a Communist patronage machine. The party could place functionaries on the payroll, who would then kick back part of their salaries. The fronts could also divert funds to pay party expenses. A third purpose for the fronts was to recruit new party members.[9]

A textbook example was the American Youth Congress. In 1934, an enterprising student at New York University, Violet Ilma, decided to gather a wide spectrum of youth groups, from the Boy Scouts to the YMCA to the Esperanto Association of North America, into one national congress. She asked Eleanor Roosevelt to be a sponsor, but received a lukewarm reply. Seeing an opportunity, the Communists attended the first congress in force and disrupted it.[10]

A campaign of slander charged Violet Ilma with having spent four months in Europe studying fascist youth movements. John L. Spivak, the Communist hatchet man involved in the Amtorg forgeries, wrote an article in *New Masses* entitled, "Who Paid Violet Ilma's Way to Nazi Germany?" In vain did Ilma protest that her mother was Jewish and her staff was Jewish. The Communists captured the American Youth Congress, which began to follow the party line. At the AYC's second congress in Detroit in 1935, Clarence Hathaway, the editor of the *Daily Worker,* said, "I am sure that the American youth, guided and led by the AYC, will be a force working for the defense of the Soviet Union and for the defeat of our own robber imperialist government."

In January 1936, William C. Hinckley, a young man from Winston, South Dakota, who worked in the Department of the Interior, was elected chairman of the American Youth Congress, which by then represented seventy-nine youth organizations, with a total membership of well over 700,000. Hinckley was a member of the Young Communist League, which had taken over the American Youth Congress. They did this by infiltrating YCL members into Youth Congress affiliates like the YMCA, the Young Democrats, Catholic Youth, and the American Jewish Congress. Hinckley represented the Christ Episcopal Church of Missouri. These infiltrators received written instructions from the Young Communist League on the line to follow in their respective groups. A directive in March 1938 urged the AYC Communists to join the Officers Reserve Corps "and thus carry from within the fight against the reactionary officers in the ROTC." The goal was to demand their replacement by officers sympathetic to labor.[11]

Eleanor Roosevelt spoke at the January 1936 National Council meeting in Washington and invited the AYC delegation to the White House for tea. Joe Lash, a member of the delegation, and later her biographer, described her patronizingly in a letter to a friend as a "good woman utterly lacking in knowledge of social forces and system. . . . It was a pleasant tea. . . . She had little cream puffs and we were waited on by butlers."[12]

Having been peppered with impertinent questions at the tea, the First Lady turned down a request to serve on the AYC advisory board. "I have heard you make statements that are not correct," she wrote the board, "and after they had been made and corrected, I heard you make them again."[13]

In 1937, the AYC paraded down Pennsylvania Avenue shouting "Schools not battleships." Demonstrators went limp in the street in front of the White House. The motorcycle police raced their cycles with open exhausts among the sit-downers. Hinckley was arrested and jailed. In the afternoon, Mrs. Roosevelt once again received an AYC delegation.[14]

———

The proliferation of fronts was astounding to behold. There were literally hundreds of them. An Abolish Peonage Committee was created "to expose conditions on southern farms." The committee brought up from Oglethorpe, Georgia, a black "refugee from peonage," Will Fleming, for a mass meeting on the South Side of Chicago. In his folksy way the Georgia sharecropper fanned class consciousness when he said that "the one-gallus* men down south— the poor whites—are my friends because they fed me and my family when [the landowner] W. T. Cunningham was starving us and working us without pay. I know that them two-gallus men like Cunningham are my enemy because they want to keep us plowing the fields until we drop dead."[15]

The decoys—famous writers, artists, and singers like Theodore Dreiser, Rockwell Kent, and Paul Robeson who could pull in nonparty members— were not hard to find. The party could count on sympathetic figures in the Roosevelt administration and draw on the pool of writers in the American Writers Congress, one of its front groups. When it first convened in New York City in April 1935, all seventeen members of the executive board were party members. At the opening session, Earl Browder, who was not known for his prose style, told the 216 delegates that "a new literature was needed to help bring about a new society [that] is not yet in existence in America, although we are powerfully affected by its glorious rise in the Soviet Union." To ensure a broad appeal for the congress, Browder pledged that writers would not have

---

* Galluses are suspenders.

to conform to a line. "We do not want to take good writers and make bad strike leaders of them," he said.[16]

At the second congress, in June 1937, with Spain in the background, Browder tightened the noose. "In relation to the two great warring camps," he said, "democracy against fascism, [the writers] will find it necessary to adjust their own work to the higher discipline of the whole struggle for democracy." In plain English, this meant that they were expected to toe the Stalinist line.[17]

In April 1938, 150 prominent writers, artists, and composers issued a statement in support of the show-trial verdicts, which sent to their deaths Stalin's closest collaborators. Among the signers were Nelson Algren, Malcolm Cowley, Dashiell Hammett, Lillian Hellman, Langston Hughes, Dorothy Parker, Henry Roth, Irwin Shaw, and Richard Wright; the actors Morris Carnovsky, John Garfield, and Lionel Stander; the painters Raphael Soyer and Stuart Davis; the composer Marc Blitzstein; the photographer Paul Strand; and the screenwriters Lester Cole, Guy Endore, John Howard Lawson, Albert Maltz, and Samuel Ornitz.[18]

Although clearly aligned with Stalinist policies, the American Writers Congress prospered, and its membership in 1938 rose to 750. FDR accepted an honorary membership with "hearty appreciation." Thomas Mann, who had won the Nobel Prize for literature in 1929, addressed the congress in 1939, but resigned soon after, saying, "The congress thinks too much about politics and not enough about literature."[19]

Malcolm Cowley, the literary editor of *The New Republic*, later had second thoughts about signing. He said he'd had doubts but kept them to himself, out of "self-protectiveness, inadequacy, and something close to moral cowardice." During the popular front period, bucking the trend was a perilous career move, as Philip Rahv, the anti-Stalinist founder of the *Partisan Review*, explained when he wrote in December 1938 in the *New Leader:* "The Stalinists and their friends, under multiform disguises, have managed to penetrate into the offices of publishing houses, the editorial staffs of magazines, and the book-review sections of conservative newspapers." The result was "unofficial censorship" of those opposed to Moscow. "The impulse to speak out has been checked time and again by careerist calculations." No one wanted to be smeared as a Trotskyite, a Franco spy, an agent of Hitler, or a tool of Hearst.[20]

Yet despite the prevailing mood and the need to comply, even inside the party independent thinking sometimes pierced through the muck. In 1934, the national teachers union was taken over by the Communists with their tactics of leverage. By 1936, the union had nine thousand members, of whom one thousand were Communists. One of the latter was Bella Dodd, born Bella Visono, the youngest of ten children of Italian immigrants. She joined the party at Hunter College, admiring the militants who went without lunch so that they could buy paper and ink for propaganda leaflets. In 1936, she marched in the May Day parade in New York, in the Communist section, with five hundred other teachers. Down Eighth Avenue they went, singing "Ye have been naught, ye shall be all."[21]

Dodd learned the front group technique of affiliation by inertia: "Dear professor, may we hear from you, if not we will add your name to the list." A list of five hundred names began to sound like a storm of protest. She did well in the party and was named legislative representative of the teachers union in Albany. But she began to doubt in 1936 when she learned that the crude oil used by the Italian armies in Ethiopia was sold to them by the Soviet Union.[22]

Dodd was expelled from the party in the 1946 purge that followed the overthrow of Earl Browder. By that time, she'd had more than enough. She had stopped using the word "comrade," having seen too many uncomradely acts. She got so mad at one meeting that she shouted, "You think like pigs." Among the charges against her were white chauvinism and applauding a speech of Browder's.

Upon reflection, Bella Dodd admitted to herself that she had used the classroom to influence her students at Hunter. "Is there a Communist geography to teach?" she wondered. "Is there a Communist math to teach? . . . A teacher teaches children. It is the things you say, the way you greet the children, the time you spend with them after hours, the books and the newspapers you recommend. . . . God help me for what I did. . . . There is no doubt in my mind that I did a great deal of harm."[23]

Granville Hicks, a literary critic who was part of the Communist cell at Harvard in the thirties, believed, like many others, that it was not a teacher's role to protect students from ideas or ways of life. Some took to drink, others to Communism. But what Hicks could not abide was the thought control in the party. His disaffection came after he wrote a book review for the *Daily Worker* in which he said that Marx and Lenin were great theoreticians. No sooner had he submitted his review than he got a wire from the party's cultural commissar, V. J. Jerome, asking "what about Uncle Joe?" Praise of Stalin had become mandatory. Hicks, who thought Stalin had corrupted the style of Russian writers, replied, "nothing doing."[24]

The Soviet government's habit of imposing a uniform style in the arts was the breaking point for a number of American intellectuals, who took for granted that in a free society, all styles must be tested against peer review, market forces, and public indifference. Dr. Norman Levinson, a math professor at MIT who belonged to the Communist cell of the thirties, broke over the party line on music. "For some reason," he said, "Stalin and his henchmen set themselves up as great critics of music. . . . But you can't bring an audience in at gunpoint."[25]

For George Mayberry, a member of the Harvard cell, frustration began with Margot Clark's Communist bookstore in Cambridge. She refused to sell *Fontamara* because Ignazio Silone was an ex-Communist. André Malraux was also on her list of banned authors. In the fifties, when the State Department was taking books off the shelves of overseas libraries, Mayberry was reminded of Margot Clark's bookstore.[26]

———

During the popular front period, the Communist Party was able to take advantage of New Deal legislation to become a force in the American labor movement. This happened in the following way: Under the National Labor Relations Act, or Wagner Act, signed by the President on July 5, 1935, employers were prohibited from interfering with employees in the exercise of their right to form unions and bargain collectively. A union chosen by a majority of a company's employees now had the right to bargain with the company in the name of all the employees. The right to strike was also protected and company unions (phony unions set up by management) were outlawed. The Wagner Act provided the legal underpinning for a huge organization drive. It was like a magic wand, which overnight created Big Labor to oppose Big Business, making America a land of great competing forces that fought each other for their share of power and wealth and political influence.

Tens of thousands of workers joined the American Federation of Labor, whose compartmentalization into separate craft unions, from carpenters to milliners, was called into question. For with the rise of mass production industries, one assembly line replaced the specialized crafts, creating a need for industry-wide unions, such as the steelworkers or the autoworkers. Thus, when there was a strike in a plant, instead of having a dozen separate unions, there was only one industry-wide union, which struck not only that plant but all the other plants as well, shutting down an entire industry.

The trouble was that the AFL was determined to protect the craft model and refused to have anything to do with the industry-wide unions.

It was no coincidence that in October 1935, only three months after the Wagner Act became law, the simmering dispute over industrial unions came to a boil at the AFL convention in Atlantic City. A majority of the seventeen-member Resolutions Committee ruled that AFL unions could have jurisdiction over only one specific craft or occupation. But for the first time in many years, a minority report was also filed, signed by six of the seventeen members. One of the six was the powerful leader of the United Mine Workers, John L. Lewis. The minority report stated that in the great mass production industries the workers were not divided by craft but were "composite mechanics." Industrial organization was the only solution, now that the Wagner Act encouraged collective bargaining, so that there could be a single union representing all the workers in a given industry.[27]

When the issue was opened for debate, Lewis shook his mane of coal-black hair and rose to speak with all the force of his Old Testament eloquence: "Heed this cry that comes from the hearts of men. Organize the unorganized!" Then the leader of the rubber workers from Akron, Ohio, took the floor to plead for an industrial charter. Florid-faced Big Bill Hutcheson, head of the carpenters union, bellowed "point of order," saying that the issue had already been settled.

"This thing of raising points of order all the time is rather small potatoes," Lewis responded.

Big Bill, who stood six feet tall and weighed close to three hundred pounds, said, "I was raised on small potatoes and that is why I am so small."

Lewis, also a heavyweight, passed Hutcheson's seat to return to the miners' table, and Big Bill growled, "You dirty bastard." An enraged Lewis advanced on Big Bill with set jaw and beetling brow and struck him with a single blow that sent him sprawling among overturned chairs. As Lewis brushed himself off, he said: "You AFL fakers are blocking a real union drive."[28]

This convention took on the symbolism of a bout not only between two overweight gladiators, but between two labor strategies. As David Dubinsky of the garment workers union put it: "The Congress of Industrial Organization was born with that one punch."[29] Lewis walked out with his 400,000 miners and six other unions in 1936, and two years later, after the CIO was expelled by the AFL, it had four million members.

John L. Lewis was swamped. He had to find trained organizers fast. He turned to the Communist Party, which was happy to oblige. Hundreds of Communist organizers streamed into the CIO. They had gone to camps and taken lessons in picketing and rioting, and how to put out a shop paper. They knew the parliamentary drill in running a local, points of order, divisions of the house, objections to consideration of the question, amendments to amendments, appeals from the decision of the chair. To those who objected that it was dangerous to let them in, Lewis replied: "Who gets the bird, the hunter or the dog?" He didn't quite see that the Communists were not retrievers. They had their own agenda, which was to use the CIO as a vehicle to push the party line.[30]

Finally, after fifteen years of wailing on the margins of the labor movement, the Communists got their foot in the door, thanks to the Wagner Act and the AFL's stubborn attachment to craft unions. The Comintern was not shy about taking credit for the great drive that built the industrial unions of the thirties. A 1938 report estimated that "in about half [of the CIO unions] our members occupy decisive elected positions, holding the leadership of something more than 25% of the total membership of the CIO. About 7,500 party members hold official positions in the trade unions, ranging from shop steward to national union presidencies."[31]

Thanks to its presence in the labor movement the party became a political force, for with its huge membership, the CIO could influence state and national elections.

—

For the American Communist Party during the popular front years of a supposedly united left, there were two triumphs, one the penetration of the CIO, and the other the civil war in Spain, where liberal disgust at the military intervention of Hitler and Mussolini played into the hands of the party. On July 17, 1936, army units led by General Francisco Franco in Spanish Morocco rebelled and crossed the Straits of Gibraltar to southern Spain. With the help of German and Italian troops and equipment, Franco declared war on Spain's popular front government.

Paul Douglas, a professor at the University of Chicago (and later senator from Illinois), recalled in his memoirs that "the Spanish army rebelled against a Republican government that did not include a single Communist in its cabinet and had only 20 Communists out of nearly 400 members of Parliament. . . . Hitler and Mussolini at once sent munitions, airplanes and pilots. . . . It seemed clear that the Loyalist government, duly elected and democratic at the start, should be helped." Congress had enacted neutrality laws, one of which provided for an embargo on arms sales to any nation at war, meaning no American weapons for Spain. "This compelled the Spanish government to accept aid from Russia," Douglas wrote.[32]

Spain became a glorious opportunity for the American party, which set up about a dozen front groups to call for the lifting of the embargo, and funnel aid to the Loyalist government. Slogans began to appear: "Dockers and seamen prevent supplies for the rebels." "Keep Hitler's hands off Spain." "Madrid is the Valley Forge of the Spanish people." On "Spanish Aid Day" young women in flamenco costume, clicking castanets, danced in the streets to collect money. In New York City alone, there were three hundred collecting stations, baskets in stores, and signs outside that said, "Help the babies of Madrid."[33]

Front group instructions for fund-raisers specified: "Have the guests sign a guest book to be used for a mailing list afterward. When pouring beer, remember that pouring in the middle of the glass gives more foam and less liquid." The inbred hoodwinking party mentality extended to bartending.[34]

The long enshrined romantic scenario of gallant Spain fighting the good war against fascist invaders, complete with marching songs and battle cries, has finally been put to rest, thanks to recently published Comintern files. The entire enterprise was a tragic mockery plotted and implemented by Stalin, who took over the Spanish government and the conduct of the war for his own ends. If nothing else, the Spanish Civil War was a lesson in the creation of a satellite state, which he would later apply to Central Europe.

On July 22, 1936, only days after Franco's invasion, a message from Moscow instructed the Spanish Communist leaders to try to form a new government that would include Communist cabinet ministers. The next day, Vittorio Codovilla, an Argentine Communist who in effect ran the Spanish Communist Party, reported that Madrid was in the hands of government forces, but that Franco held four cities and was on the attack. From Moscow, George Dimitrov, the head of the Comintern, sent instructions. The Spanish Communists should not rush ahead and create soviets. "That would be a fatal mistake," he wrote. They should work within the popular front. They should confiscate the lands of the Church and the large landowners, but not factories and business enterprises. The immediate goal was to defeat the Franco rebellion. The Communists should portray themselves as moderates and maintain the impression that the Spanish people were fighting for democracy. The government should declare its appreciation for the religious feelings of the people and refrain from occupying monasteries.[35]

On September 4, 1936, Francisco Largo Caballero, a Socialist, formed a government in which he asked the Communists to take part. By then Franco controlled half of Spain. His Moroccan troops, much feared for their custom of collecting the ears of those they killed, were airlifted to Spain in German and Italian planes.

Once Communists were in the government, the Comintern colonized Spain with its agents. By late November, more than seven hundred military advisers, most of them GRU agents, had joined the Republican army. Largo Caballero agreed to let Soviet military commissars attach themselves to Republican army units, to teach the Spaniards how to fight. In addition, dozens of Comintern agents, such as André Marty of France and Palmiro Togliatti of Italy, came to Spain to organize the International Brigades, which recruited foreign volunteers for the anti-fascist struggle.

While Franco's armies were well supplied with German and Italian tanks and planes, the Republicans, having been turned down by the United States, Britain, and France, had only Russia to turn to. In October 1936, the situation at the front worsened with the surrender of Toledo. Franco's forces advanced on Madrid.

Concerned about the collapse of the Republican front, Stalin began to send planes and T-25 tanks in October. In exchange, he demanded that the Spanish gold reserves, worth $700 million, be shipped to Moscow for safekeeping. Stalin was quoted as saying, "The Spanish will never see their gold again, as they don't see their own ears." In addition to keeping the Spanish gold, Stalin swindled Spain out of additional millions by setting a bogus rate of exchange for the purchase of Soviet weapons. The official rate was 5.3 rubles to the dollar, but for arms shipments, the Spaniards were charged at a rate of 2.5 rubles to the dollar, making everything they bought twice as expensive. For two planes alone, Stalin charged $50 million worth of gold. When it came to arms deals, the Soviets made the capitalists look like amateurs.[36]

As Franco moved on Madrid in October 1936, foreign recruits began arriving at the training camp in Albacete, in southeastern Spain, to join the International Brigades. The thousands of idealistic young men who signed up were deceived into helping Stalin hijack the Republican government. Anyone who dared criticize the brigades was denounced as a Franco agent.

A top secret memo on November 4 from the Comintern to Stalin reported that three thousand men had reached the training camp. The first brigades, hurriedly formed in November, were sent at once to the front. One of the battalions in the 14th Brigade was made up of men from a dozen nations. Their common language, they were told, was the anti-fascist struggle.[37]

From November 1936 until April 1938, when the base was abandoned, roughly thirty thousand volunteers were processed at Albacete. According to the camp commander, the largest contingents were the French (8,778), followed by the Poles (3,034), the Italians (2,908), the Americans (2,274), and the Germans (2,180). The volunteers were divided into five brigades, each with a dominant nationality: the 11th was mainly German, the 12th Italian, the 13th Balkan and Polish, the 14th French, and the 15th English and American—though, as casualties mounted, the composition changed. These International Brigades, each one led by a Comintern-appointed general, were incorporated into the Republican army, which had a total of more than two hundred brigades.[38]

Commanding the 11th Brigade was Moishe Stern, whom we last met in New York in the thirties as Mark Zilbert, then serving as the GRU chief for North America. In Spain he was a general, using the name of the Napoleonic field marshal Kleber.

With Madrid under siege, General Kleber's brigade, made up of four battalions armed with machine guns, entered the city on November 6. As Franco's air force bombed the capital, Kleber set up his headquarters in the Department of Philosophy and Literature at University City, and his German, Polish, French, and Italian battalions stretched out along the Manzanaras River. The front stabilized but his men took heavy losses. There was hand-to-hand fighting in the university buildings.[39]

When the Loyalists held Madrid, General Kleber was written up in *Mundo Obrero* as the hero of the siege. Later it was held against him that he had given interviews. He was also charged with the heresy of "Kleberism," which consisted of treating the Spaniards like second-class citizens. Summoned back to Moscow in 1938, he ended up in the gulags, where he died in the fifties.[40]

Roughly three thousand volunteers from the United States went to Spain. Of those only 1,800 returned. Party recruiters provided tickets and passports, and men who had never held a rifle were sent to the front after three weeks of training.

In May 1937, Herbert Hunt Searle, a pilot with Pan American in San Francisco, ran into a friend at a nightclub. Asked if he'd like to go to Spain, he said he didn't give a damn about politics but he'd go for the money. In New York, a man named Harry gave him a passport and a ticket on the *Berengaria*. Could it be so easy to get a passport? Searle asked. "Many people in our government are employed in our ranks," he was told.

Arriving at brigade headquarters in Albacete, the saffron capital of the world, he had to turn over his passport. The passports of the dead and missing were sent to Moscow so that they could be used by Soviet agents. As a security measure, the U.S. passport office changed from blue to green covers. The Canadians did not change theirs, which explains why Trotsky's assassin, Ramón Mercader, used a passport issued to a Canadian volunteer killed in Spain.

Searle was sent to the training base of the Anglo-American 15th Brigade at Tarazona, in northern Spain. The 15th consisted of four combat battalions, one of which was the Lincoln. He trained the men in the use of machine guns. On October 20, 1937, the twentieth anniversary of the Russian Revolution, the fifteen hundred men of the 15th Brigade paraded before two visiting American congressmen, Jerry O'Connell of Montana and John Toussaint Bernard of Minnesota, elected to a single term on the Farmer-Labor ticket. Bernard, a secret Communist who later came into the open, had as his chief aide Marion Bachrach, the sister of Ware group member John Abt. When the color guard marched past the platform carrying the red flag of the Soviet Union, the two congressmen gave the Russian closed fist salute. O'Connell cried, "Long live Russia, long live Spain and long live the Communist party."[41]

Another American who left in May was twenty-three-year-old Abraham Sobel. He was approached in Boston by a recruiter for the American Committee to Aid Spanish Democracy, who asked him if he wanted to "take a crack at Hitler." He sailed on the *Berengaria* with thirty others and on May 30 he embarked at Marseilles on the *Ciudad Barcelona*. Off Mataro, the ship was torpedoed. Of the 450 men aboard, 158 went down. "Quite a few Americans hit bottom," Sobel recalled. Sobel was on the deck when there was a sudden lurch. He jumped overboard and swam to shore. The survivors were herded into the bullring at Albacete and he was assigned the job of "mechanic chauffeur." After being wounded in the Battle of Brunete, he decided he wanted to live to see America again. He walked out of the Barcelona hospital and crossed the Pyrenees on foot, wearing out two pairs of *aspegatos*. From France he stowed away on a steamship and got home.[42]

The young Wisconsin Communist William G. Ryan contacted the Milwaukee office of the American Society for Technical Aid to the Spanish Democracy. Before leaving in April, he and his Hungarian-born wife, Alva, were given a little send-off by Mrs. Thomas Duncan, whose husband was the secretary of Governor Philip La Follette. "At the medical bureau in New York," Alva later recalled, "they gave me four packs of prophylactics. The doctor said it was to take care of our emotional life. When we got over there all we heard was give the boys a good time to keep up their morale."

At Tarazona, in Ryan's battalion, the commissar system was in place, one commissar for each officer, who could countermand orders given on the field of battle, and have the officer removed and shot. "No one ever died, so far as the pay was concerned," Ryan recalled. "The officers always saw to that."[43] They kept the wages of the dead.

The defense of Madrid, assisted by Kleber's brigade, prolonged the war for another two years. Vladimir Gorev, the military attaché of the Soviet embassy in Madrid and the GRU boss for Spain, reported in September 1936 that Largo Caballero was trying to limit Communist influence in his government. He was also reported to have privately expressed his scorn for the Soviet advisers. When Largo Caballero demanded the resignation of two Communist ministers, the Russians decided to replace him with a friendlier Premier. In May 1937, a new government was formed under Juan Negrin, who worked wholeheartedly with the Kremlin. The new regime was rigidly supervised by Stalin's agents.[44]

In February 1937, a surprise victory in the Jarama valley, north of Madrid, gave the Loyalists hope, although this battle in open country cost each side twenty thousand casualties. The International Brigades fought well against the battle-hardened Moors. In the slushy terrain of Guadalajara in March, the 11th and 12th Brigades were among the most reliable units against Mussolini's Italians.[45]

But after the huge losses at Jarama and Guadalajara, the brigades went into decline. They felt that they were being used as cannon fodder, having been sent to the front for one hundred fifty consecutive days in the toughest sectors. Absurd orders from an obtuse high command sent them into calamitous frontal attacks. At Segovia in May and June, in Brunete in July, and on the Saragosa front in August, there were mutinies and desertions. Entire battalions turned and ran. The number of self-inflicted gunshot wounds rose sharply. A concentration camp guarded by Spanish Communists was erected in the Albacete base for the recalcitrant. Between August and October 1937, four thousand men were interned there. The brigades lost one third of their men, and there were no volunteers to take their place. The losses had to be made up by Spaniards. By December 1937, in the Anglo-American 15th Brigade, of the 1,625 men and 63 officers, only 850 men and 37 officers were non-Spanish.[46]

The influx of Spaniards into the brigades created a resurgence of Kleberism, which the GRU officer Korol Sverchevsky defined as "the foul squabble about the superiority of one nationality over another." The clannish Americans rarely allowed Spaniards into their midst. They smoked their Lucky Strikes and did not offer any to their Spanish comrades, who did not have a shred of tobacco. They had their own hospital but refused to treat the Spanish wounded. Where was anti-fascist solidarity?[47]

Earl Browder went to Spain in February 1938, to breathe new life into the men of the 15th Brigade. He could not have come at a worse time. On February 27, in a snow-patched field outside Teruel, with the roar of guns in the background, Browder, wearing the commissar's long black leather coat to protect him from the icy winds that blew across the plain, told the men that their six-month enlistments would be prolonged until Franco was defeated. This news was met with boos and hooting that drowned Browder out. Raising his voice, he scorned their "unhealthy attitude" and said, "If some of you don't straighten out, you just may be sent home." Someone shouted, "Save me the first boat."[48]

To John G. Honeycomb, one of the volunteers, Browder's remarks were an insult. They had just fought a bloody battle at Teruel and seen their comrades die. Half the men of the brigade were dead. It was fine to sing songs and shout, "Bring us Franco's balls," but when it came to fighting, it was hopeless to attack fortified positions without artillery support. Honeycomb later cornered the battalion commissar, Fred Keller, in an olive grove, and told him:

"One day I will tell the world just what type of men were here and what form of sadism was practiced."[49]

In a few cases, American commissars were guilty of executing fellow Americans. Tony De Maio, a Communist organizer on the Hoboken waterfront, went to Spain in December 1936. After displaying a propensity for brutality at the Albacete detention camp, he was assigned to the Castle de Fels prison, about fifteen miles south of Barcelona. Following the disastrous Battle of Belchite in the fall of 1937, several hundred men of the brigades were hiding in Barcelona, trying to get out of Spain.[50]

De Maio and his men went around the cafés on the Ramblas looking for stragglers. One of the Americans he picked up was Albert Wallach, who was wearing civilian clothes and carrying a safe conduct pass on the letterhead of the United States consul in Barcelona. Wallach, a handsome and personable twenty-four-year-old, had arrived in Spain in 1937, but got into some unspecified scrape and was arrested and sent to a detention camp near Valencia. His father, a well-connected lawyer who knew the Secretary of State, Cordell Hull, asked the State Department to locate his son. Al Wallach escaped from the detention camp and went to see the U.S. consul in Valencia, who passed him on to the consul in Barcelona, Mr. Flood. When Wallach saw him in December, Flood allowed him to use his typewriter to type up a pass on the consulate letterhead, identifying him as a U.S. citizen.

Al Wallach's connections with the American consulate struck Tony De Maio as subversive, if not treasonable. He arrested Wallach and took him to the Castle de Fels prison, where he was kept in a black hole and charged with spying. His cell mate, Edward Palega, who had deserted from the Lincoln Battalion, recalled that Wallach was repeatedly questioned by De Maio. Wallach became so ill that he could not move from the pallet on the floor of his cell. One night, De Maio dragged him out and took him into the prison yard. Shortly after, Palega heard some shots fired. Wallach did not return to his cell and was never heard from again.[51]

When Tony De Maio testified before a congressional committee, he said he had never heard of Al Wallach. He claimed to have served in Spain in the infantry, whereas Comintern documents show that he was an officer in the SIM, the military security police, which was supervised by Alexander Orlov, a senior NKVD officer.[52]

In the Comintern files there is a report prepared by Comrade De Maio on September 26, 1938, pertaining to Wallach: "He admits that he was often questioned and as often received money from the [Barcelona] consul. He said that the military attache asked the following type of questions. What type of artillery have we, how much ammo, what are the markings, and reference to different members of the Brigade. . . . All evidence shows quite plainly that he was working as a spy." It could not be proved that De Maio, who died in 1994, committed murder, but the Comintern document shows that when he testified he committed perjury.[53]

———

By the start of 1938, the Spanish Republic had lost much of the country to Franco's forces, but still held on to Catalonia, the Basque provinces, and the area around Madrid. Stalin continued to send planes, tanks, artillery, and supplies. The Soviets had a scheme to duck America's neutrality laws by purchasing American planes, which were delivered to the U.S.S.R. and then sent to Spain. American planes ordered by the Russians were also sent to France.

On April 13, 1938, Constantine Oumansky, the Soviet ambassador in Washington, cabled Litvinov, the Commissar of Foreign Affairs, that he had seen President Roosevelt, who advised him that "one could not count on a lifting of the embargo, but that he promised to give directives not to hinder the export of any weapons to France and not to inquire about the further destination of the cargo." While obeying the letter of the embargo, FDR was willing to arm Spain through the back door. Ten DC-3s arrived in Spain via France in the fall of 1938.[54]

By then it was too late. In April 1938, the Albacete base was evacuated to Catalonia with eight thousand men, 3,500 of them sick or wounded. By mid-1938, only five thousand volunteers were still in Spain, and in October they were disbanded.[55]

By the end of 1938, Franco had cut off Catalonia from Madrid. The collapse of Barcelona marked the end of the Republic. On February 16, 1939, Kliment Voroshilov, the Commissar for Defense, told Stalin that Negrin was still asking for arms. The Russians had met the request but the arms were blocked in France. It was decided in Moscow that it would be inopportune to risk new deliveries that might fall into French hands. On March 28, 1939, Franco took Madrid and the civil war was over. After a five-month interval, Hitler invaded Poland, and World War II was on.

The Americans of the 15th Brigade returned to the United States walking tall, as if they had won the war. What better symbol of a heroic left was there than these brave young men who had risked their lives to fight Hitler and Mussolini? In their new guise, as the Veterans of the Abraham Lincoln Brigade, they were feted and applauded, and marched each spring with flags and banners in the May Day parade. Nostalgia takes the edge off reality, and the Stalinist commissars who took over Republican Spain were forgotten. And yet, the documents tell us that if Stalin had won the war, he would have installed in Spain a one-party satellite state. This would have been accomplished by liquidating the non-Communist opposition. The Spanish people were caught between two dictatorships—Stalin or Franco. Under Franco's harsh rule, Spain at least had the advantage of remaining neutral in World War II, and became a stable and independent nation instead of a Soviet puppet state. As for the veterans of the International Brigades, perhaps some of them learned this one essential rule: never volunteer.

VIII

THE DIES COMMITTEE

With its low, undulating pine forest, small clearings, two-bit towns, and dirt roads, East Texas was as Southern as Spanish moss. Beaumont, where Martin Dies Sr. opened a law office in 1897, was a thriving oil town on the Gulf of Mexico, particularly after the Spindletop gusher blasted off in 1901, producing 100,000 barrels a day. In 1909, Dies was elected to the House of Representatives for the 2nd Congressional District, which he would represent for ten years. His mostly rural and heavily black district had a small turnout because of the poll tax. Out of a population of 200,000, only seventeen thousand voted, and the Democrats always won. This was considered perfectly normal in the early-twentieth-century South. When Dies stated that white supremacy in the South "is secure and unshakable as the eternal hills," no one disputed it.[1]

Martin Senior was one of those generic Southern windbags who wore a string tie and expounded on the glories of ancient Rome. In his decade in Congress, the issue dearest to his heart was immigration—he articulated a zealous nativist conviction that most foreigners were undesirable. His speeches chastised those "beaten races . . . from Slavic and Iberic countries of Southern and Eastern Europe," though he welcomed the "descendants of the blue-eyed Angles and Saxons."[2]

Martin Senior expressed the customary beliefs of his time and place, which his son inherited. Born in 1900, with the enviable asset of his father's name, Martin Dies Jr. was the class orator at Beaumont High School. "His most notable features are his wit and his wonderful voice," said his senior yearbook.[3]

Dies was admitted to the bar at the age of nineteen and joined his father's law firm, often taking property in lieu of cash fees. By 1930, when he ran for Congress as an antitrust populist in the midst of the Depression, the district had doubled to 430,000, but winning the Democratic primary still meant winning the election. Dies ran against a six-term incumbent, James C. Box, who argued that if he wasn't returned to Washington, where he was about to be named chairman of the House Immigration Committee, the position would go to Samuel Dickstein, "a Jew from New York, born in Russia, who favors letting down the bars to all aliens."[4]

Martin Dies knew his people. He stumped hard in the backwoods hamlets, sleeping in rat-infested sheds where the farmers hung their hams. To these rural voters who barely had two quarters to rub together, he railed against the "capitalist tyranny." To the old folk who had lived through the Civil War, he waved the bloody flag, repeating in his set speech that "had these heroes in gray come home and exclaimed 'all is lost,' the South today would be ruled and governed by ignorant niggers."

Dies at twenty-nine was a big, blond, beefy fellow with a face the color of boiled ham. He appealed to the racism of white voters by promising that if elected, he would knock down Oscar De Priest, a Republican from Chicago's South Side, and the first black to serve in Congress in the twentieth century. Dies accused De Priest of "insulting the honor of the South [by] marching two buck Negroes down the aisles of Congress and introducing them as gentlemen of his race."

Dies won the July primary by one hundred votes, and never did knock down Oscar De Priest, being the sort who yells, "Let me at him" while being restrained by his friends. But he did object when Mrs. Hoover invited fifty congressional wives to tea at the White House and included Mrs. De Priest.[5]

Dies was the youngest man in the 72nd Congress. Even so, he gave the year of his birth as 1901 instead of 1900 to make himself seem younger, something Joseph McCarthy would do sixteen years later.

Dies arrived in the House at a fortuitous time, when Texans occupied positions of influence. Samuel Taliaferro Rayburn was chairman of the powerful Committee on Interstate Commerce and John Nance Garner, known as "Cactus Jack," had just been elected Speaker after serving twenty-eight years in the House. Posing as a populist with a down-home manner for electoral purposes, the sixty-two-year-old Texan was actually a conservative Democrat who owned a bank that charged usurious rates, and a pecan farm that paid its Mexican field workers a penny a pound for shelled pecans. His hatred of the Eastern establishment was matched only by his eagerness to turn a dollar. Garner, a close friend of Martin Dies Sr.'s, took Martin Junior under his wing.[6]

At the Democratic convention in Chicago in June 1932, Garner clinched Roosevelt's nomination by throwing the Texas delegation behind him. His reward was the vice presidency, which he did not really want; he said it "ain't worth a bucket of warm piss." Garner would have preferred to remain Speaker, but even more, he wanted a Democratic victory in 1932.[7]

Roosevelt's first term was a honeymoon period. Shortly after FDR's inauguration in March 1933, Dies wrote a constituent: "I am voting for the president one hundred per cent. . . . I consider it my duty to support him to the utmost." In those first whirlwind years, at the height of the Depression, and after three Republican Presidents, FDR seemed beyond reproach.[8] In January 1935, as an up-and-coming freshman congressman, Dies was named to the twelve-member Rules Committee, one of the most important in the House, since it determined which bills would come to the floor.[9]

Only later that year did Dies begin to wobble. First he voted against the Guffey coal bill, which would benefit the miners by regulating the coal industry. The bill was backed by FDR, but also by John L. Lewis and the United Mine Workers, whom Dies frowned on as being dangerous radicals. Dies broke ranks, but the bill passed anyway. He was convinced that his name was on the White House list of disloyal Democrats, although he continued to praise the President and the New Deal.[10]

Party discipline was one thing, personal advancement another. Looking for an issue to call his own, Dies fastened, like his father, on immigration and deportation. In the April 20, 1935, issue of *The Saturday Evening Post*, he began beating the drum with an article titled "The Immigration Crisis," warning that there were four million illegal aliens in the country who should be deported.[11]

Looking for evidence to confirm his suspicions, Dies attended the May Day parade in New York. "I saw 100,000 communists parade in New York on May 1," he wrote a constituent on May 15. "I did not see an American in the crowd, they openly insulted and derided everything we hold sacred. If I had my way I would deport every one of them and cancel the citizenship of those who have been naturalized."[12] Dies was finally able to give a face to the thing that he detested, and it was the face of the Communist Party, two thirds of whose members were foreign-born. The anti-alien catechism of his youth evolved into an anti-Communist crusade, a publicity-generating issue not entirely foreign to his senatorial ambitions.[13]

After the 1936 election, which returned FDR in a landslide, Vice President Garner parted ways with the New Deal. He could not abide the President's court-packing plan, which aimed to enlarge the Supreme Court from nine to fifteen members in an attempt to end its obstruction of New Deal legislation.

Nor could he tolerate the sit-down strikes in the automobile industry, which he saw as an attack on private property in defiance of the law. Instead of calling in the troops, FDR was allowing the strikes to proceed. The strikers could occupy a plant that made a single car part and cripple the entire company. Red-faced and glowering, Garner began to scold the President at cabinet meetings, telling him on one occasion: "John L. Lewis is a better man than you are if you can't find some way to cope with this."[14]

Garner was the leader of the congressional barons who brought about the defeat of the court-packing plan. In August 1937, Congress passed an alternate judicial reform bill that failed to mention naming more judges. The man who was a heartbeat away from the presidency used his influence in Congress to impede the President's policies. Martin Dies Jr. was Garner's surrogate in the House.[15]

One of the schemes devised to disable the New Deal was to have Dies, as a member of the House Rules Committee, call for an investigation of un-American activities, including the radical unions and sit-down strikes that Garner loathed. By 1938, the New Deal was sputtering after the failure of the court-packing plan, and unemployment was again on the rise. The Communist penetration of the CIO and the party's front activities were becoming increasingly transparent.

On May 10, Dies called for a special committee to investigate un-American propaganda and its diffusion.[16] Maury Maverick of Texas said it was silly to waste time on a fake sideshow, while John M. Coffee of Washington saw the committee as a covert way to attack liberal organizations. But many representatives believed that subversion was worth investigating, and Resolution 282 passed on May 26, 1938, by 191 to 41 votes in a 435-member body. Dies asked for $100,000, which the Committee on Accounts reduced to $25,000. The House Special Committee on Un-American Activities would become a standing committee in 1945, and would last for thirty-seven years.[17]

On June 6, the members were named. Dies was chosen as chairman, and the other members were John J. Dempsey of New Mexico, Arthur D. Healey of Massachusetts, Harold G. Mosier of Ohio, Noah M. Mason of Illinois, Joe Starnes of Alabama, and J. Parnell Thomas of New Jersey. Samuel Dickstein was pointedly omitted. "An investigation of this kind should not be headed by a foreign-born citizen," said Representative Joseph Shannon of Missouri.

Cactus Jack Garner predicted that "the Dies Committee is going to have more influence on the future of American politics than any other committee of Congress."[18]

Congressional committees, in existence since the dawn of the republic, were routinely used as political weapons under the New Deal, both by and against the administration. The Senate Banking and Currency Committee, for instance, investigated the Stock Exchange and banking practices in order to spur legislation to regulate their free-wheeling activities. In 1935, a Senate committee chaired by Hugo Black of Alabama (the future Supreme Court Justice), conducted a highly partisan investigation of the utilities lobby, which was intended to counter its campaign against a bill that would regulate holding companies.[19]

From the start, the Dies Committee was on a collision course with the New Deal. When the Committee on Accounts reduced his budget to $25,000, it was suggested that Dies could borrow investigators from the Justice Department. Dies made the request to J. Edgar Hoover and Attorney General Homer Cummings, but was rebuffed. Dies wrote FDR on August 24, 1938, that other committees had investigators that the Justice Department and the WPA carried on their payrolls. The precedent had been established and he needed twelve investigators. FDR replied on October 1, enclosing a letter from Harry Hopkins, who ran the Works Progress Administration, saying that he would "not be justified" in providing any more investigators. Dies was also turned down by the Department of Labor.[20]

Getting no help from the administration, Dies hired four investigators out of his budget. They were under the direction of Robert E. Stripling, a cadaverous-looking Texan with the title of committee clerk, whose father ran a drugstore in San Augustine, north of Beaumont. As the committee files show, the investigators jumped right in. On September 19, 1938, Chester "Chet" Howe reported that he was receiving "reports on every Communist meeting held in Detroit. . . . This information comes from members in good standing who cannot be exposed publicly unless a job can be found for them in another city so that they may leave immediately after testifying."[21]

The Dies Committee was the first congressional committee to take full advantage of its power to punish with subpoenas and contempt citations, and its ability to harm through insinuation and publicity. A subpoena was a scary thing, a dark and inescapable stigma. A contempt citation could result in a jail sentence, and taking the Fifth Amendment could lead swiftly to unemployment. Dies pioneered the issue of Communists in government, using it to undermine the New Deal. He polarized opinion and manipulated the press in ways that McCarthy would later emulate. The intentness of his rancor was sometimes hard to explain. Why did he call for the impeachment of Frances Perkins, the fair-minded and well-meaning Secretary of Labor, for failing to deport the Communist leader of the West Coast longshoremen, Harry Bridges, a matter that was out of her control? Pondering on Dies's unfathomable antagonism, Perkins reflected that he was a grandson of the Civil War, "cherishing those strange hidden feelings of the defeated."[22] At the same time, the Dies Committee uncovered a wealth of important information on front groups and Communists in government, creating a database for its successors. Its systematic vilification by the left was a backhanded homage to its exposure of party activities.[23]

The Special Committee to Investigate Un-American Activities and Propaganda in the United States, to give it its full name, was created to scrutinize both Nazi and Bolshevik activities, which it did, although here we are concerned only with the latter.

The HUAC hearings opened on August 12, 1938, in the second-floor caucus room of the old House Office Building, to little fanfare. But on the second day, Dies put a witness on the stand who galvanized the public and the press. He was John Frey, one of the sachems of the AFL, the aging head of the Metal Trades Department. A self-described Jeffersonian, Frey had been studying the Communist Party for many years and was far better informed than any of the Dies Committee's investigators.[24]

Frey's explosive revelations, delivered over the course of three days, provided copious specifics on the party's penetration of the CIO. He named 238 full-time Communist organizers and showed that at least ten CIO unions were Communist-dominated. Frey was well briefed on the secret plans of the party leadership, for he had an informant on the National Committee, who had attended every Communist Party convention since 1922. Frey obtained transcripts of secret leadership meetings, which discussed "the need to push President Roosevelt and his administration more to the left."[25]

The *New York Times* headline on August 14 announced: "Communists Rule the CIO." Frey, who had opposed industry-wide unions in the quarrel that led to the CIO break, and who despised John L. Lewis, said that the "sit-down strike and picketing have been used by the Communists as a training camp."[26]

Frey exposed two hundred front organizations, explaining how the party controlled them through interlocking directorates. In forty-five of those organizations, he said, fifty-two party members held 325 directorates.

Coming from a respected labor leader, and backed up by party membership books, police records, and informants high up in the party, Frey's testimony was unimpeachable. It created an instant awareness that the danger of Communist subversion was real. At the same time, it fed a little too neatly into the rumbling congressional revolt against liberal New Dealers. Dies was breaking fresh ground, for he was the first to link anti-Communist hearings with an assault on the administration.

The link was applauded in the avalanche of letters he received. From Dies's home district on October 7, 1938, G. D. Gurley wrote: "Little did the American people believe that Roosevelt was back of all this Communist stuff." On December 22, E. H. Robert chimed in: "I think you will find President Roosevelt a red-hot Communist."[27]

The liberal press, however, viewed the link as a disguised attack on the CIO and the New Deal. The *Christian Science Monitor* on November 5, 1938, saw Frey's testimony as a scheme to curb the CIO's organizing drive in Texas and other Southern states, while the *Washington Times-Herald* on December 12 called Vice President Garner the mastermind behind the committee.[28]

Along with the CIO, another irresistible New Deal target was the Federal Arts Program. Two weeks before the start of the hearings, the virulently anti-Roosevelt New Jersey Republican J. Parnell Thomas announced, "The Federal Arts project not only is serving as a branch of the Communist organization but is also one more link in the vast and unparalleled New Deal propaganda machine."[29]

The Federal Arts Program was part of Harry Hopkins's vast Works Progress Administration, which over six years found employment for eight million victims of the Depression, among whom were about 25,000 writers, artists, musicians, dancers, and theater people. No program was more derided than Federal One, as it was known.[30] Hopkins had picked Hallie Flanagan, a fellow Iowan and friend from Grinnell College, to run the theater project because she was an authority on experimental theater. But instead of calling Flanagan as a witness, the committee, between August 19 and 22, called ten disgruntled members of the Federal Theater Project, who were given considerable leeway to express their misgivings regarding the project's pro-Communist slant.

The first was Hazel Huffman, who was later hired by the Dies Committee as an investigator. Huffman had investigated the FTP on behalf of a group of nine hundred dissidents who called themselves the Committee on the Relief Status of Professional Theatrical Employees. She had written to Hopkins in June 1937 about Communist coercion in the FTP and got back a letter from an assistant saying that she should address herself to the local project offices.[31]

In her testimony on August 19, Huffman described Hallie Flanagan as a Communist sympathizer who had devoted 147 out of 280 pages in her book on theater, *Shifting Seasons*, to a eulogy of Russian theater and the Soviet Union. Mrs. Flanagan had also co-authored a play, *Can You Hear Their Voices*, adapted from a story by Whittaker Chambers and published in *New Masses* in 1931. During a drought in Arkansas, the story goes, the farmers lose their cotton crop and storm a relief station, led by a Communist. "Some people come to Communism through their minds," went one line in the play, "and others through their bellies."[32]

During Mrs. Flanagan's tenure, Huffman explained, the rule at the FTP was propaganda, promoted under the guise of "social significance." *Machine Age* was a satire on mass production. *Triple A Plowed Under* featured Earl Browder as a character. In *The Class of '29*, the cast carried a red Soviet banner across the stage as they sang a Communist marching song. In *Processional*, about a mining town in West Virginia, the American flag was torn up in front of the audience.

"It is almost unbelievable to me," Dies interjected with genuine alarm, "that they [the WPA] would use public funds intended for relief to spread Communism."[33]

Huffman claimed that of the 4,016 FTP employees in New York, few had any theatrical experience. One actor recognized a young woman and asked: "What are you doing here? You are a chambermaid at my hotel." "Well," she replied, "it is a theatrical hotel." All those on the FTP payroll, Huffman said, were coerced into joining the Workers Alliance, a Communist-controlled association that collected money for Spanish veterans or marches on Washington. Those who didn't contribute were weeded out. On the fourth floor of the WA office in New York, the walls were covered with pictures of Lenin and Stalin. Stacks of free copies of the *Daily Worker* were piled on tables next to application forms for the party and the Young Communist League.[34]

Huffman was followed by the veteran thespian Harrison Humphrey, who had played Browder in *Triple A Plowed Under.* "I left the play largely because of the propaganda," he said, "largely along Communist lines."[35]

On August 20, the actor and playwright Francis Verdi testified that in 1937, after repeated complaints, Mrs. Flanagan, who thought of him as fairminded, had asked him to investigate the FTP, a job that had taken him ten months. In his testimony, Verdi emphasized the power of the Workers Alliance. They are "subversive in their intent and their activities," he said. "They attack anyone and everyone who will not fall in with their views. . . . I have already been demoted because of my activities against the Workers Alliance."[36]

He was followed by Charles Walton, an FTP director who said the Workers Alliance controlled the casting and had sent him a middle-aged woman to play an ingenue part.

"You personally know," asked Joe Starnes of Alabama, "that large Communist elements have been placed in the casts of some of these plays?"

Walton: "Oh, continually—the cesspool must be opened sooner or later."[37]

The next witness, the actress and dancer Sallie Saunders, sought to discredit the FTP by raising the race issue. Since the party courted blacks and promoted integration, Southern congressmen and their allies found it convenient to equate all appeals for racial equality with Communism. Sallie Saunders played into that segregationist mind-set when she told her tale of woe.

While rehearsing for the musical *Sing for Your Supper,* she noticed a black man making a sketch of her while she danced. The man then called her and asked her for a date. "I got very angry and asked how he got my phone number," she recalled. "He said he took it from a petition to President Roosevelt regarding the $1,000 pay cut." She reported the incident to her supervisor, the party member Harold Hecht (later a thriving Hollywood agent, one of whose clients was Burt Lancaster). "Sallie," Hecht told her, "I am surprised at you. He has just as much right to life, liberty and the pursuit of happiness as you have."

Dies, a confirmed racist himself, broke her off, saying: "We have to be very careful about race feeling."

Sallie Saunders responded that the Communist program in the FTP was social equality and race merging.

Two months after testifying, Sallie Saunders was fired from the FTP. In an affidavit to the Dies investigator Stephen Birmingham dated October 28, she said the cause was "refusal to accept work assignment." When she was asked to join the cast of an all-Haitian show that was opening in Boston, she said she did not want to go. Evelyn Pierce, the administrator, told her that "Mrs. Flanagan is very put out with race discrimination, and you may as well know that objections against the Negroes are not recognized." She was told to report to the director of *Haiti,* Maurice Clark, who was described to her as a "deep-hued Red." Clark told her that others had begged off on the grounds that "they had a lease on this or that apartment," or that they "had obligations."

"I having no such reasons told the unvarnished truth," Sallie went on in her affidavit, "that I could not work with Negroes because of odor, which seems part of their race . . . if a Negress did my laundry, I had to air it out before I could wear it." Clark "became very angry" and told her that he had worked with Negroes all his life and they didn't smell any different than anybody else.[38]

———

In one of its many sudden changes of direction, the committee, after hearing the anti-FTP witnesses, turned to a lecture on front groups from the former fellow traveler Joseph Brown Matthews, who was destined to become the chief investigator for the committee. Known as "J.B." or "Doc," Matthews was a Kentucky-born Methodist minister, who turned to the party out of disillusion with Wilsonian idealism.

"I hope it will not appear immodest," he said in his testimony on August 20, "but . . . I was probably more closely associated with the Communist Party's united front movement than any other individual in this country." Matthews joined roughly sixty fronts and boasted that he had made five trips to Russia. "I went where I was taken and did what I was told," he explained. He was, he said, "in that life of exclamation marks: 'Help Spain!' 'Stop Fascism!' "[39]

Matthews soured on the party when Communist organizers in Norfolk, Virginia, donned Ku Klux Klan robes to terrorize Negroes so that they would join the Amalgamated Clothing Workers (a dual union). "They said they were killing two birds with one stone," he said. "That is, not only getting Negroes into the union, but able to show how brutal the Klan was in the South."

Turning to the dependence of front groups on celebrity endorsements, Matthews explained that "there is nothing simpler than to approach prominent people and get them to put their signatures to things about which they have not the remotest idea."[40]

"The Communist party," he went on, "owns outright the . . . swankiest newspaper in France, *Ce Soir*. It is little more than a year old. On the occasion of its first anniversary recently, this Communist newspaper featured greetings from Clark Gable, Robert Taylor, James Cagney, and even Shirley Temple. . . . They unwittingly serve the purposes of the Communist party. . . . Their names have definite propaganda value."

Starnes: "What about Charlie McCarthy?"

Matthews: "They have so many in everything they do not need the wooden one."[41]

The next day, headlines blared that the committee had accused the child star of being a Communist. Matthews became an easy target for mounting anti-Dies feelings in the administration. Secretary of the Interior Harold Ickes, who already had a running feud with Dies, said: "Imagine the great committee raiding her nursery and seizing her dolls as evidence."[42] Matthews was made to seem preposterous, whereas what he said was true: a number of film stars had sent congratulations to a Communist newspaper in France. J.B. had the last word, for in 1939, *Ce Soir* was banned by the French government.

———

In September, the committee returned to its demolition of the Federal Arts program by calling witnesses who had stories to tell about the Writers' Project, which apparently had also fallen under the control of Communist cliques in several locations. The project was perhaps best known for its lavishly praised American Guide series, which produced a volume on each state in the union, written by unemployed writers, some of them well known, such as Nelson Algren and Richard Wright. The guides, often running more than six hundred pages, combined social history, economic and geographical data, and folksy anecdotes, to convey a distinctive image of the state, as well as the flowing, mobile pattern of the American experience. Dull they were not, and some were controversial for their leftward slant. When the Massachusetts guide appeared in 1937 with fourteen lines about the Boston Tea Party and thirty-one on the Sacco and Vanzetti case, Governor Charles F. Hurley called for the book's seizure and for a purge of Communist writers.[43]

In three years, the New York project had five directors, one of whom, Donald Thompson, recalled: "I'm truly grateful to the Communist activists who revealed to me, way back then, what a bastard a dedicated Communist could be . . . the New York project was deliberately and often successfully harassed by the Communist Party. I knew the score well. Our Red friends loved to plot but they weren't very adroit at it."[44]

On September 15, 1938, Edwin P. Banta, a disgruntled Communist member of the New York Writers' Project, testified before the Dies Committee that his job was selling ads for the *Red Pen*, the house organ of the party writers, to restaurants and hosiery firms near the project's 29th Street headquarters.[45]

Banta told the committee that thirteen out of fifteen supervisors in the New York project were Communists. "Here we have Lou Gody, supervisor of the Great American Guide Book, who has never written a line for a newspaper, yet he passed on the writing of newsmen. . . . Mr. Kingman, in charge of the foreign language division, does not speak any foreign language."

To buttress his testimony, Banta turned over to Dies a book that his colleagues had given him when they threw a seventieth birthday party for him on March 2, 1938, in the project office. The book was *The People's Front*, by Earl Browder, and it was inscribed as follows: "Presented to Comrade Edwin Banta by the members of the Federal Writers Project Unit No. 36-S, Communist Party of America, in recognition of his devotion to and untiring efforts on behalf of our party and Communism."[46]

After his appearance, Banta was described by his erstwhile comrades as a doddering old crackpot, a portrayal that the admiring inscription seemed to belie. In addition, the book was signed by 106 of his colleagues, who penned dedications like "Yours for a Soviet America" and "Revolutionary Greetings." Banta was fired from the project and received so many death threats that he was given police protection.[47]

Banta was followed on September 15 by another defector, Ralph De Sola, a zoologist who collected rare reptiles for museums. As a project supervisor and a master writer, he wrote or edited *Who's Who in the Zoo, Birds of the World,* and *Reptiles and Amphibians.*

Joe Starnes asked: "What induced you to join the party?"

De Sola said he had opened a zoo in Miami, but it failed in 1933. "The depression hit me in my cherished enterprise in a very personal way . . . and the Communist Party had a realistic program for bringing things to a better pass."[48]

De Sola had agreed to testify, even though "everyone who has come here including myself has been labeled as a stool pigeon, a rat, a Fascist and a Trotskyite and so forth." He recalled that in June '37, the Communists on the project staged a sit-down strike, complete with cots and blankets. Men wearing red armbands called themselves the defense squad. Abe Moskowitz, who ran the sports page of the *Daily Worker,* guarded the barricaded door armed with a crowbar, under a placard that said, *No Pasaran.* A picket line outside said, "Striking Writers Support Spanish Democracy."[49]

In spite of his testimony, De Sola remained on the project, although his colleagues now called his department "the reptile's corner," and in 1939 he wrote *American Wild Life,* the best-seller of the zoological series. De Sola later became a professional informant for government agencies, and according to his own count, met with the FBI 125 times. Pressured to name Communists, he grew increasingly careless.[50]

Following the testimony of Banta and De Sola, Ellen S. Woodward, one of three Federal One directors, wrote to Dies to remind him that not one of the Federal One officials had been invited to testify. "I believe that it is the American practice," she wrote, "that all parties should be given an opportunity to be heard when an investigation of this character is underway."[51]

Her letter was ignored. Dies continued to feature witnesses hostile to the New Deal programs, in an obvious attempt to influence the November 1938 congressional elections. Nowhere was this more clear than when the committee held hearings in Detroit, where the governor of Michigan, Frank Murphy, was up for reelection. Murphy, a New Dealer loyal to the President, had averted bloodshed in the Detroit sit-down strikes of 1936 and 1937 by not sending in the National Guard. His restraint had incurred the scorn of Garner and Dies.

On October 21, less than three weeks before the election, the Dies Committee heard Judge Paul V. Gadola of the circuit court in Flint, Michigan, outside Detroit. In February 1937, Gadola had signed an injunction to evacuate the seized Flint plants, Fisher No. 1 and Fisher No. 2, but Governor Murphy prevented it from being carried out.

Dies: "You had a complete breakdown of law enforcement?"

Gadola: "Absolutely. . . . Civil authority had completely broken down." The committee found that Governor Murphy had let the riots happen under his eyes.

To accuse a governor who was up for reelection of being responsible for riots in his state's largest city was fodder for headlines. Murphy fought back with a speech in Flint. Thanks to his intervention, he said, "The strike came to an end and a quarter of a million men went back to their jobs. Not a single human life had been lost, not a liberty had been suppressed, even though we had passed through the most terrifying industrial strife in history."

Thus far, FDR had let the pugnacious Secretary of the Interior, Harold Ickes, handle Dies. But now the midterm elections were at stake. When questioned about the committee's tactics at his October 25 press conference, the President released a written statement that scathingly denounced Dies and his cohorts. "I was very disturbed," he said, "not because of the absurdly false charges against a profoundly religious, able, and law-abiding Governor, but because a Congressional Committee charged with the responsibility of investigating un-American activities should have permitted itself to be used in a flagrantly unfair and un-American attempt to influence an election."[52]

When the voters went to the polls on November 8, 1938, Murphy was one of the eleven Democratic governors who were defeated. The Republicans gained eighty-two seats in the House and eight in the Senate. Though the President still held majorities in both houses, the Republicans could now combine with anti–New Deal Democrats to control Congress. The days of a rubber-stamp Congress were over. It was a triumph for Dies and Garner against their own party. Frank Murphy, however, joined the Roosevelt cabinet as Attorney General.

With the elections over, Dies returned once again to his investigation of Federal One. On November 19, he heard several employees on the Federal Writers' Project in secret session, in order to protect them, he said, against the vengeance of the administration. The transcripts of these sessions were not published until a year later.

The most graphic of this new round of witnesses was Mrs. Louise Lazelle, the policy editor for the state guides, whose job, she explained, was to weed out partisan copy. One passage she deleted from the New Jersey guide claimed that a certain factory "was the biggest buyer of tear gas in the state." There had been one short strike at that factory where, she said, no tear gas had been used. But the passage had made it seem "that it was holding a cellar full of tear gas." Lazelle said she found "inflammatory statements rather than definite Communist propaganda."

Dies: "Did that guide invariably condemn business and industry?"

Lazelle: "Yes . . . as being the enemy."

Dies asked whether Henry Alsberg, the head of the Writers' Project, had "shaped the material for propaganda purposes."

Lazelle: "Yes, against business and against industry and against the government." The Michigan guide came in with "a terrific tirade against Henry

Ford. . . . It was too terrible and we sat on it. . . . If you quote me, it means my job."

Dies: "What are your conclusions?"

Lazelle: "The Federal Writers' Project has in its hands a splendid piece of work, but a housecleaning is absolutely necessary."

Dies: "Would you say the Federal Writers' Project is being converted into an agency to spread Communism through the United States?"

Lazelle: "I think so."[53]

It was only in December that Dies found the time to hear the three top officials of Federal One, Ellen S. Woodward, the WPA administrator in charge of the Theater and Writers' projects; Henry Alsberg, the head of the Writers' Project; and Hallie Flanagan, the head of the Theater Project.

Mrs. Woodward was a handsome woman in her forties from Mississippi, who wore organdy dresses and orchids to the "tea parties" she gave at the Mayflower Hotel, where the liquor flowed freely and the tables were piled high with canapés.[54]

Appearing before the committee on December 5, 1938, wearing white cuffs and a large white collar like a Pilgrim mother, Mrs. Woodward noted that there were three million unemployed Americans working in WPA programs; Federal One employed only 25,000. Since its inception in 1935, the Theater Project had put on 924 plays, of which only twenty-six had been criticized. More than 25,000,000 Americans, many of whom had never seen live actors on a stage, had attended project productions, which ranged from the *Haitian Macbeth* to the *Swinging Mikado*. She was forced to admit, however, that she had not read any of the plays under discussion.

Unimpressed by her statistics, Congressman Joe Starnes asked if she had read Richard Wright's essay "The Ethics of Living Jim Crow," in the book *American Stuff*, commissioned by the Writers' Project.

"No, I did not," Mrs. Woodward said.

"I want to read an excerpt," Starnes went on. "If you have a strong constitution . . . I regret very much to do this. . . . Here is one statement from page 42, 'Say, are you crazy, you black nigger?' And from page 43: 'When I was a bit slow in performing some duty, I was called a lazy black son of a bitch.' And on page 44: 'If yuh say yuh didn't I'll rip yo' gut-string loose with this fuckin' bar, you black granny dodger. Yuh can't call a white man a liar 'n git away with it, you black son of a bitch.' "

"You have got enough of that," Dies interrupted. "This is the most filthy thing I have seen."

"I just want to know," Starnes said, "if you find stuff like that rehabilitating, Mrs. Woodward."

"No, I do not," she responded. "I think it is filthy and disgusting." Thus, coarse language on the part of a black writer became equated with radicalism.

Starnes said that Viking Press had published *American Stuff* and sold more than two thousand copies.[55]

Poorly prepared, Mrs. Woodward seemed unable to offer a strong defense of Federal One. Instead, she tried to discredit the testimony of Edwin Banta by revealing that he had once been committed to a mental hospital. Dies ripped into her. "Here you have made a statement that this man is mentally deranged," he thundered. "Do you mean that you consider this man incompetent to testify before a committee?"

Woodward: "Well, I think he was not qualified."

Were the 106 out of three hundred in the New York project "who signed their original names attesting membership and belief in Communism" qualified, Dies asked. Mrs. Woodward withered under the badgering, and during the lunch break, Harry Hopkins sent over reinforcements in the form of Hallie Flanagan and Henry Alsberg.

Mrs. Flanagan, a tidy, precise, articulate woman, whom the director John Houseman once described as "the small red-haired lady with the firm mouth and the ferocity of an aroused lion," made a spirited defense. When Dies asked her what her duties were, she replied: "Combating un-American inactivity."

Joe Starnes, reading from one of her articles, said: "This is your language that I am quoting . . . 'They intend to remake a social structure without the help of money—and this ambition alone invests their undertaking with a certain Marlowesque madness.' You are quoting from this Marlowe—is he a Communist?"

Flanagan: "I am very sorry. I was quoting from Christopher Marlowe."

Starnes: "Tell me who Marlowe is, so we can get the proper reference."

Flanagan: "Put it in the record that he was the greatest dramatist in the period immediately preceding Shakespeare."

Starnes has on the basis of this exchange gone down in history as an ignorant buffoon. Yet why should a backwoods Alabama lawyer know who Christopher Marlowe was? Starnes came from a good-old-boy culture with its own icons, and Elizabethan playwrights were not among them. Would Hallie Flanagan have known who Ma Rainey was?

In the thrust and parry of the hearings, Mrs. Flanagan was at her best. When J. Parnell Thomas questioned the use of federal funds for plays like *Sing for Your Supper*, which had been in rehearsal for thirteen months, she snapped back: "May I ask whether delays are un-American?"

When Mosier asked why the Communist Party boss, Earl Browder, had been used as a character in one of her plays, she explained that "Browder appears together with Al Smith and Thomas Jefferson, not as an actual character but as a shadow on the screen."[56]

Unlike Ellen Woodward, Hallie Flanagan was well prepared and fast on her feet. Blunt without being disrespectful, a driver well in command of her vehicle, she was able to dodge a few potholes, such as Communist influence in hiring and production. She often had the committee members on the defensive, particularly Starnes.

Henry Alsberg, the national director of the Writers' Project, followed Hallie Flanagan on the stand. In an earlier incarnation as editor of the *New York Post*, Alsberg had denounced the Sisson documents as forgeries back in 1918. Two decades later he was one of those spent radicals of the twenties, all fervor gone, who had turned bureaucrat and was now responsible for getting the product of 4,500 writers into print. The frenetic manager of fifty offices staffed by 450 employees, he could be glimpsed at his desk in Washington, shouting into two phones at once, and surrounded by piles of manuscripts, which he alternately read and flung across the room.

Alsberg's method of dealing with the committee was the exact opposite of Flanagan's. Where she was tough and direct, he was ingratiating and deferential. He arrived at the hearing wheeling a library cart stacked with project publications. He admitted to having been a radical gadfly, but after editing a book of letters from prisoners in the gulag, he had become, he explained, "the arch anti-communist in America. I suffered. I was black-listed; I could not get my articles printed. To this day I am considered a reactionary."

This was something the committee, which was being attacked across the political spectrum, could appreciate. On the far left, the "Down with Dies" buttons of front groups like the American Student Union went in tandem with *Daily Worker* editorials labeling the investigation a witch-hunt. The left-wing *New Republic* derided Dies's "casual cruelties," while the American Civil Liberties Union questioned the committee's "lack of serious intent" and the "ignorance" of the members. The mainstream press underlined the disorderly proceedings. "Under a blinding glare of spotlights and a bombardment of photographers' bulbs," wrote Richard L. Stokes in the *Washington Star* on October 29, 1939, "members shout insults at each other or at the witnesses, who retort in kind. . . . More than once the audience has been permitted to rise and cheer a pronouncement of the chairman." From within the cabinet, Harold Ickes saw Dies as the harbinger of American fascism. "I cannot forget," he confided in his diary on February 4, 1939, "that Mussolini rose to absolute power in Italy as a result of a 'Communist' hunt, that Hitler did the same thing in Germany. . . . Dies can put his pieces together in the same pattern. It is not unlikely that a Communist scare will be kept fanned in this country, following which some man on horseback may arise to 'protect' us against the fancied danger."

Alsberg readily admitted that he had had problems with the Communists in the New York project. "I ever objected," he said, "to their having their literature downstairs at the door. I said the last time I was there, for Christ's sake, cannot they peddle their literature somewhere else." As for the six supervisors who had signed Banta's book, "they will have to have a trial. They will be questioned, and that is being gone into now." Troublemakers would be fired, Alsberg promised. "That is flat. We will not tolerate another rumpus in New York City."

As for the guidebooks, which were considered the greatest achievement of the Writers' Project, Alsberg insisted that he tried to keep the propaganda out, but sometimes failed. "In the case of New Jersey," he said, "it has not been violent propaganda, but it has had a little tart flavor. . . . When you read 50 pages you begin to feel those people were mocking New Jersey. There very often were wisecracks about this town and that town."

His testimony ended on a cordial note when he said: "I have always tried to maintain my independence of judgment."

Dies replied: "In other words, you . . . reserve the right to oppose the Soviet Union and Communism." Then Dies commended him for his frankness, Alsberg thanked the committee for its fairness, and the Federal One hearings came to an end.[57]

The Dies Committee hastened the demise of Federal One. In December 1938, Harry Hopkins left the WPA to become Secretary of Commerce, and Federal One lost its godfather. His replacement, Colonel Francis C. Harrington, was an Army engineer detached from the military who could not be accused of left-wing sympathies. He saw Federal One as a prodigal child in the WPA family and didn't take long to cast it out. In 1939, Clifton Woodrum, a conservative Democrat from Virginia and chairman of the House Appropriations Committee, held hearings with the announced aim "to get the government out of the theater business." Harrington told the Woodrum Committee on May 23, 1939, that he would "eliminate the operation of the inefficient arts projects" as federally sponsored programs. He fired Henry Alsberg and made deep cuts in the project staffs.

Yet it was the Roosevelt administration that quietly scuttled Federal One. In June 1939, FDR had before him a crucial $17 billion emergency relief bill that he was compelled to sign to keep the WPA going, even though one of its riders eliminated the Theater Project. Another rider stipulated that the writ-

ers', music, and arts projects would henceforth function through state sponsors, who would pay at least 25 percent of their cost.[58] Those projects limped
along under state control, and after Pearl Harbor, the writers' unit was put to
work turning out military manuals such as servicemen's recreational guides.

———

It took only five months of hearings to turn an obscure congressman from
East Texas into a nationally known figure. Dies's meaty face with the heavy
jaw and the blond hair brushed back seemed to have reserved space on the
front page. Thousands of letters streamed through his mail chute. He was
sought after to lecture and write.

Dies's congressional salary was $10,000 a year. His Texas upbringing
taught him that fame could be converted into wealth, and he found ways to
increase it. His secretary, Hazel Boies, recalled that each time there was a
hearing on the Bund or the Silver Shirts, Dies would have breakfast at the
Mayflower Hotel with the bagman for the Jewish groups. As the committee
clerk Bob Stripling put it: "If they wanted six hours of hearings, they got six
hours of hearings."[59]

On the lecture circuit, Dies would give a speech that would normally fetch
$200 and get paid $2,000, which was what he received when he spoke before
a Jewish group in Cleveland. Going after the corn-fed Nazis was also good
policy, for it made him seem evenhanded. In August 1939, leaflets signed "the
Christian Mobilizers" were distributed in New York City, saying "Dies Jew-
Controlled Committee is an Anti-Gentile Inquisition." Dies was in the curious
position of being reviled as both a Red-baiter and a Nazi-hunter.

Dies needed to arrange his bookings when his committee was not in
session. He found an agent, Ford Hicks of the National Lecture Bureau, who
took 25 percent for setting up his talks. In 1940, he earned $15,600 from
lecturing, half again as much as his salary.

He also started the Dies Foundation for Americanism, to funnel the proceeds from lectures, articles, and his book, *The Trojan Horse*, which was written by J. B. Matthews, who had gone from committee witness to ghostwriter.
Published in December 1940, *The Trojan Horse* was one of those alarmist accounts of the Red and fascist menaces at a time when "fifth columnism" was
fixated in the public mind as a result of the fall of France. Dies's thesis was
that termites on the left and the right had caused the collapse of Europe and
the same thing could happen in America. The most curious aspect of the
book's publishing history was that the four chapters on homegrown Nazi
movements were published in Germany in 1942, under the title *The Propaganda of Totalitarian-Friendly Groups in the United States*. One wonders whether

Dies ever got his German royalties. The book also had fans in Dies's home state. Roy Miller, the oil lobbyist and onetime mayor of Corpus Christi, called the book "remarkably well-written and the facts it contains are startling indeed."[60]

———

Since HUAC was a select rather than a standing committee until 1945, Dies had to introduce a resolution each year for its continuation and appropriation. The *New York Times* noted on January 8, 1939, that the committee "despite its slipshod and biased nature" seemed to "have won the support of the country and the Congress." In February, the House voted 344 to 45 to extend the committee's life. This time, Dies received an appropriation of $100,000.[61]

In an effort to seem more balanced, Dies replaced Mosier of Ohio, who was defeated in 1938, with the California Democrat Jerry Voorhis. The very prototype of the "bleeding-heart liberal," Voorhis was a pacifist and Socialist who founded schools for homeless boys and rode into Congress on FDR's coattails in 1936. Dies also named ex-FBI agent Rhea Whitley as committee counsel. He did the questioning, noticeably reducing the harangues between witnesses and committee members. Whitley didn't drift, he didn't lecture. He was a definite improvement.[62]

The Dies Committee, however, did not operate in a vacuum, but in a welter of competing agendas and political pressures. Nowhere was this better illustrated than in the case of Harry Bridges, the Australian-born head of the West Coast longshoreman's union. In Dies's persistent pursuit of Bridges the suspected Communist, there was the usual subtext of embarrassing the New Deal. FDR, meanwhile, had to shield himself against the charges that he was soft on radicals. Add to the mix the constant infighting between the Dies and La Follette committees, the one investigating the Reds and the other anti-labor groups, and the situation became a rather pungent potpourri.

When Bridges led a violent and widespread San Francisco strike in 1934, four years before the formation of the Dies Committee, even the liberal Ickes wired the White House: "Here is revolution not only in the making but with the initial actuality." In mid-1935, when a new strike broke out on the West Coast waterfront, FDR wrote Frances Perkins, the Secretary of Labor: "How does Sam Darcy [a backer of Bridges and leading West Coast Communist] get in and out of the country? I think he is not a citizen but a native of Russia. Also how about Harry Bridges? Is he not another alien?"

Pressure was building to deport Bridges, and in 1937, the immigration commissioner in Seattle told Frances Perkins that he had the evidence to deport, including the eyewitness accounts of those who had seen him at party meetings. But Perkins decided to wait for a Supreme Court decision that would affirm the legality of deportation on the grounds of party membership.

Once the Dies hearings got underway in August 1938, the committee released a statement from investigator Edward E. Sullivan, charging that Bridges was the instigator of "unbridled and unchecked Communist activity." Dies then urged Miss Perkins to launch deportation proceedings or face impeachment. In her mind, though, the charges against Bridges were offset by information she had received from the Archbishop of San Francisco. Bridges, a good Catholic, had moved his daughter from a public school where she was hounded because of her father's notoriety, to a convent school.

In June 1939, the Supreme Court decision made it possible for Frances Perkins to authorize deportation hearings, which were held that summer on Angel Island in San Francisco Bay before James L. Landis, the dean of the Harvard Law School.

In July and August, the Dies Committee investigator George Hurley monitored the Bridges deportation hearing and reported his assurances that the country would soon be rid of Harry. One of the witnesses for the prosecution was the Dies Committee informant John Leech. An ex-Communist, who had been Bridges's right hand, Leech took the stand on July 13. Hurley reported that he "really performed a fine job. It is almost a foregone conclusion that the Department of Labor will have to enter an order of deportation."

There was, however, some behind-the-scenes finagling that Hurley had not foreseen. The La Follette Committee staff, which the senator later admitted was riddled with Communists, meddled with the hearing by turning over confidential material in its files to the lawyers for Bridges. "Time and again," Hurley complained, "the attorneys for Bridges have cross-examined witnesses on the basis of evidence in their hands which could only have come into their possession through the La Follette Committee."[63]

On December 28, Landis ruled against deportation on the grounds that the evidence had not established that Bridges was a Communist.

———

On August 23, 1938, Stalin and Hitler formed an alliance that would be maintained for nearly two years. Joachim von Ribbentrop, the Nazi Foreign Minister and onetime champagne salesman, arrived in Moscow that morning and spent the afternoon closeted with a seemingly pliant Stalin. To their nonaggression pact was appended a secret protocol that partitioned Poland and Eastern Europe between Germany and Russia. After carving up Poland, the Baltic states, Finland, and the Romanian province of Bessarabia, Stalin invited Ribbentrop to a celebratory banquet, washed down with Georgian champagne and his infamous toast: "I know how much the German people loves its Fuehrer." Foreign Minister Vyacheslav Molotov made an equally infamous remark that fascism was "just a matter of taste."

A drawing was distributed to Russian army units, showing two triangles. The caption over the first said: "What did Chamberlain want?" The top of the triangle was labeled "London," while the corners at the base were marked "Moscow" and "Berlin," meaning that England wanted to push the Russians and Germans into war. The other triangle was captioned "What did Comrade Stalin do?" At the top was "Moscow," with "Berlin" and "London" in the competing corners.

The real meaning of the pact was that it saved Hitler from fighting a two-front war, while sending tremors through the American Communist Party, which was always a hostage to Soviet foreign policy. The prestige the party had gained due to its anti-fascist stance evaporated overnight. Now labeled CommuNazis, the Communists found themselves isolated from the liberal left, which fled from the front groups. Gone were the stirring days of the popular front. Membership dropped dramatically. The party, which collected 80,159 votes in the 1936 presidential election, was down to 46,251 in 1940.[64]

The rank and file was swiftly mobilized to toe the new line. Sylvia Richards, a party militant then living in Rockland County, New York, was told to join the America First Committee, an isolationist lobby, and protest against lend-lease.[65]

Roy Huggins, who was attending summer school at Berkeley, saw young Communists running around trying to retrieve the pamphlets they had laid on doorsteps, calling for a third term for FDR. The President was now a warmonger.[66]

Danny Dare, a director and choreographer who belonged to the Communist-controlled Hollywood Theater Alliance, was working on a musical called *Meet the People*. When it went into rehearsals in 1938, one of the songs was "Mr. Roosevelt, Won't You Please Run Again." Rehearsals continued into 1939, and by the time the show went on that fall, the pact was in effect and the song was replaced by a satirical sketch that showed the Senate in session:

Two gavel knocks and a voice offstage says, "The President of the United States of America."

A comedian playing FDR comes out with a fishing rod and an old fishing hat and says: "We have troubles in our country—now. We have unequal distribution of wealth—now. We have strikes and havoc on all sides—now. And I plan to do something about it—later."

Senior Senator: "I move that we appropriate $1 billion for monkey glands for overage destroyers." (Applause.)

Second Senator: "I move that we appropriate $5 billion to build factories for the under-privileged millionaires." (Applause.)

Third Senator: "I move that we appropriate $12 billion for rubber bands to stretch the Monroe doctrine." (Applause.)

Junior Senator: "I move that we appropriate $1 for relief." (Everyone gasps in horror.)

Meet the People was a huge success. It ran for a year in Hollywood before opening on Broadway. Danny Dare quit the party in disgust, as did many others. By April 1942, the Communist Party had lost half its prewar membership, as well as many prominent members of front groups. A. Philip Randolph, the influential founder of the Brotherhood of Sleeping Car Porters, quit the National Negro Congress when it disparaged FDR. Joe Lash, the fellow-traveling head of the American Student Union, was expelled from that organization for opposing the pact.[67]

—

The pact was a godsend for the Dies Committee, which had been pushed off the front page by the war. Communists could now be brought before the committee and asked to repudiate the pact. When they refused, or demurred with tortured reasoning, they made it all too clear that the party was the obedient lackey of the Soviet Union.

Earl Browder, the party Secretary, who made the cover of *Time* magazine as the apostle of "Communism is Americanism," was asked to appear before the committee. To avoid a subpoena, he complied, interrupting a national speaking tour of college campuses, and taking the witness stand on September 5, 1939.

Like Hallie Flanagan before him, the mustached and suavely dialectical Browder rattled the committee. When he saluted Marx, Engels, Lenin, and Stalin, Joe Starnes asked, "Who was the second?" When Browder asserted that the American Revolution had featured violence, Starnes exclaimed that "there was nobody in the United States slain."[68]

Browder tried to present the Communist Party as the left wing of the Democrats. "Our party has supported practically every measure of the New Deal since 1935," he said.

This led the anti–New Deal New Jersey Republican Parnell Thomas to observe: "It seems to me that the New Deal is working along hand in glove with the Communist Party." To which the New Mexico Democrat John J. Dempsey heatedly replied, "They could not play along with the Republican party because it has practically gone out of existence."

Thomas: "No Republicans would want to play with them."

Browder was less forthcoming when asked to justify the pact, saying only that there was "close harmony" between the Comintern and the American party. Parnell Thomas asked him whether it existed now that "Mr. Stalin has signed up with Mr. Hitler."

Browder: "Yes, the closest harmony and agreement exists." He denied that the American party received funds from Moscow, although it had received millions, or that it received instructions from the Soviet government. He denied that the American party sent representatives to Comintern congresses, even though he had been to many himself. He lied repeatedly, but on one occasion he told the truth, which led to his indictment and imprisonment.

When Rhea Whitley, the committee counsel, asked, "Mr. Browder, have you ever traveled under a false passport?" the reply was, "I have."[69]

Browder had visited Moscow every year since 1926, using false passports until recognition in 1933, but thought he was protected by the three-year statute of limitations. Asked for details, and after some urgent whispering from his lawyers, he took the Fifth. The leader of the Communist Party was the first to take the Fifth before the Dies Committee, pioneering this soon to be popular defense.[70]

A grand jury was convened, before which Browder appeared on October 23, 1939. He was accused of entering the United States with a passport in his name but obtained through a false statement. In his 1934 application, he falsely swore that he had never had a passport before, while in fact he had three under three different names. To get around the statute of limitations, he was indicted for renewing his passport in 1937. Tried in January 1940, he was sentenced to four years. FDR commuted his sentence in May 1942 as a gesture of conciliation toward the Soviet Union, our wartime ally.[71]

In the context of the pact, at a time when Communists and fellow travelers, by opposing aid to the Allies, seemed to be doing the work of the Axis powers, the Dies Committee grew in prestige and acceptability. It was, after all, the first to investigate Communism and fascism as the twin enemies of democracy.[72]

Dies took advantage of his wartime luster to go after his two bugbears, the New Deal and the Reds, in an investigation of government employees who belonged to the American League for Peace and Democracy, the mother of all front groups.[73]

The committee seized the league's Washington records and found that 563 federal employees were members. Among them were such high-ranking civil servants as Assistant Secretary of the Interior Oscar Chapman, who was a friend of Soviet ambassador Constantine Oumansky; Louis Bloch, a member of the Maritime Labor Board; Mordecai Ezekiel, a senior economist at

Triple A; and Edwin A. Smith and Nathan Witt, who were part of the Communist cell at the National Labor Relations Board.[74]

When the league claimed that the records had been seized illegally, Dies offered proof to the contrary on October 6, 1939: a letter from the league's chairman, Harry C. Lambertson, in which he agreed to turn over the financial records, and mailing and membership lists to the committee. Dies also read aloud a letter Lambertson had written to league members on August 25, calling the Nazi-Soviet pact a "real contribution to world peace." Laughter erupted in the hearing room, directed at an important official in a New Deal agency, for Lambertson was the assistant general counsel of the Rural Electrification Administration. On October 7, Dies announced that the publication of the list of federal employees who belonged to the league would be determined at a later date.

On the same day as Dies's announcement, Secretary of the Interior Harold Ickes confided to his diary: "The Dies Committee has been running hog-wild lately and has become a danger of the first magnitude. . . . Dies is in a fair way to build up the same kind of reputation that A. Mitchell Palmer built up in the last war. . . . He has become an actual menace. Fundamentally he is after the New Deal. He keeps saying that soon he is going to give out names of prominent New Dealers connecting them with Communist activities."[75]

The matter of releasing the names was left hanging for nearly three weeks as committee members thrashed out their conflicting views. This was the most divisive issue they had ever been presented with. In the meantime, the committee called witnesses for the league, including its president, Harry Freeman Ward, a professor of Christian ethics at the Union Theological Seminary, who would be made chairman of the American Civil Liberties Union in 1940. Ward was named in secret reports from the American party to the Comintern in Moscow as someone "who could reach a broad audience beyond the left wing circles."

Browder in his testimony a month before had admitted that the league "from the beginning was led by our party quite openly." Browder had been the featured speaker at the Second League Congress in 1934, when Ward praised his "clear historical judgment."

Before the committee on October 23, Ward argued the merits of Communism, which he called "an extension of democracy."

Starnes broke in: "In other words an improvement upon democracy?"

Ward: "It would be democracy advancing to a higher field."

Ward's description of league activities showed that it was essentially a lobby for the support of Soviet policies. Its manifesto stated that its aim was "to oppose all attempts to weaken the Soviet Union." It was subsidized by the

American Communist Party, Ward said. There were league branches in most government agencies and one in the Navy yard.

The testimony included a list of events in 1938, which showed that a government employee in Washington could build his or her entire social life around league events.

May 6: Picketing at Peoples Drug Store, 14th and U streets, in support of the New Negro Alliance campaign to force the store to hire Negro clerks.
May 8: Party at Michaelson's, 4319 15th Street, admission 50 cents, with hosts and hostesses to see that people meet people.
May 13: Spanish Committee picnic at Greenacres.
May 14: National emergency conference on civil rights legislation at the Raleigh Hotel. Plans for action to defeat various fascist bills before Congress.
And so on.

As Dies put it, the league documents "reveal a systematic effort to penetrate the government by an organization which is under the control of Communists."

Ward tried to explain why the league had backed the Nazi-Soviet pact, but Dies read a letter dated September 1 from a league member in New York that showed a certain amount of befuddlement in the ranks: "The whole state of affairs here are at sixes and sevens. People of importance are resigning. . . . I am telling people to keep quiet."

On October 24, the committee members met in a final attempt to resolve their dispute over releasing the names. Jerry Voorhis said he was against the wholesale firing of those who were identified as Reds. The job of finding and prosecuting those on the list, he said, should be left to the FBI. The Illinois Republican Noah Mason replied: "I am interested in getting rid of the Reds in government departments. . . . I have listed here 563 jobs, with salaries of up to $10,000 a year. Should we make this public or not?"[76]

To resolve the dispute, the seven-member committee went into a secret executive session the next day. John Dempsey, the New Mexico Democrat, who was against publication, went out to make a long-distance phone call. When he returned, the decision to publish the list had been made. Furious at not having been consulted, Dempsey said: "I think we have done a damnable thing."[77]

The committee then released a statement saying that the publication of the names was warranted because the government employees had maintained their affiliation with a front organization after it had been exposed as

Communist. The mail was heavy from those who said they'd been mistakenly listed or hadn't realized what they were joining. "When I joined the League," said J. H. Radabaugh, "it was in the same manner that one would become a member of the American Red Cross . . . for the promotion of world peace." Blanche Cohen said she had resigned when the league had failed to denounce the Nazi-Soviet pact, but was still listed.[78]

Outcries against publication came from all sides. In a press conference on October 27, FDR called it "this sordid procedure." An editorial in the *St. Louis Post-Dispatch* called it "in the best KKK tradition."

John Dempsey, who had been excluded from the decision to publish, objected on the floor of the House that the list was "un-American." His remarks led to an unusually acerbic debate, with Jacob Thorkelson of Montana accusing those who objected to publication of being in sympathy with subversive activities. Dempsey countered that the publication was "reprehensible." John Coffee of Washington endorsed that view, on the grounds that government employees had a right to join organizations of their own choosing. Jerry Voorhis made the point that many of those who had joined the league might not have been aware that it was Communist-controlled. The debate was ended by Noah Mason, who summed up the evidence showing the league to be a Communist front. Releasing the names, he said, was a form of "moral suasion" to prod innocent members to quit, while getting Communists out of government. The Dies Committee had first announced a year ago that the league was a Communist front, he said, giving the members notice. Dempsey retorted that a thousand years' notice was not enough for those who did not know their names were on the list.[79]

On October 28, Dies responded to the President's remark in a radio talk. What was sordid, he said, was for someone to take his salary from one government when he was being used as a tool by an organization that served the interests of another. It was sordid that there were more than five hundred such individuals on the government payroll.

What went unnoticed in the argument was that the Dies investigators found on the list one of the most productive Soviet spies inside the U.S. government. Although they could not at the time identify him as such, this was the first public exposure of Dr. Nathan Gregory Silvermaster, who gave his name to an espionage ring.

In the Roosevelt administration, however, Dies's method of mass denunciation was viewed as palpably unfair. Frank Murphy, whom Dies had helped unseat when he was the governor of Michigan in 1938, was now Attorney General. When Dies delivered his data on the league and its members to the Justice Department in late October 1939, Murphy thanked him, but noted that the government needed concrete examples of violations of law before it could prosecute. Thus, said Murphy, there was nothing he could do about the American League for Peace and Democracy or any of its members.[80]

———

In the wake of the uproar over the list, Dies continued to hold hearings on Communist influence in all sectors of American society. For the first time, though, he had to deal with hostile witnesses. Joseph Curran, president of the Red-tinged National Maritime Union, testified on October 28. Upon being told that he could not read a prepared statement, he exclaimed, "What a circus!"

"Have some respect for this committee or we are going to cite you for contempt," Dies warned.

Did the National Maritime Union carry out programs of the Communist Party? the committee counsel asked.

"We have one program," Curran said, "that is, wages, conditions, and hours.

"My stomach," he went on, "when it comes to looking for a pork chop when I am out on the picket line, does not know whether a dollar bill is red or green, as long as it buys a pork chop. . . . Those people who fed us at that time were so-called Communists."

William C. McCuistion, an ex-Communist seaman who took the stand on October 30, said the Communists had taken over the NMU when they funded the 1935 strike. When they gave Curran $3,500 to rent Madison Square Garden, he said: "Well, what is wrong with that?" They not only paid for the Garden, they provided the speakers and packed the strike committee with Reds, who used the hiring hall for recruiting. McCuistion said that when Curran tried to oppose the Reds, he was told: "You just go ahead and you will be a forgotten man on the waterfront." Consequently, Curran adopted a "we need the party" stance.

McCuistion's dramatic testimony was interrupted by an announcement that he was wanted for murder in New Orleans. Dies smelled a rat. If McCuistion was wanted, why hadn't the Washington police, also informed, taken steps to arrest him? They would probably try to arrest him when he left the committee room, in an obvious attempt to discredit a witness. "It smells to high heavens," Dies said, "and it is not only sordid but it also stinks." McCuistion was allowed to complete his testimony and go back to New Orleans to face the charges against him.[81]

———

During the pact period, the Dies Committee was particularly active. Dies went on the road, holding hearings in Chicago and Detroit. He investigated the teachers union and student front groups. His was a scattershot approach, hearing a veteran of the Spanish war one day and the ex-Communist party leader Jay Lovestone the next. It was generally conceded, however, that apart from the publication of the league membership list, the 1939 hearings were an improvement over the previous year's. Rhea Whitley, the committee counsel, was credited with keeping a firm hand on the tiller.

When the committee reconvened in February 1940, Dies announced that public hearings would not overlap with the presidential campaign. His main target would be Communists in Hollywood. This inquiry was not launched until July, when Dies went to Beaumont, Texas, as a one-man committee, to give his own electoral prospects a boost. There, on July 17, he heard the testimony of John Leech, an early Communist recruiter among the Hollywood community. In 1936, he escorted the Cultural Commissar, V. J. Jerome, to California to meet the Hollywood Reds. But Leech was expelled from the party, portraying himself as the victim of "a slander campaign." He moved to Oregon and worked on the Portland Dock Commission.

In his testimony in closed session on July 16 and 17, Leech named forty-two Hollywood luminaries as Communists, including the actors James Cagney, Humphrey Bogart, and Fredric March. Leech was one of the founders of the Hollywood Anti-Nazi League, a front that collected tens of thousands of dollars for the party coffers.[82]

On the strength of the Leech testimony, Dies went to Hollywood in mid-August, again as a one-man committee; but he was curiously subdued. His chief investigator and Texas crony Bob Stripling alleged that Dies had been paid off at a lunch with Y. Frank Freeman, the head of Paramount. The studios rolled out the red carpet for Dies, his wife, Myrtle, and two of his sons. Dies was photographed with Errol Flynn and Johnny Weissmuller, while his sons collected the autographs of a dozen stars. As Stripling put it: "Anybody who went to Hollywood to investigate Communism, they were taken up on the mountain and showed the green valley below."

In two days of closed hearings, Dies was uncharacteristically lenient and forgiving. Gone were the hectoring tone and the bullying tactics. All was sweetness and light.

On August 16, Humphrey DeForest Bogart told Dies: "I think Hollywood people are dupes for the most part. I know there are subversive activities going on . . . but I don't think those fellows knew what they were getting into. . . . Somebody entertained Browder out here. . . . I don't think that fellow knew what he was getting in for. . . . I was asked [to contribute money] but I refused, because I was suspicious."

John Leech was recalled and Dies asked: "Are you contending that Mr. Bogart was a member of the Communist Party?"

Leech: "I am. . . . I have sat in the study groups and I definitely recall Mr. Bogart's association." Leech said he was at director Frank Tuttle's home at the meeting for Browder in August 1936 and "Bogart was present."

Siding with Bogart and against his own star witness, Dies noted that non-Communists were also at the Browder party, "therefore we can exclude the Browder meeting as any evidence that Mr. Bogart has been or is a member of the Communist Party."

Leech: "With the qualification that these persons must be brought in by someone very close to the party who would vouch to keep secret what had taken place."[83]

Bogart was followed by James Cagney. Leech said that in 1934, at the time of the cotton strike in the San Joaquin Valley, one of the strike leaders, Emma Cutler, told him that Cagney was involved.

Cagney acknowledged that he had given money to the strikers. "You don't ask people what their relation is if things are tough," Cagney said, "you simply help them out." The Public Enemy was a soft touch. He had given $500 for an ambulance to Loyalist Spain. "I was raised in poverty," he said, "and by golly you can't go through life and build walls and say everything is fine for me and to hell with the other fellow."[84]

On August 17, when Fredric March testified, Dies was deferential. "We're just as anxious to defend your reputation if it is unjustly smeared or attacked as anyone could be," he said. March said he was not a Communist but he contributed to causes he felt were worthy. He was interested in Spain because "Franco stood for fascism" and had paid for an ambulance. He also joined the Anti-Nazi League.

Dies said he did not want to see March's "good name blackened."

Leech said he had seen March in August 1936 at the Browder party at Frank Tuttle's home on Rockcliff Drive. March said it was possible. Leech said March was on the list he kept of contributors to the party and that the party often used him for this or that activity. He said March had even attended some of his lectures. March said that was "a complete and unmitigated lie."

Dies: "Mr. Leech, did you ever have any reason to dislike Mr. March?"

Leech: "In spite of the 'unmitigated liar,' I have no animosity or ill feeling."

March: "Might it be possible that my name was bandied about by [Lionel] Stander and [John] Bright [two alleged Communists]. . . . That they said 'we'll take care of March, he'll do this, he'll do that' . . . might it not be wishful thinking?"

Dies: "No man can be held accountable for what someone says about him. . . . I can't in my own mind reach the conclusion that Mr. March was a member of the Communist Party."[85] Thus ended, with Dies in the role of pardoner, his foray into Hollywood.

At a subsequent hearing in New York on August 26, the actor Franchot Tone, who had attended a fund-raiser for the Scottsboro boys, the eight black teenagers sentenced to death in 1931 for allegedly raping two white women in Scottsboro, Alabama, thrown by Mary Astor, diagnosed the "bleeding-heart" syndrome when he said: "You see, when you have so much money thrown in your lap, your conscience is aroused."

Dies: "That is a very worthy feeling in any man's heart."[86]

Even though Leech had named forty-two alleged Hollywood Communists, Dies absolved them all.

On September 29, the unhappy Leech wrote the Dies investigator James Steedman that he was still awaiting his witness fees. He sure could use the money. The Portland Dock Commission had fired him. He had done everything in his power to help the committee, and in Hollywood Dies had given him "a good kick in the teeth. I'm hoping that in the end I will emerge not quite so much a son of a bitch as I'm now branded."[87]

Another witness in the Beaumont hearings was Mrs. Joe L. Maddux, who had testified with her husband, a worker at a local shipyard, regarding Communist activity in Texas. She wrote Stripling on October 2 that "since my husband Joe and I gave information to the Dies Committee, we have been unable to stay in one locality for any length of time. On his job at the shipyard my husband was discovered by the Communists and had to leave Beaumont. He is at present unable to find employment and we are in immediate financial distress. The Communists are watching us so close that my husband cannot seek employment. Is there anything within your power to make our lives less hazardous?" One way of measuring the extent of Communist influence was the intimidation of Dies Committee witnesses.[88]

—

Neither candidate in the 1940 presidential election, FDR nor Wendell Willkie, had much liking for the Dies Committee. Willkie, the president of a utilities holding company, was a Wall Street magnate. But he was also a champion of civil liberties. Improbably, in an article in *The New Republic*, he came to the defense of Earl Browder for having been railroaded by Dies. During the campaign, John Dempsey, the New Dealer on the committee, asked Dies to speak out against Willkie for siding with the Communist leader. But Dies the disloyal Democrat was more interested in discrediting FDR. Thus in October he was in Chicago charging that FDR was doing nothing about the fifth column for fear of losing a few votes. Dies claimed to have a list of 300,000 active fifth columnists and threatened to release it unless the government did something at once. In Detroit he gave the same spiel. "That was his contribution to the Democratic ticket," fumed Ickes. "It is reported that for his service Dies received compensation from the Willkie camp."[89] Even without Dies's help, on November 5 FDR crushed Willkie by 449 electoral votes to 82.

Because he was bent on censuring the Roosevelt administration, Dies ran afoul of the Justice Department and the FBI, who should have been his natural allies in the hunt for subversives. J. Edgar Hoover saw Dies as a rival and kept him at arm's length. With his investigations and his files, Dies seemed to be stepping on his turf. Hoover said that Dies suffered from "great delusions of personal grandeur."

Dies had built up good contacts with police forces all over the country, and on August 11, 1940, he received some information proving to him that Justice was soft on Communism. Homer Garrison Jr., director of the Texas Department of Public Safety, had attended a meeting of governors and state attorneys general at the Justice Department. He informed Dies that Assistant District Attorney John O. Rogge had presented Dies Committee exhibits of Nazi and Communist literature. "What significance does it have," Rogge had observed, "that there is only one panel for the Nazis and nine panels for the Communists? Does the Dies Committee weigh the two in that respect?" According to Garrison, Rogge's remarks struck the delegation of governors and attorneys general as "Commy in tenor." They complained to Attorney General Robert Jackson and the next morning Jackson apologized and spoke in direct contradiction of Rogge's previous remarks.[90]*

Matters came to a head on November 20, 1940, when Dies released his white paper on Nazi organizations. The FBI at that time was investigating the Nazi agent Manfred Zapp, to build a case for prosecution. The Dies white paper exposed Zapp and his Transocean News Service as a Nazi government outfit spreading propaganda. In so doing, Dies alerted Zapp and short-circuited the FBI inquiry. Attorney General Robert Jackson expressed his acute frustration that Dies had preempted the FBI.

Five days later, Dies fought back. He wired the President to urge that the Justice Department be made to cooperate with his committee. "There is plenty of work for all of us to do," he said, "without indulging in unprofitable disputes and childish rivalries." He felt that the Justice Department was "laboring under false impressions and giving credence to malicious rumors."[91] FDR replied that "the enforcement of illegal activities lies with the executive

* Dismissed from the Justice Department in 1947, Rogge became a fellow-traveling radical lawyer. He was a vice president of the National Lawyers Guild and a backer of the Civil Rights Congress, the legal arm of the party in racial equality cases. In 1948, he joined Henry Wallace's Progressive Party, with which he broke in 1950 over Stalin's condemnation of Tito. In the Rosenberg case, he was the lawyer of David Greenglass, who testified against his sister and brother-in-law.

branch. Carefully laid plans to break up subversive activities could be severely handicapped or destroyed by premature disclosure or hasty seizure of evidence, which might with a little more patience be obtained in a manner admissible in court, or by granting immunity to witnesses as to matters revealed by their testimony."[92]

This exchange of wires led to a meeting at the White House on the morning of November 29, 1940. From the outer office, Dies peered in at the President and said, "He doesn't look very vicious does he?" The White House prudently recorded the conversation.

For this rogue member of his own party, FDR was at his most charming, welcoming Dies in and calling him Martin, while warning him about his buckshot approach. "You have to protect innocent people," he said.

Dies mentioned the recent hearings in Hollywood: "We had quite a bit of trouble with certain movie actors who were contributing large sums of money to these organizations. . . . They had been careless and indiscreet in lending their names and prestige."

FDR chose to humor this disloyal Democrat who had gone off the reservation and campaigned against him, and who was now gumming up FBI investigations. "Of course almost everyone does that," he said, "all make mistakes. They must not be held up to the public as a whole as being sympathizers because of a contribution where it may be ignorance on their part."

FDR told Dies that the FBI was complaining that he was interfering with their cases. These suspects were "like quail," he said. "If you ever flushed them out, they would know they were being investigated and you would never get anything on them." As for the perceived Communist threat, FDR thought it was negligible. "What was the Communist vote in 1936? . . . Half a million votes [actually 80,169]. . . . Now, I would not bar from patriotic defense efforts everyone who had voted for a Communist in 1936, 1938, or 1940. Neither would you."

Dies, who had built his career on weeding out Communists, could not agree. "I would be suspicious of them," he said.

FDR: "Oh, I would check them, absolutely. But the mere fact that they voted Communist when voting for a Communist was legal doesn't automatically entitle us to say to the public 'those people are disloyal.' "

Dies finally promised to be a good soldier. "I don't want to cross the wires," he said, "regardless of anything you might have been told, and I know you have been told a great deal. I have carried on under great pressure. I have been ridiculed. I have been denounced. I have had to pay a pretty high price for what I have done. I don't want to be at cross-purpose. . . . The only thing that I ask is that the Department of Justice show some degree of cooperation in return. Here is a case: Mr. Hoover is a very excellent man, but he syndicated an article that was construed against us."*

FDR was at his avuncular best. "You have a talk with Bob," he said, speaking of the Attorney General, "and see if you can eliminate that very good example you use of Hoover saying or doing something which you take as a reflection on the committee."[93]

The fight had gone out of Dies. His bluster and antagonism vanished. Before the President he was meek, even conciliatory. "I am willing," he said, "to go every way that any man ever can to cooperate with you in this whole matter."

This era of good feeling did not last long, however, for in February 1941, Dies announced that he was compiling a list of suspects to be detained in case of war. Once again he was duplicating the duties of the FBI. J. Edgar Hoover observed in a memo on February 17: "Now that the hunt is on I imagine the OGPU agents will sit and wait for Buck Dies and his merry men to arrive."[94]

———

When the resolution to continue the Dies Committee was debated on the floor of the House in February 1941, it was approved by a vote of 354 to six and given an appropriation of $150,000. With America approaching war, and the Nazi-Soviet pact still in effect, the committee was seen, more than ever, as a safeguard against subversion.[95]

Although he was at the peak of his success, Dies was showing signs of battle fatigue. His quarrels with the administration and his perceived harassment by both the Communists and fascists were wearing him down. At the same time, he had long cherished the hope that he would one day run for the Senate. On April 9, 1941, the opportunity at last arose when Morris Sheppard, a loyal New Dealer, died of a stroke after representing Texas for twenty-seven years in the upper house.

A special election was scheduled for June to replace him. In what became known as "the screwball election in Texas," it was open to anyone who could pay the $100 filing fee. Twenty-nine candidates applied for this special Democratic primary, but only four were real contenders: Dies and three formidable opponents, the thirty-two-year-old Lyndon Johnson, a freshman congressman already seen in Washington as FDR's protégé, but little known outside his district; Gerald C. Mann, the attorney general of the state of Texas who, at

---

* Hoover, who considered Dies's Red-hunting an intrusion on his authority, floated the rumor that Dies had vice presidential ambitions. In his disparagement of the committee he used surrogates such as the editorial writer Jack Carley of the *Memphis Commercial Appeal*.

thirty-two, was a devout Christian and college football star, known through-out the state as "The Little Red Arrow"; and Wilbert Lee O'Daniel, the gover-nor of Texas, who decided in May to throw in his hat.

"Pappy" O'Daniel was one of those oddballs that the American electoral process coughs up from time to time, to remind us how circuitous the way to the voters' heart can be.[96] An unapologetic showman, the fifty-year-old O'Daniel confirmed the importance of theatrics in politics. He was a flour salesman, and to market his brand, Hillbilly Flour, he went on the radio. Be-fore long, his down-home mixture of country music, religious homilies, and advice to housewives made his show the most popular on daytime Texas radio, and catapulted him into high office. He was elected governor in 1938, after campaigning with his fiddle and banjo group, "The Doughboys," and re-elected in 1940. When the polls showed that he could win the senatorial con-test, he went on the road again.[97]

Although Dies had name recognition, his campaign was poorly funded. He spent $40,000 of his own money, whereas Lyndon Johnson, backed by Texas business interests and the White House, spent an estimated $500,000. To cut costs Dies named his wife, Myrtle, campaign manager and his nineteen-year-old son, Martin III, acted as his advance man. Not surprisingly, the campaign and the indispensable advance work were amateurish. Thinking that he could run on his committee record, he became one-note Martin, harping on the Communist threat. After a strong start, Dies began to drop in the polls. Sensing that he was losing, he went after his opponents, calling O'Daniel "a showman," Mann "a green man," and Johnson "a yes-man." On June 19, he invoked reduced circumstances. "I am not financially able to employ speak-ers, sound trucks, publicity experts, and paid hirelings," he said, "to conduct a high-pressure campaign throughout the state. I am unable to buy adver-tisements in newspapers or to place my posters on every telephone pole in the state" (as Lyndon Johnson did).[98]

With the backing of the President and the funding of his friends at the Brown & Root Construction Company, Johnson ran a strong race. He stumped hard, hired a band, and drew crowds by giving away up to $100 in defense stamps at rallies. Each rally began with a lottery, and the winners were an-nounced after the speech.

O'Daniel was the lone star of the campaign, opening each rally with his slogan, "Pappy Please Pass the Biscuits," singing songs, and talking to his rus-tic fans like an old friend. Johnson, however, was not far behind, and in the end the election turned on who could steal the most votes in the Mexican precincts. On June 28, the voters went to the polls, and O'Daniel squeaked by with 175,590 votes. Johnson trailed by a little more than a thousand, with

174,279. Dies came in a disappointing fourth with 14 percent of the vote. He was crushed, and he blamed his loss on a whispering campaign that Texas could expect less in federal handouts if he were elected, which made him more anti-Roosevelt than ever.[99]

———

When Hitler invaded the Soviet Union in June 1941, Stalin became an ally and the recipient of lend-lease. The pact period, which had allowed Dies to link the Russians and the Germans as "different cults of the same religion," as he put it, was over. Then came Pearl Harbor and America's entry into the war. Now the United States was fighting with one dictator against another. The committee announced in a report in January 1942 that it would hold no more public hearings, so as not to interfere with espionage investigations. It continued to operate, however, and continued to go after American Communists and fellow travelers, as well as pro-Nazis. It also adjusted to the wartime situation by adding Japanese-Americans to its enemies list.

On October 29, 1941, Dies had sent Attorney General Francis Biddle a list of 1,121 federal employees whom he said were members of subversive organizations. Biddle asked the FBI to investigate. On March 29, 1942, Dies released a letter to Vice President Henry Wallace charging that thirty-five members of the Board of Economic Warfare were affiliated with front groups. One of the thirty-five, Maurice Parmelee, was the author of an illustrated book entitled *Nudism in Modern Life*. The book was condemned as obscene by a U.S. District Court, but the decision was overturned by the Court of Appeals, which held that the book as a whole was not obscene. Parmelee was a harmless Utopian who predicted that "convent and monastery, harem and military barracks, clubs and schools exclusively for each sex, will disappear, and the sexes will live a more normal and happier life together." Dies transformed him into a dangerous pseudo-Communist and brought his book over from the closed shelves of the Library of Congress so that the full House could look at snapshots of nudists frolicking on the beach. There was much chortling and guffawing.

Wallace replied to the charges with the most scathing attack ever made against Dies. "We are at war," he said, "and the doubts and anger which this and similar statements of Mr. Dies tend to arouse in the public mind might as well come from Goebbels himself so far as their practical effect is concerned. As a matter of fact, the effect on our morals would be less damaging if Mr. Dies were on the Hitler payroll." Wallace's outrage, however, did not prevent Parmelee from being fired.[100]

Wallace was not the only cabinet member to reprove Dies. In April 1942, when he announced secret hearings to expose a Nazi espionage ring, Attorney General Francis Biddle ridiculed the plan. "I think that it is always a pity," he said, "to have amateurs investigate espionage."

Also, with Russia waging the war against Hitler single-handedly, Dies's sniping at the administration for being soft on Communism lost its sting. The mood of the nation evolved toward sympathy for our brave Russian ally. Merle D. Vincent, one of the federal employees on Dies's 1939 list, wrote to the congressman on October 25, 1942. He described himself as "a relatively unimportant government official," and said: "You very well know that this government and its people by cooperating with its Russian ally to crush Hitler is not embracing Communism, any more than our alliance with the people of China commits us to the use of chopsticks or Taoism." Vincent faulted Dies for questioning the loyalty of union members who were helping the war effort and invoked the two thousand maritime workers who had perished on torpedoed ships that supplied food and weapons to our allies. "Must they continue," he asked of those who had volunteered for this hazardous duty, "to sail submarine-infested seas with charges of disloyalty ringing in their ears?"[101]

In the meantime, the results of the investigation undertaken by the FBI in response to Dies's charges in October 1941, that 1,121 federal employees were members of subversive organizations, were submitted to Congress by Attorney General Biddle on September 1, 1942. The FBI found 601 cases worth complete investigations. Of these, 97 no longer worked for the government and 69 were still under investigation. As a result of the 455 completed investigations, two persons were discharged.

"As regards a large proportion of the complaints," Biddle observed, "it is now evident that they were clearly unfounded. . . . Hundreds of employees . . . have been alleged to be 'subversive' for no better reason than the appearance of their names on a mailing list." Dies cried whitewash, not without cause. The Venona transcripts have since substantiated that at least seventy-six employees of the federal government had covert relationships with Soviet intelligence during the war years.

—

Although the people of Texas had denied him a Senate seat, Dies was reelected to the House in November 1942. In February 1943, by a vote of 302 to 94, the House extended the life of his committee for the duration of the war and voted a $75,000 appropriation.

Dies had a strong mandate to continue his work, but his attacks on federal employees led Jerry Voorhis to resign. By casting too wide a net, Voorhis felt, Dies had turned the committee into an anti–New Deal forum. Voorhis now saw it as "nothing more than a political instrument of reaction."[102]

For Dies, the diminished number of hearings meant that he had to use other means in order to keep a high profile. Thus, he released material collected by his research chief, J. B. Matthews, and his staff of fourteen directly to the press or in speeches on the floor of the House.

Then, on February 17, 1943, Attorney General Biddle seemed to reverse himself by reporting to the House that the Justice Department had appropriated $200,000 to investigate 4,948 subversives, including those named by Dies. This was part of the fallout from the fear of saboteurs, such as the four who had landed in Long Island on June 13, 1942. A U-boat dropped them off with TNT and other explosives. Four days later, four more landed on Ponte Vedra Beach, Florida, twenty-five miles south of Jacksonville. By June 27, J. Edgar Hoover had caught all eight. A jubilant Biddle called FDR with the news, adding that the Nazi saboteurs had $175,000 in cash. "Not enough," replied FDR. "Sell the rights to Barnum and Bailey for a million and a half and take them around the country in lion cages at so much a head." All eight were sentenced to death and electrocuted six weeks later.[103]

In January 1944, the Dies Committee received another appropriation of $75,000, which brought the total of its funding since its inception to $625,000. Dies seemed to have thrown off the disappointment of his Senate defeat. He was his old pugnacious self, announcing an investigation of the CIO Political Action Committee, which was lining up millions of workers in FDR's bid for a fourth term. In March, he rose to the floor of the House and fired a shotgun blast at the National Lawyers Guild, the CIO political action committee, and the Blue Network, which broadcast Walter Winchell.[104]

With his millions of listeners, Winchell was covertly used by the White House to attack its enemies. Two political operatives, Tommy "The Cork" Corcoran and Ernest Cuneo, acted as liaison with Winchell, passing him items. In one item, Winchell went after anti-FDR congressmen in the "House of Reprehensibles," which included "some of the sorriest stumblebums in the nation."[105]

If he did not get equal time, Dies threatened, he would subpoena Winchell's scripts. Winchell's sponsors, the Jergens lotion people, invited Dies to speak on the radio on March 26. He called Winchell "a peddler of bedroom keyhole scandal" who wanted to "destroy Congress." Dies sent his investigators after Winchell, but all they found was that his real name was Winschel and his parents were born in Russia.[106]

In April, Dies was back in Texas campaigning for the 1944 election. On April 23, he was driving to Dallas when he felt sick. He went to Galveston for a checkup and was told he might have throat cancer. The strain of the committee work, the doubts about being able to conduct an effective campaign, the threat of a powerful coalition of New Dealers, Communists, and the CIO conspiring against him, the fear of surgery and possible death, all combined to make him quit the race. After fourteen years in Washington, he moved back to his farm in Jasper, north of Beaumont.[107]

As it happened, he did require surgery, but did not have throat cancer, and lived another twenty-eight years. Back home, he joined the 1944 dump-Roosevelt movement and backed the Republican Thomas E. Dewey–John Bricker ticket. For Dies, it was all part of the struggle in the South over who were the real Democrats: the big-government New Dealers or the good old county seat segregationists.

Dies moved to Lufkin, about fifty miles northwest of Jasper, to become a partner in a law firm there. But he missed being center stage in Washington. In 1952, when Texas failed to redraw its congressional districts following a population increase in the 1950 census, a congressman-at-large seat became available. Dies ran for it and won, returning to the House in 1953. The first thing he did was propose an increase in congressional salaries from $15,000 to $22,500, which made some of his constituents wonder if he was worth it.[108]

Dies served in the House at the same time that Joe McCarthy served in the Senate and launched his own investigations committee. Dies had labored as McCarthy's advance man, pioneering the Red-hunt in government and using his committee to smear the New Deal. McCarthy observed that Dies's "return to Congress is one of the healthiest signs of the whole election picture."

On one occasion in 1953, soon after Dies's return to Washington, McCarthy had a private talk with him and was told "to expect abuse, ridicule, and every known device of character assassination and mental torture." Later, when he was driven from the Senate, McCarthy likened himself to Dies, whom he said had been "damned and humiliated and driven from public life." "In my opinion," McCarthy said, Dies "will go down in history as a heroic voice crying in the wilderness."[109]

Back in Washington after an eight-year absence, Dies's day was past. He was not named to the House Un-American Activities Committee, which had been made a permanent committee in 1945. He was eclipsed by McCarthy, who was riding high in the Senate, as a new edition of Dies. He served three tranquil terms in the House, from 1953 to 1959. To the end, he remained an unreconstructed nativist. Speaking in 1954 against statehood for Hawaii he said: "I don't think we can assimilate this large oriental population to the extent of permitting them to have as much power and control in the United States Senate as, we'll say, the people of Texas or the people of Pennsylvania."[110]

Returning to Lufkin in 1959, Dies became a regular contributor to the magazine of the John Birch Society, *American Opinion.* From 1964 to 1967, his articles ran in thirty-five issues. In that magazine of the far-right fringe he sometimes sounded like a moderate. His views were predictable. In 1966, in an article on Vietnam, he wrote: "We must destroy Hanoi and the whole of North Vietnam if necessary." In 1966 he suffered a stroke, and in 1972 a second stroke killed him, at the age of seventy-two.[111]

Dies was the product of his turn-of-the-century East Texas background, a Southern racist who despised blacks, foreigners, and big government. He had a crude and blustering manner, a venal nature, and a second-rate mind. And yet, this simplistic but dogged ideologue, who linked Communism with the New Deal for obviously partisan motives, turned out to be surprisingly effective in uncovering the concealed activities of the party. There may have been a fair number of deluded liberals among the 563 federal employees who belonged to the American League for Peace and Democracy, but there were also a substantial number of party members and Soviet agents who worked for the government. The tactics of his enemies, for whom any criticism of the party amounted to Red-baiting, did not differ substantially from his own. Nor did his avowed patriotism preclude self-advancement or the viciously warped undermining of the New Deal. Dies may have been a flawed inquisitor, but the heresy was not imaginary. The New Deal was vulnerable to attack. Thanks to Dies, the pendulum swung from treating Communists as inoffensive reformers to recognizing them as disloyal agents of a foreign dictatorship.

The same could be said of the Dies Committee that was said of Cardinal Richelieu: that it did too much harm to be praised and too much good to be damned. Its exposure of subversion was as beneficial as its assault on the New Deal and its buckshot approach were shameful.

IX

WORLD WAR II AND
THE SOVIET INVASION
OF AMERICA

The faucet of American aid to the Soviet Union opened months before Pearl Harbor. Hitler invaded Russia in June 1941, and by mid-August the Soviet embassy in Washington had provided the White House with a shopping list twenty-nine pages long. In September, Harry Hopkins, the head of lend-lease, left for Moscow with an Anglo-American mission to discuss allocations. Stalin himself gave Hopkins the rundown: the Germans had superiority in planes and tanks, and 320 divisions to Russia's 280. Stalin knew exactly what he wanted, from tanks to barbed wire, and Averell Harriman, the head of the mission, felt that he rode them pretty hard.

By then the Germans were approaching Moscow and Hitler was already announcing that the Red Army had been crushed. No wonder Stalin was restless, chain-smoking and nervously pacing when he wasn't doodling wolves on his notepaper. But he perked up when Harriman promised five thousand jeeps. A protocol was signed on October 1, 1941, calling for shipments of up to $1 billion, financed under lend-lease. Over 150 items were listed, from tanks, planes, and destroyers, down to army boots (400,000 pairs a month) and shellac (300 tons a month).[1]

On November 7, with the Germans thirty miles from Moscow, FDR convinced Congress to grant the Soviets full lend-lease facilities. The reason, as Navy commander Admiral Ernest J. King put it, was that "Russia will do nine tenths of the job defeating Hitler." From June 1941 until the surrender of Italy in September 1943, the European war was a Russo-German war. The Russians disabled the Germans in three years of fierce fighting, taking huge losses.[2]

Between 1941 and 1946, America sent the Soviets $11 billion in lend-lease, including 3,000 planes, 581 ships, and more tanks than they could use. Also sent were entire factories, from petroleum cracking to synthetic rubber, complete with operating manuals and engineering drawings.[3]

And yet the Russians complained that they were being shortchanged. Alexander Feklisov, a KGB agent who arrived in New York in February 1941, and spent five years spying on the United States under the cover of the Soviet consulate, wrote in his memoirs that the Soviet Union received only $10 billion in lend-lease, while the other Allies got $36 billion. This, he said, was a deliberate attempt to weaken the Soviet Union by prolonging the war, in order to enrich American industrialists. The Soviet response to American generosity was paranoid suspicion.[4]

As a result of lend-lease and the gigantic logistical effort it required, Russians by the thousands streamed into the United States. This was the "Our Gallant Ally" period, when allowances were made for the country that was doing the brunt of the fighting. An estimated fifteen thousand Soviet experts visited American factories and military installations during the war.[5]

These experts belonged to the Soviet Government Purchasing Commission, which was headed by the Red Army general Leonid Rudenko. The commission sent its representatives into American defense factories and major ports. It seemed that every Soviet government agency had a branch in the United States, from the Meteorological Mission to the Seamen's Mission. Every factory producing lend-lease equipment had its Soviet team of inspectors, engineers, and military men. The West Coast ports where Soviet ships were landing to load cargo, mainly San Francisco, Portland, and Seattle, hosted Soviet teams in charge of personnel, convoy services, and repairs.[6]

While America's industrial might was producing what the Russians needed to keep more than three hundred German divisions at bay—and while we sent their troops rations that taught them to appreciate Spam—the Russians stole whatever they could get their hands on. American ships unloading lend-lease material in Vladivostok were subjected to systematic theft. A ship that made the trip several times a year had to replace, on each voyage, its ropes, blocks, and spare machine parts. It was not until the war was over, on November 28, 1945, that the People's Commissariat for the Navy issued an order that stealing had to stop.[7]

A more serious form of theft came in the pervasive spying by every Soviet agency allowed upon American soil. The war years saw bumper crops of Soviet spies. Aside from the usual diplomatic and Amtorg cover, they now had the Soviet Government Purchasing Commission, which allowed them to infiltrate KGB and GRU agents into American defense plants and military installations. They stole American military and industrial secrets just as blatantly as they were stealing the ropes and blocks off American ships. In their scope and effectiveness, the Soviet espionage operations in wartime America were without historical precedent. Never did one country steal so many political, diplomatic, scientific, and military secrets from another. It was analogous, in espionage terms, to the looting of European artworks by the Nazis. Except that in the friendly, cooperative spirit of the times, we invited them in.

———

Only since 1995, with the release of the first Venona transcripts, has irrefutable evidence of wartime Soviet espionage been revealed. The secret was kept for half a century, for it was in 1943 that U.S. Army code-breakers first began to look at the cable traffic between Moscow and its American embassy and consulates.

With the onset of war in 1939, the federal government set up an Office of the Censor, which routinely collected copies of all international cables leaving and entering the United States. The Soviets had shortwave radio transmitters in their Washington embassy and their New York consulate, but getting through to Moscow was problematic, and with the high volume of messages, they preferred to use commercial cable, convinced that their code was unbreakable. Copies of coded Soviet cables were routinely sent to the Army's Signal Intelligence Service, where they piled up ceiling-high in its Virginia headquarters on the Potomac, Arlington Hall, a wooded estate with a colonnaded mansion that had once been a girls boarding school (like Lenin's headquarters in 1917). For in the early years of the war, the army's code-breakers focused on German and Japanese messages. There was plenty to do, and the staff grew exponentially, from nineteen in 1939 to five hundred in 1946.[8]

Colonel Carter Clarke, stern-faced, brush-cut, and mustached, was chief of the U.S. Army Special Branch, which supervised the Signal Intelligence Service. Trained to act on his suspicions, Colonel Clarke in February 1943 picked up rumors of a separate peace between the Germans and the Russians. With the precedent of the Nazi-Soviet pact, this did not seem implausible, and he ordered SIS to set up a highly secret program to decipher the Soviet cable traffic, which was eventually code-named "Venona." Clarke could not have foreseen that he was launching a monumental undertaking that would endure until 1980.

It took nearly four decades to decipher 2,900 Soviet cables to and from Moscow from 1940 to 1948, and that was only a tiny percentage of the total traffic of more than a million messages, for the Soviets had five separate codes: one for its trade missions, Amtorg and the Soviet Government Purchasing Commission; one for legitimate diplomatic messages; one for the KGB and its stations in Washington, New York, and San Francisco; one for GRU (military intelligence); and one for Naval GRU.[9]

Not only did the different codes have to be sorted out, but the Soviets used the theoretically unbreakable system of the one-time pad. This consisted of turning the text into groups of numbers obtained from their codebooks and then adding a series of random numbers from a pad that could be used only once.

An axiom of cryptography is that while there may be perfect systems, there are no perfect users. In wartime, with the rise in the volume of messages from the worldwide network of Soviet stations, and with each message requiring a nonrepeatable page from the one-time pad, a crisis arose. In 1942, the foreign stations started running out of one-time pads and Moscow had to issue duplicate pages. By the end of the war, of the million Soviet messages in American hands, thirty thousand used duplicate pages, which gave the decoders something to work with, for they were able to find the same set of random numbers in more than one message. This was called "stripping off" the one-time pad.[10]

The Venona work was more laborious than that of medieval monks on illuminated manuscripts. A number of brilliant men and women were involved, not only cryptographers, but philologists, mathematicians, engineers, linguists, and people who were good at crossword puzzles. SIS eventually became the National Security Agency, which was so secretive that it was dubbed No Such Agency.

Once the code-breakers were able to strip the one-time pad numbers, they got down to the codebook groups, which they called "plain code," where the values for a given word stayed the same from message to message, producing a pattern. The work, in the words of the writer David Martin, required "a tolerance for mind-numbing drudgery and a penchant for the inspired guess."[11]

To solve the less obvious messages, the SIS had to duplicate the Soviet codebooks. A full-time "book-breaker" was found in 1945, a tall, nail-thin Mississippian with a shock of brown hair and an abstracted manner, who had made his reputation working on Japanese codes. In 1949, he was the first to decipher a Japanese word for atom bomb—*genshi-bakudan*—in a message sent shortly after Hiroshima.

This legendary figure, Meredith Knox Gardner, working in complete obscurity, spent twenty-seven years on "the Russian problem." When he finally surfaced at the age of eighty-four at the Venona conference at the National War College in October 1996, he admitted to having "a sort of magpie attitude to facts, the habit of storing away things that did not seem to have any connection." He collected arcane cricket terms in order to solve the London *Times* crossword puzzle. He had the puzzle-solving obsession that wants above all to clarify the unintelligible.[12] He was also a formidable linguist, who spoke or read not only Japanese, German, Spanish, French, and Russian, but little used languages such as Sanskrit, Old High German, and Middle High German.

In December 1946, Gardner broke into a message dated December 2, 1944, from New York to Moscow: "(xxxxxxx) enumerates scientists who were working on the problem—Hans Bethe, Niels Bohr, Enrico Fermi, John Newman, Bruno Rossi, George Kistiakowski, Emilio Segre, G. I. Taylor, William Penney, Arthur Compton, Ernest Lawrence, Harold Urey, Hans Stanarm, Edward Teller, Percy Bridgeman, Werner Ekenberg, Stassenman. . . ."[13] Here was a list of seventeen scientists, most of whom had worked on the Manhattan Project. Here was clear evidence of espionage to steal the secrets of the bomb.[14]

Over the years, Venona took its toll. Being locked up all day looking at rows of digits might seem less like a contribution to the war effort than a form of punishment. Most of the Venona decrypters were women, exempted from military service. One gave up on personal hygiene and refused to bathe. Another committed suicide. Meredith Gardner admitted to taking a drink, and after a bibulous lunch in 1972 he was involved in a hit-and-run accident, which led to his retirement.[15]

The material in the codes was far more varied than the code-breakers at first thought. It was divided by the Soviets into a certain number of "lines," one of which involved security matters among Soviet seamen. Hundreds of Russian ships landed at American ports each year to pick up lend-lease cargo. Often they spent weeks in port for repairs. Desertions were the biggest problem and each ship had "probationers" (KGB agents) on board to keep the crews in line. Due to the rising rate of desertion, vice consuls were named to Seattle and Portland.[16]

Soviet seamen were the particular province of Naval GRU, which also handled special requests, such as an artificial leg for Admiral Isakov, chief of the Naval General Staff. Naval GRU monitored all naval lend-lease activities, such as the building of twelve minesweepers and subchasers in Tampa for transfer to the Soviet navy. On June 9, 1943, the vessels carried out their sea trials, and then it was off to Murmansk with Russian crews. When four sailors deserted in Tampa, the Soviet inspector, Evgeni Khyrov, appealed to Commander Robert Frank Erdman, the officer in charge of liaison with the Soviets. With the help of Naval Intelligence, the four deserters were found on

July 17 and sent under armed guard to New Orleans, where they boarded a Vladivostok-bound Soviet tanker. Thus did the American Navy help send four Soviet sailors to certain death. But it was wartime, the Russians were our allies, and the American tradition of asylum was forgotten.[17] Soviet merchant ships had women in their crews, and on February 9, 1944, Elizabeth Kuznetskova jumped ship in Portland and made her way to San Francisco, where she was reported by the KGB to have married a taxi driver. Three agents were assigned to find her. On November 7, 1945, the KGB in San Francisco reported that the "traitor to the fatherland" had been caught and shipped to Vladivostok on the tanker *Belgorod*. Under the cover of lend-lease, the Russians carried out kidnappings on American soil.

Protracted repairs in American ports, said a Venona message, had a negative effect on discipline. Sometimes repairs took fifty days, which resulted in "demoralization and acts of treason." By July 28, 1944, desertions were troublesome enough so that the Soviet embassy in Washington was asked to detach two agents to the ports for "explanatory work" among the crews.[18]

On May 7, 1945, as revealed in the Venona traffic, Nikon Bezrukov, chief of the Soviet Government Purchasing Commission in Seattle, reported that three seamen considered above suspicion had deserted from their ship. They went to the hostel for Soviet seamen, met an unknown American, and did not return. The police detained and released them. In order to get them back, Bezrukov told the police the three had stolen $190 collected by the crew for provisions.[19]

Alexi Shakov, a purchasing commission inspector in Portland, fell under suspicion in July 1945 because his American colleagues gave him a gold watch. The conspiratorial Soviet mind could not fathom disinterested American generosity.[20]

On July 18, 1945, with the war in Europe over, the San Francisco KGB reported to Moscow that "a large percentage of seamen had been arriving sick. . . . Some deliberately conceal illness in order to get to sail abroad. Upon arrival in the ports of the U.S.A. such seamen demand hospitalization" and are thus able to desert.

Concern over the desertions reached the highest level of the Soviet government, with Foreign Minister Vyacheslav Molotov demanding a report on traitors and preventive work on the ships.[21] Though lend-lease was winding down, the desertions continued. On May 14, 1946, the *Elbeus* was in Long Beach in anchorage. Three groups of seamen were sent on shore leave. Nine went to Los Angeles. One of the nine, Timofo Gavrilov, detached himself from the others. The Soviet vice consul in Los Angeles, Tumantev, received a call from a storekeeper on Second Street that a Russian had come in and asked him to arrange a meeting with the governor. Tumantev went to the store and talked to the owner, but Gavrilov had fled when he saw the man making the call. A search was conducted in places where deserters found shelter, but Gavrilov escaped.[22]

During the years of lend-lease, a large number of Soviet sailors were so determined to escape their own country that they tried to remain in the United States, even though they knew that deserters were shot, and even though American authorities helped the Russians to catch them.

———

In the Venona traffic, a number of Soviets working in the Soviet Government Purchasing Commission (SGPC) were identified as GRU (Red Army Intelligence). The GRU chief in New York, Pavel P. Mikhailov, code-named *Molière*, in 1943 ascribed the absence of a second front in Europe to "King and the other admirals, who have the support of fascist circles, and advise a strategy to make it possible for the Russian and German armies to wear each other down."[23] In spite of American generosity, Soviet suspicions ran deep.

Other Soviet officers on the Purchasing Commission worked for the KGB. Andrey Shevchenko, an aviation engineer, was assigned to the Bell aircraft plant in Buffalo to approve planes prior to shipment. He stole classified documents concerning the Aircobra fighter (P-39), which was widely used on the Eastern Front.[24]

Once the war was over, the FBI made a few arrests among SGPC personnel. On March 27, 1946, the port representative for Seattle, naval Lieutenant Nikolai Redin, was arrested in Portland on espionage charges, as he was about to board the freighter *Alma Ata*. Arrested with him was Pavel Revizorov, the SGPC shipping representative in Portland, who shows up in another Venona message on July 26, 1944. Having gotten a local girl pregnant, he turned for advice to an American employee of the SGPC, a Russian-born woman living in Portland, Nadia Morris Osipovich. The message continued: "With the help of Nadia, the girl . . ." and then there was an undecoded blank.[25]

Yet another Soviet Government Purchasing Commission official was arrested in Portland on June 17, 1943. Captain Nikolai A. Khabalov, the assistant SGPC representative, was caught stealing a fur coat worth $1,000 from a shop window.[26] The criminal acts of our Russian guests were not limited to espionage, but included such embarrassments as shoplifting.

The greatest embarrassment for the Soviets, however, came in April 1944, when one of its Washington-based purchasing commission engineers defected. Victor Kravchenko had arrived in August 1943 and soon saw, as he put it, that "espionage was one of the most common assignments for Soviet representatives abroad." He worked in the Purchasing Commission offices at 3355 16th Street. The KGB office was on the seventh floor, behind an iron gate. Kravchenko told the FBI that on March 30, 1944, General Rudenko, the SGPC boss, had boasted that his office safe contained secret information on tank engines, navigational instruments, and plane devices. Kravchenko said Stalin was better informed on American firms than the U.S. government. "Who cared what we took," he said. "Had we taken the Empire State Building and put it on a ship, nobody would have cared."[27]

Kravchenko had seen what happened to deserters. He decided to defect with fanfare. On April 3, 1944, he held a news conference and placed himself "under the protection of American public opinion." The Soviet embassy in Washington demanded his extradition as a Red Army deserter. Harry Hopkins, who bent over backward to give the Russians everything they wanted, felt that it made "just plain sense to return a deserter to an ally who was helping to fight Hitler." He took it up with FDR, in whom the desire to help the Russians was tempered by a sense of the brutality of the regime. It was an election year, with the President running for an unprecedented fourth term. Turning a much publicized defector over to his jailers would generate unfavorable publicity. FDR told Hopkins that politically, it would be easier to send him back if the Russians promised not to shoot him. Hopkins replied that once in Russian hands no one would know if he was shot or not. FDR was unmoved by this argument, and Kravchenko escaped extradition.[28]

———

One of the charms of the Venona traffic is that it goes into squalid detail regarding lapses in its spies. So many Russians had come to America that they formed a distinct subculture, with their particular habits and predicaments, so that sometimes the KGB officers were reduced to the role of therapists, giving advice to the demoralized and the lovelorn. For example, on June 19, 1943, New York announced to Moscow the arrival of three young women "probationers" posing as students, Vera Elkina, Irina Kuritsina, and Olimpiada Tronova. By May 6 of the following year, Tronova advised her KGB control that the Soviet consul general in New York, Evgeni Kiselev, who was known as "Grand-papa," wanted to marry her. She was hesitating, and her control, Anatoly Yakovlev, wondered what to do. "Knowing Olimpiada," he reported, "we think she would try to subject Grand-papa to her influence, which would have a bad effect on the staff." Kiselev was not KGB. He was an old-fashioned music lover who invited great conductors such as Toscanini and Bruno Walter to receptions at the consulate. He also happened to be married, and his wife intended to go back to Russia with their daughter at the end of the year. What was to be done? Venona does not tell us.[29]

More KGB students arrived in February 1944. One of them, Valentin Tolstikov, code-named *Rubin,* was a student at Columbia, while his attractive wife, Maria, worked in Washington for Mikhail Serov, the assistant chairman of the Purchasing Commission. On July 26, 1944, New York KGB reported to Moscow that according to *Rubin,* Serov "persistently tried to enter into intimate relations" with his wife. Here was a case of sexual harassment that had to be settled by the KGB. *Rubin* was afraid that since Serov outranked him, he might be made a scapegoat and recalled. On July 27, a message from Moscow threatened to bring all the students home if they did not cease their endless chatter and constant griping.[30]

So many agents were operating in the United States that some were bound to be troublesome. Gregory Kheifetz, the KGB resident in San Francisco, reported on December 7, 1943, that a newly arrived agent, Mikhail Kalatozov, had been put up with his wife at the home of a pro-Soviet American, Ben Goldstein. Consular employee Elena Garbunova paid a visit to the new arrivals and found Ben Goldstein in bed with Mrs. Kalatozov. Kheifetz reported that this was not an auspicious beginning for an American assignment.[31]

Perhaps the single most severe personnel crisis the KGB had to face in America was a possible murder at the New York consulate. Vasili Polyakov arrived on May 11, 1944, with his young wife, Tamara. She died on June 12, and her death was considered strange in the extreme. An autopsy produced no result, though Polyakov in a conversation with Grand-papa Kiselev let fall the following phrase: "I cannot understand why she wanted to have anything to do with me."[32] They had come by ship from Vladivostok, and apparently they had quarreled shortly after sailing and Polyakov had wanted to put her ashore at Nakhodka, a port south of Vladivostok. After her death, Polyakov said, "I don't want to go home, I want to work here." But he was sent home on July 21, 1944. No other mention of the case was made in the decrypted Venona traffic.[33]

———

Thanks to Venona, we can follow the principal KGB agents as they go on their rounds. One was Roland Abbiat, who in 1937 had murdered Ignace Reiss on a road outside Lausanne. He was now transformed into Vladimir Pravdin, the Tass correspondent based in New York. He often went to Washington, where he hobnobbed with some of the better known American journalists, such as Walter Lippmann, Ernest K. Lindley, and Joseph C. Harsch, who were happy to help out their convivial Russian colleague.

The KGB seemed to have an unlimited faith in the store of goodwill toward Russia on the part of all Americans, so much so that Pravdin proposed in a Venona message on May 26, 1943, the recruitment of Eleanor Roosevelt. "For processing of [FDR's] wife we have . . . her great friend Gertrude Pratt, wife of the well-known, wealthy Elliot Pratt . . . patroness and guide. . . . Contacts being maintained with her by Sokirkin [First Secretary at the Soviet embassy in Washington], the official representative of the Moscow Anti-Fascist Student Committee (xxxxx). Pratt displays a great interest in life in the USSR and Soviet (xxxxx)."[34]

To think that Eleanor Roosevelt could be recruited as a Soviet spy shows a remarkable lack of insight on the part of the KGB. As the President's wife, completely loyal to his administration, and under close public scrutiny, she would never have accepted any clandestine arrangement. Through her contacts with student groups, she had experienced the deviousness of the Communists. But the misguided attempt to recruit her is interesting if only because of the mention of Gertrude Pratt, who was, at the time of the Venona message, conducting an affair with Eleanor's young friend Joe Lash, whom Gertrude would later marry. Eleanor sometimes served as an intermediary in their complicated romantic life, but this hardly qualified her for recruitment by the KGB.

Pravdin also made repeated efforts to recruit the pro-Soviet Washington correspondent I. F. Stone, who wrote for *The Nation* and other left-wing journals. Stepan Apresyan, the New York KGB resident, reported on September 13, 1944, that Pravdin had tried three times to see Stone, but each time Stone declined. Stone, said Pravdin, occupied a prominent position in the journalistic world and had vast connections. On October 11, Stone was still avoiding Pravdin, but on October 23 they finally met. Pravdin told Stone how much he valued his work. He had heard many flattering things about him. Stone was now code-named *Blini*, and Pravdin asked him "if he would give us information." *Blini* said he had noticed "our attempts to contact him," Pravdin said, particularly the attempts of people at the Soviet embassy, but he had reacted negatively, saying he feared the consequences. Pravdin replied that "we did not want to subject him to unpleasant complications." *Blini* gave him to understand that he wasn't refusing his aid but one should consider that he had three children and did not want to attract the attention of the FBI. Pravdin asked him what would be the best way to maintain a liaison. *Blini* replied he would be glad to meet but seldom came to New York. "His fear is primarily explained by his unwillingness to spoil his career," Apresyan reported. "Materially he is well secured. He earns as much as 1500 dollars a month, but it seems he would not be averse to having a supplementary income. For the establishment of business contact with him we are insisting on (xxxxx) reciprocity. For the work indeed qualified (xxxxx)."

Only one more Venona message mentioned Stone, on December 23, 1944. Pravdin had discussed the Battle of the Bulge with Stone, Lippmann, and the newscaster Raymond Graham Swing. Lippmann had spoken to Secretary of War Henry Stimson, who said that if the Germans captured Liège it would take three or four months to organize the American offensive and longer to make good the stock of equipment left behind. The breakthrough to the Rhine, set for January 1945, was stalled and the Americans were counting on the Soviet offensive in Poland.[35]

The decoded Venona messages left in doubt whether Stone had actually been recruited. In 1992, Oleg Kalugin, a retired KGB general, gave a speech at Exeter University in England. Kalugin, who was stationed in Washington in the sixties, explained that after Khrushchev's speech in 1956 denouncing Stalin's crimes, it was impossible to recruit agents on ideological grounds. Then he said, "We had an agent, a well-known American journalist with a good reputation, who severed his ties with us after 1956. I myself convinced him to resume them. But in 1968, after the invasion of Czechoslovakia . . . he said he would never again take any money from us." Kalugin later named the agent as I. F. Stone, although in his memoir he denied that Stone was an agent.[36]

———

Shortly after Pearl Harbor, on December 25, 1941, a new legal resident arrived at the Soviet consulate in New York with the modest cover job of vice consul. Vasily Zubilin, whose real name was Zarubin, was married to Elizabeth Gorskaya, the femme fatale of the KGB, famed for seducing an important Trotskyite and leading him into a trap. Zubilin, born in 1894, had a long and brilliant career in the KGB behind him, having served as a legal officer in China and Finland and as an illegal in Denmark, Germany, and France. At forty-seven, he was putting on weight, but still played tennis. His thinning blond hair was combed straight back, and his bloodshot gray eyes looked out from behind steel-rimmed glasses. Energetic and willful, he handled a number of agents himself.[37]

Zubilin's arrival in New York in 1941 signaled a shift in intelligence priorities. He had seen Stalin before his departure, who told him that with America about to enter the war, he needed to know more about its intentions and the thinking of its leaders. Concerned about FBI penetration of the American party, Zubilin wanted to cut out the party middlemen and work directly with the American spies who were supplying the information.

On the West Coast, the key liaison agent was Steve Nelson (born Mesarosh in Croatia), a party member since 1925, who had been in Spain in the Lincoln Battalion and was now doing underground work in the Bay Area. Deeply involved in atomic espionage, Nelson provided ample confirmation of Zubilin's thesis that American Communist middlemen were security-lax. The FBI had bugged his house in Oakland and his office on Market Street and found out that he was receiving information from young radical physicists who were working on the atom bomb under J. Robert Oppenheimer at Berkeley's Radiation Laboratory.

One of them, twenty-one-year-old Giovanni Rossi Lomanitz, was a big geek from Oklahoma who identified with the proletariat and joined every radical group on campus. On October 10, 1942, in a bugged conversation with Nelson, Lomanitz said he was employed in research "on a very dangerous weapon." Nelson replied that he knew about the project, which was "very important to another party member [Oppenheimer], who considered this project even more important than party work." This party member, said Nelson, was called a "Red" and had worked on the Spanish Committee and other fronts. Lomanitz said he wanted to quit the project, come out as an open Communist, and work in the shipyards. Nelson told him not to irritate Oppenheimer by quitting and not to be too open in his party activities by doing things such as distributing the party paper, *People's World.* Nelson told Lomanitz that he was considered an underground member of the party and that he must not quit "this extremely important project."

Also that October, the FBI picked up a conversation between Nelson and Lloyd Lehmann, an organizer from the Young Communist League, who was friendly with Oppenheimer. Lehmann said that a very important weapon was being developed. Nelson asked him if Oppenheimer knew he was "a YCLer," adding that Oppenheimer was "too jittery." Nelson said that Oppenheimer had been active in the party but was now inactive. "He worked on the Teachers' Committee, the Spanish Committee, et cetera, and he can't cover his past," he added.[38]

In December, the FBI overheard a discussion of Oppenheimer between Nelson and his office assistant Bernadette Doyle. Nelson said that because of his work on a special project Oppenheimer could not be active in the party. Doyle replied that the matter should be taken up by the party's state committee, inasmuch as the "two Oppys" (J. Robert and his brother, Frank) were regularly registered and everyone knew they were Communist Party members.[39]

On March 29, 1943, came the break that proved to the FBI that Nelson was at the center of an espionage network. Joseph Weinberg, another young physicist working for Oppenheimer and a Communist who had joined the party while at City College, came to Nelson's house on Grove Street in Oakland. In the bugged conversation he told Nelson that he had to see him on short notice because the team working on the project was about to be relocated to a remote site. "The professor" (Oppenheimer) had already left.

"The professor," Nelson said, "is very much worried now and we make him feel very uncomfortable."

Weinberg: "You won't hardly believe the change that has taken place."

Nelson: "To my sorrow, his wife is influencing him in the wrong direction." She had been in the party when she was young, but only for a short time. Now the project was weaning him from his old friends, as he wanted to make a name for himself. Oppenheimer's wife had been married to Nelson's best friend, who had been killed in Spain. Nelson said Oppenheimer was brilliant in his field but "when he tried to teach Marx and when he tried to teach Lenin he was way off. Oppenheimer is just not a Marxist."

Nelson then asked Weinberg for some technical information. Dropping his voice to a whisper that the bug picked up only in part, Weinberg described the "separation method" of U-235 from ordinary uranium as "that of the magnetic spectrograph with electrical and magnetic focusing." Weinberg also said that a separation plant was under construction in Tennessee (Oak Ridge).[40]

This was the first hard evidence that the young scientists working under Oppenheimer were passing the secrets of the bomb to a Soviet agent, and that Oppenheimer himself might be involved. On the evening of April 6, Nelson, now under surveillance, went to the grounds of the St. Joseph Hospital in San Francisco and was observed handing over a package to Pyotr Ivanov, the third secretary of the Soviet consulate.[41]

By March 29, Oppenheimer, accompanied by his wife, Kitty, was in Los Alamos to take up his duties as the director of the Manhattan Project. As it turned out, neither Lomanitz nor Weinberg was asked to join him in New Mexico. Lomanitz was conveniently drafted and Weinberg stayed at Berkeley as a teaching assistant.[42]

It was by accident that Oppenheimer first came to the FBI's attention. In December 1940, the Berkeley professor Haakon Chevalier hosted a discussion group, which Oppenheimer attended. The FBI had Chevalier's home under surveillance because two high-level Communists were invited—William Schneiderman, the California party secretary, and Isaac "Pop" Folkoff, a Latvian émigré and the party bagman in the Bay Area. The meeting was of particular interest to the FBI, for Folkoff had been overheard saying it was to be for "the big boys." FBI agents took down the license-plate numbers of the cars parked in front of Chevalier's house, including Oppenheimer's. By order of the Justice Department, however, Oppenheimer was never bugged, though some of the others at the meeting were.

Both Oppenheimer and his younger brother, Frank, were initially drawn into the fellow-traveling world by the women in their lives. Like many liberals, Oppenheimer was anti-Franco. In 1936, he attended a benefit for the Spanish Loyalists, where he met the green-eyed beauty Jean Tatlock, a graduate student at Stanford and a party member. Theirs was a tumultuous romance where marriage was almost proposed and breakups were common. Thanks to Jean, Oppenheimer attended party functions and met party leaders, such as Rudy Lambert, the head of the California party's labor commission, and Thomas Addis, a doctor at the Stanford Medical School and a party recruiter. The half-Norwegian and half-French Haakon Chevalier, a handsome six-footer married to a department store heiress (which did not preclude party membership), became a close friend.[43]

In 1939, Jean Tatlock left California to pursue studies in psychiatry, and a year later Oppenheimer married Kathryn Pruening, who had been born and raised in Germany. Her mother was a distant cousin of Hitler's trusted field marshal, Wilhelm Keitel. When Hitler came to power, the Pruening family moved to Pittsburgh, where Kathryn's father worked as a mining engineer. In 1933, Kitty married Frank W. Ramseyer, but the marriage was annulled after eight months. In 1934, she married Joe Dallet, a Communist organizer in Youngstown, Ohio. Kitty joined the party, taught at the Workers School, and was dues secretary for the Youngstown section. When Dallet went to Spain in 1936, Kitty went with him as far as France, where she met Steve Nelson.

Assigned to the Lincoln Battalion, Dallet was described in an evaluation as its "most disliked Commissar. . . . His patronizing air and . . . rather obvious careerist tendencies led to the dislike." On October 13, 1937, in the battle at Fuentes de Ebro on the Aragón front, Dallet was killed when he jumped out of a trench.

In 1938, Kitty met a young British doctor, Richard Stewart Harrison, whom she married on November 23. Harrison interned at a hospital in Pasadena, and Kitty met Oppenheimer at a party in August 1939. Soon after, they began an affair, and when Kitty got pregnant she asked for a divorce. On the same day that the divorce came through in Nevada, November 1, 1940, they were married in Virginia City. Oppenheimer was her fourth husband. Their son, Peter, was born on May 12, 1941.[44]

Robert's brother, Frank, became a Communist under the influence of his fiancée, Jacquenette Quann, a Canadian-born economics major at Berkeley when he was getting his doctorate in physics at Caltech. Jackie was a member of the Young Communist League, and drew Frank into her activities. They were married in 1936, and both joined the party in 1937, against Oppenheimer's advice. Frank took the party name "Folsom" and paid dues to the Pasadena chapter.[45]

Alerted by the March 29 conversation between Nelson and Weinberg, the FBI placed Nelson's house under round-the-clock surveillance. On April 10, 1943, a burly figure appeared at his door, calling himself "Cooper." It was the New York–based KGB resident Vasily Zubilin, who, though intent on tightening security, was committing a serious breach. For more than an hour they discussed the Soviet espionage apparatus in America. Their entire conversation was recorded by the FBI. Nelson complained that the Soviets in San Francisco were approaching potential spies directly without going through him. He wanted to maintain the middleman system. At one point, Zubilin handed over some cash to Nelson, and when he counted out the bills, Nelson said, "Jesus, you count money like a banker." "Vell," Zubilin replied, "after all, I used to do it in Moscow." As a result of the meeting, Zubilin was now known to the FBI.[46]

On June 12, 1943, Oppenheimer returned to Berkeley, ostensibly to recruit a personal assistant but in reality to see his old flame Jean Tatlock, who was being treated for depression at San Francisco's Mount Zion Hospital. On June 14, they had dinner at the Xochimilco Café on Broadway and afterward Oppenheimer spent the night at her apartment on Montgomery Street. He never saw her again. Jean Tatlock committed suicide in January 1944.[47]

Even though Oppenheimer had aroused the suspicion of the FBI and military intelligence with his hiring of Communist physicists and his party connections, General Leslie Groves, the military director of the Manhattan Project, issued a security clearance on July 20, 1943. As Groves put it, Oppenheimer was "absolutely essential to the project."[48]

John Lansdale, an Army Intelligence officer who worked for Groves, came to Los Alamos in early August and had a talk with Oppenheimer, who said he didn't want any Communists on the project because of their "divided loyalties." Either out of loyalty or ambition, or a combination of both, Oppenheimer's position on hiring Communists had changed. It was Lansdale's feeling that Oppenheimer's complete dedication to this momentous undertaking would not allow him to compromise its success.[49] Now that Oppenheimer was, as he put it, "inside the wire," security was tight, and he was bugged by the FBI. On August 25, back at Berkeley, he talked to an unknown man who said, "I think we should stay with the British and we will have North and South America, Africa and the Pacific with our fleet. That will leave Russia free but they can take over China."

"Yes," Oppenheimer replied, "but you have to remove that fear; that is their greatest drawback. If we remove that and the people understand Russia, Russia will not be militaristic."

"Yes," the other man said, "but here we have this weapon and while we can now force our demands and keep peace, science teaches us that Russia, within twenty-five years, or even maybe five, will also perfect defenses and weapons of their own."

"If Russia could be understood by other nations," Oppenheimer replied, "they would narrow to a nationalistic economy and we could work with them."

"Don't misunderstand me," the other man said, "I know under the Czar, people had nothing and that this new regime with its restraints on liberty is still a big step for the average person, but we don't want any part of their system."

"There is a hell of a lot we need of it," Oppenheimer replied, "and a hell of a lot we don't want."[50]

Oppenheimer's evident sympathy for Russia, a holdover from his gullible fellow-traveling days, did not, however, imply that he was willing to spy for them, as he explained in another bugged conversation in Berkeley on August 26. Although he felt that "the information about what we're doing is probably of no use because it is so damned complicated," he did not think the tight security was unwarranted. "If one means by the security problem, preventing information of technical use to another country from ecaping," he said, "I don't think it would have any effect on Russia [but] it might have a very big effect on Germany, and I am as convinced about that as everyone else is."[51] It was the Russians, however, and not the Germans, who were able to penetrate Los Alamos and steal the secrets of the bomb. The most brilliant scientist could also be the most politically naive.

Oppenheimer had returned to Berkeley on August 23 to do some more recruiting for Los Alamos. On August 26, he agreed to see the head of Military Intelligence in the Bay Area, Colonel Boris Pash. Ardently anti-Communist, Pash was the San Francisco–born son of a Russian Orthodox bishop and had gone to Russia as a young man to fight in the civil war.

Oppenheimer told Pash an intricate but distressingly vague story. Several months earlier, he said, a man who was attached to the Soviet consulate had indicated via intermediaries that he was in a position to transmit without danger of leak or scandal any information that Oppenheimer might supply. Although the procedure was explained as a way of making up for the difficulties in official communications, and although Russia was battling for her life and needed to have an idea of what was going on, Oppenheimer realized that giving information would amount to treason. He himself was comfortable with the President informing the Russians, but he did not like the idea of doing it through the back door. He felt strongly that any association with the Communist movement was not compatible with the job of a secret war project. The two loyalties just could not go together.

Prodded by Pash, Oppenheimer revealed that one of the intermediaries was the British-born chemical engineer George Eltenton, who worked at the Shell Development Company Lab in nearby San Francisco. Another was a friend on the Berkeley faculty whom he did not wish to name. Oppenheimer told Pash that Eltenton should be watched, for "he might be acting in a way dangerous to the country."[52]

Eltenton, who had spent several years as a senior physicist at the Leningrad Institute of Chemical Physics, was a true believer in the Communist cause. When the KGB resident and vice consul Gregory Kheifetz approached him in 1942 in California, he was ripe for recruitment. Later that year, it was the third secretary, Ivanov, who asked Eltenton if he knew Oppenheimer or any of the scientists at the Radiation Lab. Eltenton proposed having Oppenheimer's friend Haakon Chevalier approach him. Chevalier told Eltenton that there was no chance of obtaining any data from Oppenheimer. Now that Oppenheimer had named him, Eltenton came under surveillance.[53]

Pash sent the transcript of his forty-five-minute interview to Groves. Disturbed by Oppenheimer's evasions, he wired Groves that it was "essential that the name of professor be made available in order that investigation can continue properly."[54]

In September, when they took the same train to Washington, Oppenheimer told Groves: "I, Julius Robert, am not a Communist but I have probably belonged to every Communist front organization on the West Coast." There the matter of the unnamed intermediary rested until December 14, when Groves asked Oppenheimer to come to his office in the Los Alamos lab and ordered him to divulge the identity of the Berkeley professor. Oppenheimer named Haakon Chevalier, whom he said approached his brother, Frank, about passing secrets to the Russians. When Frank came to him for advice, Oppie told him to have nothing to do with the plan. Groves wondered whether Oppenheimer was using Frank as a red herring, and decided to inform the FBI that Haakon Chevalier had tried to recruit Oppenheimer as a spy for the Soviets. Chevalier had moved to New York to try to get a job with a wartime agency. FBI agents shadowed him and did a black bag job on his hotel room.[55]

———

In June 1943, Zubilin moved to the Washington embassy as third secretary and KGB station chief. Having been in the KGB for more than twenty years, he had the abrasiveness of the old soldier. Coarse and insulting with his staff, he drew the ire of his KGB subordinate, Vasili Mironov, who reported to Moscow that "his crudeness, general lack of manners, use of street language and obscenities, carelessness in his work and repugnant secretiveness" showed that he and his "dreadful wife" should be recalled.

Mironov went further, sending an anonymous letter typed in Russian to J. Edgar Hoover on August 7, 1943. The letter identified Zubilin as the KGB resident and named a dozen other KGB agents. In addition, the letter said that Zubilin had been involved in the Katyn Forest massacre of Polish officers, near Smolensk. The officers had been captured in eastern Poland in 1939 and moved into Russian camps. Specifically, Mironov charged that in Kozelsk, one of the camps where the Poles were detained, "Zubilin interrogated and shot Poles."[56]

Only months before, when they overran the Smolensk area, the Nazis had found the mass graves at Katyn and released the information in April 1943. The Soviets blamed the massacre on the Nazis. We now know that on March 4, 1940, Stalin ordered the KGB to shoot 14,700 Polish prisoners of war. We also know that Zubilin was sent to the Kozelsk camp in October 1939 to interrogate Polish officers and perhaps recruit some for Soviet intelligence. A survivor of Kozelsk, Professor Stanislaw Swianiewicz, recalled that "the picture of that suave, educated, and well-mannered general is still vivid among the few survivors. . . . It is hard to tell whether he should be regarded by Poles as an enemy or as a friend." The affable KGB officer loaned books to the prisoners he took an interest in and invited them to tea. His work was over at Kozelsk by early February 1940 and Zubilin was back in Moscow when in April and May, almost fifteen thousand Poles were moved to the Katyn Forest and shot into ditches. Zubilin was part of the selection process. He admitted as much in a Venona message to Moscow on July 1, 1943: "The real reasons for surveillance of me, I think [are that] the competitors [FBI] have found out about my having been at Kozelsk." The real reason was his visit to Steve Nelson, since Mironov did not write his letter until August.[57]

The FBI did not know what to make of the anonymous letter, which was not corroborated until years later, when they had access to the decoded Venona cables. Pavel Sudoplatov, a senior KGB officer and the author of *Special Tasks*, wrote that "Mironov's letter caused Zarubin's [Zubilin] recall to Moscow." After an investigation, "Mironov was arrested on charges of slander, but when he was put on trial, it was discovered that he was schizophrenic. He was hospitalized and discharged from the service." In fact, Mironov was sentenced to five years in a labor camp. When he was caught trying to smuggle out a letter about Katyn to the U.S. ambassador, he was shot.[58]

———

In September 1941, a familiar face resurfaced in New York on a forged passport—Iskhak Akhmerov, the tall, thick-lipped, wavy-haired agent with the high cheekbones and deep-set eyes who had handled Lawrence Duggan and Noel Field. His wife, Helen Lowry, Earl Browder's niece, was with him. As the illegal *Rezident*, he dealt with only the most important agents. If caught, no connection could be made with the Soviet diplomatic mission. His cover was a clothing and fur shop in Baltimore, to which he moved in 1944. In the domestic bliss of Baltimore, Helen Akhmerov gave birth to two children in rapid succession, a daughter in June 1944 and a son in March 1945.[59]

Akhmerov had been brought over to implement the new policy of taking over from the American middlemen the apparats they had formed. He was a busy fellow, forwarding 59 rolls of microfilm to Moscow in 1942, 211 rolls in 1943, 600 in 1944, and 1,896 in 1945. For his fine work, he was named "Honored Chekist" and awarded the Order of the Red Banner.[60]

Akhmerov first turned to a network run by a Russian-born American, Jacob Golos, a curious little rabbit-faced man with reddish hair and a pronounced overbite. Born Jacob Raisen in 1890, he arrived in the United States in 1910, joined the Communist Party at its founding in 1919, and worked as an organizer in Detroit and Chicago. From 1926 until 1930 he was in Moscow for special training and changed his name to Golos, which means *voice* in Russian.

Jacob Golos was put in charge of World Tourists, a party-owned travel agency in New York that sold Intourist services for visitors to Russia. On the side, he was involved in the passport racket. World Tourist actually turned a profit during the Spanish Civil War, when it provided travel documents and made travel arrangements for American volunteers.[61]

Golos had a wife and son, whom he sent back to Russia in 1936. This left him free to live the bachelor life, and in 1938 he met a native-born American Communist, Elizabeth Terrill Bentley. Later dubbed "the blonde spy queen" by the press, Liz Bentley was in fact a rather homely brunette, with a high brow, a long nose, a weak chin, and disorderly hair. But she possessed a lively personality and a romantic nature.

Bentley was born in 1908 in Milford, Connecticut, to strict parents. Her father, who ran a dry goods store, was strong on temperance. Her mother, who traced her ancestry back to a signer of the Declaration of Independence, Roger Sherman, lectured her on the maidenly virtues. Liz ignored parental advice, becoming a hard drinker and a woman of many lovers. In 1926, she went to Vassar on a scholarship and took the theater classes of Hallie Flanagan, who extolled Russia as the builder of a new society. After graduation, she taught briefly at Foxcroft, did graduate work at Columbia, then won a fellowship to attend the University of Florence. It was in Italy that she cut loose. An American fellow student recalled that at a New Year's party she was "so damned drunk she didn't know where she was" and challenged another woman to "pull down your pants and have your partner take you right on the floor." In 1934, when she presented her thesis, several fellow students later said that her faculty adviser, Mario Caselli, who had become her lover, wrote it for her.[62]

Back in New York that year, she was a confirmed anti-fascist and joined the Communist Party, becoming agitprop director of the Harlem section, and then of the Columbia University section. She signed the membership card of Clarence Hiskey, later a minor atom spy.

With her knowledge of Italian, Liz found a job in 1938 at the Italian Government Library in New York. In October, as she recalled, she met a shabby little man wearing a battered hat, Jacob Golos, who asked her to pass information on Italian fascist activities. She was soon fired, however, when the Italians learned that she had written an anti-fascist article for the *Columbia Spectator*. In 1939, with the purges having eliminated so many Russian intelligence officers, Gaik Ovakimian asked Golos to establish an agent network. Golos chose Bentley to be his assistant. He was in poor health, short of breath, suffering from chest pains, a candidate for a heart attack. His reddish hair was turning gray and his blue eyes were lifeless. This did not stop him from wooing Liz, who was eighteen years younger, and who recalled that he seduced her during a snowstorm, and that she felt herself "float away into an ecstasy that seemed to have no beginning and no end."[63]

In the 1944 profile Bentley wrote for the KGB, she said: "In addition to a strong physical attraction . . . a strong feeling of camaraderie . . . I admired him as the best kind of revolutionary." Golos trained her like a soldier at the front, she said, and sustained her in moments of disappointment. He loved her and wanted to be proud of her. Violating the rules of tradecraft, they lived together. He told Bentley that he had a wife in Russia, but that it was an arranged marriage.[64]

In 1939, Golos was arrested for failing to register as a foreign agent. At his trial, he accepted a plea bargain to a lesser charge and was sentenced to four to twelve months' probation and a $1,000 fine. Golos told Bentley that the worst thing that had ever happened to him was "to plead guilty at a bourgeois trial." He was now under surveillance, at a time when his underground work was growing, so that he delegated the handling of agents increasingly to her.[65]

In 1942, Bentley began going to Washington to see the agent Mary Price, who was Walter Lippmann's secretary. Price, an attractive young woman, tall and slender with long chestnut hair and a steady gaze, was a Communist from North Carolina. She looted Lippmann's files, passing on to Bentley material that was not in his columns, such as his schedules and sources and the texts of his interviews. Bentley stayed at Mary Price's house on Olive Avenue, and later at her apartment on I Street, and they copied the files, which she brought back to Golos.

Mary Price told Bentley that she had a source who was high up in the Office of Strategic Services. In January 1943, bedridden with viral pneumonia, Price asked Bentley to fill in for her. The source was Duncan Chapin Lee, born in Nanking of missionary parents in 1913. Lee lived in China until he was twelve, then moved to America, graduating first in his Yale class of 1935. At Oxford as a Rhodes scholar, he met and married a redheaded, left-wing Scot named Ishbel Gibb. They honeymooned in Moscow. Back in New Haven at Yale Law School, he was reported to the FBI by a neighbor in 1939 as a reader of Communist literature. He joined the law firm of Donovan, Leisure, Newton, and Lumbard, and followed his boss, William J. Donovan, into the OSS in 1942, becoming his aide. Lee also served as the legal adviser for Russian War Relief and was on the executive board of China Aid Council, a front headed by Mary Price's sister Mildred, a secret Communist.[66]

By September 1943, Duncan Lee was in Golos's apparat. On September 8, Golos told Moscow that he "works on issues of guerrilla movements, sabotage, and 'commandos'. . . . Cables coming to the State Department go through his hands. . . . All the agent information from Europe and the rest of the world also comes through his hands. He joined the party at Yale University in 1939; his wife joined the party at the same time. . . . Lee wants to work with us and pass us information . . . but can bring no documents out of his department . . . but will make notes and pass them to . . . Mary Price."[67]

When Bentley went to Lee's apartment on Dent Street to pick up his information, she found him rather fearful and reticent. One time he was on his hands and knees looking for taps on his phone line. In September 1943, he was sent on a hazardous mission to Burma to check on an OSS sabotage team. He had to bail out of his damaged plane and spent several weeks in the Burmese jungle waiting to be rescued. At the end of October, he was back in Washington. The New York station told Moscow that his "wanderings in Burma's jungles frayed him very much, and one will need some time to draw him back into active work with us."[68]

Duncan Lee's coup, in a Venona message on March 3, 1944, was to predict the D-Day landing in Normandy. He cannily guessed that the transfers of high-ranking generals indicated that "the second front will be opened between mid-May and the beginning of June."

By now, Golos's health was deteriorating. At fifty-three, he was edgy and tired. His favorite phrase was "the only peace is in the grave." On November 25, 1943, Thanksgiving Day, he and Bentley had lunch at London Terrace, then went back to their apartment, where Golos slumped in an armchair, coughed, and stopped breathing. The International Workers Order, which had its own undertakers, handled the funeral. He was buried in Long Island, next to Misha Olgin, the editor of the Communist Yiddish-language newspaper the *Freiheit*. On November 27, the *Daily Worker* ran an obituary: "One of the most notable pioneers in promoting Soviet-American friendship, Jacob N. Golos, died suddenly from a heart attack."

Bentley was devastated. Her loyalty was not so much to Moscow or to the American party as it was to Golos. After five years together, she was utterly devoted to him. In addition, she was so overworked with the agents she was running that she felt like a Stakhanovite, (a Soviet worker rewarded for his zeal). In the OSS alone, besides Duncan Lee, Bentley was running several other agents, such as Donald Wheeler, a party member in the Labor Division. The most important was Maurice Halperin, the head of the Latin American desk and a secret Communist. Halperin, whose parents had come to America from the Ukraine, had unlimited access to the OSS cable traffic. His division brazenly followed the party line, calling for an invasion of pro-Nazi Argentina, stating that the nationalist party in Bolivia was pro-Nazi, and denouncing Trotskyite activities in Mexico. Halperin kept the *Daily Worker* on his desk and no one seemed to mind. He said of "Wild Bill" Donovan, who had recruited a sizable percentage of Communists into the OSS among the Ivy Leaguers: "He was the kind of guy who could ride on two horses, one leg on one horse, the other leg on the other horse, and the horses going at different speeds, and he'd stay on both horses."[69]

When the OSS was broken up in 1945, Halperin moved to the State Department but he resigned in 1946 and became head of the Latin American program at Boston University. On November 17, 1953, Attorney General Herbert Brownell released an FBI report naming Halperin as a Soviet spy. He fled to Mexico, the start of a bizarre odyssey that took him to Russia for five years. His punishment was to be forced to live in the Socialist paradise he so admired. In Moscow he and his wife had to share an apartment with four other families. Everywhere he found misery, filth, and shoddy workmanship. Moving to Cuba, he soon tired of a regime built on exaltation and oppressiveness and left for British Columbia, where he found a teaching job.[70]

—

Mary Price was in a shaky state, having embarked upon an affair with Duncan Lee. His wife found out and made jealous scenes. Price told Liz Bentley that she could not continue as Lee's courier. Stressed out, she wanted to quit the spy business. "I want to live like a human being," she said. In an effort to help her, Bentley enlisted the support of Earl Browder, which Akhmerov saw as interference. On July 28, 1944, the New York KGB reported to Moscow on this tug-of-war over Mary Price: "Some weeks ago Bentley told Akhmerov that Browder as a result of a conversation with Mary Price had decided that Price must be withdrawn from our work. . . . In Browder's opinion Price's nerves have been badly shaken and her health is poor. . . . Akhmerov suspects pressure from Bentley who for some reason dislikes Price." Browder had the last word. Since he was the source of agents, he could also have them removed from the service.[71] Mary Price retired, moved back to North Carolina, and ran for governor on the Progressive Party ticket in 1948.

Duncan Lee continued to see Bentley. In September 1944, he advised that a list of "Reds" in the ranks of the OSS had been compiled. The list contained the names of four agents who were supplying information to the Russians. One of the names was Maurice Halperin. An instruction went out in a Venona message from Moscow on September 20: "Try through Duncan Lee to obtain [list of Reds]. . . . Tell Bentley temporarily to cease liaison with Donald Wheeler and Maurice Halperin. Give Duncan Lee the task of compiling a report on the Security Division of OSS."

Bentley put Halperin and Wheeler on ice but not Duncan Lee, who in October 1944 was named chief of the Japanese section of the OSS. She found him increasingly difficult, and wrote Moscow in late 1944 that he now had access only to reports on Japan, which he said were of no interest. Bentley wrote that he needed "special guidance—he is one of the weakest of the weak sisters, nervous and fearing his own shadow."[72] In April 1945, Moscow placed Duncan Lee "on conservation."

—

Liz Bentley also ran the Silvermaster ring, one of the most productive of the war. Shortly after the Nazi invasion of Russia in June 1941, Nathan Gregory Silvermaster, director of the Labor Division in the Farm Security Administration, contacted Earl Browder to tell him that he and a group of like-minded federal employees wanted to help the Soviet Union. Browder told Silvermaster to contact Golos, and it was this group that Elizabeth Bentley began handling in 1942, along with Mary Price and the OSS people.[73]

Silvermaster, a slight man who suffered from asthma and carried an atomizer, had a record as a Communist that went back to 1922. In 1942, he was detailed to the Board of Economic Warfare, which handled a great deal of classified war information. As Bentley put it, "whoever we had as an agent in the government would automatically serve for putting someone else in."[74]

Silvermaster was transferred to a sensitive war agency in spite of a long and notorious record as a Communist. "The overwhelming testimony from the many and varied witnesses," said a 1942 Civil Service Commission report, "indicate beyond reasonable doubt that Nathan Gregory Silvermaster is now, and has for years been, a member and a leader of the Communist party and very probably a secret agent of the OGPU." The CSC recommended that he be declared ineligible as head economist of the Board of Economic Warfare and debarred for the duration from government work.[75]

General George V. Strong, the head of G-2, wrote a letter to Silvermaster's boss, William T. Stone, pointing out that the FBI had material proving his disloyalty and asking that he be removed.

In an impassioned response, Silvermaster wrote Stone that he felt compelled to comment on the "very astonishing document concerning myself which was prepared for Gen. Strong. . . . The principal charge against me is that I was and presumably am now a Communist. This I deny categorically. . . . I have been smeared for promoting migratory labor camps."[76]

Two other high-ranking government officials weighed in to defend him: Calvin B. "Beanie" Baldwin, head of the Farm Security Administration, himself a secret Communist, and Harry Dexter White, assistant to the Secretary of the Treasury, who was a member of the Silvermaster ring. White told Acting Secretary of War Robert Patterson that Silvermaster was a loyal American.

Swayed by these men of high rank and supposed integrity, Patterson caved in. On July 3, 1942, he wrote Milo Perkins, the head of the Board of Economic Warfare, that "I am fully satisfied that the facts do not show anything derogatory to Mr. Silvermaster's character or loyalty."[77]

Of the ten or so members of the Silvermaster ring, five came from the Monetary Research Division of the Treasury Department, which had a small staff but a clubby atmosphere, where the spies hired each other, promoted each other, and wrote admiring reports about each other. One of these was William Ullmann, a colorless young man from an affluent Missouri family who shared a house with the Silvermasters off Chevy Chase Circle. Helen, Silvermaster's wife, a wiry, nervous woman who wore her dark hair tied in a knot at the back of her neck, was the daughter of Baron Peter Witte, the palace liberal in the last Czar's entourage. As Akhmerov reported to Moscow on March 15, 1944, the Silvermasters and Ullmann were sharing more than a house. Concerned about the "unhealthy relations," Akhmerov described Silvermaster as "exceptionally self-willed, stubborn, confident of his superiority over all others and behaving . . . as a dictator or fuhrer." But since he was a productive dictator, Akhmerov overlooked his arrogance and unconventional personal life.[78]

Bentley testified that she visited the Silvermasters every two weeks and sometimes spent the night. Documents borrowed from government departments were photographed in the basement, where Silvermaster had a Contax camera held in place with the lens pointing down, and a rack to hold the documents.[79]

As Bentley explained it, the real success of the Silvermaster ring came after Harry Dexter White convinced Morgenthau, the Secretary of the Treasury, to initiate an exchange of documents with other departments. "He would send information to Navy and Navy would reciprocate," Bentley said. "At least seven or eight agencies were trading information with Secretary Morgenthau . . . this plan was initiated by White because he knew the information would come across his desk." The exchange accounted for the quantity and variety of the material Silvermaster collected.[80]

On July 31, 1941, as the Germans pushed across Russia, Silvermaster reported that at a cabinet meeting, Secretary of the Navy Frank Knox had bet Morgenthau that the Germans would capture Moscow and Leningrad within a month. By May of the following year, he was reporting U.S. plane production week by week.

In a single month, October 1944, Silvermaster handed over fifty-six rolls of film. These included:

- A memo to FDR on lend-lease for the French.
- A report on the situation in Italy.
- A report on German assets in Spain.
- Instructions on the dissolution of the Nazi Party in Germany.[81]

—

After Golos's death in November 1943, Akhmerov was under instructions to take over the Silvermaster group from Bentley. Such an important source could not be left in the hands of an unsupervised American novice. Golos himself had been sloppy, but without him things could only get worse.

But Bentley was not going to give up her agents without a fight. She had developed a pride in her work and congenial relations with her spies and now these bumptious Russians were horning in.

When Akhmerov told her that he wanted to make direct contact with Silvermaster, she raised objections. In an April 29, 1944, Venona message to Moscow, Akhmerov described her reaction: "*Clever Girl* [Bentley] reported that . . . even Golos did not meet Silvermaster more than once in six months. . . . Possibly she is making this up and exaggerating. . . . She expressed an unreasoning fear that we will contact them directly."[82]

On June 25, 1944, Akhmerov reported that "now she tells me that . . . she doesn't have any other interests besides her work . . . and her life will lose its meaning without this work." Acting as a KGB "Miss Lonelyhearts," Akhmerov proposed a solution to her mood swings: "She is alone in her personal life. . . . If I could I would give her in marriage to one of our operatives . . . [or] why not send somebody from home? Send him as a Polish or Baltic refugee to South America or Canada. . . . It will bring her great happiness . . . as for our operative . . . he must be 35–45 years old, single."[83]

Over Bentley's objections, Akhmerov met Silvermaster in July 1944 at the Longchamps restaurant in New York at 34th and Fifth. When Bentley heard that Browder had told the Russians they could have Greg [Silvermaster] and his group, she confronted him. "Don't be naive," he told her. "You know that when the cards are down, I have to take my orders from them." Bentley was in shock. She felt betrayed. She now saw Browder as a conniver, a cheap and tawdry figure. KGB New York advised Moscow on July 11, 1944, that "Bentley has very much taken to heart the fact of Akhmerov's direct contact with Silvermaster, evidently supposing that we do not trust her. She is offended by Browder's consenting to our liaison with Silvermaster."[84]

As a consolation prize, Browder asked Bentley to handle a separate group of government officials, known as the Perlo group. Golos had first contacted them in 1943, but after his death, they were left adrift, due to the shortage of agents. In March 1944, Bentley was told to go to John Abt's apartment on Central Park West, where she met the core members. Victor Perlo, like Abt a veteran of the Ware group of the thirties, was now a senior economist at the War Production Board. Two others were also with the WPB, Harry Magdoff and Ed Fitzgerald. The fifth, Charles Kramer, worked for Senator Harley Kilgore's subcommittee on war mobilization. As Bentley later told the FBI, Perlo declared he would be able to supply statistical data in the aircraft field. As they discussed logistics, Perlo broke in to ask: "Is Joe [Stalin] getting the stuff safely?" Bentley thought he was a bull in a china shop. Abt, then the lawyer for Sidney Hillman's Amalgamated Clothing Workers Union, dropped out of the group.[85]

Information from the Perlo group began to arrive in July 1944. "Some months ago you wrote me to stop the connection with Perlo for a while,"

Akhmerov cabled Moscow on September 17, 1944, "because his ex-wife threatened in a letter to compromise him. I cannot afford to cease the connection. . . . It will be next to impossible to organize the group's work . . . without his active help. . . . He settles everything. . . . He is the most active in the group."[86] Yet he did tell Bentley to put Perlo on ice for a while, adding: "He will be very upset by it. He is a hypochondriac and a very nervous man. . . . We should not mention that we are doing this because of his ex-wife."[87] After a bitter divorce, a distressed Katherine Perlo had sent an unsigned letter in April 1944 to FDR, identifying the members of the Perlo group. The letter was given to the FBI, who traced it back to her and interviewed her.

By the fall of 1944, Anatoli Gromov had replaced Zubilin as legal KGB *Rezident* in Washington. Gromov wanted to get Bentley out of agent work entirely. To placate her, she was awarded the Order of the Red Star in November. She could now ride on the Moscow streetcars for free. Gromov did not have the actual medal, but he showed her a photograph of it. Bentley told Gromov he reminded her of Golos. It was difficult for a young and lonely woman to be without a man, she said. She was thinking more and more about having a family. Gromov cabled Moscow that it was urgent to find a husband for her.[88]

In December, Gromov had a showdown with Bentley. "We have at last decided what to do about all the contacts that Golos handled," he told her. "You cannot, obviously, continue to handle them; the set-up is too full of holes and therefore too dangerous. I'm afraid our friend Golos was not too cautious a man, and there is the risk that you, because of your connection with him, may endanger the apparatus. You will therefore turn them over to us; we will look into their backgrounds thoroughly and decide which ones we will keep."

"A wave of revulsion and nausea swept over me and I thought for a moment I was going to be violently ill," Bentley recalled.[89]

When Gromov saw her on September 27, 1945, she was half-drunk and barely rational. Gromov reported that the only remedy was to get rid of her, but wondered how to go about it. Accident? Suicide? A slow-acting poison in her food?[90]

Bentley was in turmoil. The Russians had badly misunderstood her nature. She had remained in the service partly out of loyalty to Golos and partly because the work gave her a sense of accomplishment. She resented it deeply when the Russians eased her out.

On a hot day in August 1945, Elizabeth Bentley went to the New Haven office of the FBI on Old Lyme Street and asked to see the agent in charge. It took some time for the bureau to respond, and it was not until October 17 that she was summoned to the New York office. She was assigned to Thomas Donegan of the Major Case Squad, a small, tightly wound agent known as "The Hat" for his habit of keeping his fedora on in the office. Bentley talked for eight hours and gave 150 names, about 40 of them government employees. She reviewed her 112-page statement, initialing every page.[91]

The FBI, which had bungled the Chambers case, was now handed by pure chance detailed information on highly placed government servants who were betraying their country. This time Hoover wasted no time. FDR had died in April. Hoover alerted the Truman White House on November 8, 1945, in a memo sent "by special messenger" to General Harry Hawkins Vaughan, military aide to the President: "A number of persons employed by the government of the United States have been furnishing data and information to persons outside the federal government who are in turn transmitting this information to espionage agents of the Soviet government. . . . The government documents were furnished to Gregory Silvermaster," the memo went on, "who thereafter photographed them and turned over the undeveloped film to a contact of the Soviets."[92]

By the time of her September 27 meeting with Gromov, at which she showed up tipsy, Bentley had already been to the New Haven FBI in August, which helps explain her agitated state. The FBI asked her to string Gromov along. Gromov in the meantime was told by Moscow to give Liz some money to build up her morale, while reducing her involvement in secret work. When Bentley saw Gromov on October 29, he gave her $2,000, which she turned over to the FBI, saying, "Here's some Moscow gold." A final meeting took place on November 21 at a New York restaurant, for upon leaving the restaurant, Gromov realized he was being followed by three men in a car and ducked into a subway station.[93]

———

Bentley's defection did more than all the wartime FBI operations to shut down the Russian espionage machine. Orders came from Moscow to destroy any remaining documents. Meetings with agents were called off. The Silvermaster and Perlo rings stopped functioning. Pravdin, Akhmerov, and Gromov were called home. Although only a courier, Elizabeth Bentley single-handedly paralyzed the Soviet spy rings. Or rather, *because* she was a courier: the one person who knew the spies at both ends.

In terms of prosecuting the spies, however, the FBI was frustrated by the requirements of the American justice system. All they had was the testimony of an admitted ex-spy, whose credentials were vulnerable to cross-examination. No stolen documents or other physical evidence could be produced.[94]

Bentley did not have any corroboration for her allegations. The Venona messages that concerned her had not yet been decoded, and even when they were, they were not released to the public. Bentley was thus vulnerable to attacks that she was a fraud and a fabulator. She testified in some detail before a number of congressional committees and was confronted with some of the agents she had named. In retrospect, now that we have the Venona material, the confrontation with Duncan Lee best illustrates the "neurotic spinster" defense that was adopted to discredit her. On August 10, 1948, Bentley and Duncan Lee both testified before HUAC. She told the story of his recruitment and their meeting. "He knew all along I was a Communist," she said, adding that she collected the couple's party dues and that his wife had asked her point-blank in the summer of 1944 whether the information was going to Russia.[95]

Duncan Lee said he knew Bentley as Helen Grant, having met her at the home of a good friend, Mary Price. He and his wife liked her at first, but "we came to the conclusion that she was a lonely and neurotic woman, that she was frustrated, that her apparent ardent liking for us was unnaturally intense. We began to feel she was an emotional weight around our necks.... As we got to know her better, her views became increasingly left-wing and intemperate and extreme.... She became a personal nuisance.... One evening she called on us and I put it to her quite bluntly that we thought we should not see her anymore." This was around October 1943. "Her reaction was quite violent. She cried, she protested that we meant a great deal to her. She was intensely fond of us and had to go on seeing us and she did carry on for about half an hour." To get her out of the house they agreed to see her in public places, "so we met her a few times in drug stores."[96]

This tissue of lies could not be refuted until the Venona messages revealed that Duncan Lee passed classified information to Bentley from 1943 to 1945, and that he betrayed his country's secrets to the Soviet Union. Lee was never prosecuted. He left for Europe shortly after testifying. Though Bentley was not without her faults, everything she told the committee was confirmed by Venona. When her book, *Out of Bondage,* was published in 1951, it got some rough treatment by reviewers. The columnist Joseph Alsop wrote in *Commonweal* that "this is a book . . . that exudes the smell of phoniness from its title page, which does not tell you who did the actual writing, to its macabre conclusion." But columnists are seldom held accountable for their derogations.

Bentley's revelations did lead to a number of loyalty investigations among the eighty government employees she had named. William Ullmann, who always received excellent reports from his superiors at the Treasury Department, resigned in March 1947.[97]

Perlo, also out of government work, was hired as an economist for Henry Wallace's Progressive Party. In combative testimony on August 9, 1948, he challenged "the lurid charges of the Bentley woman and of Chambers" as "inventions of irresponsible sensation seekers." He then took the Fifth on all questions, as did his cohorts Charles Kramer, who was now doing research for the Progressive Party, and George Silverman.[98]

———

Elizabeth Bentley found that her new occupation as cooperating witness was more stressful than being a courier-spy. The life of an agent was structured and unpublicized. She went to Washington, socialized with her contacts, picked up material, and brought it back to Golos. As a witness, she had been forced to testify repeatedly and publicly before half a dozen committees, and her word was always in doubt. Hostile witnesses called her a neurotic and a drunkard. In the spotlight's glare, she went through what she called "blue periods." In 1950, as she was about to testify in an espionage case, FBI agent Thomas G. Spencer warned that "Miss Bentley . . . may be bordering on some mental pitfall, which could be almost disastrous to the prosecution of the case."[99]

At this point, Miss Bentley sought comfort in the Catholic Church, receiving instruction from Monsignor Fulton J. Sheen. She was baptized and confirmed in November 1950. A year later her book was published. The sales were disappointing, but she was in demand on the lecture circuit, and in 1952 the FBI gave her back the "Moscow gold," the $2,000 from Gromov.

Bentley vacationed in Puerto Rico and the Bahamas and bought a house in Madison, Connecticut. She hired as caretaker and chauffeur the fifty-two-year-old John Wright, who had a record for assault and for breaking and entering. They formed a destructive pair, for she drank and he drank. When she was away, he charged his liquor to her account at Jolly's drugstore. On the night of April 30, 1952, he met her at the station when she came back from Washington. She got into her 1939 La Salle, saw that he was drunk, and took over the wheel. Along the way he grabbed it and she slammed on the brakes. He hit her in the face, knocking her out, and drove home. She did not press charges, but saw her doctor in New York the next day, who noted that "several teeth on the left side of her face were loosened, two of her lower teeth had gone through the lower part of her face, and the cuts on the inside of her mouth were badly infected." Bentley got rid of Wright, but on August 29, 1952, she sideswiped another car and failed to stop. On September 15, she lost control of her car, hit a boulder, and blacked out. The La Salle was totaled and Bentley was in bad shape. "Sometimes I think I should step out in front of a car and settle everything," she told a friend. Yet somehow she soldiered on for another eleven years, lonely and embittered that her testimony was still in dispute. She died of chronic alcoholism in 1963, at the age of fifty-five. In 1995, the release of the Venona messages corroborated every statement she had made and every name on her list, aside from a few minor glitches.[100]

———

Bentley should have been applauded, for aside from exposing the OSS, Silvermaster, and Perlo rings, she made public the identities of two spies so highly placed in government service that they acted less as filchers of documents than as agents of influence.

On April 6, 1954, Bentley testified before the Senate Subcommittee on Internal Security, which was holding hearings on interlocking subversion in government departments. Senator Homer Ferguson of Michigan asked her: "What were your avenues for placing people in strategic positions?"

Bentley: "I would say that two of our best ones were Harry Dexter White and [White House aide] Lauchlin Currie. They had an immense amount of influence and knew people, and their word was accepted. . . . Currie was a full-fledged member of the Silvermaster group, who was used not only to bail out other members when they got into trouble, but to steal White House secrets for the Soviets."

As an administrative aide who worked directly for the President, Currie was a powerful Washington insider with access to every top official from FDR on down. Bland and understated, deferential to his superiors and nonthreatening with his equals, the Nova Scotia–born Currie was a gifted economist who became a citizen in 1934, and moved from the Treasury Department to the White House in 1939.

Currie played a key role behind the scenes in carrying out FDR's China policy and was the President's envoy there in 1941. On July 10, with Currie back from China, Secretary of the Treasury Morgenthau called him regarding a message from Chiang Kai-shek's personal emissary and brother-in-law, T. V. Soong, that needed answering. "Now the president made this amazing statement," Morgenthau said. "He says he never answers directly."

Currie was quick to explain: "This is for your own ears. I have a private code [to Soong] which I never use except at the expressed direction of the president. Anything that comes or goes in that private code—I show to [Secretary of State Cordell] Hull. I'm frankly embarrassed about it all, but she thrust it in my hands when I left [China]."

Morgenthau: "Who thrust it into your hands?"

Currie: "Madame Chiang Kai-shek. . . . I put it away and never expected to use it. You just take those things uncomfortably. . . . Through commercial cable one day arrived this long message in code."

Morgenthau: "That's what happens playing around with these Soong girls."

Currie: "I went to the president most embarrassed. . . . He treated it lightly and told me to check with Cordell . . . but I'm awfully sparing in my use of it because I don't think it's quite proper. . . . I do have a few scruples you know."

Morgenthau: "We have a song around here entitled "Sing a Soong of six . . ."

Currie: "As a personal representative of the Madame in America, I'll leave it to you."[101]

Thus, one of Currie's jobs as a presidential aide was to handle coded back-channel communications between FDR and Chiang Kai-shek.

Venona corroborated Bentley's accusation that Currie was a Soviet spy, in a message on August 10, 1943, reporting that *Page* (Currie) turned over to George Silverman a White House policy paper destined for the State Department.

On September 2, Golos reported that two FBI men had visited Currie and asked him about Silvermaster being a Communist. Currie replied that he knew Silvermaster had belonged to some front groups, but that he did not know he was a Communist.[102]

By February 15, 1945, Moscow apparently felt it was not getting its full measure from the agent whom it considered to be "the master of the establishment," and asked "whether it would be possible for us to approach *Page* direct." General Fitin, the head of KGB foreign intelligence, told the New York office on March 21 that there was a "need for closer complicity between *Robert* [Silvermaster] and *Page*," adding that "*Page* trusts *Robert*, informs him not only orally, but also by handing over documents."[103]

They thought they could get more out of their well-placed agent if they handled him directly. In June, however, two months after the death of FDR, Currie handed in his routine change-of-administration resignation.

No sooner had Bentley talked to the FBI in October 1945 than the bureau began tailing Gromov, who was officially First Secretary at the Soviet embassy in Washington. An FBI report in February 1946 noted several meetings between Gromov and Currie. In 1947, the FBI questioned Currie, who admitted seeing Gromov four times, twice after leaving government service, to discuss cultural matters. Later it was learned that Currie had also met with Gromov's predecessor, Vasily Zubilin, in August 1943—when Mironov sent his anonymous letter to the FBI charging that Zubilin "has a high level agent in the office of the White House."

The FBI did not have enough evidence to indict Currie. When he testified before HUAC on August 13, 1948, he had an answer for everything. He admitted to knowing Silverman and Silvermaster. He admitted to interceding with the Board of Economic Warfare on Silvermaster's behalf, but said it was "customary procedure" for White House aides to get in touch with cabinet members on security issues. In fact, as the freshman congressman Richard Nixon pointed out, it was highly unusual for one of the half-dozen presidential aides to intervene in a security matter. Among the committee members, only Nixon brought out how feeble Currie's explanations were. When Nixon asked him if he knew Silvermaster and Silverman were Communists, Currie said he did not. At the hearing, Currie said he was now in the import-export business. In 1950, he exported himself to Colombia, bought a cattle ranch outside Bogotá, and divorced his first wife in order to marry a Colombian woman. He became a citizen of Colombia in 1958 and died there in 1993 at the age of 93.[104]

Like Lauchlin Currie, Harry Dexter White was not a member of the Communist Party. In Chambers's words, he was of the party but not in it. Also like Currie, White held a position in government where he could influence policy. Henry Morgenthau, the Secretary of the Treasury, was energetic and decisive. He had the ear of the President, as his Hyde Park neighbor and friend. Morgenthau's leadership style was to delegate authority, and in Harry White he found a workhorse who could carry any load.

Morgenthau, however, was susceptible to flattery, and White played up to him in a sometimes fawning way. He was also a great one for meetings, at which White could count on being backed up by other Soviet agents inside Treasury, such as Harold Glasser, Frank Coe, and Solomon Adler, all in the Division of Monetary Research. White and his coterie were able to manipulate Morgenthau on a number of key issues.[105]

Harry Dexter White was born in Boston in 1892 to immigrant parents from Lithuania. His father, Isaac Weiss, was a peddler who opened a hardware business. Harry was a do-gooder, a Boy Scout, and taught at the Home for Jewish Children in Dorchester. After receiving a Ph.D. from Harvard, he taught economics before joining the New Deal. A meteoric rise in the Treasury Department made him assistant secretary in 1939. Along the way, White married the Russian-born Anne Terry and had two daughters, Joan and Ruth. Short, stocky, round-faced, mustached, his appearance did not broadcast the incisive intelligence and firmness that made him so valued to his boss, though Morgenthau himself would say that he could be rude and abrupt and that he often circumvented proper channels. But on balance, White seemed like a regular fellow, whose life revolved around work, family, chess, sports such as tennis and handball, and music. Among his papers was found a collection of *Workers Song Books* with music by Hanns Eisler and lyrics such as: "The Comintern Calls You! Raise Sickle and Banner!" White did not hide his abiding admiration for the Soviet Union.[106]

White turns up in a number of Venona messages as *Jurist*. April 29, 1944, KGB New York to Moscow: "According to *Jurist*, *Hen Harrier* [Cordell Hull] in conversation with *Channel Pilot* [Henry Wallace] touched upon giving us $5 billion loan. The idea appealed to *Channel Pilot* and he discussed it with *Captain* [FDR] who recommended he go to China, where his presence could be useful."[107]

White had proposed in a March 7, 1944, memo to Morgenthau that the Russians be given a credit of $5 billion over five years, in addition to lend-lease. The idea was dropped, but on January 3, 1945, Russia asked for $6 billion repayable over thirty years at 2.5 percent interest. A Venona message on January 18 said that White had told the KGB the Soviets could get favorable terms. White persuaded Morgenthau to sweeten the pot and ask FDR for $10 billion at 2 percent, repayable in thirty-five years. Both FDR and the State Department opposed the proposal.[108]

On August 5, 1944, White told a Soviet agent that he and Morgenthau were going to London and to Normandy. It was on this trip that the "Morgenthau Plan" to turn Germany into a pastoral state was born. According to Fred Smith, a Treasury Department aide also on the trip, on the plane to London White pulled out of his briefcase a State Department memo on German reparations that foresaw the eventual reintegration of Germany into the world economy. White observed that this meant Germany would again become the heart of industrial Europe.

On August 7, White, Smith, and Morgenthau had lunch with General Dwight D. Eisenhower in his mess tent on the grounds of Southwick House near Portsmouth. This was two months after the D-Day landing, where the Americans had taken severe losses. Ike was fuming about the Germans. "The ringleaders and SS troops should be given the death penalty," he said, "but punishment should not end there." He believed the Germans were an incurably war-loving race and that they should be given no opportunity to emerge from the war as a major European power. This fell upon receptive ears, and White began to push, in his understated way, his plan to diminish Germany. "What I think is that we should give the entire German economy a chance to settle down before we do anything about it," he said. Ike made it clear that he would like to "see things made good and hard" for the Germans. The best cure would be to "let them stew in their own juice," but "choking off natural resources would be folly."[109]

Morgenthau would later say that this conversation had sent his mind buzzing. The Hyde Park farmer believed that "people who live close to the land tend to be peace-loving by nature." Why not make Germany a nation of small farmers? As Fred Smith would recall, White hatched the plan, sold it to Morgenthau, and Ike "walked into it."[110]

On September 7, 1944, KGB New York sent Moscow a message from the British spy *Homer* (Donald Maclean) on U.S. policy in Germany: "*Nabob* [Morgenthau] proposes letting economic ruin and chaos in Germany develop without restriction in order to show the Germans that wars are unforgivable. [Assistant Secretary of War John J.] McCloy points out that such a situation would be intolerable for the army of occupation."[111]

At the Quebec conference in September 1944, Morgenthau presented his plan for "converting Germany into a country primarily agricultural and pastoral in character" before British and American leaders, including FDR and Churchill, who adopted it. But in Washington, key cabinet members rebelled. Cordell Hull told FDR that the plan was bound to lead to last-ditch German resistance that would cost thousands of American lives. Stimson wrote in his diary: "I have yet to meet a man who is not horrified at the 'Carthaginian' attitude of the Treasury. It is Semitism gone wild for vengeance and . . . will lay seeds of another war in the next generation." FDR finally agreed that "Henry pulled a boner," and distanced himself from the plan.[112]

The President died in April 1945 and Truman went to Potsdam in July to meet Stalin and Churchill to discuss the fate of postwar Germany. When Truman told him he would not be going to Potsdam, Morgenthau knew his plan was scuttled and resigned. Fred Vinson succeeded Morgenthau as Secretary of the Treasury. On October 29, 1945, Pravdin informed Moscow that "although Vinson outwardly treats him in a friendly manner, White is convinced that the question of his dismissal is a matter of weeks or months. . . . Vinson never consults him."[113] White resigned from the Treasury on April 30, 1946, to become the head of the International Monetary Fund.

———

On the day after Pearl Harbor, Morgenthau announced at his morning meeting that "to make life easier for me . . . I want to give Harry Dexter White the status of an Assistant Secretary. He will be in charge of all foreign affairs. . . . I want it in one brain and I want it in Harry White's brain." A year later, White was made Treasury representative to the OSS. More classified information came across his desk than that of any other government official, including the President. Still, White could not single-handedly shape policy. The pieces in the puzzle that he did not control also had to fall into place. Thus, he failed to push through the Soviet loan or the Morgenthau Plan. But in two other schemes that helped the Soviets and the Chinese Communists, he succeeded brilliantly.

In February 1942, Congress passed a bill to lend $500 million to Chiang

Kai-shek, who was fighting half of Japan's armies. The Chinese wanted to use $200 million to buy gold bars for shipment to China, where they could be sold to mop up the local currency, the yapi, and curb inflation. On July 27, 1943, Morgenthau wrote the Chinese Minister of Finance, H. H. Kung, that "transfers from the credits for the purchase of the gold may be made at such a time and in such amounts as are allowed by existing facilities for transportation." On September 29, however, White intervened, telling Morgenthau that "we ought to be tough with the Chinese on the question of earmarking $200 million in gold for gold sales." Apparently forgetting his written promise to Kung in July, Morgenthau gave White a blank check to stall the gold deliveries.

White's stalling continued into 1944, as he pressed his case regarding Chinese graft and profiteering. He was informed by the Treasury Department representative in China, Solomon Adler, that there was a spread between the price the Chinese bought the gold at in the United States and the price they sold it at in China. The well-connected Soong family, whose bank handled the sale, was said to be raking off the profits. On December 9, 1944, White told Morgenthau: "We have stalled as much as we have dared and have succeeded in limiting gold shipments to $26 million during the past year."

Adler, as we now know, was a member of the Silvermaster ring, who turns up in the Venona traffic, code-named *Sachs*. His reports to White were highly critical. "The reckless Chinese government's conduct of its gold sales," he cabled White on March 11, 1945, "can only be described as 'frenzied finance.' " Adler advised "a negative policy towards China. . . . We should continue to send as little as possible." In fact, as Morgenthau had noted, the shipment of $26 million in 1944 did lead to a modest reduction in inflation. But Adler, in a steady stream of reports, stressed the venality, inefficiency, and hopelessness of the government, which buttressed White's case. When Adler returned to the United States after the war, he found himself under FBI surveillance, for he had been named by Liz Bentley. In 1950, he defected to Red China, where he translated Mao Tse-tung's writings into English.

Frank Coe, director of the Division of Monetary Research, was another member of the Silvermaster ring, code-named *Peak*. He prepared a briefing paper for Morgenthau, which argued that the $26 million in gold already sent was being sold to speculators, and that Madame Chiang Kai-shek herself had bought gold worth millions. Frank Coe also ended up defecting to Red China in 1953.

On May 8, 1945, T. V. Soong, Chiang's brother-in-law and financial adviser, came to Washington and showed Morgenthau his 1943 letter promising to provide up to $200 million in gold on request. Morgenthau was mortified. He had completely forgotten the letter. He called in Coe and Adler (who was back in Washington), and told them: "You were so worried about saving face. What about my face? . . . You put me in a dishonorable position and I think it's inexcusable." White was in San Francisco for the founding conference of the United Nations. When he got back on May 10, Morgenthau told him: "All the indications are that the Chinese are really going to fight. This man comes here and gets a cold shoulder. . . . I want to loosen up and show that we can be a friend to China. . . . I told them they could have two hundred million dollars' worth of gold. . . . I'm just going to turn a somersault on this thing."

On May 16, a flustered Morgenthau summoned White, Coe, and Adler, and said: "You boys have been telling me right along that Soong owns most of the stuff [the gold] and that's misleading." He was starting to have doubts about the integrity of his aides. He signed a letter to Soong authorizing a first shipment of $20 million, with the remaining $180 million to follow in three monthly installments of $60 million in May, June, and July 1945.

By the time the last shipment arrived, the end of the war was months away. Chiang Kai-shek had begun his long slide and White's embargo on the gold gave him the extra push. Certainly Coe and Adler were right about corruption in the nationalist government, but to insist on it single-mindedly in the middle of a war, with the Japanese occupying much of China, was like worrying that the lawn needs mowing when the house is on fire. A positive attitude on the part of the Treasury might have improved the Chinese economy and rekindled Chiang's fighting spirit. By 1946, the civil war with the Chinese Communists was raging. In 1949, Chiang was ousted and Mao Tse-tung declared a People's Republic of China. Failure to receive the loan in time was only part of the cause of Chiang Kai-shek's downfall, but it counted.[114]

In 1945, the Allies divided Germany into four zones, each with its own occupation currency—French, British, Russian, and American. The Treasury Department prepared to print up to 10 billion occupation marks to pay U.S. troops with. On February 11, 1945, Foreign Minister Molotov informed Ambassador Averell Harriman in Moscow that the Soviets wished to use the same currency in their occupation zone. They wanted to print it themselves, "in order that a constant supply could be guaranteed to the Red Army." And for this they needed the plates. The Treasury had never made plates available to another country. "By inviolate custom," said Alvin W. Hall, Director of the Bureau of Engraving and Printing at the Treasury Department since 1924, "bank-note makers retain possession of all plates . . . let them develop their own designs and we will help them."

At a meeting on March 7, Harry Dexter White, who was in charge of Treasury matters in the occupied areas, said that he was "loath to turn the Russian request down. . . . Russia was one of the allies, who must be trusted to the same degree as the others." But the others had not asked for plates. Alvin Hall advanced every argument he could think of. The hygroscopic ink would be adversely affected by the Russian climate. The Forbes Company, which was doing the actual printing under contract, was under heavy bond to insure against improper use of the plates.

In April, Harriman reported that the Russians would not budge. At the time, with victory in Europe a month away, the drift in American political and military circles was to promote Soviet-American cooperation in the occupation of Germany. Under pressure from White and Morgenthau, the Combined Chiefs of Staff, as well as the State Department, agreed on April 12, 1945, to make the plates available.

By June, the Russians had taken over a printing plant in Leipzig and the presses rolled. Soviet-printed marks flooded all four occupation zones as the preferred black market currency, since they were identical to American marks. The exchange rate for the American marks was ten to the dollar. A GI in the American zone could buy a pack of cigarettes at the PX for 8 cents and sell the pack for 100 black market marks. He could take the 100 marks to an Army post office and buy a $10 money order to send home, turning 8 cents into $10.

The Soviets printed millions of dollars' worth of marks, which the United States had to redeem. They financed the cost of the occupation of East Germany with the marks we gave them, until the United States stopped using and redeeming them in September 1946. At a Senate hearing in October 1953, Senator William F. Knowland of California said: "As I understand it, there are $380 million more in currency redeemed than there were appropriations for." "That is correct," replied Howard C. Petersen, assistant secretary of war. As the report of the Subcommittee on Investigations put it: "This was simply grand larceny by one government of another."[115]

Harry Dexter White first came to the FBI's attention in 1942, when the bureau was informed by the Dies Committee that he and his wife belonged to a number of front groups. When White was questioned on March 30, "he spent more time," as J. Edgar Hoover put it, "denouncing the investigations of government employees than he did in furnishing the facts." White observed that if Martin Dies "was one tenth as patriotic as I am, it would be a much better country."[116]

When White was named to the International Monetary Fund, on January 23, 1946, the FBI prepared a twenty-eight-page memo to head off his confirmation by the Senate. The memo was sent to the White House on February 1, 1946. It appeared from this memo that the only persons White saw outside office hours were Soviet agents and party members. In a bugged phone conversation, one of his daughters was recorded as saying that many of their friends believed in the same political ideas. She wanted friends she could speak freely to and not just say "what lovely weather we are having."

Among the highlights in the memo were:

- In early 1945, White saw Louis Goldblatt, the treasurer of the San Francisco longshoreman's union run by Harry Bridges and a known Communist official.
- White was said to be meeting David Karr once a week. Karr did legwork for the columnist Drew Pearson and was a former writer for the *Daily Worker*. He was later identified as a KGB agent. White visited Drew Pearson's home and was presumed to be leaking information to him.
- Guests at White's home included Harry M. Edelstein, an assistant solicitor at the Department of the Interior, active in several fronts.
- White's brother-in-law, Dr. Abraham Wolfson, was described as an active Communist.
- On December 12, 1945, White visited Alger Hiss at his home at 3210 P Street.
- On December 15, White and his wife invited Maurice Halperin of the OSS, who had been exposed as a spy, and the Silvermasters to dinner. The Silvermasters came again on December 23.
- White was a close friend of Lee Pressman, the CIO general counsel, who would later admit his membership in the Ware group. White and Pressman were neighbors in Bethesda, Maryland, and their Washington offices were close, so they drove to work together. On December 30 and 31, 1945, White and Pressman spoke at some length on the phone regarding the labor situation and negotiations with the CIO to avert strikes. Pressman said everything was going to the dogs and the White House hadn't even talked to the labor leaders. White said he would try to see Secretary of Commerce Henry Wallace.[117]

Hoover's memo described White as "a valuable adjunct to an underground Soviet espionage organization operating in Washington D.C." It was detailed in its indictment and devastating in its conclusion but it had no effect. By the time White was confirmed by the Senate Banking and Commerce Committee on February 5, 1946, Truman had not seen it. By the time General Harry Vaughan, Truman's military aide, who processed FBI communications, showed him the memo on February 6, five days after having received it, it was too late. Truman was informed that the full Senate had confirmed White that afternoon. He did not feel he could reverse the Senate confirmation. It would be better to leave White in the IMF and continue investigating him.[118]

In April 1947, White resigned from the IMF, citing ill health. He had a heart condition and bought a small farm called Blueberry Hill near Fitzwilliam, New Hampshire, close to the Massachusetts border, where he could relax.

On August 13, 1948, having been named by Bentley and Whittaker Chambers as a Soviet agent, White testified before HUAC and denied being a Communist. "My creed is the American creed," he said. He knew Silvermaster and had played Ping-Pong in his basement. "I fancied myself quite a little ping-pong player," he said. "I am recovering from a severe heart attack," White had written in a note to the committee. "I would appreciate it if the chairman would give me five or ten minutes of rest after each hour." The chairman, J. Parnell Thomas, was not inclined to let him off the hook so easily. "For a person who has a severe heart condition," he said, "you certainly played a lot of sports."

White: "I think probably one of the reasons why I suffered a heart attack was because I played so many sports and so well."

Thomas: "Mr. White, of all the persons who have been mentioned in these hearings, nine or ten worked in your department and two others are friends of yours and one is a very close friend. Now how do you account for that?"

White: "That is one of those 'when did you stop beating your wife' questions."[119]

After testifying, White went back to his farm in New Hampshire. Three days later, on August 16, 1948, he died of a heart attack at the age of fifty-six. Frank Coe, a member of the Silvermaster ring, sent a note to his wife the following day. "In my opinion," he wrote, "Harry White did not die—he was killed. He was killed slowly and cruelly by insidious slander, ceaseless investigation, and finally when his strength was gone, by public scandal."

There remained a glowing entry on White in the 1944 edition of *Current Biography*, written by I. F. Stone.[120]

—

Nineteen forty-five, the last year of the war and the first of the peace, was a year of espionage windfalls for the FBI. In early September, two months before Elizabeth Bentley revealed the identities of dozens of agents in the federal government, a short, tubby, twenty-four-year-old Russian, white as a sheet, showed up one evening in the city room of the *Ottawa Journal* and began mumbling, in heavily accented English, "It's war. It's war. It's Russia." He stood there, paralyzed with fear, until he was escorted out. The *Journal* missed the scoop of the month, for his name was Igor Gouzenko, and he was a cipher clerk at the Soviet embassy. He wanted to defect, but did not know how.

Eventually, he succeeded and was turned over to the Mounties on September 7. Five days later, J. Edgar Hoover delivered a memo to President Truman's appointments secretary, Matthew J. Connelly, saying that the Royal Canadian Mounted Police had advised him that the Soviets had an extensive espionage network in Canada. "The Soviets have made the obtaining of complete information regarding the atomic bomb the number one project of Soviet espionage," Hoover said.

"There is considerable loose talk in the office of the Soviet military attaché in Ottawa regarding 'the next war,'" the memo went on. Dr. Alan Nunn May, a British nuclear physicist, "has been identified as a paid Soviet spy of long standing. He spent some time in September 1944 at the Metallurgical Laboratory of the University of Chicago, working on the separation process for uranium."[121]

A follow-up memo was sent to the White House on September 18. "Alan Nunn May . . . has been furnishing information regarding the atomic bomb experiments," it reported. "Records of payments indicate that he was given $200 and two bottles of whiskey. . . . In addition to a small quantity of uranium 233, Dr. May furnished the Soviets with specimens of uranium 235, which were carried by plane to Moscow by the Assistant Military Attaché, Lt. Col. Peter Motinov." No fewer than twenty Canadian and three British subjects, many of them government employees, had been identified as Soviet espionage agents.[122] It was the Canadian version of the Silvermaster ring.

On October 16, Hoover was able, in another memo, to identify the defector as Gouzenko, assigned to the office of Colonel Nikolai Zabotin, the Soviet military attaché at the embassy and chief of the GRU, Red Army Military Intelligence. His assistant, Peter Motinov, was also GRU, as was the assistant attaché for air, Major Vasili Rogov.

As Hoover described it, the Soviet espionage operations in Canada were replicas of those in the United States. "The Soviets have relied on members of the Communist party for this espionage network," he explained. Spies had been recruited in the Department of External Affairs, the British High Commissioner's Office, the Department of Munitions and Supply, and the Royal Canadian Navy and Air Force.[123]

Alan Nunn May, "a shy little man with a dry sense of humor," recalled a colleague, went back to England in September 1945 and was arrested in March 1946. At his trial two months later, he confessed, sharing with the judge his moral confusion. "The whole affair was extremely painful to me," he said, "and I only embarked on it because I felt this was a contribution I could make to the safety of mankind."

Unmoved, Justice Oliver sentenced him to ten years under the Official Secrets Act. "How any man in your position," he said, "could have the crass

conceit, let alone the wickedness [to betray] one of the country's most precious secrets, when you were drawing pay for years—that you could have
done this is a dreadful thing. . . . I think you acted with degradation."[124]

At about the time of the Nunn May trial, Lavrenti Beria, head of the KGB,
sent a message to all *Rezidenturas*. "In the world of the agent networks, extensive use was made of members of the Communist Party organizations who
were known to the authorities of that country for their progressive activity,"
he cabled. "Thus Gouzenko's work as a cipher clerk . . . made it possible for the
traitor to have at his disposal state secrets of great importance. . . . Gouzenko's
defection has caused great damage to our country . . ."[125] In addition to his
duties at the KGB, Beria had been assigned by Stalin in August 1945 to head
the special committee for "all work on the utilization of the intra-atomic energy of uranium," which relied heavily on the fruits of espionage.

———

Gouzenko's defection gave the Soviets the first major scare that their espionage apparats were compromised. For the United States, it was a warning
that the Soviets were trying to steal the secrets of nuclear weaponry. By the
time of Gouzenko's revelations, atom bombs had been dropped on Hiroshima
and Nagasaki and the war was over. With Alan Nunn May's conviction, the
entire community of atomic scientists came under suspicion. J. Edgar Hoover
fixated on Oppenheimer and once again placed him under surveillance in the
spring of 1946. Oppenheimer had resigned from Los Alamos in October
1945, and was teaching at Caltech.

Deeply troubled by what he had wrought, Oppenheimer asked to see President Truman privately in October. Visibly upset, he told Truman that he had
blood on his hands. For Truman, who took full responsibility for dropping the
bomb, this was contemptible behavior. Handing Oppenheimer a handkerchief, he said, "Well, here, would you like to wipe off your hands?" When Oppenheimer left the Oval Office, Truman turned to Secretary of State Dean
Acheson and said: "I don't want to see that son of a bitch in this office ever
again."[126]

Hoover's memos to the Truman White House sought to make the case that
Oppenheimer was a disloyal Communist who may have been involved in espionage. In a memo on November 15, 1945, Hoover listed his Communist affiliations, stating that "Oppenheimer has been referred to by high Communist
party members as 'the big shot' and 'Oppie.' Communist officials have stated
that Oppenheimer was regularly registered as a member. . . . Since the use of
the atomic bomb, individual Communists in California have expressed an
interest in establishing their own contacts."[127]

Two of these Communists, Hoover said, were David Adelson and Paul Pinsky, organizers for the party-controlled Federation of Architects, Engineers, Chemists, and Technicians, which had a local at the Shell Lab in Emeryville, California, just south of Berkeley. In a bugged conversation on August 10, 1945, one day after the Nagasaki bomb was dropped, Adelson said to Pinsky: "Isn't it nice that Oppenheimer is getting the credit he is?"

"Yes," said Pinsky, "shall we claim him as a member?"

"Oppenheimer," said Adelson, "is the guy who initially gave me the push. Remember that session?" Adelson credited Oppenheimer with helping them get the FAECT local started at Shell by setting up a labor-management meeting.

Adelson (laughing): "As soon as they get the Gestapo from around him I am going to get hold of him and put the bee on him. The guy is so big now that no one can touch him, but he has got to come out and express some ideas."[128]

On March 18, 1946, Hoover sent the White House another long memo detailing Oppenheimer's activities. Upon returning to the Bay Area, he had stayed with his brother, Frank, whose house was also bugged. On New Year's Day 1946, Adelson and Pinsky came to visit. Hoover described them as "both known party members and both known contacts of Soviet representatives in the San Francisco area." (The FAECT was used as a channel for Soviet espionage.) Pinsky, whom Ivanov visited at his home in 1943, was mentioned in a Venona message as someone who could approach scientists at the Radiation Lab. The purpose of their visit was to get Oppenheimer to talk before mass meetings they were planning on the future of the bomb. They told him he was being criticized in the party "for taking an individualistic course" and for failing "to align himself with the basic trend of thought." After they had left, Frank Oppenheimer asked his brother: "Didn't you think they were pretty political?" J. Robert replied: "Well, to some extent they have to be, we just have to find out more about it."[129]

Still troubled by Oppenheimer's connection with Haakon Chevalier and George Eltenton, Hoover tried to enlist the cooperation of General Leslie Groves, who stonewalled him, saying he did not wish to compromise his relationship with the scientist. On June 26, 1946, losing patience, Hoover had his agents pick up both men and had them questioned at separate locations.

Eltenton was quite forthcoming. Sometime in 1942, he said, "when the Russians were in dire straits," he was approached by Ivanov and asked whether he knew Oppenheimer. Eltenton said he did not, but that Haakon Chevalier did. "Ivanov impressed upon Eltenton," said Hoover's memo, "that the Russians severely needed certain information and that for political reasons there were no authorized channels to obtain it." Ivanov "gave assurances that such information would be transmitted through his channels, which involved photo reproduction and [means of] transmission." Eltenton asked Chevalier to contact Oppenheimer, which he did, but Oppie refused to cooperate. That was the only request from Ivanov, who returned to Russia in 1943. Chevalier corroborated the approach by Eltenton and Oppenheimer's refusal to comply.[130]

Hoover's next move was to interview Oppenheimer, who told two of his agents on September 5, 1946, that the story he had told Boris Pash in 1943 was "a fabrication." He had been contacted by Chevalier, who had been told by Eltenton that it was necessary to furnish technical information to the Soviet Union.

In a twelve-page memo to the White House on February 17, 1947, recapitulating the Chevalier incident, Hoover stated: "Oppenheimer said that he told Chevalier that to do such a thing was treason or close to treason." He had concocted the story about his brother, Frank, to protect Chevalier's identity. Hoover added that in the September 5 interview, Oppenheimer had said that he was "so naive regarding political matters that he did not even vote, but that from 1936 to 1939 he had engaged in political matters in an amateurish way and had identified himself with many of the so-called leftist front groups and had made contributions, at least some part of which could possibly have gone into Communist party funds. He never at any time was a dues-paying Communist, but had an academic interest in the organization."

When Oppenheimer was asked about the meeting he attended in Chevalier's home on December 1, 1940, he said "he may have attended one or two gatherings at which there were present persons definitely identified with the Communist Party." He added that "he underwent a sharp change of mind and attitude at the time of the Soviet-German pact of 1939. . . . He did not reconcile the treachery employed by the Soviets in their international relationships with the high purposes and democratic aims ascribed to the Soviets by the local Communists."

Hoover informed the White House that he had turned the Oppenheimer dossier over to the Criminal Division of the Justice Department, which ruled that no prosecution would be authorized.[131]

The paradox at the heart of the Oppenheimer case was that having been placed in a highly sensitive position, he served his country loyally, while having previously maintained close ties to the Communist Party. When Communists discussed Oppie in bugged conversations, they invariably described him as a party member. Bernadette Doyle, Steve Nelson's assistant, who kept the party records in the Bay Area, said he was "regularly registered." Yet Oppenheimer, up to the day he died, denied ever having been a party member.

The paradox was resolved by Gregg Herken in his revealing book *Brotherhood of the Bomb.* According to Herken, Chevalier wrote in 1965 that Oppenheimer "wanted to maintain a certain fiction regarding some of the aspects of our past, that whole areas of our experience were to be considered as having never existed." The truth was, said Chevalier, that he and Oppenheimer had been members "in the same unit of the CP" from 1937 to 1943.[132]

This unit was a cell in the party's secret "professional section" at Berkeley. Its members were told not to take out membership cards, so Oppenheimer could rationalize that he had never been a card-carrying Communist. The cell was made up of Berkeley professors such as Arthur Brodeur, chairman of the Scandinavian Languages Department, and Paul Radin, an anthropology professor. Oppenheimer called it a discussion group but Chevalier said it was "a closed unit of the Communist Party." In 1964, Chevalier wrote a onetime member of the cell: "I had originally planned to reveal the fact that Oppenheimer had been, from 1937 to 1943, a Communist Party member, which I knew directly." But he decided not to, just as Oppenheimer had at first refused to name him.

The secret cell published a newsletter, *Report to Our Colleagues*, which was sent to faculty members at Berkeley and other colleges. Oppenheimer wrote most of it and paid for the printing, said Chevalier. It closely followed the party line. The report for April 6, 1940, during the pact period, called FDR "a counter-revolutionary war-monger" and took the Soviet Union's side in its winter war on Finland. These reports were signed: "College Faculties Committee, Communist Party of California." In his September 5, 1946, interview with the FBI, Oppenheimer seems to have lied regarding his "sharp change of mind" at the time of the Nazi-Soviet pact. In spite of his compromising activities and his repeated lies about them, Oppenheimer was instrumental in developing the weapon that won the war and the leaking of atomic secrets did not come from him.[133]

———

In his affidavit, Gouzenko also provided some intriguing though inconclusive information that pointed to a high-ranking spy in the U.S. State Department. In his September 12 memo, Hoover advised the White House that "the Royal Canadian Mounted Police received from the same source information that an assistant to an Assistant Secretary of State under Mr. [E. R.] Stettinius was a paid Soviet spy. This man's name, or nickname, is unknown at the present time."

We now know, thanks to Venona, that this assistant to the assistant was Alger Hiss. From 1941 to 1944, Hiss was the assistant to Stanley K. Hornbeck, the State Department's chief expert on the Far East, who had the title adviser on political relations. In 1944 and 1945, Hiss was the assistant to Leo

Pasvolsky, who was in charge of the State Department office assigned to work with the United Nations. Hiss had been mentioned in 1939, when Whittaker Chambers saw Adolf Berle, who jotted down in his notes: "Member of the Underground Com.—Active," but this lead was not pursued. The FBI spoke briefly to Hiss in 1942 and he told them: "There is only one government that I want to overthrow and that is Hitler's."[134]

That same year Elizabeth Bentley told the FBI that Hiss had taken over Harold Glasser from a member of the Perlo group. As Bentley would later explain the arrangement to the Senate Internal Security Subcommittee: "In 1944, I took a group of people called the Perlo group. One of the members was a Mr. Harold Glasser in the Treasury. In the process of checking everyone's past, I found that Mr. Glasser had at one time been pulled out of that particular group and had been turned over to a person who both Mr. Perlo and Charles Kramer refused to tell me who it was except that he was working for the Russians, and later they broke down and told me it was Alger Hiss. . . ." She checked with her Soviet superior, Akhmerov, who told her: "Lay off the Hiss thing. He is one of ours."[135]

Glasser, the assistant director of the Division of Monetary Research, met regularly at the Treasury Department with Anatoli Gromov, in his capacity as First Secretary of the Soviet embassy. On April 2, 1945, they were discussing the new postage stamps for occupied Germany, and as they shook hands, Glasser slipped Gromov a note based on information from Hiss. "An FBI agent told Secretary of State Stettinius that one of their agents saw documents brought to New York for photographing," it said. "Judging by the documents, only three persons had access. One of them was Hiss. The FBI man told Stettinius that 'hundreds and hundreds of documents were withdrawn'. . . . Stettinius called in Hiss and said 'I hope it is not you.'"[136]

Glasser, code-named *Ruble*, had worked for both the KGB and the GRU. Because he moved back and forth, he was slighted in the award of a decoration, which mattered greatly to him. In April 1945, Pavel Fitin, the head of KGB Foreign Intelligence, asked that *Ruble* be given equitable treatment, since he had been in the service since May 1937. While Glasser had been detached to the KGB, the "military neighbors" group [GRU] had been decorated. *Ruble* heard about it from his friend *Ales* [Hiss], who was head of the GRU group. "As the result of this transfer to our station [KGB], *Ruble* was not decorated with the other members of the *Ales* group."[137]

In 1945 alone, Fitin said, Glasser had sent thirty-four reports and also acted as a talent spotter. Some of his reports went straight to Stalin, such as discussions in London on Soviet-Polish relations; directives on disbanding the Nazi Party in the U.S. zone of Germany; a Treasury memo on lend-lease for the Soviets; and an OSS memo on stripping Germany of its heavy industry. Fitin recommended Glasser for the Order of the Red Banner.

The Venona traffic includes far fewer messages from the GRU than from the KGB. Because Hiss worked for the GRU, he is rarely mentioned. One partly decoded GRU message to Moscow on September 28, 1943, said: "the Neighbor has reported that (xxxxx) From the State Department the name of Hiss" (spelled out in the Latin alphabet).

But there is one message that clinches the identification of Hiss as *Ales.* On March 30, 1945, Gromov from KGB Washington to Moscow reported that:

As a result of [Akhmerov's] chat with *Ales,* the following has been ascertained:

1. *Ales* has been working with the GRU continuously since 1935.
2. For some years past he had been the leader of a small group of the GRU's probationers, for the most part consisting of his relatives.
3. The group and *Ales* himself work on obtaining military information only.
4. All the last few years *Ales* has been working with *Pol* [Paul— unknown agent] who also meets other members of the group occasionally.
5. Recently *Ales* and his whole group were awarded Soviet decorations.
6. After the Yalta Conference, when he had gone to Moscow, a Soviet personage in a very responsible position (*Ales* gave to understand that it was Comrade Vyshinsky) allegedly got in touch with *Ales* and . . . passed on [the GRU's] gratitude.[138]

Of the U.S. delegation at Yalta, only four went on to Moscow with Ambassador Averell Harriman and his staff. The rest returned to the United States with President Roosevelt. The four who went to Moscow were Secretary of State Stettinius, his press secretary, Wilder Foote, H. Freeman Matthews, director of the Office of European Affairs, and Alger Hiss. Three were above suspicion, but Hiss fit the bill in every particular. With the Russian penchant for providing clues in the code names, *Ales* in the Cyrillic alphabet looked like the contraction of Alger Hiss.[139]

The *Ales* message was not completely broken by the National Security Agency until August 1969. But enough of it had been broken by 1950 for the FBI to make the connection with Hiss. An FBI memo on May 15, 1950, said: "It would appear likely that this individual is Alger Hiss in view of the fact that he was in the State Department. . . . and his wife Priscilla was active in Soviet espionage and he also had a brother, Donald, in the State Department . . . Hiss did attend the Yalta Conference as a special advisor to President Roosevelt."

In 1945, Hiss was head of the State Department's Special Political Affairs Office, which was responsible for the United Nations. A glaring example of how Hiss worked against the interests of his country was provided by Spruille Braden, assistant secretary of state in charge of Latin American affairs, when he testified before the Senate Internal Security Subcommittee on March 24, 1954. Braden was a veteran Latin American hand. As ambassador to Cuba, he'd had run-ins with Lawrence Duggan.

In the fall of 1945, at about the time the first United Nations General Assembly opened in New York, Braden was negotiating with Panama for the return of 134 bases in the Canal Zone, from anti-aircraft posts to the huge Río Hato Air Base. At the opening U.N. meeting, the Russians charged that the United States had aggressive intentions in establishing military bases all over the world, giving Panama as an example. The governor of the Canal Zone at that time submitted to the State Department his annual report, how many ships came through, the tonnage, and so on. Hiss, who was handling U.N. matters, wanted to submit the Canal Zone report to the General Assembly. Braden told him that this was inadvisable, for it would open up the debate on the United States's right to be there and play into Soviet mischief-making. Ann O'Neill, the legal adviser, backed Braden. But Hiss argued that under Article 73(e) of the United Nations Charter, the State Department had an obligation to submit the report. The article stated that U.N. members were expected to transmit to the United Nations information on conditions in the territories for which they were responsible. As Braden recalled, "Article 73 addressed developing self-government, which had nothing to do with the operation of the Canal Zone. . . . There was no rhyme or reason why that should be presented to the UN. . . . It was just going to enrage the Panamanians. It was going to embarrass their government, which was already facing agitation over the bases. It would play into the hands of the Russians, with their allegations about our bases scattered all over the world. It would bring the UN into a dispute where they had no right to be. It might lead to giving them a say in the operation of the Panama Canal."[140]

Hiss, however, insisted that the report be submitted, and the matter was appealed to Undersecretary of State Dean Acheson. When Braden arrived in Acheson's office, Hiss had already been there for some time. Acheson backed Hiss. Braden was not even allowed to state his case. "I came out of that meeting boiling with rage," Braden recalled. When George Marshall succeeded James F. Byrnes as Secretary of State in 1947, Acheson asked for Braden's resignation.

As it turned out, the Panamanian Prime Minister, Ricardo J. Alfaro, spoke at the United Nations on November 14, 1946, to explain that the Panama Canal Zone was not a leased territory, but the result of a 1903 treaty that gave the United States a zone of land for the operation of the canal, with Panama retaining its sovereignty. An annuity of $30,000 was paid but it was not a lease. Alfaro said the report should not have been submitted, since the Canal Zone was not among territories classified as possessions. In rebuttal, Hiss wrote a report on the Canal Zone for the United Nations in which he called it an "occupied territory." The report was picked up by the *Washington Post* and Hiss had to apologize to Acheson. "He was very charming about it," Braden recalled. "He said that he was oh so sorry, it was just one of those things that slipped by."[141]

In March 1946, Attorney General Tom Clark and Secretary of State Jimmy Byrnes started cooperating to ease Hiss out of the State Department by leaking FBI material to Congress. On March 20, Byrnes advised Hiss that the FBI had evidence that he was a Communist and that "two separate committees on the Hill" were questioning his loyalty. Byrnes began to limit the material that Hiss was allowed to see.

Luckily for Hiss, he found an escape hatch. In the spring of 1945, he had served as Secretary General at the San Francisco United Nations Conference, attended by fifty nations, which resulted in the signing of the United Nations Charter. Efficient and unflappable, he was praised in *Time* magazine for his mastery "of incredibly complicated conference machinery." One of those he impressed was a senior adviser to the American delegation, the Republican lawyer John Foster Dulles. Knowing nothing of his security problems at State, Dulles, who was also chairman of the Carnegie Endowment for International Peace, asked Hiss to be its president.[142]

Hiss wrote to his wife, Priscilla, on January 4, 1946: "This afternoon, Mr. Dulles asked me if I would be interested in succeeding Nicholas Miraculous Butler [Nicholas Murray Butler, president of Columbia University from 1902 to 1945, who had established the endowment] at $15,000 to $17,000 a year!" Hiss told Dulles he was "very much interested," was approved by the trustees, and resigned from the State Department in December 1946. "Take this job," Acheson told him. "People will continue to raise these doubts about you so long as you are in a position where you are subject to this sort of attack."[143]

Nor did Dulles know that Hiss was still under investigation by the FBI. On June 21, 1947, agents questioned him at the endowment's Washington office. For the first time, he was asked about Whittaker Chambers, whom he denied knowing. When Dulles, who was picking up rumors that Hiss had

Communist ties, asked him about them, Hiss said that "when I was in the Department of Agriculture there were some persons who might have had some Communist sympathy, but I had with them only casual acquaintance."[144]

In 1947, in response to Elizabeth Bentley's allegations, a grand jury was convened in the Southern District of New York. Hiss testified on March 16, 1948, that he was not a Communist and did not know Chambers. Then came the historic confrontation before HUAC in August, in which the WASP establishment closed ranks to protect one of their own against the charges of a confessed Communist—an unsavory overweight apostate with bad teeth, whose very pores seemed to secrete malodorous fumes of slander.

The grand jury was still sitting, and Chambers testified on October 14, two months after making his accusations against Hiss before HUAC. He perjured himself by telling the grand jury that he had never committed espionage. Then the "Pumpkin Papers" were discovered and on December 2 HUAC subpoenaed the microfilm that was inside the pumpkin. Chambers also had sixty-four pages of typed State Department summaries that he claimed to have received from Hiss.

Truman, who wanted to discredit HUAC, which had attacked him for being soft on Communism, controlled the Justice Department through his Attorney General, Tom Clark. It was touch and go who the grand jury would indict for perjury, Chambers or Hiss. The question was, would the Justice Department be able to pressure the grand jury into indicting Chambers? Alexander Campbell, the head of the Criminal Division, who was running the grand jury, wanted to indict Chambers. Tom Clark himself privately derided the Hiss case as a "concoction of Nixon and Chambers." Richard M. Nixon had been the member of HUAC who had debriefed Chambers.

The minutes of the grand jury proceedings, which have recently been declassified, show that Chambers was saved from indictment because Hiss self-destructed. In his testimony, he became trapped in a maze of lies. When he testified on December 9, Hiss was shown a photograph of Hede Massing, whom he knew well. "Her appearance is completely unfamiliar to me," he said. Hiss repeatedly gave qualified answers, such as "I certainly do not believe that I ever saw her." One of the Justice Department prosecutors, Raymond Whearty, became so exasperated that he said: "I think we ought to have a direct answer, either yes or no, or I don't remember." Hiss then said, "I am quite sure that I have never seen her before."

When Hiss said that neither he nor his wife, Priscilla, did any typing, Tom Donegan, the other prosecutor, said: "What has been troubling us is why a family which did not type would have occasion to have so many typewriters."

When Priscilla Hiss testified on December 10, she said she and her husband were "mere acquaintances" of Chambers. Since Hiss had given Chambers his Ford, Donegan observed that it was "unusual to give an automobile to someone you barely knew."

"Why Mr. Donegan," replied Priscilla Hiss, "it wasn't very much of a gift."

When Hiss's stepson Timothy Hobson testified on December 13, he contradicted his stepfather's testimony that the typewriter was meant for his use. "I do not remember any typewriter being specifically for my use," he said.

"Frankly," Donegan responded, "I never saw a family with so many typewriters where there was no one to use any of them."

The turning point for the grand jury came on December 14, when the FBI's document expert, Raymond Feehan, testified. The FBI had found documents that were typed on the Hisses' typewriter at Timothy Hobson's former school. The FBI compared those documents to the sixty-four typewritten documents that Chambers had turned over to the Justice Department. Feehan listed the similarities, such as a defective letter *g*. When a juror asked Feehan if he had ever mistaken a Woodstock, which the Hisses had, for another make, he said: "I have spent 10 years in document work and examined hundreds of typewriting specimens, thousands, and I have never yet mistaken a Woodstock" for another make.

Hiss appeared again on December 14 and 15. A change in the frame of mind of the grand jury became evident. One juror asked him to be more specific and stop using the phrase "to the best of my knowledge." When confronted with the typewritten letters to the school, Hiss admitted that either he or his wife had typed them.

"This is the time to say what is the true story," Donegan advised Hiss, giving him a chance to come clean, negotiate a plea bargain, and avoid indictment. Instead, Hiss insisted that Chambers had snuck into his house and typed the sixty-four documents. He also tried to convince the grand jury that Chambers was mentally unstable.

Donegan responded that since Hiss had claimed he had not seen Chambers since 1936, how then could Chambers have typed up summaries of State Department documents dated 1938? One juror told Hiss that his testimony was becoming "more and more fantastic" and "went outside anything that anyone can believe."

On December 15, Hiss argued that Chambers had bribed his maid and broken into his house, but admitted that he had no evidence to offer. Whearty stated that "there appears to be no one who could be responsible for turning over these documents other than you or Mrs. Hiss."[145]

On December 15, the same day that Hiss wound up his testimony, the grand jury indicted him.

Hiss was tried twice for perjury. The guilty verdict in the second trial vindicated Chambers, who felt "the nausea of victory."[146]

Hiss was sentenced to five years. He served only forty-four months in the federal prison in Lewisburg, Pennsylvania, and many continued to believe in his innocence. With his chameleon-like ability to adapt to any environment, Hiss did his time with relative ease. He had a mind that was divided into compartments like the drawers of a bureau. With Oliver Wendell Holmes and Felix Frankfurter, he could play the establishment lawyer. With his colleagues at State, he played the impeccable diplomat. With his son, Tony, he was the exemplary father. His Soviet handlers held him in high regard as the best type of Communist. Whittaker Chambers saw in him a close friend. At Lewisburg, he got along well with his fellow inmates. Thanks to a chance introduction, he found himself under the protection of Italian mobsters, who came to him with their legal problems. In the well-stocked library, Hiss found the collected letters of Lenin's widow. At the top of a tree, Hiss the bird-watcher saw a rose-breasted grosbeak. A few weeks before his release, his fellow inmate William Remington, one of Elizabeth Bentley's agents, also convicted for perjury, was beaten to death. But Hiss left Lewisburg none the worse for wear, and spent the rest of his life playing the part of the innocent man, unjustly accused, with his usual aplomb.[147]

———

In February 1945, Kenneth E. Wells, an OSS officer in the Asian research branch, was flipping through the pages of the January 26 issue of the magazine *Amerasia* when he came upon an article, "The British Attitude Toward Thailand," that looked familiar. Upon further examination, he saw that it was lifted almost verbatim from a classified report he had written, which was distributed to Asian experts in Military Intelligence, the Office of Naval Intelligence, and the State Department.

Amerasia, a monthly with a circulation of 1,700, was edited by Philip Jaffe, a friend of Earl Browder's who wrote for *New Masses* and was affiliated with half a dozen front groups. Jaffe made his money selling greeting cards and ran *Amerasia* at a deficit. But how had he gained access to classified information?

On March 11, a five-man OSS team led by Frank Bielaski, head of the Domestic Investigation Division, staged a midnight raid on the *Amerasia* offices at 225 Fifth Avenue. One of the five was a lock-picking expert on loan from the Office of Naval Intelligence. They found more than three hundred documents stamped "Possession Is a Violation of the Espionage Act." Twenty were stamped TOP SECRET. As Bielaski recalled, "If I went down to the OSS and told them what I had seen, they just would not believe me. I therefore determined to take 12 to 14 of the documents and show them to them as proof. . . . I put those in my pocket."[148]

What looked like a major espionage case was turned over to the FBI, which placed a phone tap on Jaffe on March 14. On April 19, 1945, Andrew Roth, a lieutenant in Naval Intelligence who acted as liaison officer with the State Department, introduced Jaffe to John Stewart Service, a Foreign Service officer who had been stationed in China. Service had visited the Communist-controlled part of the country and his dispatches argued that Chiang Kai-shek was at a dead end and that the Maoists, with their austerity and lack of corruption, would win in the end. Eager to air his point of view, Service gave Jaffe some of his reports.[149]

Holding forth on May 7, 1945, in his bugged room at the Statler Hotel in Washington, Jaffe seemed quite pleased with himself. "It's very interesting that Jack Service gave—I have 19 of his reports," he told Andrew Roth, "including those three or four he had at last. He let me take them to New York, I have made copies."

"Well," Roth replied, "Jack says that they haven't been read around the Department."

The following day, in the same bugged hotel room, Jaffe conferred with Service. "What I said about the military plans is of course very secret," Service observed. "That plan was made up by [General Albert C.] Wedemeyer's staff in his absence, they got orders to make some recommendations as to what we should do if we landed in Communist territory. . . . If we landed where the Communists were, they'd be the dominant force." This was a plan to cooperate with whatever Chinese forces American troops found on the ground, upon landing on the Chinese coast to help Chiang Kai-shek against the Japanese.

As the FBI continued to collect evidence on Jaffe and his cohorts through phone taps and surveillance, Hoover, on May 21, 1945, sent a memo to the President's military aide, General Harry Vaughan. In this first mention of the *Amerasia* case to the White House, Hoover explained that Philip Jaffe was in touch with a freelance magazine writer and expert on Asia, Mark Gayn. Born in Manchuria of Russian parents, Gayn had contacts in government departments who gave him classified information, which he passed on to Jaffe. Hoover said that Jaffe claimed to have learned that Truman had on his desk a Japanese peace offer furnished through the Argentine government.[150]

On May 31, Truman was officially informed about the case by Assistant Secretary of State Julius Holmes. The President demanded a vigorous prosecution. But someone on the White House staff called Attorney General–

designate Tom Clark with an order from Truman to take no action until after the United Nations conference in San Francisco, which would last through mid-June, in order not to offend the Russians. When Clark checked with Truman, the President was incensed. He wanted to know who had given the order and insisted that the arrests take place right away. It has never been established who gave the order, although it should be noted that Lauchlin Currie, who was also getting material from Service, did not leave the White House until sometime in June.

On June 6, 1945, Jaffe, Andrew Roth, Mark Gayn, and John Stewart Service were arrested on espionage charges. Two others were arrested with them—Emmanuel Larsen of the State Department, who also leaked documents to Jaffe, and Kate Mitchell, Jaffe's co-editor, a socially registered graduate of Bryn Mawr who sometimes wrote for *New Masses*. She had a trust fund and worked for Jaffe for nothing. In fact, she had loaned him $3,500. The FBI had collected 1,772 documents from *Amerasia*'s office, 15 percent of them classified. It was easy to foresee a sensational trial—the spectacle of a high-ranking Foreign Service man behind bars in the Washington district jail was a headline all its own—but such a trial never took place.[151]

It happened that John Stewart Service, while in China, had maintained a private correspondence with Lauchlin Currie, to keep him posted on the scandals in the Chiang Kai-shek government. Currie said he needed Service's information in order to brief Roosevelt. While professing to support Chiang, Currie leaked Service's gossip to columnists like Drew Pearson. Currie felt he owed Service a favor. At the same time, he reasoned that a dramatic trial would be best avoided. Currie did not want Service to appear in court and disclose their private correspondence.

On June 11, 1945, Currie contacted Tommy the Cork Corcoran, the prominent New Deal insider who was now in private practice. As a prudent measure, Truman had, upon coming into office in April, put a tap on Corcoran's phone. Corcoran asked him what he could do to help. Currie said he would try to operate "on the side," but "if I have to, I may even come out front, but . . . I would rather not have to."[152]

Attorney General designate Tom Clark was facing a confirmation fight in the Senate. Tommy the Cork had been doing a little missionary work among key senators. Soon after talking to Currie he called Clark to tell him that he would be unopposed in the Senate. Once Clark was confirmed Corcoran worked on him and Assistant Attorney General James P. McGranery to let Service off the hook. When the possibility arose that Service would be asked to testify against his co-defendants, Corcoran called McGranery. "If that guy is ever a witness in this thing," he said, "he is through with the State Department." McGranery said the general feeling was that Service deserved "a little kick in the pants."

On July 26, McGranery promised Corcoran to "take care of it for you. Your man is Service. I got it." The next day, Tom Clark told Corcoran that Service would have no problem with the grand jury unless the prosecutors were "antagonistic," which was not the case. In a call to Service, Corcoran said, "I did want you to know I'd gone right up to the top on the damn thing." Service appeared before the grand jury on August 6 after being assured by Corcoran that "this is double riveted from top to bottom." He was not indicted. Clark had reduced the charges against the six from espionage to illegal receipt of government property.[153]

It was all rather murky and inexplicable. Why had Attorney General Tom Clark sat on the case? Why had Assistant Attorney General Jim McGranery done Corcoran's bidding? Why had the *Amerasia* prosecutor, Robert Hitchcock, been so tepid? Service, Kate Mitchell, and Mark Gayn were cleared. In February 1946 the charges were dropped against Andrew Roth. A deal was struck with Philip Jaffe that he would plead guilty to reduced charges and pay a $2,500 fine. Emmanuel Larsen got off with a fine of $500. A furious Hoover observed: "Of all the wishy-washy vacillations, this takes the prize."[154]

The prosecutors, however, felt they had a weak and tainted case. They were unable to turn any co-defendant against the others. The evidence was based in large part on breaking and entering and wiretaps. The Supreme Court had ruled in 1942 that wiretap evidence could not be used against third parties. The case never came to trial and the first espionage conspiracy of the post-FDR period ended not with a bang but with a fizzle.

———

With a face that was mostly brow, a jutting nose, thin hair, wire-rim glasses, and a somber expression, Klaus Fuchs looked the part of the introverted prodigy. Born in 1911 in the German town of Russelsheim, south of Frankfurt, he came from a long line of Protestant pastors. His father, Emil, was a Quaker who did missionary work among the poor and joined the Socialist Party.

Klaus went to the University of Kiel, where he showed brilliance in mathematics and physics. A fervent anti-Nazi, he joined the Communist Party in 1932. Although frail and myopic, he was sufficiently militant to figure on a Gestapo list of wanted Communists when Hitler came to power in 1933. He fled to England with thousands of other Germans and got his doctorate in physics at the University of Bristol. In May 1940, with the war on, he was interned as an enemy alien and sent to a camp in Canada, near Quebec. There he was befriended by Israel Halperin, who would later be named by Gouzenko as a Soviet agent. Fuchs had a sister, Kristel Heineman, who was living in Cambridge, Massachusetts. Thanks to Halperin, whose brother-in-law, the physicist Wendell Furry, was a professor at Harvard, Fuchs was able to communicate with Kristel. Furry was in the same Cambridge Communist cell as Kristel's husband, Robert Heineman.[155]

Fuchs returned to England in December 1940. His reputation as a brilliant physicist led to his being hired the following May to do research in Birmingham on a highly secret atomic bomb project code-named *Tube Alloys*. In the same way as Oppenheimer at Los Alamos, because he was needed, he obtained security clearance in spite of his Communist past. He signed an oath of secrecy and in July became a naturalized British citizen.

When Fuchs agreed to spy on the country that had given him asylum, he had an ideological reason and a personal reason. In 1941, he became convinced that the Allies were deliberately allowing Russia and Germany to fight each other. But his hatred of the Nazis was based on what they had done to his family. In 1931, his mother, depressed over the rise of Hitler, committed suicide by swallowing acid. In 1935, his father was sentenced to ten months in prison for "anti-government agitation." His brother, Gerhard, escaped to Switzerland, but Gerhard's wife and child died in a concentration camp. His sister Elizabeth married Klaus Kittowski, a Communist who was sent to a concentration camp in 1936. In despair, Elizabeth threw herself under a train. Nazism had devastated Klaus Fuchs's family and turned him into a brooding zealot with a mission to accomplish.[156]

In the Venona traffic, Fuchs first turns up in a message from GRU London to Moscow on August 15, 1941: "On 8th August, *Barch* [Simon Kremer, secretary to the Soviet military attaché at the London embassy and also GRU *Rezident*] met with a former acquaintance of Dr. Fuchs [real name used], who had moved to Birmingham on May 27, 1941, to take up his duties. . . . In three months all the material will be sent to Canada for industrial production. Fuchs will report when the opportunity occurs."[157]

In December 1943, Fuchs came to the United States as part of a fifteen-member British mission to the Manhattan Project. That month, a team of scientists at the University of Chicago under Enrico Fermi created the first sustained nuclear chain reaction. America's progress depended largely on scientists who had fled Hitler, Mussolini, and Stalin. Limited American cooperation with England led to the arrival of the British team, with Fuchs on board owing to his contributions to the theory of gaseous diffusion. He settled in New York at 128 West 77th Street and worked on calculations for the gaseous diffusion plant in Oak Ridge, Tennessee, which was intended to produce fissionable uranium. He spent Christmas with his sister Kristel in Cambridge.[158]

By early 1944, Fuchs had gathered substantial information on the plant at Oak Ridge, which he knew only as "site x." He made contact with the Soviets in New York. They assigned him to their longtime courier Harry Gold, a chemist who had been recruited in 1934. Their first meeting was described in a Venona message on February 9, 1944: "On Feb. 5th a meeting took place between *Gus* [Gold] and *Rest* [Fuchs]. . . . *Rest* greeted him pleasantly but was rather cautious at first. . . . *Rest* arrived in the United States in September [sic] as a member of the British mission on *Enormous* [code name for A-bomb]. . . . The whole operation amounts to the working out of the process for the separation of isotopes of Uranium." The message was signed *Anton,* who was Leonid Kvasnikov, in charge of atomic spying at the New York *Rezidentura*.[159]

By June 6, 1944, Fuchs had written a report entitled "Fluctuation and Efficiency of a Diffusion Plant." A Venona message sent to Moscow on June 16 said that two secret plans for the layout of the A-bomb plant had been received.

But after the June meeting with Gold near Borough Hall in Brooklyn, Fuchs missed a meeting in late July near the Brooklyn Museum and did not show up at the backup meeting on Central Park West. Gold went to Fuchs's apartment and his landlady said he had left the city.

Fuchs had been transferred that August to the most secret division of the Manhattan Project, the bomb assembly and design project in Los Alamos, New Mexico. He had not had time to tell Gold, who thought he had gone back to England. In November, Gold went to Cambridge to see Fuchs's sister Kristel, who told him her brother was in the Southwest and planned to come east at Christmas.[160]

On August 14, 1944, Fuchs settled into the secretive Los Alamos community, where mail was censored and telephones were unavailable. The compound, situated on a seven-thousand-foot-high mesa in the Jemez Mountains north of Santa Fe, was surrounded by barbed wire and guards. But for Fuchs the spy, Los Alamos was the land of opportunity. Although he was not the star of a group that included a dozen Nobel Prize winners, he had access to work on the development of plutonium as an alternative to U-235 for a bomb fuel and the implosion mechanism as a way to detonate plutonium.[161]

In February 1945, Fuchs visited his sister and passed on "a quite considerable packet," said Gold, who came to see him at her home. They agreed to meet in June in Santa Fe. This "quite considerable packet," according to Fuchs's later confession, was a report on the design of the plutonium bomb. The Manhattan Project was working on two kinds of bombs. One was the uranium bomb with a gun-type detonator. The other bomb was plutonium-based, with an implosion detonation. This was the bomb dropped on Nagasaki. At the time, it was not yet clear whether implosion could be better obtained with a high-explosive lens or with multipoint detonation over the surface of a uniform sphere of high explosives.[162]

This information was of great value to the Russians, who had launched their A-bomb research in early 1943, when Stalin named the nuclear physicist Igor Kurchatov to run the program. Kurchatov took the helm in March, in the midst of the decisive Battle of Stalingrad. Victory convinced the Russians that they would win the war and emerge as a world power. Kurchatov later acknowledged that the spy reports were important guidelines for "our research, to bypass many very labor-intensive phases of working out the problem and to learn about new scientific and technical ways of solving it." Yet despite this input, Kurchatov complained on September 29, 1944, to Lavrenti Beria, the head of the KGB, who supervised the project, that "abroad there had been created around the problem a concentration of scientific and engineering technical forces on a scale unseen in the history of world science. . . . But in our country . . . the state of affairs remains completely unsatisfactory." The Soviet leadership was not giving the research high enough priority.[163]

Nonetheless, by the start of 1945, largely thanks to Fuchs, the Soviets knew a great deal about the Manhattan Project. While Hoover was fruitlessly chasing Oppenheimer, Klaus Fuchs was taking the secrets of the bomb out of the front gate of Los Alamos in his Buick. Fuchs, who worked at the heart of the detonation problem, gave Kurchatov the solution—implosion. At their meeting on June 2 on the Alameda Street Bridge in Santa Fe, he gave Gold documents that "fully described the plutonium bomb . . . which was to be tested at *Trinity*," according to his confession. He provided "a sketch of the bomb and its components and gave all the important dimensions. . . . Full details were given of the tamper, the aluminum shell, and of the high explosive lens system." Fuchs told Gold that the U.S. planned to use the bomb against Japan and that it would produce an explosion equal to ten thousand tons of TNT.[164]

In his confession, Fuchs estimated that he had saved the Russians several years in building the bomb, or "one year at least." He left Los Alamos on June 16, 1946, and returned to England. In the meantime, the United States cut off nuclear information to the British, who decided to build their own bomb, and set up their project, Harwell, on an RAF base south of Oxford. With his Los Alamos experience, Fuchs was an obvious choice for Harwell. He was hired in the summer of 1946 and given security clearance. He later boasted, "I am Harwell."[165] Fuchs was so intent on resuming his spying for the Russians that he was given a new handler. From 1947 to 1949, he met Alexander Feklisov six times in pubs such as the Nag's Head and the Spotted Horse, and gave him formulas, graphs, and sketches. Their last meeting was in April 1949. Fuchs told Feklisov: "I hope your baby is born soon. I estimate it will take you one or two years."[166]

In 1945, when Gouzenko identified twenty Canadian agents by their real names and code names, Robert J. Lamphere of the FBI Soviet espionage squad realized that code names were a promising lead. The FBI had kept the coded KGB cables retrieved from its black bag jobs on the Soviet consulate in New York. In 1947, Lamphere turned them over to Frank Rowlett, a project director of the Venona team.[167]

Thus began the collaboration of the Venona decoders with the FBI. Venona had no investigative branch. It could decipher a message that revealed a code name, but had no way of identifying the agent behind it. The FBI could sometimes match the code name with the real name. Meredith Gardner had begun to decipher messages that showed the Soviets had spies inside the Manhattan Project. In September 1949, Gardner cracked one indicating that the Soviets had an agent in the British mission working on gaseous diffusion at the Manhattan Project, whose sister lived in the United States. By this time, Lamphere had received from an FBI man in London two captured German documents from the thirties, consisting of a Gestapo list of wanted Communists. No. 210 was Fuchs, Klaus, a philosophy student. Fuchs's name and address turned up in Israel Halperin's address book, supplied by the Mounties. His sister Kristel's address was also in Halperin's book. In September 1949, the FBI interviewed Kristel, who at that time was a mental patient in the Westboro State Hospital outside Boston. She confirmed the connection with Halperin and recalled that a man had come to see her, wanting to get in touch with her brother.[168]

The FBI opened a case on Fuchs on September 22, 1949, and alerted British intelligence. At that time, Fuchs told the security officer at Harwell that his father had been offered a university chair at Leipzig in East Germany, which might be an embarrassment to him because of his secret work. The British decided that since Fuchs had brought up the subject of his Communist background, he should be allowed to hang himself. They assigned one of their best interrogators, W. J. Skardon, an MI5 officer working at Scotland Yard, to talk to him. If he confessed, he would provide the entire case for the prosecution.

The tweedy, mustached, pipe-smoking Skardon was empathetic and avuncular, and put the jittery Fuchs at ease. Still, at first, they played a cat-and-mouse game, with Fuchs denying that he had committed espionage in two meetings on December 21 and December 30. But on January 24, 1950, according to an MI5 memo, Fuchs "under considerable mental strain and moved by a series of complex psychological factors, was persuaded to make a full confession." In his confession, which he dictated on January 30 to Michael Perrin, an atomic scientist connected with the British Ministry of Supply, Fuchs said, "I believe that the western allies deliberately allowed Germany and Russia to fight each other to death. . . . I had no hesitation in giving all the information I had."[169]

Fuchs was arrested on February 2, 1950, and tried on March 1 at the Old Bailey, under the Official Secrets Act. Lord Chief Justice Goddard presided, robed in scarlet and ermine, and venerable under his white wig. In the audience were a Tass correspondent and an FBI observer. Fuchs pleaded guilty to four counts of passing documents between 1943 and 1947 in various locations. The judge sentenced him to the maximum of fourteen years, after charging him with "the grossest treachery" and "irreparable harm." His crime was "only thinly differentiated from high treason." The entire trial lasted an hour and a half, from 10:30 A.M. until noon.[170]

In his confession, Fuchs had not given away the names of his contacts. Lamphere was after the man who had visited Kristel. In her deposition to the FBI in 1945, Liz Bentley had described ten meetings in 1940 with a minor Soviet agent, Abraham Brothman, who ran an engineering firm in Queens. She picked up blueprints, which she brought to Golos. The FBI questioned Brothman in May 1947. He explained that passing out unclassified blueprints was his way of drumming up business. He knew Bentley as "Helen." "Sometime in 1940," he said, "Helen stopped coming to my office and another individual named Harry Gold came . . . and said he represented Golos." Brothman had made the mistake of identifying Gold as a courier for Golos. A worried Brothman called Gold and said "the FBI were here . . . they know everything. . . . They have a photograph of you and me in a restaurant. . . . Someone has ratted! . . . It must have been that bitch Helen!" Gold was questioned on the same day as Brothman and told the FBI he had worked two years for Golos as a consultant and was now working for Brothman in his Queens laboratory.

Focusing on Gold, Lamphere found that some of the personal details he had told Brothman were identical to those that the man who came to see Kristel had told her. Lamphere was eager to talk to Fuchs in London and show him film and photographs of Gold. Only in May 1950 did the British allow the meeting. On May 20, Lamphere spent an hour with Fuchs in the cold and dreary Wormwood Scrubs prison. At thirty-nine, Fuchs was sallow-skinned and stoop-shouldered, with receding hair and teeth stained yellow from nicotine. He told them that the man he knew as Raymond might have been Jewish, that he was a chemical engineer and a resident of Philadelphia.[171]

In the meantime, in February 1950 Gold saw in the paper that Fuchs had confessed. Dispirited and fatalistic, he waited for the FBI to arrive. On May 17, two agents interviewed Gold for nine hours. They filmed him and took still photographs for Lamphere to show to Fuchs. On May 22, they searched his apartment in Philadelphia, which Gold thought he had sanitized. But the moment came when agent Dick Brennan pulled from behind a book a folded street map of Santa Fe. On the cover, it said "Land of Enchantment," and inside, Gold had highlighted Alameda Street. Brennan asked: "So you never went west of the Mississippi? How about this, Harry?"[172]

Gold crumpled and said, "Yes, I am the man to whom Klaus Fuchs gave information on atomic energy." Corroboration came in London on May 24, when Fuchs identified a still photo of Gold, saying, "That is him, my American contact."

For nine years, Fuchs sewed mailbags with the other inmates at Wormwood Scrubs. His fourteen-year sentence was reduced for good behavior and in 1959 he was reunited with his eighty-five-year-old father in Leipzig, where he was received with honors and appointed deputy director of the Institute for Nuclear Physics near Dresden. He married and lived a normal family life, with no need for the controlled schizophrenia of spying. In 1979, he was awarded the Karl Marx Order for his scientific work. He died of lung cancer in 1988.[173]

As for Harry Gold, his KGB handlers had committed a blunder equal to the repeated use of the one-time pads, by making him a courier for agents in two different networks. This was breaking an essential rule of tradecraft, that each network must be compartmentalized, and that no person should have access to more than one.

Under questioning on June 2, 1950, Gold revealed that he had another source in New Mexico, a GI who lived on High Street in Albuquerque, married with no children, whom he had contacted on the same June trip when he saw Fuchs in Santa Fe. He had paid the GI $500 for his information. The GI was a draftsman or a machinist at Los Alamos with a Bronx or Brooklyn accent. Harry had met his wife, whose name he recalled was Ruth.

FBI agents checking personnel records at Los Alamos found a David Greenglass, who had a wife named Ruth and who lived in Albuquerque at 209 North High Street. Gold was shown two photographs of Greenglass. At first, like Fuchs, he was not sure. But on June 15, he positively identified some more recent snapshots. That same day, Greenglass was brought in for questioning. He confessed, implicating his wife and his brother-in-law, Julius Rosenberg. When he identified Gold, Fuchs started a chain reaction that led from Gold to Greenglass and from Greenglass to the Rosenbergs. From the arrest of Fuchs in February 1950 to the arrest of Julius Rosenberg on July 18, less than six months elapsed.[174]

There was ample corroboration in the Venona traffic concerning the Rosenberg spy ring. Remembered as a spy of atomic secrets, Rosenberg was more importantly the leader of a ring of well-placed agents who furnished military and scientific information.

In 1946, Meredith Gardner had begun to break some key messages and by the summer of 1947 he had uncovered the outlines of a massive Soviet espionage effort. Lamphere and the FBI were brought in to help identify the code names in 1948.

The first message mentioning the Rosenberg ring was sent to Moscow on May 5, 1944: "*Antenna* [a code name for Rosenberg suggesting knowledge of radio] proposed for recruitment a *Zemliak* [Fellow Countryman or party member], 25 years old, living in *Tyre* [New York]. . . . Took courses at Cooper Union . . . worked for two years in the Signal Corps lab at Fort Monmouth but was discharged for union activity. He now works at Western Electric." His name was given in the Latin alphabet as Alfred Epaminondas Sarant. "Do you sanction?" the message asked.[175]

Sarant was a young and rather hotheaded Cooper Union–trained electrical engineer who shared a Greenwich Village apartment with Joel Barr, another of Rosenberg's recruits. Both had worked on military radar at the U.S. Army Signal Corps lab at Fort Monmouth and both had been dismissed, Sarant for disruptive union activity and Barr for party membership. Barr and Sarant got jobs with Western Electric developing a top secret radar bombsight.

By mid-November 1944, Rosenberg's code name had been changed from *Antenna* to *Liberal*. KGB New York reported that *Liberal* "has safely carried through the contracting of *Hughes* [Sarant], who is a good friend of *Meter* [Barr]." The KGB proposed to "pair them off and get them to photograph their own material, having been given a camera for this purpose." *Liberal* would pick up the film and deliver it to the KGB.

A December 13, 1944, New York to Moscow message said that *Hughes* [Sarant] had "handed over 17 authentic drawings relating to APQ-7." This was a secret airborne radar system developed by MIT and Western Electric, where they worked.[176]

After the war, Sarant moved on to the physics lab at Cornell and Barr went to France to take graduate courses. When Greenglass was arrested in June 1950, Barr vanished. In July, Sarant was questioned by the FBI. Then he too vanished, with the wife of one of his close friends in Ithaca, Carolyn Dayton, who left behind two small children. Sarant left behind a wife. Years later, it was learned that Barr and Sarant were doing scientific work in Leningrad, Barr as Joseph Berg and Sarant as Philip Staros. Barr helped build the first Soviet radar-guided anti-aircraft gun, which was used by the North Vietnamese against American planes. He died in Moscow in 1998. Sarant, who had worked on computer research for the Soviet military, died in 1979.[177]

On July 26, 1944, KGB New York advised Moscow that *Antenna* had gone to Washington for ten days. There he visited his old school friend Max Elitcher (real name used), who was working for the Bureau of Standards, where he was head of the section for warships with guns of over five-inch caliber. Rosenberg described him as loyal, reliable, levelheaded, and able. His wife was also a Communist, and worked for the War Department as a psychologist. Elitcher had all the necessary equipment for taking photographs. New York asked Moscow for clearance on Elitcher.[178]

Because Elitcher's name appeared in clear text, this message led to the identification of Rosenberg as *Antenna*. The cryptanalysts did not know who *Antenna* was; neither did the FBI. But they knew Elitcher. The Office of Naval Intelligence had started investigating him after he attended a rally in 1941 of the Communist front group American Peace Mobilization. He had also attended a secret caucus of Communists employed by the Bureau of Standards. When the FBI questioned Elitcher in 1950, he broke. He admitted to having been a Communist and confessed to being an old friend of Rosenberg's going back to City College days, when they were both electrical engineers. Rosenberg had tried in vain to recruit him in the summer of 1944 in Washington. Elitcher added that Morton Sobell, another City College friend, was a member of Rosenberg's network. Elitcher had accompanied Sobell in New York when he dropped film off for Rosenberg.[179]

Another member of the City College engineers' group whom Rosenberg recruited was William Perl, born Mutterperl. On September 14, KGB New York reported to Moscow that *Gnome* [Perl] had been paid only expenses until recently. Judging by the material received, he deserved remuneration "no less valuable than that given the rest of *Liberal's* group, who were given a bonus by you. Please agree to paying him 500 dollars." This was signed [Stepan] Apresyan, then head of the KGB New York station.

Perl had matured into a brilliant aeronautical scientist, who during the war worked for the Air Force on a number of secret projects, at Langley Field in Virginia and at the Lewis Flight Propulsion Laboratory in Cleveland. In 1950, he was under consideration for a post with the Atomic Energy Commission and underwent a loyalty check. The FBI came to call on July 20. Had he sublet the vanished Al Sarant's Morton Street apartment at one time? Perl was called before a federal grand jury and denied under oath that he had ever known Julius Rosenberg. Tried for perjury in May 1953, by which time he was a physics instructor at Columbia University, Perl was found guilty and sent to prison.[180]

Fourteen Venona messages concerning Perl corroborate that he was a valuable and productive agent. Among these were:

On May 10, 1944, Perl reported on a long-distance fighter under development by Vultee Aircraft.

On May 20, 1944, he reported on a jet engine under development by Westinghouse.

On October 22, 1944, KGB New York advised Moscow that *Gnome* (Perl), who was now in Cleveland, was so valuable an agent that they proposed to send a liaison team there to handle his material. *Liberal* recommended *Linza* (Michael Sidorovich), whom he described as: "Fellow Countryman, was volunteer in Spain, lives in western NY. . . . *Liberal* had known him since childhood, including political work, says he and wife are devoted. Wife is dressmaker who can open shop in city for cover. . . . *Liberal* says *Linza* ready to renew contact with us."[181]

On December 20, 1944, KGB New York reported to Moscow that Sidorovich and his wife had sold their New York home and moved to Cleveland. *Liberal* had gone to Cleveland to arrange the introductions. Sidorovich and his wife, Ann, received a $500 bonus for making the move.

———

On September 21, 1944, a message from KGB New York to Moscow first brought up Ruth Greenglass. *Liberal* recommended the wife of his wife's brother as possibly providing a safe apartment. She was twenty-one, a *Townswoman* (U.S. citizen), and a *Gymnast* (Young Communist League) since 1942. Her husband, David, had been called up and was now working at the *Enormous* plant in Santa Fe.[182]

David Greenglass had been inducted into the Army in April 1943, leaving behind his bride. Both were devoted, dues-paying party members. David got to Los Alamos in August 1944, and wrote Ruth that he was working on a top secret project—"not a word to anybody about anything except maybe Julie [Julius]." Greenglass was working in the laboratory of George Kistiakowsky, head of the Explosives Division at Los Alamos, making models of bomb parts. Ruth made plans to visit her husband in New Mexico in November, when he had a five-day furlough. Julius, who had already proposed to Moscow that Ruth be involved in his activities, told her that she should ask David if he would pass on information. Ruth didn't like the idea, but Ethel said if it was something Davey wanted to do, why not let him decide?[183]

In mid-November 1944, the newlyweds were reunited at the Hotel Franciscan in Albuquerque. Toward the end of her stay, Ruth brought up Julius's request. They talked it over, pulled in the two directions of alarm and eagerness, and decided to comply. David gave Ruth some information to take home about the layout of Los Alamos and the scientists there.

As David Greenglass later recalled, "Julius Rosenberg was the type of man that was charming, hard, and a wonderful salesman. The proverbial salesman who could sell refrigerators to Eskimos. He had many facets to his personality. . . . He also had a certain ruthlessness. . . . One of the things I was particularly working on was the high explosive lens mold. . . . He told me the Russians were very interested."[184]

On November 27, 1944, the cryptographer Meredith Gardner tackled a Venona cable that gave him insomnia. The message to Moscow was responding to a request for more information on Ethel Rosenberg. "First name Ethel," the cable said. "Twenty nine years old, married five years. Finished secondary school. A Fellow Countrywoman since 1938. . . . Knows about her husband's work and the work of *Meter* [Barr] and *Nil* [unidentified agent]. In view of delicate health does not work. Is characterized positively and as a devoted person."[185]

This cable used the same spell code as a previous message Gardner had cracked, which had given the names of the scientists at Los Alamos. He fastened on the name Ethel. He had the E and the L, and in between there was a three-letter group. Finally he decided that since the Soviet cable traffic included a lot of English words, the most common three letter word was "the." This intuition was on target, for the name was E-the-L.[186]

On December 16, 1944, KGB New York reported to Moscow that "*Osa* [Ruth] has returned from a trip to see *Kaliber* [David]. *Kaliber* expressed his readiness to help. . . . He said the authorities of the camp were openly taking all precautions for preventing information about *Enormous* falling into Russian hands. This is causing serious discontent among the progressive workers. . . . In mid-January *Kaliber* will be in *Tyre* [New York]. *Liberal*, referring to his ignorance of the problem [the A-bomb] expresses the wish that our man should meet *Kaliber* and question him personally." Signed [Leonid] Kvasnikov, the KGB man in charge of atomic espionage.[187]

Julius Rosenberg's handler was Alexander Feklisov, the same man who would later handle Klaus Fuchs in London. Code-named *Kalistrat*, this young KGB agent had been in New York since 1941. He met Julius some fifty times; the two men liked each other, and became friends. Julius Rosenberg carried out his spying with adolescent eagerness, once hailing Feklisov with a loud "Hello, Comrade." Feklisov advised caution; he told him to stop seeing his

Communist friends and not to subscribe to any Communist newspapers. Rosenberg lived for Soviet military victories and admired the partisans who harassed the Nazi regiments in the dead of winter. Feklisov told him he was a partisan in his own way, taking risks, and gave him a Leica with a special lens for microfilming documents.

They often met at the Automat on 38th Street and Broadway, which had no waitresses and two exits. On December 24, 1944, both men arrived carrying packages. Julius did not take money. He said he loathed the rich and looked forward to the day, predicted by Lenin, of gold-plated urinals. But this was Christmas, and Feklisov gave him an Omega stainless steel watch, a brown crocodile handbag, and a teddy bear. Julius had a present for Feklisov, a brown box weighing about fifteen pounds. Inside it was a top secret proximity fuse, a small radar unit that was placed inside an artillery shell, exploding the shell when it came close to the target. The Russians considered the proximity fuse second only in importance to the atomic data. An astounded Feklisov asked him how he had obtained it. Julius explained that as an inspector for the Signal Corps, going from plant to plant, he had found a rejected proximity fuse in the workshop at Emerson Radio. He replaced the defective parts, put it in his briefcase, and walked out with it. Who was going to inspect the inspector? When the U-2 flown by Francis Gary Powers was shot down over Sverdlovsk on May 1, 1960, it was with a proximity fuse.[188]

In January 1945, Greenglass came to New York on a two-week furlough and prepared some sketches of the implosion lens mold, which corroborated what Fuchs would tell the Soviets: that the Los Alamos scientists were committed to a plutonium-fired, implosion-type detonation.

On January 8, Kvasnikov notified Moscow that "*Kaliber* has arrived in *Tyre* on leave. He has confirmed his agreement to help us. . . . He has given us a hand-written plan of the layout of Camp-2 and facts known to him about the work and the personnel. The basic task of the camp is to make the mechanism that is to serve as the detonator. Experimental work is being carried out on the construction of tubes of this kind and experiments are being tried with explosives."[189]

One evening during David Greenglass's furlough, his brother-in-law called and said there was someone he wanted him to meet. Rosenberg seemed to exercise a Svengali-like influence over Greenglass. He hopped into a car and went as instructed to 42nd Street and First Avenue, where Rosenberg was waiting. A stranger appeared, wearing a hat with the brim down. He was Anatoly Yatskov, a specialist in scientific intelligence at the KGB station, chosen to debrief Greenglass. He asked questions about the mold design, and soon realized that Greenglass did not have the scientific background to understand the research going on in New Mexico. He had an adequate enough visual memory to draw a rough sketch of the lenses he was working on, but could not explain their use. Still, he was an additional source at Los Alamos.

When Greenglass left, Yatskov took Rosenberg to a cafeteria to discuss how to proceed. "Many soldiers' wives stationed at Los Alamos live in Albuquerque," Yatskov said. "It would be best if Ruth moved there as well." That way, Greenglass could leave the compound on weekends to see his wife. [190]

In February 1945, Ruth moved to Albuquerque to be with her husband, who commuted the ninety miles from Los Alamos on weekends. In June, Harry Gold showed up in Albuquerque with the password "I come from Julius." Greenglass was discharged from the Army on February 28, 1946, and joined his brother-in-law in New York to found a firm called G&R Engineering.

In June 1950, when Harry Gold identified him as a Soviet agent, Greenglass told his story to the FBI. He didn't want to turn in his own flesh and blood, he later explained, but realized that Julius and Ethel wanted to be martyrs. Ethel's mother had gone to see her daughter in Sing Sing. "Why do you persist in your cause?" she pleaded. "Think of your children. Think of what you are doing to them." Ethel said, "You are not my mother. Leave. I don't want to have any more to do with you." Ethel was five feet and one hundred pounds of pure obstinacy. David thought that "to martyr yourself for a completely erroneous ideological cause was the most ridiculous thing a person could do." [191]

At their trial in March 1951, Julius and Ethel Rosenberg were convicted on charges of espionage. The misfortune of the Rosenbergs, aside from their propensity for martyrdom, was that they were arrested shortly after the outbreak of the Korean War. Had the Venona messages been deciphered sooner, had the FBI been able to get to Fuchs faster, their trial might have taken place before Korea. As it was, Judge Irving Kaufman acknowledged the importance of the timing at the sentencing hearing on April 5. "The issue of punishment in this case is presented in a unique framework of history," he said. "Putting into the hands of the Russians the A-bomb years before our best scientists predicted Russia would perfect the bomb has already caused, in my opinion, the Communist aggression in Korea . . . and who knows but what millions of people may pay the price of your treason." Thus, the Rosenbergs were irrationally labeled as potential mass murderers. [192]

Before handing out the death sentence, Judge Kaufman had sounded out the views of the FBI. On April 2, 1951, J. Edgar Hoover replied with a memo saying that a death sentence for a wife and mother with no previous criminal record would be perceived as cruel and vindictive. It would generate "a psychological reaction on the part of the public that would reflect poorly on the FBI." Others in the FBI and the Justice Department agreed. Thus, Judge Kaufman imposed the death penalty over serious objections from the Justice Department. He called Ethel Rosenberg a "full-fledged partner" in her husband's treason. But where was the evidence? Judge Kaufman claimed that the Rosenbergs had given the Russians the secret of the bomb, but this was not the Russian view. Kurchatov, the chief Russian atomic scientist, would later say that Fuchs's material had been "exceptionally important," while Greenglass's notes had provided little more than corroboration.[193] General Leslie Groves himself, in charge at Los Alamos and not partial to spies, later said: "I think that the data that went out was of minor value." If any one man was responsible for hastening the Soviet bomb, it was Klaus Fuchs.

Kaufman's double death sentence, viewed in the light of Klaus Fuchs's sentence of fourteen years, reduced to nine, was out of all proportion, an immoderate Cold War reaction bordering on hysteria.

The appeals process spent itself, and President Eisenhower refused to grant clemency, as pickets crowded in front of the White House. In June 1953, a final effort was made to enlist the cooperation of the Rosenbergs. Attorney General Herbert Brownell sent John V. Bennett, Director of the Bureau of Prisons, to tell them that their sentence could be commuted if they confessed. An unrepentant Rosenberg told him: "My wife is awaiting a horrible end for having typed a few notes!"[194]

On June 16, three days before their execution, Eisenhower offered this curious reason for refusing clemency to Ethel Rosenberg in a letter to his son, John: "If there would be any commuting of the woman's sentence without the man's, then from here on the Soviets would simply recruit their spies from among women."[195]

On June 19, ten thousand gathered in Union Square for the death watch. The tabloid headline read: "Spies Fry Tonight." People cried, speakers spoke, improvised choirs sang "Let My People Go," and a collective wail arose upon the news that the Rosenbergs had been taken to the execution chamber.

Meredith Gardner saw the headlines and was shaken from his world of mathematical conundrums. "I thought it was a great tragedy," he recalled. "I was very much downcast. It was a very unpleasant thing to feel that I was a link in the chain of events that got them there."[196]

The real tragedy was that Venona was kept secret for so long. It was kept even from President Truman, who, had he been privy to it, would not have seen Communists in government as merely a partisan issue. Venona was kept secret because its postwar customers, the FBI, the CIA, and Military Intelligence, wanted the cryptanalysts to keep identifying the spies behind the code names. The Venona decrypts found 349 American citizens and residents who had a covert relationship with Soviet intelligence. Of the 349, 171 were identified. The other 178 were known only by their code names. Who was *Achilles,* involved in scientific spying at the University of Chicago? Who was *Nile,* an asset of the New York KGB office, who in 1944 was paid a monthly stipend? Who was *Randolph,* a journalist based in New York who went often to Washington? Hiding behind code names were Soviet agents who might still have policy jobs, in the military or in the State and Defense departments, promoted as time went by. Thus, even though the Soviets had changed their codes after the war, having been tipped off by the British agent Kim Philby, the search for agents known only by their undeciphered code names went on for years. It was not until 1977, with diminishing returns in the work's operational value, that William P. Crowell, the acting chief of the Venona group in the National Security Agency, decided that their work was done. The Venona program was shut down in October 1980.[197]

Even then, the secret was kept for another fifteen years, due in part to the mind-set of the SIGINTers, the Signals Intelligence veterans, with their "band of brothers" tradition. They had spent years breaking the code and the fact that no one else knew about it was a source of pride. They took pride too in being invisible, and hated press attention. In addition, making Venona public required the agreement of the principal agencies involved: the CIA, the FBI, and the NSA, who took their time conducting their internal debate. It was not until 1995 that Venona was disclosed. Over the next two years, 2,900 partially decrypted messages were released, with blanks and abbreviations.[198]

Soviet espionage harvested a full crop of spies during the war years, when the acronym agencies, in dire need of personnel, seldom bothered with loyalty checks. The old-line departments like State and Treasury were also infiltrated by agents at a policymaking level, such as Harry Dexter White, Lauchlin Currie, and Alger Hiss.

The penetration of the Manhattan Project was a spectacular coup. As John Earl Haynes and Harvey Klehr put it in their authoritative book, *Venona,* the Soviets during World War II conducted "an unrestrained espionage offensive against the United States . . . of the type that a nation directs at an enemy state." During the war, the Communist Party U.S.A. had fifty thousand members, a recruitment pool that was dipped into often. These American Communists formed a phalanx of ideological sympathizers who used the rationale that Russia was our ally and that we should help them defeat the Germans.

If the Venona messages had been released in a timely way, the swing of the pendulum to hysterical anti-Communism could perhaps have been avoided. In the case of the Rosenbergs, the existence of an espionage ring would have been proven beyond dispute, cutting the ground from under the protest movement. The books arguing their innocence would have been exposed as diatribes. At the same time, Venona provided evidence that Ethel was far from a full-fledged partner in her husband's espionage. For a message of November 27, 1944, said plainly that Ethel, "in view of delicate health, does not work." Sentencing Ethel to a lesser charge would have helped defuse the protests.

Had Venona been released, the decrypts would have corroborated Liz Bentley in every particular. The doubts that hung over her testimony would not have stood up. All those whom she named, from Duncan Lee to Silvermaster to Perlo, would have been prosecuted and probably convicted. Instead, they went free.

Had Venona been released, the confrontation between Chambers and Hiss would have left no doubts regarding Hiss's spying. As it was, Chambers was denounced for everything from having bad teeth to being a pathological liar. Even after Hiss's perjury conviction, the case was not decisively cleared up and a number of books were written claiming that Hiss was innocent. The whole matter remained under a cloud, which only Venona could have lifted.

A few dupes and opportunists still argue that Venona is a forgery and that Hiss was blameless.[199] But why would hundreds of cryptanalysts labor for half a century to produce 2,900 pages of forged decrypts? Anyone who has spent time studying Venona transcripts will come to the conclusion that these partly broken messages in their abbreviated cablese with their multiple code names and their bizarre prose style would be impossible to forge. It's inconceivable that men like Meredith Gardner, who spent their entire careers decoding Venona, could have been party to a forgery.

If further proof is needed, it comes from the KGB itself. "SIS ace Meredith Gardner was able to break the five main coding systems used by NKVD *Rezidenturas* in America before 1946," Alexander Feklisov wrote in his memoirs. "Between 1946 and 1952, Gardner decoded—partially or completely— about 2,200 [sic] secret messages that uncovered many operations and identified many Soviet intelligence officers and agents. . . . For the most part, I must admit that, apart from a few errors, the decrypted messages are genuine."[200]

The climate of the postwar years that brought about McCarthy rested on doubt and uncertainty as to the extent of Soviet espionage in the United States. It was in such a climate that demagogues and political opportunists could move in and make hay. The timely release of Venona could have shown the American people the true extent of Soviet espionage, which was far-reaching, while showing also that by 1950, when Senator McCarthy got going, it was all but over with. The wartime secrets had been stolen, the networks had been dismantled thanks to Bentley and Gouzenko, and the Soviets had lost the ideological rationale of a Russia at war, which fostered recruitment. The release of Venona would have nipped McCarthyism in the bud, for the true facts about real spies would have made wild accusations about imaginary spies irrelevant. Only in the absence of Venona could McCarthy feed on collective fears regarding immense conspiracies and treacherous leaders. Venona would have revealed unstinted spying, abetted by the American party. It would have led to the prosecution of disloyal public servants. It would have stifled the outcry that Communists were the innocent victims of Red-baiting and witch-hunts, and shown that McCarthy was inconsequential to the issue he rode to fame.

X
___

TRUMAN
TAKES CHARGE

The Russians did not like Harry Truman. They saw him as an accidental President, raised unelected into the highest office due to FDR's death. The proletarian Soviet rulers displayed a streak of snobbery regarding Truman's petit-bourgeois origins. They much preferred the aristocratic, manorial Roosevelt, magnetic and mellifluous, while Truman was brusque and plainspoken. Through the filter of their reductive dogma, the Soviets saw the rookie President as the figurehead of Wall Street imperialism.

This came out with alarming clarity in a Venona message from the KGB man in New York, Vladimir Pravdin, to KGB Moscow on May 26, 1945, ten weeks after the end of the war in Europe. He said there was an organized campaign on the part of reactionary circles to "get hold" of *Sailor* (Truman) and bring about a change in policy toward the U.S.S.R. "The most reactionary section of the press welcomes *Sailor's* accession to power," he advised. *Sailor* was friendly with such Republican reactionaries as Robert Taft and Burton K. Wheeler and was notoriously untried and ill-informed on foreign policy. Averell Harriman, the former ambassador to Moscow, was singled out as "one of the bitterest anti-Soviet propagandists. . . . He does not shrink from any chicanery." The head of the United States delegation to the Reparations Commission in Moscow, Edwin Pauley, represented the interests of Standard Oil. Pravdin said his appointment was a gesture of friendship from Truman to the oilmen.[1] Harriman's "chicanery" upon his return from Moscow in April 1945 had been to warn Truman that the Soviets wanted to take over Eastern Europe and penetrate Western Europe.

The same hostile tone was evident in a message sent to Moscow on June 14, 1945, from the KGB *Rezident* and Soviet consul in San Francisco, Mikhail Vasilov, reporting on the founding conference of the United Nations. "Dulles and other partners of the firm Sullivan and Cromwell," Vasilov cabled, "are known for their support of Franco and German cartels and for their leading role in the America First organization. Apart from the known pro-fascists such as [J. Edgar] Hoover, Wheeler, Vandenberg and others, there are the like-minded persons of [Thomas E.] Dewey and others who feel the next war will be against the USSR . . . forming a coalition of Anglo-American conservatives."[2] Senator Arthur Vandenberg of Michigan was on the American delegation, and the Republican lawyer John Foster Dulles was an adviser. The irony of Vasilov's comments on the reactionary makeup of the delegation was that it was riddled with Soviet spies. Harry Dexter White was the Treasury representative, reporting his observations to the San Francisco KGB station, and Alger Hiss was the secretary general of the conference.

Political arteries were hardening. Gone was the wartime friendship lubricated by lend-lease. America for the Soviets had reverted to its old role as class enemy. The postwar Venona traffic was less concerned with espionage than with preparing an ideological foundation for the Cold War. It is tragic to surmise that this farrago of half-baked information was shaping Soviet foreign policy.

The Big Three gathered in Potsdam, a suburb of Berlin, in July, to draw the map of postwar Germany. It was there on July 16 that Truman received the news of the first successful A-bomb test in the New Mexico desert. Stimson wrote in his diary that Truman was "tremendously pepped up by it. . . . It gave him an entirely new feeling of confidence." Truman in his diary wrote: "Believe Japs will fold up before Russia comes in. I am sure they will when 'Manhattan' appears over their homeland."[3]

Truman waited a week before he casually approached Stalin and said: "We have a new weapon of unusual destructive force." Stalin nodded without surprise and thanked him for the information. He already knew about the bomb. Marshal Georgi Zhukov, who was also at Potsdam, later wrote in his memoirs: "Stalin . . . pretended he saw nothing special in what Truman had imparted to him. . . . On returning to his quarters, he told Molotov about his conversation. Molotov said, 'they're raising the stakes.' Stalin said, 'we'll have to talk with Kurchatov about speeding up our work.' "[4]

On August 6, the bomb was dropped on Hiroshima, destroying that large city and killing seventy thousand. Truman gave a radio broadcast to advise the nation: "Three hours ago an American airplane dropped one bomb on Hiroshima and destroyed its usefulness to the enemy. . . . The Japanese began the war from the air at Pearl Harbor. They have been repaid many fold. It is an atomic bomb. It is a harnessing of the basic power of the universe. The force from which the sun draws its power has been loosed against those who brought war to the Far East. . . . The fact that we can release atomic energy ushers in a new era in man's understanding of nature's forces."[5]

Churchill once said that war, first and foremost, is about "who does the dying." Pre-bomb U.S. military policy was a two-phase invasion of the Japanese home islands, to begin in November 1945. "I asked General Marshall what it would cost in lives to land on the Tokyo plain and other places in Japan," Truman wrote in explanation of his decision to Professor Cates at the University of Chicago on January 12, 1953. "It was his opinion that such an invasion would cost at a minimum one quarter of a million casualties and might cost as many as a million men on the American side alone, with an equal number of the enemy. The other military and naval men present agreed. . . . I ordered atomic bombs dropped on the two cities on the way back from Potsdam, when we were in the middle of the Atlantic Ocean."[6] For Truman, the arithmetic was irrefutable: better to have several hundred thousand Japanese dead than a quarter of a million Americans or more.

Truman found himself in a postwar quandary that was far more complex than wartime, when you knew who your enemy was and you fought him openly, with full support at home. In this new situation, there were no open hostilities, but pinpricks and probes in different parts of the world, with the use of surrogates, masterminded in Moscow.

Stalin still thought in the outdated terms of a *cordon sanitaire* to protect Russia from German invasion routes. He plunged into the game of grab—Poland, the gateway for the German armies; Hungary, Romania, and Bulgaria, who had fought alongside the Germans. Once Stalin had annexed Eastern Europe and established police states on his perimeters, would that lead to further probes? Stalin probed in Turkey, where the Dardanelles, connecting the Black Sea with the Mediterranean, would give Russia a warm water link to Western Europe. He probed in Iran, by sending in troops and backing an Azerbaijani uprising in the north. But on May 8, 1946, he wrote one of the Azerbaijani leaders that keeping troops in Iran was a mistake, for then "why couldn't British troops stay in Egypt, Syria, Indonesia and Greece?"[7] This was good old Metternichian balance of power politics. The Russian troops pulled out. Stalin lost Iranian oil concessions.

Truman knew that an American response was in order, for Europe was too war-weakened to react. On July 12, 1946, he was having a drink with his naval aide and fellow Missourian Clark Clifford, and with George Elsey, Clifford's aide. Congressional elections were coming up in November and Truman's popularity was sagging. At one point, Truman said he was tired of being pushed around by the Soviets, who were chiselers. He wanted a statement on Soviet aims, which Elsey, who had a master's in history from Harvard, was assigned to produce. Elsey asked for input from other departments, including the Army, the Navy, and the Joint Chiefs of Staff.

The reports that Elsey drew upon were a litany of Soviet transgressions. The Navy said that instead of destroying eleven German submarines and several destroyers in their zone of occupation as agreed upon, the Soviets had added those vessels to their fleet, enlisting their officers by force. Their aim was "to become a first-class sea power." America had to prepare with its own naval buildup.

The State Department listed Soviet violations of international agreements. In their zone of Germany, they had imposed one-party rule and were manufacturing war matériel, including airplanes, instead of complying with the agreement to eliminate the German war potential. In Hungary, Romania, and Bulgaria, they had violated Yalta by failing to form governments by free elections. This was also true in Yugoslavia and Poland. In all those countries, the governments represented the will of the Soviets rather than the will of the people. In violation of lend-lease, the Soviets had turned over goods to Poland and other countries in Eastern Europe and had failed to return naval vessels loaned to them.

The Joint Chiefs of Staff sent Elsey a list of violations of military agreements. When the Soviets found American prisoners of war captured by the Germans, they sent them to Odessa in boxcars instead of releasing them. The United States was not allowed to evacuate the sick and the wounded. Only after repeated protests were they freed. In partitioned Korea, Soviet roadblocks were found south of the 38th parallel in May 1946. In Romania, the Soviets seized the entire navy as war booty. The Joint Chiefs concluded that "the present military policy of the USSR is to establish a perimeter of the Soviet-dominated states . . . the Soviets . . . are building up their war potential and that of their satellites to the end that they will be capable of defeating the western democracies. . . . Once they embark on a plan of armed aggression it can be expected that their immediate objective will be the seizure of military control of most of Eurasia." Their aim was "eventual world domination." The United States "must maintain sufficient strength" and "develop new weapons . . . to prepare for a major war."

In preparing his report for the President, Elsey had to abide by the assumptions of the Joint Chiefs that since the Soviets sought world domination and routinely violated agreements, the United States could not permit any further increment of Soviet power. He had no choice but to call for an increase in military capabilities, an upgrade in the atomic arsenal, and the promise of assistance to countries threatened by Russia. Elsey's report lay the groundwork for the Cold War standoff between the two powers, each of which suspected that the other wanted its destruction, and for the doctrine of containment first proposed by George Kennan.

Forgotten in the argument was America's nuclear deterrent. We now know from the work of Soviet historians that the Elsey report misread Stalin's intentions. As Vladislav Zubok and Constantine Pleshakov wrote in *Inside the Kremlin's Cold War*, "the bomb destroyed Stalin's expectations of being second to none among the world's great powers. . . . Stalin in 1946 restrained revolutionaries, not only in Iran, but also in Greece and other places where he did not want to promote premature confrontations with the British and the Americans. . . . Stalin wanted a breathing spell in order to rearm." The surprise for Stalin was "that the Cold War started before he could get his Bomb."[8]

———

In support of Stalin's postwar foreign policy, the American Communist Party pursued a vigorous anti-Truman line. With the President's agreement, J. Edgar Hoover authorized massive wiretaps. By the end of the war, he had also infiltrated the party, and was able to report on its activities to the White House.

On November 8, 1945, Hoover reported that the party's education director in Illinois, David Englestein, had stated that "The United States has abandoned the late president's foreign policy and is now launching upon a program of secret use of the atomic bomb." It was the duty of all Communists to agitate for the return of American soldiers, which would give the Soviets a free hand in Eastern Europe.[9]

Gone was the laxity of the war years, when defecting Soviet sailors were returned to their ships. On April 1, 1946, Hoover reported the arrest of a Soviet naval officer, Lieutenant Nikolai G. Redin, who had bought the blueprints of a destroyer tender from an undercover officer in Naval Intelligence. At the State Department, Undersecretary Dean Acheson advised the Justice Department: "Arrest him by all means if you have the goods on him. Then the Russians will disown him. But if he is acquitted the Russians will charge a frame-up and begin arresting Americans in Russia."[10] During the war, the State Department had not permitted the arrest of Soviet spies, even when they were caught red-handed.

Hoover also kept a close watch on the members of wartime spy rings who had not been prosecuted and were still employed by the government. On March 18, 1946, he reported to the White House that Harry Magdoff, a member of the Perlo ring, code-named *Kant* in Venona, was working at the Department of Commerce. In a bugged conversation, Magdoff expressed his loyalty to Henry Wallace, the Secretary of Commerce. If Wallace ever left the Commerce Department to strike out on his own, Magdoff would go with him, he said, even if he had to work for half his present salary. The person whom he was talking to observed: "You really have got religion."[11]

Charles Kramer, another member of the Perlo group, with the Venona code name *Mole,* was working for the Office of Price Administration, Hoover reported to the White House on May 31, 1946. Hoover described him as "a known espionage agent."[12] Kramer had been on loan to Senator Claude Pepper's Wartime Health and Education Subcommittee. Pepper, a left-leaning Florida Democrat, condemned his own administration as too severe on the Soviets. In a speech written by Kramer, he "advocated the destruction of all the United States facilities capable of producing the destructive forms of atomic energy," Hoover said. On May 1, Hoover added, Kramer had "surreptitiously disposed of various Communistic materials in a refuse can near an isolated bus stop in the vicinity of his residence in Arlington, Virginia."[13] Kramer was also asked to help the campaign of one of the few Communists elected to the House of Representatives, Hugh DeLacy of Washington state. Hoover said they discussed a presidential bid for Claude Pepper at the 1948 convention, in order to make the Democratic Party "our kind of party."[14] Truman wasn't responsive to Hoover's information, for at that time he had other priorities.

———

Despite its shrill anti-Truman line, the American Communist Party was in the process of self-destructing. Earl Browder, after the *Time* magazine cover story and the wartime invitations to meet with high officials in the State Department, began to see himself as a mainstream political leader. He predicted in a pamphlet, *Victory and After,* that the wartime alliance between the Soviet Union and the United States would continue after the war. He said he would even be willing to shake hands with J. P. Morgan to promote unity. He said America was not ready for Communism and bid adieu to class warfare. In May 1944, he dissolved the American Communist Party and replaced it with the Communist Political Association, which he saw as the left wing of a broad coalition within the two-party system.

The founding convention of the Communist Political Association took place in late May 1944, beneath portraits of FDR, Churchill, and Stalin. Infatuated with his own rhetoric, Browder hailed the nine thousand Communists serving their country in the armed forces. The party, with 63,000 members, seemed strong and vibrant. In the CIO, the Communists controlled unions with a total membership of 1,370,000 members.[15]

In Moscow, the Browder line was seen as heretical. In April 1945, Browder was lambasted in a French Communist journal, to make it look as if Moscow was not directly involved. The article derided his "erroneous conclusions" and deviant Marxism. Who was Browder to rewrite Marx? In effect, the article was an announcement that the Soviet drive toward world revolution would continue unabated in the postwar period.[16]

The fallout from the article destroyed Browder. For fifteen years he had been portrayed as a fount of wisdom, despite his wooden prose and plodding mind. Overnight, he became a despised heretic, vilified by those who had salaamed. At a meeting of the National Committee in June 1945, Browder sat alone in a corner, a leper without a bell, while others asked forgiveness for having followed his "opportunistic line." William Z. Foster took charge as party chairman at a special convention in July. Eugene Dennis, a Comintern-trained Stalin loyalist born Francis Waldron in Seattle, was named General Secretary. On February 5, 1946, Browder was expelled from the party as a "social imperialist." Those who failed to recant were expelled for "petit bourgeois anarchism."[17]

This was another one of those turning points, like the Nazi-Soviet pact, which many party members could not stomach. Babette Lang, a Communist in Los Angeles from 1942 to 1946, recalled that when the article on Browder came out, she thought, "Gee, this is kind of a fast shuffle. We were told there was no connection between the American party and the Russian party . . . and I didn't like the idea we were taking directives from the Russians. I lost heart in the whole thing. I didn't like the direction. I just felt washed out."[18]

Meta Reiss, the story editor at Paramount, left the party after Browder's banishment, recalling a statement of Ignazio Silone, who said that in the party there was no such thing as an adversary in good faith. The minute you disagreed, they began to call you names. "This is a dangerous policy, there is no independent thinking among the rank and file," she said.

Others were beyond saving, such as the scriptwriter and prominent Hollywood Communist of the forties Richard J. Collins. "The situation was that a man who loved Browder on Monday hated him on Thursday," he recalled. After Nemmy Sparks, the district organizer for Los Angeles county, had listened to Collins's views, "I was stripped of my epaulets. . . . A good many people after the Browder episode wanted to get out."[19]

After Browder's removal, the purge was on, as Hoover reported to the White House on September 25, 1946. The CPUSA National Committee had received a letter from the French Communist Party "asking that a list be compiled of all party functionaries including those in the trade unions. . . . There should be submitted complete biographical data concerning each individual. . . . Questionnaires were sent out . . . covering personal background data . . . education . . . activities in the Communist party . . . and full reports on participation in strikes, lockouts, demonstrations, arrests."[20]

———

In the November 1946 congressional elections, the Republicans swept both houses. Some saw their victory as a postwar desire for change, others as a reaction against the policies of the New Deal, still others as the result of shortages, in cars, in houses, in meat and sugar, in nylon. Truman, whose popularity had dropped to such a point that he did not campaign, saw the election as a sign that he lacked voter appeal. He was "terribly downcast," according to his adviser Clark Clifford. No Democratic congressman had asked for him. They had played old recordings of FDR's fireside chats instead.[21]

The results were a disaster for the Democrats. The Republican seats in the Senate went from thirty-eight to fifty-one and in the House from 190 to 246. After sixteen years of Democratic rule, the pendulum had swung. The Republicans had gained control of both houses for the first time since 1930.

Truman foresaw two difficult years, two years of political maneuvering. The 1946 campaign was not only a blow to the presidency, it paved the way for McCarthyism when Republican candidates denounced the Democrats as dupes of the Soviets. The Republicans lumped together their two favorite issues, anti-Communism and anti–New Dealism, which turned out to be a successful strategy.

In campaigns around the country, Republican candidates ran on their unvarying opposition to the New Deal. Ohio Republican John M. Vorys patted himself on the back for eight years of fighting against "New Deal incompetence, waste, graft, extravagance, and bureaucracy." Senator Kenneth S. Wherry of Nebraska made his slogan "the defeat of the New Deal." Other campaign slogans included "Got Enough OPA?" and "To Err Is Truman."

The next step was to link the New Deal with Communism. William Jenner, a small-town Indiana lawyer with a Manichaean mind, incapable of shadings, ran for the U.S. Senate in 1946 on a platform that New Deal liberalism was "a form of Communistic radicalism." He made the preposterous accusation that seventy thousand known Communists were on the government payroll. In Oklahoma, the Republican candidate George B. Schwabe warned of "the imminent danger of Communism." In Nebraska, Senator Hugh Butler charged the Democrats with failing to rid the labor unions of Communists. Endorsing the line, the Republican National Committee lamented "the infiltration of alien-minded radicals" in the federal government. Personal attacks on Truman added a nasty note. Jenner said Truman liked to go to football games for the pleasure of seeing someone else fumble.[22]

The first set-to between the President and the 80th Congress took place in January 1947. A new agency had been formed, the Atomic Energy Commission, and Truman wanted a civilian to head it. He plucked from the Tennessee Valley Authority its energetic head, David E. Lilienthal, and named him chairman of the AEC on November 1, 1946. TVA was one of those large-scale New Deal programs repugnant to right-wing Republicans. In addition, the long-time Tennessee senator Kenneth "Old Mack" McKellar held a grudge against Lilienthal for refusing to allot him patronage jobs.[23]

The stage was set for a stormy confirmation hearing before the Senate part of the Joint Committee on Atomic Energy. Lilienthal's nemesis, the seventy-six-year-old McKellar, tiny but fierce, who had been in the Senate since 1916, was not a member of the joint committee, but was extended the privilege of attending the hearings.

On January 17, 1947, when the hearings opened, a pessimistic Lilienthal wondered why he had risked his name, his health, and his livelihood in such a hostile environment. McKellar rambled irrelevantly, declaring that "Macedonian scientists" under Alexander the Great had been the first to split the atom.

On February 4, McKellar asked Lilienthal about his thoughts on Communism, and he replied with an eloquent affirmation of his faith in democracy. His remarks impressed the senators, many of whom wanted to shake his hand. Red-eyed, the veins on his forehead bulging, McKellar asked Lilienthal where his parents were born. He had forgotten the name of the village in Austro-Hungary, which was now Czechoslovakia, but replied, "in the vicinity of Pressburg." McKellar thought he had scored a point because Czechoslovakia was now under Soviet influence. Lilienthal was disgusted by the "snide pretense that masked McKellar's obviously anti-Semitic ploy."[24]

The issue of anti-Semitism came up again in a Hoover memo to the White House on February 17, 1947, which reported a phone conversation between the Democratic fixer Thomas Corcoran and Bennett Clark, a former senator and a friend of Truman's going back to World War I, who was now a judge. Clark told Corcoran that he had asked Senator Vandenberg, the powerful Michigan Republican, not to support Lilienthal.[25]

"The story of how Lilienthal, like Peter, denied himself thrice, ought to be circulated," Corcoran said.

Clark said: "You can't go putting something in the paper that the president of the United States told me more or less in confidence. I mean—it's an embarrassing thing to do. I mean—if I could do it casually, I might just say, 'well,

Lilienthal says he isn't a Jew,' and they'd say, 'well how do you know,' and I'd say, 'he told the president.' The president told me: 'I asked him point blank.' I don't want to put the president in the position of a Jew baiter or anything of that sort." Judge Clark said he had urged Senator Vandenberg not to lead any crusade for Lilienthal.[26]

On March 28, with Lilienthal's confirmation still in doubt, Senator Bricker of Ohio attacked him with the "piddling criticism of a witch-hunting mind," Lilienthal wrote in his diary. Vandenberg told him that the hearings reminded him of "a lynching bee." Lilienthal asked himself: "Why not chuck the whole business?"[27]

When the full Senate debate opened, Senator Vandenberg saved the day with a strong pro-Lilienthal speech, and he was confirmed on April 9 by a vote of 50 to 31, with moderate Republicans crossing the aisle. But it had been a grueling, three-month process, a portent of confirmations to come.

———

At the same time that the confirmation hearings were going on, Truman launched the containment policy formulated by George Kennan with his aid package to Greece and Turkey. This was also the birth of a Cold War consensus in Congress on issues of national security. Clark Clifford reminded Truman that Congress had to be scared into bipartisan support. The danger had to be exaggerated in terms of "which of the two systems currently offered the world is to survive."

Truman planned to present the aid program before a joint session of Congress on March 12, 1947. On March 10, Clifford predicted that Truman's speech would make people realize "that the war isn't over by any means."

On March 12, Truman followed Clifford's advice to stoke the furnace of crisis. "Should we fail to aid Greece and Turkey in this fateful hour," he said, "the effect will be far-reaching to the West." All those in the House chamber where the joint session was held rose up in applause. In subsequent hearings, the Republican Representative Albert M. Cole of Kansas summed up the feeling of Congress when he said the question was not whether Greece was democratic but whether "Russia is a threat to the peace of the world . . . and whether Greece is the military strategic point at which to stop such aggression." On April 22, the Senate passed the $400 million aid package by 67 to 23 and on May 9, the House passed it by 287 to 107.

———

Between 1945 and 1950, in the first five years of the Truman administration, and before McCarthy made his mark as a Red-hunter, the American Communists, already weakened by Browder's ouster, felt the full weight of all three branches of government bear down on them as never before. The measures enacted by and under Truman made the party a walking corpse.

The President who destroyed the party did not believe in what he called "the bugaboo" of Communism. In a letter to the onetime governor of Pennsylvania George H. Earle on February 28, 1947, Truman wrote: "people are very much wrought up about the Communist 'bugaboo,' but I am of the opinion that the country is perfectly safe so far as Communism is concerned—we have too many sane people."[28]

For Truman, Communism was not a danger to the country, but a potent political issue that the Republicans were using against him. After the 1946 election, Marquis Childs wrote in the *Washington Post* that the Communist issue had swept the Republicans to victory. The lesson was not lost on Truman. His strategy was to take the issue away from Congress. He prepared for the 1948 presidential election by mounting a loyalty program that would be the domestic panel of his containment policy. If you opposed the Soviet menace abroad you could not ignore it at home. In this way he would outflank the Red-hunters in Congress.

On March 21, 1947, Truman issued Executive Order 9835, requiring a loyalty check of more than two million federal employees, and creating a loyalty bureaucracy of more than six thousand. This was a program of vast proportions, involving not only the employees in place, but also the half-million new employees a year who were brought in because of turnover. Each government department and agency had a loyalty board. The Post Office had five regional boards, the Army had eighteen, the Air Force eighty-six, and the Navy three hundred, some on ships. For appeals, a twenty-three-man Loyalty Review Board was set up, operating in panels of three, and made up of "successful citizens of judicial temperament who have the confidence of all groups." A staunch sixty-seven-year-old Republican, Seth Richardson, who had served as assistant attorney general under President Hoover, was named head of the review board.

To fund the programs, Truman asked Congress for $16 million for the Civil Service Commission, which went back to 1883, and would conduct the loyalty boards, and $9 million for the FBI, which would run the field investigations. Congress, showing where its sympathies lay, granted $7 million for the FBI and $3 million for the Civil Service. Clifford noted that "President feels very strongly anti-FBI. . . . Wants to be sure and hold FBI down, afraid of Gestapo." But Clifford told Truman that the FBI was better equipped to fingerprint the huge number of employees and to conduct field investigations on those who required them, and that it had better-trained agents than the Civil Service Commission. The FBI allotted 975 agents to the task.[29]

The way the boards worked was that after receiving FBI reports of derogatory information, they asked suspected employees to prepare their defense. At their hearing, employees could appear with or without counsel and could introduce witnesses and affidavits. The suspects were never told who their accusers were, for the FBI insisted on protecting its informants. Critics complained that there was an unfair presumption of guilt, as the accused could not see the charges and had no access to the secret reports. The board then decided, on the basis of the charges and the employee's testimony, whether there were "reasonable grounds" to determine disloyalty. If removal was recommended, the employee could file an appeal before the Loyalty Review Board, and was suspended without pay in the meantime. But what were "reasonable grounds"? They varied from board to board.

Although there was abundant criticism that the loyalty boards were just another form of witch-hunt, the most remarkable thing about them was how few employees were found to be disloyal. As of June 30, 1949, 2,541,717 employees had been fingerprinted. Of those, 10,368 were given full field investigations, of which 8,323 were deemed worth completing. Of that number, 785 employees resigned prior to a hearing. Of the remainder, 5,450 went before a hearing, and 5,118 were cleared. Of the 332 who were not cleared, 102 were fired and the others were in stages of appeal. One hundred and two out of 2.5 million was a minuscule percentage. There were far more resignations than there were dismissals.

As Seth Richardson, the head of the review board, told a Rotary Club lunch on March 31, 1949: "Does that sound like a bloodthirsty outfit maliciously trying to railroad people out of the government? . . . They say we are corrupting the morale of employees. . . . I say that is tommyrot." Eleanor Bontecou, who wrote an authoritative book on the program, concluded that "in very few cases can the conduct of the hearings be called unfair in the sense that the board members displayed the animus of witch hunters."[30]

Sometimes the questions of the board members bordered on Big Brotherism, as when a proofreader for the Government Printing Office was asked what he meant when he said, "some day things will blow up with a bang." He said he had meant that there would be another Depression. He read the *Daily Worker* and had Communist friends. The board recommended dismissal.[31]

Another employee was asked: "How did that Communist literature get into your home?"

"The *Daily Worker* was given to me as a free subscription," he said. "I read everything that came along. . . . Now I'm afraid to read anything. Twenty years from now they'll be asking 'Why did you read the *Wall Street Journal?*' "

Board member: "You can determine pretty well what kind of individual one is by the company he keeps." The employee was dismissed.[32]

As Walter Gelhorn, who wrote a book on loyalty and science, put it: "The inconspicuous ichthyologist in the Fish & Wildlife Service knows many secrets, but they are secrets of the speckled trout."[33] Most of those fired for disloyalty were small fry. The big game, such as Alger Hiss, Noel Field, and Lawrence Duggan, had by then left government service.

On June 5, 1947, while receiving an honorary degree at Harvard, General George Marshall presented the plan that bears his name. Congress had to be convinced that massive aid to Europe was vital and more than two hundred congressmen went abroad to see for themselves. In September, Moscow launched the Cominform, successor to the Comintern, whose main task was to disrupt and obstruct the plan. Obstruction might also come from Congress, so Truman called a special session on November 17 to get it through. These were not small sums. Five hundred ninety-seven million dollars was needed to help France, Italy, and Austria through March 1948. When conservative Republicans wanted to reduce the amount to $400 million, Senator Vandenberg said that would be like "throwing a 15-foot rope to a man who is drowning 20 feet from shore." The bill passed, not for humanitarian reasons but as a Cold War measure.[34]

One unintended consequence of the Marshall Plan was to divide the CIO, whose Communist unions opposed it on Cominform instructions. Philip Murray, president of the CIO, invited Marshall to address the October 1947 convention in Boston, where Communists attacked the plan as a plot to rebuild Europe as an anti-Soviet bastion. Marshall, the first Secretary of State to address a labor convention, called on the delegates to support aid to Europe in a world faced with the choice between freedom and dictatorship.

Henry Wallace, the Secretary of Commerce, was seriously out of step with the Truman administration. He seemed to be pursuing his own foreign policy. According to his diary, he had lunch on October 24, 1945, with Anatoli Gromov, who under the cover of First Secretary at the Soviet embassy was the KGB station chief in Washington. Given Wallace's "man in the moon" eccentricity, it's debatable whether he knew Gromov's real occupation. Wallace had set up the meeting, which was reported to Moscow, where it was considered important enough to reach Foreign Minister Molotov, who penciled in the instruction: "It must be sent to Comrade Stalin!"[35]

In his diary, Wallace wrote that "Gromov did most of the talking. The Russians are deeply hurt at the various actions of the United States relative to the atomic bomb, Great Britain, Argentina, and eastern Europe. . . . He can't understand why we let Argentina get away with all kinds of anti-democratic programs while at the same time we insist on democracy in the Balkan states."[36]

According to the writer Allen Weinstein, who uncovered Gromov's report to Moscow, Wallace did his share of talking, proposing, as if speaking for the President, that the United States invite a group of Soviet scientists to visit their American colleagues in the field of nuclear energy. Wallace told Gromov he was trying to get control of atomic energy for military purposes transferred to the United Nations Security Council, but that he was opposed by the War Department. As for Truman, Wallace went on, he was "a petty *politico* who got his current post by accident." There were two groups "fighting for Truman's soul," Wallace told Gromov, one clustered around Attorney General Tom Clark and Secretary of State Jimmy Byrnes, which was "extremely anti-Soviet," and a smaller group centering on himself that wanted good relations with the U.S.S.R. Wallace told Gromov: "You could help this smaller group considerably, and we don't doubt . . . your willingness to do this." Gromov was dumbfounded that Wallace had gone "beyond the fragile boundaries of discretion" by asking for Soviet support for a cabinet clique. In Russia, that would have been treason.[37]

One might ask, what did all this have to do with commerce? Wallace was off the reservation. On September 12, 1946, in a foreign policy speech at Madison Square Garden, he said: "I realize that the danger of war is much less from Communism than it is from imperialism." On September 20, Truman fired him over the phone and wrote in his diary: "The Reds, phonies, and 'parlor pinks' seem to be banded together and are becoming a national danger. I am afraid they are a sabotage front for Uncle Joe Stalin."[38]

An embryonic pro-Wallace third party group, the Progressive Citizens of America, was formed on December 29, 1946. Hoover told the White House: "Its objectives closely follow those of the Communist Party." The Progressive Citizens of America, Hoover reported on April 3, 1947, held a Wallace rally on March 31 at Madison Square Garden. Harlow Shapley, the fellow-traveling Harvard astronomer, sarcastically welcomed FBI agents in the audience, then added: "Hey, there's someone with a subversive look. Back up the wagon, J. Edgar, we got him." Jo Davidson, the sculptor, fellow traveler, and co-chairman of the PCA, said Truman's aid to Greece and Turkey had brought about a national crisis. Wallace said Truman was helping undemocratic governments and by what right did we interfere? The event collected about $30,000. Hoover reported that the comedian Zero Mostel sang a song making fun of government investigators. Nineteen thousand attended and there was an overflow crowd of three thousand that listened to the broadcast outside the Garden.[39]

On June 17, 1947, Hoover reported to the White House that a special meeting of the California Communist Party had been held in San Francisco on May 28 to make plans for the inauguration of a Wallace for President third party movement. William Schneiderman, the California chairman of the party, told the twenty Communists attending the meeting that to get a third party on the ballot in California they needed petitions signed by about 300,000 voters. Schneiderman said the party leadership had decided to undertake the campaign for signatures. Schneiderman further stated, Hoover reported, that when Henry Wallace was in Los Angeles on May 19, he held a secret conference with his advisers and "left the door wide open for the organization of a third party."[40]

Wallace was about to throw his hat in the ring. Hoover reported on August 18, 1947, that he had recently said at a high school in Norwalk, Connecticut, that he planned to "head a third party of independent voters." "Let's not worry about Communism," Wallace told his audience. "Let's make democracy work. . . . The life of Christ is strangely parallel to the doctrines of Communism."

Wallace announced his candidacy on December 29, 1947. Two weeks later Hoover reported to the White House that the day after the announcement, the American Communist Party's National Secretariat held a special meeting to "start the ball rolling" by organizing national pro-Wallace groups. "We believe," said someone at the meeting, "that we will roll up between seven million and nine million votes for Wallace. This will be just enough votes to defeat Truman and prepare the way for the election of a progressive president in 1952."[41]

On January 19, 1948, Hoover reported to the White House that Arnold Johnson, the chairman of the party's legislative bureau, had gone to California on January 10 to spend two weeks organizing the petition drive there. He conferred at length with Schneiderman, who said the drive had gotten off to a slow start because of resistance in the trade unions. As of January 1, only 150,000 signatures had been collected. Schneiderman had mobilized California's three thousand Communists, who were said to be devoting up to fifteen hours a week to filling petitions. To qualify for the ballot they had to have 280,000 valid signatures by February 26. To be on the safe side, the goal was set at 450,000.

The Communists felt, Hoover went on, that "the whole Third Party movement in the United States will be wrecked if the Progressive Party is stopped in California." Conversely, there was a feeling in the national leadership that "the Communist Party may disintegrate if kept exclusively on Third Party work for too long a time at the expense of Communist party . . . activities."[42]

It is indisputable from Hoover's reports, based on his infiltration of the party at a high level, that the Progressive Party was the brainchild of the Communist Party, which launched it, staffed it, micromanaged it, and found a willing spoiler in Henry Wallace, who mistook Communist backing for mass appeal. Wallace, who had reached the highest level of government as FDR's running mate in 1940, now lent himself to a scheme to defeat the party he had once belonged to.

Wallace was an easy mark, a political naïf who saw no duplicity in his backers. Absentminded and muddled, he fell asleep at meetings and was glad to let others make the decisions. When first approached, he was editor of *The New Republic*, whose offices were as crowded as Grand Central Station with Communist-controlled delegations falling over each other to entreat him, and tell him he had three million fans. His main speechwriter was Lewis Frank, who led the pro-Communist caucus in the American Veterans Committee. Another speechwriter who came on board later was the Soviet agent Charles Kramer, who wrote the line denouncing J. Edgar Hoover as an "American Himmler." Also in the Wallace camp were Marion Bachrach, the sister of John Abt and a longtime Communist, and Victor Perlo, head of the spy ring named after him. Wallace's campaign manager was Calvin B. "Beanie" Baldwin, a secret Communist.[43]

No sooner had the left wing of the CIO begun a hesitant mobilization for Wallace than its president, Philip Murray, who saw that the third party goal was to defeat Truman, opened his offensive. At a meeting of the CIO executive board in January 1948, a resolution was proposed that it was "unwise to inject a third party into the political scene in 1948." Another resolution pledged to support the Marshall Plan. Both resolutions carried by a vote of 33 to 1. They were the first indication that a parting of the ways had been reached with the Communist-controlled unions. Two weeks later, Murray fired Lee Pressman as general counsel; he went to work for the Wallace campaign. Murray also fired Harry Bridges as CIO regional director for Northern California and denounced the Progressive Party as a creature of the Communists.

In their rush to launch the Wallace movement, the Communists did not foresee that the price of a third party was the loss of labor. By taking over the campaign, they marginalized both Wallace and themselves. Through the willing instrument of Wallace, they carried out the Cominform order to oppose the Marshall Plan.[44]

The Progressive Party drove away "captive liberals." For the columnist

Max Lerner, Wallace's defense of the Czech coup in February 1948 was the last straw. Dwight Macdonald wrote that "Wallaceland is the mental habitat of Henry Wallace . . . a region of perpetual fogs . . . whose natives speak Wallese, a debased provincial dialect." Americans for Democratic Action, a conclave of anti-Communist liberals formed in 1947, recruited some of the defectors.[45]

———

Communism was a major issue in the 1948 campaign, but a three-sided one, with the two major parties denouncing Wallace and each other. Truman at first skirted the issue in the hope of stifling it, but it would not leave him alone. That summer, HUAC launched its investigation of Communists in government, featuring sensational testimony by Liz Bentley and the Chambers-Hiss duel. Even though the hearings had merit, Truman saw them as a Republican tactic to besmirch his record three months before the election.

At a press conference on August 5, 1948, Truman made the remark that launched a thousand angry letters. At that time, newsmen did not have to identify themselves, so no one knew who asked the loaded (and perhaps planted) question: "Mr. President, do you think that the Capitol Hill spy scare is a red herring to divert public attention away from inflation?"

Truman: "Yes, I do." And he went on in his irrepressible style: "The public hearings now under way are serving no useful purpose. On the contrary, they are doing irreparable harm to certain people, seriously impairing the morale of federal employees, and undermining public confidence in the government. And they are simply a red herring. . . . They are slandering a lot of people that don't deserve it."

On August 13 at another press conference, Truman was asked: "Congressman Mundt . . . said the committee's work will make you eat your statement word by word. You still think it's a red herring, sir?"

Truman: "Yes I do . . . the strongest type you can smell."[46]

By this time, the letters were flying into the White House. Mrs. Gean Kimball Byrne of Burbank, California, wrote on August 16: "The American people are desperately worried about the Communist infiltration. . . . Please, Mr. President—no more 'red herrings.' "

Cliff B. Engeswick of Sheboygan, Wisconsin, wrote on August 7: "You seem to be shielding some of the proven to be Communists by gathering the records into the White House. . . . I am a world war veteran. . . . Clean up the federal government and free it from poisonous subversion."

Ira Baer of New York City wrote on August 20: "Your charge 'red herring' is unfair. . . . I am beginning to question whether we are not becoming a nation of weaklings, cow-towing [sic] and scraping to a lot of damn lying Communists." This was obviously an issue that had struck a nerve, as Senator McCarthy would discover two years later.[47]

On August 16, White House aide George Elsey met with Attorney General Tom Clark to devise a counterattack strategy. In a memo to Clark Clifford on the same day, Elsey described the strategy as endeavoring to impeach the testimony of Bentley and Chambers. "Justice should make every effort to ascertain if Whittaker Chambers is guilty of perjury," Elsey wrote. It should also proceed with an "investigation of Chambers' confinement in a mental institution." It should "make it clear that Miss Bentley was not successful in transmitting secret material to the Russians which they did not already have."[48]

It was the smear season, with the White House acting to discredit the two witnesses who did the most to expose Soviet espionage in the United States. In August, HUAC smeared the President in its interim report, alleging that it had been "hampered at every turn by White House obstructive tactics," such as Truman's refusal to release loyalty files on government employees to the committee.

On September 1, Truman's Republican challenger, Thomas Dewey, accused the President of allowing "Communists and fellow travelers" to gain high position in the government.

At his press conference the following day, Truman was asked: "Governor Dewey said yesterday that cleaning the Communists out of Washington was a national job of great urgency, and one that could be tackled as soon as a Republican president could get it done."

Truman: "I think Mr. Dewey's intention is to eliminate the Democrats from government, not the Communists." (Laughter.)

Q: "It has been charged that you are protecting Communists."

Truman: "That is just a lie out of the whole cloth. . . . I never protected a disloyal person in my life."[49]

Smelling a vote-getting issue, the Republicans upped the decibels. On September 25, the Republican national chairman, Hugh Scott Jr., said that Truman showed "indifference to Communist penetration at home."

Truman's riposte, which came in Oklahoma City on September 28, was to deflect the Republican charges by portraying the Wallace third party and the Republicans as allied against him. "The Communists feel," he said, "that by backing the third party they will take votes away from the Democratic ticket and thus elect a Republican president. The Communists want a Republican administration because they think that its reactionary policies will lead to the confusion and strife on which Communism thrives."

Against all odds, Truman won the election with 24,105,812 votes to Dewey's 21,970,065. Wallace got 1,157,140 votes, fewer than Strom Thurmond's Dixiecrats, who were challenging Truman in the South. Wallace was finished, and resigned from the Progressive Party in 1950 when it condemned the U.S. defense of South Korea.

The most serious damage to the Communist Party resulting from the Wallace fiasco was its hastened expulsion from the CIO. Philip Murray now had a friend in the White House and was spurred to clean his own house. At the Cleveland convention on October 31, 1949, the resolution committee reported amendments to the CIO constitution. One barred Communists from membership on the executive board. Another gave the board the authority to expel by a two-thirds vote an affiliate pursuing Communist policies. Both passed.[50]

On the day after the convention, William Steinberg, a member of the CIO executive board, filed charges against ten unions suspected of being Communist-controlled. Four three-man committees were named to conduct the hearings. To determine whether those unions had followed the zigs and zags of the Moscow line, their house organs and public statements were examined. If they had slavishly toed the line during the Nazi-Soviet pact by lobbying against the extension of the draft, and then reversed themselves when Hitler attacked Russia in 1941, they were purged. So were unions that backed Wallace in 1948.

All ten unions were purged. The CIO lost more than a million members, but got many of them back by raiding the unions they had expelled. The troops that the Communists had been able to muster in CIO unions were now a ghost army. The party's greatest success, creating a true mass base by colonizing the CIO, was now part of the debris of its self-defeating policies.[51]

———

The Communist Party was under a hail of attacks, from congressional committees, the CIO, and the Truman loyalty program. But now came the strategy that drove it underground. In June 1940, Congressman Howard W. Smith, a conservative Democrat from Virginia, had cobbled together various failed bills and came up with the Smith Act, which would make it illegal to advocate or teach the forcible overthrow of the government or to belong to a group advocating or teaching such action. The Smith Act passed the House by 382 to 4 and the Senate by voice vote, and FDR signed it into law on June 28, 1940. Its critics called the Smith Act the first federal peacetime sedition statute since 1798, and warned that it gave prosecutors sweeping powers to punish dissenters protected by the First Amendment.[52]

The Smith Act was not used against Communists during the war. The idea of reviving it seems to have come from the FBI. On January 27, 1948, Hoover wrote Attorney General Tom Clark that he "might wish to consider the prosecution . . . of the Communist Party" under the Smith Act. Such prosecution, he explained, would "result in a judicial precedent being set that the Communist Party . . . is illegal. . . . Once the precedent is set, the members and adherents can be dealt with as violators." In plain English, the Smith Act could be used to put Communist leaders on trial and send them to jail.

Clark, however, felt that the Smith Act was a poor tool for judicial action. As he testified before HUAC on February 5, 1948, "Adequate proof against the individual is most difficult to adduce . . . because of the shifting program and character of the party line."

That spring, the FBI assembled a massive legal brief to press its case, 1,350 pages and 546 exhibits. The purpose of this anti-Communist compendium, Hoover wrote Clark, was to "establish the illegal status of the Communist Party of the United States of America." On April 15, Assistant Attorney General T. Vincent Quinn brought the FBI brief to John F. X. McGohey, the U.S. attorney for the Southern District of New York, and asked him to determine if a case to indict could be made before a grand jury under the Smith Act.[53]

On April 29, McGohey went to Washington for a five-hour meeting with Clark and Quinn. The Attorney General opened the meeting by asking: "What are you going to do about Commies?" McGohey said, "It was possible to support charges of violation of the Smith Act," but that he would need two months to prepare the case for a grand jury.

In early May, Hoover provided McGohey with a list of seventeen Communists against whom charges could be brought. The Justice Department sent McGohey five assistants to speed things along. A grand jury was called into session in New York on June 22. After being presented with evidence of their violations, it voted on July 20, 1948, to indict the twelve members of the party's highest body, the National Board, who were also on the larger National Committee. One of them, however, William Foster, the party's national chairman, and a major figure since its early days, had his case severed due to a heart ailment and was freed on bail pending his recovery. Hoover was furious, for the sixty-seven-year-old Foster, long under surveillance, was maintaining a romantic liaison with a woman in Buffalo, which did not seem to affect his heart. FBI agents intercepted Foster's love letters and reported to Hoover that "while the Communist Party was scurrying to protect its very existence, its National Chairman . . . took time out . . . to carry out an apparent personal escapade." In 1960, Foster suffered a stroke and was declared unfit for trial. When he died a year later, he was eighty years old.

A memo stamped SECRET on July 23 expressed Hoover's indignation that only twelve had been indicted. The same evidence, he believed, could have been used to indict the fifty-five members of the National Committee and many more. Failure to do this, Hoover said, gave the party time to "protect members" and to make it "practically impossible for the government to locate vital [membership] records." Hoover recalled his initial success in 1917, when one hundred Wobblies had been indicted in a single swoop. He noted that "the IWW was crushed and never revived. Similar action at this time would have been as effective against the Communist Party."[54]

The eleven defendants on trial represented the crème de la crème of the party: Eugene Dennis, a florid, burly man with a small, hesitant voice, was General Secretary; a Minnesota Finn born Arno Gus Halberg, Gus Hall, was the party's future leader; Robert Thompson, thick-necked and verbose and a decorated World War II veteran, was head of the New York party; Gil Green (born Greenberg in Chicago's Jewish ghetto) was the leader of the Illinois party; Carl Winter (born Weisburg), head of the Michigan party, flabby and soft, had visited Russia eight times. There were two black defendants: Benjamin Davis Jr., the tall, broad-shouldered chairman of the party's legislative committee, twice elected to the New York City Council, and Henry Winston, the organizational secretary. Russian-born Irving Potash of the furriers union was awaiting deportation, as were Jack Stachel, a longtime party leader and trade union expert, and the Scottish-born John Williamson, all three noncitizens. John Gates (born Regenstreif), the editor of the *Daily Worker,* was a Spanish Civil War veteran.[55]

The trial, which lasted from November 1948 until October 1949, turned out to be the longest criminal trial ever held in the United States up to that time, largely because of the defense lawyers' delaying tactics. The party was hoping to win over public opinion through its usual propaganda outlets, which took time to organize. In the meantime, the lawyers for the Smith Act Eleven swamped the court with frivolous motions.

The judge, Harold Medina, the son of a well-to-do Mexican businessman, had gone to Princeton and Columbia Law School, where he taught for twenty-five years. He had only been on the bench for eighteen months, and this was his first criminal case. Over the years, he had acquired a reputation as abrasive and short-tempered, and the defense lawyers, particularly Harry Sacher, Abraham Isserman, and Richard Gladstein, tried to make him lose his judicial composure with their guerrilla tactics: motions to delay on the grounds that the public was inflamed; that the judge was prejudiced; that Foster's illness meant the whole case should be postponed; that in the Southern District of New York there were not enough workers and blacks to serve on juries; that the police in Foley Square, in front of the federal courthouse, were intimidating prospective jurors. It was becoming interminable. As soon as Medina denied one motion they filed another, buying time until the protests worked—the Committees for the Defense of the Eleven, the barrage of mail, and the pickets around the courthouse.[56]

The trial opened on November 1, 1948, but the motions and stays and jury selection took up four months, so that the defendants were not brought into Room 110 of the courthouse until March 7, 1949. Seven women and three blacks were on the jury of twelve, whose forewoman, Thelma Dial, was a black housewife.

The trial took place in a circus atmosphere, inside and outside the courtroom. Outside, pickets marched around the traffic island across from Foley Square, shouting "Adolf Hitler never died, He's sitting at Medina's side." On May 22, 1949, Secretary of the Navy James Forrestal jumped to his death from the Navy hospital where he was being treated for depression, and the placards said "Medina will fall like Forrestal." Medina's home phone would ring and a voice would say "Jump" and hang up. Delegations came daily to see him, such as Mothers of Purple Heart Veterans and Consumer Union housewives, all under Communist discipline. At first he gave up his lunch hour to receive them, until he saw the groups as part of the effort to wear him down, along with the hate mail. Eventually there was a backlash against the blatant Communist attempts to strong-arm the legal system. The *New York Times* called for a law banning the picketing of federal buildings.

Inside the courtroom, all was *Sturm und Drang*, with hyperactive lawyers leaping to their feet and defendants screaming. At one point, Harry Sacher said: "I have sat here and watched Your Honor scratch his head, pull his ears, smile, and do other things which have had the effect of negating what we say." It was calculated insolence, thought Medina, repeated daily.[57]

Wanting a show trial, the defense rejected the First Amendment defense that advocacy was protected under free speech and instead made an elaborate defense of Communist theory. The method was called "labor defense," a series of swift and repeated attacks, the trial as political theater, a chance to indict the system and turn the tables on the judge. Guilt and innocence were immaterial; the idea was to make a stand and mobilize sympathizers.

To avoid chaos, Medina decided to get tough. When John Gates refused to answer questions on May 24, he was sentenced to thirty days for contempt, starting at once. In the ensuing uproar, Gus Hall shouted, "I've heard more law in kangaroo courts." He was remanded to jail for the duration of the trial. Then Henry Winston jumped to his feet and shouted "more than 500 Negroes have been lynched in this country," and Medina remanded him to jail as well. Two more defendants, Carl Winter and Gil Green, were cited for contempt and sent to jail, so that only six of the original eleven were left in the courtroom.[58]

The prosecution relied on thirteen ex-Communist witnesses, several of whom were FBI infiltrators. They testified that they had been taught that the party's goals could only be achieved through violence. The chief witness, Louis Budenz, had grown up in Indiana in a German-Irish Catholic family. Disillusionment over the Depression nudged him into the party in 1934. As managing editor of the *Daily Worker* during the war years, Budenz knew the eleven men in the dock rather well—Jack Stachel, whose greatest pleasure was correcting others on small points of doctrine; Gene Dennis, with his hectoring, lecturing gobbledygook; Gil Green, who was jubilant in 1944 when American troops were driven back in the Battle of the Bulge while the Red Army was making rapid advances into Germany. Budenz defected from the party in 1945 and became a frequent witness before congressional committees. At the Smith Act trial, he said: "The Communist Party of the United States is basically committed to the overthrow of the government of the United States. Socialism can only be attained by the violent shattering of the capitalist state."

The Smith Act was loosely worded, and so was the indictment. The prosecution did not have to show any overt act of subversion and chose instead to expound at length on Marxist-Leninist texts that called for the violent overthrow of capitalism. The defense played into the prosecution's hands by acting like hysterics instead of invoking the protection of the First Amendment.

Medina was not impressed by Sacher's closing argument on September 29: "The early Christians used false names. They met in secret. They thought in secret. . . . If these prosecutors were contemporaries of Jesus they would have Jesus in the dock." It was a curious line of reasoning for a party that proclaimed its atheism.[59]

On October 15, 1949, Medina instructed the jury, which took one day to reach a guilty verdict. Medina then said: "Now I turn to some unfinished business." He charged five defense lawyers with contempt and gave them sentences ranging from thirty days to six months. The defendants were led out in handcuffs, as Medina had revoked their bail. Overnight, Medina became a national hero and received five thousand letters of congratulation. He moved up to the U.S. Court of Appeals and prosecutor McGohey was named a federal judge.[60]

On the day of sentencing, October 20, McGohey asked for a maximum of ten years. "Today," he said gravely, "in the atmosphere of the Cold War, the potential danger of these men as the leaders of a subversive group is probably incalculable." Medina gave them five years and a $10,000 fine, with the exception of Thompson, who got three years in view of his war record—he was a platoon leader in New Guinea, had killed a lot of Japanese, and was awarded the Distinguished Service Cross. Thompson said he took "no pleasure that this Wall Street judicial flunky has seen fit to equate my possession of the DSC with two years in prison."

The defense lawyers appealed the case, alleging a biased jury and judicial misconduct, and citing Medina for "sustained manifestations of hostility." A three-judge appeals panel, consisting of Learned Hand, Thomas Swan, and Harrie Brigham Chase, heard the case on June 21, 1950. Two days later, North Korea launched its invasion of the South. On August 1, the appeals panel voted unanimously to uphold the verdict. Learned Hand wrote the opinion, in which he said: "The trial was punctuated over and over again with motions for mistrial, often for patently frivolous reasons . . . and often in most insulting language. . . . At times, it is true [Medina] rebuked the attorneys; at times, he used language short of requisite judicial gravity; [but] the record discloses a judge, sorely tried for many months of turmoil, constantly provoked by useless bickering, exposed to offensive slights and insults, harried with interminable repetition . . . who showed . . . self-control and forbearance."[61]

The case was then appealed to the Supreme Court. Truman had named four new Justices to the bench, making it his own: Secretary of the Treasury Fred Vinson, Attorney General Tom Clark, Harold Burton, the ex-mayor of Cleveland, and Sherman Minton, a Truman crony and a former senator from Indiana. These four upheld the Cold War consensus that existed in the other branches of government. There were only two dissenters: William O. Douglas and Hugo Black, while the other three, Felix Frankfurter, Stanley Reed, and Robert H. Jackson, were FDR holdovers who provided the swing votes. The Truman court could have tackled McCarthyism at the line of scrimmage. Instead, it stayed on the sidelines and gave its imprimatur to executive acts and the findings of congressional committees in a number of key decisions.[62]

On June 4, 1951, Tom Clark, writing for the majority, upheld the right of any community to fire employees who failed to sign a loyalty oath. The case, *Garner v. City of Los Angeles Board of Public Works*, concerned civil service employees who in 1948 had refused to sign a loyalty oath. Clark ruled that "past conduct may well relate to present fitness . . . past loyalty may have a reasonable relationship to present and future trust."[63]

Thus, the Smith Act came before a court that was prone to rule in favor of the government on matters of internal security. A majority was in place that did not look leniently at the Communist Party in a time of national emer-

gency. The two dissenters, Black and Douglas, were First Amendment abso-
lutists who believed in firm judicial checks against the slightest violation of
civil liberties. Douglas had called Truman's loyalty program "the most intensive search of ideological strays that we have ever known."[64]

Black believed the government should step in when people did something,
not when they said something, and the Smith Act defendants had not been
charged with any overt act. To the claim that the party might destroy America, Black responded pithily in the round-robin conference notes in February
1951: "The goblins'll get you." For Douglas too, contemporary forms of free
speech, whether burning the flag or a draft card or belonging to the Communist Party, were protected.[65]

The court heard arguments as the Chinese crossed the Yalu River into
North Korea in November 1950. It was a difficult time to be dispassionate. On
June 4, 1951, the court affirmed the lower court ruling by a vote of six to two,
Tom Clark, who had been Attorney General at the time of the Smith trial, re-
cusing himself. Vinson wrote the decision, saying that "no one could conceive
that it is not within the power of Congress to prohibit acts intended to overthrow the government by force or violence." Black wrote in the margin: "Of
course—but these people were not convicted for acts." Vinson's reply was dis-
missive: "the government does not have to wait until the putsch is about to be
executed, the plans have been laid, and the signal is awaited."[66]

In his dissent, Black wrote that the court had found "these miserable merchants of unwanted ideas" guilty of plotting the overthrow of the government "without a shred of evidence." Douglas, also dissenting, wrote that the
Smith Act required "the element of intent—that those who teach the creed
believe in it. . . . Not a single seditious act is charged in the indictment. . . . The
fact that their ideas are abhorrent does not make them powerful." Was the
American Communist Party so potent that it had to be suppressed simply for
articulating its platform? Douglas was far from convinced. It was to his mind
"the least thriving of any Fifth Column in history."[67]

The Smith Act convictions may have been a punitive Cold War judgment,
but they were an effective one, dismantling the party leadership and driving it underground. The Supreme Court decision unleashed a storm of new
arrests—on June 4, and June 20, nineteen second-string party leaders were
arrested in New York. On July 26, fifteen were arrested in California. More
were arrested in August in Baltimore, Pittsburgh, and Cleveland. Juries
ground out Smith Act convictions and the arrests continued until 1956, for a
total of 126, of whom ninety-three were convicted.

The original eleven defendants had been granted bail by the court of appeals while awaiting the Supreme Court decision. When the court upheld,

they were ordered to start serving their sentences on July 2, 1951. But when the second wave of arrests came on June 20, the party decided that it needed at least some of its top leaders at liberty. So four jumped bail—Gus Hall, Robert Thompson, Henry Winston, and Gil Green.

Gus Hall fled to Mexico, swimming across the Rio Grande like a wetback, but in the opposite direction. In October 1951, he was arrested in a Mexico City hotel and taken back across the border, straight to Leavenworth Prison. Bob Thompson was nabbed in August 1953 in a cabin in the high Sierras, near Twin Heart, California. He was taken to the federal detention center in New York City to await trial for bail-jumping. In October, a deranged Yugoslav immigrant being held for deportation struck him on the head with an iron bar, fracturing his skull. A metal plate was inserted under his scalp, but he was never the same.[68]

Gil Green and Henry Winston, both hiding out in Chicago, were never caught, but in 1956 they turned themselves in. While serving his sentence in a federal prison in Terre Haute, Indiana, Winston was operated on for a brain tumor; he came out of the operation blinded. In 1961 he was released on a clemency order signed by President John F. Kennedy. As for Gil Green, he called himself John Swift, dyed his curly hair red, and put wax in his nostrils to make them flare. A party dentist inserted plastic dentures over his lower back teeth to fill out his sunken cheeks. He moved from place to place, staying with party sympathizers. In 1956, he was sentenced to three additional years for jumping bail. At Leavenworth, where he was sent to serve his sentence, he was reunited with Gus Hall, who'd lost a lot of weight due to stomach ulcers.[69]

The Smith Act prosecutions bankrupted the Communist Party, both financially and politically. The cost of the first trial was $50,000, and the appeals cost $110,000. The forfeited bail added up to another $80,000, and bail was set higher for the next wave of arrests. The party was forced to let its paid employees go, after which it could no longer function effectively. It was so fearful of informants that instead of recruiting new members, it formed its own loyalty boards and purged thousands.[70]

The remaining members were divided between an open party of sixteen thousand and an underground party with three layers of depth—the "deep freeze," who changed their names and lived covertly; the "operative but unavailable," who secretly saw only each other; and the "deep deep freeze," who stayed out of party matters entirely. The party was now powerless and isolated from the mainstream. The momentum of a purposeful social movement was replaced by the isolation and adventurism of the underground. It was what the party called the "five minutes to midnight policy."[71]

Barbara Hartle, one of the top Communists in Washington state, was ordered to go underground in 1950. As she later recalled, it was "an impossible situation for a person of my temperament and attitude." A native of the small sawmill town of Godfrey, on the banks of the upper Columbia, she had joined the party in 1933 while running a circulating library in Spokane. Much to her sorrow, she sold it in 1937 on orders from the party to become an organizer in Seattle.

In June 1950, she was told to take the name Margaret S. Johnson, move to Eugene, Oregon, and stay on ice as a reserve leader, ready to replace those who might be arrested. She worked as a waitress at the River Toad Café and stayed in touch with the party through a courier. She came to like her calm and ordered life; instead of one emergency after the other she could sew and crochet and read the classics. In her solitude, away from "orientation" seminars, she began to see how blind she had been, how mentally enslaved. When she had been a full-time worker in Seattle, separated from her railroad worker husband, the party had urged her to get a divorce right away: if she went back to her husband, they would lose a full-time district functionary. She had left her family back in Spokane, but she obeyed the party, as in so many other things, when they told her a divorce was necessary.

Once Barbara Hartle went underground, she thought of leaving the party. She was in a no-man's-land, at odds with herself, when she was arrested in Eugene on September 17, 1952, on charges of violating the Smith Act. She was instructed by the party not to water down principles in order to secure acquittal. Convicted on October 10, 1953, she was sentenced to five years, and only then did she break with the party. While serving her sentence at Alderton Prison near Seattle, she agreed to appear before HUAC. On June 14, 1954, in the custody of a matron from the U.S. Matron's Office, she named dozens of Communists in the Washington state area.

Francis E. Walter of HUAC said of Mrs. Hartle: "After doing what she did, the least this committee could do would be to suggest to the Board of Pardons that she be released." Another member of the committee, Kit Clardy, added: "Strangely enough, she asked us not to do anything. She said she made a mistake and wanted to pay for it." After serving more than a year of her sentence, she was paroled and became a chicken farmer.[72]

———

Although the American Communist Party was brought to its knees under Truman, the President himself was ambivalent about the new security measures. He had in a sense been forced into the loyalty program after the 1946 congressional elections. Wary of its implications, he wrote Eleanor Roosevelt that he did not want the program to turn into a witch-hunt. He did not instigate the Smith Act prosecutions, but went along with them in a presidential election year to shield himself from Republican accusations that he was soft on Communism.

Yet the President, having narrowly defeated Thomas Dewey in 1948 to serve a second term, had to contend with the ripple effect of foreign affairs on domestic politics. With every inimical Soviet move, the anti-Communist thermometer rose and conservative congressmen introduced anti-subversion legislation. There was a glut of bills, to deport, to identify, to require the registration of, to redefine treason. On April 29, 1949, Clark Clifford sent a memo to Truman advising him to restrain the conservative elements in the government. "It is one thing to take basic counter-espionage and security measures," he wrote. "It is another thing to urge or tolerate heresy hunts at every stump and crossroads, to smoke out and punish non-conformists of every shade and stripe. . . . We are moving to riddle the barn door in order to hide the knothole."[73]

Truman did not disagree with his advice, but his hands were tied as he confronted, in the second half of 1949, two major foreign policy setbacks.

On August 29, 1949, a Soviet bomb was successfully tested. Now Stalin could threaten the United States with atomic weapons, just as the United States could threaten the Soviets. There was a real danger now of war through miscalculation, as well as a fundamental change in the political equation. The Soviets might take greater risks, thinking the United States would back down rather than face a nuclear war. A sense of foreboding soon spread from the confined circles of national security experts to the public at large. A-bomb shelters were built in basements stocked with canned food and schoolchildren crouched under their desks with their hands over their heads in safety drills. The dangers of radiation entered the popular imagination. The two adversaries were now "scorpions in a bottle," as Robert Oppenheimer put it.

The American response was National Security Council report 68, an alarmist document which stated that the Soviet Union was "widening the gap between its preparedness for war and the unpreparedness of the free world. . . . The United States now faces the contingency that within the next four years the Soviet Union will possess the military capability of delivering a surprise atomic attack of such weight that the United States must have . . . increased air, ground, and sea strength, and atomic capabilities . . . to survive the initial blow." Truman responded by expanding the production of American bombs, from 200 in 1949 to 290 by the end of 1950 and 841 by 1952. He also gave the green light to the development of a hydrogen bomb.[74]

The second setback came on October 1, when the People's Republic of

China was proclaimed in Peking. In August 1945, Soviet troops had arrived in Manchuria to launch a second front against Japan. But after the mushroom cloud over Nagasaki ended the war, the Soviets handed over their captured military hardware to the Maoists. General George Marshall returned from a mission to China in 1946 saying that the Chiang Kai-shek regime was like "corroded machinery that does not function." On February 20, 1948, when he was Secretary of State, he appeared before the House Foreign Affairs Committee in executive session and said: "We cannot afford, economically or militarily, to take over the continued failures of the Chinese government, to the dissipation of our strength in more vital regions." Stated plainly, aid to Europe would produce results, aid to China would not. Mao crossed the Yangtze River in April 1949 and occupied Shanghai. In June, he announced the "lean to one side" doctrine, aligning himself with the Soviets. By October, Chiang Kai-shek and the remnants of his government and his army had fled to Formosa. The hope that Mao Tse-tung would become an Asian Tito was blasted when he went to Moscow for a two-month visit and signed a treaty of mutual assistance.[75]

The Republicans, frustrated after their loss in the 1948 election, now had two more sticks to beat Truman with: the Soviets had stolen the secrets of the bomb through espionage and he had allowed the Communists to seize China.[76]

———

Truman had been planning to recommend the dissolution of the House Un-American Activities Committee after his reelection, but he had to abandon his plan after Hiss was indicted for perjury in 1949. When Hiss was convicted in January 1950, Richard Nixon took the floor of the House to praise HUAC's role in uncovering the evidence. He quoted from a classified FBI report of November 1945, which informed the White House about the spy ring, implicitly scolding the Truman administration for not pursuing the lead.

It was J. Edgar Hoover's practice, in presidential election years, to serve the man he saw as the President to be—in 1948 this was not Truman, but Dewey. Thus he covertly helped Dewey in his campaign, passing on data from FBI files, and making himself agreeable in the hope that Dewey would keep him on as FBI Director.[77]

Although Truman relied on Hoover for wiretaps, he disapproved of the man and his methods. Shortly after coming into office, in April 1945, he told his budget director, Harold Smith, that he wanted the FBI scaled down to prewar proportions. Smith replied that it "was not altogether appropriate to be spending federal funds merely to satisfy curiosity concerning the sex life of Washington bureaucrats and members of Congress."[78]

Truman's antipathy toward the bureau was nurtured and reinforced by his friend Max Lowenthal. He had known Max since his first committee assignment on Interstate Commerce as a freshman senator in 1935, when Lowenthal was chief counsel. Lowenthal had spent the last three years of the war as a consultant to the Board of Economic Warfare, run by Henry Wallace. Once Truman was President, Lowenthal, now a lawyer in private practice, wrote him letters telling him what a great job he was doing. He also took the line, to which Truman was receptive, that the postwar spy scare had been concocted by his political enemies. In a letter on June 10, 1949, he wrote: "A dispatch reported your comment that all these spy excitements arose out of a natural desire for headlines. . . . What have your opponents got left. . . . The only thing is hysteria. . . . People can stand just so much of this superabundance of spy scares, and no more. . . . Your opponents play the spy stuff and the police control measures, come Hades or high water."[79]

Lowenthal had been working for some years on a critical study of the FBI, and wrote Truman on June 16, 1949: "The newspapers have been getting suspicious about what is really being accomplished at the FBI. . . . Some of them are veering around to the view given in print by Hanson Baldwin, military expert of the *New York Times*, that with respect to internal counter-espionage, the FBI is only so-so. . . . The facts bear out the conclusions stated by [Supreme Court Justice] Louis D. Brandeis . . . that it takes brains to discover deeply hidden facts, and for this, detectives are not much good."[80]

In June 1950, Louis Nichols, the FBI liaison with Congress, reported that he had learned from one of his press contacts that "the president has made up his mind to let the director go" but was advised not to do "anything rash" in view of Hoover's popularity, for it would hurt the Democrats in 1950 and 1952.[81]

On July 20, 1950, Hoover got wind of Lowenthal's book and wrote Truman that "Max Lowenthal is working on a book in which he is reported to have taken the position that World War I and II were unnecessary and that the United States should not become involved in World War III." Hoover had it all wrong, for the book was a history of the FBI since its beginnings. In an effort to disparage Lowenthal, Hoover noted that his parents were born in Lithuania and that "several strong allegations have been received alleging Communist Party membership on the part of Lowenthal." One informant said he had placed large numbers of Communists in government employment. He was said to belong to several front groups, such as the National Lawyers Guild and the American Committee for the Protection of the Foreign Born.

Truman sided with his old friend, forwarding Hoover's memo to Lowenthal on July 25, with the comment: "I thought you would be interested in the inaccuracy of the letter." On July 31, Lowenthal thanked Truman and observed: "How can we rely on him [Hoover] to locate foreign agents and ascertain what they do when he can't get a simple fact about the book right?"[82]

Hoover was caught with his facts wrong, which did not stop him from trying to prevent the book's publication once he was alerted to its title, *The Federal Bureau of Investigation*, in a forecast in *Publishers Weekly*. Critical items were planted with friendly commentators such as Walter Winchell. FBI agents visited bookstores to pressure them not to stock the book. On September 1, 1950, Michigan Congressman George Dondero made a speech on the floor of the House in which he called Lowenthal, who was "not unknown at the White House," a traitor for trying to destroy the FBI. He had "pawns" in the government who helped him to "spy more effectively," said Dondero. But not even the attacks from Hoover and inimical congressmen were able to lift the book from total neglect when it came out in the fall.

Lowenthal sent Truman bound galleys on September 1, in which Truman wrote copious comments in the margins. Lowenthal remarked that "some day I hope to tell you the stories of the attempts to stop the book, through the operations of the staff of a House Committee." A staff member had come to his home in Connecticut late at night and "scared the daylights" out of his wife. "This was followed by a visit to my publishers [William Sloane Associates], and 'casual' comments indicating that it might be unwise to publish the book." Truman replied on September 8 that "it seems that they really used police state methods to prevent the publication of this book but I am glad you are going through with it."[83] By 1950, the President had already been alerted to the dirty tricks used by unscrupulous congressmen—but there was more to come.

XI

JUDGE JOE

Wisconsin became the thirtieth state in 1848, the same year that a revolution in Germany brought thousands of immigrants to America. Many of them found their way to the sparsely settled state, and so did Poles, Scandinavians, and Irish, all looking for cheap land. From County Cork in southern Ireland, a dairy region famous for its butter, with a fine harbor to set sail from, came Stephen McCarthy. In 1859, he bought 160 acres at the northern tip of Lake Winnebago, near the town of Appleton, poised between Green Bay and Milwaukee. By moving to Wisconsin, he was able to buy a bigger spread than he could ever have owned back home. When he had settled down, he found himself blessed with a multinational pool of single women to pick from. He married a German frau, Margaret Stoffel, twenty-one years his junior, and had ten children, two of whom became nuns.[1]

One of the ten, Timothy, born in 1866, worked on his father's land until he was thirty-five, then inherited 143 acres, which he cleared for a farm of his own. In 1901 he married Bridget Tierney, known as "Bid," whose parents also came from Ireland. They had seven children in rapid succession: Mary Ellen in 1902, Olive in 1904, Stephen in 1905, Billy in 1907, Joseph on November 14, 1908, then Howard and Anna Mae. These early settlers brought with them the habits and talismans of the Old World. Women were breeders, children were farmhands, the father ruled his dairy fiefdom with its cows and horses and fields of oats and barley. Life turned on fifteen-hour days and devout Catholicism: beads before bed, the Holy Name Society, and Sunday mass.

An early settler described Wisconsin as "a young buffalo, who roams over his beautiful prairies and reclines in its pleasant groves with all the buoyant feelings of an American freeman." He might have been describing Joe McCarthy, the only one of Tim's seven children to shed the halters of his immigrant grandparents and break away from his cramped Wisconsin upbringing to embark on a larger life. The three girls married, Steve became a factory worker, Billy a truck driver, and Howard a farm auctioneer.[2]

The Underhill Country School, a mile away from the McCarthy farm, was the proverbial one-room schoolhouse where all eight grades studied together. The McCarthy children were not expected to go on to high school. Joe graduated at fourteen, already thick in the chest, but clean-cut, with none of the jowly, predatory look of his adult years. In the stern McCarthy clan, Joe was like a vein of quicksilver in a block of granite, voluble, restless, independent, entrepreneurial. He launched his own chicken business at the age of fifteen and soon had two thousand laying hens. He bought a truck and drove his eggs and broilers to the Chicago market, even though he was not old enough to drive. But one time he overloaded the truck, which tipped over on a curve, sending the cages full of chickens splintering across the road. He persisted for four years, until in 1928 he was bedridden with pneumonia and his entire flock died.[3]

Part of the entrepreneurial spirit is the imperative of success, which must be maintained in one's mind at least. On June 2, 1942, when Joe McCarthy applied for a commission in the Marine Corps, he wrote the recruiting officer in Milwaukee, Major Saxon Holt: "I did not immediately enter high school. I worked for a farmer about 10 months and saved enough money and entered the poultry business in a small way. I continued until 18 years of age in the poultry business, at which time I had a flock of approximately 8,000 chickens."[4]

In May 1929, Joe found a job as manager of a Cash-Way grocery store in the town of Manawa, population seven hundred, about twenty miles northwest of Appleton. He was off the farm, making his mark as a go-getter, a backslapper, a greeter, determined to know everyone in town. As he wrote Major Holt: "A chain grocery to which I had been selling eggs then employed me to open a store at Manawa. Within two months I had the largest volume of any one of their 29 stores." In fact the chain had nineteen stores and the store in Appleton had a much bigger volume.[5]

Joe was by now twenty years old, and the moment of his final break from family tradition came when the Cash-Way job began to seem like a dead end. He made the mortifying decision to go to high school, where he would be in class with thirteen- and fourteen-year-olds. At Little Wolf High in Manawa, he found a sympathetic principal, Leo Hershberger. Joe arrived on September 9, 1929, for the opening day of classes and sat with the forty-three freshmen. "I would have sold out for two cents on the dollar," he later said. But he was driven, and accustomed to working dawn to dusk. By Thanksgiving he was a sophomore, by midyear a junior, and in March 1930 Hershberger announced that he would graduate in June. As Joe wrote Major Holt: "I completed the four-year high school course in one year and graduated on the Honor Roll with an average of slightly over 90." Even when the achievement was genuine, there was the compulsion to embellish. He was on the Honor Roll, but poor grades in Latin brought his average below 90.[6] Principal Hershberger wrote on his report card: "Joe graduated in one year. He waded through and actually covered the work by will power, unusual ability and concentrated work!!" The weekly newspaper, the *Manawa Advocate*, reported the activities of this prodigy. His fame spread as far as Milwaukee when he was written up by the *Journal*.[7]

When Joe McCarthy applied to Marquette University in Milwaukee, he answered yes to the question on the application: "Did you attend four years of high school?" In a concentrated way, he had, and Hershberger helped him complete the form. Joe spent five years at Marquette, two in the engineering school (1930–1932), and three in the law school (1932–1935). Herbert Hoover, then President, had been an engineer, but Joe found the law less exacting, and more suited to his nature. He worked his way through school, finding jobs in the midst of the Depression years. He sold a caulking compound for doors and windows door-to-door and pumped gas at Standard Oil stations. As he wrote Major Holt: "In 1933 I got a job with the Standard Oil Company, selling gas, servicing cars, etc. (Won the company's annual tire sales contest)." Whatever he was doing, he had to be the winner.[8]

When Joe graduated from law school in June 1935, he hung out his shingle on Main Street in Waupaca, a town of five thousand and a county seat, about thirty miles west of Appleton. He stayed there only eight months, for in Shawano, a larger town forty miles north of Appleton, Michael Eberlein was looking for a partner. An established lawyer, Eberlein had run as a Republican for state attorney general in 1930 and would run for the U.S. Senate in 1940. He lost, being considered arrogant and overbearing.[9]

In 1936, Joe was a Democrat, pro-FDR and pro–New Deal. Wisconsin had a three-cornered political system, thanks to the Progressive Party, founded by the La Follette political dynasty. Robert M. "Old Bob" La Follette was a U.S. senator from 1905 until his death in 1925. In 1936, one of his sons, "Young Bob," was U.S. senator and his other son, Phil, was governor. Wisconsin politics came down to battles between conservative Republicans and La Follette Progressives, with the Democrats running a poor third. But Joe announced in

July for district attorney on the Democratic ticket. He won only 577 votes in the September primary, trailing Progressive Louis Cattau and Republican Ed Aschenbrenner. On the campaign trail Joe gave fourteen speeches in two days in October, praising the President and cursing his opponent, Alf Landon, whom he called "William Randolph Hearst's puppet from Kansas . . . hare-brained, illogical, and senseless."[10]

In his campaign for district attorney, McCarthy charged that the incumbent, Louis Cattau, held a second job in violation of a county ordinance. Cattau said that Joe had misstated the facts. His other job as secretary of the Shawano County Fair, he claimed, did not violate the spirit of the ordinance. Cattau did, however, hold a salaried outside job, even if it took up little time. McCarthy put Cattau on the defensive, and did much better in the election, with 6,175 votes for Cattau, 3,422 for Joe, and 2,842 for Aschenbrenner. The lesson was that the politics of personal attack worked. The media had printed his statements verbatim without checking the facts. For example, he'd told the local paper in Shawano that he had several years' experience with the Milwaukee law firm of Brennan, Lucas, & McDonough. That was the second lesson: He could lie and get away with it. The third lesson was that he would get nowhere as a Democrat. He dropped out of party activities.[11]

It was not in Joe McCarthy's nature to long remain as second fiddle to Eberlein. Thoughts of a judgeship may have been inspired by FDR's 1937 plea for younger judges in the midst of his court-packing plan. Looking around for a vulnerable incumbent, McCarthy found Edgar V. Werner, the circuit judge for the 10th District, which consisted of three counties, Shawano, Langlade, and Outagamie. Werner was sixty-six and had been riding the circuit for twenty-four years. Pompous and condescending, he was disliked by lawyers. He had been reversed often by the Wisconsin Supreme Court, and was so inefficient that he had piled up a huge backlog of cases.[12]

The 10th Judicial District was largely rural, and McCarthy, in his three-month campaign in 1939, visited farmers and their families. He knew how to talk to them about crops and climate. He sent out thousands of postcards showing a little boy holding a baseball bat, captioned: "Let's Play Ball." But more potent than these Currier & Ives methods was his attack on Werner's weak spot. The standard biographical source for lawyers, the Martindale-Hubbell directory, listed Werner's date of birth as 1866, which would have made him seventy-three. As a candidate in 1916, Werner had added seven years to his age in order to seem more mature. But now the deception, repeated in edition after edition, backfired. McCarthy told everyone that Werner was seventy-three and would be eighty when his new term ended. He ran ads in the local papers accusing Werner of lying about his age. Werner produced a birth certificate that showed he was born on July 24, 1872, in Black River Falls, Wisconsin, which made him sixty-six in February 1939. But he was not as effective in broadcasting his defense as McCarthy was in attacking him. Shortly before the election, Joe ran an ad under the headline: "What About This Age Question?" In April 1939, McCarthy won, by 15,164 votes to Werner's 11,219. Once again, the lesson was: dirty tricks work. At thirty, Joe McCarthy was the youngest man ever elected a circuit judge in Wisconsin.

McCarthy was sued for making a false statement about Werner, but the suit was declared without merit. On January 2, 1940, he took over his district, with its backlog of 250 cases, shuttling to the seats of his three counties—Appleton for Outagamie, Antigo for Langlade, and Shawano for the county of the same name. He worked nonstop on the backlog, on the principle that "justice delayed is justice denied." He was praised for streamlining his district.

In recently opened McCarthy papers at the Marquette University archives, Joe comes across as a fair-minded and compassionate judge. At the same time, he was laying the groundwork for a political career by cultivating lawyers and officeholders, and gaining name recognition by giving speeches.

In January 1940, Joe tried his first murder case, in Antigo. James Blaine Skidmore, a farmer in Langlade County, had a son and a daughter, both engaged. The date was set for a double wedding. As McCarthy later put it, the daughter "felt that her fiancé was entitled to some special privileges, with the result that she became pregnant." The fiancé jilted her, and took off for Michigan to work in a lumber mill. Her brother got married on the appointed date, and the wedding dance was held as planned. The ex-fiancé drove down with several friends to what should have been his own wedding. Since it was a cold night, the men consumed some liquor on the way. What happened next was in dispute. James Skidmore claimed that his daughter's former fiancé had threatened him and he shot him in self-defense. But the jury found Skidmore guilty of murder in the first degree and sentenced him to life. Six years later, when McCarthy was back on the circuit after serving with the Marines in the Pacific, Skidmore appealed to the governor of Wisconsin for executive clemency. McCarthy supported the appeal, writing Governor Walter S. Goodland on April 23, 1946: "Had the case been tried by the court I frankly would have found him guilty of some form of manslaughter. . . . I am inclined to believe that Skidmore shot him . . . as a result of derogatory remarks made by the ex-fiancé to Skidmore about his daughter. . . . I could easily understand how a father might well become so incensed as to warp and twist his judgment to the point that he would kill. . . . Skidmore was a rather frail man, and the fiancé was a husky, strapping fellow."[13]

A review of some of McCarthy's divorce cases reveal him as a caring judge who took the time to mitigate the hardships caused to the children, a sharp contrast to the prevailing view that he was a specialist in quickie divorces. In the case of *Wollenberg v. Wollenberg,* Mrs. Wollenberg was on relief and the two children were with her parents. One was anemic and needed medical attention, and McCarthy wrote Mr. Wollenberg's lawyer, Robert Fisher, on March 9, 1940, that the father should pay some reasonable amount in child support until the case came to trial. Fisher replied on March 12 that "when Wollenberg tried to see his children on two occasions, he was visited by a police officer and told not to annoy. . . . It is pretty hard to tell a man to contribute for support when he receives that kind of treatment. He is almost desperate in wanting to see the children. . . . While he did little or no drinking before, he is now making a fool of himself. . . . He has a $300 back grocery bill, but I will see what I can do." McCarthy was able to obtain some child support from Mr. Wollenberg.[14]

In case after case, McCarthy kept the interests of the children uppermost. In August 1940, when Kenneth C. Schomann of Oconto was charged with nonsupport, Joe at first put him on probation. When he learned that Schomann was living with another woman in Appleton, by whom he'd had several children, he had him brought in and sentenced him for violating the court's order. In September 1940, in *McMeekin v. McMeekin,* in Antigo, the husband's lawyer, E. A. Morse, wrote to Judge McCarthy: "I am convinced that if McMeekin wants to really try he should be able to make much more money than he is now. His spirit and ambition seem to be just completely gone, however. His attitude seems to be that he would just as soon spend his time in jail." McCarthy brought the defendant into court, and when he promised to do some sincere job hunting, he suspended the matter for thirty days. But when the thirty days were up and McMeekin still had not paid the $115 he owed for child support, McCarthy committed him to the Wisconsin General Hospital for observation. A parade of deadbeat dads came before Judge Joe, who was usually able to get them to cough up.[15]

When there was no contest, McCarthy could expedite divorces. But a case such as *Smurawa v. Smurawa* took years to settle. The parents were separated, and fought over custody. The boys, Arthur, eleven, and Sylvester, nine, were staying with Andrew Smurawa's brother outside Pulaski. On July 16, 1941, Helen McDonald, a Shawano County children's worker, wrote McCarthy that "Arthur still holds a bitter hatred toward his father."

McCarthy arranged for the father to pay $25 a month so the children could attend the Guardian Angel Boarding School near Green Bay. When more bickering ensued over the parents' visiting rights, McCarthy wrote Father Henry C. Head, the director of the school, that "with extreme bitterness of feeling between the father and the mother, I wonder if it is wise to let either of them take the children away from school."[16]

McCarthy granted the divorce on January 16, 1942, at Shawano, but no provision had been made for Lottie Smurawa's support. She wrote to McCarthy that he was her "only hope." She had married Smurawa at the age of fifteen, she said. "He never acted as a husband that would love his wife but was always rude and mean. I was just a slave to him. He treated me as the worst dog around. When he got drunk he would grab the knife and tell me to get out. It was unbearable. For seven years we were like strangers. Sometimes I begged God to let me die." McCarthy made sure the husband paid her $20 a month ($200 in 2003 dollars).

In July 1940, Joe went to some trouble to get a man released whom he had sent to Waupun state prison for drunken driving. When he learned that the man, Clifford Brandt, was working in a tavern, McCarthy sent him a compassionate reprimand, perhaps because he was a drinker himself, perhaps because, as a good Catholic, he believed in the possibility of redemption. "If we could keep you away from drink you would turn out to be a damn good man," he wrote. "I do wish you would not make it any more difficult for yourself and everyone concerned by working in a tavern where you certainly will do considerable drinking unless you are a superman."[17]

———

McCarthy had by now completed his switch from Democrat to Republican. That summer, Wendell Willkie was running against FDR, who had already been President for two terms. Joe wrote Willkie on August 10, 1940: "Last spring at the age of 29, by an overwhelming majority, I was elected the youngest circuit judge ever to hold office in the United States." He now wanted to apply as campaign manager for Willkie "in all of the so-called borderline or questionable states in your election. . . . In view of the shortness of time between now and election day, I would suggest . . . that we meet and go over this matter at the very earliest possible moment." For some reason, Willkie did not jump at the chance, and lost the election in November.[18]

As a jurist, McCarthy was alert to mitigating circumstances, but had a tendency to shoot from the hip. He often went to other districts to fill in for absent judges, and in June 1940, he presided over a case in neighboring Oconto County. The defendant, Harvey Hanks, had held up a country store there in November 1932, with his brother, Edward. Armed with guns, they had bound and gagged the owner and his two brothers, pistol-whipped them, and taken $1,204 in cash from the till. Hanks fled Wisconsin and was convicted of burglary in Michigan in 1935 and sentenced to one to seven. Released in 1938, he was soon reconvicted on a counterfeiting charge. Again released, in February 1940, he was remanded to Wisconsin to stand trial for the 1932 armed robbery. The Oconto jury sentenced Hanks that June to three to four years.

When Hanks applied for executive clemency in March 1941, McCarthy wrote a letter to the state Board of Pardons. Hanks's crime, he said, took place "during the heart of the depression. While this boy and his brother were living in a dilapidated car somewhere in Oconto county, they robbed an old gentleman while armed. . . . I believe that he was a victim of the depression—not so much a criminal at heart as a young man lacking in strength of character." His subsequent criminal record was that "which might be expected from a young man running away from his original crime. . . . I would not oppose granting executive clemency." On April 6, Hanks wrote McCarthy to thank him. He now knew, he said, that there were people outside "who care about someone who had fallen into the rut of a criminal," and he no longer felt that "everyone has it in for me."[19]

But executive clemency was denied after the Oconto County district attorney, Harold W. Krueger, wrote to the Board of Pardons, pointing out that Hanks's attitude in the county jail "was that of a hardened, confirmed criminal." On the way to the penitentiary, he had remarked "this is easy. I'll be out in about three years doing bigger jobs." "This man is a habitual criminal," Krueger said. "The longer he is kept confined, the better off society will be." Krueger added that at the time of the robbery, Hanks had not been living in an automobile, as he had led Joe to believe. "The fact is he was living with a brother-in-law, but I did not put him on the stand in the trial for the reason that this brother-in-law was afraid of his life in case he testified."[20] In this case, it seems, a clever conman was able to play on McCarthy's sympathies for victims of the Depression.

Under the pressure of his court duties, McCarthy was drinking heavily, which may have contributed to driving his Buick in April 1941 into the back of another car. He told his insurance company, Western Casualty and Surety in Fort Scott, Kansas, that he had misplaced the name and address of the gentleman whose car was hit. One of his friends sent Joe as a prank a letter purportedly from the Reverend B. Hallock, D.D. "No doubt you have heard of me and my great work in the cause of temperance," the reverend wrote. His better known talks were "Down with the Drink Evil" and "There Is No Alcohol in My Veins." His constant companion on his lecture tours, said the reverend, was Herman Fontescue, who "used to sit with me on the platform, and I would point him out to the audience as a horrible example of the ravages of drink . . . drooling at the mouth, his hair unkempt and matted, and staring at the audience through bloodshot eyes." Herman had passed away, "and a mutual friend has given me your name, and I wonder if you would consent to accompanying me on my fall and winter tour to take poor Herman's place."[21]

In April 1941, Joe's brother Billy was drafted and sent to Camp Grant, Illinois, even though he had flat feet. Joe planned to drive down with his parents. "Mother is like a three-year-old with a new toy," Joe wrote Billy on April 21. "She calls up every day to see that nothing happens to my car." Billy was in the medical corps, which Joe said "was no damn good." Joe told him to "use a little sales work," contact his commanding officer, and tell him about his radio and mechanical experience. On May 9, Joe wrote Billy that he'd heard they weren't drafting anyone over thirty. "I am keeping my fingers crossed and hoping for the best," he added, in marked contrast to the eagerness to enlist he later displayed.[22]

McCarthy had heard so many divorce cases, that although still a confirmed bachelor, he considered himself an authority on marriage. In May 1941, he visited a friend in Detroit, Leroy G. Peed, a successful fifty-four-year-old businessman who had recently married an attractive twenty-seven-year-old woman. The new Mrs. Peed, Ann, confided in Joe that her husband was distant and did not demonstrate affection. Absorbed in his work, he paid scant attention to the bride half his age. Since McCarthy was a judge, she told him she wanted a divorce so that she could marry a younger man. On May 21, 1941, Joe wrote her a letter that reflected his strict Catholic upbringing, with its pieties about the evils of divorce. "I fear you are due for a rude awakening once you have divorced Roy," Joe said. "Divorcees, even young and extremely beautiful divorcees, are not considered by men as the best marriage prospects. Ann, you are frankly slightly beyond the most marriageable age. Religious beliefs will automatically remove a large number of eligible men. . . . Divorcees, many of them with money, beauty, etc., are a dime a dozen. . . . You will simply be joining that vast and unenviable group of disillusioned, unsuccessful women. . . . Christian dogma indicates that we are put here to be well, happy and useful. . . . You have miserably failed to find any means to make yourself really useful. . . . Now I know you can't take in washing. . . . But children will go a long way to solving many of your problems. . . . If you can't have your own, then for God's sake adopt some. . . . Children will give you and Roy some joint interest. . . . If Roy refuses to have children or to adopt some, then I would say . . . possibly the best thing you could do is get a divorce." He hoped he hadn't sounded too brutal.[23]

McCarthy was not shy about giving advice, and on June 12, 1941, he wrote to James R. Bailey, a young lawyer in Cedar Rapids, Iowa, who had asked him to come down and help him defend a client in a murder case. "The job is not to convince the jury that the defendant is not guilty," he wrote, "nine times out of ten they are guilty or they wouldn't be on trial, but rather it is to sell your client to the jury and convince them that they are doing somebody a great favor by letting him off. If you can't sell your client, then set the stage so that the principal figure is not your client but his mother, his wife, or better yet the child. . . . Don't dwell on the facts surrounding the killing any more than you have to. Spend the time showing his past life, lack of opportunities, financial difficulties etc. . . . Take off several days and check on the background of each juror: Married or single; number and age of children; is their home life happy or otherwise; whether or not they have ever been in trouble; religion and lodge connections; be able to recognize them by name." The law according to McCarthy was not exactly the law according to Blackstone. It was more on the order of "if justice prevails, we'll file an appeal."[24]

On September 8, 1941, Joe wrote his brother Billy that "mother has been gradually failing since you left. . . . She has about one chance in ten of ever recovering. . . . It is merely a matter of time." Bridget McCarthy had hardening of the arteries and Joe reported on September 11 that he had just come from the hospital and "death may come at any minute. . . . She still recognizes everyone most of the time. . . . Sometimes she calls Howard Bill and me Howard." Bridget McCarthy died a few days later at the age of seventy-one. On October 2, Joe wrote Billy: "Tim is well. Howard is building a new steel silo. . . . I am going out to drive the corn binder. . . . Tim is saving some good fat roosters for you when you return." Joe sent $30 to Father John S. Jolin at St. Mary's College in Kansas, to say low masses for his mother.[25]

McCarthy cultivated members of the press, among them John Wyngaard, a syndicated columnist based in Madison. Wyngaard wrote the occasional speech for him but balked in November 1941 when he asked for an antiwar harangue. Wyngaard suggested that Joe write to the isolationist America First Committee, and "they'll send you a truckload of nonsense." In early December 1941, Joe and Wyngaard spent a week in Washington, seeing the sights and paying calls on Wisconsin congressmen. This was McCarthy's first visit to the capital, and a reporter for several Wisconsin newspapers, Virginia Imlay, interviewed the judge on his impressions.

The interview took place just before Pearl Harbor. According to the notes of John Wyngaard, who was present, McCarthy delivered an isolationist tirade against the war. "My contact with the would-be greats has merely confirmed and crystallized the thoughts which I have long held," he told Imlay. "I was appalled at the rapidly increasing momentum of our march toward war. . . . One of our Wisconsin congressmen said 'my voters know how I feel, so why should I worry?' If we get into war, the fault will lie with the administration and it will perhaps mean the end of the Democratic party." McCarthy also disparaged the arguments of the Wisconsin congressmen, which he said were based on their opinions of Hitler and Hirohito and their political theories. Only once had he heard "a careful weighing of the advantage of a British victory against the cost in human lives and political and social upheaval. One of course does not feel that our representatives are evil or dishonest men, but merely weak men . . . who lack either the force of character or the intelligence to assume even a semblance of leadership—men who are weather-cocks swaying in the breeze of public opinion." McCarthy was playing to the isolationist sentiments of Wisconsin's German population, but the interview, which ran on December 6 in the *Shawano Evening News*, the *Appleton Press-Gazette*, and the *Green Bay Press-Gazette*, could not have come at a worse time. On the heels of his antiwar diatribe came Pearl Harbor, and America was at war. In addition, he had smeared the Wisconsin congressmen who had befriended him in Washington, and his remarks were published in their districts.[26]

A response was not long in coming. On December 9, Joshua L. Johns, the representative for the 8th District and the chairman of the Wisconsin Republican delegation, wrote McCarthy, urging him to deny the remarks he had made. "I am sure you want the good will of the Congressmen of Wisconsin instead of their ill will," he wrote.

The representative for the 6th District, Frank Keefe, who had invited Wyngaard and McCarthy over to his house for dinner, objected to the passage about the congressman who had said "why should I worry?" Virginia Imlay's article had Joe adding, "In fact, I could detect an undercurrent of glee in his voice when he contemplated what he considered his own smug and clever position."[27]

Keefe said that McCarthy's remarks were "a direct indictment of every representative in Congress from Wisconsin and make no exceptions. . . . You have put every representative from Wisconsin into the same class. To say that I am amazed is putting it mildly. . . . You should remove this stigma from the members of the Wisconsin delegation. Until I hear the contrary I shall assume that you were entirely misquoted."

Reid F. Murray of the 7th District recognized himself as the congressman whose remarks had "an undercurrent of glee." He wrote McCarthy that he and Keefe and Johns "all have sons in the service who are now in combat units, and I would hate to think that anyone would get any glee out of their own sons, or anyone else's, being killed in the war. . . . No normal person . . . could make such an inference."[28]

Instead of accepting the responsibility for his fatuous remarks, McCarthy blamed the messenger for the message. He complained to Virginia Imlay that "what was given as a general observation of official Washington was distorted into a vicious condemnation of our Wisconsin representatives. For the life of me . . . I can't understand why you . . . dressed up my statement. Mr. Murray informs me that I have credited him with some brainless statement in regard to war. . . . The only comment I made about Mr. Murray was that I was rather amazed at the way he had made himself into an authority on agricultural questions during the short time he was in Washington."[29]

But John Wyngaard's notes, which he kept and which can now be found in the Marquette archives, show that Imlay's article was substantially accurate. McCarthy had some fence-mending to do. He wrote all three congressmen to tell them he hated to think they could believe he had made the vicious comments that had been attributed to him. To Keefe he said: "You know I have been accused of a lot of things, Frank, but never of being a damn fool." To Murray and Johns: "I value the friendship of you gentlemen enough so that I wouldn't jeopardize it by an act from which nothing could be conceivably gained."[30]

Virginia Imlay's article was an early example of the self-destructive gene in McCarthy's makeup. He was already planning to run for the U.S. Senate. Why did he feel compelled to denigrate three Republican congressmen who could have become valuable allies, but who now believed, as Murray put it, that Joe was not a "normal person." It was like the old story about the scorpion who hitches a ride on a frog's back to cross a river but stings the frog halfway over. "Why?" asks the dying frog. "It's my nature," replies the drowning scorpion.

Now that the war was on, McCarthy began to consider military service as a helpful career move, even though state and federal judges were exempt from the draft. Carl Zeidler, the "boy wonder" mayor of Milwaukee, made front-page news when he joined the Navy. But Joe did not want merely to enlist as a buck private. He thought he should have an assignment commensurate with his high station. In March 1942, he applied to the legal division of the War Production Board, thinking that a wartime alphabet agency could employ his talents, without the risk of combat. He got a letter back saying that his application had been received, but there were no vacancies. The legal division consisted of fewer than sixty lawyers, and already it had nine hundred applications on file.[31]

In the meantime, Judge Joe had another messy divorce on his hands in Shawano. In October 1941, Grace Whiting had sued in his court for divorce on the grounds of cruel and inhuman treatment. Her husband, Herbert, countersued on the grounds of adultery. The couple had six children. At a hearing on January 5, 1942, Mrs. Whiting admitted to adultery. Solomon-like, McCarthy granted custody of the three youngest children to the wife and the three oldest to the husband. Mr. Whiting wanted a trial, but Joe said a trial was a waste of time and money and they should agree to a default judgment. Mr. Whiting was upset that the court had granted custody of his three minor children to his wife in spite of her adultery. He filed an affidavit of prejudice, asking for another venue. On February 5, Mr. Whiting's lawyer, D. W. Goodnough, argued that the case should be tried before another judge.

McCarthy tried to be fair to both parties, down to the last letter of the law. On February 25 he wrote Mrs. Whiting: "I should note that you have been skimming the milk which your husband sent you, to make butter. You, of course, cannot do that. The orders were to give you sufficient milk for the children to drink and not for butter making."

Grace Whiting wrote him on March 24, 1942, that she was now viewed as "a tainted woman" and wanted to take her three youngest and move to another county. "By my husband's one-sided stories," she said, "I'm afraid I won't be thought very highly of here, and I'd like to go where I can make a new start." McCarthy told her on March 26 that she was free to move. In the meantime, Mr. Whiting's lawyer applied for a writ of mandamus in Wisconsin Supreme Court, ordering Joe to honor the affidavit of prejudice. He agreed on March 26 to let another judge try the case, so as not to waste time "to decide who is entitled to an old coat or an old dress." Judge Arnold F. Murphy of Marinette County in northern Wisconsin was assigned the case, but on May 16, McCarthy intervened one last time, writing D. W. Goodnough that his client had refused to bring his wife the sewing machine, in accordance with the court order. He would be brought in for contempt of court, unless the machine was delivered by May 19. Mrs. Whiting also wanted her flower bulbs. "Why don't you write him, Dave," McCarthy asked, "and get a little tough so as to convince him to quit acting like a small boy."

McCarthy wrote Judge Arnold Murphy on May 16 to fill him in. He explained that this "was one of those criss-cross affairs, the husband was going out with the wife of one of the neighbors and the wife was going out with the husband. . . . Apparently the wife was a little hard up for the 'attention' that her mentally affected husband could not supply." McCarthy had wanted to expedite matters, he said, but the husband had insisted on a jury trial and filed his affidavit. McCarthy said that he had been under observation for a mental disorder. It's an open question whether his remarks prejudiced Judge Murphy in the case, but the divorce was granted.[32]

All around him that spring of 1942, Joe saw his friends leaving for the war. On March 25, he wrote Frank Boylson at Camp Papago in Phoenix: "It seems that just about everybody I know from the whole state is in the army now. . . .

Men are so scarce I will soon have to start dating my secretary. . . . I broke my ankle and have been somewhat handicapped in getting around." McCarthy was accident-prone, having been in several car crashes, and now a broken ankle. By April 29, his ankle cast was off, but on June 21, he was involved in another accident in Slinger, about twenty miles north of Milwaukee. By his account, he'd picked up two hitchhikers when a car driven by someone named Francis Flynn pulled in front of him, weaving back and forth and forcing oncoming cars to go into a ditch to avoid him. Joe said he decided to pursue Flynn, who was obviously drunk, and take his car keys. He honked his horn and Flynn swerved into the middle of the highway and slammed on his brakes. Joe crashed into the back of his car. A policeman arrested Flynn for drunken driving and took him to the county jail. McCarthy wrote the Jaeckel insurance agency to collect damages, plus medical expenses for injuries to his shoulder and back. While recovering, he ordered from the Doubleday One Dollar Book Club *The Imperial Soviets,* the first sign of an interest in Communism.[33]

Joe's close friend Urban Van Susteren, a lawyer whom he had named divorce counsel for Shawano County, applied for active duty in the Army Air Force in early 1942. He told Joe, "Be a hero—join the Marines." When Joe seemed hesitant, Van Susteren asked: "You got shit in your blood?"[34] On June 2, 1942, McCarthy sent his application to Major Saxon Holt in Milwaukee, giving his qualifications for a commission. With his customary bragging humor, he wrote his brother Billy: "If I can get in now, I can clear the whole mess up rather quickly." On June 4, he went to the recruiting office to meet Major Holt and gave an impromptu press conference in which he said that he wanted to enlist "as a private, an officer, or anything else. . . . I want to join for the duration." Major Holt told the *Milwaukee Journal:* "Sure, here was a fellow who was ready to give up $8000 a year to work for us at $21 a month."[35]

On June 10, McCarthy wrote the Central Wisconsin Life Insurance company to reinstate a lapsed policy, but noted that "the thought occurs that your company might not be willing to do that because of the fact that I am going in the Marines, where I understand the mortality is very high."[36]

McCarthy was given a leave of absence without pay by the Board of State Circuit Judges, so that when he was released from the Marines he could go back on the bench. On August 6, he wrote Van Susteren, now a second lieutenant at Lowry Field in Denver, that he had received his commission as a first lieutenant in the Marines and was leaving for Quantico on August 12. "I'm mighty happy that I didn't get an unimportant job like second lieutenant. I understand you bastards are about a dime a dozen."[37]

McCarthy was in the Marines for thirty months, from August 1942 to February 1945. When he enlisted, he was thirty-three years old. From August until December 1942, he was in boot camp in Quantico, huffing and puffing over the obstacle course alongside eighteen- and nineteen-year-olds in an echo of his high school ordeal. "That first week's training at Quantico I thought I'd die," he later said. From December 1942 to April 1943 he was stationed in El Centro, California, as intelligence officer for Marine Scout Bomber Squadron 235. On March 31, the squadron left for Pearl Harbor for more training, then embarked on June 12 for the South Pacific aboard the seaplane tender *Chandeleur.* On board ship, much of Joe's time was devoted to drinking and playing poker. On June 22, the *Chandeleur* crossed the Equator, which called for the traditional ceremony of shellbacks (veteran sailors) hazing pollywogs (those crossing the Equator for the first time). The pollywogs, including Joe, had to appear barefoot on the boat deck in pajamas and overseas caps before an enthroned shellback costumed as Neptune and holding an electric trident. The shellbacks chased them with paddles and hoses as Neptune speared them with the trident. As one of Joe's shipmates recorded the incident in his diary, "McCarthy . . . was going down a ladder with a bucket fastened to his foot when he slipped. His other foot caught on a lower rung—an iron pipe, a few inches from the steel bulkhead—and he fell backward, injuring his foot. . . . Three bones were broken and I watched them put a cast on his foot." When the cast was removed with acetic acid, Joe's left leg was burned, which left an ugly scar.[38]

On July 3, 1943, the *Chandeleur* landed at Espiritu Santo, the largest of the New Hebrides, a chain of twelve islands in the Southwest Pacific, about one thousand miles east of Australia. The New Hebrides hadn't been invaded by the Japanese and served as a major Allied base. McCarthy's dive-bombing squadron was first stationed on the small island of Efate to the south.

On September 1, 1943, Marine Scout Bombing Squadron 235 was stationed at Guadalcanal's Henderson Field and began flying combat missions. All organized resistance on the Solomon Islands, about 750 miles north of the New Hebrides chain, had ended in mid-February 1943. As intelligence officer, Joe had a desk job, quizzing the returning pilots on the success of their missions.

McCarthy had learned to fire the twin machine guns on the dive-bombers and sometimes went on missions as tail gunner, or with a camera to take aerial photographs. Penn Kimball, the PR officer on Guadalcanal, was supposed to get stories into hometown newspapers, and wrote one on Joe's six missions. The stories were slugged "an advance Marine base," so when the Wisconsin papers used them, Joe sounded like quite a hero, though all he'd done was go along for the ride. McCarthy got so much play that he came up to Kimball waving a sheaf of clippings and said "this is worth 50,000 votes." He made no secret of his plan to run for the Senate and had painted "McCarthy for Senator" on the side of a truck. These so-called missions, Kimball recalled, were actually against the rules, for Joe was not "in a flight status." "To my knowledge," Kimball said, "he never fired a shot in anger."

In October 1943, Joe wrote to one of his friends, Judge Arnold F. Murphy, asking him to look into whether an officer in the Marines could be a candidate for public office. Murphy replied on October 11 that "the Milwaukee papers have kept the general public pretty well informed as to your doings. . . . Your friends are legion and they are all very proud of you." He was looking into the eligibility question.[39]

The number of McCarthy's combat flights varied as widely as the number of Communists in the State Department he later named. In 1944, in his failed Senate campaign, he said fourteen. In 1946, in his successful Senate campaign, he said seventeen. When he applied for retroactive medals in 1951, he said thirty-two.

Somehow, Joe got a squadron section leader, Major Everett E. Munn, to recommend him for a citation. Munn's letter noted that "On 22 June 1943 Captain McCarthy suffered a broken and burned foot and leg. He however refused to be hospitalized and continued doing an excellent job as Intelligence Officer, working on crutches. Captain McCarthy has flown numerous combat missions over targets defended by intense anti-aircraft fire, and acted as a rear seat gunner in a dive bomber, performing the duties of an aerial photographer and observer, and taking excellent pictures of enemy emplacements, thereby gaining valuable information and contributing to the success of subsequent strikes."

June 22 was the date of the shellback hazing aboard the *Chandeleur*, but Munn's letter made it sound as if Joe had broken his foot as the result of a combat mission. It's amazing that Munn would write such a letter, since he knew that the squadron had not arrived at its Pacific station until July 3. But it's also possible that Joe had written the letter himself, for as Major Glenn A. Todd, the squadron's executive officer, wrote the author Thomas C. Reeves in 1977: "Intelligence officers had very little work to do so we gave them all sorts of odd jobs. They wrote citations for awards." Munn's letter, forwarded to Chester A. Nimitz, commander in chief of the Pacific fleet, resulted in a citation signed by Nimitz in the spring of 1944 for "meritorious and efficient performance of duty as an observer and rear gunner of a dive-bomber . . . in the Solomon Islands area from Sept. 1 to Dec. 31, 1943." Such citations were pro forma, and Nimitz signed thousands of them during the war without checking on their accuracy. But it was valuable for McCarthy, for whenever doubts were raised regarding his combat record and battle wounds (Why had he not received a Purple Heart?), he could refer to the citation, even though the Pentagon later confirmed that he was never wounded.[40]

In 1951, while preparing the ground for his 1952 reelection campaign to the Senate, McCarthy, by then a major in the reserves, applied retroactively for the Distinguished Flying Cross, which was awarded to those who had flown at least twenty-five combat missions. To substantiate his claim, he offered his own flight logbooks. He did not send in the actual logbooks, but typed up extracts dated September 22, 1951, listing thirty-two missions, all between September 22 and December 20, 1943, while he was on Guadalcanal, except for one in April 1944 and one in May 1944.

When his application was processed, however, an endorsement from the Marine Corps Commandant to the Navy Board of Decorations and Medals noted that "only nine of the strikes and flights listed by Major McCarthy in the enclosed Strike/Flight data sheets could be substantiated by the War Diary of Marine Scout Bombing Squadron 235."

Although Joe had only nine confirmed flights, the Secretary of the Navy, Dan A. Kimball, approved the Distinguished Flying Cross for "daring bomb attacks on enemy installations." In addition, McCarthy was awarded the Air Medal and four gold stars for "heroism and extraordinary achievement" in other missions.[41] The citation made no mention of his injury. Major Todd, his executive officer, later said that McCarthy could not possibly have flown thirty-two missions. Todd himself had flown only fourteen and Major Munn, the section leader, fewer than twenty.[42]

In April 1944, Joe filed by mail to run in the Wisconsin Republican primary in August for U.S. senator, against the Republican incumbent Alexander Wiley, a popular senator in office since 1938. McCarthy had been assured by his friends back home that he was eligible, though he would not be allowed to discuss political issues while in uniform. He wangled a leave back to America in July, pleading, as he told all and sundry, his leg injury, and was on the West Coast on July 13.[43]

McCarthy had a month before the August 15 Republican primary, where he was entered in a field of four. Alexander Wiley, running for a second term, was heavily favored. McCarthy was the gallant interloper, representing service to the nation rather than partisan politics. Resplendent in his Marine uniform with little stars and ribbons, he crisscrossed the state with his usual manic energy, apologizing that regulations barred him from discussing issues. He would in fact have been hard-pressed to discuss postwar monetary and foreign policy, or domestic issues such as labor agitation and demobilization.

He told the Milwaukee League of Women Voters on August 3: "I wish I could discuss the importance of maintaining a strong Army and Navy . . . but I may not do so because I am in the same position as the boy who wrote home that censorship prevented him from saying it was raining and he was in a foxhole."[44] As he spoke, some of the worst fighting of the war was going on in Iwo Jima and Okinawa, but gallant Joe was thousands of miles away, running on the myth of his war record: the exploits of Tail Gunner Joe, the dive-bombing judge.

In Shawano on July 25, he displayed his self-deprecating humor: "I don't know how many Japs I got but I ruined a lot of coconut trees." On August 1 at the Shawano Club, when asked to tell about his wound, Joe said he had hurt his leg "while helping to remove a pregnant woman from off a submarine."[45] His campaign took on the primary colors of a Jack and Jill book. See Joe run. Run, Joe, run. See Joe wrapped in flag. See Joe bomb Japs. See brave wounded Joe. Senator Wiley won with 153,570 votes, but Joe came in second with 79,380, which wasn't bad for a novice.

After the primary, McCarthy, now a captain, returned briefly to Marine barracks at the air station in El Toro, California, resigned his commission, and was released in February 1945. On February 9, he wrote Colonel Robert Richards in El Toro that "when I have a few free moments I start to get lonesome for the Marines. . . . The local papers were quite generous upon my return . . . generally conceding that I might have had some little help in winning the war in the Pacific. . . . My friends marvel at the fact that there has been no noticable slow-up in the Pacific theater since my return."

On March 13, 1945, McCarthy wrote Captain Urban Van Susteren, who was on an Army base in Syracuse, that "I have been doing a great deal of speaking-fence-building for 1946. Frankly I am getting damn good at speaking." He was averaging 1.4 speeches a day, on everything from Dumbarton Oaks to peacetime conscription, and building up his campaign machine for 1946.[46]

Van Susteren was getting married in Syracuse on June 23 and Joe was best man. Marjorie, the bride, wanted him to wear his blues. As for his own plans, Joe confided that "I am farther from marriage than I have been for a long time. Either I'm growing old or the Tropics have boiled out the small amount of ambition which I have ever had along that line."[47]

In April 1945, McCarthy won uncontested reelection as circuit judge. But his time on the bench was bedeviled by a bizarre situation he had gotten into at the El Toro air station. In September 1944, Carl Pederson, a sergeant at El Toro, bought a Dodge sedan on the installment plan through the Vaughn Finance Company in Los Angeles. He defaulted on the first installment, but had his wife request an extension, which was granted. When he missed his extension, the car was repossessed on November 29, 1944. Pederson then paid $210.75 and got his car back, but missed the next payment. He appealed to the tail-gunner-judge for advice. McCarthy decided that Pederson was the victim of shady practices. The car had been sold above the ceiling price, he said. Pederson had signed a blank contract, after which exorbitant interest rates had been inserted. This was not the way to treat a fellow Marine.

McCarthy advised Pederson to keep the car and pay no more on his account until his interest payments were reduced. Richard Vaughn of Vaughn Finance wrote the commanding officer at El Toro on January 17, 1945, that they would have to repossess the car again and this time Pederson would not be allowed to reclaim it. Vaughn added: "We are at a loss to account for Capt. McCarthy's exceedingly uncooperative attitude." Joe estimated that the fair price Pederson still owed on the car was $354.58. On January 25, Pederson turned over that sum to Joe to keep in escrow. He advised Pederson to take the car out of state so that Vaughn could not repossess, then left El Toro to return to Wisconsin, while keeping up with the case by correspondence.

On April 20, 1945, McCarthy wrote Lieutenant Daniel Scully in the legal office at El Toro, enclosing a letter for Vaughn Finance. "You will recognize that the contents of this letter are mostly the byproducts of the farm,"* he wrote Scully. "If Pederson just sits tight, the finance company will finally get sick of the deal. . . . At least we shall have discouraged them from making like contracts with other returning Marines." Pederson was still using the car on and off the base, and there was no word from Vaughn. Scully was waiting to see if the finance company would accept Joe's offer of $354.58.

But Richard Vaughn was not "sick of the deal" and replied to McCarthy's letter on April 24, 1945: "I am wholly at a loss to understand your persistence in interfering with Pederson's performance of his contract. . . . I am furthermore amazed to find you to be a member of the judiciary, in that you are so singularly lacking in the qualities usually associated with a person occupying such a position. Your advice to Pederson has accomplished nothing for Pederson, it has done nothing but cost Pederson money by way of late charges. Your continued improper advice to Pederson will cost Pederson more money. . . . Have done with this nonsense and instruct him to pay the sum of $272.80 in late charges."

In the meantime, Pederson had taken the car out of California. McCarthy wrote Vaughn on May 12: "The car was removed on my advice, but only after the lawful balance was placed in trust for payment." He made Vaughn an

---

* By the "byproducts of the farm," McCarthy meant bullshit.

offer "good for 30 days" to pay the $354.58 he held in escrow. McCarthy then wrote Pederson: "I assume that they will believe the car is now in my possession in Wisconsin. . . . Don't pay them a cent until they agree to $354.58."

On June 8, 1945, Vaughn wrote McCarthy that the balance owed was $844.35. "The contract balance is Mr. Pederson's, not yours or anyone else's. . . . If you, through ignorance . . . are in possession of Mr. Pederson's encumbered automobile and are concealing the same, may I suggest that you inquire into the consequences for such actions." On June 18, McCarthy raised his offer to $365. "Not one cent more than the above shall be paid," he said.

That summer, Pederson was released from the service and he and his wife drove the Dodge to their home in Henneville, Michigan. The Pederson case dragged on into 1946, for Vaughn was unable to locate either them or the car.

The Walker collection agency in Los Angeles eventually found the car and had it seized by the sheriff. On September 7, 1946, Mrs. Pederson wrote McCarthy: "We don't want to seem anxious, we know how busy a man of your standard can be. You're quite the public eye now and believe me we are proud of you." Joe was then in the midst of his Senate campaign. Mrs. Pederson said they wanted to get the whole thing over with so they could have their car again. Carl wasn't working and they had moved in with his brother. The car was parked outside the sheriff's office. "We do want our car back," she said, "we are at a loss without it and will need a car when our new arrival comes in December."[48]

There the correspondence ends. McCarthy was too busy campaigning to pay much attention to the Pedersons. There is no indication that he returned the $354.58 he was holding for them. McCarthy had gone on a quixotic crusade to defend a serviceman against a finance company, but his efforts ended with their car being seized and with the Pedersons owing close to $1,000, at a time when the husband was unemployed and the wife was expecting. As Vaughn had written him, Joe did not evaluate the consequences of his acts.

———

Joe was getting fan mail, and on May 10, 1945, he replied to an admirer in Manitowoc, Marjorie Miley. "While in the combat area, I suffered a broken and burned foot in a plane crash, which incidentally, was partly responsible for my being placed on inactive status." His foot still bothered him, and in July he went to the Mayo Clinic in Rochester, Minnesota, to have it looked at. To Mary Lou Van Ness, a girl he'd met in the South Pacific, he wrote: "Have spent a stretch up at Mayo Clinic and got the leg patched up as good as new—the one that prevented our dancing." In Appleton, he went on, they tried to get

Bing Crosby or Bob Hope to honor the survivors of the Iwo Jima flag raising, but "decided that the next best bet was to have McCarthy do the honors." If there was a trace of modesty in Joe, it was well hidden. He was a human bullfrog, always croaking about his achievements, most of which were exaggerated or fabricated.[49]

———

Nineteen forty-six was a year of triumph for McCarthy. It brought him to the national scene as the destroyer of the La Follette dynasty and the Progressive Party, returning Wisconsin to two-party politics, and it brought him to Washington as a senator. Young Bob La Follette was not so young anymore, having served in the Senate since 1925. He seldom came to Wisconsin, where he was known as "the senator from Virginia," having once owned a house there, though he now lived in Washington. His sister-in-law complained in 1945 that he was "making the 'Record' but ignoring the home fires."[50] Young Bob was in poor health from a streptococcal infection, suffered from depression, and drank too much. He approached the 1946 election without enthusiasm. The Progressives were now a minority third party and conservative Republicans controlled the state GOP. Thomas Coleman, a steely but soft-spoken Madison businessman, ran the party through his Republican Voluntary Committee. He hated the La Follettes, who had backed FDR in the thirties, and later recalled that the high point of his life was when Young Bob lost the primary in 1946.[51]

In January 1946, McCarthy jumped into murky political waters when he pursued the Republican nomination for U.S. senator. Would Young Bob, the incumbent senator, run as a Progressive, a Democrat, or a Republican? Joe's mail was encouraging. On February 18, C. A. Nelson wrote: "Wisconsin should be represented by a resident of Wisconsin, not by one whose home is in Virginia but claims residence once every six years—the election-year dusting off of the old farm mortgage, still on record in Dane county, and waving it wildly before 'you poor tillers of the soil.' " McCarthy felt he could count on the votes of those who saw Young Bob as an absentee senator.

On February 15, Roy J. Morgensen, the editor of the *Badger Sportsman*, a monthly devoted to fish and wildlife, wrote: "You are running under the banner of the only political party we have left in this country. . . . The other major party is now a European combination." McCarthy could count on the isolationist vote.

On February 18, he heard from A. J. Langholfe, president of the Lutheran Altenheim Society of Wisconsin: "It will be my utmost desire to help defeat the Champion Faker La Follette from Fairfax county, Virginia. How can any

American of German extraction support a senator who toyed with the New Dealers to remake America according to the Moscow-Finkelstein pattern?" McCarthy could count on the German vote, with its anti-Semitic overtones. He also had the veterans groups behind him. George Reddick in Wabeno wrote him on February 7: "There are plenty of other power blocks, paper industry, strikes by labor, so why in the hell shouldn't there be veteran power blocks. . . . You are young, you are a veteran, you have the oomph we need."[52]

The Progressives met on March 17, 1946, in Portage to decide whether they would run as a third party, go over to the Democrats, or join the Republicans. Wisconsin was now a Republican state, and Young Bob realized that if he wanted to win, he would have to win as a Republican. The delegates voted 284 to 77 to join forces with the GOP, but in so doing, made enemies. The Democrats, who saw the Progressives as brethren, felt betrayed. Organized labor cursed La Follette for joining the party of reaction and "labor haters" like Senator Robert Taft. Conservative Republicans, who had fought the La Follettes for years, did not welcome the return of this far too prodigal stepson. An influential former Progressive and former Democratic congressman, Thomas R. Amlie, said of Young Bob's return to the GOP: "The only thought that comes to mind is the 11th verse of the 20th chapter of Proverbs, "as a dog returneth to his vomit, so a fool returneth to his folly."[53]

Such a kaleidoscopic situation was made to order for a newcomer like Joe. The key was the convention of Thomas Coleman's Republican Voluntary Committee, which was meeting in Oshkosh on May 4 and 5. RVC endorsement for McCarthy would be a giant step toward winning the primary. He formed a "McCarthy for Senator" club, with Urban Van Susteren as executive secretary. Still on the circuit court, he solicited support on his "Circuit Court Chambers" stationery, which he had ordered only after deciding to run. His eligibility was being contested on the grounds that the Wisconsin constitution barred a circuit judge from holding any other office during the term to which he was elected. McCarthy sought advice from a lawyer friend, William McCaslin, in Grand Rapids, Michigan, where Homer Ferguson had been elected senator from the circuit court, even though Michigan had a similar provision. McCaslin replied on March 4, 1946, that the question of eligibility had not been raised for Ferguson: "It was deemed elementary that he had the right to run because the federal constitution superseded the state statute, which was seen as a deterrent to the seeking of higher office." The state had never intended to keep circuit judges from acquiring higher office, which would be unconstitutional. Thanks to the precedent of Homer Ferguson, McCarthy decided he was on safe ground.[54]

He also had to contend with voters suspicious about his war record. On

April 16, he sent his "only copy" of the Nimitz citation, which he wanted back, to Oshkosh lawyer Charles Nolan, who had been told that Joe had never been a rear seat gunner. On the same day he sent a copy to Dr. G. M. Shewoelter, the Republican county chairman in Green Bay, writing him: "Some of my political 'friends' have told you that a minor injury which I received in the Pacific in the combat area was supposedly fictitious and was sustained by me in a cab accident in Washington, and that as a result your feelings toward my candidacy were not overly friendly." McCarthy observed that "there was definitely nothing heroic in the case of my injury—just one of those damned unfortunate things."[55] The recipient was supposed to think that Joe was at the same time modest and plucky.

McCarthy was now thirty-seven, and concerned about his appearance. On March 28, he wrote Martha's Beauty Salon in Oshkosh: "I find that I am again rapidly becoming bald. The scalp treatments which you used to give me either did some good or I have a powerful imagination. . . . I would like a few more."[56]

At the May convention of the Republican Voluntary Committee in Oshkosh, "Boss" Coleman backed McCarthy, who won the RVC endorsement handily, by 2,339 votes to 298 for the Milwaukee lawyer Perry Stearns, with La Follette trailing badly. Joe wrote Francis M. Higgins on May 14: "The entire machinery of the Republican organization is now committed to support me." To Hal Beaton he wrote: "La Follette was definitely looked upon as a renegade. Although he claims to have returned to the Republican party, he is disliked and on the outside."[57]

La Follette and McCarthy would slug it out in the Republican primary on August 13, 1946. On May 27, Joe told Mary Lou Van Ness at Paramount Pictures in Hollywood that the campaign was progressing nicely. "I feel quite confident that come January, I shall furnish the steak and champagne in Washington." To get the Republican Voluntary Committee endorsement, "I personally contacted practically all of the 2,845 delegates from every hole and corner of the state." He had the first six delegations solid and "when it appears that a candidate has the endorsement cinched, other counties jump on the bandwagon, so that I got an overwhelming vote on the first ballot. . . . Out of the 2,845 delegates, I received 2,339."[58]

In the three months between the RVC convention and the Republican primary, McCarthy crisscrossed the state, whereas La Follette remained in Washington until shortly before the election. Joe often wore khaki Marine Corps shirts to save wear and tear on his other clothing, as he put it. He'd come to a town, and walk up and down Main Street, drawing a crowd, and hit the bank, the barber shop, the drugstore, and the hotel. He had an amazing ability to remember names and to suit his remarks to his audience. To young Republicans in Eau Claire he blasted American appeasement in foreign affairs and to a blue-collar audience in Milwaukee he said, "I do not subscribe to the theory that a war with Russia is inevitable." On the courthouse steps in La Crosse, he said union activities would have to be curtailed, while in factory towns he showed up in overalls and told the workers he was one of them.[59]

Having already courted the ninety thousand German-born voters in the state, McCarthy sent out thousands of postcards to Catholic voters in June and July. The Catholic hierarchy got behind him. Father Dick of Central Catholic High School in Green Bay sent letters to every convent in Wisconsin that said: "Venerable and dear Sister Superior: Ordinarily, I don't deal in politics. A certain Joseph R. McCarthy . . . is running for senator in the coming primaries. . . . He is a personal friend of mine . . . and a good Catholic. . . . My purpose is not to dictate in any way your voting. . . . If you have no objections, I would like you to tell your community about Judge McCarthy. I assure you it will be a personal favor to me. . . . Sincerely in Christ." Father Dick reported to Joe that some convents planned to cast their entire vote for him.[60]

Ten days before the primary, Young Bob La Follette arrived in Wisconsin as if the nomination was his by birthright. He didn't seem to care whether he won reelection or not. When McCarthy asked for a debate, Young Bob ignored him. Nationally known reporters who disdained to take a close look at the primary took it for granted that La Follette would win. James Reston of the *New York Times* wrote on election eve that Young Bob "is expected to prove tomorrow . . . that a man can bolt the Republican party and get away with it."[61] But in La Follette's absence, one thousand Young Republican volunteers, who called themselves "the Flying Badgers," had distributed McCarthy campaign literature to every town in Wisconsin of more than five hundred, blanketing the state in two hundred cars and three airplanes.

McCarthy won the primary by the thin margin of 207,935 to 202,557. Young Bob's defeat was blamed on labor's defection, for he was beaten in the labor strongholds of Milwaukee, Kenosha, and Racine, dotted with big factories like Allis-Chalmers, and employing many foreign-born workers. The story was floated that CIO Communists helped elect the arch anti-Communist McCarthy, but the CIO *News* ignored both La Follette and McCarthy. The Flying Badgers and La Follette's flabby campaign were more to the point.[62]

McCarthy had won the primary by 5,378 votes, not exactly a landslide. But he was credited with finishing off the La Follette dynasty, which had ruled Wisconsin for forty-six years, ever since Old Bob had been elected governor in 1900 as a Republican, then founding his own Progressive Party in 1911. His was one of those third-party dynasties that sometimes emerge in a state to bedevil the two-party system. When the La Follettes backed the New Deal in the thirties, the Progressive Party lost much of its influence.

R. G. Sayer, the manager of the Wausau Lumber Company, sent a note to Raymond Moley, the former FDR brain truster, now a columnist, who was at a loss to comprehend La Follette's defeat. "For many years, Mr. La Follette only represented a minority of the voters in Wisconsin," Sayer wrote. "He voted with the 'New Deal' and the labor unions. . . . At the end of the recent session of Congress he voted to retain the wartime ceiling on the price of dairy products, and this act sealed his fate. . . . The people were not voting for Mr. McCarthy but against the New Deal."[63]

McCarthy was now a national figure, receiving congratulations from the conservative Republican Senator Styles Bridges of New Hampshire: "Your election in November is assured. It is going to be a pleasure to be associated with you in the Senate." Philip H. Willkie, son of Wendell, whose 1940 campaign Joe had offered to run, wrote that "I particularly liked the fact that you stressed La Follette's isolationist record and made that the issue of the campaign."[64]

As the Republican candidate for the U.S. Senate, Joe was now under greater scrutiny. On August 24, Mr. and Mrs. A. W. Larson of Milwaukee wanted to know if there was any truth to the rumor that Joe was drunk one night while on the radio and was cut off on the air. George J. Reid, a printer of "snappy cartoons" in Milwaukee, put out a broadside entitled "Here's News," showing a hatchet-wielding Carry Nation with the message: "Carry Nation was born in Bone-dry Kansas. Alf Landon was born in Bone-dry Kansas. Howard J. McMurray [McCarthy's Democratic opponent in the Senate race] was born in Bone-dry Kansas. Don't let McMurray start ruining Wisconsin in 1946. Elect Joseph McCarthy U.S. Senator and Save Wisconsin."

Reid's spoof made it seem that McCarthy was running on a ticket devoted to hard drinking. Joe called Reid to protest on August 27 and Reid wrote to him the next day: "Your ravings sounded like one gone plain nuts. You acted the part of a common hoodlum. . . . You Mr. McCarthy no doubt know the taste of Bourbon. . . . Your nomination is a fraud. . . . You did not act rational. . . . When you called I thought you were pickled and you were trying to tickle me with your pickle."[65]

Joe wrote on August 30, asking for the names and addresses of all those who got the Carry Nation cartoon. "This cartoon is the most unintelligently underhanded and unfair a piece of campaign literature as I have ever seen in the state of Wisconsin," he said. Reid said that he had distributed a thousand of the cartoons and planned to focus on the counties where breweries were located. He had a new cartoon in mind: "Sooner vote for a yellow dog than Joseph McCarthy." Joe threatened legal action.

Realizing that in the political arena he was fair game for all manner of vilification, McCarthy longed for the uncomplicated camaraderie of the Marines, which would never come again. One of his Marine buddies, John McLellan, wrote on August 30 that he wanted "the job you promised me in '44—caretaker of federal cemeteries in the Solomon Islands." His letter awakened Joe's nostalgia, and he replied that he would always remember the bull sessions at noontime and the swims on Bougainville beach. He still felt a strong link with the boys.[66]

After knocking off La Follette, McCarthy's campaign against McMurray was something of an anticlimax. Joe referred to him as "a nobody" and predicted he would win by 250,000 votes. McMurray was a professor of political science at the University of Wisconsin who had served one term in Congress. Aldric Revell, the Madison *Capital Times* columnist, wrote that he was a pompous egghead who "couldn't pass a mirror without gazing into it with soulful love." In a debate with McCarthy, McMurray said: "I am a university professor, with a doctor of philosophy degree from our state university, the highest degree the university can give." Joe deflated him with his reply: "I'm no professor—just a farm boy."

McMurray called McCarthy "Two-Job Joe," since he had not resigned his judgeship, and the *Capital Times* raised the issue of quickie divorces. Joe had granted two divorces in 1946 to couples whose lawyers had made small contributions to his campaigns. In both cases, the divorces were uncontested but had been filed in Milwaukee, where the court was backlogged. So the lawyers came to Appleton and got judgments from McCarthy, in March and September 1946. There was no substance to the charge that McCarthy was running a divorce mill. As we have seen, he tried contested cases scrupulously. But McMurray capitalized on the quickie divorce issue, which he said had harmed Wisconsin's judicial system. McCarthy replied that "the Milwaukee cases I tried had been pending for at least six months while efforts at reconciliation were being made. Are those quickie divorces?"[67]

Joe was also seen as representing Wisconsin's business elite behind a smoke screen of being pro-farmer and pro-labor. He was backed by American Action Inc., a reactionary pro-business organization, and went to Chicago in September to pay a visit to Colonel Robert McCormick, the virulently anti–New Deal owner of the *Chicago Tribune* and a member of American Action. The *Tribune* backed McCarthy.

It was in his campaign against McMurray that McCarthy first came to grips with the issue he would make his own: Communism. He called his opponent "communistically inclined" and a "little megaphone" of the "Communist-controlled CIO-Political Action Committee." He went no further than conservative newspapers such as the *Appleton Post-Crescent*, which wrote in an editorial on October 9: "The Democratic Party has made love to these commies, sloppily kissed them in public."[68]

McCarthy was the Republican candidate in a Republican state in a Republican year, and won by the impressive margin of 620,430 to 378,777. On November 18, he resigned as circuit judge. A suit contesting his eligibility was dismissed.

At the age of thirty-eight, Joe was going to Washington, where he would be the youngest member of the Senate. Not only had he won the election, he had manufactured a legend, as the farm boy, chicken farmer, and grocery store manager who had made it through law school. As the youngest circuit judge ever elected. As the patriot who resigned his draft-deferred judgeship to enlist in the Marines as a buck private. As a tail gunner in a dive-bomber who took part in thirty-two strikes in the South Pacific and was seriously wounded in combat. As the intrepid campaigner who toppled the La Follette dynasty, a task that no other Republican was willing to undertake. As a manly, never-give-up, fist-banging, don't-tread-on-me, hundred percent American, with no airs about him, who pressed his pants under the mattress at night and sharpened his razor on the callused palm of his hand when he got up in the morning. He came across as a Frank Capra hero, a Mr. Deeds or a Mr. Smith, though he turned out to be more like a character in an Elizabethan tragedy, a modern Dr. Faustus.

XII

SENATOR JOE

A cold rain was falling on Washington when Senator Joseph McCarthy arrived at Union Station in early December 1946 and made his way to his downtown hotel room. The Republican 80th Congress would convene in January, but he decided to make his presence felt right away. Having toppled La Follette and won election to the Senate before reaching his fortieth birthday, Joe was a changed man, with intimations of invincibility. His inflated ego made him believe that he was as good as any other senator, if not better, as if the Senate chamber were a boxing ring, with the other senators lined up to be knocked down or out in the title bout.

On December 3, McCarthy called a press conference at the Capitol, to give his views on the coal strike. Away with the notion that freshman senators should keep a low profile. The lesson that life had taught him was "Go for it! And whatever you do, you'll get away with it." Washington was no different from Shawano, only bigger. Wasn't all politics local? His proposal was hardly new, for President Truman had been cursed by labor for proposing a similar measure during the railroad strike. Joe wanted to draft John L. Lewis and his mineworkers into the Army. If they still refused to work, they'd be court-martialed, with "penalties ranging up to and including the death sentence."[1]

From the start, McCarthy took an anti-labor stance, and positioned himself as the tool of special interests. He was sworn in on January 3, 1947, into a Senate that had fifty-one Republicans and forty-five Democrats, and assigned to the Banking and Currency Committee, chaired by Charles W. Tobey of New Hampshire.

His first battle in the Senate had to do with sugar, which was still rationed nearly two years after the end of the war. The sugar-producing states, which included Wisconsin and its beet growers, wanted an end to controls, while the sugar-consuming states like Vermont and New Hampshire, where house-wives used large quantities of sugar for their annual canning, wanted an eq-uitable distribution of sugar that did not favor sugar-hungry industries such as the makers of soft drinks.[2]

In March, the Wisconsin legislature sent a joint resolution to the Banking and Currency Committee urging the removal of all controls on sugar. McCarthy was named to a subcommittee headed by Senator Ralph Flanders of Vermont to study the question. He co-sponsored a bill to end sugar ra-tioning at once. His research showed that there was plenty of sugar to go around.

Tobey asked for thirty-five pounds a year per housewife. In the debate on March 27, the freshman senator and the chairman snapped at each other in a pointless argument over how many pounds of sugar housewives should be allotted. McCarthy worked himself up into a lather, calling Tobey's amend-ment "fictitious," "ambiguous," and "deceptive," and recalling that in his childhood, "My mother, who had seven children, used to get 100 pounds of sugar to put up her fruits and berries." A bill was passed to end sugar ra-tioning by October 31, 1947, and when it became clear that McCarthy was right about abundant sugar supplies, the date was advanced to August 30. McCarthy had won his first victory but with his hectoring he earned the en-mity of two powerful senators.[3]

Back in Madison, the anti-McCarthy *Capital Times* dubbed the junior sena-tor "Pepsi-Cola Joe," charging that he was the tool of the soft drink company. He was a friend of Pepsi-Cola president Walter Mack, who wanted decontrol so that he could increase his production. He was also a racetrack crony of the Pepsi-Cola bottler Russell M. Arundel, the owner of an island off Nova Scotia where he entertained in style. In December 1947, Arundel signed a six-month note for $20,000, which Joe used as collateral to help secure a loan at the Appleton State Bank. Though it looked like a payoff, Joe reimbursed the note.

Pepsi syrup was not going to put McCarthy on the map. He was a junior senator in search of a cause, which he found in housing. In 1947, there was an acute housing shortage. The Depression had curtailed residential building and the war had diverted contractors into defense work. By 1947, the veter-ans were back, living in attics, cellars, boxcars, and chicken coops. A baby boom made the need for decent and affordable housing all the more urgent.

Many congressmen favored federal loans for contractors, but there were sharp divisions over public housing for the poor, who could not afford down payments. Surprisingly, one of those who favored public housing was Mr. Republican, Robert Taft. One of his friends had taken the Ohio senator on a tour of the Cincinnati slums in 1937, up unlit staircases, through overcrowded hovels, in and out of garbage-strewn alleyways. Taft became a convert to public housing, and joined with two Democratic senators, Robert Wagner of New York and Allen Ellender of Louisiana, to present a bill in November 1945 with a goal of 1.25 million housing units over the next ten years, as well as low-interest loans for 500,000 public housing units. Taft was startled to find himself under attack as a Socialist by the real estate lobby for his modest espousal of public housing. The TEW bill, as it was known, passed the Senate without a roll call on April 15, 1946, but a conservative coalition in the House Banking and Currency Committee refused to hold hearings on the bill.[4]

In the summer of 1947, Congress set up a Joint Committee on Housing, made up of fourteen members of the Senate and House Banking Currency committees, to investigate the housing shortage. As one of the seven members from the Senate side, McCarthy opposed public housing, calling the projects "deliberately created slums," and "breeding grounds for Communism." The joint committee met on August 19, 1947, to elect a chairman, which according to time-honored congressional protocol should have gone by seniority to Senator Tobey. But by pushing through a motion that no proxy votes be counted, McCarthy got Ralph Gamble of New York, a spokesman for the real estate lobby, elected chairman, with himself as vice chairman. Tobey, who was tangling with Joe for the second time, observed of the joint committee, "This child was born of malpractice. I hope the forceps didn't hurt it."[5]

The joint committee divided into subcommittees and held hearings in thirty-three cities, compiling testimony from 1,286 witnesses that would cover seven thousand pages. McCarthy became an expert on such arcane issues as gypsum lath and cast iron oil pipes. His real role in the hearings, however, was to serve as a paid propagandist for makers of prefab housing and to put public housing in a bad light. There was big money to be made in prefab, which public housing would cut into.[6]

Behind the scenes, McCarthy was making deals with prefab builders, according to the testimony of Robert C. Byers in his bankruptcy hearing on August 1, 1951, in U.S. District Court in Columbus, Ohio. Byers had launched a company to build ten thousand "Miracle Homes" for returning servicemen. In the fall of 1947, Joe came to Columbus to address the Association of Building Standards. The mayor was there, as well as other prominent Columbus citizens. He arrived an hour late, saying he'd had quite a night, losing all his money in a crap game.

At Byers's hearing, the bankruptcy trustee, John S. Dunkle, asked: "You state that most of this money was spent in the operation of the business, and for parties. Let's take the party that was held at the Seneca Hotel two years ago. The one that Senator McCarthy was present at. Do you know who paid for that party?"

Byers: "It came out of our treasury, one of our companies, I think Bob Byers & Son."

Dunkle: "How much did you pay Senator McCarthy at that time for coming here?"

Byers: "Five hundred dollars." [$5,000 in 2003 dollars.]

Dunkle: "Was that his only compensation?"

Byers: "Not quite. He had a little extra. Some whiskey, and some entertainment. . . . I understand my son took him up to the Deshler [Hotel] and took $5500 from him in a crap game . . . but he never paid."[7]

As Byers explained in a sworn affidavit unconnected with the bankruptcy hearing, since McCarthy was vice chairman of the Joint Committee on Housing, he could do no wrong. After the first payment in 1947, Byers gave him $500 in cash and Joe said, "Charge this to advertising and don't show my name on your books." With the next $500 payment, Joe said, "Put it down as a loan and later charge it off."

"It was a disgusting sight," Byers went on, "to see this great public servant down on his hands and knees, reeking of whiskey, and shouting, 'come on babies, papa needs a new pair of shoes!' Someone brought in a gal and he said, 'That's the baby, I'll take care of her just as soon as I break you guys.' The baby in question sat patiently on the bed awaiting her chances for a ten-dollar bill. . . . The next morning bright and early he inquired the closest route to the nearest Catholic church."[8]

McCarthy held hearings in Columbus, focusing on those who had sold housing materials in violation of wartime regulations. He put the head of the Guden Lumber Company on the stand for selling plasterboard on the gray market. Byers said Joe then told him: "He is softened up now and will be easy to handle." Later Byers talked to Guden, who was in a rage. "All that shit is after is money," Guden said. "If I ever get a chance at that bastard, I'll fix his clock." Joe told Byers: "In politics there are only two types of people, those you can use and those from which you want to steer clear, and the trick is to separate the sheep from the goats."[9]

McCarthy couldn't do much for Byers, whose real estate license was canceled and who was indicted for selling stocks without a license. Byers felt that Joe had betrayed him. But Joe had found greener pastures. In October 1948, he met Carl G. Strandlund, the president of Lustron, a company in Columbus that made all-steel prefab housing. Strandlund retooled a fighter plane factory that turned out twenty-six houses a day. They came in kits with three thousand pieces that could be assembled in less than a week, and presto, you had an all-steel house, from the studs to the walls to the shingles on the roof. It was rodent-proof, termite-proof, and fireproof. It never had to be painted, for the walls were made of porcelainized steel panels in pastel colors. Billed as the House of Tomorrow, using wartime technology to solve the housing shortage, Lustron was subsidized by the Reconstruction Finance Corporation to the tune of $37,500,000 in loans.[10]

Eager to share his expertise on housing, McCarthy had been working on a book on the subject. He sent his research assistant, Jean Kerr, to the Housing and Home Finance Agency to gather information. Joe pitched an article to Lustron, which agreed to publish it as part of a booklet. Although the article did not promote Lustron's prefabs, Strandlund was happy to have the vice chairman of the Joint Housing Committee in his corner.

At a press conference in February 1949, McCarthy announced that he had authored a thirty-seven-page article called "Wanted: A Dollar's Worth of Housing for Every Dollar Spent." His article would appear in a booklet published by Lustron called *How to Own Your Own Home.* Asked what he had been paid for the article, he said, "It's embarrassingly small. Besides, I had to split it with ten people who helped me." It later came out that he had been paid $10,000.

Lustron went out of business because its houses were overpriced. Unassembled houses with two bedrooms and one thousand square feet were no bargain at prices up to $10,000. The company closed in 1951, after manufacturing 2,500 kits. Today, fifty survivors are listed in the National Register of Historic Places.[11]

In January 1949, Senate Democrats introduced a housing bill calling for the construction of more than a million public housing units over a seven-year period. A compromise was reached at 810,000 units over six years. McCarthy backed the bill, which passed the Senate and the House in the spring of 1949, showing, if nothing else, that Congress works by a wearing-down process.[12]

———

When Truman won the 1948 election, the Democrats regained control of both houses of Congress. Burnet R. Maybank, an old-fashioned Democratic senator from South Carolina, became chairman of the Senate Banking and Currency Committee, and one of the first things he did was bump Joe, confiding to a fellow senator, "He's a troublemaker, that's why I don't want him."

McCarthy retained his seat on the Expenditures in the Executive Departments Committee and was assigned to the Committee on the District of Columbia, the Siberia of committees. Joe wrote Taft on January 7, 1949, that "I am the only Republican singled out for no major committee, which . . . will be extremely embarrassing to me in my state." Taft, who was chairman of the GOP policy committee, declined to help the upstart who had obstructed his housing bill.[13]

—

Mulling over the collapse of the "Thousand-Year Reich" in a bunker near Frankfurt on December 12, 1944, Hitler summoned his generals (who were asked to leave their weapons at the door) and announced a mighty offensive in the West. The Allied armies had forty-eight divisions on a six-hundred-mile front from the North Sea to Switzerland, but were stalled on the German frontier west of the Rhine. Hitler's plan was a counterthrust in the hilly, wooded, snow-clad region of the Ardennes, in southern Belgium and Luxembourg. The Germans could split the First and Third U.S. armies and blitz their way to Antwerp, the Allies' main port of supply.[14]

The German generals in the bunker on that day saw a stooped, puffy-faced man with trembling hands, but though they thought the plan was a delusion, they could not shake his resolve and were left to carry out his order. On December 15, the Fifth and Sixth Panzer armies launched parallel attacks on a seventy-mile front along the German border between Aachen to the north and Trier to the south, in foggy weather and snowstorms that grounded Allied planes for five days. This final offensive on the Western Front, which lasted a month until the Germans were routed, became known as the Battle of the Bulge.[15]

With a fluid front and the element of surprise, the Germans swiftly thrust into Belgium. One unit, the 1st SS Panzer Regiment "Adolph Hitler," known as "The Blowtorch Regiment," moved into Belgium to Büllingen, and by December 17 had reached a crossroads two miles south of the small town of Malmédy, about twenty miles from the German border. The 1st SS Panzer was a battle-hardened regiment of about 1,500 men, some of whom had served on the Russian front or been concentration camp guards. Its leader, twenty-nine-year-old Lieutenant Colonel Joachim Peiper, took a forward detachment beyond Malmédy to the town of Stoumont, leaving his second in command, Major Poetschke, in charge.[16] On December 17, 1944, with the 1st SS Panzers holding the Malmédy crossroad, an American unit of about 150 men from the 785th Field Artillery Observation Battalion left from Spa, the headquarters of the U.S. First Army, and headed for St. Vith, a town twenty miles south of Malmédy, close to the German border. When they reached the cross-road, they came under heavy fire from the 1st SS Panzers. Outnumbered and outgunned, and above all, astonished at finding Germans there, they surrendered. Sergeant Kenneth Ahrens recalled being stopped by German tank fire, jumping out of his jeep, and crawling into a ditch. "They kept us pinned down until we were captured," he said. "It was a complete surprise. We threw up our arms and gave up. They pushed us all into a cow pasture. Practically my entire company was lined up in that field. I was thinking about spending Christmas in some camp in Germany." After searching them and taking their watches, rings, and wallets, the SS lined up tanks on the edge of the field twenty feet away. "A man stood up on top of a tank with a pistol and fired, and all hell broke loose. They opened up their machine guns and sprayed us," Ahrens said.[17]

SS men moved through the field, finishing off the wounded at point-blank range, then saying *Tot* and moving on. Private Kenneth Kingston lay face down in the field. A German reached for his watch and felt his pulse. He pulled out his pistol and aimed at Kingston's head. Just then another SS called him, giving Kingston time to make a slight adjustment so that the bullet missed his head.[18]

Seventy-two bodies were found, while about thirty escaped and fifty were missing. It was the worst massacre of Americans in the European war.

On May 7, 1945, the Germans surrendered and the war in Europe was over. The Allies divided Germany into four zones of occupation, with the United States taking the three southern provinces of Hesse, Bavaria, and Bade-Württemberg. Aside from the international trial of Nazi leaders at Nuremberg, each occupying power had its own method of dealing with war crimes. The Russians stood suspects up before firing squads or sent them to Siberia. The U.S. Army conducted a series of trials of individual offenders at Dachau, site of the concentration camp, outside Munich. These were mainly German soldiers charged with the torture or murder of captured Allied troops, who were tried by military courts-martial, which produced a total of 426 death sentences. Of these, General Lucius D. Clay, the military governor of the U.S. zone, commuted, set aside, or reduced all but one hundred.[19]

The War Crimes Group of the Judge Advocate's Office did not at first know which Nazi units were involved in the Malmédy massacre. Thousands of German prisoners of war were scattered in American, British, and French camps, in hospitals, and in labor detachments. By order of General Eisenhower, all war crimes suspects were assembled in the Zuffenhausen camp near Frankfurt and screened. A high priority was given to finding the troops who had committed the Malmédy massacre. It was a difficult job, for Peiper had sworn his unit to secrecy. Interrogators developed a route of march and Order of March for December 17, 1944, and identified the SS 1st Panzers. They built up a roster with the most likely triggermen. Major Ralph Shumacker, of the Judge Advocate's office, recalled that "the atmosphere in Zuffenhausen was that of a division reunion. They could not be questioned there, as they would construct their stories among themselves."[20]

Those involved, between four hundred and five hundred, were moved in the fall of 1945 to a prison in the small town of Schwabisch Hall, about thirty miles northeast of Stuttgart. They were placed in a separate cell block and isolated from each other so that they could not corroborate alibis. A special unit guarded them and they were questioned for four and a half months by German-speaking U.S. Army interrogators.[21]

The interrogators built their case from one rank to the next, starting with the privates, who incriminated the sergeants, and so on. They used what they called the "*Schnell* procedure," which consisted of questioning the suspect in a room with three "judges" at a table that resembled an altar, covered with a cloth. On the cloth were placed lighted candles and a crucifix, to emphasize the sanctity of the oath and create a sort of Black Mass effect.[22]

In one case, the man on top of the tank who fired first was identified by the only officer to survive the massacre, Lieutenant Virgil T. Lary, as an SS private named Fleps. One of the interrogators, William Perl, went into Fleps's cell and said: "We know you fired those first shots. We are not interested in that. We want to know who told you to fire them." Fleps replied: "Hans Siptrott."[23]

Perl, a member of the Vienna bar who fled Austria for America in 1940, found a chink in the wall, which was that some officers were hated by their men. To one officer, Friedrich Christ, he said: "If you lie it is not good. We know everything. You are hated by your own soldiers and they will talk against you. The other officers have confessed." Perl kept it up until Christ broke, saying: "I only repeated the order I got from Poetschke." And then he recited the order: "The impending battle will be the decisive one . . . and we will have to behave towards the enemy in a way that causes panic and that the rumor of our behavior will precede our units. . . . So that our enemy will be frightened to meet us. . . . In this connection, no prisoners should be taken." The Malmédy massacre was part of a deliberate strategy of murdering prisoners of war in order to establish a reputation for terrorism.

Eventually, there were enough confessions to make cases against seventy-three of the SS held at Schwabisch Hall, who were moved to Dachau to stand trial in May 1946. Under the standards of American military justice, they were provided with defense lawyers, some German and some American. The defense team was headed by Colonel Willis M. Everett Jr., an Atlanta lawyer who had no criminal or trial experience, having worked in his father's law firm since 1921.[24]

The trial opened on May 16 and lasted until July 16. The court consisted of eight judges, seven of them senior officers, with the president a brigadier general, and the eighth a so-called law officer. Eleven lawyers, six Americans and five Germans, were on the defense team.[25]

One of them, Lieutenant Colonel John S. Dwinell, felt the defense had a case, based on extorted confessions. But when the defense put the accused on the stand, "they were like a bunch of drowning rats, turning on each other, and clutching at straws. They would say, 'No, I was not at the crossroads, but so and so was there.' " So the defense stopped them from testifying, because "they were so panicky they were saying things to perjure themselves." Only nine of the seventy-three took the stand, and as a result, the accused were unable to introduce the evidence that might have helped their case.[26]

Colonel A. H. Rosenfeld, the lawyer on the eight-man court, noted that Everett "during the entire course of the trial took no part in the examination. He simply introduced the witnesses and then sat down. He took very little part in the conduct of the trial." Nor did he ever ask to go to Malmédy and reconstitute the incident. It was obvious to Rosenfeld that Everett had botched the defense.[27]

On June 16, the eight judges deliberated for two hours and twenty minutes before returning guilty verdicts against all seventy-three defendants. After the verdict was announced, each defendant had two minutes to plead mitigation: "I have a wife and three children . . . My grandfather is very very sick . . . I am the sole support of my large family . . . If I hadn't followed orders I would have been shot in the back." Rosenfeld recalled that only one of the supposedly hardened and unrepentant SS said: "I did what I did because I wanted to do it and I would do it again." The sentencing was on a case-by-case basis. Forty-three were sentenced to death, twenty-two to life, and the remaining eight to lesser sentences.[28]

Everett complained bitterly that the mistreatment of the accused at Schwabisch Hall Prison had not been taken into consideration. He saw the verdict as a stain on his record. Even after returning to the United States, Everett was a man obsessed. He began collecting affidavits from the imprisoned Malmédy SS, via their German lawyers. Of course, the urgent interest of those sentenced to death and life imprisonment was to get their sentences commuted. Thus, Benoni Junker's affidavit on January 19, 1948, said he had been beaten at Schwabisch Hall and that he repeatedly heard cries for help and shouts of agony. Gustav Sprenger's affidavit, dated January 21, 1948, said: "I was taken before the *Schnell* court. I was told to be ready at any time for hanging. I was beaten by an American guard. Finally, I said Yes to every-thing." Friedrich Christ's affidavit, dated January 22, 1948, said: "At first Lt. Perl threatened me with perjury. . . . Then he threatened me with hanging. . . . I was no longer a master of my own judgment. . . . I was told my mother would receive a form message about my hanging and that she would not get any work and thus no ration card and she would starve." Other affidavits, col-lected by the German lawyers and sent to Everett, told of beatings with clubs, matches lit under fingernails, broken jaws, and injured testicles. Nearly two years after the trial, and after having been convicted and given heavy sen-tences, the SS murderers of captured Americans were suddenly remembering harsh treatment at Schwabisch Hall.[29]

Everett appended these uncorroborated and highly suspect affidavits to the petition that he sent the U.S. Supreme Court on May 11, 1948, asking to have the Malmédy verdict vacated for lack of due process. When he spoke in his pe-tition of "wrongdoers," he did not mean the SS, but the American team at Schwabisch Hall. With Justice Robert Jackson abstaining, since he had served as chief U.S. counsel at Nuremberg, the court was tied 4 to 4, which meant that it declined to hear the appeal. Everett complained that he had spent $30,000 of his own money preparing his petition.[30]

It was not entirely spent in vain, for the petition revived interest in the Malmédy trial. In Germany, General Lucius Clay commuted thirty-one of the forty-three death sentences, arguing that American jailers had "used very rough methods to get the first breaks. . . . That so bothered me that I cut the death sentences to life imprisonment."[31]

In July, Secretary of the Army Kenneth C. Royall named a three-man com-mission to conduct a survey of the 139 remaining death sentences meted out at all the Dachau trials, including the twelve Malmédy death sentences. The three were Texas Judge Gordon Simpson, Charles E. Lawrence of the Judge Advocate's Office, and E. L. van Roden, a judge at the Orphan's Court in Delaware, Pennsylvania. They spent six weeks in Germany in the fall of 1948, and heard thirty-three witnesses. The Simpson Commission recom-mended that the twelve remaining Malmédy death sentences be commuted, and General Clay commuted six of them. The other six were commuted in 1951, after West Germany became a federal state and custody of the prison-ers was handed over to the Germans.

Upon his return, Judge van Roden began giving speeches at Rotary Clubs and making lurid charges based on Everett's affidavits, which he had made no attempt to corroborate. Van Roden before the war had endorsed a pro-Nazi and anti-Semitic book, which accused FDR of being surrounded by Jews like Felix Frankfurter, Henry Morgenthau, and Bernard Baruch. He was a poor choice for Secretary Royall's commission. Van Roden knew a fellow who worked on the *Chester Times*, James Finucane, who was also on the staff of a pacifist and isolationist group called the National Council for the Prevention of War. Van Roden told his tale of tortures and threats, all based on the SS affidavits, to Finucane, who put out an inflammatory press release in mid-December 1948. By this time Finucane was in touch with the German lawyers, who had their own axes to grind, and was getting letters from convicted SS men.[32]

The press release was distributed to members of Congress, who called for an investigation. William Langer of North Dakota, a pacifist and isolationist, made two speeches on the Senate floor regarding this terrible miscarriage of justice. On January 17, 1949, *Time* magazine ran a story stating that Everett's petition "reads like a record of Nazi atrocities," equating the U.S. interrogators at Schwabisch Hall with Nazi war criminals.

In February 1949, *The Progressive*, a liberal magazine in Madison, Wisconsin, ran an article under Judge van Roden's byline called "United States Atrocities in Germany." The article said that interrogators at Schwabisch Hall were "posturing as priests" and that "all but two of the Germans in the 139 cases we investigated had been kicked in the testicles beyond repair."

"Our investigators," said the article, "would put a black hood over the accused's head and then punch him in the face with brass knuckles, kick him, and beat him with rubber hose." The article concluded that "American investigators who abused the power of victory and prostituted justice to vengeance should be . . . prosecuted."[33]

———

McCarthy's career in the Senate was stagnating in 1949, after his forays into sugar rationing and housing, and he needed an issue that would reignite his popularity in Wisconsin. He was now branded as a troublemaker, bumped from the Banking and Currency Committee, and could no longer rely on his career as a Marine or his upset of La Follette to sway an audience. He had always courted the German vote by taking extreme pro-German positions. On November 3, 1945, when he was laying the foundation for his 1946 Senate campaign, he sent the *Green Bay Press-Gazette* the text of a radio talk he was giving on November 13, in which he planned to say that "by the subterfuge of refusing to declare the war ended, even though Germany has long since surrendered unconditionally, we are using the soldiers of our former enemy as slave labor. By turning over our German prisoners to France, we are actively dealing in white slaves; and perhaps I will call attention to the recent stories to the effect that roughly one hundred thousand German prisoners of war are slowly dying in France because of malnutrition; and call attention to the Polish demand for an additional fifty thousand German slave laborers to work inside her Silesian coal mines."[34]

McCarthy sent a copy of his talk to his friend at the *Chicago Tribune*, James Maxwell Murphy, on November 15, with the comment: "You will note that I did not touch on the question of our trying the German leaders, whose only crime was attempting to win the war. I could well have made the comparison of our methodical terror bombing of refugee-crowded cities in Germany and compared the men responsible for that practice with the so-called German war criminals. However, I decided to restrict myself to a condemnation of the treatment of the clearly innocent GI Joes of the German army."[35]

These were truly stupefying remarks coming from a soon-to-be United States senator who had fought in World War II, albeit in the Pacific Theater. Were the German troops, who slaughtered 5,700,000 Jews in death camps, who executed tens of thousands of hostages in occupied lands, who massacred fifty thousand in the Warsaw Ghetto, and who systematically murdered captured Allied airmen, "innocent GI Joes"? McCarthy's comparison of Allied bombing with Nazi war crimes was an echo of Colonel Peiper's remark to an American interpreter that the Malmédy massacre could be justified or excused because of the bombing of German cities.

McCarthy delivered his radio talk shortly before the start of the Nuremberg trial, which revealed the extraordinary scope of Nazi extermination techniques. One of the prominent Wisconsin businessmen of German origin who denounced the Nuremberg trial was Walter Harnischfeger, who owned a company that made construction machinery such as traveling cranes and who also built prefab housing. He said in 1948 that the trial was "worse than anything Hitler did. It beats Dachau." Harnischfeger before the war was close to Bundist groups and sympathetic to the Nazi regime. One of his nephews, Frederick von Schleinitz, was said to have an autographed copy of *Mein Kampf* and wore a swastika watch chain.[36]

On April 12, 1942, the Fair Employment Practices Commission ordered eight Midwestern companies holding war contracts to stop discriminating against workers because of race or religion. The Harnischfeger company was one of the eight. The FEPC charged that Harnischfeger refused to employ Negro or Jewish Americans and ran ads asking for "gentile, white, and Protestant" help. After the war, Harnischfeger made frequent trips to Germany to campaign against the dismantling of German factories for reparations.[37]

McCarthy's connection to Harnischfeger was arranged by Tom Korb, who was the industrialist's general counsel. Korb was a close friend of Joe's going back to Marquette, when they double-dated and both had gas station jobs.

When McCarthy launched his Senate campaign in 1946, Korb joined his team. "I will do whatever I can," he said, "to resist losing Republican votes in the Fourth District" of Milwaukee, where Korb lived. Then on September 18, Korb wrote his college chum that Harnischfeger was inviting 150 Milwaukee industrialists to lunch, to "educate" them regarding the new public relations program of the National Association of Manufacturers. "Would you like to be my guest at this luncheon?" Korb asked. "We will not put too much emphasis on your presence. You will not be at the speaker's table, but will sit in the background with me. Word will get through the audience and you will have the opportunity of meeting many of those upon whom you will rely for support." On September 23, Korb invited McCarthy to attend a dinner in the Harnischfeger plant cafeteria to honor the employees who had worked there twenty-five years or more, of whom there were about 130. "You may be called on to say a few words, but they will not be political," Korb instructed. Harnischfeger was part of a group of seventy wealthy Wisconsin businessmen who funded McCarthy's campaign. When he was elected, Harnischfeger sent him a telegram of congratulations.[38]

Joe was intent on remaining in Harnischfeger's good graces, for even after the election, he relied on him for financial help. In 1947, when he was having problems with his notes at the Appleton State Bank, he wrote his friendly banker, Matt Shuh, on May 9: "I have made complete arrangements with Walter Harnischfeger . . . to put up sufficient collateral to cure both our ulcers, but as luck would have it, I was completely laid up in the Naval Hospital under a 'No Visitors' rule when Harnischfeger came through Washington. He left for Europe and won't be back for about a month."[39]

In 1950, a *Capital Times* reporter wrote in an interoffice memo: "For some time, McCarthy's patron in Wisconsin among the big industrialists has been Walter Harnischfeger . . . who has very close connections with elements in Germany that were close to the Hitler crowd." At a meeting in Madison in 1948, the reporter went on, Harnischfeger spoke "in a state of rather advanced intoxication," and said that "Germany was once again being turned back to the masses."[40]

In February 1949, after the publication of van Roden's article on the mistreatment of the SS defendants in *The Progressive*, the uproar over Malmédy came to the attention of several Senate committees. McCarthy, who was on the Special Investigation Subcommittee of the Committee on Expenditures, thought it was the proper venue for Malmédy, since it had handled the case of Ilse Koch, "the Bitch of Buchenwald," married to the camp commander. But Senator Millard E. Tydings of Maryland, the chairman of the Armed Services Committee, quickly preempted McCarthy's subcommittee and announced hearings in April 1949.[41]

Smelling Pentagon influence, Joe feared that the armed services hearings would be a whitewash. He also sensed an issue that would appeal to the Wisconsin German vote and particularly to his backer Harnischfeger. When a subcommittee of three was named—Chairman Raymond E. Baldwin of Connecticut, Estes Kefauver of Tennessee, and Lester C. Hunt of Wyoming—McCarthy was invited to attend the hearings and given permission to ask questions of the witnesses.[42]

Tom Korb arrived in Washington, on leave from the Harnischfeger company, to act as McCarthy's unpaid administrative assistant for six weeks to help him in his daily preparation and write his press releases. The hearings provided a revealing glimpse of what McCarthy would later become in his anti-Red crusade. He adopted as gospel the contentions of SS men trying to escape long sentences, and did his best to besmirch the reputation of the Army. This was in fact the first Army-McCarthy hearing, with McCarthy as incorrigible then as he would be later.

"I am here informally," McCarthy said as he arrived on opening day, April 18, in Room 212 of the Senate Office Building, but he quickly took over the proceedings. Of the three senators on the Baldwin subcommittee, Kefauver was rarely present and Hunt seldom opened his mouth. Thus the hearings became a duel between Baldwin, a senator of the old school, courteous and reasonable, and McCarthy, who fought bare-knuckled and below the belt.

Baldwin noted that about eighty American soldiers were "slaughtered in cold blood, in total violation of all accepted rules of civilized warfare. . . . Young men who were entitled to expect that if they fell into the hands of the enemy, they would be treated as prisoners of war."

McCarthy jumped in at once: "Every member of our committee realizes the gruesomeness of the crime. . . . There is no desire to see anyone who is guilty go free." But he wanted to check out reports on "how confessions were obtained. . . . Mock trials . . . physical force . . . taking ration cards away from the families of prisoners. . . . Was this 'American Justice'?"

Secretary of the Army Kenneth Royall took the stand and noted that in nearly all murder cases, the defendants claimed their confessions were coerced. People were getting excited about the statements of German prisoners without hearing the other side.

McCarthy: "I was in the Marine Corps and feelings ran high that . . . it was important to protect the rights of prisoners."

Royall: "These were not prisoners of war. . . . They were criminals who had been apprehended."

McCarthy: "You don't know whether they are criminals or not until they are convicted."

Royall: "They are charged with war crimes."

McCarthy said that if convictions were improperly obtained, "it would be a tragedy. . . . It would do to American prestige over in Europe infinite damage. . . . Doing everything we accuse the Russians are doing."

Royall (losing patience): "I do not want to leave unchallenged the statement that we are following procedures that are analogous to those in Russia. That is not a fact."

On April 20, the chief prosecutor at the Dachau trial, Lieutenant Colonel Burton E. Ellis of the Judge Advocate's Office, took the stand. He said the policy at Schwabisch Hall Prison was to isolate the prisoners until they confessed. Only much later, after the trial was over, did they complain of how confessions were obtained. Ellis admitted there had been mock trials, conducted rapidly in German in a cell with candles and crucifix, but said they were not all that effective.

McCarthy: "It makes me rather sick down inside to hear you testify what you think is proper or improper."

Ellis said he had seen two mock trials. In one, after saying *nein, nein* for ten minutes, the man confessed. The mock trials were a tactic to elicit confessions, Ellis said. It was a nice-cop, tough-cop routine where the nice cop said "you have got to give him a chance to tell his story."[43] Ellis insisted that the charges of physical coercion were patently false.

Major Dwight F. Fanton, the officer commanding the interrogators, had issued an order on February 7, 1946, stating that "any ruse or deception may be used in the course of interrogation, but threats of physical violence . . . should be scrupulously avoided."

McCarthy: "When we were out in the Pacific, we used to pick up Jap diaries, and in it they told exactly what happened to our men, who were held by Japs, and there were threats of running tractors over people, we found out what the Japs did to our boys. . . . If you are trying to get a confession out of someone, you might get exasperated and shove him around."[44]

When Kenneth Ahrens, one of the Malmédy survivors, took the stand, McCarthy objected that "this would appear to put those of us who feel this thing should be investigated in the position of defending the actions of those storm troopers. . . . It would inflame the public and get away from what our army was doing." But Baldwin insisted that Ahrens's testimony was a necessary corrective to the statements of the SS.

Ahrens said that when the SS started firing at 1:00 P.M., "I turned around and fell flat on my face. I didn't dare look around. I was hit in the back. I could hear them walking amongst the boys that were lying there. Some of the boys weren't dead and there was a lot of moaning and groaning. You would hear a stray shot here and a stray shot there. Making sure there was nobody left alive. That went on like a little while. . . . I mean time was like years. . . .

They must have thought I was dead. Troops were going back and forth on the road. . . . And every once in a while, a tank or half-track would roll by and turn their guns on us, just for a good time. I mean, they were laughing." At dusk, Ahrens started running and made it to the woods, and got picked up by an American jeep.

Senator Hunt: "If any of those SS troops during the trial was pushed against the wall, would you consider they were being mistreated?"

Ahrens: "I certainly would not. I often wish I would have a chance to push them up against the wall."

Hunt: "Do you think that six out of 73 who may be hung for the killing . . . seems to be a very serious penalty?"

Ahrens: "I certainly do not."

McCarthy: "This provides part of a Roman holiday here. . . . I think it is so entirely improper. . . . It is an attempt to inflame the public and intimidate members of this committee."

McCarthy was attacking the reputation of the Army and defending SS murderers. Running out of patience, Baldwin told him: "I have given you every consideration and every courtesy." When Joe kept harping on the mock trials, Baldwin said: "I want to give you every latitude I can, but it does seem to me we are wasting time."

And yet McCarthy persisted. On April 29, he said he was getting "a flood of mail from men in that area," that is letters from imprisoned SS forwarded by their lawyers. "The two men who were most referred to as sadistic are Perl and Thon." McCarthy was using SS affidavits to build a case againt the U.S. interrogators.

James J. Bailey, the court reporter at the Dachau trial, buttressed McCarthy's case when he testified that Perl "had a really sadistic, brutal streak. . . . He was an Austrian whose wife had been in a concentration camp." Bailey said he had seen Perl knee men in the groin.

McCarthy eagerly elaborated: "You know it was claimed that these men sentenced to death were crippled for life because they had been kicked in the genitals."[45]

On May 4, Judge van Roden, whose inflammatory article in *The Progressive* was partly responsible for the hearings, took the stand. He said he felt the confessions were coerced. He also repeated the claim that "some of them had been injured in the testicles."

"There will be testimony here to the effect that of the 139 men who were sentenced to die," McCarthy shot in, "about 138 were irreparably damaged, being crippled for life, from being kicked or kneed in the groin." Bailey, who had been there, said quietly, "In my opinion, that is a gross exaggeration."

But McCarthy wasn't listening. He continued his rant: ". . . Convicted with these fake confessions, these fake hangings, the kneeing and kicking to get confessions. . . . I believe it would be a mistake to continue executing these men."

Baldwin: "I am wondering what chance for an appeal and review the men who gave their lives at Malmédy crossroads and were shot had?"

McCarthy: "What about those 15 or 16 year-old boys [SS] who were kicked in the testicles, crippled for life. . . . Shall those men of the losing nation have a fair trial? . . . The Army acted with the utmost malice."

It was at this point that, under questioning by the subcommittee counsel, the retired Marine Colonel Joseph M. Chambers, van Roden provided the most shocking surprise of the hearing. McCarthy had repeatedly cited van Roden's article as evidence of injuries to the testicles. But van Roden admitted that though the article had appeared under his byline, he had not written it. It was written by his journalist crony Finucane, who had made most of it up. Van Roden explained: "Now in the next paragraph, where it says, 'All but two of the Germans, in the 139 cases we investigated, had been kicked in the testicles beyond repair,' I did not say that. What I said was that all but two were recommended for commutation to life imprisonment. . . . I do not know how many may or may not have been kicked or kneed in the testicles. . . . That figure is absolutely wrong."[46]

Upon having his argument deflated, McCarthy left the hearing room, knowing that his case was in shreds. But he recovered when Dwight Fanton, the chief of the Schwabisch Hall interrogators, took the stand on May 5. McCarthy had learned that Fanton, a graduate of Yale Law School, was a member of Senator Baldwin's Bridgeport law firm. This was more ammunition he could use to label the hearings a whitewash. Fanton refuted the "vicious charges" made in Everett's petition and likened his description of the mock trials to "an Orson Welles dramatization." Accounts of beatings and starvation were "pure fabrications," he said. Violence would only have thwarted the urge to confess.

Joe jumped in with his usual pugnacity: "Is it true that you couldn't have convicted a man unless you beat the hell out of him in a cell?"

Fanton: "Wait a minute there."

McCarthy: "I am going to get this from you if I have to keep you here a week."

Senator Hunt: "Let's be a little more courteous with the witness. Let's not attempt any browbeating."[47]

Fanton, however, refused to be browbeaten. He had closely observed the interrogators and their techniques, he explained, and had seen no duress. Perl, he said, had been a lawyer in Vienna, and "was quite above sadism and taking unfair advantage."

On May 17, William Perl, who in civilian life was an industrial psychologist, testified that he was "strictly instructed not to promise immunity. . . . There was no physical force whatever used."

McCarthy said: "I think of the 10 interrogators he is one of the three accused of most of the brutality." He then proceeded to charge Perl with making false statements, and proposed that he take a lie detector test. "That is the only way we can close this matter," he said.

Perl: "If it is so reliable, we should have used it from the beginning. Why have a trial at all? Get the guys and put lie detectors on them. 'Did you kill this man?' The lie detector says 'Yes,' go to the scaffold. If it says 'No,' go back to Bavaria."

McCarthy: "I think you are lying. I do not think you can fool the lie detector. . . . You are not smart enough to beat it." Baldwin said it would accomplish nothing to give Perl a lie detector test.

McCarthy: "That's certainly an unusual statement on the part of the chair."

Baldwin: "It is not the purpose of this committee to protect anybody." The statements of mistreatment had come from the affidavits of SS prisoners. They too should take the test.

McCarthy went into his snarling mode: "The chair seems to be afraid of the results of that test. This committee is afraid of the facts and is sitting here solely for the purpose of a whitewash of the Army. It is inexcusable for the chairman not to allow the tests."

Baldwin maintained his composure. "Let us keep this thing on an even, level tone," he said. "Let me remind the senator that he was invited to sit in on these hearings. He has been permitted . . . to cross-examine witnesses. . . . To be faced with the charge that we are trying to whitewash anybody—"

"The committee does not want the facts," McCarthy cut in. "The committee is afraid of the facts, and the committee is sitting here to whitewash those involved. . . . Over in the House, Alger Hiss was asked whether he would submit to a lie detector test and he did not have the courage to." This was another of his tactics, to compare two unrelated cases to establish a spurious connection between Alger Hiss and William Perl.

Senator Hunt said he did not want to set aside his own judgment "for a mechanical machine."

McCarthy said he felt thwarted. "I was very disturbed when I found out the chairman of this subcommittee was the law partner of one of the men who was in charge of the Malmédy trials. I felt the senator should not sit as chairman of this committee. . . . I felt the committee was trying to protect the men charged with wrongdoing."

Baldwin: "I am surprised at the senator's charges . . . he has had every opportunity to go into the thing very thoroughly."

McCarthy caught himself. He had gone too far, questioning the ethics of the committee chairman who had permitted him to sit in on the hearings. Changing course, he said: "I have a tremendous amount of admiration and considerable affection for the senator from Connecticut." The chair had done much to oblige him.

Back on the stand, Perl said that Wichmann, an SS who shot an American sergeant in the back, "was the only one who actually repented of his crime."

McCarthy: "You did lie in order to get confessions. Tell me, yes or no."

Perl: "I would like to protest against the use of the word 'lie.' If an American officer is trying to find who killed 400 of his co-soldiers and uses perfectly legal methods, that is not a lie."

McCarthy: "Give me some other word I can use so that I will not insult your sensibilities, will you? What word can I use?"

Perl: "Winston Churchill in the House of Commons in 1906 referred to a 'terminological inexactitude.' "

On May 18, with Perl still on the stand, McCarthy called him "a master of evasion." Joe returned to his favorite topic, damaged testicles. The affidavit of Rieder, who had been sentenced to death for killing a Belgian woman, said he had been kicked in the testicles. Rieder had not taken the stand at the trial, and Perl insisted the affidavit was false. "I never kicked him," he said. "I do not think it ever happened."[48]

Baldwin had to remind Joe not to use uncorroborated allegations.

McCarthy: "I think I am competent to ask my questions."

"Do you think it is fair for the chair to ask a question?" an exasperated Baldwin responded.

Joe kept badgering Perl, and coming back to the lie detector, and comparing Perl to Alger Hiss, then saying Perl was lying.

Baldwin: "That is a very serious charge to make against a man who wore the Army uniform of the United States."

McCarthy: "One hundred and eighty million men wore the uniform, senator. I wore it too. I do not claim it made me better or worse."

Baldwin had finally reached the breaking point. "Wait a minute," he said. "You have done a lot of talking here. . . . We are not going to prejudge this case in any way."

McCarthy heedlessly repeated that Perl had obtained false confessions.

On May 19, all three members of the subcommittee, in a united anti-McCarthy front, expressed their opposition to the lie detector as "a marked departure from Congressional procedures." All the members of the full Armed

Services Committee were also opposed. "It would be unfair to subject them," they said of Perl and the other interrogators, "unless we also subjected their German accusers."

McCarthy was disgruntled, but struggled on. The prosecutor, Lieutenant Colonel Burton Ellis, was back on the stand on May 19. Joe asked him why Pletz, an SS man charged with killing captive Americans from a machine gun mounted on his tank, had had his sentence reduced from life to twenty years.

Ellis said it was his age—he was twenty-one. Even though "he was charged with the most unwarranted murder of American boys. . . . Out of pure viciousness he mowed down fifteen or twenty."

Eyeball-to-eyeball with Ellis, McCarthy argued that he had let Pletz off because he was not guilty. "Is it not a fact that you were deliberately deceiving us?" he roared. "It is obvious that this man is not telling us the truth."[49]

Then Joe added his own peculiar line of reasoning: "What if he were 22? What if he were 21 and a half?" With his outbursts and his bizarre defense of the SS, McCarthy had become the focus of the proceedings. Among the witnesses who refused to be intimidated by his tactics was Ralph Shumacker, an assistant prosecutor at the Malmédy trial. "There are those who have become quite sympathetic to the German nation," he said. "I have viewed the rows of white crosses and Stars of David which mark the graves of those victims who cannot speak. They were mute testimony to the righteousness of our nation in bringing to justice those who needlessly and with sheer delight took their lives."

Shumacker added that "Perl was an excellent interrogator. . . . He was always thinking of some trick or some new angle. . . . It was always a matter of cleverness." Bailey, the court reporter, on the other hand, "was drawing on his imagination."

On May 20, Joe was back at his most rambunctious, charging that "American Army officers in charge of war crime trials were in effect tearing a page from the books of Hitler and Stalin in order to get confessions." He said that Ellis "had received the Legion of Merit for his prostitution and perversion of justice before the world." The interrogators were "refugees from Hitlerism," a coded term for Jews. Baldwin's refusal of a lie detector test indicated "a whitewash of the Army officers involved."

At this point, McCarthy announced that he was abandoning his own sinking ship. The hearings had "degenerated into such a shameful farce," he said, "that I can no longer take part in them."

Baldwin's response was as levelheaded as Joe's had been offensive. "Mr. McCarthy has lost his temper and with it his sound impartial judgment," he said. "The chairman does not propose to have any of the exaggerations on the part of the junior senator from Wisconsin affect his judgment. More than 120 unarmed and surrounded American soldiers were brutally shot down in cold blood by German SS troops. To this day, no one has been executed for this crime. . . . The junior senator from Wisconsin has proceeded from the assumption that the charges made . . . have all been proven and that the Army is guilty. Oddly enough, he has been quick to accept and espouse the affidavits made by convicted war criminals two years after the completion of the trials. . . . He has overlooked the fact that affidavits of this type have little or no value in an American court. In the meantime, he has stated that he believes American officers testifying under oath were not telling the truth . . . though no proof was offered. . . . He accepted the unsupported affidavits of German SS troopers, some of whom unquestionably were guilty of the cold-blooded murder of American POWs, as against the sworn testimony of American officers."[50]

Baldwin's words were like the spanking of an unruly first-grader. McCarthy, his brow spotted with perspiration, responded with a threat. "I might say that the day is going to come when the chairman is going to bitterly regret this deliberate and very clever attempt to whitewash," he said. "I think it is a shameful farce, Mr. Chairman, and inexcusable." With that, he said "Goodbye, sir," and stomped out of the hearing room, leaving the subcommittee to proceed without his disruptive presence. McCarthy's career as an apologist for the SS and a mouthpiece for his pro-Nazi backer Harnischfeger was over, but in his attack on the Army there would be a reprise.

After recessing over the summer, the subcommittee traveled to Munich in September with several doctors, who examined fifty-nine SS men in Landsburg Prison. About ten had old war wounds or skin rashes, but there was no evidence of the allegations made in the affidavits. Lieutenant Colonel Edwin J. Carpenter, who had investigated the allegations after the trial, testified that "those statements were made to delay the execution of the sentence of the court."[51]

Thus ended the Malmédy hearings, during which McCarthy provided a subplot that showed him at his posturing, blustering, wrongheaded worst. But even then he was not done. In July, when the hearings were recessed, he took the Senate floor and accused Baldwin of a whitewash, which led the Armed Services Committee to pass a resolution expressing confidence in Baldwin, "because of the unusual, unfair, and utterly undeserved comments . . . that had been made." The resolution was signed by Senate leaders such as Democrats Lyndon Johnson and Millard Tydings, and Republicans Styles Bridges and Leverett Saltonstall.

In mid-October 1949, Baldwin delivered the subcommittee's final report. "I am convinced the Army did the best job it could," he told the Senate.

McCarthy broke in repeatedly, exclaiming that "the system of justice . . . was fundamentally wrong," and that "a conquering nation which has the power of life and death over people must be very meticulous in protecting these liberties."[52] Baldwin had said prior to the hearings that he would resign his Senate seat in mid-term to take a judicial appointment in his native state. McCarthy's behavior gave him no incentive to change his mind. What was behind this behavior? Why so much passion to defend SS murderers? To revive his flagging career? To pay a debt to his German backers in Wisconsin? Because he was not equipped with the usual restraints? Dwight Macdonald, then a *New Yorker* writer, reflecting on the hearings in a letter to a friend, called Joe "a master-hand at doubletalk. . . . He couldn't resist falsification. . . . Something pathological there."[53]

Les Fossel, one of Baldwin's aides, later said that "most of the Americans charged were Jewish, and there was an undercurrent of anti-Semitism in the whole business. . . . One indication of why Joe got interested is that he blossomed out with a new administrative assistant, Thomas W. Korb, who was Harnischfeger's legal counsel." Fossel related an exchange that was not in the transcript. Marine Colonel Joseph Chambers, the committee counsel, confronted Joe with false passages in his statements and said, "You just lied, you son of a bitch." "Sure I did," Joe replied, "but I got away with it, didn't I?" Fossel said of Joe: "Take any good, genial Irishman, remove his conscience, and you've got McCarthy."[54]

The hearings had not helped Joe. Among his fellow senators he was viewed as a loose cannon. Back home, he was relentlessly attacked by the *Capital Times*, which he denounced as "lower than a darky with a shovel and hoe."[55] He was generally viewed as unlikely to win reelection in 1952.

XIII

RED-HUNTER JOE

When Senator McCarthy launched his anti-Communist crusade in 1950, Soviet espionage was in the doldrums and the American Communist Party was crippled by the measures taken under the Truman administration. McCarthy arrived on the battlefield after the battle was over to finish off the wounded. His main target was the State Department, whose three major Soviet spies were gone: Lawrence Duggan committed suicide on December 20, 1948; Noel Field was behind the Iron Curtain; and Alger Hiss was a convicted perjurer. There had been more important spies in the Treasury Department, but Harry Dexter White died of a heart attack in 1948, and the members of the Silvermaster and Perlo groups were out of government service. Plenty of Soviet spies had infiltrated the U.S. government, but most of them were gone, and McCarthy was left with marginal cases, which he tried to inflate.

The collapse of the wartime networks, due largely to Whittaker Chambers and Elizabeth Bentley, left the KGB men in America empty-handed. Two experienced agents, Pravdin and Gromov, were replaced in 1946 by Grigory Dolbin, who was under diplomatic cover. He spoke no English and controlled no agents. By the summer of 1947 he was able to read the Washington papers without a dictionary, and reported "a bitter anti-Soviet campaign in the country."[1] In December, he was replaced by Alexander Panyushkin, the Soviet ambassador. Just as Joe began beating the drum, Panyushkin presided over a nonexistent agent network. In a 1950 analysis of the Washington station, the KGB said: "Since the middle of 1949, it practically stopped work on finding recruiters and new agents. It followed the line of least resistance, either drawing to our work people largely known by their connection with the U.S. Communist Party, or trying to use as agents officials from Eastern European countries."[2] A March 1950 memo from KGB boss Sergei Savchenko said: "Bentley gave away more than 40 most valuable agents to American authorities . . . [who] worked in key posts in leading state institutions, the State Department, the Treasury Department, etc."[3] These agents were impossible to replace. Panyushkin griped in October 1950 that he could not recruit any agents given the "current fascist atmosphere in the U.S. . . . We work here in an atmosphere . . . of almost 50 agents exposed long before us."[4] The number of dedicated radicals willing to spy for the Soviet Union now that it was no longer a wartime ally had shrunk dramatically. Moscow complained that espionage was at a standstill, but to no avail. One illegal, Rudolph Abel, arrived in New York in 1948, but in the eight years before his arrest, he never recruited anyone.

The decline of the agent networks went in tandem with the collapse of the American Communist Party, beginning with the ouster of Browder from the leadership. Once he was gone, so was the principal liaison between the KGB and the American party.[5]

A memo from Stephen Spingarn in May 1950 to President Truman outlined how the administration had been able "to counter and neutralize Communist activities in this country." Spingarn, the White House aide in charge of internal security, said that the FBI "had placed ever-increasing emphasis upon the activities of Communists in our midst." This had led to prosecution in the courts in cases such as Judith Coplon, Alger Hiss, Harry Bridges, Gerhardt Eisler, and the Hollywood Ten.

The government "has dealt a most forceful blow to the Communist conspiracy," Spingarn asserted, "by vigorously prosecuting all of the important leaders of the party" under the Smith Act. Spingarn reported that the government "has under very active investigation the cases of over 1,000 citizens with a view to revocation of citizenship and deportation on grounds of subversive activity."

As a result, Spingarn noted, FBI figures showed a decline in party membership from 74,000 in January 1947 to 53,000 in May 1950. (This was before the Supreme Court upheld the first Smith Act convictions in 1951, at which time the party went underground and the open membership dwindled to sixteen thousand.) The FBI cited "a drop-off in every aspect of the party's campaign within the labor movement," and "financial duress" due to legal costs.

To Spingarn, the FBI figures had "a tremendous wallop." He wanted Truman to use them "for a major address . . . and not just a whistle-stop occasion. These figures are the best proof that the Communist movement in this country is on the wane . . . due to the vigorous action which the administration had taken."[6]

In adopting the anti-Communist cause, McCarthy was a latecomer playing on a paradox—that as the party declined, alarm about it mounted. Truman had seen this in January 1949, when he told Clark Clifford that "the hysteria-mongering branch of the Republican party is the brains of this [anti-Red] movement." He named Karl Mundt and Richard Nixon in the House and Homer Ferguson in the Senate.[7] Spingarn saw it too, writing in a memo on January 31, 1950, of "a crusade or holy war entirely devoted to attacking Communism. . . . The holy war type of fight tends to make the single policy of anti-Communism the test of American patriotism. This would qualify some very curious people as our friends," such as those who say that "Franco is the leading European anti-Communist."[8]

This anti-Communist "holy war" was partly partisan politics, a rallying cry for the Republicans, out of office since 1933. It was fueled by frustration. But there was also a feeling in the population at large that the government was awash in treachery, which it had been, though it no longer was. This lag in perception made McCarthyism possible. The revelations in the Venona transcripts, had they been made public, would have made McCarthy's charges irrelevant. But given the paucity of information, the espionage issue was ripe for exploitation.

———

McCarthy had many estimable qualities and followed a well-trod American path, that of the farm boy who succeeds in politics thanks to midnight oil and pluck, with more than a pinch of unscrupulousness thrown in. So far, a standard Horatio Alger story. As a judge, he went beyond the call of duty to help some of those he had sentenced to jail, and looked out for the children of divorce. He was a generous man, who donated fairly large sums to a seminary in Burma. But he was also careless about money, and a liar of pathological proportions. As he rose in politics, he abandoned whatever scruples he may have had and gave in to expediency. He was like a character in a medieval morality play, fought over by an angel and a devil. Once elected to the Senate, the impulse for power and gain took over. He used his office to collect money in underhanded ways. By failing to abide by the Senate's code of conduct, he alienated influential senators. His first three years in the Senate were undistinguished, and in 1950 he was a man in need of an issue, with a problematic election coming up in 1952. As it happened, his timing could not have been better, and he quickly became one of the leading figures of his party. But although he gave his name to an ism, his rise and fall took a mere five years, from the Wheeling speech in February 1950 to his censure in December 1954. Three years later he was dead, not yet fifty.

—

When McCarthy embarked on a crusade against Communists in the State Department, he was following a well-trod path. In the summer and fall of 1945, a number of wartime agencies were disbanded, and those employees who did not move back into the private sector were transferred to the State Department. In August 1945, the State Department had 13,372 employees on its rolls. The wartime agencies added another 12,797: 7,482 from the Office of War Information; 1,013 from the Office of Strategic Services; 1,273 from the Foreign Economic Administration; 1,797 from the Surplus Property Administration; and 1,232 from the Office of Inter-American Affairs.[9]

Jimmy Byrnes, then Secretary of State, recalled in his memoirs that the number of State Department employees "was almost doubled by the transfer to it of all or part of the war agencies. The transfer of these agencies did not make me very happy. The job of acting as 'undertaker' for war agencies necessarily is a bad one. The most capable people are impelled to leave. . . . Morale sags and the problems multiply." The State Department, however, felt that the recruitment policies of the interim agencies did not meet its standards, and by March 1947, all but four thousand of the hand-me-downs had been screened out.[10]

General William J. Donovan's OSS posed a particular problem, in that he had hired a number of Soviet agents. Liz Bentley had identified half a dozen, among them Duncan Lee and Maurice Halperin. J. Edgar Hoover knew of others, and wrote in a memo in October 1946: "The OSS was a breeding ground for Commies."[11]

When the OSS was disbanded on September 20, 1945, the Research and Intelligence Branch went to the State Department, and the Counterintelligence Branch went to the War Department, where it was renamed the Strategic Services Unit. The SSU chief, Colonel William Quinn, knew he had inherited some Communists, as well as lock pickers and counterfeiters. In October, he asked J. Edgar Hoover to vet the 2,500 OSS newcomers, whom he cut down to nine hundred.[12]

In the State Department, half of the thousand OSS transfers were kept after screening. They were placed under the command of Colonel Alfred McCormack, who was named special assistant in charge of research and intelligence. McCormack, a partner in the distinguished law firm of Cravath,

Henderson & de Gersdorff, had served in Military Intelligence (G-2) during the war.

In his memoirs, Dean Acheson, then undersecretary of state, wrote that the Research and Intelligence section "died almost at once as the result of gross stupidity." In plain English, this meant that when the OSS was abolished, Acheson saw a window of opportunity for State to take the lead as the department in charge of intelligence; that opportunity was lost when the CIA was formed on September 18, 1947. Acheson thought the State Department had muffed its chance, but there was more to it than that.[13]

Ostensibly, there were two camps inside the State Department, one of which, led by Acheson and McCormack, wanted to build up a centralized intelligence unit. The other camp, led by the officers in charge of the geographical divisions, fought to maintain their existing intelligence capacities. But what was presented as a jurisdictional dispute had a strong security component.

Byrnes had named, as his assistant secretary in charge of administration, his law partner and South Carolina crony, Donald Russell. With his direct line to Byrnes, Russell had precedence over Acheson. J. Anthony Panuch, an anti-Communist hard-liner, was Russell's assistant in charge of security. Panuch worked closely with Raymond E. Murphy, who ran a mysterious State Department Office called EUR/X, devoted to the study of worldwide Communist subversion. This Wizard of Oz–like character, known only to a handful inside State, performed such tasks as debriefing Soviet defectors.

Murphy warned Panuch that prior to the demise of the wartime agencies, the Communist-controlled United Public Workers of America had only one member inside the State Department. After the transfer, the membership rose to between one hundred and two hundred. The chairman of the UPWA local, Peveril Meigs, advocated striking against the federal government. "This means that the Department now has a first-class headache," Murphy wrote Panuch, since Congress was placing riders on all appropriations bills, stating that no part of the funds could be used to pay the salaries of employees who sanctioned the right to strike against the federal government.[14]

Panuch went on the offensive, fearing that a centralized intelligence agency inside State, made up of retreads from the OSS, would present serious security problems. On November 14, 1945, he passed on to Don Russell a memo from one of Colonel McCormack's fellow officers in Military Intelligence, which said that he had been "a vigorous leader of a pro-Communist group within G-2, [who] permitted officers with known Communist leanings (as reported by the FBI), to sit in positions where they could influence the trend of intelligence."[15]

Panuch's memo on McCormack was leaked to the House Military Affairs Committee. On March 14, 1946, Andrew Jackson May, the committee chairman, charged that employees with "strong Soviet leanings," who had been forced out of the War Department were now at State. May added that he had complained strongly to Byrnes. "We named the names of the personnel involved and there are many of them," he said. Others on the committee said there were about fifteen, one of whom was McCormack.[16] On March 20, in a letter to May, McCormack called the allegations "a tissue of lies, created by irresponsible and evil men with evil purposes." It was clear, he said, that the committee had been listening to a former Army officer who was out to get him.[17] Acheson in his memoirs called May's remarks "the first pre-McCarthy attack."

The upshot of the McCormack fracas was the scuttling of the Acheson plan for a centralized intelligence agency. On April 22, 1946, Byrnes decided against it and Colonel McCormack resigned. Then, when General George Marshall replaced Byrnes as Secretary of State in January 1947, keeping Acheson as undersecretary, the first thing Acheson did was fire Panuch. John Peurifoy, one of Acheson's protégés, took his place.[18]

Once awakened, concern in Congress over Communists in the State Department did not let up, particularly at appropriations time. In June 1947, the Senate Appropriations Committee questioned Secretary of State Marshall. The committee report stated: "It is evident that there is a deliberate, calculated program being carried out not only to protect Communist personnel in high places, but to reduce security and intelligence protection to a nullity."[19]

In the House, John Taber, a Republican from upstate New York, first elected in 1922, was chairman of the Appropriations Committee. "I saw a cartoon the other day called 'the Sabre Dance,' " Truman once said, "in which they showed a big man with a sabre cutting off the heads of all the appropriations. . . . Well, I named it the 'Taber Dance.' "[20] Taber was now just as concerned with Communists in government as he was about budget cuts. He named a subcommittee to hold hearings in January 1948 on appropriations for the departments of State, Justice, Commerce, and the federal judiciary.

The chairman of this subcommittee was Karl Stefan, a Nebraska Republican born on a farm near Zebrakov, Bohemia, whose parents had settled in Omaha when he was one year old. Educated at the YMCA night school, he had worked as a telegrapher, newspaper editor, and radio commentator. A congenial, hearty fellow, whose standard joke was that he could make you an admiral in the Nebraska Navy, he was elected to the House in 1934.

The 1948 hearings on the State Department, which was asking for $214,918,000, had to do with such matters as representational allowances and the bearing of climatic conditions on post rotations. The committee sent a team over to State under the direction of its chief investigator, Robert E. Lee, to collect data on the value of services performed as compared to the cost in tax dollars. In the course of their work, they stumbled on the loyalty files. Lee and his men spent four months poring over the files and came up with 108 suspect cases, which they summarized for the Stefan subcommittee hearings. These cases were by no means exhaustive, "just dipping in here and there," as Lee put it. Lee sneaked in as the curtain was dropping, for on March 13, 1948, Truman directed all federal departments to withhold personnel security and loyalty files from members of Congress.[21]

On January 26, Stefan questioned Hamilton Robinson, the head of the Office of Controls. With 782 employees, Controls was a grab bag of six unconnected divisions including munitions, visas and passports, and security. Robinson had the right background for State—the Taft School, Princeton, and Yale Law School. From 1942 to 1946, he had worked with John Foster Dulles at Sullivan & Cromwell. In less than four years in the Army, from 1942 to 1946, he had risen from first lieutenant to lieutenant colonel. He had glowing recommendations as an administrator.

Stefan had summaries of the 108 loyalty cases unearthed by Lee in front of him and began throwing random cases at Robinson, using numbers instead of names. Here was no. 102, who was involved in the *Amerasia* case. He had taken the side of the Chinese Communists in a roundtable discussion at Northwestern University and was a great admirer of Russia. His investigation was pending.

Robinson: "It is a tough determination. . . . To damn a man's career for the rest of his life."

Stefan: "I suppose it would be a bar to employment if they were interested in maintaining the American way of life."

Robinson: "That is a sort of a funny question."

Taber (who was sitting in on the hearings): "I do not think it is funny."

Stefan continued to list the cases. One was an associate of suspected spies, but had been cleared by the State Department loyalty board. Another boasted that he was a Communist. One had written an article on Russia called "Toward a Classless Society."

"I am just a man from the prairies of Nebraska," Stefan said, "asking why these people are on the payroll."

Robinson said he had to be sure "that somebody is not getting a dirty deal."[22]

Stefan then turned to no. 52, a high State Department official. This was John Carter Vincent, who as chief of division of Chinese affairs was influential in guiding postwar China policy. According to his State Department loyalty file, Vincent had been observed on October 25, 1947, contacting a man in Washington. The man then went to the Soviet embassy. At this time, a telegram from Truman to Chiang Kai-shek was picked up by Moscow before it was sent from Washington. The inference was that Vincent had passed Truman's wire to a Soviet agent. In another incident, Vincent's raincoat was found by guards in a State Department men's room. In a pocket were some papers in Russian. Vincent later explained that he had gone out to lunch on a rainy day, and, not having brought his own raincoat, he grabbed one he saw in the outer office, which had been hanging there for weeks. But if that was the case, why didn't he put it back where he found it?[23]

To the committee, John Carter Vincent's explanation sounded fishy. John Taber observed: "I have not been as much disturbed for a long time."

"We are continually told," Stefan said, "that there are people with disloyal leanings in various branches of the government." How many in the State Department, he asked Robinson, had been terminated since the loyalty program had gone into effect?

Robinson said that in 1947 his office had opened 255 cases, of which 136 were closed. Of the 136 closed cases, 33 had resigned, 15 were dismissed, and 88 stayed on the job. All those dismissed were from wartime agencies. The dilemma, he said, was that employees had rights, "and you cannot lean over too far one way because you are a witch hunt or too far the other way because you are harboring Communists. So you are caught in a squeeze."

Despite its detection of laxity, the redoubtable House Appropriations Committee cut only $17 million from the State Department budget, or about 7 percent. In his report on February 27, 1948, Stefan concluded that "the committee does not feel the department has been as diligent as it might have been in the selection of its personnel."[24] This was an understatement, for both Taber and Stefan were incensed over State Department practices, which they assailed on the floor of the House.

There was enough concern in Congress to launch yet another hearing on State Department security practices. On February 2, 1948, J. Edgar Chenoweth of Colorado, the chairman of the House Committee on Expenditures in the Executive Department, decided to hold hearings on the State Department's Office of Controls.

When those hearings opened on March 10, 1948, the first witness was Hamilton Robinson's boss, John Peurifoy, the undersecretary for administration. "I have been shocked," he said, "deeply, by the revelations of the Canadian white paper [on Gouzenko]. . . . But I cannot believe that the only alternative is to be swept off our feet by the gossip mongering and character assassination which so often accompanies personal investigations. I am also disturbed by the present tendency to extend the highly questionable theory of 'guilt by association' to lengths that amount to a travesty of traditional American justice."[25]

At the Stefan subcommittee hearings in January, Hamilton Robinson had revealed that sixty-four of the 108 suspects on the Lee list were still employed by the State Department. Peurifoy on March 10 stated that the number was down to fifty-seven. This was one of the numbers that McCarthy would brandish in his speeches in February 1950.

Peurifoy then explained how he had come to hire Hamilton Robinson to head the Office of Controls and what an exemplary manager he was. The only thing his FBI screening under the Truman loyalty program had turned up was that he had a second cousin who had been investigated for Communist activities and who had been in the State Department from 1944 to December 1946.

This second cousin, Robert Talbot Miller III, was no. 12 on the Lee list, where he was described as "in all probability the greatest security risk the Department has had."

When Hamilton Robinson testified before the Chenoweth Committee on March 10, he was asked about his association with Robert Miller. He said that Miller had been the best man at his wedding, but "since I have been in Washington, I have seen very little of him. He calls up once or twice a year for lunch. Since I accepted this job as Director of Controls, I have had absolutely nothing to do with him."[26]

The committee did not know it, but Miller was a Soviet agent of some importance, identified by Elizabeth Bentley to the FBI. After graduating from the Kent School and Princeton, Miller became a freelance newspaper correspondent in Europe. In 1934, he was the Moscow stringer for the *Chattanooga News*. There he met and married Jenny Levy, an American girl who worked for the English-language *Moscow Daily News*. In 1937, they left Russia and Miller worked as a press agent for the Spanish Republicans.

Two years later, Miller teamed up with two American veterans of the International Brigades, Jack Fahy and Joseph Gregg, to found *Hemispheric News*, which supplied American newspapers with copy from Latin America. As it turned out, all three were Soviet agents. Fahy is mentioned in Venona as an operative for Naval GRU.[27] Liz Bentley told the FBI in 1945 that Jacob Golos had recruited Robert Miller and Joseph Gregg via the American Communist Party. She had handled them as separate agents: neither knew the other was KGB. In 1941, *Hemispheric News* was absorbed by a wartime agency, the Office of Inter-American Affairs. When it was disbanded in 1945, Miller and Gregg transferred to the State Department. Miller rose to the position of assistant chief of research and publication. In July 1946, J. Anthony Panuch, the diligent security chief later fired on the recommendation of Dean Acheson, urged Miller's dismissal, based on FBI reports. Upon being questioned, Miller said he had met Bentley socially as Helen, but did not know her last name. With the FBI closing in, Miller resigned in December 1946.[28]

The Chenoweth Committee hearings concluded on March 12, having barely scratched the surface. In closing, Chenoweth said: "I will tell you very frankly there is a feeling of suspicion in this country that somewhere in the State Department Communists exercise influence. . . . Do you think that we would be able to round up enough people . . . whose loyalty is unquestioned to work there, without having this constant criticism and complaint?"[29]

Fred Busbey, an Illinois Republican on the Chenoweth Committee, felt that the hearings had been concluded prematurely. There were a few things he wanted to get off his chest, and one of them was that Hamilton Robinson was incompetent and should not be running the Office of Controls. On March 25, 1948, he gave a speech entitled "What's Wrong with the State Department" on the floor of the House.

It was highly improbable, Busbey said, that Robinson did not know about his cousin's activities. He had in fact told some members of Congress off the record that after taking over the Office of Controls he had lunch with Miller at least a dozen times and that in his opinion Miller was probably a Communist and perhaps a Soviet agent.

In October 1946, when Miller was looking around for another job, he applied to the Central Intelligence Group (precursor to the CIA) for a position. The CIG wrote to Robinson, asking for a reference. Instead of warning the CIG about his cousin's Communist connections, Busbey said, Robinson gave this sarcastic reply: "According to the telephone book, his phone number is Ordway 1420."

Did this kind of behavior, Busbey asked, qualify a man for passing on the security and loyalty of twenty thousand State Department employees? Busbey wasn't saying that he was disloyal, but that he was unqualified for the job. "The State Department as an outpost in foreign policy should be inviolable," Busbey concluded. "It should be like Caesar's wife, and it is utter nonsense to be confronted with case after case of reasonable doubt only to find Mr. Robinson clearing him or waiting for proof of an overt act."[30]

———

In 1948, with a presidential election coming up, the furor over Communists in the State Department receded. One of Truman's campaign planks was "the do-nothing 80th Congress." On his whistle-stop tour in October, he went after individual congressmen. In Auburn, he had John Taber in his sights for using "a butcher knife . . . on appropriations that have been in the public interest." With Truman's victory, the Democrats gained solid majorities in both houses of Congress—54 to 42 in the Senate and 263 to 177 in the House.[31]

When McCarthy revived the Reds issue in February 1950, he relied heavily on the work done by the two House committees in 1948. Since Truman had roped off loyalty files from the Congress, his basic text became the Lee list.

It was the practice of Republican congressmen to fan out across the country in February and give Lincoln Day speeches. As a junior senator without any important committee assignment, McCarthy drew a less than alluring five-city tour, starting with the West Virginia Republican Women's Club on February 9 at Wheeling. Forced on tour, he decided to turn it into a tour de force, focusing on the issue that he hoped would revive his reputation.[32]

McCarthy needed some research help with his Lincoln Day talks. He knew a reporter at the *Washington Times-Herald,* Jim Waters, who put him on to the paper's Capitol Hill man, Ed Nellor. Having covered the Hiss case in 1948, Nellor was familiar with the issue. In addition, he had exactly what Joe needed, a copy of the Lee list, with fifty-seven cases pending as of March 1948.

Following the 1945 transfer of the wartime agencies, statements had been made on the floor of the House that "hundreds if not thousands of employees have been eliminated from the State Department by the screening committee because of Communist leanings or activities of membership." Responding to these statements on August 1, 1946, Secretary of State Jimmy Byrnes wrote Representative Adolph Sabath of Illinois that they were incorrect. Byrnes explained that of the roughly four thousand employees kept by the State Department, three thousand had been screened. In 284 cases, a recommendation against permanent employment was made. Of the 284, 79 had been terminated. That left 205, as of August 1946. Byrnes did not give their names. Nor did McCarthy know how many of these 205 were still in the State Department more than three years later or how many had been cleared.[33]

Joe set out on his five-city tour with a lot of undigested information. It was all new to him, and he got a little confused. He had a valid case to make, documented by two House committees in 1948, that security risks were allowed to remain in the State Department. But he spoiled his case by overstating it and jumbling the numbers in the Mixmaster of his mind.

At 5:00 P.M. on February 9, 1950, Paul J. Miller, the program director of station WWVA in Wheeling, received a copy of Joe's speech. "I have in my hand," it read, in a line soon to become notorious, "a list of 205—a list of names that were made known to the Secretary of State as being members of the Communist Party and who, nevertheless, are still working and shaping policy in the State Department." That evening, when McCarthy spoke in the Colonnade Room of the McLure Hotel before an audience of 275, WWVA taped the speech and broadcast it later, from 10:00 to 10:30 P.M. The tape was later erased to be reused on the *Wendy Warren* show. The next day Frank Desmond of the *Wheeling Intelligencer* reported on the speech, using the 205 figure.[34]

The rest of his speech had been cobbled together from old newspaper clips about the spread of world Communism, the loss of China, and the treachery of Alger Hiss. He gave a few, rather stale names, such as Gustavo Duran, who had left the State Department and found a job at the United Nations, and Julian Wadleigh, who had also left the State Department and had recently written a series in the *New York Post* called "Why I Spied for the Soviet Union."

Though his facts were often wrong, McCarthy's timing could not have been better. Mao Tse-tung had recently taken power in China, with Chiang Kai-shek fleeing to Formosa. Hiss had been found guilty of perjury in January 1950 and sentenced to five years in prison. Klaus Fuchs had been arrested in England and had confessed shortly before the speech. The notion of a fifth column, which had given the Russians the secret of the bomb, was on American minds. McCarthy was tapping a well of resentment, and in a way, he was right by analogy, for the secrets of the bomb *had* been stolen. His remarks were picked up by the Associated Press and ran in roughly thirty papers. Continuing westward on his five-city tour, he was in Salt Lake City on February 10, where he changed the number of State Department Communists to fifty-seven, the number of cases still pending on the Lee list in 1948, when John Peurifoy disclosed it in his testimony before the Chenoweth Committee that March. On February 11 in Reno, at the Mapes Hotel before four hundred Republicans, he stuck to fifty-seven. The Reno *State Journal* reported on February 20, that "Senator McCarthy, who had first typed a total of 205 employees of the State Department . . . scratched out that number and mentioned only 57 card-carrying members."[35]

After the Reno speech, McCarthy sent a wire to President Truman, charging that a State Department spokesman had denied his claim that State was harboring fifty-seven Communists. He instructed Truman to "pick up your phone and ask Mr. Acheson how many . . . he failed to discharge . . . after lengthy consultation with Alger Hiss." Joe wanted Truman to "demand that Acheson give you . . . a complete report on all those who were placed in the department by Alger Hiss. . . . Failure on your part will label the Democratic party of being the bed-fellow of international Communism."[36] On the basis of an outdated list, Joe was making outlandish charges with bad grammar.

Infuriated by McCarthy's eight-hundred-pound-gorilla tactics, Truman wrote but did not send this reply: "This is the first time in my experience, and I was ten years in the Senate, that I ever heard of a Senator trying to discredit his own government before the world. You know that isn't done by honest public officials. Your telegram is not only not true and an insolent approach to a situation that should have been worked out between man and man, but it shows conclusively that you are not even fit to have a hand in the operation of the government of the United States."[37] The battle was joined between the pugnacious President and the boorish senator, which could only help the one with the lesser position.

In Las Vegas on February 13, the figure remained fifty-seven, as it did on the 15th in Huron, South Dakota. On his home turf in Milwaukee on February 16, McCarthy was told that Truman had said at a press conference that Joe had not spoken a word of truth. This was balm in Gilead, for every denial required a response, every headline led to another headline, like a game of Ping-Pong, and Joe finally mentioned the Byrnes letter and the list of 205.

Elated by the media attention on his five-city tour, McCarthy decided to press his charges on the floor of the Senate. Again, he relied on the Lee list. But by now, he had become a magnet for people with tales to tell. So he had some new cases, which were not on the Lee list, probably provided by J. Anthony Panuch, whom he mentioned flatteringly in his speech, or by Robert L. Bannerman, another State Department security man no longer in office.[38]

McCarthy did not want to admit that his cases came from a House committee report dating back to 1948. He jumbled the numbers on the Lee list and interspersed them with his other cases. At this point he declined to give any names. His eighty-one cases, mostly from the Lee list, were a tangle of valid security threats, garden-variety liberals, and persons with tenuous connections to the State Department. He found it impossible to separate the quest for improved security from the temptation to discredit the Truman administration. McCarthy was pulling the loyalty issue back into the spotlight at a time when it might loom large in the 1950 elections. Thus, his speech turned into a partisan dogfight that lasted six hours.

When he arrived on the Senate floor in the late afternoon on February 20 with his bulging briefcase, only a sprinkling of senators were present. If he had been allowed to present his eighty-one cases without interruption the proceedings would have taken about an hour. But the interruptions came fast and furious, with cries of "will the senator yield." This was one of the reasons for his messy recitation, for the delays and arguments made him lose his continuity; some numbers he skipped while others he repeated.

One of the senators present was the Senate Majority Leader, Scott Lucas of

Illinois. "If I had said the nasty things that McCarthy said about the State Department," he had recently stated in Chicago, "I would be ashamed all my life." McCarthy reprimanded him for his remark, calling him the "alleged Democratic Leader." All he wanted to do, Joe said, was "to root out the fifth column in the State Department."[39]

Lucas demanded that McCarthy name the 205 card-carrying Communists he had spoken of at Wheeling. Joe trumpeted: "I will not say on the Senate floor anything I will not say off the floor." This was a remark he would come to regret.

The Democrats present acted like objection-raising defense lawyers: Where did he get his cases? Why did he not name names? Why did his numbers keep changing?

McCarthy replied that his cases came from sources inside the State Department. "If there were not some good, honest, loyal men," he said, "men who are willing to risk their positions, I would not be able to give this report tonight." As for the names, he said somewhat disingenuously that since they had not been charged with anything, it would be unfair to name them. This led to accusations that he did not have them.

Commenting on the small number of senators present, Senator Harley Kilgore of West Virginia said: "The wet season is driving the pintails north." By 7:30 P.M. only fourteen cases had been read. The Republicans demanded a quorum and senators trooped in from dinner, one of them in white tie and tails. The Senate went into a night session as McCarthy battled to list his cases, and by the time he was done it was close to midnight.[40]

Without the names, McCarthy's list was unverifiable, particularly since he often distorted or exaggerated the information in his summaries. Now that we know the names, it can be divided into four categories: those who were no longer or had never been in the State Department; liberal Democrats; suspected loyalty cases; and Soviet spies. But Joe was incapable of making distinctions. His level of vehemence was the same for all categories.

After McCarthy's speech, Carlisle H. Humelsine, the assistant secretary of state for administration (who had replaced John Peurifoy), stated that of the eighty-one cases, only forty were still employed in the State Department. Seven on the list had never been employed there. Among these were Harlow Shapley, a Harvard astronomer and ardent fellow traveler, who had been named in 1947 to the National Committee for UNESCO, for which he was paid $10 a day plus transportation expenses; Frederick L. Schuman, a prolific pro-Soviet author and professor at Williams, who had once lectured at the State Department; and Dorothy Kenyon, a municipal court judge in New York City, who had been named in 1947 to serve as American delegate to the

United Nations Commission on the Status of Women. Her three-year tenure was up before Joe made his speech. McCarthy called this humanitarian assignment "a high State Department position," insinuating that she was a policymaker with access to classified information.

McCarthy said that Kenyon belonged to twenty-eight Communist fronts. She had indeed belonged to twelve, some without her permission, some from which by her own admission "I got out as fast as I could," and others where "I did not like the company I was keeping." She was one of the many liberals who were gulled into joining fronts during the Spanish Civil War. She was on record for denouncing the Nazi-Soviet pact in 1939, and clashing with the Soviet delegate on the U.N. commission. But in McCarthy's version of events, she was guilty of deep-rooted Communist activities.[41]

Among the more murky cases of reasonable suspicion was Joe's case no. 2, John Carter Vincent, who had been observed contacting an apparent Soviet agent. McCarthy claimed in his summary that the major portion of his loyalty file had been removed. Vincent, one of the architects of the State Department's Asian policy, was accused of favoring the Chinese Communists. Cleared five times by the State Department loyalty board, he was removed from the Asian desk and sent to Bern, Switzerland, and Tangier, Morocco. In 1953, when John Foster Dulles was Secretary of State, he was forced to resign.

Peveril Meigs, no. 3 on Joe's list, joined the State Department in September 1945 and was assigned to the Joint Intelligence Study Publishing Board. He was the head of a United Public Workers local that advocated striking against the government and followed the Soviet line. The State Department allowed him to resign in 1948 because it did not want to court problems with the union. He joined the Department of the Army and was suspended by the Army loyalty board and discharged the same year.[42]

As for Soviet agents, there were at least two. One was Robert T. Miller, case no. 16, and Hamilton Robinson's second cousin, whom Liz Bentley had identified as one of her "singletons." "This individual's file is perhaps the largest physically of the State Department loyalty files," McCarthy said. "The file reflects that this individual furnished material to known Soviet espionage agents and that he had contacts with a long list of Communists and suspected Soviet agents." Miller had resigned in December 1946.

The second Soviet agent was Mary Jane Keeney, who had transferred to State from the Federal Economic Administration. Her downfall came about because she kept a diary. She and her husband, Philip, became known as "the librarian spies." In 1937, they were fired from the University of Montana Library for radical activities. They moved to Berkeley, where according to Mary Jane's diary, they were members of the Marin County Communist cell. During the war, Philip was a librarian for the OSS, while Mary Jane worked for the Board of Economic Warfare and the Federal Economic Administration. According to Venona, they were recruited by the GRU in 1940. In 1945, however, they were transferred to the KGB. In a black bag job, the FBI copied her diary, which described their KGB control, Sergey Kurnakov, whom she called "Colonel Thomas." When Kurnakov went back to Russia in December 1945, Philip Keeney's comment was recorded in a diary entry: "It is wonderful for him that he is returning. It makes me green with envy." Philip went to Tokyo to help reconstruct the Japanese library system. Facing a loyalty investigation in 1948, Mary Jane Keeney left the State Department for the United Nations, from which she was soon fired after U.S. protests. She and her husband opened an art film club. They were never prosecuted for their espionage, which had been uncovered thanks to Venona and the FBI break-in.[43]

There was another "category" on Joe's list, the one that defied simple explanation. Esther Caukin Brunauer, case no. 47, had joined the State Department in 1944. The following year, she was assigned to the United Nations founding conference in San Francisco as assistant to New York Congressman Sol Bloom. McCarthy charged that she had been "the first assistant to Alger Hiss," which she had not. He said, "This is one of the most fantastic cases I know of," and in some ways it was.

Esther's husband, Stephen, was a chemist in the Explosive Research Division of the U.S. Navy, where he headed a large staff of scientists conducting secret work. Stephen Brunauer admitted to having joined the Young Workers' League in 1927, describing it as "a glorified social club with dances and picnics and infrequent participation in picket lines and strikes." He soon left. In a letter of support, Senator Joseph Ball of Minnesota described him as "perhaps the most violently anti-Communist person I know."

Stephen Brunauer was Hungarian-born, and had a brother still living there. In 1946, the Navy asked him to go to Budapest on a secret mission. He was instrumental in arranging the escape of a number of scientists to the United States, where they did outstanding work for the Navy.

Esther, meanwhile, had been assigned to the State Department Division of Internal Security, even though she had Communist associations. In 1946, according to a loyalty board report, she was named head of a State Department delegation that was supposed to observe the A-bomb tests on the Pacific atoll of Bikini. For this she needed a special red security pass from the Navy, which would give her access to classified data. But the officer in charge told her she could not have one. She persisted, to no avail. So she told a WAVE in her office to go pick up the pass for her, which aroused the suspicion of the security division. She ended up not going to Bikini.[44]

In 1948, Esther Brunauer was brought before the State Department loyalty board on charges of being "in sympathetic association with the Communist Party, to have supported its policies, and to have been a member of the American Friends of the Soviet Union." At the hearing, when she was asked whether she knew about the red passes, she said: "I did not, no sir. If I did, I don't remember it now, sir."

She was then told: "The situation concerning the issuing of the red pass apparently reached a point where it was pushed upstairs so that Vice Admiral Blandy and Admiral Hussey talked about it. They ruled that you were not going to be cleared for the Bikini tests. . . . That conflicts directly with what you have testified today."

Brunauer: "I have no recollection. . . . I was a terrifically busy person, heading up the bureau group for the Bikini tests. So I cannot recall what sort of passes were needed. . . . What you see at Bikini is nothing, you see a big blow. What is important is the record, the reports."[45]

Esther Brunauer was cleared, but transferred to the State Department liaison staff with UNESCO. She was in the UNESCO job at the time McCarthy listed her in his February 20 speech. His information came from the Lee list, culled from the State Department loyalty board files. "A reliable informant," said her Lee list dossier, had reported both Brunauers to be Communists. In addition, Esther had "recently contacted a subject of a Soviet espionage case."

In April 1951, her husband, Stephen, was suspended by the Navy. Carlisle Humelsine, the assistant secretary in charge of administration, privately told Senator Millard Tydings of Maryland: "I understand he is a drunk, and that three times lately they've found him laid up with other women. He's a bad security risk, though there's no hint of disloyalty."[46] Stephen Brunauer resigned rather than go before the Navy's loyalty board.

Following her husband's suspension, Esther was suspended by the State Department. In September, new charges were brought against her: that she was active in party organizations in the twenties and thirties, and that she had been affiliated with nine front groups in 1935 and 1936. Esther Brunauer was dismissed on June 16, 1952.

The matter of the red pass loomed large in Esther's file. She had clearly lied to the loyalty board. As for Stephen, why had he resigned instead of defending himself at a hearing? If drinking and adultery were the criteria, there would have been dozens of cases. Here was a man who had attained a high position in the U.S. Navy and made vital contributions to national security. The loyalty boards worked in mysterious ways. He found a job in private industry in the Midwest.

Though there were no important spies left in the State Department in February 1950, there was a need to tighten up security. Was it not possible to find applicants without Communist backgrounds and connections to work in the department that conducted our foreign policy? This had been the heartfelt cry of the two House committees who had done the spadework in 1948 that McCarthy was now riding to national recognition. Had he culled his list, had he come out with the names, had he studied the files more carefully, he would have made a more forceful case. Instead, he concealed his sources and sought to overwhelm his Senate colleagues with the bogus momentousness of his findings.

———

Only one of Joe's eighty-one cases, no. 54, resulted in the indictment of a State Department employee. This was Val Lorwin, who served in the labor section. "This individual," McCarthy said, "has been connected with a number of Communist front organizations and was active in attempting to secure the issuance of a non-immigration visa to a French Communist leader."

At the time, Lorwin was a labor economist in Paris, and he granted visas recommended by the American ambassador, so that French labor leaders could attend an international conference. In the thirties, Lorwin had been a Norman Thomas Socialist, but he was soon fed up with the party's "wornout phraseology" and quit when he began to work for New Deal agencies such as the Labor Department and the War Production Board. In 1935, while still a member, he had a friend from Cornell, Harold Metz, staying in his house in Washington. Fifteen years later, after Lorwin had been named by McCarthy, Metz came forward and filed an affidavit on July 10, 1950, stating that Lorwin had been a Communist in 1935 and had shown him his party card. Metz said he had seen some "strange-looking people" in Lorwin's house.[47]

Lorwin testified at a State Department Loyalty Board hearing on December 20, that the "strange-looking people" were members of the Socialist Southern Tenant Farmers Union. He said that he had shown Metz his Socialist Party card, which was red, and that Metz had mistaken it for a Communist card, which at the time was a black-bound booklet. In February 1951, Lorwin was suspended as a security risk, but his case was reopened as colleagues told of his fine work in the OSS and the State Department. On March 28, 1952, Lorwin was cleared by the loyalty board, but since he had long been under suspension with no salary, he had resigned and taken a teaching job at the University of Chicago.[48]

In the meantime, Metz's statement came to the attention of the Criminal Division of the Justice Department, whose head, James M. McInerney, asked for a further investigation. The case was assigned to James Gallagher, who argued that there were grounds for an indictment. Others in the department doubted his wisdom in pursuing an insufficiently developed case, but on January 7, 1953, Gallagher's request to present the case to a grand jury was approved by Attorney General James McGranery, who had been criticized by Republican senators for not being a vigorous prosecutor.[49]

Gallagher appeared for one hour before a grand jury in Washington on December 2, 1953, and an indictment was returned on December 4, charging Lorwin with perjury before the State Department loyalty board in December 1950. The case presented serious difficulties in that it was Lorwin's word against Metz's. Gallagher had hoped that two FBI informants would testify at the trial, but the FBI told him that one had relied on hearsay and the other had been misquoted.[50]

Concerned over the weakness of the case, William A. Paisley, chief of the Trial Section at the Justice Department, examined the grand jury minutes and was shocked to find that Gallagher had lied to the jurors, telling them that he had corroboration from two FBI informants, each of whom would identify Lorwin as a Communist. In addition, Gallagher had not called Lorwin before the grand jury, saying that his whereabouts were unknown, and that it was pointless in any case, since he would only take the Fifth like other Communists. Gallagher knew at the time that Lorwin had denied under oath that he was a Communist. The only person called before the grand jury was Metz, who repeated a conversation that went back eighteen years.[51]

Paisley recommended that the indictment be dismissed. The trial, which was about to begin, was postponed until June 7, 1954. Confronted with his misrepresentations, Gallagher said he was hoping at the time that the FBI would make some witnesses available. He said it was better to indict on slight evidence than to appear before a Senate committee to explain why he had not obtained an indictment.

On May 24, 1954, Gallagher was suspended and placed on annual leave, a mirror image of the suspended Lorwin. On May 25, Assistant Attorney General Warren Olney III moved to dismiss the indictment. On May 27, Olney fired Gallagher.[52]

In an explanatory letter to Senator William Langer, chairman of the Judiciary Committee, Attorney General Herbert Brownell said that Metz might have been confused about whether the card he had been shown was Socialist or Communist. "Both were anathema to Mr. Metz," Brownell said, though "there is some evidence that Mr. Lorwin . . . was active in the Socialist Party in opposing the plans of the Communists. . . . The description of the card . . . given by Mr. Metz is more consistent with membership in the Socialist Party rather than the Communist Party. . . . It is because of this extraordinarily delicate balance that at least some corroboration for Mr. Metz' recollection is considered necessary."

Senator Estes Kefauver of Tennessee offered to introduce a bill to pay for the cost of Lorwin's defense. Lorwin said he did not want that, although there was no way of "restoring several years of my own and my wife's life, or the unblemished reputation which even the government's admission of error can never make quite clear." To a friend, Lorwin wrote, "I was thankful that we have no children."[53]

The lesson of the Lorwin case was that McCarthy was beginning to have imitators. Gallagher had wanted to chalk up a case, and make his name as a Red-hunter, and was willing to lie to a grand jury to do it. This match of the unscrupulous and the self-seeker was McCarthy's greatest legacy.

Such was the fallout from McCarthy's speech on February 20, 1950, to which Truman responded in a press conference three days later that he was the one who had eliminated subversives in government. But many newspapers, from Honolulu to Washington, simply echoed Joe's charges that there was a spy ring in Washington.

McCarthyism was catching fire. By March 1950, the donations and the mails were heavy: "Why don't you get the rats out of the State Department?" Drew Pearson noted in his diary for March 21: "Sentiment for McCarthy seems to be building. . . . Sen. Taft amazed me by admitting that he was egging McCarthy on." Senator Wayne Morse told a newsman: "Taft and McCarthy are practically sleeping together."

When Joe's old antagonist William T. Evjue, the editor of the Madison *Capital Times,* visited Washington that spring, he was amazed to see how Joe was lording it over everyone. Someone told Evjue: "The only way to bring Joe McCarthy to his knees is to roll out a set of bones."[54]

———

Not everyone, however, was jumping on the McCarthy bandwagon. Even in the Senate, that citadel of tolerance, there were rumblings of discontent. The first senator to speak out on the Senate floor against Joe, although obliquely, was also the most junior senator of the ninety-six, having arrived in Washington that January to fill out the term of the departed senator Raymond Baldwin of Malmédy fame. He was William Benton, Rhodes scholar, vice president of the University of Chicago, millionaire advertising man in the firm of Benton & Bowles, and chairman of the board of the *Encyclopaedia Britannica.* After the war, he had served as assistant secretary of state for public affairs.

Benton was biding his time, feeling at first that he should leave Joe to the elders. But after the February speech, he began to think it was absurd to charge the Truman White House with being soft on Reds when it had done so much to bring down Communism. He felt that he had a duty to speak out in support of Secretary of State Dean Acheson, whose department was being splattered with mud. On March 22, 1950, Benton delivered his maiden speech before rows of empty seats. Only a handful of supportive Democrats were there to hear him say that "harrying and tormenting Dean Acheson until he quits his great post is not the cure to the problems of the Department. You don't cure a man's headache by cutting off his head." Benton was the first senator to attack McCarthy on the floor of the Senate, calling him a "hit and run propagandist on the Kremlin model."[55]

The other insurgent who dared to buck the trend was the only woman in the Senate, Margaret Chase Smith, Republican of Maine. She had come to the Senate in 1949 after serving eight years in the House and was on the Executive Expenditures Committee with Joe, who flattered her and told her she was his candidate for Vice President in 1952. But as time went by, she saw the Senate floor become a forum for slander. She believed in senatorial courtesy, which McCarthy constantly flouted. She was a hardworking legislator, who attended roll calls and was prepared for hearings, whereas McCarthy was sloppy and shot from the hip. She lived by the rules, guarding seniority, whereas McCarthy had no respect for rules. She liked facts and clarity, whereas McCarthy was a great obscurer and twister of facts. She thought his February 20 speech was character assassination.[56]

Senator Smith decided to make a "Declaration of Conscience" on the floor of the Senate, and rounded up six other moderate Republicans to sign it with her—George Aiken of Vermont, Charles Tobey of New Hampshire, Oregon's Wayne Morse, Irving Ives of New York, Edward J. Thye of Minnesota, and Robert Hendrickson of New Jersey. On June 1, 1950, she rose and read her declaration. "Certain elements of the Republican Party have materially added to this confusion in the hopes of riding the Republican Party to victory through the selfish exploitation of fear, bigotry, ignorance, and intolerance," she said. Smith and the other six called for an end to "totalitarian techniques." Only one other Republican senator, H. Alexander Smith of New Jersey, expressed support for Smith's declaration, but she got a lot of ink and was on the cover of *Newsweek*. Joe promptly labeled the eight senators "Snow White and the Seven Dwarfs."[57]

The most concerted attack on McCarthy, however, came in the form of a Senate hearing. One of the more relevant remarks during Joe's marathon speech on February 20 was made by the Republican senator from Massachusetts, Henry Cabot Lodge, who said that he would "make a motion to have a subcommittee of the Foreign Relations Committee take up every single one of the accusations which the senator from Wisconsin makes."

"I was hoping the senator would," Joe said.[58]

On February 22, Resolution 231 was adopted by the Senate, calling for a full investigation of whether persons disloyal to the United States were or had been employed by the Department of State. On March 8, 1950, a subcommittee of five opened hearings in the marble-columned Senate Caucus Room. The chairman was the Maryland senator Millard Tydings, a conservative Democrat whom FDR had called "a betrayer of the New Deal," but who was now in the position of helping Truman discredit McCarthy. The other Democrats were eighty-two-year-old Theodore F. Green, a wealthy Wilsonian from Rhode Island, and Brien McMahon of Connecticut, one of the chorus of hecklers on February 20. The two Republicans were Lodge and the conservative, pro-McCarthy senator from Iowa, Bourke Hickenlooper. The subcommittee sat until July 7 and called thirty-five witnesses to determine whether the State Department had retained disloyal employees.

It became clear on the first day of the hearings that Tydings intended to put McCarthy on trial and dismiss his evidence. In this, he had the full support and cooperation of President Truman. Tydings wagged his finger at Joe and said: "You are in the position of being the man who occasioned this hearing, and so far as I am concerned you are going to get one of the most complete investigations in the history of the Republic." Lodge complained that the hearings reminded him of a "kangaroo court."[59]

McCarthy provided Tydings with 112 names, including thirty-seven that were not on the Lee list, obtained from his sources at the FBI and in the State Department. But instead of conducting a full investigation, Tydings dealt only with nine cases whose names Joe had made public. They included the two fellow travelers who were not in the State Department, Harlow Shapley and Frederick L. Schuman, the liberal judge Dorothy Kenyon, and Esther Brunauer. All nine were given the opportunity to refute McCarthy's charges.

Esther Brunauer testified on March 27 that since McCarthy had named her, she and her family had been getting threatening calls, such as "Get out of this neighborhood, you Communists, or you will be carried out in a box." She also testified that she and her husband had been friends of the Soviet agent Noel Field since 1928.

Senator Hickenlooper asked about the Brunauers' connection to a Hungarian diplomat, Ferenczi. Esther said she had met him at a UNESCO conference in 1947 in Mexico City. On his way back to Hungary Ferenczi dropped in on Stephen Brunauer in Washington and asked him if the Rockefeller Foundation could help Hungary's scientific institutions. According to Esther, her husband replied that since Hungary was a Communist regime, there was little likelihood of help. Having been given the brush-off, Ferenczi then discussed with other members of the Hungarian legation in Washington whether to reveal Stephen Brunauer's past Communist affiliations, but decided against it. The Tydings Committee did not pursue the issue further although it could well have asked how Esther Brunauer knew about these discussions concerning her husband.[60]

The high point of the hearings came when McCarthy named Owen Lattimore, the director of the Walter Hines Page School of International Relations at Johns Hopkins University and an expert on Mongolia, a field he had almost to himself. Lattimore had so little to do with the State Department that Dean Acheson recalled in his memoirs: "Dr. Lattimore had never been connected with the Department and I did not know him." He was an academic, sometimes tapped for government service. In 1941, FDR had sent him to China on the recommendation of Lattimore's good friend, the Soviet agent Lauchlin Currie, to advise Chiang Kai-shek. In 1942, he was named head of the Pacific Bureau of the Office of War Information, with a staff of five hundred, and in 1944 he accompanied Henry Wallace on his trip to Siberia.[61]

That was good enough for McCarthy, who on March 13 called him a "pro-Communist" and "one of the principal architects of our Far Eastern policy." Four days later, Tydings declared that McCarthy had not provided the committee with the name of a single Communist. Piqued, Joe responded by naming Lattimore as "the man whom I consider the top Russian espionage agent in this country," and Alger Hiss's onetime boss "in the espionage ring in this country." Both of these accusations were preposterous, but Joe, as usual, was going for headlines. On March 21 in executive session he told the committee that Lattimore "will be the biggest espionage case in the history of this country ... the top Russian spy." He told reporters, "I am willing to stand or fall on this one." Senator Taft, sensing a promising issue in the upcoming congressional elections, said: "The greatest Kremlin asset in our history has been the pro-Communist group in the State Department."[62]

McCarthy followed up on March 30 with another marathon speech on the floor of the Senate, where he was protected from libel suits. This one lasted four hours, and was largely devoted to Lattimore, whom he called "one of the top Communist agents in this country." He was now prepared to give the Senate material proving that Lattimore was a Soviet agent and a Communist Party member. "I realize that this is an extremely shocking statement," he said, explaining that he was getting his information from "certain loyal and disturbed government employees." He said he was swamped with letters from "thousands of disturbed Americans, urging that this house-cleaning—perhaps I should say rodent-destroying—task be continued."[63]

By overstating his case, McCarthy spoiled it, although Lattimore had much to answer for, not as a spy but as part of a network of Asian experts who followed the Soviet line. Born in 1900, he was raised in China, where his father was a teacher. In the twenties, he traveled extensively through China and into Mongolia, a vast landlocked highland country wedged between China and Russia. After more than two centuries of Chinese colonization, Mongolia became a People's Republic in 1921, with the help and guidance of the Soviet Union. This sparsely populated land of nomadic herdsmen advanced directly from feudalism to Socialism, bypassing capitalism. In 1921, there were two doctors in the entire country, and a 2 percent literacy rate. The Soviets built hospitals and schools. The Mongols adopted Soviet laws, Soviet courts, Soviet Five Year Plans, and the Soviet one-party system. Nomads for a time were allowed to keep ownership of their herds, while collective farms and state-owned industries were introduced. Mongolia, in effect, became a satellite of the Soviet Union.

In his books, Lattimore took the position that Mongolia was an independent state free from Russian domination. Mongolia was "set free by the non-exploitation policy of the Soviet Union," he wrote in *Inner Asian Frontiers of China*, "the granting of loans without interest, economic aid, technical help, and the creation of an army trained and equipped by the Soviet Union." For Lattimore, the Mongols were a distinct people saved from extinction by a benevolent Soviet intervention.[64]

Other scholars saw Lattimore's claims as special pleading. After 1926, the Soviets did not allow foreigners into Mongolia. A Soviet visa, which had to be approved by Soviet Military Intelligence, was needed to go there. This ban on visitors was hardly consonant with the thesis that Mongolia was independent. Nicholas N. Poppe, the China-born professor of Oriental languages at the University of Leningrad from 1925 to 1941, and the head of Mongolian studies in Russia, met Lattimore in the thirties. Lattimore was by then the editor of *Pacific Affairs*, the journal of the Institute of Pacific Relations, an influential think tank with foreign branches, including one in the Soviet Union. Lattimore came regularly to Russia to confer with the IPR members, some of whom were Soviet intelligence officers who used the IPR to collect information.

In order to enhance his chance for a visa, Poppe said, Lattimore lobbied the well-connected IPR member V. E. Motylev, who was in charge of the much awaited *Soviet World Atlas*, commissioned by Lenin in the early twenties. It finally appeared in 1937. Poppe said it was "a Marxist-Leninist cartographic picture of the world," divided into Socialist and Imperialist camps. "One map shows Mongolia completely absorbed and integrated in the Soviet economic and political system. It is a Soviet satellite." Lattimore reviewed the *Atlas* in the September 1938 issue of *Pacific Affairs* and said it "commands full intellectual respect." But even with Motylev's help, Poppe said, Mongolia remained closed to Lattimore. Poppe himself was not allowed to go there.

By 1949, Poppe had moved to America and taught at the University of Washington in Seattle. He told a congressional committee that Lattimore "wrote of Mongolia as a democratic country which has made magnificent progress and so on . . . but this is not the end of the story. The deportation of Mongolian Buddhists, Lamaseries, the destruction and annihilation of the Mongolian government, the execution of the Mongolian ministers, the forced collectivism, the deportation of many to the Soviet Union, are rather negative phenomena. . . . I cannot call such a system a democratic one. In 1932 the entire population revolted againt the Soviets. Many members of the Mongolian People's Army took the side of the revolters and this rebellion was suppressed by the Russian Red Army. Tanks and aircraft were rushed from Russia to Mongolia." Lattimore gave "a greatly distorted picture," Poppe said. Since he could not tour Mongolia in the thirties, he got the material for his book "in Soviet papers."[65]

Igor Bogolepov, who was assistant chief of the League of Nations Division in the Soviet Foreign Office, recalled meeting Lattimore at the Moscow IPR headquarters in 1936. Maxim Litvinov, the Foreign Office Commissar, had told Bogolepov that Stalin wanted to get Mongolia into the League of Nations (which the Soviet Union had joined in 1934), but the situation was still not ripe. They had to mobilize foreign writers and journalists. Then, as if to himself, Litvinov asked, "Lattimore, perhaps?"[66]

Lattimore went to see the American ambassador, William Bullitt. "An inspiring thing has happened," he told Bullitt, "the Mongols have achieved full independence." "Was there no Soviet control or Red Army there?" Bullitt asked. None whatsoever, Lattimore replied. He asked Bullitt to write FDR at once and make the case for recognizing the People's Republic of Mongolia, which would help to get it into the League of Nations. Bullitt thought that was an amazing request, for having Mongolia in the League would only give the Soviets an additional vote.

Bullitt knew more about Mongolia than Lattimore realized, for he was a longtime friend of Lev Karakhan, the deputy commissar for foreign affairs. In 1934, Karakhan was sent to Mongolia to put down another uprising. Upon his return, he went to the American embassy and told Bullitt in confidence that it had been a small matter, since the Soviets ran the army and the police with OGPU agents. "All I had to do," he said, "was oversee the purge. In a country of nomads, there are only 300 or 400 people who count. All I did on a given night was to have about 400 seized by our OGPU men, and I had them shot before dawn and installed the people that the Soviet government wanted, and Mongolia is now completely ruled by the OGPU." After having hundreds shot, Karakhan found himself at the wrong end of a firing squad during Stalin's purges.[67]

In his self-appointed role as defender of the Soviet faith, Lattimore offered a tortuous absolution of the purges in an editorial in *Pacific Affairs* in September 1938. "Verbatim records of the trials are entirely credible," he wrote. "A great many abuses have been discovered and rectified. . . . Habitual rectification can hardly do anything but give the ordinary citizen more courage to protest, loudly, whenever he finds himself victimized by 'someone in the party,' or 'someone in the government.' That sounds to me like democracy." Nicholas Poppe had a slight correction. "The Soviet Union," he said, "is a democracy with concentration camps."[68]

It was on the trip with Henry Wallace that Lattimore outdid himself as a one-man pro-Soviet claque. On May 22, 1944, they crossed the Bering Strait from Alaska to Siberia in a C-54 transport. On May 24 they reached the port city of Magadan on the Sea of Okhotsk, in deepest Siberia, where forty below was considered mild. A city of forty thousand, Magadan was the capital of the Kolyma district and the headquarters of the Dalstroi, or Far Northern Construction Trust, which Wallace described as "a combination TVA and Hudson's Bay Company." The trust operated one hundred mines, most of them gold, over a four-hundred-mile-long area, with a work force of 300,000. Wallace and his entourage, which included John Carter Vincent as his State Department adviser, visited a hog farm and heard the Red Army Choir sing at the Magadan House of Culture. Wallace found the people he met "not unlike our farming people in the United States."[69]

On May 26, he visited two Kolyma gold mines, where the men dug up piles of gold-bearing rocks. They were on a three-year contract, Wallace was told, and were paid two thousand rubles a month. After seeing the mines, the Dalstroi director, Ivan Nikishov, took Wallace for a walk in the taiga. "He gamboled around like a calf enjoying the wonderful air immensely," Wallace wrote in his diary.[70]

After Siberia, the Wallace caravan moved to China. They were back in Washington on July 10, having covered 27,000 miles in fifty-one days. In the December 1944 issue of *National Geographic*, Lattimore published a glowing account of Siberia entitled "New Road to Asia." In the gold mines of the Kolyma valley, he found "instead of sin, gin and brawling of the old-time gold rush, extensive greenhouses growing tomatoes, cucumbers, and even melons, to make sure that the hardy miners get enough vitamins!" The miners in the photographs he took did indeed look strong and healthy. Nikishov and his wife, Lattimore said, "have a trained and sensitive interest in art and music and also a deep sense of civil responsibility."

Wallace said that Siberia reminded him of the American Far West, with its pioneers. He did not realize that the tens of thousands of "settlers" in the Kolyma valley were not there voluntarily. Kolyma was part of Stalin's vast system of gulags, which exposed, better than any other feature, the criminal underpinnings of the Soviet state. The vast penal complex of Kolyma went back to the thirties, when Stalin made gold mining a priority to pay for the purchase of Western machinery. The city of Magadan had been built by prisoners, as had the roads linking it with the camps. In 1939, the 140,000 Kolyma convicts extracted 35 percent of all the Soviet gold produced that year. Hours were long, rations were short, and conditions were harsh. The death toll was estimated at one third of the prisoners per year.[71]

In June 1951, an article appeared in the *Reader's Digest* entitled "Eleven Years in Soviet Prison Camps." It was written by Elinor Lipper, who had been an inmate in the Kolyma gulag at the time of the Wallace visit. "No other visit," she wrote, "ever aroused so much excitement as Henry Wallace's visit to Kolyma during the war. The NKVD carried off its job with flying colors. Mr. Wallace saw nothing of this frozen hell with its hundreds of thousands of the damned . . . the wooden watchtowers were razed in a single night . . . the prisoners had three successive holidays, for during his stay, not a single prisoner was allowed to leave the camp." Wallace had admired the 350-mile road that ran from Magadan northward over the mountains. "Tens of thousands of prisoners had given their lives in building it," wrote Lipper. Wallace had described Nikishov as "gamboling about." "It is too bad," she continued, "that Wallace never saw him 'gamboling about' in one of his drunk rages, raining filthy, savage language upon the heads of exhausted, starving prisoners." The entire population of Kolyma "is made up of victims of political oppression." The smiling miners that Lattimore had snapped were NKVD gulag guards. The fruit and the vegetables he had seen in the greenhouses were for the staff.

When a subcommittee of the Senate Judiciary Committee held hearings on the Institute of Pacific Relations in 1951, Wallace testified on October 17 and acknowledged that he had been duped on his visit to Magadan. "I was not going out of my way to find slave labor," he said. "The Russians were going all out to impress me."[72]

As for Lattimore, after the war he turned against Chiang Kai-shek as China teetered on the edge of civil war. He called the Kuomintang "the war party," as if the Chinese Communists were the party of peace. When Mao Tse-tung ousted Chiang in 1949, Lattimore became a target for the "Who lost China?" camp in Congress.[73]

At the time of the Tydings hearings in March 1950, when McCarthy made his charges, Lattimore was in Afghanistan on a mission for the United Nations. He returned to testify before the committee on April 6, taking an hour and forty minutes to read a ten-thousand-word statement in which he gave as good as he got. He called McCarthy "a willing tool" of the China lobby, "the simple dupe of fanatical persons." He detailed his brief assignments for the State Department: a speech as part of a lecture series; in October 1944, a two-day panel discussion on China; in 1945, three months on a reparations mission to Japan. That was it. He denied all of McCarthy's charges.

Joe was in need of reinforcements, and on April 20, 1950, the cavalry came to the rescue in the form of Louis Budenz. The fifty-eight-year-old Budenz had left the party in 1945 and become a professional witness. He made a living and a reputation by naming those he had known in the party, and sometimes, those he had not known.[74]

On April 20, 1950, Budenz testified before the Tydings Committee that Lattimore had been part of a Communist cell in the Institute of Pacific Relations. This was quite a surprise, since less than a month before, Budenz had testified at another hearing that he knew four hundred concealed Communists, of whom he named quite a few, but not Lattimore. He also admitted that he had never met Lattimore or told the FBI about Lattimore. Apparently, Lattimore was a recent discovery. On April 21, J. Edgar Hoover pointed out in a memo to Attorney General J. Howard McGrath that Budenz had never previously mentioned Lattimore, though he had been grilled about *Amerasia.* But the FBI did not inform the Tydings Committee of its doubts.[75]

Another ex-Communist, James Glassner, who had been managing editor of the *Daily Worker* when Budenz was labor editor, told the FBI that Budenz was "fabricating smears against Lattimore" and that his remarks should be discounted as "emanating from a psychopathic liar." As Senator Dennis Chavez of New Mexico put it: "I do not think he knows the truth from falsehood any more."[76]

———

As the Tydings hearings proceeded, McCarthy seemed to be stealing the show. His strategy of throwing out charges daily was harvesting headlines such as "McCarthy Names Reds," "McCarthy Calls State Department Envoy Red," and "Has McCarthy Struck Red Gold?" Intended as an investigation of McCarthy's accusations on the floor of the Senate, the hearings were turning into Joe's pulpit. In the *Christian Science Monitor,* Richard L. Strout described the Tydings Committee as "close to the breaking point" as McCarthy admonished, lectured, and reproved it. "If he can only make it stick it will be a major blow to the Truman administration."[77]

Tydings, whose effort to chastise McCarthy had the President's blessing, asked Truman for help "to hold the line and prevent public smear sessions." Truman had said on February 24 that he would not comply with committee requests to subpoena loyalty files. But Tydings desperately needed to see the files that McCarthy kept ranting about in order to discredit him. On March 16, White House aide Donald Dawson told Truman that Tydings wanted the files turned over "as soon as possible." That way, instead of relying on "one-sided extracts" revealed by McCarthy, committee members would be able to inspect the full files and decide whether or not his charges were trumped up.[78]

On March 30, 1950, at the Little White House in Key West, Truman was still mulling over what to do, at a time when the polls showed that 50 percent of the people held a "favorable opinion" of Joe. Sitting in a wicker chair with reporters around him in a circle, he angrily called McCarthy "the greatest asset that the Kremlin has."

Joe's attacks were partisan politics as usual, Truman believed, for "the Republican party has endorsed the antics of Mr. McCarthy."

Tydings saw Truman at Blair House on April 28, and explained why his committee needed to see the files that McCarthy had obtained from the Lee list. The next day, Truman told his assistant press secretary, Eben Ayers, that Tydings "has in mind to finish the discrediting of McCarthy." An investigator named Lee, Truman continued, who was a Republican, had "abstracted or stolen" some loyalty files and furnished them to McCarthy. Tydings was hoping to bring these facts out, which "may go so far as to result in the Senate acting to throw out McCarthy."[79]

Tydings was calling the White House half a dozen times a day. Truman was with Ayers when he took one of his calls on April 29. Ayers recalled that "after he hung up the president commented that Tydings was the most nervous individual he ever saw."

In its May 15 issue, Newsweek reported a secret meeting in Tydings's apartment to plot a strategy to destroy McCarthy. Among those present were the committee counsel, Edward P. Morgan, and John Peurifoy, now deputy undersecretary of state, who agreed with the President's decision to release the files. The object of the meeting, said the article, was "the total and eternal destruction" of McCarthy. The strategy was to show that "his sensational accusations stemmed from a two-year-old trial of State Department 'suspects' already examined by four congressional committees which remained unimpressed."[80]

Truman made the files available on May 4. On May 10, several committee members, including Henry Cabot Lodge, trooped down to a White House office where the files were piled on a big table under guard. Reading them was a laborious process. These were raw files with sometimes as many as thirty FBI interviews in a single case. It took Tydings two days to get through a dozen files. Lodge found that "the files alone did not furnish a basis for reaching firm conclusions of any kind. . . . The files which I read were in such an unfinished state" that to go through them "would be a waste of time."[81]

Tydings realized that his plan to confront McCarthy with material from the files was not feasible. He called the White House daily to explain that the files were more than they had bargained for. He was looking for a way out. At a staff meeting on May 25, Truman said: "He got himself into it, now it is up to him to get out of it." On June 8, Truman said that "Tydings has given every indication of being in a state of panic and of lacking any backbone or courage in dealing with the situation." Tydings wanted Truman to give him an escape hatch by announcing that the committee should complete its study of the files by June 21. Truman said he would do no such thing, for it would only result in charges that the President was trying to bottle the files up.[82]

Thus it was that, unable to confront McCarthy over the Lee files, the committee drifted into an investigation of the *Amerasia* case. Once again, McCarthy made wild charges that turned the hearings into a carnival. A terminal weariness set in and on June 25 the invasion of South Korea provided a new and far graver crisis. On June 28, in a closed session, Tydings said: "I think our work is pretty well concluded, if you want my opinion."

Bourke Hickenlooper, one of the two Republicans on the committee, begged to differ. "I don't think it was ever started, Mr. Chairman," he said. The other Republican, Henry Cabot Lodge, said there were too many unanswered questions, any of which, such as the hiring of "sexual perverts" by the State Department, "would be good for six, seven, or eight months." On this partisan note, the hearings ended.[83]

The 313-page Tydings report, released on July 20, was signed by the three Democrats on the committee, but not by the two Republicans. The report was an indictment of McCarthy's charges and methods. It described his selection of cases from the Lee list as "twisted, colored and perverted." There were three cases of mistaken identity. The charges were "a fraud and a hoax perpetrated on the Senate of the United States . . . the most nefarious campaign of half-truths and untruths in the history of the Republic."

The report denounced the Republican members of the committee, Hickenlooper and Lodge, for failing to examine the files made available by the President. Lodge had looked at a dozen and Hickenlooper only at nine. Nonetheless, the report concluded that the review of the loyalty files had failed to turn up a single Communist. The idea of a "spy ring" at the State Department was "preposterous," it said. The charges against the China hand John Carter Vincent were called "absurd." Regarding Lattimore, McCarthy was accused of a "distortion of the facts on such a magnitude as to be truly alarming." In the case of John Stewart Service, who had handed over classified documents to Philip Jaffe in the *Amerasia* case, the report said: "We must conclude that Service was extremely indiscreet," but this was insufficient "to brand him . . . as disloyal, pro-Communist, or a security risk."[84]

The report concluded that McCarthy "has stooped to a new low in his cavalier disregard of the facts." It was itself cavalier, however, for it included some serious misstatements. It said that all McCarthy's names came from the Lee list, whereas thirty-four did not. It said: "The sub-committee of the House Appropriations Committee . . . which considered the 108 memoranda, did not regard them as of sufficient significance even to submit a report concerning them or the loyalty of the State Department personnel generally."

But the Stefan subcommittee had issued a report on February 27, 1948. Far from clearing the State Department, it had repeatedly expressed its alarm at the laxity of its security procedures. When the Appropriations Committee chairman, John Taber, presented the findings of the Stefan subcommittee to the House in March, he said they "indicated a very large number of Communists on the rolls of the State Department."

The Tydings report said that the Chenoweth Committee on Expenditures in the Executive Department had also "indicated their satisfaction" with the loyalty situation. This was the committee that had grilled Hamilton Robinson, whom one of its members, Fred Busbey, called incompetent on the floor of the House. Clearly, the committees cited by Tydings had reported the opposite of what he had them saying.[85]

On July 20, when the full Senate debated the Tydings report, the air was electric with partisan energy. When Tydings strode in, wrote the reporter for *The New Republic,* the Democrats were "positively growling for revenge. . . . You could hear a hoarse, angry mutter." For two hours Tydings thundered against McCarthy, calling him a charlatan guilty of exploiting his office. When William Jenner of Indiana denounced Tydings for "the most scandalous and brazen whitewash of treasonable conspiracy in our history," Tydings responded: "You will find out who has been whitewashing—with mud and slime, with filth . . . at the expense of the people's love for their country."[86]

In the full Senate, the Tydings report was adopted with a vote along party lines. Facing reelection in Ohio that fall, Taft kept his troops in line. Joe knew he could count on the Taft Republicans, for he had become the standard-bearer for his party.

With the assistance of President Truman, the Tydings investigation developed into a Democratic scheme to discredit McCarthy. Joe greatly assisted the scheme with a number of unfounded accusations, but the Tydings Committee failed to consider the genuine problem of State Department laxity and falsified its report.

Lattimore's troubles were not over. In 1952, the Senate Internal Security Subcommittee opened hearings on the Institute of Pacific Relations. Lattimore was at the heart of those hearings and testified for twelve days. His sarcasm and arrogance did not endear him to the committee. At the outset, he qualified the committee's output as "a nightmare of outrageous lies, shaky hearsay, and undisguised personal spite." Genuinely surprised, committee member Arthur V. Watkins asked: "Why do you start out abusing us?"

J. G. Sourwine, the committee counsel, asked: "Does your ego compel you to the conclusion that the committee is after you?" "Not my ego," Lattimore replied, "my epidermis."

Later on, Lattimore corrected Sourwine on his grammar. Sourwine asked: "Do you want to make a distinction here between being unbiased and being unable fairly to appraise the facts?"

"I will rejoin the split infinitive," Lattimore replied. "Unable to appraise the facts fairly." In fact, "unable fairly to appraise" was not a split infinitive.

Lattimore managed to antagonize every senator on the committee. He called William Knowland, an admirer of Chiang Kai-shek, "the senator from Formosa."

When Democratic Senator Willis Smith of North Carolina asked him a question about McCarthy, Lattimore asked: "Is your argument, senator, a *post hoc, ergo propter hoc?*"

Smith: "I am asking you in plain language."

Lattimore: "I should say that Senator McCarthy is a graduate witch-burner."

Smith: "I am going to retain my composure . . . regardless of his truculence and his petulance or his arrogance."[87]

Lattimore's testimony led to an indictment for perjury on such trivial counts as his failure to remember the date of a lunch with the Soviet ambassador, Constantine Oumansky. On May 3, 1953, a federal judge threw out four of the seven counts. The Court of Appeals sustained the dismissal on July 8, 1954. The Justice Department obtained a new indictment on October 7, 1954. On January 18, 1955, the same judge, Luther W. Youngdahl, threw out the indictment again, and the Justice Department dropped the prosecution. A more pertinent but unstated charge would have been: boorishness before a Senate subcommittee.[88]

—

On June 24, 1950, President Truman was spending a quiet weekend at home in Independence. After an early dinner and small talk on the screened porch with his wife and daughter, he went to bed at nine. Acheson called Truman at 9:30 P.M. Missouri time: "Mr. President, I have very serious news. The North Koreans have invaded South Korea."

Acheson summoned the United Nations Security Council for an emergency meeting on Sunday, June 25. The Security Council passed a resolution 9 to 0, calling the invasion "an act of aggression" and demanding the withdrawal of North Korean forces to the 38th parallel. There was no Soviet veto because the Soviet delegate was boycotting meetings to protest the denial of U.N. membership to the People's Republic of China.

On June 30, with the fall of Seoul and the South Korean army in tatters, Truman ordered U.S. ground forces in Japan to Korea, under the command of General MacArthur and under the U.N. umbrella. With these decisive actions, Truman saved South Korea and started a war that lasted three years and left 33,629 Americans dead.

The Korean War instantly validated and magnified McCarthy's appeal. He could go on distorting the truth in speech after speech, but a growing number of Americans were prepared to believe him when he linked the war with the State Department whitewash. On July 2, 1950, he said that "American boys are dying in Korea" because "a group of untouchables in the State Department sabotaged the aid program" for Asia.[89]

On July 12, Joe gave vent to his bile in a letter to President Truman: "Today American boys lie dead in the mud of Korean valleys. Some have their hands tied behind their backs, their faces shot away by Communist machine guns. . . . They are dead because the program adopted by this Congress [to arm Korea] to avoid such a war . . . was sabotaged."[90]

Joe was on a roll. In Madison, the Republican boss Tom Coleman saw him as the hope of the GOP. He did not think McCarthy's charges were overdrawn, and praised him for his tenacity and determination. Joe wrote Coleman that he thought Communism in government would be a major campaign issue in the fall. "Had we won a quick, speedy victory in Korea without many casualties, the administration might have been bailed out," he said. The implication was that for a Republican triumph in the fall of 1950, it was better to have a long war with a high number of American casualties.[91]

———

During the campaigns that fall, Joe was in demand all over the map. He gave more than thirty speeches in fifteen states, although not up for reelection himself until 1952. This gave him plenty of time to go after his enemies in the Senate, such as Scott Lucas in Illinois, Brien McMahon in Connecticut, and Millard Tydings in Maryland. McCarthy attacked them by name, saying at a

Republican rally in Hyattsville, Maryland: "Lucas provided the whitewash when I charged there were Communists in high places. McMahon brought the bucket; Tydings the brush."[92] It was amazing how an accusation repeated often enough became embedded in people's minds, for Joe had not found any Communists in high places, he had only made it sound as if there were some. In November 1950 McCarthy reached the apogee of his cometlike trajectory; he seemed bathed in an aura of political invincibility.

The result for the Democrats was a loss of five seats in the Senate, among them Scott Lucas and Millard Tydings. But they still held the Senate by two votes. In the House they lost twenty-eight seats, but kept a comfortable majority. It was not a disaster, but it hurt. The true importance of the campaign was the adoption by Republicans of the scare tactics pioneered by McCarthy.

Egregious misconduct in the Maryland campaign came under the scrutiny of the Senate Subcommittee on Privileges and Elections, which held hearings from February 20 to April 11, 1951. This would be the second year in a row that McCarthy was investigated by his colleagues. The members were Guy M. Gillette of Iowa (chairman), Thomas Hennings Jr. of Missouri, Mike Monroney of Oklahoma, Robert Hendrickson of New Jersey, and Margaret Chase Smith of Maine.

Facing Tydings in Maryland, John Marshall Butler, a Baltimore lawyer who had never run for office, was happy to have Joe and his staff plan his campaign. Also on board was Ruth McCormick "Bazy" Miller, niece of the colonel and editor of the *Washington Times Herald*. She brought in Jon Jonkel, a public relations man from Chicago, as campaign manager. Running against a well-known incumbent cost money, and Joe helped raise it, getting $10,000 from Texas oilman Clint Murchison alone.

As Jonkel put it at the hearing: "We took advantage of every leak in Tydings' canoe." Maryland was a Democratic state, but in 1950 the party was split. "That was the biggest stripe on the barber pole," Jonkel said. They started out with one-inch ads that said "Be for Butler," to give him name recognition. Then they ran some radio spots with the sound of brakes squealing and the message "stop wasting government money," to put Tydings on the defensive.[93]

Roscoe Simmons, a black evangelist from Illinois who wrote articles in the *Chicago Tribune*, was imported for six weeks to get out Maryland's large black vote. Tydings was unpopular with blacks, for he opposed civil rights measures. As the Baptist preacher James T. Boddie put it at the hearing: "We didn't receive any of the crumbs, much less a slice." "I spoke in saloons," Simmons said, "I spoke in churches, I spoke under trees and on street corners, I spoke in the fields." His slogan was "Back to Good Old Dixie."[94]

The crowning achievement of the McCarthy-assisted campaign was a four-page tabloid called *From the Record,* ostensibly put out by "Young Democrats for Butler," a shell group formed in mid-October. Half a million copies of the tabloid inundated the state a few days before the election, run off by the *Times Herald* printer at a modest cost of $1,440.

A front-page headline said "Tydings Group Held Up Arms." "One of the fundamental reasons for our early failure in the Korean war," said the story, "is being charged to the Senate Armed Forces Committee headed by Tydings. . . . Congress appropriated $87,300,000 to arm the South Koreans. . . . Only $200 of this money was spent before the North Koreans attacked. It was spent for baling wire." This was one of Joe's familiar and disproven refrains. On page 3, another article was headlined "Tydings Committee Blamed for High Korean Casualties." The article noted 343 casualties from Maryland alone.

On page 4, there was a composite photograph of Browder and Tydings, captioned: "Communist leader Earl Browder, shown at left, in this composite picture, was a star witness at the Tydings Committee hearings and was cajoled into saying that Owen Lattimore and others were not Communists. Tydings answered, 'Oh thank you sir.' " The picture of Tydings had been taken in 1938, that of Browder in 1950.

Frank Smith, the chief editorial writer for the *Times Herald,* testified that it was Bazy Miller "who came up with the composite idea. We got out pictures showing Browder talking and Tydings listening. . . . It was not a fake. . . . It was not a fraud. It was not proposed to deceive anyone. It was plainly marked composite. . . . A white line down the middle clearly indicated it was two pictures." But most people who saw it thought it was one picture.

Garvin Tankersley, the *Times Herald* photo editor (soon to marry Bazy Miller), said: "We wanted to show that Mr. Tydings did treat Mr. Browder with kid gloves. . . . No secret on that."[95] Those responsible for the tabloid seemed proud of their accomplishment. There was not a hint of apology in their testimony.

McCarthy told Tom Coleman, who called the composite picture "inexcusable and needless," that he had nothing to do with it. He was generally credited with the Butler victory, though there were signs that Tydings had worn out his welcome in the disaffection of the labor vote, the Catholic vote, and the black vote.

The subcommittee report, released on August 2, 1951, said that "the Maryland campaign was not just another campaign. It brought into sharp focus campaign tactics and practices that can best be characterized as destructive of fundamental American principles." The tabloid "ignored simple decency and common honesty." The composite picture was a "shocking abuse of the spirit and intent of the First Amendment."

———

Joe ended the year with two more mishaps, one a flirtation with the lunatic right, the other a brawl at a black-tie affair with a famous columnist. On November 9, 1950, Secretary of Defense George Marshall offered the job of assistant secretary for manpower to a woman, a small but stylish woman who wore jangling bracelets and high heels, and who had also held a dozen government jobs in the fields of labor and manpower—Anna M. Rosenberg, born in Hungary in 1901. Marshall needed someone capable of handling the manpower problems resulting from the Korean War.

Almost at once, the extreme right wing launched an anti-Anna campaign. On November 10, the right-wing commentator Fulton Lewis Jr. said on the radio that Anna in her youth had belonged to a John Reed Club. He had it from J. B. Matthews, the former Dies Committee researcher, who was now in private practice with his files and had distributed a nine-page sheet listing Rosenberg's alleged front affiliations. Benjamin H. Freedman, a Jewish right-winger in New York, printed 25,000 copies of Matthews's charges. There was some hesitation as to whether they had the right Anna Rosenberg, but on November 27, a memo from Matthews said: "There is not the slightest doubt that this is *the* Anna Rosenberg" cited in the Dies hearings. On November 29, the Armed Services Committee met to consider the nomination. Rosenberg testified that she was not the person cited. There were forty-six Anna Rosenbergs in New York, she said, which was why she always used her middle initial, M. After a session that lasted an hour and ten minutes, all thirteen senators voted to confirm.[96]

But her foes did not give up. Freedman flew to Washington to see the anti-Semitic Mississippi Congressman John E. Rankin, who denounced Anna M. on the floor of the House. The anti-Semitic demagogue Gerald L. K. Smith, who was organizing his own campaign, teamed up with Freedman, who by this time had gotten on to Ralph De Sola. We last met De Sola as a witness before the Dies Committee, testifying about Communists in the Writers' Project. He then launched a career as a professional witness, and boasted that he had met with the FBI 125 times. But he was spread so thin in his eagerness to provide leads that he began mixing people up. He claimed to have met Anna Rosenberg at Communist front meetings. Freedman flew to Washington on December 4 with a signed statement from De Sola, which he presented to Georgia Senator Richard Russell, who had replaced Tydings as chairman of the Armed Services Committee. Freedman asked that the confirmation hearings be reopened.

In the meantime, the Reverend Wesley Smith, still another anti-Semite, who refused to concede that Christ was a Jew, passed on to Joe some anti-Anna evidence. Joe saw not only a promising "Communist in government" issue, but a way of attacking Marshall, whom he considered responsible for the loss of China because of his ill-fated mission there in 1945.[97]

Joe sent an investigator, the ex-FBI man Don Surine, to New York to check out De Sola, who identified a 1936 photograph of Anna M. Rosenberg as the woman he had known.[98]

On December 5, 1950, the Armed Services Committee reopened the hearings, which lasted through December 14. The face-off at the hearing between De Sola and Anna Rosenberg took place on December 8. Senator William Knowland of California asked De Sola how he could definitely identify someone he had seen fifteen years before, but De Sola was positive. He had seen Anna at a meeting "in the late summer and fall of 1934 and 1935."

Rosenberg: "And I spoke to you?"

De Sola: "Yes, you spoke about what an excellent device the John Reed Club had been for a sounding board for Communist propaganda and as a recruiting ground."

Rosenberg: "Mr. De Sola, I don't believe that any human being wants to do what you are doing purposely. You came into the room and you said, 'this is the woman.' You never looked at me. Do you know what you are doing to me?"

De Sola: "I am looking at you and I am looking at you now. . . . We stood up when we talked. Would you mind standing up?"

Rosenberg: "I will stand up. Now tell me, am I the woman in the John Reed Club?"

De Sola: "Yes, ma'am you are; I am sorry to say so. . . . I am sorry to see that we have a Secretary of Defense who had to be assisted by a Communist. I am sorry for our country."

Rosenberg: ". . . I have never seen this man in my life. . . . I have no recollection of ever seeing his face."

With the appearance of other witnesses, De Sola's credibility unraveled. De Sola had claimed that James McGraw, a project supervisor on the Writers' Project and a Communist, had told him that Anna Rosenberg had recruited other Communists for the project. But when McGraw testified, he affirmed under oath that he had never been a Communist. He had been the superior of De Sola, whom he judged to be "a person of extreme dishonesty who would stop at nothing for bits of notoriety in which he could stand out." De Sola had mentioned the former FBI agent George J. Starr as someone who could corroborate his testimony. When Starr testified, he seemed well disposed toward

De Sola, but had to admit that they had never discussed Anna Rosenberg or the John Reed Club.

De Sola saw himself as a heroic figure, another Whittaker Chambers, and he said in his defense that "the very brilliance of Mrs. Rosenberg, her record of achievement, as fine if not finer than that of Alger Hiss, is in itself a threat." He succumbed to the built-in flaws of the professional witness trade. When you started out, you had an inventory of names, but when your inventory ran out, and you were still in demand, you got careless because you didn't want to disappoint. When the FBI was unable to track down any of those whom he claimed would corroborate his testimony, they stopped using him.[99]

The Armed Services Committee quickly confirmed Anna M. Rosenberg. When the confirmation came before the full Senate, even McCarthy voted for her. The by-products of the confirmation were that De Sola was finished as a paid informant and that McCarthy was linked to right-wing crackpots. As Hoover wrote Senator Mike Monroney on April 3, 1951: "Edward K. Nellor, leg man for Fulton Lewis, planned and executed the Anna Rosenberg smear for Lewis and Sen. Joseph R. McCarthy." After the hearing, the FBI found the Anna Rosenberg cited by the Dies Committee in California, where she had moved years before Ralph De Sola said he had met her.[100]

On December 12, 1950, Louise Tinsley Steinman, the well-connected daughter of an Ohio newspaper publisher, held a dinner dance in the ballroom of Washington's Sulgrave Club in honor of Senator James H. Duff of Pennsylvania. Whether she did it to be provocative or without thinking, she invited both Drew Pearson and McCarthy and sat them at the same table. More than any other newspaperman, Pearson was an almost chronic pain in Joe's epiderm.

The most influential of the syndicated columnists, Pearson was also the first to take on McCarthy, right after the Wheeling speech, when he wrote that "every man on the McCarthy list has already been scrutinized" by other committees. "Sen. McCarthy is way off-base." After that, the muckraking Pearson never let up, in his column "Washington Merry-Go-Round" or in his weekly radio program. During the Tydings hearings, Pearson discredited McCarthy's main witness, the ex-Communist Louis Budenz, by revealing that "Budenz was married to two women at the same time" and had "three children born out of wedlock." By June 1950, Pearson had devoted more than forty columns in full or in part to the disparagement of McCarthy, dredging up such matters as the Lustron payment and Joe's tax problems.[101] At that time Joe approached Pearson's leg man, Jack Anderson, and told him, "I'm going to have to go after your boss. I mean no holds barred."[102]

As Pearson sat down with his wife at Louise Steinman's dinner, he was dismayed to see McCarthy on the other side of the table. "I'm going to tear you limb from limb" was Joe's greeting, referring to a speech he planned to make on the Senate floor.

"How is your income tax case coming along? When are they going to put you in jail?" Pearson asked. Joe jumped up from his chair, went over to where Pearson was sitting, grabbed the back of his neck with his thumb and forefinger, and said "You take that back." Pearson started to get up, but Mrs. William McCracken, the wife of a Washington lawyer, told him, "Don't be a fool. Sit down. Can't you see he's been drinking? Don't embarrass your hostess." During the rest of the dinner and dancing, Pearson kept an eye on Joe, who always had a glass in his hand.[103]

When Pearson and his wife left the ballroom and went down to the cloakroom, Pearson gave his check to the attendant and reached into his pocket for change. Joe came up behind him, pinned his arms, wheeled him around, and kicked him in the groin, saying: "Keep your hands out of your pockets. . . . No guns," as if he thought Pearson was armed. Then he said, "Take that back about my taxes." Richard Nixon arrived and pulled them apart, saying, "Break it up like old New England Puritans." Frank Waldrop of the *Times Herald* recalled getting a call late that night from a drunken Joe, bragging that he'd kicked Drew "in the nuts." Again this interest in damaged testicles.[104]

On December 15, McCarthy gave a two-hour speech in the Senate, most of which was a compilation of the indignation expressed about Pearson by other congressmen and public officials. Protected by Senate immunity, he called Pearson a "Moscow-directed character assassin." He told loyal Americans to notify the Communist's radio sponsor, the Adam Hat Company, that "anyone who buys an Adam hat, any store that stocks an Adam hat, anyone who buys from a store that stocks an Adam hat, is unknowingly and innocently contributing at least something to the cause of international Communism." Adam Hat caved in, but other sponsors stepped into the breach.[105]

Pearson filed a $5.1 million libel suit against McCarthy and asked for heavy damages for the unprovoked Sulgrave Club assault. Pearson's lawyer was William A. Roberts, who had been present at the Sulgrave. When Roberts took a wide-ranging pretrial deposition from McCarthy on September 26, 1951, there was a tense moment when he asked about Thomas Korb having been in Joe's office at the time of the Malmédy hearings. McCarthy said Korb was there to see that justice was done to the accused SS. "The Germans were given a mock trial," said Joe, "fake convictions, a fake death sentence. . . . It was stuff to make you vomit." Roberts replied: "What makes me vomit is what the Nazis did."[106]

The libel case dragged on until combat fatigue set in, when it was dropped in 1956.

The year had been a busy one for Joe. He was now a national figure, at the cost of some credibility and considerable criticism from some of his fellow senators.

McCarthy's apex in irresponsibility came with his attack on June 14, 1951, on George Marshall, in a sixty-thousand-word speech on the Senate floor. Why attack Marshall, the least self-serving of men, aide to General John Pershing in World War I, Army Chief of Staff in World War II, Secretary of State from 1947 to 1949, and now Secretary of Defense? There was no rational reason to go after this American icon. Perhaps Joe the giant-killer wanted to cut down to size one of the few American statesmen held above reproach.

Joe did not write the three-hour diatribe, which showed enough knowledge of diplomatic and military history to twist it out of shape. Later, in his deposition before William Roberts, he would declare: "I can hardly say that I am the author of it." The principal author was Forrest Davis, a deeply conservative onetime editorial writer for the *Cincinnati Enquirer.* McCarthy by himself would never have referred to "the great Swedish Chancellor Oxenstiern" or quoted Shakespeare.

It was an outrageous rant, in which Marshall was made the villain for everything from Pearl Harbor to backing a premature second front in 1942 to the loss of China and the Korean War. Marshall, "this grim and solitary man," was behind every incident in American foreign policy since the war. It was the "single cause" explanation that mental health doctors attribute to paranoid minds.

McCarthy's discussion of the Marshall Plan was particularly ludicrous. He had voted for the Marshall Plan, he said, but now saw that it had made the United States "the patsy of the modern world." He wondered what had prompted Marshall and answered his own question—it was Earl Browder's book on the Teheran conference, *Our Path in War and Peace.* Here was McCarthy recommending a book by the leader of the U.S. Communist Party because he found in it "the blueprint for . . . indiscriminate benevolence abroad comprehended in the Marshall Plan," this "massive and unrewarding boondoggle."[107]

Joe was not arguing facts, but "a conspiracy on a scale so immense as to dwarf any previous such venture in the history of man. A conspiracy so black that . . . its principals shall be forever deserving of the maledictions of all honest men." Quoting from *Macbeth,* he said of Marshall: "I am in blood steeped so far, that should I wade no more, returning were as tedious as going o'er."[108] A more pertinent Shakespearean phrase would have been: "This is a tale told by an idiot, full of sound and fury, signifying nothing."

Marshall refused to comment. If he had to explain that he was not a traitor at this point in his life, he told friends, it was not worth the trouble. He retired that September at the age of seventy-one, perhaps disgusted with the political climate, as Senator Baldwin had been before him. His final task as Secretary of Defense, at the insistence of Anna Rosenberg, was to review a squad of servicewomen. In 1953, he won the Nobel Peace Prize.[109]

Following Joe's tirade, a slight drop in temperature could be noticed among his Republican claque, a slight distancing to avoid contamination. On October 22, 1951, at a press conference in Des Moines, Senator Taft said bluntly: "I don't think one who overstates his case helps his own case. . . . His extreme attack against General Marshall was one of the things on which I cannot agree with McCarthy."[110]

While Joe, with his pit bull tactics, made many senators reluctant to tangle with him, there was one senator who was not afraid, because he was not a professional politician, and did not have his entire ego invested in reelection. This was Senator William Benton of Connecticut, who could act on his visceral dislikes without fear of retribution.

On August 3, 1951, the Gillette subcommittee report on the Maryland election was released. Reading the report at his home in Southport, Benton, who was a member of the parent Rules Committee, felt that something should be done about McCarthy or the momentum would be lost. There was a case to be made here, under a Senate resolution adopted on April 13, 1950, that any senator indulging in dishonest election practices was subject to expulsion. If he did not follow up, all would evaporate in the haze of Washington's dog days.

Benton decided to take matters a step further, for the report charged McCarthy with being "a leading and potent force in the election," and called his tactics "odious." He would take the floor on Monday, August 6, and move for Joe's expulsion. He knew that his motion would not pass. A resolution to expel an incumbent senator for unworthy conduct was unheard of. For one thing, senators did not like to take action against other senators—after all, it was a club. For another, expulsion required a two-thirds vote while censure needed only a majority. But Benton wanted to dramatize the issue and perhaps spark a debate.[111]

On the afternoon of August 6, 1951, Benton introduced a resolution asking the Rules Committee to conduct an investigation to determine "whether or not it should initiate action with a view toward the expulsion from the

Senate of . . . Joseph McCarthy." Benton suggested that "the Senator from Wisconsin should at once submit his resignation from this body. . . . If the Senator refuses to resign . . . then I suggest that at least he refrain from taking any further part in the activities and procedures of the United States Senate until my resolution has been received and reviewed by the Committee on Rules and Administration and until action has been taken upon it by the Committee and by the United States Senate itself."

Fat chance! Joe countercharged on August 7 that "Benton has established himself as a hero of every Communist and crook in and out of government." A number of senators had come up to Benton after his speech and told him they admired his courage, but could not back him openly. When the radio commentator Martin Agronsky praised Benton, he lost fifteen local sponsors.[112]

Benton's resolution was referred to the Subcommittee on Privileges and Elections, the same one that had looked into the Maryland election. Benton now had to present an indictment and settled on ten cases where McCarthy had lied to the Senate. Senators, however, do not expel one of their own for lying. If they did, how many would be left? They only took action for offenses against the Senate itself. Since 1871, there had been eight cases of expulsion, but not one senator expelled.

When McCarthy spoke on August 9, offering up an encore of his old accusations, Benton's challenge seemed to have put some backbone in a few of the other senators, for there was quite a fracas. Joe was still harping on his February 1950 names, and said that twenty-nine of them were pending before the loyalty board. He had written "The Red Dean" Acheson to take steps against them, but had received a reply from Deputy Undersecretary of State Carlisle Humelsine on July 25 saying that he was mistaken—the twenty-nine were in varying categories. Some were being processed by the loyalty board. "Your indiscriminate lumping together of names . . . is tantamount to holding hostage the reputation of these employees," Humelsine wrote.

McCarthy then said he was about to be "damned from hell to breakfast. . . . I understand that one senator would like to see the Senator from Wisconsin expelled from the Senate because he exposed our friend Millard Tydings."

Joe went on to attack Philip Jessup, ambassador-at-large for the State Department, and one of his nine public cases before the Tydings Committee, for testifying at Hiss's second trial that his reputation for loyalty and veracity was "outstanding" and for "signing a petition to destroy our atom bombs."

That was too much for Ernest McFarland of Arizona, the Senate Majority Leader, who rose to say: "I have sat on the floor of the Senate and heard men charged by innuendo and inference, with disloyalty and even with high

crimes . . . without any substantial evidence. . . . I have heard one senator, by
innuendo and insinuation, charge a high official of this government, a man
who has served his country for a lifetime with distinction and honor, with
being a traitor or near traitor. . . . To attempt to refute such charges merely
dignifies the assertion. . . . It is beneath the dignity of members of the Senate
to smear anybody. When the name of any member of the Senate becomes an
adjective for mud-slinging . . . we have come to a time when a halt must be
called."

Herbert Lehman of New York sided with McFarland: "The process of making charges . . . under the protection of Congressional immunity is a form of
character assassination which all of us must abhor and condemn." Philip Jessup, Lehman added, "deserves much better of his fellow citizens than the
shabby and dastardly treatment which is accorded him here."

Senator Kenneth Wherry of Nebraska told Lehman he was out of order
under Senate Rule 19, that one senator could not impute improper motives
to another. Lehman said he would substitute the word "cowardly" for "dastardly."

McCarthy said he was sure the Majority Leader did not wish to label "a
once great party as a party which stands for the protection of Communists
and crooks in government."

McFarland: "I am not going to be goaded into a colloquy with the junior
Senator from Wisconsin."

Joe said he was tired of those Democrats "who get up and scream to high
heaven, 'Joe McCarthy, you are smearing these poor innocent Communists.' "
(Applause from the galleries.)[113]

Without mentioning McCarthy's name, President Truman on August 14
called on the American people to put an end to hate-mongers "who are trying
to divide and confuse us and tear up the Bill of Rights."

At that time, in the Truman White House, a debate was simmering on the
correct tactics to employ against McCarthy. At a meeting on August 24, 1951,
the recently appointed press secretary, Joe Short, who had replaced Charlie
Ross, took the line that the State Department habit of replying to each and
every charge that McCarthy made was counterproductive, and he asked the
President's permission to "tell State to lay off." George Elsey, the assistant to
Truman's special counsel, Charles Murphy, who had replaced Clark Clifford
in 1950, thought he spoke for most of the White House staff in saying that "a
forceful, direct rebuttal to McCarthy's lies and reckless charges is necessary.
The 'be quiet and it will go away' approach did not work." In a memo to Murphy, Elsey wrote, "I do not think we should stand by and let Short put the lid
on State without having a thorough airing of the situation." The trouble was

that the forceful rebuttal did not work either, for this was not a case of who was right, but of partisan politics, with a presidential election a little more than a year off.[114]

In the fall of 1951, the Gillette subcommittee was stuck with the Benton resolution. Guy Gillette hoped that it would quietly fade away, but Joe did not allow that to happen: he went on the attack. On September 18, he released a letter to Thomas Hennings of Missouri, questioning his qualifications to sit on the subcommittee. His law partner, John Raeburn Green, was the lawyer for a Smith Act defendant, John Gates, an editor of the *Daily Worker* "who was recently convicted of plotting to overthrow the government of the United States." Hennings replied in a speech on the Senate floor on September 21 that Green had been assigned the case by the U.S. Supreme Court. He had taken the appeal without a fee, and the American Bar Association had praised his action as "advocacy . . . at its noblest." (John Gates left the party in 1956, calling it "a corpse.") Joe's attack on Hennings strengthened the resolve of the subcommittee, which voted on September 24 to hear Benton and rejected McCarthy's request to cross-examine.[115]

At this point, Margaret Chase Smith began to have second thoughts about serving on the subcommittee. She was tired of leading the charge with nobody following. Her "Declaration of Conscience" in 1950 had placed her on McCarthy's hit list. He was the ranking Republican on the Senate Investigation Subcommittee of the Government Operations Committee and bumped her in January 1951. Smith was named to the Rules Committee and assigned to Privileges and Elections, where she helped conduct the investigation on the Maryland election. She had received no support from her party on her "Declaration of Conscience." Even among the Democrats, few stood up to Joe. Why should she, a Republican, stand alone and see her record in the Senate distorted by his fulminations? On September 24, she wrote Carl Hayden, the chairman of the Rules Committee, that she no longer wished to serve on the subcommittee taking up the Benton resolution.[116]

On September 28, 1951, the hearings began, with Benton establishing McCarthy's "pattern of conduct" and presenting his ten cases, from Lustron to Malmédy to Tydings and Marshall. Benton told the committee it was dealing "with a senator thought to be of unsound mind." When Gillette asked McCarthy if he wanted to respond, he replied on October 4: "Frankly, Guy, I do not intend to read much less answer Benton's smear attack. I am sure you realize that the Benton type of material can be found in the *Daily Worker* almost any day of the week."[117]

Gillette, though a loyal Democrat, was of the timorous persuasion and did not want to offend anyone. Joe badgered him in a letter on December 6, saying that the subcommittee "spends thousands of taxpayer dollars for the sole purpose of dragging up campaign material against McCarthy" and was "guilty of stealing just as clearly as though the members engaged in picking the pockets of the taxpayers."

The Subcommittee on Privileges and Elections began to unravel when Smith quit. She was sensitive to Joe's charges that the subcommittee's actions would hurt the Republican Party as well as himself. The New Jersey Republican Robert Hendrickson yearned to switch to the more placid Library of Congress Subcommittee, which had a vacancy. He probably would have bolted had McCarthy not approached him in the Senate cloakroom to tell him patronizingly, "You're doing the right thing by resigning, Bob. It's the only thing to do with your prejudices." More than once, events would have gone Joe's way if he'd kept his mouth shut. Hendrickson soldiered on, writing his brother on January 25, "I do not feel that I can run out in the 'midst of a trial,' so to speak, despite Joe McCarthy's wishes to the contrary."[118]

On April 10, the Senate voted 60 to 0 to allow the subcommittee to continue its work. McCarthy introduced a resolution to enlarge the scope to include Senator Benton, which was approved, so that he too was investigated. Then Joe dared Benton to make his charges off the Senate floor, which Benton did, and Joe sued him for $2 million (but dropped the suit in March 1954).[119]

In May 1952, the committee focused on the Lustron deal. Benton wrote a friend that he was doing "a dirty, unpleasant job, knowing that it was a lot easier for a group of people to corner a skunk and kill him than for one man to do it." On May 7, Joe wrote Benton that he wanted the case advanced on the calendar. His reason was "that shortly before you appointed yourself to lead the fight to smear and discredit McCarthy, the Communist Party through its then secretary Gus Hall (who has since been jailed), proclaimed the need to rid our country of the fascist poison of McCarthyism. . . . That there is no question that the aim and objective of the Communist Party and Benton are the same insofar as McCarthy is concerned . . . the only question is whether it is knowingly or through stupidity."[120]

McCarthy had adopted an ipso facto method of logic that branded anyone who criticized him a Communist. On July 30, he made his only appearance before the subcommittee, wheeling in a cart stacked with books and documents and offering "62 different exhibits" to prove that Benton was "paralleling the Communist Party line down to the last period." In fact, he presented twenty-four exhibits, which proved nothing. One of them alleged that Benton had the *Britannica* printed in England to avoid union wage scales. Benton said in his rebuttal that Joe had just displayed the pattern of fraud and deception that should be grounds for his expulsion.[121]

On September 9, 1952, Herman Welker resigned from the subcommittee, calling it "a political vehicle for the Democratic party." The next day, Gillette resigned, telling Benton that "McCarthy just threatened me. He says that if I continue to press the investigation, he's going into Iowa and campaign against me and defeat me." Although Gillette was not up for reelection until 1954, he saw himself as the next Millard Tydings. Mike Monroney went to Europe on a holiday, which left a subcommittee of two, Hennings and Hendrickson. Carl Hayden, the chairman of the parent Rules Committee, volunteered to make it a threesome.

But on November 12, when the hearings resumed, Hennings was nowhere to be found. He was known to go on benders, and on November 13 Benton located him in New York in room 1627 of the Plaza Hotel. He had been seen the night before at a popular nightclub, guzzling martinis.[122] The problem now was to get Hendrickson, a Republican, to sign the report. He worried that the criticism of McCarthy would hurt the party. But once again, Joe helped him make up his mind.

In December, McCarthy called Hendrickson's home in New Jersey. His twenty-one-year-old daughter answered and told Joe that her father was in Washington. He refused to believe her and started snarling that Bob had better come to the phone. Hendrickson told Benton that Joe "gave her a mean time." Hendrickson's doubts evaporated, and after a six-martini lunch with Hennings on January 1, 1953, he signed the report, which was released on January 2, the last day of the expiring 82nd Congress.[123] Mike Monroney of Oklahoma, the subcommittee member who had left for Europe, had always said, "The way to get at Joe is where does he get his money?" The report focused on his finances, calling the Lustron fee for the booklet on housing "highly improper" and chiding him for using contributions for his anti-Communist crusade to buy soybean futures. But it sidestepped the issue of expulsion, saying that it should be taken up by the entire Senate. Thus Benton's challenge ended with a pratfall. McCarthy was disruptive, but he was not yet intolerable. Hendrickson had managed to get some embarrassing material cut out of the report. McCarthy thanked him by saying he was "the only man who has lived so long without brains or guts." At the start of the 83rd Congress, William Jenner became chairman of the Committee on Rules and Administration, and suppressed the report. But it became the basis for McCarthy's later condemnation.

The farcical voyage aboard the leaky tub Privileges and Elections, from which one senator after another jumped ship, had lasted nearly a year and a half. At the Republican convention in Chicago on July 7, 1952, a bitter affair that dashed the hopes of Harold Stassen and Robert Taft (who died in 1953),

Eisenhower was nominated on the first ballot and chose as his running mate Richard Nixon, who acknowledged that anti-Communism was his "road to the ticket."

Later that month, the Democrats met in Chicago and nominated Adlai Stevenson, who did not espouse the anti-Communist crusade. He said he had no interest in "nervously looking for subversive enemies under the bed and behind the curtain."[124]

In July 1952, McCarthy was operated on for a herniated diaphragm, which required the removal of a rib and a twenty-four-inch incision. He had a scar from his stomach to his shoulder blade. The operation gave him chronic pain, and his painkiller came in a bottle. He kept it in his briefcase and re-porters saw him drinking whiskey before breakfast. His pal Urban Van Sus-teren, with whom he stayed in Appleton, saw that "his best friend was now the bottle." He'd swallow a handful of baking soda to ward off a hangover. "He was like a one-man slum district," Van Susteren recalled.[125]

Despite his weakened state, McCarthy traveled to ten states to campaign for his friends: To Arizona to stump for Barry Goldwater, who defeated Joe's Senate foe Ernest McFarland. To Nevada, Washington, Wyoming, and Mon-tana. To Michigan, Missouri, and Indiana. To West Virginia and Connecticut, where he made three anti-Benton speeches. In Bridgeport, he announced a repetition of the Maryland campaign. The entire Republican hierarchy was there to greet him. In Westbury, he told his audience that Benton "was worth a hundred million dollars to the Kremlin." One state he avoided was Massa-chusetts, where Henry Cabot Lodge was fighting off John Fitzgerald Kennedy. Lodge repeatedly asked him to come, but Joe Kennedy told his friend McCar-thy to stay away, which he did. Ike came to Boston to praise the incumbent Re-publican senator at a pre-election rally, but his coattails were not long enough to save Lodge.[126]

On August 22, Ike was in Denver on his whistle-stop campaign and said that he did not support "Un-Americanism" and "the unjust damaging of reputations." When a reporter mentioned Marshall, he said, "I have no pa-tience with anyone who can find in his record anything to criticize." Joe's at-tack on Marshall had included a blast at Ike for not taking Berlin in 1945. He accused Ike of stalling and letting the Russians capture the German capital. Ike proposed to his aides that they make the Wisconsin tour an occasion for a Marshall tribute. The aides were divided. Some said "don't tangle with Joe," while others suggested staying out of Indiana and Wisconsin, since going there would mean photo ops and podium stances for the two senators who had vilified Marshall, William Jenner and Joe McCarthy. Ike decided to go, and on September 8 he was in Indianapolis with Jenner, who had called Marshall "a front man for traitors." When Jenner introduced him, he grabbed Ike's hand and raised it. One of Ike's speechwriters described him as "almost purple with rage." "If he puts his hand on me once again, I'm going to knock him right off that platform," Ike said.[127]

When Ike's train chugged through Michigan, Tom Coleman came aboard and warned him not to offend Joe on his home turf. Ike nonetheless asked his speechwriter, Emmet John Hughes, to insert a defense of Marshall in his Milwaukee speech. On October 2, when the train was stopped for the night in Peoria, Wisconsin Governor Walter Kohler flew there with Joe. The next morning, Kohler took aside Ike's aide, Sherman Adams, to warn him of the effect any jibe at McCarthy could have on the state ticket. Truman had carried Wisconsin in 1948. Adams asked Ike to drop the remarks defending Marshall, which he did. Kohler told Ike: "When you call on the Pope, you don't tell him what a fine fellow Martin Luther is." When Ike spoke in Green Bay, Joe was on the platform with him. Ike said, "I'm going to say that I disagree with you." Joe replied, "If you say that you'll be booed." "I've been booed before and being booed doesn't bother me," Ike said. But he toned down his remarks. "I want to make one thing very clear," he told his audience, "the purpose that he and I have of ridding this government of incompetents . . . and above all of subversives . . . are one and the same. Our differences apply not to the end result but to the methods." Without endorsing McCarthy by name, Ike repeatedly called for the election of the entire Republican ticket. In Appleton, his hometown, Joe came bouncing out of the rear car to introduce Ike, who said the country needed "every single man . . . on the ticket here in Wisconsin from the governor himself through the Senate and the House."[128]

Ike did not want to say anything that would split the party, and political necessity was part of the reason he backed down. But there was another reason, and to understand it we have to go back to October 1950, when General Walter Bedell Smith was named Director of the CIA. Smith had been Eisenhower's chief of staff during the war and the two were close friends. As CIA chief, Smith wanted to improve relations with the FBI, and he often invited the FBI liaison, Sam Papich, in for private chats. On July 17, 1952, shortly after Ike's nomination, Smith told Papich that "Ike has not fully found himself and will continue to be somewhat nervous and unsure of himself." From one soldier to another, Ike had told Smith "that he was not going to be hoodwinked by politicians."[129] Smith had a way of putting his foot in his mouth. During a discussion with several other CIA men on the value of the polygraph test, Smith said that the FBI had given a lie detector test to a veteran agent with sixteen years' service, only to find that the man was a lifelong homosexual. "When old Edgar heard about it, he almost dropped dead," Smith said. The story got back to Hoover, who was not happy that malicious rumors about the bureau were spreading through Washington thanks to the CIA Director.[130]

Smith had been ambassador to Moscow after the war, and became friendly with William Benton, then in the State Department. When McCarthy sued Benton for libel, Smith was subpoenaed to give a deposition on September 29 and 30, 1952, to say what he thought of the Marshall Plan. Asked his opinion of Marshall, he said, "You are asking the molehill to comment on the mountain." As for the Marshall Plan, Smith said, "one of my Western European colleagues stated to me that the Marshall Plan was a stroke of genius." The deposition ranged over other topics, and Smith said at one point, speaking in a blunt and soldierly way: "I know there were Communists in the State Department. . . . I believe there are Communists in my own organization. . . . I believe that they are so adroit and adept that they have infiltrated practically every security organization of government."[131] This comment was picked up by the press, creating quite a flare-up. Here was the head of the intelligence department in the Truman administration appearing to corroborate McCarthy's statement about Communists in government. In addition, he was a close friend of the Republican candidate. All Smith had meant was that vigilance was needed, but the media made it sound as if the CIA Director, whose job it was to gather intelligence, saw massive Communist subversion in the government.

On September 30, Smith called Eisenhower and Stevenson and said it would be deplorable if the CIA was used for political capital a month before the election. On October 2, 1952, he wrote Truman to tell him how distressed he was. He was afraid that Truman would now be charged with failing to take aggressive action against the Communists. One of his staff officers had spoken to Francis Walter of the House Un-American Activities Committee, who wanted Smith to testify, he told Truman. Walter said that the Democratic members of the committee felt that Smith's deposition "was the result of disloyal connivance on my part to injure your position," Smith went on. This feeling stemmed from his close association with Eisenhower. "I cannot stomach this implication of disloyalty," Smith said. He repeated and underlined his loyalty to the President.[132]

On October 13, 1952, Smith appeared before HUAC and explained that he had not meant to imply that the State Department "was riddled with Communists." He knew only of two.

Francis Walter said that his statement about Reds in the CIA "disturbed all of us." Could he elaborate?

Smith said, "we have discovered one or two . . . but not in the United States . . . this thing has been exaggerated." Smith explained that "it would be foolish and fatuous to assume that somewhere we do not have penetration."[133]

An FBI memo on October 8, 1952, recounted that Smith had told Papich, the FBI liaison man, "that's what happens when you talk too much." He admitted that he'd placed himself in a jam, but Ike got him off the hook by instructing that Smith's testimony not be used in any Republican speeches. The congresswoman Clare Boothe Luce had wanted to give Smith's remarks some prominence in a radio talk on Truman and Communism, but was told to keep a lid on it. "On the occasion of Eisenhower's recent talk in Wisconsin," the FBI memo said, "Eisenhower had planned to make complimentary references to Gen. Marshall . . . but he refrained from doing so after McCarthy agreed not to make any references to Smith's testimony in Washington. . . . Gen. Smith stated that despite the fact that Eisenhower and McCarthy have reached some form of working agreement, the relationship between the two men is far from being friendly."[134] Ike had generously saved his old friend's hide by muzzling Joe, in exchange for which he cut out the Marshall paragraph in his Milwaukee speech on October 3. Ike actually sounded like McCarthy, warning about Communists in government and praising those who had "the sense and the stamina to take after the Communists themselves."

After Ike was elected, he moved his old comrade-in-arms from the CIA to the State Department, as assistant secretary.

———

As for McCarthy, he won the Republican primary on September 9 against the little known Leonard F. Schmitt, a former district attorney, by 515,481 to 213,701, which reinforced his faith in his vote-getting powers. In the election he was running against Thomas Fairchild, who had been elected attorney general in 1948. But Joe didn't bother to campaign in his own state. Instead, he toured other states, and garnered headlines by making scurrilous remarks about Adlai Stevenson. In a speech in Chicago on October 27 that was carried by 550 radio and 55 television stations, he said that Stevenson "would continue the suicidal Kremlin-shaped policies of this nation." He stressed Stevenson's character reference to Hiss and called him "Alger—I mean Adlai." On another occasion, he said that if he were put on Stevenson's campaign train with a "slippery elm club," he would beat some Americanism into the Democratic candidate. This was something new in campaign rhetoric—the threat of bodily harm.

On November 4, 1952, Ike won 55 percent of the vote, or 33 million popular and 442 electoral votes, carrying thirty-nine states. The Republican ticket also won slim majorities in Congress, 48 to 47 in the Senate and 221 to 213 in the House. One of the reelected Republican senators was Joseph R. McCarthy, who beat Fairchild by 870,444 to 731,402. In Wisconsin, however, Joe trailed the ticket, running 100,000 votes behind Ike and 139,000 votes behind the reelected Governor Kohler. James Doyle, the leader of the state's Democratic Organizing Committee, released a statement that said:

"To President Eisenhower: Our full and fervent support in the task of building peace.

"To Senator McCarthy: War unto the death."[135]

This statement turned out to be literally true, for Joe did not live to serve out his second term.

One of the casualties of the 1952 election was William Benton, who lost to his Republican opponent, William Purtell. Benton realized that he was known as "the fellow who's against McCarthy," but did not blame his defeat on Joe. It was Ike's popularity. He took cold comfort in having lost by 89,000 votes, while Stevenson had lost Connecticut by 129,000. John Bailey, the Democratic chairman in Connecticut, said, "McCarthy obviously didn't beat Bill Benton in Connecticut. Eisenhower beat Benton. The general was very, very strong in Connecticut. In 1950, McCarthy came into Connecticut three times to speak against Benton, who won."[136]

After the 1952 election, the GOP controlled the federal government. Why should McCarthy continue his flawed crusade? Why attack a fort you occupied? Joe had his own reasons and announced in December that he had only scratched the surface, placing himself on a collision course with the President of his country and leader of his party.

XIV

DECLINE AND FALL

In his State of the Union message on February 2, 1953, President Eisenhower said he intended "to clear the air of that unreasoned suspicion that accepts rumor and gossip as substitutes for evidence. . . . The primary responsibility for keeping out the disloyal and the dangerous rests squarely upon the executive branch."[1]

Washington pundits reasoned that with the Democrats out of the White House, and Communists out of the government, McCarthy's attacks would subside. Senator Taft, the Republican leader, with a majority of 48 to 47, tried to lateral the Communist issue to William Jenner, chairman of the Senate Internal Security Subcommittee, which was given exclusive jurisdiction over government subversion. McCarthy became chairman of the supposedly inoffensive Committee on Government Operations, which had, however, an Investigation Subcommittee that he would tailor to his purpose.[2]

Joe's first target was James B. Conant, the president of Harvard, that anti-McCarthy enclave, whom Ike had named High Commissioner to Germany. On February 3, 1953, he wrote the President to list his objections. Conant was opposed to parochial schools. He was permissive about Communists in education. In 1944, he had spoken in favor of destroying the industrial capacity of West Germany, as advocated in the Morgenthau Plan. Normally, McCarthy said, he would plan an all-out fight on the Senate floor, but because of Ike's "overwhelming popularity," he feared that his all-out fight would fail. Thus, while he would vote against Conant, he had decided to make no public statements against him. Conant was confirmed in February.[3]

McCarthy's opposition to a routine appointment was a signal that far from wanting to cooperate with the new administration, he hungered for confrontation. The method was the same as with Truman: make charges, grab headlines, increase his power base. The first "knock-down fight," as Secretary of State John Foster Dulles called it, came over the Bohlen nomination.

When Ike took office, there was no American ambassador in Moscow. George Kennan had been declared persona non grata in September 1952, when he said, while on a stopover in Berlin, that the Soviet Union reminded him of Nazi Germany. To replace him, Ike chose the career service officer Charles E. "Chip" Bohlen, who had been to Yalta with FDR, and who was considered one of the top experts on the Soviet Union.

Bohlen's nomination went to the Senate on February 27, and the Foreign Relations Committee scheduled hearings on March 2, 1953. Bohlen defended the Yalta agreement, which was anathema to conservative Republicans, who blamed Yalta for the loss of Eastern Europe and China. At the same time, there were rumors of "derogatory material" in Bohlen's security file. Ike persuaded Senator Taft to back the nomination, out of party loyalty. The Foreign Relations Committee vote, however, was delayed for a second round of hearings. On March 5, Stalin died, giving the appointment some urgency.

On March 13, Dulles spoke to presidential aide Sherman Adams, who said, "we are on very shaky ground." Dulles asked if that meant the "morals" charges were being aired, and Adams said yes, though he didn't want to fire anybody over a rumor.[4]

On March 16, Dulles worked the phones, enlisting support in Congress. He told Taft that Bohlen might not be in Moscow very long, perhaps only a few months. He then called Bohlen, who was home quarantined with the measles, to tell him there was no weakening of Ike's determination. The Bohlen confirmation was turning into a major test of executive power versus congressional obstruction.[5]

On March 17, Dulles saw Hoover, who admitted that most of the case against Bohlen was based on rumor, but that it was not yet possible to give him a complete security clearance. Wavering, Dulles told Ike that if he decided to dump Bohlen, he could do it on those grounds. Ike said he could also do it on "health," though that would look bad too. Dulles said the best line to take before the committee the following day was to tell the truth about what was in the report and if they didn't want to go along, the responsibility for destroying Bohlen's reputation would be on their shoulders. Ike expressed surprise at Hoover's attitude. "Let's never propose an appointment before we have all these clearances before us," he said. "We don't want to get into this again."[6]

Dulles was so worried on March 18, the day of the second hearing, that he refused to ride in the same car as Bohlen or have his picture taken with him. But Taft had done the spadework, and Bohlen was approved unanimously, 15 to 0. Even Homer Ferguson of Michigan, who felt strongly about Yalta, went along. McCarthy angrily predicted that the President would withdraw the nomination if he saw "the entire file on Bohlen."

On March 19, the State Department security chief, R. W. Scott McLeod, a hard-liner who was a friend of McCarthy's, decided to resign. He had brought derogatory material on Bohlen to Dulles, who had failed to act on it. Dulles said that if he resigned now he would probably cause a floor fight on Friday when the nomination came before the full Senate. Sherman Adams, Ike's chief assistant, told Dulles that McLeod was under the influence of McCarthy, "which might make him a bit hazardous." Dulles said if he quit there would be repercussions. He might testify before the McCarthy committee, on television.[7]

On March 20, an account of McLeod's conversation with Dulles appeared in the Washington morning newspapers. Dulles told McLeod: "This story could only have emanated from you and I consider that this constitutes a gross breach of security." Jim Hagerty, Ike's press secretary, was so upset he said there were only two courses, that McLeod should resign or Dulles should resign. Dulles said the characters were minor but the issues were great, for they would determine whether McCarthy and Jenner could dominate the executive branch of this government. McLeod was obviously in touch with McCarthy. Sherman Adams said, "If the boy does not come clean you cannot keep him," but to remember the explosion that would come on the Hill. Dulles talked to McLeod, who seemed repentant. Dulles said Ike had authorized him to demand his resignation, but he was willing to make a fresh start. McLeod said he would write a letter of apology that Dulles could show the President. Dulles told Adams, "We will watch him and keep him somewhat on trial." The explosion on the Hill was averted.[8]

On March 21, McLeod told one of Dulles's aides that McCarthy had called him, wanting him to testify. McLeod said, "You are not going to make headlines out of my blood." In any case, Dulles had told McLeod that as security officer he was not cleared to testify before a congressional committee. McCarthy told reporters: "I know what is in that [Bohlen] file. I have known what's in his file for years."

Joe wasn't bluffing. He had obtained a copy of the Bohlen file as well as a copy of the security file of Bohlen's brother-in-law, which was more explosive. Charles Thayer, the blue-eyed, round-faced West Point graduate, had joined the Foreign Service in 1937 and had been posted to Moscow. During the war, while in the OSS, he was assigned to the Tito partisans in Yugoslavia, and by 1945 he was chief of the U.S. military mission in Belgrade. Later that year, he was transferred to Vienna, and when the OSS was disbanded, he joined the State Department and became the head of radio broadcasting at the Voice of America.

In 1948 and 1949, D. L. Nicholson, chief of the Division of Security in the State Department, conducted a security investigation of Thayer, which collected statements from more than a dozen informants he had worked with over the years. The report consisted of an abundance of colorful detail regarding Thayer's homosexuality. He was also accused of being pro-Tito to the detriment of American interests when he served in Belgrade, and of enriching himself through black market activities. Although there was no reason that Bohlen should have been tarred by the conduct of his brother-in-law, the disclosure of the security report would not have helped his confirmation. At the time of the hearings, Thayer was consul general in Munich. When McCarthy summoned him back to Washington to testify, he resigned "to pursue a career in writing." Later, a State Department spokesman admitted that he had been dismissed "on the basis of morals charges."[9]

Joe had prepared two speeches for the full Senate debate, and he asked Nixon which one he should use, the "real dirty one" or the "pretty rough" one. Nixon advised the latter, and on March 23, McCarthy refrained from bringing up Charlie Thayer. He did, however, use the Malmédy ploy of asking for a lie detector test for Dulles and McLeod, "to get to the bottom of this very confusing picture." An angry Taft scotched that idea, but agreed in a compromise to review Bohlen's FBI file with the Democratic senator from Alabama, John J. Sparkman, who had been Adlai Stevenson's running mate in 1952 and was considered above reproach.

On March 24, Taft reported that he and Sparkman had looked over the summary, which was "unusually complete, 25 pages, single-spaced." Taft told the Senate that "Mr. Bohlen was a completely good security risk in every respect." At the end of three days of debate, he was confirmed by a healthy majority of 74 to 13. What had been at stake was not only Bohlen's appointment to Moscow but Eisenhower's ability to govern. After the roll call Taft sent word to Ike: "Don't ask me to wheel any more Bohlens through the Senate."[10]

Until 1953, McCarthy had made explosive speeches, but had not conducted a single investigation, though the Senate had investigated him three times, over the Lee list, the Maryland election, and the Benton resolution. Now he was chairman of the Committee on Government Operations, which until

1953 had been called the Committee on Executive Expenditures. The committee had a Permanent Subcommittee on Investigations, formed in 1946, which had a broad mandate to look into government departments for malfeasance.[11]

McCarthy obtained a budget of $200,000 for his committee operations and went about beefing up his staff. On January 2, 1953, he hired as chief counsel a precocious twenty-five-year-old named Roy Cohn. The son of a judge, Cohn had graduated from Columbia Law School at the age of nineteen, and had to wait until he turned twenty-one to pass his bar exam. Hired as an assistant U.S. attorney, he cut his teeth on some big cases—Smith Act, Remington, Rosenbergs. As special assistant to Attorney General James McGranery, he worked on the Lattimore perjury case and presented the case of American Reds in the United Nations to a grand jury, which returned no indictments.[12]

When he hired Cohn, McCarthy told him: "They're all trying to push me off the Communist issue. The sensible thing for me to do, they say, is start investigating the agriculture program to find out how many books they've got bound upside down at the Library of Congress. They want me to play it safe. I fought this Red issue; I won the primary on it. I won the election on it, and I don't see anyone else around who intends to take it on. You can be sure that as chairman of this committee this is going to be my work. And I want you to help me."[13]

Cohn, who had no legislative experience, ran the hearings like a prosecutor before a grand jury. The sleepy look that his eyes conveyed was a disguise—he was ferociously ambitious, and all too conscious of his own merit, which made him at times abrasive. He tended to push people around, until they pushed back. Cohn brought with him the agent of McCarthy's doom, in the form of a twenty-six-year-old beach boy type, the tall and wavy-haired David Schine. The son of a self-made hotel and movie theater magnate, Schine had attended Harvard, where he was known for his black Cadillac convertible, his electric piano (he wrote songs), and his hiring of secretaries to attend classes and take notes. Essentially, Schine was Cohn's dumb blonde.

McCarthy's friend Joe Kennedy was looking for a berth for his twenty-seven-year-old son, Bobby, a recent graduate of the University of Virginia Law School, where he had invited McCarthy to speak. Having written a paper on the supposed sellout at Yalta, Bobby would fit right in, except that he couldn't stand Cohn, who was brash and high-handed. Bobby resigned on July 29, although he returned in February 1954 as counsel for the three minority Democrats. In his 1960 book, *The Enemy Within*, Robert F. Kennedy wrote that "with two exceptions, no real research was ever done. Most of the investigations were instituted on the basis of some pre-conceived notion by the chief counsel or his staff members and not on the basis of any information that had been developed. Cohn and Schine claimed they knew at the outset what was wrong; and they were not going to allow the facts to interfere. Therefore no real spade work . . . was ever undertaken. I thought Senator McCarthy made a mistake in allowing the Committee to operate in such a fashion, told him so, and resigned."[14]

With Roy Cohn at the helm, McCarthy's investigations came fast and furious, a good dozen in 1953. The other members of the subcommittee—the Republicans Karl Mundt, Everett Dirksen, and Charles E. Potter, and the Democrats John L. McClellan, Stuart Symington, and Henry M. Jackson—served on a number of other committees, and often did not attend. In addition, the three Democrats boycotted the hearings from July 1953 to January 1954, in protest over McCarthy making his own rules. Thus, with McCarthy in the habit of calling hearings at short notice, or outside Washington, he was often the only senator present. He was able, as his critics put it, to operate as a one-man committee, as judge, jury, prosecutor, and press agent, all in one.[15]

McCarthy developed the method of first holding executive sessions, which were closed to the public and the press, and where he could rant at will, berating witnesses and making wild charges. The transcripts of these hearings, more than eight thousand pages, were opened in May 2003 after being sealed for fifty years, and offer a wealth of new insights into McCarthy's tactics.[16]

The closed hearings were dress rehearsals for productions that sometimes never saw the stage. Even when they led to open hearings, some of the witnesses in the closed hearings did not make the grade, if they defended themselves effectively or failed to advance the chairman's case. After a closed hearing, McCarthy would brief the press, often making headline-grabbing claims that were at variance with what had taken place. In 1953, 117 executive sessions were held behind closed doors, and 395 witnesses were heard. To bring in these hundreds of witnesses, McCarthy was said to be signing blank subpoenas like traffic tickets. Many witnesses had no time to prepare or find a lawyer, for the subpoena might arrive hours before the hearing.[17]

Contrary to what has been believed until now, McCarthy did not launch his hearings with the Communist issue. He had other agendas. His first closed hearing was an example of how he used his chairmanship of a congressional committee to get back at his enemies. This vendetta closed hearing on January 15 and 16 was an attempt to smear two longtime enemies: Senator Wayne Morse, the Oregon Independent who had signed Margaret Chase Smith's "Declaration of Conscience" in June 1950 and persistently criticized McCarthy, who called Morse "the senator from Junior"; and Edward P. Morgan, the chief counsel on the Tydings Committee. Morgan, a former chief inspector in the FBI, had gone to Wisconsin in 1952 to campaign against McCarthy's reelection. On November 2, he appeared on television in Milwaukee and revealed that McCarthy had used a forged Civil Service Commission report on security studies in a Senate speech. Stung, McCarthy responded on election eve that Morgan had posed as an FBI agent, even though he had left the bureau in 1947 (which Morgan had pointed out), and called his attack a "new low in campaign degeneracy." Wisconsin Democrats considered Morgan's TV appearance the most effective tactic of their failed campaign.[18]

In this January hearing, McCarthy attempted to link Morse and Morgan to a disreputable fixer and lobbyist, Russell W. Duke (born Dutko), and to show that both men had improperly and perhaps illegally sought favors from government agencies on Duke's behalf. Duke was a resident of Oregon who had made friends with Senator Morse and introduced him to Morgan.

"Duke was one of those individuals who have a thousand things on the fire," Morgan explained in his testimony. Although he was not a lawyer or an accountant, Duke dealt in patents, in oil leases, and in tax cases. Morgan testified that Duke had a criminal record for robbery, that he had once tried to kill himself, and that he threw his wife down the stairs.[19]

Nonetheless, Morgan handled some of the tax cases that Duke steered to him. One case involved an Oakland druggist named Shafer who owed $500,000 in taxes and penalties and was indicted for tax evasion. Morgan took the case for a $20,000 contingency fee, but could do nothing for him and did not collect. Another case involved a San Francisco woman, Inez Burns, who kept a large sum of cash in her basement, but did not declare it. She told Internal Revenue that rats had eaten the money "and it became gummy and so forth," Morgan testified. Morgan had better luck with a Chinese doctor in Portland, Ting David Lee, who had inherited a large sum from relatives in China and was assessed a $100,000 fine. A letter from Duke to Morgan was introduced in which Duke said, "As you know, Senator Morse's office has taken the matter up." Evidence was presented that Morse had introduced a private bill on Dr. Lee's behalf. Morgan was able to settle Dr. Lee's $100,000 assessment for $6,000, and received a large fee, as did Duke. Morgan said of Duke's letters, one of which claimed that "Morse will go along 100 per cent": "Either the man who wrote it was drunk and on goofballs or he was demented."[20]

When Duke testified, he had severe memory lapses. He explained that in 1950, he had been in an explosion and had suffered "a malignancy in the upper antrum" that affected his memory. "Sometimes I will blank out for a couple of weeks at a time," he said. "With excitement, I hemorrhage." After testifying, Duke fled to Canada, so that he would not have to testify again. That was the end of the Duke hearings.[21]

Nothing could have been further from Communists in government than the closed hearing on January 26, which was concerned with the "Stock-piling of Strategic Materials." "Today we are talking . . . about the feather-buying project," McCarthy explained. "At first blush, it does not seem that feathers are a strategic product, but I understand you just cannot fight a war without them. You need them for the sleeping bags, the flying jackets."

The problem was that most of the waterfowl feathers had come from China, but when China went Communist, feather imports were curtailed. The hearings investigated irregularities in feather contracts and went into arcane discussions on whether the government had been cheated by imports from Eastern Europe that had too little goose and too much duck. It all sounded a bit like a Marx Brothers movie.[22]

In late January, there was a closed hearing on "File Destruction in the State Department." Since 1950, State had been McCarthy's pet target, but this time he made a point of saying he did not wish to go into the Communist aspect. On January 28, he called Secretary of State Dulles to let him know he was in-vestigating the filing system, but "not from the Communist angle." Dulles replied that he knew from experience "that once anything is filed here it's lost." Dulles asked if there was any bad intent, but Joe said it was mostly wastefulness and inefficiency.[23] McCarthy instructed Cohn that he wanted to focus on the removal of files, not Communism and subversion. He did not want any duplication with Senator William Jenner's Senate Internal Security Subcommittee.

The information on the files came from a whistle-blower, John Matson, a State Department security officer. Matson had his own problems, which raised the general question of the reliability of whistle-blowers. His boss, John W. Ford, chief of the Division of Security and Investigation, said in a state-ment to the McCarthy Committee that Matson was on probation due to lack of judgment, a persecution complex, and the slanting of reports.[24]

In his testimony on January 26, Matson said that derogatory material was surreptitiously removed from the files and not returned. No slips were en-tered, so you never knew who took what. "Another case," Matson said, "was a man named Victor Purse . . . who asked for the file of a previous Foreign Ser-vice inspector, who had been fired after admittedly being a pervert, and Purse removed information which indicated the reason for which he was fired." This was not Communism, but cronyism.

McCarthy, who routinely accused Foreign Service personnel of being "powder-puffs," said: "We will not make the names of any of the perverts public . . . but I would like to have that name. . . . Apparently a number of the perverts who lost their jobs in the State Department showed up in Paris in jobs that paid better. . . . So at some time it will be necessary to get the names of all the four hundred some homosexuals who were removed from the State Department."

Matson: "This particular man is Thomas Hicock. Unfortunately this man a week later committed suicide [in 1952], so he is out of the picture. He had been in the Foreign Service for over 18 years."[25]

When Helen Balog, the supervisor of the Foreign Service file room, testified on January 27, she reported that one of her file clerks had warned her, "If you go down there and tell them anything, it will cost you your job."

"I want you people to protect me," Balog told the committee. "I do not want you to divulge anything I have said." Of course, that was one of the purposes of closed sessions—secrecy, unless McCarthy leaked to the press. Balog confirmed that documents were removed from the files. One document, she said, was "a medical report on a man that was a psycho case." Another was a letter of recommendation from Owen Lattimore, whom Joe had once called "the top Russian spy," which had mysteriously vanished. Joe said the letter was removed at a time when the State Department was defending Lattimore "as an innocent, abused individual."[26]

It came out that one reason derogatory material was removed was so that the members of the Foreign Service Promotions Board would not see it when they asked for the files, the idea being that men should not be denied promotion on the basis of allegations. Robert J. Ryan, assistant chief in the Division of Foreign Service Personnel, admitted removing allegations of homosexuality.

McCarthy: "Do you not think a promotion board should know whether a man is 'queer' or not before they promoted him?"

Ryan: "If it was proved he was a 'queer,' he would have been fired, senator."

McCarthy: "You don't mean to say that all the homos are out now, do you?"

Ryan: "We are certainly doing the very best we can to get them out of the State Department."[27]

In five days of open hearings in February, McCarthy uncovered some serious sloppiness in the handling of files, but, as he had alerted Dulles, it had nothing to do with Communists. Some files, such as Philip Jessup's, could not be found. Some were taken out and not returned. He focused on John Stewart Service, who in 1949 was cleared to withdraw files. Helen Balog said he had asked for the keys so he could work there at night, after she went home.

McCarthy: "And the next morning you would have no way of knowing whether he took one piece or a hundred pieces or a thousand pieces of material."

Senator Charles E. Potter: "With the record that Mr. Service had for documents sticking to his fingers, it is like putting an arsonist in charge of a match factory."

As a result of Joe's investigation, the file system was revamped.[28]

Prior to the open hearings on the State Department files, McCarthy continued his pursuit of homosexuals in government in a closed hearing on February 2, misleadingly titled "Violation of Export Control Statutes." This was perhaps the most shameful of his closed hearings, in which a decent and honorable public servant, who happened to be a concealed homosexual, was gratuitously vilified. The inquisitor in this case was Roy Cohn, himself a concealed homosexual at the time, who later died of AIDS, which added to the hypocrisy of the proceedings.[29]

Eric L. Kohler had been controller of the Tennessee Valley Authority from 1938 to 1941, and held other government jobs until 1949, including controller of export controls under the Marshall Plan. He was a prominent accountant who had written a textbook and taught at a university. The supposed purpose of the hearing was to investigate the shipment of Marshall Plan goods to Austria and from there to the Soviet Union, which Kohler knew nothing about.

From the start, however, the inquiry focused on Kohler's private life. "While I understand the staff has material reflecting your morals," McCarthy said, "I am not interested in your morals, except insofar as it might result in a security risk. . . . There is to be no publicity here in anything having to do with your morals. . . . We are of course interested in . . . the question of being able to blackmail a man because of something he has done in the past. We know that is a definite threat."

Then Cohn said: "Let me ask you this, Mr. Kohler. You are a homosexual, are you not?"

Kohler: "Well, that has been stated . . . I am perfectly willing to admit that I am, for the purposes of your private record here. . . . [But] I think it is very easy to do a man irreparable harm, because agents can go to his friends and try to find out. . . . Something like that has been done in my case. It is very sad."

Cohn: "Now, Mr. Kohler, would you tell us whether or not you have brought about the employment of any homosexuals in the United States government?"

Kohler: "I have never mingled them in my official capacity."

Cohn produced a letter written by Kohler.

"You first describe a man by the name of Bill," Cohn said, "with whom you had sexual relations. You then proceed to say, 'Bill . . . became the head of one of the units of the U.S. Bureau of the Budget'."

"He was not a homosexual in any sense of the word," Kohler said.

Cohn: "You say in your letter that you had sexual relations with him."

Kohler: "Yes I did. But I don't think that proves he was a homosexual."

McCarthy pressed Kohler to give the man's name, which Kohler declined to do.

McCarthy insisted, saying that his refusal "indicates the danger of having anyone with this, what I refer to as an affliction or mental aberration, handling secret work. . . . It shows how easily they could be blackmailed into giving out secret information."

Kohler said the man's name was William Cooper, and that he now taught at the Carnegie Institute of Technology.

Then more of Kohler's letters to his homosexual friends were read at the hearing. Kohler described going to parks and other places in New York City looking for "fairies and queers." He said he liked to seek out hustlers on 42nd Street.

Senator Henry "Scoop" Jackson: "You have accepted these proposals when you have been solicited?"

Kohler: "On these few rare occasions." He said he'd had "sporadic relationships" with men for over twenty years.

McCarthy promised him that the press would not be informed as to his testimony and that the whole session was off the record. Nothing about Kohler surfaced. But was this kind of gay-bashing the proper function of a congressional committee, even in the fifties?[30]

Thus far, McCarthy's closed hearings had produced only one open hearing, on the State Department files, and that one was less than dramatic. He was hiding his light under a bushel, though that was about to change with the Voice of America hearings. Created during the war as part of the Office of War Information, the Voice of America relied heavily on refugees who spoke the forty-six languages used in its broadcasts. Anti-Communist employees leaked the names of suspected Reds to members of Congress. This promised to be fertile ground for McCarthy, who leaked a preview of coming attractions to one of his fair-haired reporters, Willard Edwards of the *Chicago Tribune*. The story, which ran on February 13, the day of the first closed hearing, said: "A Senate investigation of Communist influences in the Voice of America here has uncovered amazing evidence of a conspiracy to subvert American policy in this nation's radio propaganda broadcasts abroad. Closed-door questioning has developed a picture of such alarming proportions that executive sessions have been ordered. . . . Subpoenas are fluttering on desks in Union Square and more than 100 witnesses have been lined up for questioning," out of a total of 1,400 employees.[31]

The closed session on February 13, however, did not live up to the billing, for it was not about Communist subversion, but about millions of dollars allegedly wasted in the construction of two transmitters, one in North Carolina and one in Dungeness, Washington, known as Baker East and Baker West.

David Schine, who was not a lawyer, and who was listed as "chief consultant," questioned the witnesses, starting with Lewis J. McKesson, the engineer who had blown the whistle on the overruns, which he estimated at $31 million. McCarthy had to reprimand Schine, who had no legislative experience, but was being brought along by his crony Roy.

Senator Scoop Jackson asked McKesson: "So the waste, in connection with Baker West, is in the location of the project? Not so much in what they are doing?" Schine butted in: "May I clarify that, senator? There is waste within the project itself, too." "I think Senator Jackson wants the witness to answer that," McCarthy interjected. Schine was learning the ropes, but never questioned any witnesses in open session.[32]

The Voice of America was now part of the State Department. All of the State Department's propaganda efforts—the libraries, the radio broadcasts, the magazines, and newsreels—came under an umbrella subagency called the International Information Administration. No sooner had McCarthy's closed hearings begun, than John Foster Dulles accepted the resignation of Dr. Wilson M. Compton as head of the IIA. In 1953, there were 189 libraries with two million books, while the VOA broadcast fifty hours of daily programs in almost as many languages. After Eisenhower's election, a new policy emerged that books should represent "a balanced collection of American thought." This classified directive was leaked to McCarthy, who smelled blood and launched his investigation.[33]

Under the "balanced collection" policy, books by Communist authors were stocked in the overseas libraries. At the closed hearing on February 13, one of those authors testified. Howard Fast was that odd man out, a flag-waving Communist who wrote popular novels based on American history. One of his books, *The Unvanquished*, about George Washington, had been read by Eleanor Roosevelt on a record for the blind.[34]

McCarthy asked Fast to name his books, but added: "You see, I do not happen to be a reader of your books, so when you name them, I have difficulty."

"If you are interested in American history," Fast replied, "it might be important to read them."

Fast complained about the manner in which his subpoena had been served. At one in the morning, he said, his bell rang and a voice said: "I am the assistant counsel for the Senate Committee on Operations and I want to talk with you, Howard."

"I don't know you from Adam," Fast said he replied. "Beat it or I will call the police."

"At 1:30 A.M. there was a pounding on the door and a ringing of the bell, which woke my children and terrified them, in time-honored Gestapo methods . . . and here was this offensive character again, and this time for the first time he said he had a subpoena."

McCarthy: "Would you say they were GPU tactics or NKVD-type tactics also?"

Fast: "This action I find offensive and unworthy of any arm of the government of the United States."[35]

In another closed hearing, on February 14, McCarthy tried to find examples of subversive behavior in the Voice of America staff. What he found was the usual griping that takes place in any office and the usual eccentric behavior. Larry Bruzzese, a features editor, said: "I have consistently heard remarks, sneering, and derogatory statements, about America in general, on the part of four or five fellows in the Italian service."[36]

Nancy Lenkeith, who had worked in the French service, said the acting chief, Troup Matthews, had tried to recruit her for a Marxist collective he wanted to set up in Rockland County. He said he wanted "people with no dogmatic religious beliefs." Marcelle Henry, also on the French desk, was known for her anti-American attitude, according to Lenkeith (Henry was fired that May). In one of her scripts, Lenkeith said, Henry wrote: "The Americans are incapable of serious thought. They are children who struck oil, light-headed and cheerful."

McCarthy: "In other words, the type of material being beamed out as the Voice of America would sound more like the voice of Moscow."[37]

McCarthy's televised open hearings began on February 16 and went into policies under the "balanced collection" order. Roy Cohn presented a February 3 State Department instruction: "Similarly, if like Howard Fast—he is known as a Soviet-endorsed author—material favorable to the United States in some of his works may be given a special credibility among selected key audiences." This memo gave Joe a chance to have a tantrum before the television cameras, charging that the International Information Administration was supporting subversion.

McCarthy was seen in the press as scoring points on the Eisenhower administration. William S. White of the *New York Times* reported that "no greater series of victories by a congressional body over a senior executive department in so short a time is recalled here."[38]

The State Department reaction was not long in coming. On February 19, Carl McCardle, John Foster Dulles's press secretary, and Herman Phleger, Dulles's legal counsel, issued Policy Order No. 9:

"Librarians should at once remove all books and other material by Communists, fellow travelers, etcetera, from their shelves." It was a repudiation of the "balanced collection" order, and it gave McCarthy the ammunition he needed, for he could now send a team overseas to make sure it was being enforced.[39]

The closed hearings continued in counterpoint to the open hearings. In a closed hearing on February 23, McCarthy found a likely subversive in Reed Harris, the number two man at the Voice of America. In the report on the hearing later put out by the subcommittee, Harris was described as having written "blatantly pro-Communist material" while at Columbia University, "some of which was reprinted in the *Daily Worker.*"[40]

At the February 23 hearing, Alfred Puhan, a program manager, accused Harris of trying to eliminate the entire VOA Hebrew language service, which was beamed to Israel. At a time of anti-Semitic purges behind the Iron Curtain, Puhan felt that was unwise. "I think it was a stupid decision, a stupid order," he said.

McCarthy tried to get him to say it was more than a stupid decision, it was sabotage on the part of Reed Harris. Senator Scoop Jackson: "It does seem a little ridiculous to close up the Hebrew desk at a time when the Russians have, for the first time since the Czars, come out on a positive anti-Semitic tone." This was an issue VOA should hit hard, he said, to make the Russians look bad.

Harris testified that the decision on the Hebrew language had been made not by him but by the Program Allocations Board, for budgetary reasons, and that it was later rescinded.

Ignoring Harris's explanation, McCarthy thundered: "If I were a member of the Communist Party and I wanted to protect the international Communist movement from the results of this anti-Semitic program . . . would I not recommend the elimination of the Hebrew language desk at that time?"[41]

McCarthy also brought out that while at Columbia, Harris had written a book on the commercial side of college football, called *King Football*. McCarthy said the book aped the Communist line and that Harris had been suspended from Columbia.

Harris explained that he had been the editor of the *Columbia Spectator*, which he had tried to turn into a crusading newspaper. "We thought we were being very brave," he said. He wrote an editorial on mismanagement in the student dining halls, which were run by the sister of Columbia's president, Nicholas Murray Butler, and that was what caused his suspension. Harris went on to work for the Federal Writers' Project in the *American Guide* series, but resigned in a protest over Communist infiltration. Nonetheless, McCarthy described his testimony as "of a very disturbing nature."[42]

Finding no subversives, McCarthy on February 16 vented his fury on a vivid VOA review of the film *They Drive by Night*, which said, "A big-assed female dish wiggles across the truck's path and the trucker whistles and waves, and for some reason the dames always go for the truckers. The smile goes out, the hand waves."

"Why on God's earth," McCarthy asked, "do you feel justified in paying for this kind of thing? Do you think this describes America?" Joe the compulsive gambler, drinker, and skirt-chaser was transformed into Joe the guardian of morality.

In an open hearing on March 3, McCarthy set up Reed Harris, the IIA deputy administrator, as a scapegoat, even though he now repudiated his book as "too one-sidedly sarcastic, too bitter, too know-it-all." Aside from exposing the underside of college football, Harris had defended the right of Communists to teach in the universities.

Senator Jackson said: "I do not think it is any crime that you expressed very liberal views during the depth of the depression. . . . [Wendell] Willkie did that when he was in college."

When McCarthy questioned Harris, he waved the book on football as if it were a Communist tract.

Harris: "Each time you hold up that book and wave it, you make it sound a little worse."

McCarthy worked himself up to a point where he could hardly speak, saying: "You repeat over and over that you have been cleared to do this job. Now, I am not comparing you to him, but you understand that Alger Hiss was also cleared."

Harris: "Mr. chairman, this is really a fantastic thing to do." McCarthy said he was not comparing him to Hiss and then did just that.[43]

After being mangled on television, Harris resigned on April 14. Not only did McCarthy fail to find any Communists in VOA, he forced the resignation of a man with a strong anti-Communist record. Harris was reinstated in 1961, when Edward R. Murrow became the head of the U.S. Information Agency.

The repercussions of the VOA hearings went beyond changes in policy and employees unfairly forced from their jobs. On March 5, Raymond Kaplan, a forty-two-year-old Voice of America engineer, jumped in front of a truck and was killed near the MIT campus in Cambridge. Kaplan was the liaison man between MIT and the Voice when the sites for the Baker transmitters were chosen. The coroner ruled that he had killed himself out of fear that he would be called before the McCarthy Committee. In a letter he left for his wife and son, he wrote: "I am the patsy in any mistakes made. . . . Once the dogs are set on you, everything you have done since the beginning of time is suspect. . . . I can't take the pressure any more."[44]

His co-workers, however, could not believe his death was a suicide. He had seemed eager to testify and had made a hotel reservation in Washington in case he was held overnight. How could he have been killed by a truck that was going twenty miles an hour, and why had the letter to his wife and son been found on his person in a stamped envelope, unmailed? McCarthy summoned a co-worker, Dorothy Fried, to testify in a closed session on March 10. "It seems impossible," he said, "that a man would commit suicide with that background." Miss Fried replied: "Well, it is my opinion that he exaggerated his own importance in his own mind. He made this California survey [on the location of Baker West] . . . but the decision came from Washington."[45]

A closed hearing on March 10 seemed to have as its only purpose payback against critics of McCarthy. David Cushman Coyle, a contract writer for the Publications Bureau of the State Department, was fired on the day that he appeared before the committee. His crime was not the pamphlets he had written, such as "East Germany Under Soviet Control," but his friendship with Lowell Mellett, who wrote a column called *On the Other Hand* for the Scripps-Howard chain. While relaxing over drinks at their club, Coyle had told Mellett that he had called the police to complain about a neighbor's barking dog, and the police said they could do nothing unless he gave his name. Coyle said the police told him: "We don't want to have all sorts of paranoiacs complaining about their neighbors unless there is really something to it, so we want to have your name."[46]

Mellett saw a way to use Coyle's anecdote in a column called "The Right to Confront Accusers." He imagined someone saying: "What's to prevent [an accuser] turning in a report to my department, saying that a lot of funny things had been going on at my house, with suspicious characters slipping in and out; that they had reason to suspect my loyalty isn't all it should be? So I'd be investigated. Government can't take any chances. And it wouldn't, especially if my neighbors had the forethought to take their cock-and-bull story to Senator McCarthy first and get him into the act."

Questioned by McCarthy, Coyle said: "I have told Mr. Mellett that I didn't approve of the methods used by the McCarthy Committee and I thought he ought to get after it. I think it is an undesirable thing to have a man like Matson [the whistle-blower in the State Department files investigation] to be protected in his job when he has made himself a nuisance to his fellow workers. . . . There is nearly always a neurotic or a paranoiac or some guy that is always being ill-treated, and nothing so stymies an organization as to have the neurotic have a rich uncle." (After Matson testified, he was demoted, but the committee urged that he be returned to his job.)

McCarthy: "We have been informed . . . that one of your principal functions was to give the background and make the contacts to promote attacks upon the effort to expose Communists in the State Department. . . . If that was your function, we intend to get to the bottom of it."

Coyle: "I was fired this morning. . . . Presumably because I had been called by Mr. McCarthy."[47]

On March 24, 25, and 26, the hearings turned to the information centers abroad and the books they used. James Allen (aka Sol Auerbach), the foreign editor of the *Daily Worker,* who had once served as a Comintern agent in the Philippines, was the author of *World Monopoly and Peace,* a book praising the Soviet Union's superiority in all things, which was available in the International Information Administration libraries.

Senator Everett Dirksen of Illinois: "So a student in Bombay goes into the library and he picks up one of your books . . . and he sees, 'the Soviet Union is the only world power which is neither aggressive nor potentially aggressive.' "

When Allen repeatedly took the Fifth, Joe said: "I might say that if you were in a Russian court today and you were asked whether you were an American spy and you said 'I refuse to answer relying on my constitutional privilege,' your life insurance would be awfully high" (laughter).

Earl Browder's book, *Communism in the United States,* was also available in some overseas libraries, and when Browder testified and took the Fifth, Senator Karl Mundt said he was amazed, since Browder "has been in, and ousted, and in, and ousted several times."

Browder: "My life has been disorganized since 1950."

McCarthy: "If you had your way in this country, many lives would be disorganized."

Senator John McClellan of Arkansas: "I suggest you ask the questions without lecturing the witness each time."[48]

The Russian-born William Marx Mandell, who had written four books, such as *Democratic Aspects of the Soviet Government,* some of them available in the libraries, was a particularly truculent witness. "This is a book burning," he said. "You lack only the tinder to set fire to the books as Hitler did years ago." Mandell took the Fifth repeatedly. Hiding behind the provision against self-incrimination tended to invalidate his emphatic defiance. One of Mandell's books was *Soviet Far East and Central Asia.* Dirksen asked him if he had ever been to those areas.

Mandell: "I was not in that area. Einstein was never inside the atom. He seems to be able to understand it." Mandell said his books were in the overseas libraries as a form of "slick propaganda," to give the impression that the United States tolerated a variety of views. Instead of looking into books, the committee should "discover how Sen. McCarthy saved 170,000 bucks on a $15,000 salary," a reference to his tax problems.

McCarthy: "One more Communist calling names means nothing."[49]

On March 26, Langston Hughes, the prominent black poet, sixteen of whose books were available in fifty-one libraries, testified that he had broken with the party. Long ago, he had written some militant poetry such as "Good Morning, Revolution" and "Put Another 'S' in the USA to Make It Soviet."

Roy Cohn noted a recent sketch called "When a Man Sees Red," a satire on HUAC. Hughes explained that "one of the members of the committee called a Negro witness by a very ugly name." People in Harlem called that "playing the dozens," and felt the committee was unfair to Negroes.

McCarthy: "Do you feel that those [early] books should be on our shelves?"

Hughes: "I was certainly amazed to hear that they were."

He said his early work did not represent his current thinking. In his latest book, *Montage of a Dream Deferred,* he had written, "America is young, big, strong, and beautiful, and we are trying very hard to be as the flag says, One Nation, indivisible, with liberty and justice for all."

Joe said he had heard a lot of screaming from witnesses about being mistreated. Had he been mistreated?

Hughes: "I was agreeably surprised at the courtesy and friendliness with which I was received."[50]

On March 27, Bernhard J. Stern, a teacher at Columbia, and the author of seven books available in sixty-three overseas libraries, including *Understanding the Russians,* was called in. When he was asked if he was a member of the Communist Party, he took the Fifth.

Senator Stuart Symington of Missouri asked him if he could think of anything the Kremlin was doing that he disagreed with. He said he couldn't, "right off the bat."[51]

McCarthy: "The witness puts me in mind of a divorce case I tried once as a judge, and the wife was on the stand telling what an awful husband she had. I asked her if she had any faults. She said, 'Yes, I have my faults.' And I said, 'name one.' She said, 'Judge, I can't think of any off hand.' "

Stern: "That is a very clever anecdote, but I am not a divorcee."[52]

The hearings were interrupted in early April 1953, so that Cohn and

Schine could go to Europe and tour overseas libraries to hunt down books by Communist authors. Their much publicized seventeen-day spree turned out to be a public relations disaster.

The tour opened in Paris on April 3, 1953, where Ambassador Douglas Dillon confided to the *New York Times* columnist Cy Sulzberger that the two men had summoned embassy personnel to their hotel, and asked them whether they got enough backing from their ambassador. They seemed bent on digging up dirt on the American embassies in the countries they visited.[53] The joke passed along in the embassies was "see you tomorrow come Cohn or come Schine."

On April 7, the pair arrived in Germany, where they spent nine days. West Germany had been declared a Federal Republic in 1949, but there was still a United States High Commissioner's office, known as HICOG, which ran a large-scale library program to combat the Communist propaganda barrage from East Germany.

The newly appointed High Commissioner, James B. Conant, was not in Germany at the time, so on April 7 in Bonn, Cohn and Schine saw the deputy chief of public relations, Theodore Kaghan, who in his youth had written anti-fascist plays and signed a Communist Party nominating petition. But while serving in Austria from 1947 to 1951, he had shown himself to be a staunch anti-Communist.

Nevertheless, Cohn and Schine zeroed in on Kaghan, who had made the mistake of calling them "junketeering gumshoes." During the meeting, Cohn quizzed Kaghan aggressively on his Communist background and accused him of leaking stories about them to the press and of assigning them a so-called escort who was actually a spy. Kaghan noted that "Cohn doesn't look at you; he looks all around you, as though he wasn't really interested in you."[54]

The next day, in Berlin, Cohn announced that a "top American official" in Germany would be recalled to Washington to testify to the McCarthy committee about his plays. Kaghan told the *Manchester Guardian* on the same day that "I have spent more time superintending anti-Soviet broadcasts, pamphlets, newspapers and news agencies than Sen. McCarthy and his two traveling spies have spent in school."

John J. McCloy, the High Commissioner prior to Conant, from 1949 to 1952, had brought along an associate, his old Wall Street crony Benjamin Buttenweiser. He told McCloy's biographer, Kai Bird, that while Cohn and Schine were in Bonn, HICOG bugged their hotel room, revealing evidence of homosexual conduct, or what Buttenweiser euphemistically called "pillow fights."[55]

In Frankfurt, the *Abend Post* reported playful behavior: "In the hotel lobby, it was observed that Mr. Schine batted Mr. Cohn over the head with a rolled up magazine, then both of them disappeared into Mr. Schine's room. . . . Later their chambermaid found ashtrays and their contents strewn throughout the room. The furniture was completely overturned."

On April 15, Cohn and Schine were in Vienna for a day and a half, which the Socialist newspaper *Arbeiter Zeitung* said was "exactly long enough to receive denunciations." On April 19, they came to London, and were so badly ridiculed in the British press that they stayed only five hours and flew back to New York.

And so ended what seemed like the spring vacation of two rowdy fraternity brothers. Only in Washington were their antics taken seriously. On April 23, Dr. Robert Johnson, the new head of the International Information Administration, announced the dismissal of 830 Voice of America employees, as part of a "retrenchment program," at a savings of $4.3 million.[56] For "retrenchment," you could read, "McCarthy probe."

Brought to Washington from Germany, Theodore Kaghan testified in closed session on April 28. He admitted signing a nominating petition for a leading Communist, Israel Amter, in 1939, because "I thought he had a right to be on the ballot." He had gone to several party meetings because his roommate at the time was a party member, but had not become one himself. At the University of Michigan, he wrote anti-racist plays that followed the party line, from which McCarthy read excerpts.

McCarthy asked him about his phrase "junketeering gumshoes."

Kaghan: "They were going about a very serious business in a very superficial way. . . . They avoided me and then they went up to Berlin and they made a statement to the press that I had Communistic tendencies. . . . By their activity they reflected discredit on this committee and the Senate. . . . The overall situation they created was one of giving the Germans a chance to jump on the United States for doing things which the Germans did not understand."[57]

On April 29, Theodore Kaghan testified in open session. His real sin, he said, was having called Cohn and Schine "junketeering gumshoes." Kaghan added: "We were prepared to give them a complete picture of what we were doing. . . . They didn't come to the briefing." Kaghan said Cohn and Schine had made themselves ridiculous, and "the result was a raft of press comments and cartoons throughout the German press, which . . . cast aspersions on the whole operation of the committee here." As for his youthful flirtation with the party, Kaghan said: "I had a case of political chickenpox, which you are trying to make into an incurable disease."

On May 11, Kaghan resigned, saying: "When you cross swords with Sen.

McCarthy, you cannot expect to remain in the State Department."[58] He became the United Nations correspondent for the *New York Post*.

Although the tarring and feathering of Theodore Kaghan was shameful, and although they left Europe trailing the mockery of the European press, Cohn and Schine did not leave empty-handed. Their sources in Frankfurt told them that in 1945, under the occupation, Allied press control officers had recruited local newsmen to jump-start a democratic German press. The only qualification was that Nazis were banned. Two of these press control officers, one American and one British, had recommended Communist newsmen to the board that licensed the postwar newspapers.

Their names were James Aronson and Cedric Belfrage, and they were brought before the committee in a closed session on May 13. Aronson was a Harvard graduate, radicalized by the Spanish Civil War, who moved ever leftward when he worked for the *New York Post* and the Sunday department of the *New York Times*, until in 1948 he founded the *National Guardian* with his wartime pal Belfrage.[59] The *Guardian* obediently followed the Soviet line and was known as the organ of nonparty Stalinism. Belfrage, who worked for British intelligence in New York during the war, was a Soviet agent mentioned in Venona. He reported what he picked up to the New York office of the KGB. He gave the KGB an OSS report on the Yugoslav partisans that had been passed to the British. He reported the movements of his boss, Sir William Stephenson, known as *Intrepid*.[60]

At the closed hearing, Aronson, who was apparently not a party member, took the Fifth when asked if he was, "on strong principle."

Senator Stuart Symington asked: "If you did not have strong principles, you would say you were not a member of the Communist party?," which was apparently the case.

Cohn said the *National Guardian* was "a magazine under Communist control following the Communist line and having on its staff a considerable number of members of the Communist party." He asked Aronson whether he had made a speech at a Communist rally in the last few weeks saying that he had helped set up German newspapers that followed "the democratic line," but that the State Department was trying to make them "reactionary." Aronson took the Fifth.

When Belfrage was asked if he was a party member, he replied: "Any answer I might give to that would be used only to crucify myself and other innocent persons."[61]

On May 14, when Aronson and Belfrage testified at a public hearing and repeatedly took the Fifth, an immigration agent was in the hearing room, invited by McCarthy. The next day, two immigration agents came to the

Guardian office and arrested Belfrage, who was not a U.S. citizen, on a deportation warrant. He was taken to Ellis Island as a "dangerous alien," then released on appeal, and finally deported in August 1955. Belfrage portrayed himself in books and articles as a victim of persecution, and McCarthy did not live to learn that he had uncovered a Soviet spy and been instrumental in his deportation.[62]

In questioning left-wing figures in the arts, McCarthy went beyond those writers whose books were in overseas libraries. In a closed hearing on May 26, he questioned the composer Aaron Copland on the grounds that he had gone to Italy on a Fulbright professorship in 1951, which had been funded with government money.

"I spend my days writing symphonies, concertos, ballads," Copland protested. "I am not a political thinker." And yet Copland had been unusually generous in allowing his name to be used by a number of Communist fronts. His name appeared on appeals against the deportation of Harry Bridges, on petitions for the dismissal of charges against Smith Act defendants, and on committees for world peace conferences.

Copland came across as the prototype of the absentminded composer when he admitted that he was himself taken aback when a congressman introduced a list of the organizations that had used his name into the *Record.* "I was absolutely amazed at the number of entries in connection with my name," he said.

He then tried to explain that his commitment to the plight of humanity was connected to his artistic impulses as a composer. "I was moved by specific causes," he said, "to which I lent my name. Musicians make music out of feelings aroused out of public events."

Senator Karl Mundt did not see the connection. "I can't follow that line of argument," he said. "I don't see how that line of reasoning makes sense with a hatchet man like Bridges."

Copland: "A musician, when he writes his notes, he makes his music out of emotions and you cannot make your music unless you are moved by events. If I sponsored a committee in relation to Bridges, I may have been misled. . . . There was something about his situation that moved me."

Copland's analysis of the artistic temperament was lost on Senator Mundt, who replied: "When you get to Browder and Bridges, I think musicians have to go by the same code as governs other citizens."[63]

As the hearings proceeded, the State Department sent overseas libraries lists of proscribed books by such authors as Howard Fast, Langston Hughes, Edgar Snow, and Jean-Paul Sartre. John J. McCloy, the former High Commissioner to Germany, who had deliberately included books critical of America in the *Amerika Haus* libraries, in the conviction that diversity of material was the key to their popularity, was informed that librarians in Germany had actually burned some of the forbidden books. On June 14, he went to Dartmouth, where President Eisenhower was giving the commencement address. As Ike was waiting to go on, McCloy told him about the book burnings. "And the value of those books," he said, "was that they were uncensored. They criticized you and me and Dean Acheson and anyone else in government."[64]

Many of Ike's supporters had been urging him to speak out about the censoring of books, and he finally did when he told the graduating class: "Don't join the book-burners. Don't think that you are going to conceal faults by concealing evidence that they ever existed. Don't be afraid to go in your library and read every book as long as any document does not offend our own ideas of decency. That should be the only censorship."

The hearings came to a close in July, without having found any traitors. Although Joe failed to achieve the dismantling of the overseas libraries and the Voice of America, the administration was divided about their future. At a cabinet meeting on July 10, 1953, Charles E. Wilson, the Secretary of Defense, argued that the federal government should not be in the library business. Vice President Nixon saw no reason why Congress should fund general-purpose libraries. John Foster Dulles said it depended on who was in charge. In August, a new agency was formed, separate from the State Department. The United States Information Agency incorporated the overseas libraries and the Voice of America. The main result of the hearings was to erode much of the goodwill that had been created abroad by the libraries. These libraries also loaned records, and Roy Cohn proposed at one point that the music of the fellow-traveling Aaron Copland should be banned. If you were going to ban books, why not ban music as well?

During the course of these 1953 closed hearings, the level of McCarthy's frustration mounted as witness after witness took the Fifth. To refuse to answer a question because it might incriminate you was a formidable defense. There was no way of getting around it, no matter what Joe tried. He started out by lecturing: "You understand that the privilege cannot be taken lightly, it can only be taken if you honestly feel that a truthful answer might tend to incriminate you." Then he threatened: "You are ordered to answer that question. . . . The Committee must decide in each instance whether you have the right to refuse to answer. . . . If you refuse to answer whether you truthfully feel, that you honestly feel, that the truthful answer would incriminate you, you could be held in contempt." Finally, he would try to shame the witness by saying "I personally have respect for the Communist who has enough guts to stand up and say, 'Sure, I am a Communist and here's why I am a Communist.'. . . A frank and honest answer cannot hurt you." This was not quite true, since a frank and honest answer might lead to a loss of employment. But in spite of McCarthy's hectoring tactics, not a single witness who appeared before his subcommittee was imprisoned for perjury, contempt, espionage, or subversion.[65]

As we now know from the Venona transcripts, a number of spies did appear before him in the closed hearings. One was Frank Coe, who testified on June 3 on what was called "the Austrian incident." In 1949, Marshall Plan officials said that the high exchange rate for the Austrian shilling worked against the nation's financial stability and in favor of the Russian occupation forces. Objections to devaluation came from the International Monetary Fund, whose secretary was Virginius Frank Coe.[66]

Frank Coe had been named as a Soviet agent as early as 1939, on the list that Whittaker Chambers turned over to Adolf Berle. During World War II, he was assistant director at the Treasury Department's Division of Monetary Research, which was headed by Harry Dexter White. He was a member of the Silvermaster ring, and was named in 1945 by Elizabeth Bentley. Coe was an agent for the KGB, whose code name *Peak* appears in four deciphered Venona messages. When White was named Director of the International Monetary Fund in 1946, he brought Coe with him. Interviewed by the FBI, Coe denied any part in Soviet espionage or Communism. In 1952, he took the Fifth before a Senate committee and was asked to resign from the IMF, an agency of the United Nations.

McCarthy had first named Coe on October 27, 1952, when he was campaigning against Adlai Stevenson. He said that Stevenson was unfit to serve because Alger Hiss and Frank Coe had recommended him as a delegate to a conference of the Institute of Pacific Relations ten years before. "Why, why," he asked, "do Hiss and Coe find that Adlai Stevenson is the man they want representing them at this conference?" In fact, Stevenson did not attend the conference.

When he testified on June 3, Coe was in the position of having recently lost his job for taking the Fifth. He was going around, like a leper without a bell, looking for work. "I have been out of the country seeking employment," he said. "I have been to Canada, I have been to Mexico, I have been to Cuba and Nassau."

When McCarthy asked him if he had blocked the devaluation of the Austrian shilling, Coe said the objection had come from the Czechoslovakian delegation of the IMF.

On all other questions, such as whether he had known Alger Hiss and Lauchlin Currie, he took the Fifth.[67]

In 1956, Coe emigrated to Communist China and worked for Mao Tse-tung's government as a translator. In 1959 he wrote articles praising Mao's massive purge of the year before as an ideological purification that would help increase economic production.[68]

———

With McCarthy, Eisenhower continued to act, in military terms, by attacks on the flanks. An opportunity to employ this approach arose on June 22, when Joe named J. B. Matthews executive director of his subcommittee. There was enough material in J.B.'s files to launch ten investigations. But on July 3, 1953, the right-wing *American Mercury* came out with an article by Matthews called "Reds and Our Churches," which opened by saying, "The largest single group supporting the Communist apparatus in the United States is composed of Protestant clergymen." Many were the anti-McCarthy sermons in pulpits that Sunday. The Protestant clergy constituted a powerful lobby, and they flooded the Senate with demands for Matthews's departure.

In the White House, as speechwriter Emmet John Hughes recalled, there was a little drama "suggestive of how much in government may have to be achieved by indirection." Deputy Attorney General William Rogers saw the Matthews flap as a chance to curb McCarthy, and assured Hughes that he had Nixon's blessing. As Rogers put it, "With all the Protestants up in arms, even a buddy of McCarthy's like Karl Mundt can hear the Lutherans screaming back in the Midwest." The method was to "encourage" a telegram of protest to the President from the National Conference of Christians and Jews in New York, to which Ike could respond with a strong censure of McCarthy and J.B. But they had to act fast, before Joe realized what a liability Matthews was. Sherman Adams agreed to the plan and Hughes drafted the President's reply.[69]

On July 9, Hughes waited anxiously for the message of protest from New York, which called Matthews's charges "unjustified and deplorable." By the afternoon, Hughes heard rumors that Joe was about to fire Matthews, which would make Ike's reply moot. Rogers called from Nixon's office on the Hill: "For God's sake, we have to get that message out fast or McCarthy will beat us to the draw." Adams approved Hughes's draft and took it in to Ike, as Hughes stood in front of the news ticker in press secretary Hagerty's office waiting for the bulletin on the President's statement. On his way to announce Matthews's resignation, McCarthy stopped by Nixon's office, where Rogers stalled him with questions on his investigation, knowing Joe's tendency to ramble. Finally Joe said, "Gotta rush now—I want to be sure I get [out] the news of dumping Matthews." But Ike had won the race against the clock. His statement asserted that "irresponsible attacks that sweepingly condemn the whole of any group of citizens are alien to America."[70] As White House Special Counsel Bernard Shanley put it in his diary, "this was the first real nail in the McCarthy coffin."[71]

Joe counterattacked by announcing an investigation of the CIA. On July 9, Roy Cohn demanded the appearance before the subcommittee on that day of William Bundy, a CIA analyst who was Groton, Yale, and Harvard Law as well as Dean Acheson's son-in-law. He had contributed $400 to Alger Hiss's defense fund. CIA Director Allen Dulles did not want him to testify, because airing the contribution would give McCarthy the ammunition to smear the CIA. Bundy had to be sent beyond the reach of a subpoena, and Dulles told him to leave at once for his parents' house on Boston's north shore.[72]

On July 10, all the committee members except Everett Dirksen met in Room 347 of the Senate Office Building to discuss the Matthews flap and the Bundy disappearance. Beyond these issues, the committee was in crisis. The staff was quitting, unable to put up with Roy Cohn's abrasive ways. Ruth Young Watt, the chief clerk, later recalled that "everything was in shambles . . . because everybody was at cross-purposes." The three minority members were furious that they had not been consulted on the Matthews appointment. McCarthy, they felt, ran a one-man committee, holding hearings at short notice, when they had other obligations, and forgetting to inform them who the witnesses were. They arrived at the July 10 secret meeting determined to make their voices heard.[73]

"Let me first," McCarthy said, "if I may, give you a report on the meeting with Dulles. . . . I talked to him last night and he suggested holding up calling Bundy . . . and he could come over and give us his views on the case. He [Bundy] contributed to Alger Hiss's defense fund on two different occasions— $200 each. He is not an extremely wealthy man . . . so that would be a very sizable contribution." (One reason for the contribution was that Bundy's father, Harvey, was vice chairman of the Carnegie Endowment for World Peace, where Hiss was employed, and his father had solicited actively for Hiss's defense.)

Bundy was up for a "Q" clearance, and his security file, with the Hiss donations, had been leaked to the subcommittee. On July 9, Cohn had called Walter Pforzheimer, the legislative counsel at the CIA, and said, "He is up for a top security clearance and we wonder whether he should be approved."

McCarthy went on: "Mr. Cohn called the liaison between the CIA and the Senate, Mr. Pforzheimer, and asked to have this man appear. . . . Pforzheimer called back and said Bundy was away on vacation and he didn't know where he was. Roy suggested that it was rather unusual that the CIA would not know where its top operators were. . . . Roy then talked to Allen Dulles and he took the position that no employees of the CIA could appear before any Congressional committee. I thought that was a bit unusual. . . . If they say . . . that calling an employee of the CIA will endanger their operations, I think we should lean over backwards to go along with them . . . but a man who has a record of this kind [Bundy] must appear. Dulles was down in my office this morning and I asked him how it would endanger his operations if Bundy were called. He made no claims at all that we were going to endanger his operations. He took the position that we should not call any of his people. He said, 'Well, other intelligence agencies in the world would know we were calling his men.' We pointed out to him how ridiculous his stand was, how ridiculous I thought it was."[74]

Symington: "I don't think anybody has the right, except the president, to refuse to testify before a Congressional committee. Possibly the Supreme Court. . . . But here is the problem you have got with respect to Bundy—I have heard he is a Republican [he was a liberal Democrat]—Hiss has fooled an awful lot of people. His lawyer for the first part of the trial . . . John Foster Dulles. . . . There were lots of people fooled by Hiss and this boy might have been fooled by him too. . . . Many good Republicans were fooled by Hiss."

McCarthy: "Bundy, according to Dulles, only met Hiss once and he is not a wealthy man and $400 is a lot of money."

McClellan: "Maybe he took up a collection."

Jackson: "Was he a classmate of his at Harvard?"

Mundt: "I understand Bundy was a member of Acheson's firm."

Jackson: "I assume Mr. Dulles is going to talk to the president . . . to know what the policy of the administration is going to be regarding calling of witnesses."

Mundt: "It might be better to can everybody in the past administration."

McClellan: "This is a pretty sensitive thing. . . . We should proceed with the utmost caution. . . . They are gunning for you [McCarthy] and shooting at you every chance they get, so keep it a committee action. Have him [Dulles] come here and sit down and talk to us."

McCarthy: "I gathered in talking to Dulles this morning the thing he resented most is that he hadn't been approached directly."

Symington: "Well, we didn't know anything about it except from the newspapers. . . . It is a little embarrassing to have a newspaper man call you up and say we are going to interrogate Bundy. . . . Isn't there some way we could be apprised in advance?"

Jackson: "We didn't have the name. I asked who was coming up."

Cohn: "On these authors, we subpoena maybe 50 and five show up."

McClellan: "The point is, Roy . . . can't you arrange an appointment for a day in advance?"

Cohn: "This . . . was a very emergency situation."

Then, out of the blue, McCarthy asked for the authority to hire and fire staff. "The Matthews thing was unfortunate," he said. The Democratic members of the committee had put out a statement. "Maybe it was a political move and you had to do it," McCarthy said.

Symington: "I think it is pretty obvious we had to do it pretty quick."

McCarthy: "I hope the committee will give me authority to employ and discharge employees."

McClellan: "Set a meeting one day next week . . . and we will go into it. . . . We are entitled to have some members of the staff assigned to us as a minority group and this committee moves so darn fast. . . . I have got to have somebody . . . to help us."

McCarthy: "I have no objection to assigning a staff member to the minority."

Mundt: "I don't like to see you pick on Joe and pull the rug from under him, but I shall certainly vote to let you fellows have part of the staff. Hoey did turn it down." (Clyde R. Hoey, the North Carolina Democrat who had chaired the subcommittee from 1949 to 1952, in the Truman years, had declined to give the Republican minority a staff member.)

McCarthy: "If the minority wants somebody, they should have somebody."

McClellan: "You know the work load here is two or three times as heavy as under Hoey."[75]

Symington: "I want to find a fellow who thinks senators don't work hard after six months of this."

McCarthy returned to having the authority to hire and fire. The Democrats did not want to give it to him after the fallout over Matthews, and McClellan repeated that they should set up a meeting to discuss it.

"I have the press waiting out here," McCarthy insisted. "Other committees have given the chairman the right."

Symington said Joe was forcing the issue after having been pressured to fire Matthews: "I only said I would like to see Mr. Matthews leave the committee. . . . I expressed dissatisfaction with one member . . . and you are building a very broad issue out of it."

McCarthy: "I have no thought or desire to take any arbitrary action in employing or discharging. [But] I can't operate if each time I hire or discharge someone I have to round up several members."

This was a specious argument, since hirings and firings did not take place that often and other members could be paged and reached by phone. McCarthy had created a furor with his poor choice of Matthews, and in spite of that he was claiming the right to hire and fire, which only reinforced the conviction of the minority that he was running a one-man committee.

Symington pointed out that Joe had hired Matthews without the approval of the full committee. He did not want Joe to hire whomever he wanted.

Mundt said they had to hire a new staff director now that Matthews was gone and added, "I think the chairman should choose him."

Symington said it should be subject to the approval of the committee.

Mundt: "I don't want to vote on every staff member."

Symington said it was like the president of a company who had to be accountable to his board of directors.

Mundt then moved a resolution that the chairman should have the right to hire and fire staff, and that the chairman should assign a staff member to the minority.

Symington: "If another Matthews comes up and writes another article, I want the right to oppose it."

Digging in his heels, and knowing that he had the majority on his side and Everett Dirksen's proxy in his pocket, McCarthy said: "I intend to have a vote before I leave today. I have taken too much kicking around."

They voted on Mundt's motion along party lines, 4 to 3, including Dirksen's proxy.

Then McCarthy said that Matthews, who felt he had been smeared in the press, wanted to appear before the subcommittee to defend himself.

McClellan said that bringing him in would inevitably lead to an investigation of the clergy.

Mundt agreed that it would be "in extremely bad taste," and Potter concurred.

"The last thing I am going to do is investigate the clergy," McCarthy said.

It was agreed that Matthews would not appear and the meeting adjourned. Frank Carr, the head of FBI Subversive Activities in New York, was named to replace Matthews.[76]

The three Democrats, in protest over McCarthy's peremptory takeover of hiring and firing, decided to boycott committee hearings, which they did for the rest of the year. This dramatic move brought further opprobrium upon McCarthy's head. The Democrats in the Senate viewed the boycott as a proof of his misconduct. Senator Burnet R. Maybank, an influential member of the Southern bloc, said there was no "place in our government for domineering one-man rule regardless of political affiliation." In the *New York Times*, William S. White wrote: "To boycott one's fellow senator is about as grave a step as can be imagined. To lose face in the club that is the Senate is, sometimes, actually to lose all."[77]

Allen Dulles went to the Hill on July 10 and met with the Republican members of McCarthy's subcommittee, the three Democrats having staged a walkout over the Matthews flap. Dulles said, "Joe, you're not going to have Bundy as a witness." He took the position that if CIA men were forced to testify, their sources of information would dry up. Later, John Foster Dulles called his brother and asked how he had come out. Allen said it was something of a draw. He did not make any statement to the subcommittee, but McCarthy was in an ugly mood, having been slapped down pretty hard when Bundy failed to appear. The general tenor was that the CIA was neither sacrosanct nor immune from investigation.[78]

Nixon then brokered an agreement between Allen Dulles and McCarthy. If Joe promised not to summon any CIA personnel, the CIA Director would order an internal review of Bundy. Joe asked, "But what about his contribution to Hiss?" Nixon replied, "Joe, you have to understand how those people in Cambridge think. Bundy graduated from the Harvard Law School, and Hiss was one of its most famous graduates. I think he probably just got on the bandwagon without giving any thought to where the bandwagon was heading." With Nixon's help, the CIA stonewalled McCarthy. It was another crack in his veneer of impregnability.[79]

Unperturbed by the departure of its three Democrats, McCarthy's truncated subcommittee continued its investigations during the Washington summer, when most senators were back home mending fences. In mid-August 1953, he conducted a brief open hearing that was probably the high point of his investigative career, for he actually found a security risk. The Government Printing Office had 7,300 employees, some of whom handled classified material. The FBI had a file on one of the binders, Edward Rothschild, who had been charged during the war with stealing classified data and trying to organize a Communist cell within the Government Printing Office. His wife was also in the party. The FBI gave the GPO loyalty board the names of forty informants prepared to testify against Rothschild, but none were called and he was cleared. The FBI continued to provide evidence in 1951, but in 1953 Rothschild was again cleared.[80]

The hearings opened on August 17 in Room 318 of the Senate Office Building, when Mary Stalcup Markward, who had been undercover six years for the FBI, testified that she had known Esther Rothschild as a Communist in a white-collar cell, the Thomas Jefferson Club.

James B. Phillips, a bindery operator, said the classified material was kept in a safe and you had to be cleared to handle it. He had seen Bertha Lomax, a stitching machine operator, put classified material in the pocket of her dress. Phillips reported her and she was fired.

On August 18, Phillips resumed his testimony. This time he said that Edward Rothschild had invited him to a cell meeting, to which he had gone once, but not again.

Charged with stealing a Merchant Marine codebook during the war, Rothschild took the Fifth. Joe had his wife's party card, evidently obtained from the FBI. She too took the Fifth. McCarthy told the Rothschilds: "Your refusal is telling the world that you have been selling secrets and that you have been engaged in espionage."

Another witness, Cleta Guess, who had sat next to Rothschild at the GPO plant during the war, recalled that he would sit behind his big machine reading the *Daily Worker*. "If someone came, he'd fold it up and put it in his left back pocket. One night, you could see part of the name of the paper sticking out and I was laughing up my sleeve."

"There was one book that had an aircraft diagram that Eddie was interested in," Cleta Guess went on. "I saw him on a few occasions put a pamphlet in his right pocket." To show how lax security was, "I took several things home so we could establish that you could take them out. They never looked in your purse. You can pin anything down to your dress. . . . I remember a secret code for the U.S. Merchant Marine" that Rothschild had. "I had a cousin in the convoys. . . . Going to Russia with provisions. . . . I thought to myself, if this goes to the enemy poor Johnny might be blown up." She went to the FBI, but Rothschild was cleared.[81]

After the hearings, Rothschild was suspended without pay and later removed, ending a career of more than twenty years with the Government Printing Office. Whenever McCarthy's foes claimed that he had never found a security risk, he could point to Edward Rothschild.

———

In mid-July 1953, Senator McCarthy asked General Miles Reber, chief of Army Legislative Liaison, to try to get a direct commission for Schine on the basis of his education and prior service in the Merchant Marine, for Schine was about to be drafted. On July 15, Schine called General Reber's office and asked if he could drop by the Pentagon that afternoon and "hold up my hand." He was told to submit an application for a commission and came by to fill it out, saying he was in a great hurry and wanted to be sworn in right away. He was sent to the Pentagon dispensary for a physical. On July 23, his application was rejected as "not qualified."[82]

On August 5, 1953, the FBI liaison agent Sam Papich went to see General Walter Bedell Smith, now an assistant secretary of state, on one of his regular visits. Smith mentioned the various headaches he was having in the department. He had been visited on several occasions by Roy Cohn, who had advised Smith that his "running mate," David Schine, had recently been classified 1-A, and that Cohn and Senator McCarthy were very much interested in obtaining a commission for Schine in the armed services. According to the FBI account of the meeting, "Cohn asked General Smith if he could intercede with his contacts in the Army in order that a commission could be obtained without Schine being involved in any basic training. General Smith stated that he informed Cohn that this would be almost impossible to do. He stated that Cohn's request was very unusual and . . . that Senator McCarthy could be placed in an embarrassing spot if news ever leaked out that the Senator and Cohn were endeavoring to obtain special privileges for Schine. According to General Smith, Cohn was not at all impressed by the General's comments and inquired what the possibilities would be of arranging a position for Schine in the CIA." Cohn added that he was "not enthusiastic" about placing Schine there, "because Senator McCarthy had found the CIA to be a very 'juicy' target and the Senator would not want to be left in the position where he would be obligated to Allen Dulles." Smith said that "if Cohn so desired, he would approach Allen Dulles . . . who would not be particularly cooperative in view of the recent conflicts with McCarthy." Smith pointed out that Dulles "has a son who was seriously wounded in Korea last year and it was very doubtful that Dulles would try to arrange a position for Schine in order that he could avoid military service."[83]

—

On September 29, 1953, at St. Matthew's Cathedral in Washington, forty-five-year-old Joseph McCarthy married his assistant, twenty-nine-year-old Jean Kerr, tall, auburn-haired, and as beautiful as she was stubborn and tough-minded. Gone was the confirmed bachelor, always on the go, shooting craps till dawn, with a bottle in his briefcase, sleeping in rumpled clothes. Here was a new Joe, freshly shaven, in striped pants and morning coat, walking down the aisle of the cathedral and taking communion at the nuptial mass as Washington's political elite looked on. Vice President Nixon and his wife, Pat, were there, as were Allen Dulles, Sherman Adams, Secretary of the Army Robert Stevens, and a herd of congressmen from both sides of the aisle, including John F. Kennedy. Nine hundred well-wishers crammed into the cathedral, and 3,500 more waited outside, as if for a matinee idol at the premiere of his movie. Among the cabled congratulations came one from Pope Pius in the Vatican, conveying his "paternal and apostolic" blessings. Cheers greeted the newlyweds as they emerged on the steps of the cathedral and ducked into a waiting limousine under showers of rice.[84]

Gossips whispered that Joe had gotten married to stifle rumors that he was a homosexual. Drew Pearson was said to have a drawerful of affidavits to that effect, but he had not published anything. Joe had made an even feistier enemy in Las Vegas during the 1952 campaign when he called the contentious publisher of the *Sun*, Hank Greenspun, an ex-Communist and an Army deserter. Greenspun paid him back by running articles that Joe was gay. "It is common talk among homosexuals in Milwaukee who rendezvous at the White Horse Inn," one of them read, "that Sen. Joe McCarthy has often engaged in homosexual activities."[85]

In June 1953, William Evjue of the *Capital Times* in Madison wrote Drew Pearson that the homosexual issue was bothering Joe. Evjue had heard from Herman Edelsberg, director of the Anti-Defamation League, whom Joe had met at the Carroll Arms Hotel, that "McCarthy opened up the discussion of the thing that was troubling him. . . . It was the homo story that was printed by . . . Hank Greenspun. . . . McCarthy asked Edelsberg if he thought it would be advisable to start a criminal libel suit against Greenspun. . . . Edelsberg pointed out that McCarthy would be compelled to take the witness stand and to refute the charges made in the affidavit of the young man, which was the basis for Greenspun's story." McCarthy decided that suing would do more damage to his reputation than not suing, because of the attendant publicity.[86] William Benton, who although out of the Senate continued to plot McCarthy's downfall and was prepared to use almost anything against him, wrote his assistant John Howe that he thought the charge of homosexuality was "phony."[87]

———

Prior to his honeymoon, McCarthy had launched closed hearings on Communist infiltration among Army civilian workers. The Army was his preferred target after the State Department, perhaps because he had been humbled in 1949 at the Malmédy hearings.

On September 2, with the usual hyperbole, he told reporters that he had uncovered two civilian employees in the Quartermaster Corps whose jobs enabled them to keep track of troop movements to Korea. "If the picture continues to develop," he said, "it would appear to be a very serious threat to military security."[88]

One of the employees was Doris Walters Powell, a black woman on maternity leave who worked as a procurement clerk, processing accounts for the food that was sent to Army camps. When she testified in closed session on August 31, she said she had worked on a Harlem newspaper, *The People's Voice*, which had been taken over by the black Communist leader Doxey Wilkerson, but that she did not think of herself as a Communist. She was only a secretary.

McCarthy: "I know you are not as dumb as you are trying to make out."

Powell: "I received a card—something I had to get into a meeting with Wilkerson. . . . I got very unpopular when I found out it was a Communist organization. . . . I wanted to get the paper for the benefit of the Negro people . . . and this group were found to be Communists." Following her testimony, Doris Walters Powell was suspended by the Quartermaster Corps and eventually let go.[89]

On September 1, Captain Donald Joseph Kotch, a security officer in the Quartermaster Corps, was ordered by McCarthy to produce the loyalty file of Doris Walters Powell, which he refused to do. Under Truman's 1948 order, still enforced under Eisenhower, the loyalty and security files of government employees could not be released to congressional committees.

Kotch said Powell did not have access to any classified files. McCarthy kept insisting that knowledge of food shipments would tell you about troop movements.[90]

Another Quartermaster Corps officer, Colonel Ralph M. Bauknight, was questioned by David Schine, still listed as "chief consultant." Bauknight said of Powell: "I can't believe this employee could possibly apply the ration factor and determine strength." To say that Powell knew about food shipments to Korea was "verging on the impossible." From New York, the food was not sent abroad but to ports of embarkation. In addition, Bauknight said, "All classified material is under lock and key."

Schine: "You think a Communist could be of value to the party at the procurement end?"

Bauknight: "I don't understand what contribution a Communist could render by knowing procurement information."

McCarthy then leaked false information to the press that Powell had had access to classified material for three years.[91] After newspapers repeated his allegations, Powell lost her job.

On September 2, when Colonel Wendell G. Johnson, head of Military Intelligence with the First Army on Governor's Island, stonewalled McCarthy on the loyalty files, Joe lost his temper: "The case is such a flagrant one," he said, "that whoever cleared her was either incompetent beyond words, abysmally incompetent, or he was of the same stripe that she is. . . . We will order you to produce the names of those who cleared her. I am getting awfully sick of the stalling around I have had in the last few days. This is the case of a Communist working on and handling secret material."[92]

McCarthy also used the closed hearings on Army civilian workers to conduct one of his vendetta performances. The target this time was his sparring partner Drew Pearson, whom he wanted to catch receiving classified information. He discovered that an official on the Munitions Board, H. Donald Murray, had leaked information to one of Pearson's legmen, Fred Blumenthal. When Murray testified on September 8, he explained that his boss, John D. Small, the chairman of the Munitions Board, was upset over a Pearson column that said the board was bogged down. Small asked Murray to have a talk with Pearson and "get him off his neck." Murray saw Blumenthal and asked him to stop publishing half-truths. Thereafter, Blumenthal saw Murray regularly to get leads on stories and check facts.

McCarthy charged that Murray was being blackmailed by Blumenthal, who threatened to run a false story so that Murray would give him the correct story as the lesser of two evils. Murray denied it, and there the matter rested, for there was no open hearing. McCarthy told the press that a former employee of the War Munitions Board had given secret information on tanks and planes and weapons to an associate of Drew Pearson's, Frederick G. Blumenthal.[93]

Pearson was concerned enough to mention in his diary for October 24 that he planned to write his editors and sponsors to be prepared for possible Justice Department action. This was a war of nerves, he said. The rumors had been spreading since Walter Winchell had mentioned Murray in a broadcast. But he felt he could weather the storm for publishing restricted information. He looked up the columns "McCarthy has been yelling about," which had to do with General MacArthur's poor intelligence during the Korean War retreat in 1950, as well as "the column on tank turrets, which came from Don Murray, Jack Small's assistant in the Munitions Board. Frankly, I don't think that a jury would ever take action on those."[94]

McCarthy's probe of Army employees created ripples that reached up to Secretary of the Army Robert Ten Broeck Stevens, the product of Andover and Yale, who had inherited his father's prosperous textile business. Tall and affable, with gray hair combed straight back and a ruddy complexion, he usually wore double-breasted gray flannel suits. He had served as an officer in World War II and had been an early backer of Eisenhower. Stevens was a mild and reasonable man who believed in accommodation; pitting him against Joe was like throwing a goldfish in the same pond as a barracuda.[95]

On September 17, 1953, Stevens told Fred Seaton, an assistant secretary of defense, "I still continue to have my fingers crossed. . . . I agreed to give him the names in that one case. I refused on the loyalty files. . . . I feel at the moment that Joe is very strong for the Army. . . . I think we are getting along well with Joe. I don't know how long it will last." Stevens named a special liaison officer to handle McCarthy, John G. Adams, a lawyer from South Dakota who had served in Europe as an Army officer during the war, a likable fellow with a sense of humor.[96]

On September 9, Deputy Attorney General William Rogers called Stevens to ask: "How are you getting along with Jumping Joe?"

Stevens: "I am not the kind of a fellow to go around borrowing trouble. I am perfectly willing to give way on small things, but when it comes to Executive Orders of the president, we are going to stand tightly."

Rogers: "I think half of the battle is to have a good relationship with him."[97]

In the ongoing Army hearings, McCarthy had fastened on a pamphlet called *Psychological and Cultural Traits of Soviet Siberia,* charging that Military Intelligence (G-2) had distributed this "clearcut" Communist propaganda to thirty-seven commands in 1952. General Richard C. Partridge, the head of G-2, testified on September 21, 1953, but seemed woefully unprepared. Partridge said the pamphlet was "a good, honest attempt."

McCarthy: "Do you know that this book quotes from Joe Stalin or not."

Partridge: "I don't know that it quotes from Joe Stalin or not."

McCarthy: "Don't you think you are incompetent to testify? . . . I don't want someone here who knows nothing about this document and just giving us conversation."[98]

Bob Stevens attended the hearing and saw one of his general officers get bulldozed. General Partridge was soon reassigned to an obscure post in Europe.

Another target of the Army hearings was Fort Monmouth, the Signal Corps facility in New Jersey. This sprawling two-thousand-acre base with about 9,600 military and 7,500 civilian employees included the top secret Evans Signal Laboratory, a research center for radar (radio detecting and ranging), an advanced World War II weapon for locating hostile targets. It was the investigation of subversives at Monmouth that brought Joe back from his honeymoon in October 1953.

The commander at Fort Monmouth, General Kirke Lawton, was secretly passing information to McCarthy about suspected Communists, but officially he was under orders not to let anyone at Monmouth talk to the subcommittee. On October 2, Roy Cohn and another of Joe's investigators, the portly and cherub-faced Frank Carr, met with Stevens in his Pentagon office to discuss the Monmouth blackout order. Always obliging, Stevens picked up the phone in front of them and called General Lawton to say: "I authorize you to give permission. . . . Make people available. . . . I do not want to put any strings on that. But don't show them the files."

Lawton: "Now I am clear."[99]

By October 12, McCarthy was back, presiding over five days of closed hearings in New York's federal building. He questioned about twenty-five former and current civilian employees at Fort Monmouth, many of whom repeatedly took the Fifth. General Lawton suspended those who still worked there and invoked the privilege. McCarthy announced the suspensions as they occurred. He told the press that he had uncovered a trail of "extremely dangerous espionage," which dealt with "our entire defense against atomic attack."[100]

On October 14, Aaron H. Coleman, who had been suspended prior to testifying, said that he was a radar specialist who had worked at Monmouth for fifteen years, with an interruption of two years in the Marine Corps during the war. In 1946, upon returning to Monmouth, he had taken home classified documents to catch up and been suspended for two weeks for "carelessness in the custodianship of documents."

"Do you know," McCarthy asked, "that some of these secret documents are missing and have shown up in East Berlin in the Russian laboratories?"

Coleman had known Julius Rosenberg at City College. In 1938, he said, Rosenberg had taken him to a meeting of the Young Communist League, saying that he should not have a closed mind. He left after an hour and a half, he said, after telling Rosenberg, "this isn't a democratic organization." "I was convinced the Communist Party was dominated by Moscow," Coleman said.[101]

As for the documents in East Berlin, it turned out that a twenty-three-year-old defector who had worked in the Pirma lab in East Germany as a mechanic had claimed, once he reached the West, that he had seen microfilms of blueprints that came from the Evans lab at Monmouth. An Air Force investigation concluded that the defector's information was unreliable and that the microfilmed documents had been turned over to the Soviets under wartime lend-lease, when Soviet representatives were stationed at Fort Monmouth and had access to classified documents. Undeterred, McCarthy announced that he was sending an investigator to Germany to interview the defector.[102]

After the session with Coleman, McCarthy told the press that the recently executed Rosenberg had formed a Communist spy ring at Monmouth while working there as a technician in 1942 and 1943. "An ex-Marine officer," he said, "may have been the direct link between the laboratories and the Rosenberg spy ring." But the only crime McCarthy could charge Coleman with was attending a Communist Youth League meeting, and in 1958 he was reinstated at Fort Monmouth.[103]

A glaring example of the way Joe twisted the evidence that came out at closed hearings was his statement to the press on October 16 that "the most important development" of the Monmouth hearings had just taken place. McCarthy said that a witness had broken down and cried after "some rather vigorous cross-examination by Roy Cohn. I have just received word that the witness admits that he was lying and now wants to tell the truth."

The witness was Carl Greenblum, an electronics engineer at the Evans lab. "I am very sorry that we had to call you," McCarthy told him on the morning of the 16th, "I understand that your mother died just a couple of days ago. . . . A matter of considerable importance came up . . . and we decided we had no choice."

McCarthy asked Greenblum if he had been in a car pool with Julius Rosenberg during the war. Greenblum said he didn't recall, adding: "Rosenberg was somebody who I just did not like the looks of." They had been in Signal Corps class together, but "I never had anything to do with him." Greenblum mentioned another Monmouth employee, Joseph Levitsky, as "a radical" who had known Rosenberg.

McCarthy, a few moments before so solicitous, now thundered at Greenblum: "I don't know whether Joseph Levitsky is lying or you are" about the car pool. "One of you is. I am referring this to the Attorney General . . . to determine who the perjurer is and have him indicted."

Greenblum, already shaky, began to weep. "Don't be upset about it," Cohn told him, "and don't be nervous about it. . . . You have had a tragedy in your family. . . . Why don't you go out and have lunch and think the whole thing over . . . and come in after lunch?"

McCarthy: "Suppose you come back at three this afternoon. . . . Will someone show the young man to the door?"[104]

It was during the lunch break that McCarthy spoke to the press. When Greenblum returned in the afternoon, he said: "I am all right now. . . . I want to start afresh. . . . I want to explain the circumstances of coming here and trying to hide an association with Levitsky, whom I know to be a Communist . . . because he told me he was a Communist." He said Rosenberg was friends with Levitsky. When they discussed the Rosenberg case in 1951, Greenblum said, Levitsky told him: "There but for the grace of God go I." After the hearing, Joe told reporters that a witness had been heard to remark: "I was in the Rosenberg ring and but for the grace of God there go I." Levitsky, who had been fired from Monmouth, testified on October 17. He took the Fifth and refused to identify the people in the car pool. Joe said he would be cited for contempt. Greenblum was fired and someone painted a hammer and sickle on the side of his house. In 1958, a federal district court ordered him reinstated.[105]

As part of his "get along with Joe" campaign, Stevens organized a trip to Monmouth on October 20. In a phone call to J. Edgar Hoover on October 19, he said: "I am going up tomorrow to Monmouth with McCarthy. . . . I think perhaps he is willing to turn this [investigation] back to the Army so that . . . we can follow it from here on in."

Hoover: "Naturally they are interested in publicity, and sometimes that comes a little faster than the facts do. I think it required a great deal of patience. You ought to be qualified to become ambassador someplace."[106]

The visit to Monmouth was uneventful, except that when they got to the Evans lab, which required security clearance, Stevens ruled that elected officials could join him, while Roy Cohn had to wait outside with John Adams. Feeling humiliated, Cohn paced up and down, saying, "This is war! . . . They let Communists come in and kept me out!" At lunch, Stevens apologized.

Schine did not go to Monmouth, and the next day, Stevens called him to say, "I am sorry I missed you yesterday."

Schine: "I was all set to go and the pilot told me at the last minute that the fog wouldn't permit the plane to take off."

Stevens said he had reviewed Schine's case with Secretary of Defense Charles Wilson "and it adds up to this: Neither he nor I can see an appropriate way to avoid the basic training. . . . It is my honest conviction that that is the wise thing to do, Dave, and then there is an excellent chance that we can pick you up and use you."

Schine: "I certainly am happy to know that you are both thinking about it. . . . We will probably have to talk this over at greater length sometime."[107]

In mid-October, McCarthy and Adams were riding uptown on the subway after the hearings, and Adams was surprised to hear Joe griping about Schine, whom he said was of absolutely no help to the committee, and only interested in getting his picture in the papers. It had reached the point where he was a complete pest. Joe said he was anxious to see him drafted and hoped that nothing would interfere. "Send him wherever you can, as far away as possible," he said. "Korea is too close." Joe asked Adams not to repeat what he had just said to Cohn.[108]

On October 27, Schine was about to be drafted and sent to Fort Dix for basic training. Cohn called Stevens and said, "On our young friend . . . it will be next Tuesday. We would like him around for awhile . . . he could be furloughed for a couple of weeks. And I am thinking of this CIA thing again—have you given it any further thought? . . . I talked to Joe and I talked to Dave, and they would be willing. The question is, could the people over there pick him up right away?"

Stevens: "Do you want me to talk to Allen Dulles?"

Cohn: "I would appreciate that. . . . Tell him we have this problem here, and how does it fit over in their place?"[109]

Schine was inducted on November 3 and Stevens gave him fifteen days to conclude "important committee work." But when the press got wind of it, the temporary duty in New York was canceled and he actually got on a bus from 39 Whitehall Street on November 10, 1953, arriving at the reception station at Fort Dix that evening.

McCarthy was still demanding the loyalty files of the Monmouth suspects, thirty-three of whom General Lawton had suspended by late October. Stevens gave Adams the folders of the thirty-three and asked him to evaluate them. Adams reviewed the cases and eventually had twenty-five reinstated. On October 28, Fred Seaton called Stevens and said: "On Joe's request for those loyalty records . . . that now does become a matter of principle."

Stevens: "I am just going to tell Joe no in a nice way. . . . I am working well with McCarthy and I will say yes to stuff that makes sense and no to what does not. . . . We may have to go up to [Defense Secretary] Wilson, and he may go on up to the president. . . . I have had this out with Joe since I started on the job. . . . Joe does not have too many friends in the administration, so the fact that I am going to turn him down will not upset the relationship."

Seaton: "I think you have done a magnificent job."

Stevens, much of whose time was absorbed in appeasing Joe, said: "I am disappointed I haven't got him off our back now."[110]

According to Adams, McCarthy for the first time joined with Cohn in urging Stevens to give Schine a New York assignment. He proposed "we assign Schine" to study pro-Red leanings in West Point textbooks. Stevens said he could arrange for Dave to complete his committee work over the weekends and after training hours.

Joe said this would be satisfactory, but under no circumstances "would there be a whitewash of the Army situation."[111]

It was becoming evident that the Monmouth hearings, despite Joe's repeated claims of espionage, were coming up empty, and yet he doggedly kept calling witness after witness, to little effect. On November 4, outside the hearing room, the admittedly Communist lawyer Victor Rabinowitz started chatting with a young woman about to testify, who said that she did not have a lawyer. Rabinowitz, who was there on behalf of another witness, offered to represent her as well. Her name was Sylvia Berke and she had worked for the Signal Corps in 1943. In 1946 and 1947 she had joined the party when she worked for the Distributive Processive Workers of America, a Communist-controlled union. She was now a clerk at a public school in the Bronx.[112]

Sylvia Berke told Rabinowitz that she planned to take the Fifth, even though it would mean losing her job at the school. Rabinowitz said he would appeal to McCarthy's sympathy for a mother raising a small child and separated from her husband. He waited for Joe to come out of the elevator. With his customary geniality, McCarthy threw his arm around Rabinowitz and said "Hello Vic! What can I do for you?" Rabinowitz asked if Sylvia could be excused. It was unnecessarily cruel, he said, to deprive a woman in her circumstances of her profession.

"It's all right with me," McCarthy said, "but you'd better take it up with Roy." Cohn, who was standing ten feet away, blurted out: "Nonsense. We can't withdraw the subpoena. This woman possesses a great deal of information concerning subversive activity at the Signal Corps. She's one of the most important witnesses in this investigation."[113] Sylvia Berke took the Fifth, though she said she was no longer a party member.

On November 9, an article in the *Washington Post* said, "Nothing . . . indicates that there is any known evidence to support a conclusion" of espionage in the Monmouth hearings. This story had been leaked by Adams, and was based on the cases he had studied describing past associations. At a press conference on November 13, Stevens confirmed that the Army had been "unable to find anything resembling current espionage at Fort Monmouth." The *New York Times* headline said: "Stevens: No Spies at Monmouth."

On November 17, 1953, Stevens and Adams invited McCarthy, Cohn, and Carr to lunch at the Merchants Club in lower Manhattan. After downing a double Manhattan, Joe accused Stevens of "calling me a liar before the whole country." He then ordered another double. Stevens said he had been misquoted and suggested that Joe should investigate the Air Force and the Navy instead of the Army.[114]

McCarthy's public hearings, based on evidence collected in the closed hearings, "Army Signal Corps: Subversion and Espionage," opened on November 24 in Washington, because in New York there was a newspaper strike. As the only senator in attendance (the other Republicans claiming other priorities), Joe was unrestrained, asking such questions as "What have you got against this country?" and "Do you think that if Rosenberg was properly executed, you deserve the same fate?" There were ten public hearings until the end of the year, and five more in February and March 1954. Of the thirty-four witnesses, twenty-five took the Fifth on Communist connections, but there was no sign of espionage.

Stevens had another matter on his mind. He had heard disturbing reports on General Lawton, the commander at Monmouth. Lawton had given some restricted lectures at the post theater. In one, he had said that many of the military who violated regulations were graduates of City College, Columbia,

MIT, Harvard, and the University of Wisconsin. The implication was that these colleges tended to indoctrinate students with leftist ideas. In other lectures, he had endorsed McCarthy's investigation and said that all those who took the Fifth were Communists.

Stevens told Adams that he wanted to transfer Lawton out of Monmouth. "He is apparently so much in the good graces of Joe that if we should remove him, Joe wouldn't like that. . . . I want to put somebody new on it."

Adams: "Where are we going to put all these generals?"

Stevens: "What do you mean?"

Adams: "We take Lawton and we take Partridge."

Stevens: "Anybody who is incompetent is going to be replaced and I don't give a damn whether we have a place for him or not. . . . If what I have heard turns out to be true, I am going to relieve him immediately."

On November 25, Adams told Stevens that he'd talked to McCarthy about firing Lawton "and they think it would be interpreted as a direct slap." Joe wanted Stevens to hold off.

Stevens: "I will try to hold off."

Adams: "About the colleges—Joe says unfortunately that happens to be true."

Stevens: "It is not up to any army officer to make a speech of that kind."

Lawton stayed on, but was denied promotion.[115]

The only Army officer who spoke out against the Monmouth hearings was retired Brigadier General Telford Taylor, who had been chief Allied prosecutor at the Nuremberg war crime trials and was now in private practice. On November 27, he spoke to the West Point Debate Council and Forum and denounced the probe as a "shameful abuse of Congressional investigative power" that posed a threat "to the morale and efficiency of the Army." In a dig at Secretary Stevens, he observed that the German officer corps had been destroyed because it took up "false notions of playing politics with demagogues."

McCarthy responded on December 5 with a leaked copy of Taylor's confidential civil service form, which carried the notation "unresolved question of loyalty." Joe demanded to know who had invited Taylor to address West Point cadets and announced that he would subpoena Taylor. On December 8, however, McCarthy held a closed hearing on "The Case of Telford Taylor" at which Taylor did not testify. The witness was Philip Young, Chairman of the Civil Service Commission.

"Last week," McCarthy said, "I commented upon a man, Telford Taylor, who is not with the government. . . . I pointed out that I have long had information that his loyalty files had been flagged. . . . Nevertheless, someone at

West Point called this man over to indoctrinate or speak to the cadets." Joe asked Young if he had checked Taylor's file. Young said it was flagged for loyalty, which was "purely a warning notice. The flag itself may not mean the individual was disloyal."[116]

Soldiers in their first four weeks of basic training at Fort Dix were not given weekend passes, except in an emergency. But Stevens agreed that on the first four weekends, Private Schine could have passes for committee business, plus an extra evening or so. Very quickly, Schine's absences got out of hand. He had a car and a driver to take him to Trenton and New York. Fort Dix was eighty miles from New York; there was no way to check on whether his absences were devoted to committee work. The favoritism shown to Schine had an adverse effect on the morale of the other trainees in his unit, Company K of the 47th Regiment. Schine himself spread stories around the camp that he was on a secret mission.

On December 8, 1953, the post commander at Fort Dix, General Cornelius Ryan, called Adams to say that Schine was leaving the post nearly every night and that he had been seen in Trenton in a social situation that had nothing to do with committee work. On one occasion, he did not return to the base until 4:55 A.M. Ryan said he intended to terminate the weekday evening passes. He was afraid Schine would fall asleep at the rifle range and shoot someone.[117]

It came out in the dossier the Army gathered that Schine avoided guard detail, barracks-cleaning parties, and weapon-cleaning parties. He paid his fellow soldiers to clean his rifle. He never served a full day on Kitchen Police. He was allowed to leave training to take phone calls. There were thirty thousand soldiers at Fort Dix, but Schine got all the attention.

On December 17, with the closed hearings on again at Foley Square, McCarthy and Cohn and Adams had lunch at Gasner's, near the courthouse. Pat Kennedy joined them with her boyfriend, Peter Lawford. Again they discussed Dave, and Roy worked himself up into fits that out-tantrumed Joe. It seemed to Adams that Cohn had gained complete ascendancy over Joe.

Why was Cohn so obsessed with keeping Dave by his side? Roy was a closet homosexual, although later in his life he was flamboyantly promiscuous and died of AIDS in 1986, at the age of fifty-nine. Roy later denied that he and Dave were lovers, but the crusty senator from Vermont, Ralph Flanders, said, "It was an unsavory relationship. I got evidence of that later in Europe . . . anybody with half an eye could see what was going on."[118]

Roy Cohn had reached a position of power on McCarthy's committee while still in his twenties, and he found that losing his temper and making threats helped him get his way. Experience taught him that he could intimidate high figures in the administration, and particularly the insipid Secretary of the

Army. But power was currency, and why spend it on Schine? He was ready to go to improbable extremes to keep Schine around because to the physically unappealing Cohn, Schine was the Golden Boy, the complement he needed.

There is direct evidence in a handwritten memo by Fred Seaton, assistant secretary of defense, that Cohn and Schine had a homosexual relationship. At the time of the 1954 Army-McCarthy hearings, when the Army investigated Schine, Seaton wrote in an unsigned memo on his letterhead that Schine's chauffeur in December 1953, when he was at Fort Dix, had been interviewed. The unnamed chauffeur, wrote Seaton, "stayed on a month or so . . . at Fort Dix, ordered to drive 45mph—law 25. . . . When drove Schine to New York or other places annoyed at driving back 4–5 A.M. . . . Drove Cohn to Fort Dix several times." Seaton said the chauffeur was "ready to testify," though he never did. He would testify that he drove Cohn and Schine to Philadelphia and to "joints in New York," and that they "engaged in homosexual acts in back of car." The rest of the memo, released by the Eisenhower Library, has been blacked out.[119]

In tests at Fort Dix, Schine had been disqualified for the infantry because of a defect in his back. Other tests showed an aptitude for training as an assistant criminal investigator. The plan at this point was to send him to Provost Marshall School at Camp Gordon, Georgia, where he would remain for nearly five months. While there, he would have no special permission to leave the post.

Knowing that 90 percent of inductees were given overseas duty after training, Adams called Cohn and asked: "Roy, what will happen if Dave gets an overseas assignment?"

Cohn: "Stevens is through as Secretary of the Army."

Adams: "Oh come on, Roy, can that stuff."

Cohn: "We'll wreck the Army. . . . The Army will be ruined . . . if you pull a dirty, lousy, stinking, filthy, shitty double cross like that."[120]

At Fort Dix, Schine missed KP over New Year's, and was told that he would draw KP on a weekend to make up for the one he skipped. When General Ryan sent Schine a telegram ordering him to return, Cohn called the general to protest the telegram.

————

At the start of 1954, the continued boycott of the three Democrats jeopardized the subcommittee's appropriation. McCarthy was often the only member who attended closed hearings. Sometimes, when he was not present, Cohn or Schine presided. When Schine presided, Cohn addressed him as "Mr. Chairman." Cohn and Schine did not operate by the normal rules that govern committee staff. They rented their own offices. Schine made long-distance calls to his friends to notify them about televised hearings. Schine signed McCarthy's name on a letter to the Senate Rules Committee for permission for him and Cohn to use the Senators' Baths, a pool and steam room for senators. Permission was not granted.[121]

In January, Carl Hayden of Arizona, the ranking Democrat on the Senate Appropriations Committee, threatened to cut off the McCarthy subcommittee's funds for lack of a "majority vote." Senator Guy Gillette of Iowa asked the Senate to restrict overlapping of the McCarthy subcommittee with other committees. McCarthy called these efforts "a vote against the exposure of spies and saboteurs," adding that it was "a natural thing for left-wing Democrats to try to stop the exposure of treason." At a closed meeting on January 14, McCarthy agreed to the Democrats' demands for a minority counsel, and they picked Robert Kennedy. New rules were established that the hiring and firing of staff members must be confirmed by a majority and that no public hearings would be held if the minority unanimously objected. Under those conditions, the Democrats returned to the fold on January 25. In the full Senate, only one senator voted against the subcommittee's appropriation—J. William Fulbright, whom Joe called "half-bright."[122]

The year of McCarthy's demise, 1954, opened with one of his most inane investigations, into the promotion of an Army dentist. Roy Cohn called John Adams on January 4 to tell him that the committee knew about a Communist dentist at Camp Kilmer, New Jersey. During the Korean War, there was a shortage of doctors and dentists, and Congress passed a law to get them into service. Irving Peress, a dentist in Queens with Communist affiliations, was one of those drafted under the Doctors and Dentists Act, on October 15, 1952, with the rank of captain. On his loyalty questionnaire, he wrote "constitutional privilege," which was a way of taking the Fifth. Assigned to Camp Kilmer in March 1953, he was promoted to major in October with hundreds of others, according to their standing in private practice. In the ensuing outcry over "Who Promoted Peress?," the answer was the Doctors and Dentists Act. But owing to bureaucratic foul-ups, the Army did not react promptly to the tip-off on his loyalty form.

Secretary of the Army Stevens was still mired in the Schine affair. On January 14, 1954, he thanked Joe "for that marvelous cheese" and asked, "Would it be out of order to buy you a cocktail that you might name?"

"I would favor that very much," Joe said. They met that evening at the Carroll Arms and Stevens told Joe what Schine's routine would be at Camp Gordon. His tour would last five months. Stevens left on January 17 on a month-long tour of military bases in the Far East.

Roy Cohn was on vacation in Boca Raton, staying at a Schine-owned hotel when on January 18, he learned from Frank Carr that Schine would be in Georgia five months. He called Adams to ask if this was true and was told that it was.

The next day Adams got a call from Carr saying that Joe wanted to quiz six Army loyalty board members. He wanted these witnesses, even if he had to subpoena them. Carr said that Cohn had blood in his eyes over Camp Gordon. To Adams, this could only mean that Cohn was using the loyalty boards to punish the Army for sending Schine to Georgia.[123]

Adams realized it was time to counterattack. One of the lawyers on his staff had drafted a letter outlining the reasons why the Army could not turn over loyalty board members to the committee, which was known around the office as "The Fuck You Letter." On the afternoon of January 21, Adams took the letter to the Justice Department and walked into Attorney General Herbert Brownell's large, wood-paneled office. To his surprise, aside from Brownell and his deputy Bill Rogers, four top White House advisers were there— General Jerry Persons, the congressional liaison officer; Henry Cabot Lodge, the United Nations delegate; Gerald Morgan, special counsel; and Sherman Adams, chief of staff.

Brownell told Adams to sit down and recount the story of the Army's struggle with McCarthy. When he had finished, Sherman Adams, who had seemed to be dozing, looked up and asked: "Have you a record of this?" John Adams said he didn't. "Don't you think you ought to start one?" the White House chief of staff asked. Here was another opportunity, as with the J. B. Matthews article, for the White House to mount an anti-McCarthy offensive surreptitiously.[124]

On January 23, Adams walked through an early morning snowfall to his office at the Pentagon and got his Dictaphone and dictated his notes on the incidents with Schine. He underlined what he called "the continuous bracketing of requests for special treatment of Schine with discussions of investigations against the Army."

As Adams was contending with the Schine case, the Peress investigation was also moving along. On January 23, one of Cohn's staffers called General Ralph Zwicker, the commandant at Camp Kilmer. Zwicker gave the committee the name of the Communist dentist. Irving Peress had been given an honorable discharge on January 18, but had chosen to stay in the Army until March 31, being entitled to up to ninety days leeway. On January 27, Cohn called Adams to tell him the committee wanted Peress to appear. Adams did not realize Peress was still in uniform.

When Peress testified at a closed hearing on January 30, he took the Fifth. Joe called him a Communist. Peress went back to Kilmer and asked to have his discharge moved up. He was discharged on February 2. Joe charged a cover-up. He wanted Peress court-martialed. In what was essentially a case of bureaucratic bungling and paper-shuffling from base to base, McCarthy purported to see "deliberate Communist infiltration of our Armed Forces."[125]

On the evening of February 17, McCarthy and his wife, Jean, were in New York for the hearing the next day in Room 110 of the U.S. courthouse in Foley Square. A taxi in which Jean was riding was struck by another car and she had to be hospitalized. Joe had a sleepless night. The next morning, he had a splitting headache. Even though Peress had been discharged and appeared in civilian clothes, McCarthy had hauled him in to put pressure on the Army to produce members of its loyalty boards.[126]

When the televised hearings opened, Joe questioned Peress, lost his temper, and began to rant at the Army for giving Peress an honorable discharge. He then demanded that the officer who had signed the discharge appear that afternoon. "I think here you have the key to the deliberate Communist infiltration of our armed forces, the most dangerous thing," he said. "And the men responsible for the honorable discharge of a Communist are just as guilty as the man who belongs to the conspiracy himself." It was another one-man hearing, where Joe could vent his bile at will. Peress, whom Joe repeatedly called "a Communist conspirator," quoted from Book Seven of the Psalms: "His mischief shall return upon his own head and his violence shall come down upon his own pate."[127]

During the recess at lunch, Joe went to Flower Fifth Avenue Hospital to see Jean and learned that her fractured ankle would remain in a cast for weeks, which did not improve his frame of mind. He returned to the afternoon closed hearing with his head still throbbing and his nerves frayed. According to John Adams, special counsel for the Army, he calmed them with Old Grand-Dad.

Appearing before him were General Ralph W. Zwicker, the commandant at Camp Kilmer, and his assistant chief of staff, Lieutenant Colonel Chester T. Brown. Zwicker, who had been suffering chest pains, was accompanied by a medical officer, Captain W. J. Woodward.

McCarthy started with Brown, who refused to answer questions about Peress's loyalty status.

This set Joe off, and he said: "I will listen to Communists refuse to answer; I will listen to no army officer protecting a Communist and you are going to answer these questions or your case will come before the Senate for contempt. . . . I am sick and tired of it."

Colonel Brown still refused to answer.

"I am going to let the public see you, sir . . . protecting and covering up

Communists," Joe said. He was so angry that he asked that the room be cleared of everyone but the witness.

"I want," Joe fumed, "the American people . . . to see our army officers sitting here, refusing to give the facts about traitors and spies. . . . Any man in the uniform of his country who refuses to give information to a committee of the Senate . . . that man is not fit to wear the uniform of his country. . . . He is in the same category as the traitor whom he is protecting. . . . I am going to ask the Senate to have you cited for contempt."[128]

Then it was General Zwicker's turn. Ramrod-straight and leathery-faced, Ralph W. Zwicker was an authentic World War II hero, who had not been shooting at coconuts. He landed with the first wave on D-Day as commander of the 38th Infantry Regiment. Picking up the carbine of a fallen man, he led his regiment up the bluffs under heavy fire and won the Silver Star for gallantry in action.

Zwicker, having seen Colonel Brown mauled, was unresponsive from the start, denying any knowledge that Peress was a Communist and taking a swipe at the committee by observing that it had unearthed no new evidence.

Joe worked himself up into a rage. "Don't be coy with me, General. . . . Don't you give me double-talk. . . . I am going to keep you here as long as you keep hedging and hemming."

Zwicker: "I am not hedging."

McCarthy: "Or hawing."

Zwicker: "I am not hawing, and I don't like to have anyone impugn my honesty, which you just about did."

McCarthy: "Either your honesty or your intelligence, I can't help impugning one or the other."

Why, Joe asked, had Zwicker not prevented the discharge of Peress, knowing he was a Communist?

Zwicker said the question was irrelevant and that he could not give a constructive answer.

McCarthy: "You are ordered to answer, General, unless you take the Fifth Amendment. I do not care how long we stay here, you are going to answer it."

Zwicker: "Do you mean how I feel toward Communists?"

At that point, Joe seemed to snap. He was like a man with Tourette's syndrome, who can't control his vocal outbursts.

"Anyone with the brains of a five-year-old can understand that question."

Zwicker: "Start it over, please."

The reporter reread the question and Zwicker said: "I do not think he should be removed from the military."

McCarthy (more and more agitated): "Then, general, you should be removed from any command. . . . [You are] not fit to wear that uniform, General. . . . It is a tremendous disgrace to the Army to have this sort of thing." McCarthy ordered him to come to a public hearing on February 23, saying: "I want the public to see just what kind of incompetent persons the army has in its officer corps."[129]

The closed session with Zwicker, parts of which were leaked to the press, proved to be a milestone in McCarthy's demise. It shocked and alarmed McCarthy loyalists in the media. His staunch backer the *Chicago Tribune* wrote: "We do not believe Senator McCarthy's behavior toward General Zwicker was justified and we expect it has injured his cause of driving the disloyal from the government service." The pro-McCarthy columnist David Lawrence called it "a bad mistake on the senator's part."[130]

On February 19, Stevens called General Zwicker to say, "I deeply resent the comments Sen. McCarthy made to you yesterday. . . . I wanted to tell you how much I think of you."

Zwicker: "If any other officer's character is impugned as mine was yesterday, and higher authority do nothing to refute those statements, the loyalty of the officers to the Department of the Army is going to vanish. . . . He called me everything you can imagine in the book. . . . I hope I can wrap this rascal up."[131]

With the J. B. Matthews flap, McCarthy had the Protestant clergy against him. After his mugging of General Zwicker, he had against him the Army, the veterans, a growing part of Congress, and a man who had spent most of his adult life in uniform—Eisenhower.

On February 20, Stevens called McCarthy, who was in Albany. "I went on the Hill yesterday and called on various members of your subcommittee," he said. "I went because I was upset by the reports on Gen. Zwicker."

McCarthy: "I have had a most insulting session with the general. . . . Are you going to keep from us the names of the officers who protected these men?"

Stevens: "I am going to try and prevent my officers from going before your committee. . . . I don't believe we can afford to let splendid officers with outstanding combat records to be abused." For once, Stevens was showing some backbone.

McCarthy: "You just go ahead and try it, Robert. I am going to kick the brains out of anyone who protects Communists. . . . I don't give a goddamn whether an officer is a general or what he is, when he comes before us with the ignorant, stupid, insulting aspect of those who appeared, the American people will know about it."

Stevens said he would not allow General Zwicker to appear in open session.[132] Thus, the Zwicker hearing was postponed.

On February 20, Stevens told James Reston of the *New York Times:* "We cannot maintain the morale of the Army with this kind of thing."

Reston: "I have seen what has happened to my friends in the Foreign Service, they are not reporting accurately, they are not sticking their necks out. . . . That's what will happen to your officer corps, if they are beat on the head by this character."

On February 21, Stevens released a statement that he had instructed General Zwicker not to appear. "I am unwilling for so fine an officer as General Zwicker to run the risk of further abuse." Stevens received hundreds of telegrams of congratulation, one of which said, "At last the dragon has met St. George."

On February 24, Stevens accepted an invitation to have lunch on the Hill with the four Republicans on the committee—Mundt, Dirksen, Potter, and McCarthy—in the Capitol office of Everett Dirksen. Stevens was hoping to get a written agreement that there would be no further abuse of Army witnesses. Instead, he was persuaded to agree to a "Memo of Understanding" that was seen as a capitulation to the committee. He agreed to make Zwicker available if the committee wanted him. He agreed to give the committee the names of everyone involved in the promotion of Peress. McCarthy told newsmen: "Stevens could not have surrendered more abjectly if he had gotten down on his knees."

The White House was in shock, seeing its plans unravel. Jim Hagerty noted in his diary: "McCarthy-Stevens broke wide open today . . . Stevens . . . giving Joe everything he wants—names etc. Stevens called me late at night (10 P.M.) to say he wanted to release his statement and then resign—told him to cool off overnight. But we sure were dumb. Someone let Stevens walk right into a bear trap, and now I'll have to work like hell to get him out of it—what a job."[133]

Bernard Shanley, the special counsel, said in his diary: "Stevens . . . has messed up the situation completely. . . . Most people believe that someone in the White House urged this capitulation on Stevens. . . . To go there alone, without advice and without an attorney, was like committing suicide."[134]

Upon returning to the Pentagon after lunch, Stevens took a call from Lodge and said: "I went up and had lunch at their request. . . . It may be a tenuous armistice, I don't know."

Lodge: "Between you and me, this is all preliminary to an attempt to destroy the President politically. There is no doubt about it. He is picking on the Army because Eisenhower was in the Army. . . . This is basically an attempt to destroy Eisenhower. They are going to try to win as many votes as they can on this Communist issue in the fall. The same crowd that supported Taft at the

[1952] convention are now revolving around Joe." Lodge said Ike had asked him to call Stevens. "You have that documentation there on boy S, and I think you ought to get that in shape for publication."

Stevens: "We are doing that."

Lodge: "That would be a devastating thing."[135]

That call on February 24 was the turning point, with Ike himself, acting through Lodge, asking for the publication of the Schine report. As Hagerty noted on February 25, Ike had worked on Dirksen, who "will work on committee to get Cohn fired, stop one-man committee from meeting, and strip some of his power by saying subpoena could only be issued by majority vote."

Hagerty described Eisenhower as "very mad and getting fed up—it's his Army and he doesn't like McCarthy's tactics." He quoted Ike as saying: "This guy McCarthy is going to get into trouble over this. I'm not going to take this one lying down. . . . It won't be long before he starts using my name instead of Stevens'. He's ambitious. He wants to be president. He's the last guy who'll ever get there if I have anything to say."[136]

————

In a closed hearing on March 4, with Senator Charles Potter presiding, the Subcommittee on Investigations convened on the topic "Alleged Threats Against the Chairman." The witness, William J. Morgan (born Mitrano), was a lieutenant colonel in Military Intelligence, in the Reserves, with a doctorate in psychology from Yale. During the war, he was in the OSS and served with a British team that picked agents to operate in Nazi-occupied territory. He had parachuted into France to train guerrillas. In the early days of the CIA, he had developed tests for CIA recruits.

In 1953, he was working for C. D. Jackson, Eisenhower's special assistant for psychological warfare. In September, at a meeting with his superior at the Psychological Strategy Board, Horace Craig, who was on the CIA payroll, they discussed Senator McCarthy. Craig said that the senator's influence was the most important factor in negating the activities of the United States abroad. Both men had served in the OSS under "Wild Bill" Donovan. "You know," said Craig, "what his suggestion would be?" Morgan said he did not. Craig said that Donovan would have assigned an agent to penetrate the McCarthy organization. They went on discussing how to get rid of McCarthy, and Craig said: "It may be necessary to liquidate Senator McCarthy as was Huey Long. There is always some madman who will do it for a price."

"I was quite stunned," Morgan told the committee. He was not sure whether Craig was serious, but to be on the safe side, he got in touch with the committee investigator, Don Surine, which led to the closed hearing.

"At the time," Morgan said, "I thought, 'he must be losing his mind.' "

McClellan: "A man in government service making remarks like that, it might go to his fitness to continue to serve as a public servant."[137]

There was, however, no public hearing on the matter.

———

John Adams had the forty-page Schine report sitting in a drawer. He had shown it to Sherman Adams, several senators, some Army officers and newsmen. He thought of the report as a stick of dynamite with the fuse burning. Struve Hensel, the Defense Department counsel, asked Adams to rewrite it in chronological order. To Adams, this meant it was about to be released. He reordered it as a "Chronology of Events."[138]

Tuesday, March 9, was a red-letter day in what could now be called the dump-McCarthy movement. In a plan conceived in the White House and confided to his diary by Jim Hagerty, Senator Charles E. Potter, a World War II veteran who had lost both legs to German shrapnel and who was upset by Joe's treatment of Zwicker, was enlisted to ask Secretary of Defense Wilson for the Schine record. "That ought to start the ball rolling to get rid of Roy Cohn," Hagerty wrote. The White House did not yet realize that the report would have a far more dramatic result.

Potter, a Republican from Michigan, spoke to his old friend, Secretary of Defense Charlie Wilson, who said "the man has gone too far. No one in this world is safe from his slander." Potter said Stevens should have stopped him a long time ago. "That's right," Wilson said. "But you know Stevens as well as I do. If a gunman held him up in an alley, he would hand over his wallet and then write the man a check to buy a new suit of clothes." Potter wrote Wilson a letter asking for the Schine report.[139]

Also on March 9, seventy-three-year-old Ralph Flanders, the Vermont Republican who had been tussling with McCarthy since the sugar rationing debate in 1947, spoke out against him on the floor of the Senate. Flanders did not fear Joe's vengeance, for he was retiring when his term ran out. Portraying McCarthy as an outlaw, Flanders said: "He is doing his best to shatter the party whose label he wears. . . . What is his party affiliation? One must conclude that his is a one-man party, and that its name is 'McCarthyism.' . . . He dons his war paint. He goes into his war dance. He emits his war whoops. He goes forth to battle and proudly returns with the scalp of a pink Army dentist."[140]

Ike had long said that the McCarthy problem must be solved in the Senate, and here was a respected Republican senator taking Joe on. Ike wrote Flanders: "I think America needs to hear more Republican voices like yours."

The most damaging blow to McCarthy on March 9 came not from the White House or the Senate but from the television studio of the CBS network. At 10:30 that night came the half-hour program *See It Now*, hosted by Edward R. Murrow, with "A Report on Senator Joseph R. McCarthy." Murrow did not intend it as a balanced report; he did a cut-and-splice job, so that Joe would convict himself out of his own mouth. The network was concerned about loss of sponsors and other reprisals, given McCarthy's funding by the corporate right wing and his sub rosa ties to radical right hate groups. But Murrow got the green light, if grudgingly. McCarthy was captured in his frothing rants, brandishing "secret evidence," and beating down witnesses.

Murrow ended the program with an editorial: "This is no time for men who oppose Senator McCarthy's methods to keep silent. . . . The actions of the junior senator from Wisconsin have caused alarm and dismay amongst our allies abroad and given considerable comfort to our enemies. . . . He didn't create the situation of fear; he merely exploited it, and rather successfully. Cassius was right: 'the fault, dear Brutus, is not in our stars, but in ourselves.' "

After half an hour of McCarthy-bashing, this was a curious conclusion, which did not blame the senator for his misdeeds, but the large segment of the population whose alarm had brought him fame. A number of commentators noted that Murrow was a latecomer to the McCarthy melodrama. Other broadcasters, such as Martin Agronsky in his radio program on ABC, had gone after Joe earlier and suffered for it. Agronsky lost half of his 120 sponsors, but remained on the air, despite the complaints of affiliates, thanks to his network's president, Robert Kintner, who told him: "Keep it up."

In terms of impact, however, Murrow's timing could not have been better. His program came at a time when public opinion had started to turn against McCarthy. His Gallup Poll rating had fallen from 50 to 46 percent, and would keep falling. His core constituency of Midwestern Republicans was beginning to wonder whether he was an asset or a liability. In this changing climate, the Murrow program mobilized the fragmented but growing anti-McCarthy forces. It touched off the largest response ever generated by a network TV program, starting with thousands of phone calls and telegrams to CBS and continuing with national press coverage, much of it favorable.[141]

It was now possible to see the Senate turning against Joe, like a battleship turning in the Atlantic, so slowly that it barely seemed to move. On March 11, Adams heard from Charlie Potter that a secret meeting of Republican senators had been held, which included McCarthy, William Knowland of California, and John Bricker of Ohio, "and they laid it on pretty violently, recommending the termination of one of the staff members and to get off the Army's neck," as Adams told Stevens.

March 11 was also the day that the Schine report was released, listing forty-four counts of improper pressure on the Army from July 1953 to February 1954. "It's a pip," Hagerty wrote. "Shows constant pressure by Cohn to get Schine soft Army job, with Joe in and out of threats."

The report was a devastating attack on McCarthy, who was charged with allowing a staff member to blackmail and bully the Army. Potter, in close touch with the White House, called for an executive session of the subcommittee to determine the facts, adding that if the report was accurate, "Mr. Cohn should be removed immediately." The three Democrats on the subcommittee also called for a meeting.[142]

McCarthy's response was to hurriedly draft eleven memos that seemed to place blame on the Army and backdate them, in order to mount a defense. The memos purported to be accounts of conversations among his staffers accusing the Army of blackmail. Copies of the memos were distributed and taken at face value. On March 12, Karl Mundt asked for an impartial Senate committee to investigate both the Army's and McCarthy's accounts. Four days later, the subcommittee met in executive session and thrashed out a solution: the subcommittee itself would conduct a full inquiry. McCarthy, the object of the inquiry, would remain on the committee, but would step down as chairman. Mundt would take his place.

On March 24, 1954, Eisenhower told Jim Hagerty that it was "inconceivable" that McCarthy should serve on the subcommittee investigating his row with the Army. He had informed Mundt, but "you can't trust that fellow. He plays everything against the middle." The next day, before his press conference, Ike told Hagerty: "I'm going to say he can't sit as a judge. . . . I've made up my mind you can't do business with Joe and to hell with any attempt to compromise."[143]

But in his press conference on March 25, Ike spoke in more balanced tones. "In America," he said, "if a man is party to a dispute, he does not sit in judgment on his own case, and I don't believe that any leadership can escape responsibility for carrying on that tradition."[144]

Finally, it was decided that McCarthy would step down as a member of the committee. Idaho's Henry Dworshak would sit in his place. McCarthy would, however, be allowed to cross-examine witnesses and to subpoena them. This last point was of particular concern to the President, who feared that Joe would start reeling in government officials as witnesses, whether they were in the White House, the Army, or on federal commissions.

On April 6, 1954, McCarthy made a televised appearance to respond to the Murrow program. In the course of his remarks, he made headlines with a new charge: the development of the hydrogen bomb had been delayed for eighteen months while Russia was advancing with a similar project. "If there were no Communists in our government, why did we delay?" he asked. "Our nation may well die because of the eighteen-month delay." McCarthy's remarks caused alarm in the White House. Jim Hagerty wrote in his diary on April 7 that "Joe was skating pretty close to the Oppenheimer case. We have to move fast before McCarthy breaks the Oppenheimer investigation and it becomes our scandal. It's just a question of time before someone cracks it wide open and everything hits the fan."[145]

What scandal was Hagerty referring to? To understand the concern in the White House, we must go back to Oppenheimer's activities after the war, when he became known as "the father of the A-bomb." In 1946, the legislation that created the Atomic Energy Commission to administer the nation's nuclear program also set up a General Advisory Committee, which would serve as a brain trust for the AEC. Oppenheimer was named chairman of the GAC in 1947, the same year that he became the director of Princeton's prestigious Institute of Advanced Studies.

In 1949, President Truman asked the Atomic Energy Commission for a report on whether to proceed with the hydrogen bomb. On November 7, the advisory committee chaired by Oppenheimer reached the unanimous decision that the hydrogen bomb should not be developed. Two days later the AEC voted 3 to 2 against the bomb. Aside from his moral objections, Oppenheimer did not think the "super" was feasible. In the rancorous debate that ensued, scientists were split into two camps. Overriding the AEC, Truman decided on January 31, 1950, to go ahead, on the grounds that if the Russians had the capability we had to beat them to it.[146]

Oppenheimer continued to oppose the "super," while scientists who backed the bomb charged that the advisory committee was dragging its feet. Edward Teller, "the father of the H-Bomb," told the FBI in early 1952 that he would "do almost anything to see [Oppenheimer] separated from the General Advisory Committee because of his poor advice and policies regarding national preparedness and because of his delaying of the development of the H-bomb."[147]

On March 26, 1952, in a memo to the White House, Hoover, who continued to consider Oppenheimer a security risk, opposed his upcoming reappointment in June as chairman of the GAC. Aside from his Communist associations, Hoover said, he had received some disturbing information regarding Oppenheimer's wife, Kitty. According to Hoover, "she uses intoxicants to excess and when her husband is out of town she frequently calls R. F. Tessein, late at night, to come to her house and drink with her." Tessein was Oppenheimer's chauffeur at Princeton.[148]

That June, Oppenheimer was forced off the General Advisory Committee.

He was, however, given a year's contract with the Atomic Energy Commission as a consultant, which meant that he could keep his "Q" security clearance. On November 1, 1952, at Eniwetok, one of the Marshall Islands, the, hydrogen bomb was tested and a small coral island was vaporized.

There matters would have rested had it not been for a young man named William Liscum Borden. A World War II bomber pilot, Borden was obsessed with the probability of a nuclear war and America's need for nuclear supremacy. After graduating from Yale Law School, he was hired by Senator Brien McMahon, chairman of the Joint Committee on Atomic Energy, to be its executive director, at the age of twenty-eight.

Borden, who had written a pamphlet on the possibility of a nuclear Pearl Harbor, fixated on Oppenheimer as the chief obstacle to the hydrogen bomb. In compiling a dossier on the scientist, Borden became convinced that he was a Soviet agent. In May 1953, with the change of administration, he left the joint committee and devoted his time to the updating of his material on Oppenheimer.[149]

In the meantime, on March 12, 1953, McCarthy and Roy Cohn met with Hoover to discuss an investigation of Oppenheimer. Hoover, whose case against the scientist was based on wiretaps, tried to dampen the senator's enthusiasm. Oppenheimer, he said, "has been one around whom the scientists of our country have usually rallied whenever there has been any question raised about loyalty and integrity." Whatever Joe's committee did, he said, "should be done with a great deal of preliminary spade work. This is not a case which should prematurely be gone into solely for the purpose of headlines."[150]

For the moment McCarthy did not pursue his Oppenheimer leads. Borden, however, did, and on November 7, 1953, he wrote Hoover that "more probably than not, J. Robert Oppenheimer is an agent of the Soviet Union. . . . He has worked tirelessly . . . to retard the United States H-bomb program."[151]

Borden's letter touched off the most controversial security investigation of the Eisenhower years, one in which the President became deeply involved. On November 30, 1953, Hoover sent copies of Borden's letter, along with an updated FBI dossier on Oppenheimer, to Secretary of Defense Charles Wilson and to Lewis Strauss, the chairman of the Atomic Energy Commission.

On December 2, Wilson called the President. "Have you seen the new report of J. Edgar Hoover on Dr. Oppenheimer?" he asked. Ike said he had not. "Well, Lewis Strauss and I have received copies directly from Hoover, and it's the worst one yet. Lewis told me that McCarthy knows about it and might pull it on us."[152]

In a diary entry dated December 2, Ike wrote: "In a telephone call Charlie

Wilson states that he has a report from the FBI that carries the gravest implications that Dr. Robert Oppenheimer is a security risk of the worst kind. In fact, some of the accusers seem to go so far as to accuse him of having been an actual agent of the Communists.

"I instructed him [Wilson] to notify the attorney general [Herbert Brownell] at once. The attorney general will examine the evidence to determine whether or not an indictment should be sought. . . . The sad fact is that if this charge is true, we have a man who has been right in the middle of our whole atomic development from the very earliest days it began."[153]

Ike considered the Oppenheimer matter grave enough to call a high-level meeting in his office the next day. In attendance were Secretary of State John Foster Dulles, Secretary of Defense Charles Wilson, CIA Director Allen Dulles, and Robert Cutler, Director of the National Security Council.

Ike wanted Oppenheimer's top secret "Q" clearance suspended, but he wanted it done secretly. If the news leaked to McCarthy that Oppenheimer was a security risk, he could use it to smear Eisenhower for harboring Communists. In addition, Ike wanted to place "a blank wall" between Oppenheimer and "all government operations."[154]

Ike realized, he wrote in his diary on December 3, that "the overall conclusion has always been that there is no evidence that implied disloyalty on the part of Dr. Oppenheimer. However, this does not mean that he might not be a security risk. . . . If this man is really a disloyal citizen, then the damage he can do now compared with what he has done in the past is like comparing a grain of sand to an ocean beach. It would not be a case of merely locking the stable door after the horse is gone; it would be more like trying to find a door for the burned-down stable."[155]

The initiative for an investigation of Oppenheimer now shifted from the President to Lewis Strauss, the chairman of the Atomic Energy Commission. Strauss was not a scientist, but a self-made millionaire investment banker and onetime aide to Herbert Hoover. During the war, he was a deskbound admiral, working on procurement. In 1947, Truman named the security-conscious Strauss as one of the five commissioners on the Atomic Energy Commission. He often clashed with Oppenheimer, who was on the advisory committee, on such matters as the sharing of atomic information and the development of the hydrogen bomb. In their discussions, Oppenheimer adopted a patronizing tone that Strauss resented.[156]

In July 1953, Strauss was named chairman of the AEC. When the Russians tested a hydrogen bomb in August, Strauss wondered why Oppenheimer had written in the July issue of *Foreign Affairs* that they were four years behind. Strauss, like Borden, began to fixate on Oppenheimer and asked the FBI to help him find evidence of his disloyalty. Strauss was outraged by the information he collected from various sources—that Oppenheimer had padded his GAC expenses; that he had found a job for Earl Browder's son at the Institute for Advanced Studies; that he had had an affair with the wife of one of his colleagues at Berkeley, the physicist Richard Tolman, who later joined him in Los Alamos.[157]

Strauss was one of the recipients, in early December 1953, of the FBI dossier and the Borden letter. When Charlie Wilson asked him if he thought Oppenheimer was a Communist, he said: "I do not know that he is a Communist but I do know that he is a liar." Then Eisenhower ordered the suspension of Oppenheimer's clearance. On December 10, at an AEC meeting, Strauss announced the suspension. One of the other commissioners suggested convening a Personnel Security Board hearing. Strauss instructed the AEC general counsel, William Mitchell, to draw up a statement of charges based on the FBI and Borden material. Mitchell and his staff drew up a list of thirty-eight charges, ranging from Communist associations to the Haakon Chevalier incident to the delay of the H-bomb.[158]

Oppenheimer, who had been traveling in Europe, returned on December 13. At a meeting with Strauss on December 21, he was shown a list of the charges. His contract as a consultant was up the following June. The question arose whether it would be better for him to resign now and avoid a loyalty hearing. Oppenheimer was in shock, telling friends: "I can't believe what is happening to me!" The AEC had suspended the clearance of and filed charges against the most prominent scientist in the country. On December 23, Oppenheimer wrote Strauss that he could not resign, for that "would mean that I accept and concur in the view that I am not fit to serve this Government, that I have served for some 12 years. This I cannot do."[159]

Both sides spent the next two months preparing the case. Oppenheimer's lawyer was Lloyd Garrison, while the lawyer for the loyalty board was the combative prosecutor Roger Robb. He had the advantage of knowing his adversary's strategy, for Strauss had persuaded Hoover to tap Oppenheimer's home and office phones in Princeton, in violation of the attorney-client privilege. One of the wiretaps described Oppenheimer as "very depressed . . . and has been ill-tempered with his wife." The wiretaps also overheard Oppenheimer discussing his dilemma with sympathetic columnists such as James Reston and Joseph Alsop.[160]

The three-member Personnel Security Board consisted of Gordon Gray, president of the University of North Carolina, a millionaire lawyer who owned two newspapers and a radio station, and who belonged to clubs that Oppenheimer could not join; Thomas Morgan, the son of a North Carolina tobacco farmer, and president of Sperry Gyroscope; and Ward Evans, an expert on explosives for the Bureau of Mines and chairman of the Chemistry Department at Northwestern.[161]

On January 31, 1954, David Lilienthal, who had experienced some trouble himself at his confirmation hearing as the first chairman of the Atomic Energy Commission, pointed out in his diary that "the new factor" in the Oppenheimer case "is the increasing wildness of the McCarthy method of 'investigating' such things. . . . It seems to me that the fellow who made the atomic bomb possible should come out of this furor with a good record. . . . The Oppenheimer experience . . . is the very essence of these fearful times."[162] What Lilienthal did not know was that President Eisenhower himself had set in motion the process that would result in a hearing with forty witnesses and thousands of pages of evidence, which would tarnish the career of one of America's most distinguished scientists. And that this was done out of Ike's fear that if he did not act, McCarthy would let loose the hounds of calumny.

McCarthy did attack on April 6, with his charge on the delay of the H-bomb, but without naming Oppenheimer. Ike responded the next day at his press conference that there had been no delays. "We've got to handle this so that all of our scientists are not made out to be Reds," he told Jim Hagerty. "That goddamn McCarthy is just likely to try such a thing." But Joe did not try anything, for he was busy with his own problems, with the Army-McCarthy hearings about to start. They opened on April 22, and ran concurrently with the Oppenheimer loyalty board hearing, which had begun on April 12, in a barracks-like prefab structure on Constitution Avenue, across the street from the AEC headquarters. All the old accusations were repeated, while character witnesses lined up to defend Oppenheimer, who sat in the back of the room on a leather couch, smoking his pipe.[163]

When he admitted lying in the Chevalier incident, Robb asked, "Why did you do that, sir?"

Oppenheimer: "Because I was an idiot."

Robb: "He told not one lie in 1943 to Col. Pash but a whole fabrication of lies."[164]

Oppenheimer said that on his trip to France the previous December, he had dined with his old friend Haakon Chevalier at his apartment in Montmartre with his new wife, Carol. Chevalier was translating books by André Malraux into English and the next day he introduced the author of *Man's Fate* to Oppenheimer.

This was too much for Eisenhower, who observed: "How can any individual report a treasonable act on the part of another man and then go and stay in his home several days? It just doesn't make sense." Ike could not conceive that a man could remain friends with someone who had tried to lure him into espionage.[165]

On May 6, the hearing ended, and on May 23 the loyalty board voted 2 to 1 that Oppenheimer was a security risk and should not have his "Q" clearance reinstated. Ward, the explosives expert, voted in his favor. Lilienthal wrote in his diary: "His crime was that he did not show the proper 'enthusiasm' about the H-bomb program." On June 29, the five-member Atomic Energy Commission upheld the board by 4 to 1. Lilienthal, who had resigned as chairman in 1950, found the decision "unutterably sad."[166] Senator Clinton P. Anderson of New Mexico, who was on the Joint Committee on Atomic Energy, later accused the AEC of bowing to "the McCarthy hysteria."

Oppenheimer was permanently removed from public service, and died in 1967, at the age of sixty-three, of throat cancer. Eisenhower, whose haste to protect himself launched the inquiry that censured the scientist, might have pondered the opinion of his old friend John J. McCloy, who had been assistant secretary of defense during World War II. "I am very distressed, as I assume you are," McCloy wrote Ike on April 16, 1954, "over the Oppenheimer matter. . . . I feel that it is somewhat like inquiring into the security risk of a Newton or a Galileo. Such people are themselves 'top secret.' . . . In 1941, there were so few people in the United States who had the highly refined mind . . . to operate in these abstruse fields, that I suppose we would have put a pro-German to work . . . or even a convicted murderer. Such people were few and far between and I cannot escape the conviction that this man . . . was responsible for our pre-eminent position in the field of nuclear weapons."[167] But Eisenhower felt he had to ward off an unscrupulous demagogue, which did not leave him the luxury to consider Oppenheimer's scientific contributions.

———

Televised by NBC, the Army-McCarthy hearings opened on April 22, to determine whether improper pressures had been applied on the Army by McCarthy and vice versa. The subcommittee consisted of four Republicans and three Democrats, with McCarthy operating as a free radical. Lawyers had been hired: for the committee, Ray Howard Jenkins, a no-nonsense criminal lawyer from Knoxville who had defended six hundred murder suspects; for the Army, the tall and natty Boston lawyer Joseph Nye Welch, who, at sixty-three, concealed behind a mild and sometimes bumbling manner a subtle intelligence and a folksy eloquence.

The Army-McCarthy hearings were a seminal moment in the American experience, a seemingly routine congressional hearing transformed into a mass spectacle, thanks to television. Imagine the Burr-Hamilton duel tele-vised, or the Lincoln-Douglas debates, or more recently the Yalta conference. A mesmerized nation (or at least those who owned TV sets) watched the hear-ings unfold in the form of a classical tragedy, as the protagonist was gradually brought down by the flaws in his own character.

In the marble-columned Senate caucus room, gray figures appeared on the flickering screen, sorting papers and whispering—the cherubic Stevens, the reptilian Cohn, the rumple-haired Dirksen with little elephants on his tie, the thin, bony-faced McClellan, son of a tenant farmer, the quizzical Welch with his bow tie askew, and the balding, jowly, smirking McCarthy—all actors improvising their lines in this unrehearsed drama.

At 10:00 A.M. on April 22, the big oak doors swung open and more than five hundred spectators and participants crowded into the capacious caucus room, with its high ceilings and Corinthian columns flanking the scaffolding erected for the TV cameras. The subcommittee members sat on one side of a long mahogany table, with McCarthy and his cohorts, Cohn and Carr, at one end. At 10:35, when the cameras started rolling, Chairman Karl Mundt ex-plained that the issue before them was whether McCarthy and his aides had "sought by improper means to obtain preferential treatment for one Private G. David Schine," and whether the Army had held Schine "hostage" to try and "force a discontinuance of further attempts . . . to expose Communist in-filtration in the Army."[168]

Mundt asked the committee counsel, Ray Jenkins, to call the first witness. Joe interrupted to raise a point of order, which became his device for injecting himself into the proceedings. From the start, he would establish a pattern of guerrilla tactics, hit and run, harassment and evasion. This first time, it was an irrelevant demand that the charges filed by Adams and Stevens should not be labeled "Filed by the Department of the Army," since they were civilians. "Point of order" became a national catchphrase, thanks to television, which helped turn McCarthy into an object of ridicule.[169]

The hearings seemed to divide into a drama in five acts, each with its own climax. The first witness called to the stand was General Miles Reber, the Army chief of liaison on Capitol Hill, with thirty-five years of Army service. General Reber began to explain that he had received a phone call from Schine on June 15, 1953. McCarthy raised a point of order—this was hearsay, be-cause the call was not directly to him. "Mr. Schine seemed to have an attitude of haste and impatience," Reber continued, "about getting a commission." Reber said that he also received two calls a day from Cohn. "He was persis-tently after me. . . . I recall of no instance under which I was put under greater pressure."

McClellan: "If someone insists, that is a request, is it not, for preferential treatment."

Reber: "Yes, sir."

At this point McCarthy made one of his slimy inferences. Did General Miles Reber know that when Cohn and Schine went to Europe, his brother Sam Reber, who had been deputy high commissioner under Conant, "repeatedly made attacks upon them and appointed a man to shadow them throughout Europe."

When Jenkins objected that McCarthy's remarks were irrelevant, he went on: "I realize the normal feelings which a man has for his brother [who] . . . made vicious attacks on Mr. Schine and Mr. Cohn. . . . General, when you had this great success in helping promote Schine to the extent that he is a private, don't you think you should have at least told me about the fact that you were the brother of the man who had all this difficulty?"

Reber said he was not aware of his brother's difficulties.

McCarthy: "Are you aware that your brother was allowed to resign when charges that he was a bad security risk were made against him?"[170]

Reber, pounding his hand in his fist: "I do not know and have never heard that my brother retired as a result of any action of this committee." (According to Benjamin Buttenweiser, who served in Germany under McCloy, Cohn had unearthed a rumor that Sam Reber had had a homosexual episode at Harvard, and by threatening to make it public, forced his resignation.[171] Given Cohn's proclivities, Reber's mishap was ironic.)

Having no defense against Reber's testimony, McCarthy had resorted to character assassination. Senator Henry "Scoop" Jackson wondered whether they would "be trying members of everybody's family before we get through." This was Act One, with McCarthy playing the villain behind the door, ready to pounce on the unsuspecting witness. The attack on Reber revealed one of the keys to McCarthy's mentality. He was incapable of believing that a man might be acting out of a sense of duty or what he thought was right. There had to be an underhanded, spiteful motive. In other words, Joe believed everyone was like him.

In the afternoon, Stevens took the stand for the first of what would be thirteen days of testimony. He said that the Schine case had been discussed with McCarthy's staff in more than sixty-five phone calls and nineteen meetings. There was "no record that matches this persistent, tireless effort to obtain special consideration and privileges for this man," Stevens said. Stevens gave chapter and verse on Schine's antics, how he hid in a truck cab on rainy days, how he left drill practice to make phone calls, and how he avoided KP.

At this mention of KP, Senator Potter asked: "Would you elaborate on this because it happened that I, in my first 24 hours in the Army, I served 17 hours on KP, and I have a little personal interest in how [Schine's avoidance] could be done."[172]

By the end of the fourth day, Stevens was through testifying. But McCarthy, who had been permitted unlimited cross-examination, kept him on the stand for nine more days. When he wanted to make a speech, he simply said "point of order," which others called points of disorder. As John Adams put it, Joe was in effect conducting a filibuster, while Stevens sat there, looking uncomfortable but managing to keep his temper and remain polite, never raising his voice.

———

In the midst of the televised sessions, Senator Mundt continued to hold closed hearings in his office, to clarify material that came up in the testimony of witnesses. On April 23, he heard George Sokolsky, the Hearst columnist. Short and plump, with a thick head of hair, Sokolsky had gone to Russia in 1917 to cover the revolution for a New York news service; the experience turned him into an anti-Communist conservative. He was close to J. Edgar Hoover and had a productive working relationship with the FBI. He was practically an unpaid member of McCarthy's staff, sending him documents, writing his speeches, giving him advice, and flattering him. As John Adams put it, "Sokolsky became a fixture in the McCarthy camp." He recommended Roy Cohn to Joe as counsel. After Schine was drafted, Sokolsky called Adams repeatedly to suggest that the Army should be "practical" and "reasonable" and "use common sense" in its treatment of Schine. Army records showed that Sokolsky also contacted Stevens to recommend a reduction in Schine's basic training so that he could enter the Counterintelligence Division school at Camp Gordon.[173]

In Mundt's office, Sokolsky was asked about the November 17 lunch at the Merchants' Club, which he had attended with Roy and Joe and Stevens. It was "a very gay, hilarious, convivial luncheon party," he said. Sokolsky was asked if he had heard Stevens say that they should go after the Air Force or the Navy rather than the Army. "At one point, Secretary Stevens said, 'Why do you pick on me?' " Sokolsky replied. " 'Why don't you pick on some other branch of the government?' Senator McCarthy threw his arm around his shoulder and he said, 'That is the trouble with having friends. If you and I were not friends, I could proceed with this investigation [Fort Monmouth] more effectively.'

"It was all said in a jovial manner," Sokolsky went on. "On November 17, Mr. Stevens seemed to be very pleased with me. He asked me to come see him the next time I am in Washington. . . . I was in Washington on Nov. 24 so I went to see him. . . . He told me he was in great difficulties and . . . that he was embarrassed by it and it might ruin his career. . . . He made the point that . . . McCarthy . . . seems only to pick on him. . . . We also discussed David Schine . . . and that he could not arrange for Schine to have only eight weeks of basic training. . . . If they only had sense enough to let him alone, and not put pressure on him, he at the end of 16 weeks would arrange for Schine to have a satisfactory job, possibly in New York. I commented that I didn't care whether Schine had eight or sixteen weeks . . . and he showed me a letter from his son, who had been promoted to corporal . . . without his assistance . . . and I said that anything should be done to avoid this kind of quarrelsome relationship . . . and this type of unpleasantness."

Sokolsky denied brokering a deal to send Schine to Camp Gordon, but said that in a conversation with Adams in February, he had observed that "I thought it a very good thing for Schine to be down there and get hardened up, and he said he wished he were in Iceland, and I said . . . 'Better send him to Paris.' "[174]

Another witness, Iris Flores, appeared in Mundt's office the next day. In a memo, Willard Edwards of the *Chicago Tribune*, who was coaching witnesses and otherwise making himself useful during the hearings, explained to Cohn that Miss Flores "is one of Dave Schine's girlfriends, No. 1 on the list at the present time. She is the one to whom Dave made several phone calls a day during his Fort Dix stay. . . . The Army has insisted on questioning her to determine if Dave misused his pass privileges for feminine entertainment when he was supposed to be engaging on committee business. . . . She was Dave's companion on New Year's eve and her testimony would be that she fretted the evening away while Dave pored over committee records in preparation for the annual report. That was fine but would anyone believe it?"[175]

Miss Flores, a striking twenty-nine-year-old brunette from California, who was now living in New York, gave her occupation as "inventor." She had designed "a brassiere gadget" that she had placed with I. Newman and Sons, a girdle company. "I have dedicated the last three years to working on my inventions," she said. "I have two patents right now. One is for a complete line of brassieres . . . and the other is a brassiere shaper."

Had she received daily calls from Schine at Fort Dix? "I am in and out of my house so much that I miss a great many calls," Miss Flores said. "I am on these inventions." Had she had time to see Schine? "We had a quick dinner and very late at night because he was always busy . . . it was always hurried." She saw him on Christmas Day, even though, she said, "I spent a great deal of time in bed because I had laryngitis." She saw him again at Cohn's house on New Year's Eve. "We had a cold supper and then . . . they were reading all kinds of papers. Mr. Cohn gave him lots of things to read."

A couple of times, she said, she drove out to Fort Dix with Schine in a chauffeur-driven car and then drove back to New York, "because he was so terribly tied up." "He is a very quiet boy," Miss Flores said, "he doesn't like night clubs and this business [in the] newspapers is ridiculous. . . . He dines quietly. . . . After all, one has to eat, you know." One time, they went dancing at the Plaza. She was asked if she and Schine were engaged. "I don't have a ring," she said.[176]

———

On April 26, committee counsel Ray Jenkins, who liked to play Perry Mason, brandished a photograph taken in the fall of 1953 at McGuire Air Force Base, showing the Secretary of the Army and Private Schine smiling at each other.

Jenkins: "Mr. Stevens, isn't it a fact that you were being especially nice and considerate and tender of this boy Schine?" The public relations officer at McGuire thought there was something funny about the picture, and looked through his files for the original, which showed a third person, Colonel Jack Bradley. It was Bradley that Stevens was smiling at.

The next morning, Army counsel Welch had a blowup of the uncropped picture and made a point of order of his own, saying that "a doctored photograph [was] produced in this courtroom as if it were honest."

McCarthy, sensing danger (shades of the Tydings-Browder photo), issued a point of order to shut Welch up.

Seeing a chance to catch Joe off balance, Welch inflated the doctored photo into a major issue that lasted several days and produced hundreds of anti-McCarthy headlines. By the time the hearing got back on track, Welch had succeeded in planting the suspicion that Joe and his aides relied on trickery and fakery to make their case.[177]

On April 28, McCarthy tried to show that the charges against Schine were trivial—so what if he had his shoes commercially polished, if he wore a fur-lined hood and special boots with straps and buckles on the side? "Dave has a size 12 or 13 foot," Joe said, "so he went downtown and bought a shoe. . . . It is all ridiculous in the extreme. What do you think?" he asked Stevens.

Stevens: "I think you would like to have had him something other than a private." (Applause.)

The hearing was not turning in Joe's favor, which made him even more enraged. He bellowed at Chairman Mundt, insulted Stevens, and griped about other committee members. He was coming across, as his friend Senator Jenner of Indiana put it, as "the kid who came to the party and peed in the lemonade."

On April 30, there was more discussion of the doctored picture, a copy of which Schine had kept at Fort Dix. One of McCarthy's investigators, James R. Juliana, said, "I never knew what hung on Schine's wall."

Welch: "Did you think it came from a pixie? Where did you think this picture that I hold in my hand came from?"

McCarthy: "Will counsel for my benefit define—I think he might be an expert on that—what a pixie is?"

Welch: "I would say, senator, that a pixie is a close relative of a fairy. . . . Have I enlightened you?"

Joe had stepped right into that one, allowing Welch to raise the homosexuality issue by inference.[178]

The doctored photograph was Act Two. On the evening of May 3, Charlie Potter paid a secret visit to Eisenhower's living quarters at the White House to brief him on the hearings. Potter's account made Ike so mad that he slammed his fist on the desk.

"It would be funny if it were not so degrading," Potter said. "It all depends on what Joe happens to be thinking at the time. Or maybe it depends on the phase of the moon."

"Psychopathic, yes," Ike said.[179]

———

On May 5, in Room 248 of the Senate Office Building, the *New York Times* columnist James Reston testified in a closed session about a front-page story on February 26, regarding Stevens's lunch with members of the subcommittee. Reston said that after the lunch, Stevens had met with Army Chief of Staff Matthew B. Ridgway and Deputy Secretary of Defense H. Struve Hensel, who had briefed Stevens before the lunch on the type of questions he might be asked. Stevens told them he was satisfied with how the lunch had gone. But Hensel had a copy of the ticker, which seemed to have a damaging communiqué from Stevens. Reston later asked Hensel why no one had advised Stevens that the statement to which he had agreed would be taken as a surrender. Hensel replied with the story about Finnegan, who was at the bar, full of booze. Since he had already had his drink, there was no point in asking whether his credit was good.

The next day, Assistant Secretary of Defense Fred Seaton, a former Nebraska newspaper publisher, was questioned in closed session about what had come to be known as "the memorandum of misunderstanding." Seaton said that at 4:30 P.M. on the afternoon of the lunch, he got a call that a meeting was in progress. Stevens said he felt the memo had achieved the purpose of the proper treatment of witnesses, but that the reaction on the ticker was negative.

"I had a lot to do with that luncheon," said Senator Mundt, who was presiding at the closed session. "And I just wonder what in the dickens could have happened, because . . . he certainly left here in the friendliest of moods, and we had all the difficulties patched up, and we had a big area of understanding . . . [and then] the clouds opened up and the hailstones started coming down. . . . I was wondering if at this meeting [of Stevens and his aides] it was suddenly decided to tear that memorandum into shreds and come out swinging."[180]

Seaton: "These early press reports took a very dim view of it." What he did not say was that the early press reports had been influenced by McCarthy's boast to reporters that Stevens could not have surrendered more had he crawled on his hands and knees.

In his 1991 memoir, *Deadline*, Reston described McCarthy's technique as "desperately bold and cunning." He knew "that big lies produced big headlines. He also knew that most newspapers would print almost any outrageous charge a United States senator made in public."

———

Act Three of the Army-McCarthy hearings could be called "The Purloined Letter." On May 4, McCarthy thrust at Stevens a two-and-a-quarter-page letter from J. Edgar Hoover to General Alexander Bolling, head of Army Intelligence, dated January 26, 1951, and giving the names of thirty-five Fort Monmouth employees suspected of subversion.

Stevens was stunned. He had never seen the letter.

Welch: "I have an absorbing curiosity to know how in the dickens you got hold of it. . . . We will find that letter . . . if we have to keep 14 colonels up for 14 nights. I cannot erase from my mind this sense of impropriety."

An overnight check revealed that a fifteen-page letter had in fact been sent by Hoover to Bolling. McCarthy's version seemed to be a summary, with the same information and language. Joe denied it came from Hoover, but refused to reveal his source, except to say, "This came to me from someone within the army . . . an officer in the intelligence department . . . a young patriot."

Welch said McCarthy's letter was "a carbon copy of precisely nothing . . . a perfect phony." Attorney General Brownell ruled on May 6 that the letter constituted an unauthorized use of classified information.

McCarthy responded with bravado: "I would like to notify those two million [government] employees that I feel it is their duty to give us any information they have."

A furious Ike told Hagerty: "This is nothing less than a wholesale subversion of the public service. McCarthy is making the same plea of loyalty to him that Hitler made to the German people."[181]

"Any man who testifies as to the advice he gave me," Ike told Hagerty, "won't be working for me that night." His reasoning was that the people he had appointed, such as Sherman Adams, had "no political existence" beyond the President. Thus, he issued an order that no witnesses could testify about conversations with employees of the executive branch. That way, no word would leak out regarding the key meeting of January 14 when Sherman Adams had asked John Adams to keep a record of Schine's preferential treatment, which would have revealed the White House's deep involvement.

Two weeks into the hearings the strain on Joe began to show. He spent the day at the Senate caucus room and then more hours at the office to prepare for the next day, sometimes until after midnight. His activities were well irrigated, according to John Adams and Mark Catlin, a friend from Appleton and a Washington lobbyist. Adams said Joe usually had a bottle of bourbon in his briefcase and started his drinking in the morning. Catlin said that at night Joe drank straight vodka. Both estimated he drank about a quart a day. He often got by on two or three hours sleep.

On May 12, forty-two-year-old John Adams took the stand and described in detail Roy Cohn's abusive and obscene language. When Schine was inducted, Adams said, he told Roy that "the national interest requires that Schine be treated just like every other soldier." Roy exploded and said, "If it's the national interest you're interested in, I'll give you a little bit. . . . We'll hold a series of hearings and point it out to you." Adams recalled that "this was the subject which caused the degeneration of an otherwise friendly relationship."

Two days later, Adams said: "I often pleaded with Cohn and Carr to let the soldier alone, to let him be a soldier."

McClellan: "Why did you not agree to appease by sending him up to West Point to read textbooks?"

Adams: "I guess as good a reason as any is that we had 25,000 men killed in Korea who didn't have the money or the influence to get themselves a New York assignment. . . . When the day comes when the people of this country begin to mistrust the Selective Service System, Congress will take it off the books."

McClellan: "Is it unusual for a call to come into . . . the Secretary of the Army requesting that a private be kept off of KP?"

Adams: "It is so unusual, sir, it is nothing short of fantastic."[182]

On May 27, it was finally Roy Cohn's turn to testify. He had been coached to appear meek and respectful, in order to make a good impression, which went against the grain. On May 28, Ray Jenkins gingerly broached the Cohn-Schine relationship.

Jenkins: "We have friends whom we love, I do. And the relationship between you and Dave Schine had been very close for two years."

Cohn: "Yes, sir. He is one of a number of good friends that I am proud to have."

Jenkins: "And you perhaps double-dated?"

Cohn: "We have been on double dates, sir."

Jenkins kept at it: "You and this boy, Dave Schine, were almost constant companions, as good, warm, personal friends, weren't you?"

Cohn: "The truth is that we were and are good friends. He is one of my many good friends. I hope you will not ask me to scale which one is a better friend."

Jenkins was not about to pry beyond this. He found greener pastures in Schine's work habits. What exactly did Schine do for the committee, he asked? What made him so indispensable?

Cohn said he interviewed witnesses in the Voice of America investigation and worked on "related matters."

Did Cohn keep a file on the work that Schine did? Jenkins asked.

Cohn: "To a limited extent, sir."

Jenkins: "Do you mean to tell us that Dave Schine . . . did not, after his conference or interview with each witness, make a memorandum for the file?"

Cohn: "No, sir . . ."

Where did Schine keep this information? Jenkins asked.

Cohn: "A good deal of it, sir, was information which he had in his mind."[183]

On June 1 on the floor of the Senate, Senator Flanders fired another round at McCarthy, prompted perhaps by Eisenhower's comments. Flanders wondered aloud about "the strange tenderness he displayed for the Nazi ruffians at Malmédy. . . . His anti-Communism so completely parallels that of Adolf Hitler." As for the hearings, said Flanders, "Irrelevant mysteries are served up each day like the bakers' breakfast buns. . . . But . . . the real heart of the mystery . . . concerns the personal relationship of the Army private, the staff assistant, and the senator. . . . The staff assistant seems to have an almost passionate anxiety to retain . . . the Army private." Then he called Joe "Dennis the Menace" and asked: "Does the assistant have a hold on him, too? Can it be that our Dennis, so effective in making trouble for his elders, has at last gotten into trouble himself?"

McCarthy came fuming into the hearing room, saying he had just been over on the Senate floor. "I have been very patient with the senator from Vermont as he has engaged in his diatribes over the past number of weeks," he said. "I have felt that he is a nice, kind, old gentleman. I wondered whether this has been a result of senility or viciousness."[184]

The hearings then turned to the eleven memos purportedly dictated between October 2, 1953, and March 11, 1954, to Joe's secretary, Mary Driscoll, known for her efficiency and precision. She was also loyal, and testified that she had typed the memos on the stated dates.

Did she keep her shorthand notebooks? Jenkins asked. No, she never did. Did she place the memos in a file? Yes, she did, in a file that said "Investigations Committee."

At that point, Joe Welch, the lawyer for the Army, asked if he could have the chair by the witness, the chair Cohn was sitting in to coach Mrs. Driscoll and to pass to her scribbled notes from McCarthy.

Mundt: "That would seem a bit unfair."

Welch: "I thought it would be a convenience if I sat near her as I examined her." (Laughter.)

Welch began by asking innocuous questions and then focused on the typewriters, for the memos had been typed on three different typewriters. Did she know which typewriters had been used?

Mrs. Driscoll: "I don't recall. . . . A typewriter is a typewriter and I don't pay attention to the type of typewriter."

Welch: "You are a paragon of virtue. My secretaries are always kicking about them and wanting a new one."

Welch went through the memos. In the final memo, dated March 11, 1954, Frank Carr said he was "searching the files for the memoranda concerning Schine." But Mrs. Driscoll had said she kept all the memos in one file.

Welch: "You had them all together, did you not?"

Mrs. Driscoll: "Maybe I overlooked one."

Welch: "I think I must now ask to have them . . . examined and expert opinion taken as to their authenticity."

McCarthy angrily waved his finger at "this man Welch . . . this very, very clever little lawyer," who was heckling this "young lady." Welch was in fact six foot three, four inches taller than Joe, and Mrs. Driscoll, the sister of the TV anchor David Brinkley, was a grandmother in her fifties.[185]

Such was Act Four, which failed to solve the riddle of the eleven memos. "Of all the documents presented," said committee member Charles Potter, "these were the most mysterious, the most important, the most unbelievable." Only years later did Willard Edwards, the *Chicago Tribune* man who became a trusted McCarthy aide, reveal that "the senator's own lack of files was a handicap. His staff, relying on memory, had good reason to suspect a distortion . . . of facts to support the Army's case. So a decision was made to translate memories into typed memos, back-dated."

The final act in the drama came in a single day, for everything that followed was an anticlimax. On the afternoon of June 9, Welch made fun of Cohn's eagerness to catch Communists.

Welch: "Mr. Cohn, if I told you now we had a bad situation at Monmouth, you would want to cure it by sundown, if you could, wouldn't you?"

Cohn: "I am sure I couldn't, sir."

Welch: "When you first met Secretary Stevens, you had in your bosom this alarming situation about Monmouth, is that right? And you didn't tug at his lapel and say, 'Mr. Secretary, I know something about Monmouth that won't let me sleep at night?' . . . And whenever you learn of them from now on, Mr. Cohn, I beg of you, will you tell somebody about them quick?"

McCarthy saw a chance to use Welch's mocking remarks against him. If Welch wanted information right away, Joe could tell him "that he has in his law firm a young man named Fisher whom he recommended, incidentally, to do work on this committee, who has been for a number of years a member of an organization which was named, oh years and years ago, as the legal bulwark of the Communist Party [the National Lawyers Guild].

"Mr. Welch has such terror and such a great desire to know where anyone is located who may be serving the Communist cause, and to know it before sundown, that we are now letting you know. I have hesitated bringing that up, but I have been rather bored with your phony requests to Mr. Cohn here that he personally get every Communist out of government before sundown.

"I get the impression that while you are quite an actor, you play for a laugh. I don't think you yourself would ever knowingly aid the Communist cause. I think you are unknowingly aiding it when you try to burlesque this hearing."

Welch then found words that would be deposited in the nation's memory bank: "Until this moment, senator, I think I never really gauged your cruelty or your recklessness." Yes, Fred Fisher had belonged to the Lawyers Guild while at Harvard Law and some months after. He was now secretary of the Young Republicans League in Newton while working for Welch's firm, Hale & Dorr. On April 3, when Fisher and another young aide, James St. Clair, had come to Washington, Welch had warned them over dinner that if there was anything in their background that could hurt the case, "speak up quick." Fisher mentioned membership in the Lawyers Guild. Welch told him, "Fred, I just don't think I am going to ask you to work on this case."

"So, Senator, I asked him to go back to Boston. Little did I dream you could be so reckless and so cruel as to do an injury to that lad. . . . He shall always bear a scar needlessly inflicted by you. If it were in my power to forgive you for your recklessness and cruelty, I would do so. I like to think I am a gentleman, but your forgiveness will have to come from someone other than me."

If McCarthy had been capable of self-control, he would have let the incident end there. Welch had made his point, which was to show Joe up as an unscrupulous bully, and that was enough. But Joe was by nature incapable of strategic retreat. He had to counterattack, saying, "Mr. Welch talks about *this* being cruel and reckless. He has been baiting Mr. Cohn here for hours. . . . I just give this man's record . . ."

Welch: "Senator, may we not drop this? We know he belonged to the Lawyers Guild and Mr. Cohn nods his head at me. I did you no personal injury, Mr. Cohn."

Cohn: "No, sir."

Welch: "Let us not assassinate this lad further, senator. You have done enough. Have you no sense of decency, sir, at long last? Have you left no sense of decency?"

Cohn was shaking his head and trying to get Joe to stop. For Cohn on June 7 had made a deal with Welch that his side would not mention Fred Fisher if Welch dropped the issue of Cohn's draft status, where he had managed through various stratagems to avoid service in World War II and Korea. Cohn wrote in his 1968 book, *McCarthy*, that "McCarthy approved the deal."

But Joe was like a linebacker who flings himself at the quarterback and cannot halt his momentum even though the ball has been released. "Mr. Welch has been filibustering this hearing," he went on, "talking day after day about how he wants to get anyone tainted with Communism out before sundown. I know Mr. Cohn would rather not have me go into this. I intend to, however. Mr. Welch talks about any sense of decency. . . . It seems that Mr. Welch is pained so deeply he thinks it is improper for me to give the Communist front record of the man whom he wanted to foist upon this committee. . . . But there is no pain in his chest about the unfounded charges against Frank Carr; there is no pain there about the attempt to destroy the reputation and take the jobs away from the young men who were working in my committee."

Welch: "Mr. McCarthy, I will not discuss this with you further. You have sat within six feet of me and could have asked about Fred Fisher. . . . If there is a God in heaven, it will do neither you nor your cause any good." (Lengthy applause.)

It was 3:45 P.M. To deflate the tension, Mundt called a five-minute recess. Welch, milking the scene for the TV cameras, walked out with his head bowed. Thus ended the final act of the drama, although the hearings would continue until June 17.[186]

Charlie Potter, who was serving as Ike's informant, had watched "in horror and disbelief," as he later wrote, "as McCarthy's pure hatred of Welch poured out. Welch made a boorish clown out of McCarthy and a fumbling adolescent out of Cohn." Potter saw Joe as emotionally unbalanced, an overage delinquent who liked smashing windows, stealing hubcaps, and defacing the sides of buildings with graffiti.[187]

McCarthy was a diminished man, having brought down the furies upon himself. In Wisconsin, even the tail-wagging Republican papers called his behavior on June 9 "inexcusable" and "brutal." The *Wisconsin State Journal*, a stalwart supporter since 1946, wrote that "in one black second . . . McCarthy . . . wrecked it all. He blew his angry head of steam and cast out an ugly smear on a young man who had no connection with the case. It was worse than reckless. It was worse than cruel. It was reprehensible."[188]

In the nation at large, Republicans who had seen McCarthy as a vote-getter now saw him as a liability. Even before June 9, White House mail was running strongly anti-Joe, with congressional elections coming up in the fall. From Ohio, Representative George H. Bender, the Republican candidate for the Senate, warned Ike on May 7 that "McCarthyism has become a synonym for witch-hunting [and] star-chamber methods." From New Hampshire, the national committeeman Frank J. Sulloway wrote Sherman Adams on May 17 that "if we don't do something about McCarthy, we are going to lose a lot of votes." From Iowa, the Republican leader Jim Sherman wrote Adams on February 22, 1954, that Republicans could not win in November without the help of "many Democrats and 'liberal' Republicans." Palmer Hoyt of the *Denver Post* wrote Eisenhower on May 24, "It is now time for the Republican party to repudiate Joe McCarthy before he drags them all to defeat." Once a Republican Galahad, McCarthy was now an albatross.[189]

On June 11, in the midst of the hearing, Senator Flanders came into the caucus room, made his way past the spectators and cameramen to the long table, and handed McCarthy a letter. Joe read aloud: Flanders planned to make another speech about his activities as soon as he could get the floor and would be glad to have him present.

McCarthy then commented aloud on the letter: "Number 1, I will be unable to be present because I am testifying. Number 2, I don't have enough interest in any Flanders speech to listen to it. Number 3, . . . if you have nothing except the usual smear, gleaned from the smear sheets, then . . . I think you should do it here under oath."

Mundt: "I am sorry, we can't permit this kind of feuding to go on here."

Flanders: "I retire under compulsion."

McCarthy: "I have no feud with Mr. Flanders. I have said . . . it was not the result of viciousness but perhaps senility." Later, he told reporters: "I think they should get a net and take him to a good quiet place."[190]

McCarthy would have done well to pay closer attention, for the Vermont senator that afternoon introduced Resolution 261 to remove him from his committee chairmanship unless he answered the questions raised by the Hennings report, which dealt mainly with McCarthy's finances. The Flanders resolution proved to be the opening salvo in the McCarthy censure, for it charged him with being "in contempt" of the Senate.

Later that day, Senator Scoop Jackson, who was being advised by the minority counsel, Bobby Kennedy, brought up a pamphlet Schine had written on psychological warfare. Schine proposed: "We must create a 'Deminform' or association of democratic parties."

Jackson: "Isn't that word 'Deminform' pretty close to 'Cominform'?"

McCarthy: "Let's be fair, Mr. Jackson."

Jackson: "He has 'higher clergy, pastoral letters.' Is he going to infiltrate the clergy?"

McCarthy: "You know that he is talking about fighting Communism."

Jackson: "Look, under 'Community Leaders,' he has the Elks and the Knights of Columbus. I don't know whether they have an Elks Lodge in Pakistan."

McCarthy: "You apparently think this is humorous."

Jackson: "Let's turn to 'Periodicals.'. . . He has . . .'Universal appeal—pictures, cartoons, humor, pinups.' What kind of program is he going to carry out for the use of pinups. . . . We can all laugh at that one, I think."[191]

There was so much laughter that the session was adjourned. It was more than Cohn could stand to see his protégé being ridiculed. He had watched in silent anger as Bobby Kennedy handed Jackson the documents he was using to make Dave a laughingstock. As they rose to leave, a furious Roy came face-to-face with Bobby and told him he was "full of crap." They shouted at each other and Roy said, "Apparently there is only one way to settle this," and started to swing, but the two featherweights were soon separated, and so ended their famous nonfight.[192]

On June 17, after thirty-six days, the hearings ended. "This is a little like June week on the college campus," Senator Dirksen said, "when we utter our valedictories and say goodbye to all the amazing things that were a part of this legislative venture. We have plowed the long furrow."[193]

If the end was like a college graduation, what was the lesson to be learned? Potter, perhaps the most balanced member of the committee, said in a press statement that he believed McCarthy and Cohn were guilty as charged of bringing improper pressures on the Army, but that Secretary Stevens's performance had been "degrading." The hearing made clear that Cohn and McCarthy had bullied and blackmailed the Army into pampering Schine, for reasons that had more to do with Cohn's pathology than Schine's "expertise," and that Stevens had cravenly appeased McCarthy.

Most remarkably, all the hubbub had been caused by one man's obsession for another man. These were not matters of state, but of personal gratification. Add to that Cohn's arrogance, his need to prove himself by pushing people around, his sheer *chutzpah* in making obscenity-laced threats, and his political cunning placed at the service of obtaining favors for his boyfriend.

Seldom had men in high office been drawn into such insignificant matters. Never before had the basic training of an Army private become a test of the Army's integrity. Never before had the power and resources of a congressional committee been applied to such a trifling end.

Roy Cohn resigned on June 19 and went into private law practice. Schine remained at Camp Gordon. McCarthy's reputation was in shambles. Eisenhower privately congratulated Welch, who told the President that at the very least the hearings had managed to keep Joe on television long enough (187 hours) so that the public could get a good look at him. In the September 1 subcommittee report, all seven senators agreed that Cohn had extended his authority, that McCarthy had let him, and that Stevens was guilty of appeasement. By that time the planet had turned, and Joe had other problems.

———

On June 11, Flanders had made his speech on the Senate floor asking that McCarthy be removed from his committee chairmanship. There was little support for this approach, mainly because Southern Democrats did not want any tampering with the seniority system. Deciding on a change in strategy, Flanders on July 16 proposed another resolution that called for censure. This, he said, was more in keeping with the procedures by which the Senate had previously disciplined one of its own members. Walter F. George, the dean of the Southern Democrats, said on July 17, "This is something I can go along with."

Historically, since 1850, there had been only three cases of censure in the Senate. In the first, on April 17, 1850, Thomas Hart Benton of Missouri clashed in a debate on the Senate floor with Henry Stuart Foote of Mississippi. Benton rose angrily from his seat and strode toward Foote, who drew and cocked his pistol (in those days senators were armed and did not always check their weapons in the cloakroom). Other senators intervened and Foote surrendered his gun. The matter was referred to a select committee, which censured both men for being seriously at fault.

Tempers flared again on February 2, 1902, when the two senators from South Carolina, Benjamin R. Tillman and John L. McLaurin, slugged it out on the Senate floor. "Pitchfork Ben," an intemperate segregationist, who favored lynching and the disenfranchisement of blacks, and who had been exposed in shady land deals by President Theodore Roosevelt, attacked his colleague for backing the President. They fought until separated, and their punishment was censure.

In the only nonviolent case, in 1929, Senator Hiram Bingham of Connecticut was censured for hiring a lobbyist on the payroll of the Connecticut

Manufacturers Association to advise him during Finance Committee hearings on a tariff bill.[194]

The vote on Flanders's new resolution did not take place until July 30, 1954, since a number of senators were away campaigning for the primaries. The content of Flanders's Resolution 301 was: "Resolved, that the conduct of the Senator from Wisconsin, Mr. McCarthy, is contrary to senatorial tradition and tends to bring the Senate in disrepute, and such conduct is hereby condemned."

A number of senators thought the resolution was too vague and general, and asked for a bill of particulars. This led to specific charges being added in the form of amendments. Flanders himself added thirty-three. Then Senator Knowland, the Majority Leader, proposed that a select committee of three Republicans and three Democrats be named to hold hearings on the resolution. The resolution and the committee were adopted by a vote of 75 to 12.

On August 5, Vice President Nixon, after consultation with Minority Leader Lyndon Johnson, announced the committee members. The chairman would be Arthur V. Watkins, a skinny, austere, sixty-seven-year-old Mormon from Utah; the other Republicans were Francis Case of South Dakota, a one-time newspaper editor, and the seventy-year-old Frank Carlson of Kansas, a farmer and stockman. The Democrats were Edwin Johnson, who had come to Colorado as a homesteader and who had been in the Senate for seventeen years; the courtly John Stennis of Mississippi; and the jovial Sam J. Ervin Jr. of North Carolina. The two Southerners liked to say, "Salt down the facts. The law can wait!"

On August 2, hoping for another Army-McCarthy circus, Joe demanded the right to cross-examine. Watkins told Flanders: "We are not unmindful of his genius for disruption." The Watkins Committee ignored McCarthy as it drafted its own rules, limiting the number of witnesses and the right to cross-examine. There would be no television. Nor would there be the chummy ambiance where everyone sat at the same table. McCarthy and his lawyer, Edward Bennett Williams, would sit at a small table facing the committee. Joe was a juggler robbed of his pins.

On August 24, 1954, Watkins announced that the committee had boiled down the forty-plus amendments into thirteen charges divided in six categories: McCarthy's finances; his abuse of colleagues; his contempt of a Senate committee; his acceptance of classified information; his telling government employees to break the law; and his abuse of General Zwicker.[195]

Public hearings were set to begin on August 30, 1954, in the celebrated caucus room of the Old Senate Office building. On August 29, the committee held an executive session to lay down the rules, which McCarthy and his lawyer attended. One rule provided that McCarthy and Williams could not be heard at the same time. Williams agreed that McCarthy would do no talking except when testifying.

Seeming agitated, Joe brandished a news clipping from the *Denver Post* and demanded to know what the committee was going to do about it. The clipping, dated March 12, 1954, was an interview with committee member Ed Johnson, who was quoted as saying that "there was not a Democrat in the Senate who didn't loathe Senator McCarthy." Watkins said the committee would study the matter.

The next morning, the room was packed, but no cameras were rolling. Watkins had also banned smoking, so the air was cleaner. Most of the day was spent on legal matters, but as the time for recess approached, Senator Johnson spoke up to deny the quote in the *Denver Post*. Williams asked to have read into the record some material connected to the article. Watkins said he didn't want to "clutter up the record" with a lot of "extraneous matter."

Then Joe said he wanted to ask a question. Watkins would not let him, under the rule that he and his lawyer could not both jump in. "We are not going to permit both of you to argue this matter."

McCarthy: "Just a minute, Mr. Chairman, just a minute."

Williams kept asking for more information on the Johnson interview. Watkins kept saying it was not material to the hearing.

McCarthy: "I should be entitled to know . . ."

Watkins: "The senator is out of order."

McCarthy: "Can't I get Mr. Johnson to tell me . . . ?"

Watkins: "The Senator is out of order."

McCarthy: "Whether it is true or false?"

Watkins: "The Senator is out of order. . . . We are not going to be interrupted by these diversions and sidelines. We are going straight down the line. The committee will be in recess." He pounded the gavel until Joe shut up.[196]

Thus, in the first day of the hearing, Watkins showed McCarthy who was boss. He was not going to tolerate any interruptions. If he had not enforced the rules from the start, McCarthy would have trampled roughshod over the committee.

There were nine public hearings, the last one on September 13. They were far less dramatic than the Army-McCarthy confrontations, for they consisted mainly of placing into the record McCarthy's remarks and letters. Joe was absent most of the time and wasn't allowed to speak when he showed up. So he took his case outside the hearing, holding press conferences to attack the committee.

The sixty-eight-page unanimous committee report, released on September 27, recommended censure on two counts. One was the Zwicker incident, which the committee called "reprehensible." The other count was contempt of the Gillette-Hennings subcommittee in 1951 and 1952, which had convened in response to Senator Benton's resolution asking for McCarthy's expulsion. This was seen as an offense against the Senate. McCarthy had been asked on five separate occasions to appear before the subcommittee, but had appeared only once. He had repeatedly denounced the subcommittee. He had defamed Senator Hendrickson by calling him "a living miracle without brains or guts."[197]

It was decided to postpone the debate on censure until after the elections on November 2, 1954. The Republicans lost seventeen seats in the House and two in the Senate. The Democrats had gained control of both houses, which meant that whatever the outcome of the censure motion, McCarthy would lose the chairmanship of his committee in January 1955.

The Republican senators returned for the censure debate in a chastened mood, some of them thinking that Joe was partly responsible for the GOP defeat. The committee report was presented to the Senate on November 8, and two days later the censure debate began. Watkins made his presentation, but McCarthy interrupted, defending himself on Watkins's time and grandstanding to the galleries.

McCarthy resorted to his customary trickery. He had prepared a speech so vile that, had he delivered it, he would have been in flagrant violation of Rule 19: that the motives of a senator could not be impugned. So instead of making the speech, he had it inserted into the *Congressional Record.* "If I lose on the censure vote," the speech said, "it follows, of course, that someone else wins . . . the Communist Party. . . . It has made a committee of the Senate its unwilling handmaiden. . . . In writing its report it imitated Communist methods. . . . It did the work of the Communist Party."[198]

Watkins was astonished to see some of Joe's cohorts taking up the same line. Jenner of Indiana charged the select committee with "ignoring the activities of a conspiracy against the junior Senator from Wisconsin. . . . The strategy of censure was initiated by the Communist conspiracy." Jenner suggested that "some members of the Senate might be secret Communists." Barry Goldwater of Arizona said that "those unknown engineers of censure" were engaged in a "merciless fight to destroy a United States senator and the fight against Communism."

The freshman senator Clifford Case, a liberal Republican from New Jersey, responded that the committee had been told, "Here is a job you have to do. Are we going to welsh on it because we fear that the *Daily Worker* will say, 'That is a little water on our wheel'?"[199]

On November 14, Watkins got some support from two of the Democrats on the committee. Senator Ervin, who had thus far remained silent, was aroused by Joe's undelivered speech to say on *Meet the Press* that his remarks were "pretty solid ground" to expel him from the Senate for "moral incapacity." If he believed what he said, he was suffering from "mental delusion." Senator Stennis, genuinely shocked by Joe's attack on Watkins, told the Senate that he threw "slime and slush" at all senators who criticized him. Unless the Senate voted censure, Stennis said, "something big and fine has gone out of this chamber . . . something wrong has come in and got accepted."[200]

Three days later, Watkins spoke for an hour and a half. He mentioned McCarthy's "hit and run attacks," and pointed out that Joe had called him a coward. "I am asking all my colleagues: What are you going to do about it?"

When he had finished, the Senate broke into applause. Watkins felt so weak he had to find a couch in the cloakroom to lie down on. The junior senator from Utah, Wallace F. Bennett, introduced a motion to add to the censure the charge of abusing the chairman of the select committee.

On November 17, McCarthy went into Bethesda Naval Hospital to treat a bruised elbow, which had developed into bursitis. The Senate agreed to adjourn until he was back on the 29th. Edward Bennett Williams came to the hospital with Barry Goldwater to ask Joe to work out a compromise by writing letters of apology to Watkins and Hendrickson. With one arm in a cast, he threw the pen across the room and started cussing. He yelled so much that the floor nurse called for a doctor. Williams noticed that Joe kept a bottle of bourbon under the mattress.[201]

On November 29, with McCarthy back, the Senate agreed to limit debate and vote two days later. There was some opposition to the Zwicker charge. The Senate, jealous of its prerogatives, including the right to insult witnesses, was hesitant to approve any measure encroaching on them. It would only approve offenses against itself. Lyndon Johnson, now Majority Leader, stopped by Watkins's chair and said, "Arthur, you are going to have to drop the Zwicker matter. There are at least 15 Democratic senators who will not vote for the censure resolution if the Zwicker charge is part of it." And so it was dropped, leaving the charge of contempt for the Gillette-Hennings subcommittee, plus the recently added charge of abuse of the Watkins Committee.[202]

The debate dragged on into December 2, what with three compromise resolutions that went down to defeat. That evening, amid cries of "Vote! Vote!" censure was voted 67 to 12, with McCarthy voting "present" and 16 absentees—among them John F. Kennedy, whose father was a good friend of Joe's, and the Wisconsin Senator Alexander Wiley, who decided he would be better off traveling in Brazil. Voting for censure were all forty-four Democrats, the Independent Wayne Morse, and twenty-two Republicans. The Republican Party was split right down the middle between old guard and Eisenhower moderates.[203]

A vindicated Benton commented on December 2 that there had never been a senator like Joe, "who impugned the honesty of many of his fellow senators without a tincture of sustaining fact." If there were five other senators like him, Benton thought, the Senate would be unable to function.[204]

Lyndon Johnson was glad his tactics had prevailed. "Joe's just a loud-mouthed drunk," he told his aide Bobby Baker. "Hell, he's the sorriest senator up here. Can't tie his goddam shoes."[205]

As for the President, his strategy of letting the Senate handle McCarthy had paid off, while Truman's method of matching him punch for punch had helped to raise his stature. Of course the Eisenhower White House had prodded matters along, but discreetly. Ike, however, was not sure censure was enough, writing his friend Clifford Roberts on December 7 that "the number of senators who voted against censure indicates that the so-called splinter group may constitute almost half the party. . . . McCarthy is operating at the same old stand."[206]

Quite soon it became clear that the Senate floor was no longer a forum, or even a haven, for McCarthy. Watkins felt that the post-censure transformation of Joe could not be entirely explained "by his poor health, his heavy drinking, his losses in the market, or even his broken spirit, caused by a turncoat press. The answer lay deeply within the heart of the man." Once out of the spotlight, he was like a plant without sunshine or water. The backslapping, crowd-pleasing, overconfident, reporter-pursued Joe was no more. The only thing he had left was his mean streak; now, when he passed Watkins's desk on the way to the cloakroom, he would hiss with whiskey breath, "How is the little coward from Utah?" Other times, however, he was friendly and polite. Watkins concluded that his day-to-day behavior depended on his bourbon intake.[207]

As for Senator Flanders, who had once been in Coventry himself, he noticed that when Joe got up on the Senate floor to speak, there was a move for the door. If senators were gathered in the cloakroom and Joe joined the huddle, it dispersed. At lunch, if he sat at a table, the others would finish their bean soup and their sandwich and get up and leave. Joe thrived on being popular and well liked. When he became unpopular and disliked, he withered.[208]

———

In January 1955, McCarthy turned over the chairmanship of the Committee on Government Operations to the Democrat John McClellan.

Although diminished and disheartened, he was incapable of changing, even though the world around him had changed. Stalin had died in March 1953, and the Korean War had ended that July. McCarthy could no longer use in his oratory the American boys dying in battle. In 1955, there was peace abroad and prosperity at home. This was not an inviting context for Joe, who applied chaos theory to politics.

If there was no genuine crisis, he would fabricate one. As Ike had put it, he was back "at the same old stand." On March 11, 1955, he wrote the President an abusive letter for not obtaining the release of eleven U.S. airmen held by Communist China. Hagerty confided to his diary on that day: "All of us on the staff, including the president, will make it a point not to have any comment whatsoever on anything McCarthy says or does. We have him relegated to the back pages of the papers and he knows he is not news anymore. Consequently, he is desperately trying to get back on the front pages. . . . The best treatment for McCarthy is to ignore him. That is the one thing he cannot stand and if we continue this sort of silent treatment, he will blow his top and sink still lower in political importance."[209]

In June 1955, Eisenhower was preparing for the first summit conference since Potsdam, ten years before. The summit, to be held in mid-July in Geneva, would bring together the so-called Big Four, the United States, U.S.S.R., Britain, and France. With Stalin's death and the ascension of Nikita Khrushchev, Soviet foreign policy was more flexible. The new Soviet posture of "competitive co-existence" required some adjustment on the American side.[210]

But such a gathering, signaling a thaw in the Cold War, was an alarm bell for McCarthy, and another opportunity to bash the Eisenhower camp. Joe went before the Foreign Relations Committee on June 20 to present a resolution that the fate of the satellite nations should be a subject for discussion at the Big Four conference.

On June 21, when Ike met with the leaders of both houses, there was a brief mention of Joe's resolution. Ike told the congressional leaders that he would of course bring up for discussion those things that caused international tensions, such as the captive states. He added that he could know more about Europe in five minutes than McCarthy could in fifteen years. Nixon told him not to take the resolution seriously. Ike said there was a story going around Washington: "It's no longer McCarthyism, it's McCarthywasm."[211]

The debate by the full Senate a few days later gave Joe an unpleasant surprise. Majority Leader Lyndon Johnson said, "The issue is very simple. It is whether the president of the United States shall be sent to Geneva with a gun at his head."

Joe watched dumbfounded as his onetime allies on the Republican right jumped ship. When Senator Knowland agreed with Johnson, McCarthy told him that he was "shocked and disappointed" by his position. An angry Knowland replied, "I'll place my record in opposition to Communists against yours any day."

McCarthy said it was characteristic of the Democrats "to whine and whimper whenever the red-hot stove of Communist aggression is touched."

But Bourke Hickenlooper of Iowa, another faithful McCarthyite, said: "I do not agree that they are appeasers of Communism."

When Joe questioned Eisenhower's ability to negotiate with the Russians, his once devoted acolyte, Jenner of Indiana, asked, "Wherein have the president or congress given comfort to the Communists?"

Even the senator who was called "McCarthy junior"—Herman Welker of Idaho—turned against Joe, perhaps concerned about his chances for reelection. There was a decided change in climate, with the Republican senators making a show of unity in preparation for the 1956 presidential election. The Senate voted against the resolution 77 to 4, which left McCarthy virtually alone.[212]

Roy Cohn, who visited Joe regularly, now found him "at home, sunk deep in his armchair, staring into the fire." Keeping up the battle against Communism, he said, was as futile as "shoveling shit against the tide."[213] And yet he kept shoveling, for after Ike had returned from the summit, basking in the "spirit of Geneva," Joe attacked him in a speech on August 1, saying he had made agreements that sold out nationalist China and South Korea. He charged that Eisenhower had made a deal at Geneva to trade the offshore islands Quemoy and Matsu for the eleven American POWs. Amazingly, it was Senator Knowland, known as "the senator from Formosa," who came to the defense of the administration. Afterward, Knowland called Secretary of State Dulles from the cloakroom and said that at first he was determined to let Joe's speech go unchallenged. But it was so extreme in nature that Knowland could not let it pass. He told Joe that he had spoken to the President and the Secretary of State and that "there was no such thing as a deal of this sort or selling out of any of our allies with whom we have mutual defense treaties." Dulles told Knowland he was "on sound ground." Dulles had himself issued a statement that "we had made no political promises or concessions to obtain release."[214]

McCarthy did not seem to realize that he was spinning his wheels. He continued to act as if his pronouncements mattered. On September 21, 1955, he wrote Ike a windy five-page letter that was yet another request for the release of government security files to congressional committees. "The left-wingers are having a field day at the expense of the nation's safety," he said.[215]

In 1956, when Eisenhower was up for reelection, Joe continued to pester him. On February 16, he wrote the President to complain about a U.S. district judge in Boston, Bailey Aldrich, who in October 1955 had presided over the trial of Leon J. Kamin for contempt of Congress. Kamin had been cited by Joe's committee during its investigation of defense plants. He had been employed on a secret radar project while being a paid official of the Communist Party.

McCarthy questioned Kamin at a hearing in Boston on January 15, 1954. When Kamin took the Fifth, Joe cited him for contempt. At the contempt trial in Boston on November 21, 1955, when Joe appeared in the courtroom to testify, a member of the jury clapped. Judge Aldrich at once dismissed the jury and declared a mistrial. He then dismissed four of the six counts against Kamin. On January 5, 1956, he dismissed the other two counts on the grounds that in investigating Communists in privately owned defense plants, the subcommittee was outside its jurisdiction.

Joe was "taken aback," he wrote Eisenhower in February 1956. After the trial, he had commented that the judge's decision was "ridiculous," and then let the matter drop. But now he had some important new information from the *New Bedford Standard-Times*. On August 2, 1955, two months before the Kamin trial, Governor Christian Herter had nominated Judge Aldrich as a trustee of Massachusetts Memorial Hospital. Aldrich was sent a non-Communist affidavit card to sign, but wrote Herter that it was against his principles to sign it. He would rather forgo the post on the hospital board than sign the card. The governor's executive council ruled that no exception could be made. Finally, on September 13, after being told that failure to comply would cause great embarrassment to the Herter administration, Judge Aldrich signed.

"What are we to say," Joe asked Ike, "of a federal judge who rebels against signing a statement that he is not a Communist and agrees to sign it only after severe pressure has been brought to bear . . . and then proceeds to sit as judge and jury in the trial of a man charged with contempt of Congress. . . . He should have disqualified himself on grounds of prejudice. . . . That he should have gone ahead and tried the case is disgraceful."[216]

It was Eisenhower's policy now to ignore McCarthy's communications. But the Aldrich incident is instructive in showing that the Communists in government issue had lost steam. That a Boston judge should defy the Red-hunters was a replay of events in the 1920 Red Scare.

Back home in Wisconsin, Joe was also on the skids. His old friend John

Wyngaard, in his column *Under the Capitol Dome,* said he was no longer in touch with his constituents. He no longer had any say in the management of the Wisconsin Republican Party. His chances for reelection in 1958 were poor. "The Communists in government issue which served him so mightily during his heyday has been exhausted."[217]

As if to corroborate Wyngaard, Attorney General Herbert Brownell wrote Eisenhower on October 8, 1956, that "Communist leaders now publicly declare that the party has suffered such heavy organizational losses and its influence has declined to such a low point that the party is confronted with a critical situation." Prosecution under the Smith Act had resulted in the convictions of 108 top Communists. Twenty-two others were awaiting trial. The *Daily Worker* had closed its Washington bureau. The exposure of Communist Party fronts had led the party to abandon the concept of broad front organizations. It was going back to infiltrating existing organizations. The labor unions had expelled Communists from their ranks. The loyalty security programs had rid the government of disloyal employees, and 169 subversive aliens had been deported.[218]

What was McCarthy's contribution to this dismantling of the Communist Party? Except for inducing hysteria in the general population, little or nothing. The party had been made irrelevant by the anti-subversive measures of the Truman and Eisenhower administrations and by information supplied by the House Un-American and Senate Internal Security committees—not by the McCarthy Committee, which uncovered a few snippets here and there, but on balance made a lot of noise to little purpose. The headlines promised much more than Joe could deliver.

In November, the presidential election came at a time of international turmoil. On November 3, 1956, the Red Army invaded Hungary, creating another trauma of soul-searching among those perhaps fifteen thousand American Communists still in the party. On November 5, French and British paratroopers dropped on Suez. November 6 was election day, and Eisenhower defeated Stevenson by a 10-million-vote margin, twice the 1952 margin. The Eisenhower landslide made McCarthy seem increasingly inconsequential.

In 1956, in the eyes of those who knew him, Joe was a "sick pigeon." The vocabulary of his rhetoric had always relied on pugnacious vitality. He presented himself as a "fighter," "scrapper," "brawler," "slugger," "battler," whose moves were "savage uppercuts," "bare-knuckled jobs," "fist-clenching," and "hard-hitting slugfests." But now he became a commuter to Bethesda Naval Hospital, leaning on his wife's arm and slow in movement, suffering from back trouble, heart trouble, elbow trouble, stomach trouble, knee trouble, hernia trouble, and above all, drink trouble. Van Susteren said that by 1956 he drank a bottle a day, which takes serious application. By the summer, he was in and out of detox. When he was hospitalized in September, his wife told reporters it was for treatment of an old knee injury received while helping to repair a plane on Guadalcanal. In late September in Appleton, he suffered from delirium tremens and saw snakes leaping at him. Van Susteren called his doctor in Washington, who said two thirds of his liver was gone and he would soon die unless he stopped drinking.[219]

In December, the Wisconsin congressman Alvin O'Konski told the Washington reporter Ronald May off the record that he had seen Joe twice in northern Wisconsin and both times he was drunk. "I remember one time at Land O' Lakes," O'Konski said, "McCarthy was so drunk he didn't know what day of the month it was." O'Konski said that Joe had terrible nightmares and woke up screaming—in other words, delirium tremens. It was too much even for his wife, Jean, who had become a pretty hardened character, O'Konski said.[220]

But despite his drinking, and despite his pariah status, Joe was not a quitter. On January 4, 1957, the day after the opening of the first session of the 85th Congress, he rose to say that he wanted to introduce into the *Congressional Record* the newsletters that he had sent his constituents. Holding one in his hand, he said, "This one has some facts on the censure vote. . . . I had and have the utmost contempt for the Gillette Committee and also for the Watkins Committee. . . . The greatest example of cowardice that the Senate has witnessed in its long history was when senator Watkins . . . refused to answer my questions. . . . It was a disgrace to the state of Utah and a disgrace to the United States." Some of the senators present wondered if he had been drinking.[221]

McCarthy's wife, Jean, a Presbyterian who had converted to Catholicism when they married, arranged that January, with the help of Cardinal Spellman, for the adoption of a five-week-old girl from the New York Foundling Home, whom they called Tierney. Howard Rushmore, an ex-Communist who had served on Joe's staff, ran into him at Eisenhower's inauguration on January 21, 1957. Joe took Rushmore home to see his daughter, who was sound asleep in her crib. He seemed thrilled, but slightly in awe of this small presence.

Adopting a daughter did not stop Joe's drinking. His skin developed a yellow pallor, a sign of jaundice and liver damage. Hearing reports of his health, the *Milwaukee Journal* prepared his obituary. Adding to his woes was financial trouble. He had invested in the Green Bay Uranium Company. In 1956, the company was liquidated and its director fled to South America. Joe had been thinking of buying a ranch in Arizona, but that was now a pipe dream.[222]

On April 28, McCarthy was admitted to Bethesda Naval Hospital with a severe liver ailment. Four days later, on May 2, 1957, he died of "acute hepatic failure." He had drunk himself to death. His wife, Jean, was at his bedside. He was forty-eight years old.

———

In a tribute to McCarthy, his friends in the media emulated his hyperbolic style. George Sokolsky said he had been "hounded to death." Fulton Lewis Jr. called it "an organized lynching." Lewis in his broadcast recalled the tender side of Joe, carrying Tierney in his arms, or "dancing capers" to make her smile.[223]

On May 6, after a requiem mass at St. Matthew's Cathedral attended by two thousand, the flag-draped casket was taken to the Capitol with a forty-eight-Marine honor guard and carried into the well of the Senate chamber for a funeral service, an honor rarely granted. A brief service was followed by the Senate chaplain's eulogy.

After the Senate service, McCarthy's body was flown to Austin Straubel Airport in Green Bay. A cortege of thirty-five Marines drove the twenty-eight miles to Appleton, with onlookers watching along the route. On May 7, with twenty-one senators in attendance, McCarthy was buried next to his parents in St. Mary's Cemetery, on a spruce-shaded bluff above the Fox River. Everett Dirksen, one of the senators watching Joe's remains being lowered into the ground, as he stood on the hillside above the riverbank, with the wind whispering in the trees, wondered: "What is the worth of a person's days?"

On August 14, at a memorial service in the Senate chamber, McCarthy's colleagues had their final say, respecting the tradition of not speaking ill of fallen colleagues.

Lyndon Johnson: "Joe McCarthy had a rare quality, which enabled him to touch the hearts and the minds of his fellow men."

Karl Mundt: "He made a great circle of enemies because he refused to quit."

William Jenner: "Joe McCarthy was human. He had weaknesses, like the rest of us. When he was cut with knives, he bled. But he had a fighting heart. . . . When men he admired seemed to desert him, he broke."

Bourke Hickenlooper: "McCarthy was like a dentist who starts drilling one's tooth. Every once in a while, he strikes a sensitive nerve and the patient jumps."

Barry Goldwater recalled that Joe came often to Arizona because he had asthma. They fished and played poker. "I must say that he was not good at either one. . . . I have eaten his cooking. I must say the same as I did about his fishing and poker."[224]

His wife, Jean, who had to answer hundreds of letters, wrote the Catholic Action Guild on May 22 that Joe had given his life "because he exhausted himself physically for love of his fellow being. . . . When Joe used to come home to Appleton, he saw the heart and soul of this country standing along the roadside on the 30-mile drive from Green Bay."[225]

Jean was now raising her daughter alone, and wrote a friend on August 9: "Tierney is cuter than ever—and wiser! She has six teeth now and can stand up when she gets a grip on the crib railing."[226]

In a comment from an ordinary citizen, John Hoffman of Green Valley, California, wrote Senator Flanders on June 4: "Some say McCarthy was a great American. If America is a land of intolerance, of untruth, of win at any cost, of character assassination, of deceit and treachery and turmoil, McCarthy stands high on the list. . . . Were McCarthy the symbol of Americanism, we would want none of it."[227]

But Dirksen's question remained unanswered: What is the worth of a person's days?

It would be pleasant to remember the compassionate judge who saw to it that the children of divorce were provided for and who tried to rehabilitate the young men convicted in his court. But when he reached the national stage as a senator in 1946, tail gunner Joe revealed the twin engines that propelled him, ambition and greed. His equipment did not include sound judgment, or honesty, or fair-mindedness, or truthfulness, or integrity, or any kind of moral compass. He did marshal energy and cunning at the service of his aspirations. As someone who liked to quote *Macbeth*, he should have pondered this line: "Vaulting ambition, which o'leaps itself and falls on the other side."

McCarthy had an unanchored, compulsive personality, excessive in its verbal expression and appetites, without any capacity for restraint or instinct for self-examination. He was like the ball in a roulette wheel, jumping haphazardly from slot to slot. He had a certain oratorical bravado combined with a messy mind. Despite the pad of blank subpoenas in his pocket, and the briefcase bulging with documents, he was usually wrong on the facts. He was essentially an opportunist who believed in little but his own advancement, a hollow man, all in surfaces. He was interested in Communism to the extent that he could make himself into the number one anti-Communist, just as he was interested in sugar to make a name for having ended rationing. He had no worldview or understanding of foreign affairs, but picked up fragments and slogans as ammunition for his administration bashing—not only under Truman, but under a President of his own party.

His strongest trait was a hatred of authority, whether of the presidency, the Army, or the State Department. Where did that chip on his shoulder come from? Order of birth, anarchist rage, feelings of inferiority? It's too late to place him on the analyst's couch, although the media endeavored to fill the gap. For him, party loyalty meant nothing, nor did the public good or the merit of the issues. The only thing that counted was to score points and defeat your opponent, by bluffing and lying. McCarthy made the fascinating discovery that he could attack anyone and the newspapers would print it. He was locked in a symbiotic embrace with the media, until it finally turned against him.

In a variant on the old Teddy Roosevelt remark, "He's a dictator, but he's our dictator," the groups that coalesced around Joe, the Republican right, the right wing of the Catholic Church, the American Legion, and all the paranoia-nourished fringe groups and super-patriots, came together saying, "He's a bully, but he's our bully."

In an attempt to straighten the zigzag course of his mismanaged ship, McCarthy hired Roy Cohn as helmsman. But Cohn was so besotted with David Schine that he was willing to use the power of investigation to coerce the Army into doing his bidding. Unable to control his overbearing aide, McCarthy was brought down by him.

Once in private practice, Cohn was often reprimanded for unethical conduct and was tried and acquitted in 1964, 1969, and 1971, on charges of conspiracy, bribery, and fraud. He was disbarred in 1986. Cohn would be brought down by AIDS in 1985. The arrogant little squirt with friends in high places, the show-off with the orange tuxedo, wasn't showing off anymore.[228]

As for the object of his affection, Schine died on June 19, 1996, at the age of sixty-nine, when a single-engine plane piloted by his son crashed in Burbank, California. After getting out of the Army, Schine went into his father's hotel business and did a little film producing. He had five children with his Swedish wife, Hillevi, who was Miss Universe of 1955. Only in his relationship with Cohn had he momentarily departed from a basic ordinariness.

Who could have predicted that censure would be a fatal blow? But with censure, Joe lost his credibility, which was the same as losing his self-respect, for if no one else believes you, how can you believe in yourself? The longer he remained in the Senate, the more senators he alienated. Even those who had first hailed him as a serviceable battering ram eventually feared he had turned into a torch who would set fire to them all. His poisonous spirit of revenge, against Tydings, against Benton and Flanders and Watkins, made him some enduring enemies, and it was those enemies who had the last word. As Arthur Watkins put it, "When he lost his credibility and standing . . . he collapsed like a pricked balloon." McCarthy had called Watkins a coward, but he was the real coward, because he couldn't handle a setback. Once exposed, he drank himself to death, as if knowing in his dark heart that he was a fraud.

With McCarthy's death, the burr under the administration's saddle was gone, the hysteria over a moribund Communist Party dropped to a murmur, and the burgeoning conservative movement lost its greatest encumbrance.

XV

McCARTHYISM

Postwar McCarthyism existed long before Joe came on the scene in 1950. Joe was what Lenin called a "tailist," latching on to a spontaneous grassroots movement, born out of the dimly understood reality of America's postwar global role. The postwar equation consisted of two inimical great powers, one of which had a subversive group in the other's midst, masquerading as a political party. No one yet knew about Soviet espionage. Russia did not have the bomb. But the threat of another nuclear power was alarming, particularly in the light of Soviet expansion in Eastern Europe.

The veterans, many of whom had fought on the same side as their Russian allies in Europe, were among the first to express their anxiety about the changing balance of power. In St. Louis in January 1946, American War Dads issued a pamphlet called *The Communist Cancer,* which stated that "there is no such thing as an American Communist." The Communist Party in Missouri at that time counted fewer than five hundred card-carrying members.

Missouri State Senator Horace C. Williams, a Republican from the Ozarks, rose on the Senate floor in January 1947 and fanned the air with the Christmas issue of *Towertime,* the University of Missouri campus publication. He objected to the cover, which showed Stalin dressed as Santa Claus going down a chimney, to illustrate an article about politicians exploiting the Red Scare.[1]

In Peoria, Illinois, in 1947, a Paul Robeson concert was canceled and the city council passed a resolution barring the appearance of "any artist or speaker who is an avowed propagandist for un-American ideologies."[2]

Early in 1947, one of the first state imitators of the House Un-American Activities Committee was formed in Washington State, where the Democratic Party had veered to the left, electing the secret Communist Hugh DeLacy to the House from 1944 to 1946. The seven-man Joint Legislative Fact-Finding Committee on Un-American Activities was chaired by State Senator Albert F. Canwell, a onetime deputy sheriff. Another senator on the committee, Thomas Bienz, said in March 1947 that "probably not less than 150 on the University of Washington faculty are Communists or sympathizers." The university's Board of Regents promised to fire all subversives, and the Canwell Committee held hearings in July 1948. In September, the university filed charges against three professors who had refused to testify and three others who admitted past membership, but declined to discuss their colleagues. Raymond Allen, the university president, recommended dismissal for all six.

On January 8, 1949, the tenure committee voted 7 to 4 to fire the first three as "agents of Communism," and to place the other three on two-year probation. On January 22, the Board of Regents affirmed the ruling. The rationale was that a Communist teacher must believe and teach what the party line decrees. Even if he taught a nonsensitive subject such as home economics, a Communist teacher could not be trusted. Nor would one want a member of the Ku Klux Klan teaching anthropology.[3]

Each university was a small fiefdom that settled the problem in its own way. There was no uniform, standardized policy. But the premise that Communists should be excluded from government and from American political life was often extended to the universities. Even a liberal college such as Antioch in Yellow Springs, Ohio, fired a math professor, Robert Rempfer, for distributing a clemency petition for the Rosenbergs. It became a common practice for universities to fire faculty who took the Fifth before congressional committees. The committees then brought them in deliberately for that reason.

By 1949, twenty-two states had adopted oaths of allegiance for teachers.[4] By then, the anti-Communist rhetoric had been notched up following the Hiss-Chambers-Bentley spy revelations of 1948. The Truman loyalty program also shaped public awareness, as the loyalty oath fad spread to radio stations and other private establishments.

In Sunfield, Michigan, in July 1949, the Congregationalist minister, Albert W. Kauffman, who also taught high school Latin and English, wrote a letter to the magazine *Soviet Russia Today*, saying: "I oppose the capitalist ideology that is promoting war against Russia." The Michigan American Legion picketed Kauffman's church. On December 4, the Sunfield Board of Education fired him for bringing "unfavorable publicity" to the school. One board member said, "It's pretty bad when our basketball team comes out on the floor and the opponents say, 'Here come the Commies.' "[5]

In 1947, lagging behind the Midwest, Harvard had a John Reed Society sponsoring lectures on Marxism. One of the speakers was John Gates, the legislative director of the Communist Party (who quit the party in 1958). This was the last stand of the united front at Harvard. By 1950, Harvard had an unnamed faculty member (probably McGeorge Bundy), who was listed by the FBI as a Confidential National Defense Informant. There were two sound reasons for Harvard's cooperation with the FBI. One was that it kept congressional committees at bay. The other was that Harvard's Russian Research Center did classified work for the Air Force's Air Targets Division. Clyde Kluckhohn, the director of the center, agreed to brief the FBI on its work. The assistant director, H. Stuart Hughes, who had been active in the Wallace campaign, was dropped. Once the universities became involved in classified government work, national security preempted academic freedom.[6]

Aside from organized groups with a voice in society, such as the universities, the veterans, and the churches, there were anti-Red freelancers. Anyone with a letterhead could jump in. In 1949 in Norwalk, Connecticut, Suzanne Silvercruys Stevenson launched the Minute Women of the U.S.A. She was a Belgian-born sculptress married to an Army colonel. The Minute Women were anti-labor, anti–income tax, and pro-segregation. They wore on their starched bosoms red, white, and blue pins with the slogan "Guarding the Land We Love." By May 1952, they claimed to have half a million members in 104 chapters in forty-six states. Calling herself "the Paul Revere of the Fair Sex," Mrs. Stevenson traveled from chapter to chapter giving set speeches, such as "The Public Schools Are Honeycombed with Communists."

No chapter of the Minute Women was more ardent than the one in Houston, Texas. There, members enrolled in classes at the University of Houston to ferret out subversive teachers. They managed to get several prominent educators fired.[7]

———

In October 1947, three years before McCarthy got started, HUAC investigated Reds in the film industry. Hollywood was a world of its own, confined, stratified, and self-absorbed. It was a glittering, money-grubbing, ego-driven town. John Bright, who co-wrote five James Cagney movies, including *Public Enemy*, recalled that when he arrived in 1929 "there was no left-wing movement at all." He was one of the original four secret Communists in the Hollywood section of the party, which in the thirties grew to three hundred. John Howard Lawson, the voluble Cyrano-nosed playwright, became the commissar of the

Hollywood Communists. He lectured to young actors, telling them that their performances had to advance the class struggle. "If you are merely an extra playing a member of a country club," he said, "play it in a way that will invite prejudice against the class represented. If you are an extra in a street scene of a tenement district or in any poor surroundings, play your part to excite sympathy."[8]

Communists were instrumental in the founding of the Screen Writers Guild, which won certification from the National Labor Relations Board in 1938. Aside from obtaining financial advantages, the Guild took away from the studios the right to designate the screenwriter on the credits. Through its ability to place members on the board, the party controlled the Screen Writers Guild until the fifties.

There was a period of radical chic in Hollywood from the mid-thirties to the mid-forties, when women in evening dresses joined longshoremen on the San Diego docks to picket a ship bound for Japan with scrap iron, and when Norma Shearer in a sequined gown toasted the victors of Stalingrad.

This was the period when being a Communist could help your career. Nathan Benoff, a comedy writer for the radio program *Duffy's Tavern,* came to Paramount in 1943 to break into films and met the writer and director Robert Rossen (*All the King's Men*). Rossen asked Benoff to "come out to a meeting of the party and meet a lot of big writers." Benoff joined as a form of social promotion, but stayed in only a few months. "I dipped my toe, I dunked it, and I ran," he recalled.[9]

Another writer, Bart Lytton, had joined the party in New York in 1935, but dropped out when he moved to Hollywood. In 1944, he was approached by the RKO writer George Beck, considered by some to be an opportunistic Communist (he later cooperated with HUAC).

"Say, what is this about you?" Beck asked. "I understand you were expelled. You'd better get it cleared up, because if you don't, your name is mud in this town."[10]

Concerned about Beck's warning, Bart Lytton got in touch with the party organizer, Elizabeth Glenn, who told him that charges had been filed against him. "Apparently I had done everything but set fire to my mother," he said. As the months went by, or dissolved, in movie parlance, friends dropped him, dinner dates were canceled at the last minute, and when he came into Guild meetings, backs were turned. "A very competent rumor factory was at work. . . . The smear tactics they later accused the HUAC committee of were tactics they were masters at." Lytton lost jobs. He was astonished at the party's influence. He had been a prolific and successful writer, but now he couldn't find work, he was red-listed. He had a nervous breakdown.[11]

One way that the Communist writers justified the hack work they did for the studios was to claim that they could influence the content of films. This dogged effort to infiltrate the party line into scripts could reach ludicrous levels. Bernice Fleury, who worked on animated cartoons for Warner Bros., recalled cell meetings where they discussed how to have more socially conscious cartoons. (Bugs Bunny panhandling for carrots?) She left the party in disgust.[12]

Many of those in the industry, whether Communist or not, scoffed at the idea. In the production process, films passed through too many hands, and political messages would be weeded out. As the director Edward Dmytryk said, "You would have to go through the line, and you would have to have a chain of Communists from beginning to end."[13]

One of the more talented screenwriters, Dalton Trumbo, who survived the blacklist, argued that if content had not changed, HUAC would not have come to Hollywood. At the same time he admitted that the accomplishments were puny. Even the anti-fascist films had cheap sentiment and shallow characterizations.[14]

At the core of the content conundrum were the Communist writers' low feelings of self-worth. They worked in an industry that catered to the bourgeois consumer society they professed to scorn. As they tanned themselves by their pools in Beverly Hills, they reflected on their quandary. They had been co-opted by the capitalist society they were supposed to be combating, and were prostituting their talent as hired hands for the studios. To reclaim their integrity, they became more strident in their party activities.

Edward Dmytryk, who testified before HUAC on April 25, 1951, gave what was perhaps the most probing analysis of the Hollywood Communist mentality. "In Hollywood more than anywhere else in the world you hear the word 'break,' " he said. "A successful person in Hollywood will never say 'I got there by hard work and personality.' He will say 'I got the breaks.' So there is a lingering feeling that their success is not deserved. They make so much money that they look around for some organization that will validate them. The party lays very clever flytraps."[15]

Such was the context for the October 1947 confrontation between HUAC and the Hollywood Ten. The wealthy but self-despising Hollywood hacks finally had a chance to prove their radical mettle. Since seven of the ten were writers, they could play at being heroes by writing scripts for themselves. When the U.S. marshal came to the RKO studios and handed subpoenas to Dmytryk and writer Adrian Scott, they got in touch with the liberal lawyer Bartley Crum. But the others retained the Communist lawyer Ben Margolis, who devised a strategy that would follow the party line rather than help the witnesses. Margolis brought in the CIO counsel and longtime Communist Lee Pressman to tell them they were on the barricades of the battle for freedom and must stick to their guns.[16]

Margolis turned the hearings into a show trial abounding in disruption and confrontation. On the five-day train ride to Washington, he coached the Ten for twelve hours a day, conducting mock cross-examinations and drilling them in the techniques of agitprop.

Alvah Bessie, the only one of the Ten to have served in the International Brigades, later said: "Mr. Parnell Thomas [the HUAC chairman] was correct in that there was a strong party organization in Hollywood. There must have been 200 or 300 people in the talent and craft sections alone, not counting the backlots and so forth."[17] All the Ten later admitted or were shown to be party members.

When the hearings opened in Washington, screenwriter John Howard Lawson testified on October 27 and started yelling: "I am not on trial here . . . this committee is on trial."

Thomas (mildly): "We don't want you to be on trial."

Lawson kept yelling and Thomas said, "You are just making a big scene for yourself and getting all 'het up.' "

Lawson kept it up until he was removed and held in contempt. He was described as having written for the *Daily Worker* since 1934 and having defended the purge trials. His party card, No. 47275, obtained from the FBI, was read into the record.

The next day, Trumbo testified and said he understood they had his membership card. "I would like to see what you have," he said.

Thomas: "Oh you would! Well you will pretty soon."

Trumbo: "This is the beginning of an American concentration camp." (Disturbances in the audience.)

Trumbo made so much noise he was cited for contempt like Lawson, which seemed to be the goal.

And so it went. Albert Maltz had written *Pride of the Marines*, starring John Garfield as a Jewish soldier wounded at Guadalcanal. In a hospital scene, he gave what was known among party screenwriters as "the ya-ya speech," which condemned America as the home of inequality and racial discrimination. "My name isn't Jones, so I can't get a job," and so on. To protect himself, the screenwriter had another character respond with the "I love these rocks and rills" speech. Before the committee, Maltz made his brave little speech: "I would rather die than be a shabby American, groveling before men whose names are Thomas and Rankin, but who carry out activities in America like those carried out in Germany by Himmler." This was the same man who had groveled before the cultural commissar V. J. Jerome to recant an article saying that writers should sometimes pursue artistic rather than political goals. Maltz then threw a little tantrum and called HUAC staff member Robert Stripling a "Quisling." His party card was read into the record as were his fifty-eight party affiliations.[18]

Bartley Crum later said that as the histrionics mounted, he could feel the audience in the hearing room lose sympathy for the witnesses. The HUAC committee members kept their composure while the Ten ranted. These frustrated showoffs, so conniving and secretive in their party activities, and so clamorous in their denunciations of the committee, made complete fools of themselves. But that was what Margolis intended, as he wrote his fellow defense lawyer Robert W. Kenny: "We shall undoubtedly receive many setbacks. Only by proper utilization of each stage of the proceedings, and of setbacks themselves, can a case like ours achieve the necessary public support. . . . Then the public can understand what the fight is about. . . . The presentation of these issues will advance our objectives even though the court rules against us."[19] It could not have been said more clearly. The true purpose of the hearings was to create sympathy for the party rather than to defend the Ten charged with contempt. The more setbacks the better!

The Ten didn't realize that they had been thrown to the wolves to improve the party's image. They were found guilty of contempt on May 5, 1948. The Court of Appeals upheld in June 1949, saying: "It is absurd to argue . . . that questions asked men, who, by the authorship of the scripts, vitally influence the ultimate production of motion pictures seen by millions, which questions require disclosure of whether or not they are or ever have been Communists, are not pertinent questions." In April 1950, the Supreme Court declined to review the case. The flaw in the argument was "vital influence." Trumbo may have thought, as he put it, that he was "using art as a weapon for the future of mankind," but nine times out of ten the studio system blocked out the message. As Samuel Goldwyn said, "If you want to send messages, use Western Union."

To take Trumbo as an example, by December 1947 the producers had decreed a blacklist of the Ten. Trumbo was getting letters addressed to "Traitor Trumbo," "Jew-lover Trumbo," and "Red Rat Trumbo." Suspended by MGM, he had to mortgage his home. He asked his agent, George Willner, who pioneered the use of fronts and pseudonyms for blacklisted writers, for "a polish job."[20]

In June 1950, his appeals exhausted, Trumbo went to jail at the federal pen in Ashland, Kentucky. It wasn't such a bad place, he wrote his wife, Cleo, with fresh vegetable salad daily from the prison farm, and newspapers and magazines.

By 1952, Trumbo had sold his ranch and moved to Mexico, where there was quite a colony of blacklisted screenwriters, including John Bright and Albert Maltz. Trumbo wrote a script about a boy and a bullfight, called *The Brave One*, under the name Robert Rich. In March 1956, when the Oscars were handed out, Robert Rich was nowhere to be found. By this time, the black market was flourishing like a green bay tree, which led to the collapse of the blacklist in films. Trumbo was returned to his prior eminence. On May 26, 1957, he wrote Murray Kempton that "having made no public announcement when I joined the Communist Party, I naturally made none when I departed from it [in 1956]. . . . Why did I leave? . . . The XXth Congress furnished the opportunity [though] I never believed in the perfection of the Soviet Union. . . . So I don't feel impelled to penitential cries."

The question was, how did Trumbo reconcile his many years in the party with his love of money? He said that he had lost an estimated $1 million because of the blacklist. His friend John Bright told him it was deeply immoral to mourn the loss and accused him of "ideological corruption." The Hollywood blacklistees had subverted art and honesty by selling the status quo through mass hypnotism, Bright said. Their political activity derived in large part from a recognition of their guilt. And then they wept when they were deprived, not of bread and milk, but of Cadillacs and minks.[21]

Trumbo saw America as a nation of money-grubbers, but he was one himself, with a veneer of militancy.

Another question was, between those who took the Fifth and those who named names, where was personal honor? The privilege stated that no one is bound to accuse himself. Thus, taking the Fifth meant you had something to hide. Why else would answering incriminate you? As Supreme Court Justice Hugo Black put it, "If there is nothing to conceal, then why conceal it?" Taking the Fifth naturally produced an assumption of guilt, to the extent that it could not be introduced in a subsequent court proceeding as evidence. In congressional hearings, Communist witnesses routinely used the Fifth to avoid perjury on the one hand and telling the truth on the other. As Carl Beck wrote in *Contempt of Congress*, taking the Fifth promiscuously "makes a mockery of a constitutional privilege established for the protection of the individual from the arbitrary exercise of power. By subverting this privilege, these witnesses eroded its efficacy and contributed to the rejection by the public of the worthwhileness of the self-incrimination plea."

And what of non-Communist witnesses taking the Fifth out of principle, or to defy the committee? As the "friendly" witness Abe Burrows, co-author of *Guys and Dolls*, told HUAC on November 12, 1952, "Communist Party members, in the Fifth Amendment, discovered a way to refuse to answer the questions of the committee without being cited for contempt, and they would like everyone who is called, and that includes non-Communists, to refuse to answer this committee."

The spectacle of literally hundreds of witnesses taking the Fifth with robotlike regularity made a poor impression. When they invoked the founding fathers, there was something unclean about it. Will Lee (aka William Lubovsky) of the American Theater Wing told HUAC: "I stand on the right as given to us by James Madison and his associates."

Why could they not tell the truth? The answer was that if you admitted membership, you would have to name others, which made you a stool pigeon. But between the posturing cardboard heroes who took the Fifth and those who named names, the former were cowards afraid of admitting their allegiance, while the latter were doing their duty as citizens under oath before a congressional committee. Some of the latter were opportunists trying to avoid the blacklist, but others had left the party and felt it was proper to expose its underhandedness.

Frank Tuttle, a well-bred Yale graduate of the thirties, was the veteran director of seventy pictures when he testified before HUAC on May 24, 1951. He was one of the early joiners, from 1937 to 1947, and part of the cell in the Directors Guild. He named names, and when he was asked why he had turned informant, he said, "All decent people, who share this dislike for informers, if they think about this carefully, will agree with me that at this particular moment [of the war in Korea] it is absolutely vital [to inform] . . . with ruthless aggression abroad in the world, the aggressors are as ruthless with their own people as they are with those they consider their enemies."[22]

Another reason for informing was that it was the lesser of two evils. The choreographer Jerome Robbins was a compliant witness when he testified on May 5, 1953, hoping perhaps to skirt the issue of his homosexuality. He was also disillusioned with the party, which he had been a member of from 1943 to 1947, in the "theatrical transient group." Robbins recalled that at one of the early meetings someone asked him in what way dialectical materialism had helped him create his ballet *Fancy Free*. "I found the question a little ridiculous. . . . The ballet is about three sailors on shore leave in New York. . . . The purpose was to show how American material and American spirit and American warmth . . . could be used as an art form." But in the party, "you are constantly told to make your art carry a political message." He attended another meeting where Martha Graham was called "the face of fascism." "I have the highest respect for this woman," he said. "This floored me . . . this procedure to label things fascistic, bourgeois, decadent." Robbins named those in his cell and was congratulated by the committee, one of whose members, Clyde Doyle, said: "Use that great talent that God blessed you with to promote Americanism."

Robbins: "Sir, all my works have been acclaimed for their American quality particularly."

Doyle: "I realize that, but let me urge you to even put more of that in it where you can appropriately." Robbins did, in *West Side Story*.[23]

The actor Sterling Hayden, who had a contract with Paramount, said he joined the party as a reaction to his dislike of Hollywood. He felt "kind of lost, not being an actor by inclination," and he was introduced to Isaac "Pop" Folkoff, whom Hayden thought of as "an old warrior in the class struggle," and who was actually the West Coast liaison man for the KGB, and a senior leader of the California Communist Party, born in 1881 in Latvia. Hayden joined the party after the war and was given the assignment of swinging the Screen Actors Guild behind a strike. "It was the stupidest, most ignorant thing I have ever done," he recalled. He was dismayed by the Communist belief "that they have the key, by some occult power, to know what is best for people." He got out in 1946 and gave the committee quite a few names, including that of the actor Will Geer, who was married to Hal Ware's niece Herta, making her the granddaughter of Mother Bloor.[24]

Jerome Robbins and Sterling Hayden were not subjected to a campaign of vilification for naming names. The one emblematic informer, dragged through the mud for half a century, was Elia Kazan. It could only have been the revenge of mediocrity on talent.

When he first appeared before the committee in executive session on January 14, 1952, Kazan refused to name names. But HUAC leaked his refusal to the *Hollywood Reporter*, and the pressure began to mount. Spyros Skouras, the president of Twentieth Century Fox, implied that if he didn't name names, he wouldn't work. Darryl Zanuck, the producer of *Viva Zapata!*, which Kazan directed, told him, "Name the names for Chrissake, who the hell are you going to jail for?"[25]

Kazan thought of Albert Maltz, who had never shaken off the party shackles, and Budd Schulberg, who had been attacked by the party for writing *What Makes Sammy Run?*, which was viewed as anti-Semitic. When they were shooting *Zapata* in Mexico, the Film Technicians union was Communist, and its president, Gabriel Figueroa, showed the script to the comrades, who said it needed work. Kazan began to think of all the times he had been bullied by the party—maybe it should be driven out of its hiding places.

Part of Kazan did not like giving names, but another part asked, "Why should I be in the cold?" He finally did it as an act of cleansing, to wipe out seventeen years of posturing. Not to forget the practical side. Why should he give up his right to work to protect a party he now despised?[26]

On April 10, 1952, Kazan testified before HUAC after writing the committee a letter that said: "I have come to the conclusion that secrecy serves the

Communists. . . . The American people need the facts and all the facts. . . . It is my obligation as a citizen to tell everything I know."

Kazan said that he had been a party member for nineteen months in a Group Theater unit that included Morris Carnovsky, Clifford Odets, J. Edward Bromberg, and three or four others. Kazan quit the party when he saw that the cell was trying to take over Group Theater as a mouthpiece for "socially conscious" plays. A Communist organizer was brought in from the automobile workers in Detroit to show him the error of his ways. "My fellow members looked at him as if he were an oracle," Kazan recalled. "That was the night I quit."[27]

After his testimony, Kazan got hate calls and hate mail. "I became an easy mark for every self-righteous prick in New York and Hollywood," Kazan recalled. When he was snubbed by his former colleagues, he thought, "What doesn't kill you makes you stronger."[28]

In the year 2000, at the age of eighty-nine, Kazan was finally awarded an honorary Oscar, but remained a magnet for controversy. Martin Scorsese and Robert De Niro applauded him, but Nick Nolte and Ed Harris, who were babes in arms at the time of HUAC, sat on their hands. Sean Penn, who was not yet born at the time, signed a full-page ad in *Variety* saying that Kazan had "validated the blacklist," which had begun in 1947, four years before Kazan's testimony, and which required no validation.

Anti-Kazan demonstrators picketed the Dorothy Chandler Pavilion in Los Angeles, where the Oscar ceremony was held. Among them were two blacklisted writers: Bernard Gordon, a journeyman who wrote such screenplays as *Earth vs. the Flying Saucers* (1956) and *Zombies of Mora Tau* (1957). He had been blacklisted in 1947 and wrote scripts under the name Raymond T. Marcus. Gordon thought Kazan had "damaged the Hollywood community." Another demonstrator, Robert Lees, had joined the party in 1939 and scripted Pete Smith shorts, as well as *Juke Box Jenny* and *Bachelor Daddy.* He had been named by Sterling Hayden and was summoned before HUAC on April 11, 1951. On the train trip east, he was coached by his lawyers, Ben Margolis and Robert Kenny, and rehearsed his answers. He was so learned in the techniques of the Fifth that he took it when asked the name of his collaborator of seventeen years, Fred Rinaldo. His testimony, which lasted for an hour and a half, was a veritable deluge of Fifth Amendment responses. And now he was demonstrating against Kazan, whom he thought should apologize. But apologize for what? For telling the truth and giving seven or eight names that were already known, or for being the director of *Gentleman's Agreement, A Streetcar Named Desire, A Face in the Crowd,* and *On the Waterfront?*

In the HUAC hearings, the confrontational style pioneered by the Ten in

1947 persisted in the fifties. While the committee was pilloried for its witch-hunts, the conduct of some of the witnesses was overlooked. The soapbox style was still evident on April 8, 1953, when the blacklisted actor and writer Ned Young testified. "Do you seriously think you can pound the truth in the dust with that gavel," he asked the committee chairman, Donald L. Jackson.

Jackson: "If you don't think I resent sitting here day after day and being abused by men of your stripe, you are in error."

Young: "How low can you get? I think you are a contemptible man."

Jackson: "I am proud to be called contemptible by people like you, sir."

Young: "This is costing me my livelihood. I will never work again. . . . I think this is just rotten."

Not only did Young work again, he won the Oscar for best screenplay in 1958 for *The Defiant Ones*, directed by Stanley Kramer, which he wrote as Nathan E. Douglas. It was the story of two escaped convicts, one black, one white, chained to each other.[29]

Young was followed by Sol Kaplan, a composer who had adapted Tchaikovsky into songs for a TV special called *The Magic Nutcracker*, and who said every member of the committee was "a bigot, a perverter, and a devil on earth."

Jackson: "This is entirely aside from the question."

Kaplan: "I am not your Charlie McCarthy. . . . Your ventriloquism does not work for me."

Jackson: "No. I would pick another dummy."

Kaplan: "You are very strong with blackjacks in your hand."

Blacklisted, Kaplan wrote ditties for television commercials. One of his clients was the Ford Motor Company. Despite his convictions, Kaplan ended up as a capitalist tool, writing "Got it made, got it made, with the '62 Fords on parade."[30]

———

By the time Joe came on the scene with his Wheeling speech in February 1950, McCarthyism was in full swing. To blame it all on McCarthy, said the Ohio newspaper publisher Edward Lamb, "is like blaming the temperature on the thermometer." McCarthy, who concentrated on Communists in government, became an enabler for the others, a cheerleader who sanctioned grassroots anti-Communist activism. The political component, as Hubert Humphrey explained it in *The Education of a Public Man*, was that "the Republicans had been out of the presidency since 1933 and they were desperate to regain political power. . . . They used the anguish and distress of the Korean war and fed the irrationality of Senator McCarthy."

In the *Washington Post*, the cartoonist Herblock showed Joe climbing out of a sewer dripping mud, but in many parts of the country he was hailed as a hero. The oil millionaire Hugh Roy Cullen called him "the greatest man in America."[31]

The period to which McCarthy gave his name sanctioned the blacklist racket, although that too was launched before he came on the scene. For it was in 1947 that three former FBI men started American Business Consultants (ABC), which put out a newsletter called *Counterattack*, listing entertainers and union officials with alleged party connections. *Counterattack* charged $24-a-year subscriptions as well as clearance fees for those who wanted them. This was private enterprise at its worst, trading in reputations, and fostering the principle that people should be fired because of a rumored affiliation, or some trivial act such as sending Mother Bloor a card on her seventy-fifth birthday. Entertainers on radio and television were easy targets because the sponsors could be intimidated and could in turn intimidate the networks.

In June 1950, only months after McCarthy's Wheeling speech, American Business Consultants published a 213-page book called *Red Channels*, which listed 151 supposedly Red-tinged actors, writers, producers, and directors. The cover showed a red hand seizing a microphone. The Hearst press jumped in—"Red Infiltration of TV, Radio Bared"—and *Counterattack* plugged its product: "A copy of *Red Channels* should be in every American home . . . next to the radio or TV set." Many of those named were blacklisted.[32]

It was a dirty little business, exposing people, often on flimsy grounds, and getting paid to expose them by the ad agencies and networks who subscribed to your publication, and then getting paid again to help clear those who were named.

One casualty of *Red Channels* was Philip Loeb, the short, doleful actor who played the suffering father on *The Goldbergs*, a sitcom about a middle-class Jewish family in the Bronx. He had seventeen front group listings in *Red Channels* and was dropped from the show. Loeb was a widower with a schizophrenic son, whom he had to move from a private to a state hospital. On September 11, 1955, at the age of sixty-one, he checked into the Hotel Taft, took some pills, and never woke up.

The blacklist racket was booming, with room for expansion. Vincent Hartnett, a graduate of Notre Dame who had served in Naval Intelligence, was at American Business Consultants, compiling material for *Red Channels*, but left in 1952 to launch his own publication, *Aware*. He worked closely with the grocer Laurence Johnson, who owned five supermarkets in upstate New York, decorated with cracker barrels, old piggy banks, and campaign buttons.

Hartnett fed names to Johnson, who then called the networks to say he would boycott the products of their sponsors.

One of Hartnett's techniques was to study old photographs of May Day parades with a magnifying glass, to see who he could spot. A letter would follow, "Have you changed your views?" If you had, he could clear you for a fee. If you hadn't, you would be listed in *Aware*. His treatment of the actress Kim Hunter was typical. When he named her in 1952, she was blacklisted. Her press agent then asked Hartnett what she should do. He said he could review her entire record for a fee of $200. He also helped her write her mea culpa, in which she said: "It was only after I had made several errors in judgment that I was finally alerted to a clearer and more intelligent understanding of the insidious working of the Communist conspiracy."[33]

———

One of the by-products of the McCarthy era was the rise of the undercover witness. Undercover FBI agents were extremely effective in identifying Communists in the Smith Act trials and in HUAC hearings, though this had little to do with espionage. It was part of the sometimes overzealous effort to dismantle the Communist leadership under the Truman and Eisenhower administrations. In the period from 1952 to 1954, the Justice Department had eighty-three informers on its payroll, thirty of whom were regularly used as witnesses in congressional hearings and Smith Act trials.[34] The "professional witness," who made a living informing on the party affiliations of those he had known, was prone to stretch the truth and behave inappropriately in order to stay in business.

Armando Penha, an undercover FBI man in New Bedford, Massachusetts, apparently seduced a young woman, enticed her into joining the party, where he was a section organizer, and then named her as a Communist. Olga Garczynski, a punch press operator at the Royal Brand Cutlery company, was a member of the party from 1953 to 1956. At the time, Penha, a married man with children, was courting her. On March 19, 1958, she testified at a HUAC hearing that "whatever Mr. Penha told me to go to, I went. He dragged me into this mess. If it wasn't for him, I wouldn't be in this mess. . . . In 1957, he didn't come up to the house any more, so that was the end of whatever dirty work that he wanted me to do." As a farewell gift, Olga sent a birthday card to Penha's two-year-old daughter, Susan, with a note enclosed for his wife. Penha made a pro forma denial: "I did not court her or any other female Communist sympathizer or dupe."[35]

In Cleveland in 1948, a black woman who had joined the party decided to go undercover for the FBI when she discovered that the local cells were segregated. Julia Clarice Brown had thought the party furthered civil rights, but when she was assigned to the southeast section, she found that she could not attend meetings there because it was all white. On paper, she was a member of the southeast section, but she attended meetings at the northeast section.

When she testified before HUAC in June 1962, the committee counsel, Alfred M. Nittle, said: "This is an astounding assertion. . . . You say there was segregation practiced by the Communist Party?"

Brown: "I complained to Benjamin Davis when he came to Cleveland. . . . He didn't like it and one day he spoke on it, but it didn't do any good. They still didn't allow me in the south-east section."

Her first assignment was to be the chauffeur for Freida Katz, the head of the Civil Rights Congress, a front group. Brown went to plants and passed out leaflets on police brutality and lynching. In 1948, she helped collect the 75,000 signatures Wallace needed to get on the ballot in Ohio. She got to know a lot of Cleveland Communists, and she was happy to turn them in once she realized that while giving lip service to civil rights they practiced segregation.[36]

Mary Stalcup Markward, who operated the Rainbow Beauty Shop in Washington, and who went undercover in 1943, recalled at a hearing in June 1951 that her work in the party ostracized her husband. "He was facing all the hardships of lack of association with friends, and the gossip and so forth."

Mrs. Markward made the point that undercover agents often rose quickly in party ranks, thanks to their simulated motivation. She was elected chairman of the Northeast Club in 1944, then to the city committee, then city treasurer, then to the Maryland District Committee, before quitting in 1949. She testified in McCarthy's 1953 hearing on the Government Printing Office. The party hierarchy was studded with FBI informants, whose ability to gain information depended on their performance as promotable Communists.[37]

———

The freelance ex-Communist professional witnesses included all manner of dubious characters, but none so bewilderingly eccentric as Harvey Matusow. Born in the Bronx in 1926, the son of a cigar store owner and a Russian-born mother, Matusow joined the Army at the age of eighteen, in 1944, serving in France and Germany. It was in the Army that his propensity for not telling the truth was first exposed. He said he could speak French, Spanish, Italian, and German. But when he was handed a passage from a book in German, he couldn't translate it.[38]

Mustered out of the Army in 1946, Matusow was back in New York and drifted into the party, which gave him "a feeling of belonging." Soon he became a paid employee, working in party bookstores and as a switchboard operator at party headquarters. In the summer he went to Camp Unity in Wingdale, New York: lectures in the morning and hootenannies in the evening with party songbooks. On the grounds, a boulder with Lenin's face sculpted into it, a Communist Mount Rushmore. Matusow was in the youth group, which in 1948 morphed into Youth for Wallace. He worked for People's Songs, which ran the cultural part of the campaign. Short, stocky, dark-haired, brash, and garrulous, Matusow was the salesman type. In 1948, he won a trip to Puerto Rico for selling the most subscriptions to the *Sunday Worker*.[39]

In 1950, he was living with an African-American divorcee and took a job with a Harlem collection agency. The party accused him of "white chauvinism" and demoted him. In a fit of pique, Matusow went to the New York office of the FBI in late March and said he was a disillusioned Communist who wanted to be an undercover informant. He was paid $75 a month to cover expenses and named several hundred persons he knew in the party. Assistant Attorney General William F. Tomkins later said that corroboration had been found for 90 percent of those he named.

In the summer of 1950, Matusow met Craig Vincent at a party affair at the Hotel Albert in New York City. Vincent operated a dude ranch for comrades in the mountains of New Mexico and was recruiting guests. Matusow was invited and went in July. The San Cristóbal ranch was eighteen miles north of Taos. Vincent, a Communist lawyer who had run the Wallace campaign in Colorado in 1948, had opened the place in 1949. On March 17, 1950, in Denver, according to congressional testimony, Communist leaders decided that the ranch would be operated for the party. When he testified before the Senate Internal Security Subcommittee in June 1953, Vincent took the Fifth when asked if the ranch was an adjunct of the party.[40]

With its 160 acres at 7,900 feet, and its unspoiled mountain scenery, San Cristóbal was a place where stressed-out party functionaries could unwind in the company of their own kind, sing Spanish Civil War songs, and visit Indian pueblos. One of the regulars was Clinton Jencks, an organizer with Mine, Mill, and Smelter, a Communist-controlled union that was ousted by the CIO in 1950, after a trial that ruled "the Communist Party is in direct control of the union's leadership and dictates to that leadership the policies it shall adopt."[41]

Tall, rangy, and flaxen-haired, Clinton Jencks was sent to southwestern New Mexico in 1947, where he was known by the Mexicans who worked the copper and silver mines as "El Palomino." Jencks merged the scattered Mine, Mill locals into one big local, 890.[42]

At the San Cristóbal ranch in the summer of 1950, Jencks met Harvey Matusow, who was trying hard to be the life of the party, calling square dances and singing his repertoire of people's songs. He also turned over the names of the guests to the FBI office in Albuquerque. Matusow chatted up Jencks, telling him he was thinking of moving to New Mexico. "It is a good idea," Jencks said (according to Matusow). "We can use more Communists out here." Matusow said that Jencks told him he was in touch with Mexican Communist organizers, with whom he was plotting to curtail the production of copper for the Korean War effort. At that time, the party line was "let's stop war production."[43]

After Matusow's stay at the ranch, the party caught on to his undercover work and expelled him in January 1951 as "an enemy agent." At loose ends, Matusow, who was in the Air Force Reserve, asked to be called to active duty as a staff sergeant. He was sent to Wright-Patterson base near Dayton, Ohio, where he remained from April to December 1951. Always strapped for cash, he sewed chevrons on the uniforms of the NCOs, at two bits a chevron.[44]

Matusow didn't fit in at Wright-Patterson. His fellow airmen shunned him because he was bumptious. He was treated for manic depression. In August, he spent two weeks at the base hospital with a nervous breakdown. He was diagnosed as a "schizoid personality . . . manifested by nomadism, eccentricity, seclusiveness, moderate stress of a break with Communist party."

In September, he went to the chaplain, William Coolidge Hart, and said he wanted to clear his name and expose the Communists in New York. The chaplain sent him to the public information officer on the base, Martha Edmiston, a youthful forty, with cropped hair and a fresh complexion. Martha and her husband, John, a reporter on the *Dayton Journal Herald,* had been undercover FBI agents who had infiltrated the Ohio party in 1940 and 1941 and testified before HUAC in July 1950.

Matusow came across to Martha as humble and sincere. She and her husband decided to show him the ropes. An effective witness had to abide by a number of rules:

Don't name anyone unless you can substantiate it.
If you mention a name and that person is in the room, turn around to face the person.
Play your big cards one at a time.
In each appearance, open up areas for further questioning to assure continuity of employment.

The Edmistons tried to help Matusow overcome his crude mannerisms, which they believed he had picked up in the party—his terrible table manners, his overbearing treatment of waiters, his interrupting the conversation of others, and his insistence on being the center of attention.

Martha Edmiston put Matusow in touch with the Dayton FBI and with the Ohio HUAC in Columbus. Word went out to HUAC in Washington, who sent a veteran investigator, Don Appell, to debrief him. By October 1951, Matusow had completed a seventy-one-page affidavit, which Martha Edmiston later said was "probably the first and only time he told the truth."[45]

In November 1951, the Edmistons shepherded Matusow to Washington to appear in a closed session of HUAC. They shared a suite at the Congressional Hotel. The day before the hearing, John Edmiston saw Matusow primping and asked, "Where are you going now, Buster?"

"I think I will drop over and see if I can get in touch with Senator McCarthy," Matusow said.

"Hold it a minute," John said. "You are here on subpoena from the House Un-American Activities Committee. You have no business going around dabbling with other congressional committees. . . . If you do that it is going to be the kiss of death."

That was good advice. For although McCarthy had made his name as a Red-hunter by the end of 1951, he had yet to conduct a single investigation. All he had done was make speeches, usually on the floor of the Senate, where he was protected from libel. He was the ranking Republican on the Committee on Expenditures in the Executive Departments, which had a subcommittee on investigations, and which was renamed Committee on Government Operations in 1952. Only in 1953 did he launch his first investigation.

The House Un-American Activities Committee, on the other hand, had a long track record as the leading instrument of unbridled anti-Communism in Congress. It pioneered the Communists in government issue, which McCarthy later exploited. HUAC also directed its fire at the New Deal liberals, labor leaders, intellectuals, and artists. One of its members, John Rankin, was an outspoken racist who once called Walter Winchell "a little slime-mongering kike." Another, J. Parnell Thomas, went to prison in 1949 for padding his payroll with nonexistent employees. But HUAC also broke some big cases with Elizabeth Bentley and the Hiss-Chambers confrontation. HUAC made the reputation of the future President Richard Nixon, who maintained a covert liaison with the FBI. As he wrote in his memoirs: "We had some informal contacts with a lower-level agent that proved helpful to our investigations." "Lower-level" was unduly modest, for the help came directly from J. Edgar Hoover, who provided reports on upcoming witnesses and the party cards of the Hollywood Ten. With its sensational hearings and its popular booklets, such as *Spotlight on Spies* and *100 Things You Should Know About*

Communism, HUAC helped to create the climate in which McCarthy prospered. Starting in 1950, Joe drove HUAC from the headlines, and after his censure in 1954, HUAC suffered collateral damage, fading into obsolescence until its discontinuance in 1975.

On November 26 and 27, 1951, Matusow, in a new Air Force uniform, testified on Communist youth groups in a closed session of HUAC, which was a dress rehearsal for the public hearing. After that first visit to Washington, the Edmistons saw Matusow transformed from the unassuming airman who wanted to clear his name into an overbearing egomaniac convinced of his own importance. Back at the base, he threw his weight around and already saw a movie in the works, in which he would star. On December 17, he was released from active duty.

Matusow returned to Washington to testify in an open hearing on Communist youth groups on February 6 and 7, 1952. On the first day, when the hearings recessed at noon, he learned that King George VI of England had died. "What a hell of a break for me," he told the Edmistons. "The king had to die on my day of triumph. Pushed me right off the front page."[46]

Prior to testifying, Matusow had sold his story to the *New York Journal-American*, a paper in the Hearst chain, splitting the $750 fee with the Edmistons. He went to New York to confer with the Hearst reporter Howard Rushmore, who wrote the story as an "as told to" four-parter. Rushmore was an ex-Communist who had quit his job as movie reporter for the *Daily Worker* after refusing to pan *Gone with the Wind*. He committed suicide in January 1958 after murdering his estranged wife.

In the meantime, the Justice Department decided to use Matusow as a witness in the Smith Act prosecution of sixteen second-string Communists in New York City. Roy Cohn, the prosecutor, questioned Matusow, who knew most of the defendants, in New York on December 21, 1951. Could Matusow link any of them to statements advocating the forceful overthrow of the government?

On July 21, 1952, Matusow took the stand for five days of testimony. One of the defendants was Alexander Trachtenberg, the head of the party's publishing arm, whom Matusow had met when he worked in the bookstores. Cohn wanted to connect Trachtenberg to a book by the prosecutor in the purge trials, Andrei Vyshinsky, *The Law of the Soviet State*. Matusow told Cohn that he had discussed the price of the book with Trachtenberg. Cohn said that wasn't good enough. Roy then pointed to a passage that would help his case and asked Matusow to tie Trachtenberg in. When Matusow testified on July 22, he said that Trachtenberg had told him the Vyshinsky book dealt with "the establishment of socialism, how the diametrically opposed classes could be eliminated."[47]

To prove Trachtenberg's intent, a passage in Vyshinsky's book was read to the jury, stating that "violent seizure of authority by the proletariat . . . is the most important thesis of Marxist-Leninist doctrine." Matusow quoted another defendant, George Black Charney, as saying that "Puerto Rico is being used as a military base for the United States and an independent Puerto Rico would help destroy those bases and cripple the Caribbean defense." The Smith Act defendants were convicted. Judge Edward J. Dimock gave Matusow credit for providing the crucial evidence that convicted Trachtenberg and Charney.[48]

It was also in July 1952 that McCarthy, who was up for reelection, was operated on for a stomach hernia, which removed him from the campaign trail. Joe asked Matusow to pinch-hit for him and make some speeches in Wisconsin. He sent Matusow to the McCarthy club in Milwaukee, where he was astounded by the cash that was pouring in, thousands of letters with bills in them. Joe came home to Appleton and Matusow saw him at Van Susteren's, going heavy on the bourbon. Whenever he was asked if he wanted another, Joe said: "Well, you can put it this way—Yes." At 4:00 A.M., having drunk "a sea of bourbon," Joe in his undershirt said, "I'll show you my scar for a quarter," displaying a slash like a railroad track dividing his torso in two. He stumbled to bed just before sunup.[49]

In September, McCarthy sent Matusow on a western tour in states like Montana and Washington, where he wanted to defeat the Senate incumbents Mike Mansfield and Scoop Jackson. Harvey followed the Edmistons' advice of playing his big cards one at a time, and when he ran out of big cards he pulled them from the bottom of the deck. In Great Falls, Montana, he made headlines with the claim that "the Sunday section of the *New York Times* alone has 126 dues-paying Communists. On the editorial and research staffs of *Time* and *Life* magazines are 76 hard-core Reds. The New York Bureau of the Associated Press has 25." Matusow seemed to be following Joe in the numbers racket.

Matusow had now found his calling, as a professional witness. If he was not subpoenaed, he volunteered. In July 1952, Don Connors, an ex-FBI agent on the staff of Senator McCarran's Internal Security Subcommittee, proposed that an investigation of the Mine, Mill, and Smelter union would "lend itself to a particularly good hearing in a western state this fall." If the hearings were timed with the November elections, they would help conservative candidates in the Rocky Mountain states. Hearings were scheduled for October in Salt Lake City.

When Matusow heard that his pal Jencks from San Cristóbal was due to testify at the Salt Lake City hearings, he volunteered to testify against him. The issue for Jencks boiled down to his signing of a Taft-Hartley affidavit in

1949. Union officials who refused to sign affidavits stating that they were not Communists were denied the services of the National Labor Relations Board for certification and collective bargaining. To get around the problem, the party adopted a "resign and sign" strategy, telling the members to quit the party and sign the affidavits, though in some cases they remained secretly in the party. Jencks had signed the affidavit on August 17, 1949, which meant that if he had remained in the party, he had committed perjury.

Matusow arrived in Salt Lake City to testify on October 6, 1952, thinking: "I have to make this good . . . I have to hit the headlines." He identified Jencks as a Communist on the basis of their conversations in San Cristóbal in the summer of 1950, after Jencks had signed the affidavit. Matusow said Jencks was planning a strike to "cut down production for the Korean War effort."

Jencks admitted to being at the ranch, but took the Fifth when asked if he had met Matusow and conversed with him. In the committee report, Chairman McCarran recommended that the Justice Department prosecute Jencks and other Mine, Mill officials for perjury. Only Harvey and one other witness had placed Jencks in the party in 1950, after he had signed the affidavit.[50]

With his Jencks testimony, Matusow reached the upper strata of professional witnesses. He was asked to a party at the New York home of Doc Matthews, who had also testified at the Salt Lake City hearings and who lived in a penthouse on West 24th Street. He was invited to the Washington home of Arvilla "Billie" Bentley, who lived on Fox Hall Road, next door to Averell Harriman. Arvilla was divorced from the Texas millionaire Alvin Bentley, a major donor to McCarthy's campaigns. Matusow was annoyed because Billie had refused a "*Life* Goes to a Party" offer. He might have gotten his picture in *Life* in this regular feature of the magazine.[51]

In November 1952, the Hennings Committee was investigating McCarthy's finances. Arvilla Bentley had been subpoenaed to answer questions about the $7,000 she had loaned McCarthy. If she was under oath, she would have to tell about the money she'd given Joe in the anti-Tydings campaign in Maryland in 1950. Matusow took Bentley to Nassau in November to duck the subpoena. Although she was quite a bit older than Matusow, and although he was a self-described "mess" at five foot six and 230 pounds, a romance blossomed. She gave him a $300 set of golf clubs.

When Matusow got back to Washington, he sold the story of Bentley's flight to Drew Pearson for $250, which did not stop him from marrying her in March 1953. Harvey and Arvilla shared a love of gambling, and made Las Vegas their second home. "We were partners at the dice table," he recalled. He once ran eight passes in a row, making eight and six the hard way.

Arvilla wanted him to give up testifying, thinking it was undignified. But

Harvey had some unfinished business: in April 1953, he testified before a federal grand jury convened in El Paso, Texas, which indicted Jencks for perjury.

The marriage quickly unraveled. Harvey and Arvilla fought constantly and in August 1953 went to Reno to get a divorce. Harvey did not contest it, and in the property settlement he got to keep the Buick station wagon. On the day they were divorced, Harvey struck Arvilla in the face in a Reno garage. "She hollered for somebody to call a cop," he recalled, "but then got up and walked away." The marriage had lasted four months. Harvey bummed around the Southwest in his Buick, working at odd jobs.[52]

On August 24, 1953, Matusow wrote McCarthy from Reno: "When I testified at the trial of the 16 Communist leaders in New York, the defense said, 'You'd do anything for a buck.' I denied it, but he was right. My testimony was honest but that was about the only thing that was." Matusow thought of writing a book and began to work on it that fall. The working title was *Blacklisting Is My Business*. In his outline, chapter eight was described as "Dude ranch for comrades. In New Mexico near Los Alamos."

At the Jencks trial in El Paso in January 1954, Matusow was the star witness. He repeated the testimony he had already given twice, at the Salt Lake SISS hearings and before the federal grand jury in Texas. Jencks did not take the stand and the jury took twenty-two minutes to find him guilty of perjury for swearing falsely to a Taft-Hartley affidavit. He was sentenced to five years and appealed. His lawyer was Nathan Witt, a member of the Ware group of the thirties, who did the work of the party when he was on the National Labor Relations Board. At the trial, Witt demanded that the FBI submit the reports that Matusow had made regarding Jencks, to see if they jibed with his testimony. But the prosecutor said they were confidential, and the trial judge, Robert E. Thomason, denied Witt's motion. Then Witt filed a motion for a new trial, upon which Judge Thomason ordered him to take the stand and asked him if he was a Communist. Witt took the Fifth, as he had done previously before HUAC. Judge Thomason said: "No lawyer who claims the privilege can practice in my court."[53]

Matusow was trying to work on his book, but he didn't have any money. None of the publishers he contacted would give him an advance. On April 27, 1954, he was in Peacock Alley of the Waldorf-Astoria appearing on a radio program, when he spotted the fellow-traveling Methodist Bishop G. Bromley Oxnam, executive secretary of the Methodist Federation for Social Action, a front group disowned by the Methodist Church that had been investigated by HUAC. Matusow approached Bishop Oxnam as a sinner wanting to confess and told him, "I have lied again and again to these committees and I want to ask for forgiveness." That June in a speech in Westminster, Maryland, Oxnam mentioned that Matusow "sought me out twice to say he had a religious experience and wished someone would undo 'all the lies I have told about so many people.' "[54]

Bishop Oxnam's remarks came to the attention of Angus Cameron, who had been let go as editor-in-chief of Little, Brown in September 1951 after taking the Fifth before HUAC. Cameron had been chairman of the Progressive Party in Massachusetts in 1948, and treasurer of the National Wallace for President Committee. He was a trustee of the Samuel Adams School in Boston, identified by the Attorney General as a party front. As an editor, he was known for having turned down George Orwell's satire of the Soviet Union, *Animal Farm*.

After leaving Little, Brown, Cameron teamed up with the Communist writer Albert E. Kahn to found Cameron & Kahn, a firm that published pro-Soviet and anti-American books, which were sometimes subsidized by such Communist-controlled unions as the furriers.

It happened that Cameron knew Bishop Oxnam, having attended De Pauw University in Greencastle, Indiana, of which Oxnam was president. Cameron alerted Nat Witt, the general counsel of Mine, Mill since 1941, to Bishop Oxnam's remarks that Matusow had lied in his testimony. When Witt was given a copy of Oxnam's remarks that August, he saw opportunity knocking.[55]

From February to June 1955, the Senate Internal Security Subcommittee held hearings on "The Significance of the Matusow Case." Nathan Witt testified that "I followed closely any developments relating to a possible recantation on Mr. Matusow's part." On September 13 or 14, 1954, Witt said, he discussed the possibility of a subsidy for Matusow's book with his fellow Mine, Mill lawyer John T. McTernan.

Jay Sourwine, the staff director for SISS, asked: "Was it then Mr. McTernan's suggestion that by doing such you might eventually facilitate the securing of an affidavit from Mr. Matusow to support your motion for a new trial [for Jencks]?"

Witt: "We didn't spell it out that way, but that was clearly the thinking of both of us." They had already drafted the affidavit, based on Bishop Oxnam's statement that Matusow had admitted lying. Witt presented his plan on September 20 to the Mine, Mill leadership, which agreed to subsidize the book. Then Witt conferred with Albert Kahn, who agreed to publish it. Thus, Witt, Kahn, and Cameron agreed to make an author out of Matusow. The money would come from the pockets of the Mine, Mill rank and file, and from the cash in the Jencks defense fund.

In October 1954, Matusow was drifting around the Southwest, knowing nothing of these plans. He was, as usual, broke, and living by his wits. He was in Taos when Albert Kahn reached him on October 20 and offered to publish his book. Kahn proposed a $900 advance in weekly installments of $50. Aware of Matusow's instability, Kahn kept him on a short leash. Kahn sent him a plane ticket to New York, where the contract was signed on October 26.[56]

Cameron & Kahn came to Matusow when he was destitute, and after his book had been rejected by mainstream publishers. They had already made a deal with Mine, Mill to subsidize it. Mine, Mill agreed to buy six thousand copies of the book, and Canadian Mine, Mill pledged to buy another five thousand. A first payment of $1,250 was sent to Cameron & Kahn in October. In January 1955, Mine, Mill sent another $2,000.

The book was written in three months, or rather it was extracted by Witt in taped conversations at his home in Croton-on-Hudson. Several chapters in Matusow's original outline were omitted, such as "My Red Marriage" and "Communist Arms Smuggling Ring Within the U.S. Army." The aim of the book was to have Matusow recant his testimony and obtain new trials for Jencks and the Smith Act Sixteen. In key instances, the material in the book was at variance with Matusow's taped comments, which were introduced at the 1955 SISS hearings.

On a tape dated December 14, 1954, Kahn said: "Now let me ask you this example—'cause I think this could come in well. You say in your testimony you met one of the Vincents at a Communist party at the Albert Hotel."

Matusow: ". . . I knew Vincent was a party member and I said so. I knew Jencks was a party member and I said so. I can't say here that Jencks wasn't a party member after he signed the [Taft-Hartley] affidavit because I know that he was."

Kahn: "Why do you say you know he was?"

Matusow: ". . . Jencks officially resigned from the party. . . . But to my mind it made him no less a Communist because he put a piece of paper down and said I'm no longer a member. . . . Jencks was still under Communist party discipline. . . . He didn't change his thinking because he issued that scrap of paper."[57]

A certain alchemy was at work that transformed what Matusow said into its opposite. Matusow turned in his drafts, which were rewritten by Kahn and Cameron, who had the power to withhold his weekly payments if he did not behave.

In January 1955, while the book, retitled *False Witness*, was being printed for publication the following month, Matusow signed two affidavits. In one, he recanted his testimony on Jencks, saying: "There was no basis for my stating that Clinton E. Jencks was a member of the Communist Party at the time I stated so in court. . . . I testified falsely when I appeared in Salt Lake City on Oct. 8, 1952, before Sen. McCarran." In fact, he had by his own admission on the tapes testified truthfully, but was now lying to satisfy his employers.

Matusow also provided an affidavit on his Smith Act testimony, saying that Roy Cohn had asked him to fabricate remarks made by Trachtenberg and others. This affidavit was closer to the truth, for Matusow had been coached by Cohn.[58]

At the end of February, *False Witness* was published, with a helping hand from the columnist Stewart Alsop. Cameron shrewdly picked him because he and his brother Joe had written articles denouncing the use of paid government informants. Alsop's syndicated column of January 28, 1955, said that "legal lying by such professional informers as Matusow . . . has been tolerated by all three branches of the American government." Alsop found *False Witness* "inherently credible" and called the witness business "a profitable one, courtesy of the American taxpayer." This imprimatur from a leading establishment columnist launched the book.

Publication was synchronized with a campaign for new trials, which might be seen as the party's Last Hurrah, at a time when 134 Communist leaders had been indicted under the Smith Act, with eighty-three convictions. Thanks to Matusow, the party could claim that all Smith Act trials were rigged. Party leader William Z. Foster wrote Eisenhower on February 25, calling for the suspension of Hoover and Brownell for using perjured informants. *People's World*, the Communist newspaper in Los Angeles, launched a petition drive on February 10 calling for an end to the use of paid informers. Matusow gave a press conference at the Biltmore under the auspices of Friends of the Soviet Union. There he was in his gray suit recanting, with his éminence grise Nat Witt behind him. It seemed as if the party's fortunes were riding on his book.[59]

When Matusow appeared on February 21, 1955, in the klieg-lit room 318 of the Senate Office Building, before the Senate Internal Security Subcommittee, he swore that what was in the book was true. He had kept diary entries, though he did not have his diary with him. Perhaps it was at his parents' home.

In the tapes with Kahn, Matusow was asked: "When you named these 200 individuals . . . as members of the Communist Party, were you sure of your own knowledge?"

Matusow: "I believed at the time that all of the people who I testified about were actually dues-paying members. . . . I identified people, and 15 percent fit into the category of hearsay."

But now, at the SISS hearing on February 21, Matusow perused the list of the 244 he had named and said "some aspect of my testimony regarding each of these individuals is false."

As for the Vincents, whom he had told Kahn were Communists, he now said, "I didn't know them as Communists." In his outline, he had called San Cristóbal "a dude ranch for comrades," but now he said he did not know it was operated by the party.

Matusow told the committee that he now had a comedy act, which he performed at the Champagne Room on MacDougal Street in Greenwich Village, calling himself Dimitri. His act was to recount the Army-McCarthy hearings as if calling a baseball game.[60] On March 7, Albert Kahn testified, modestly calling himself "the most widely read non-fiction writer in the United States, abroad." He also made repeated professions of devotion to the Fifth Amendment.

Kahn was the author of *The Great Conspiracy,* which was required reading for American POWs in North Korean prison camps. Igor Bogolepov, a onetime division chief in the Soviet Foreign Office, had testified on April 17, 1952, at the Institute of Pacific Relations hearings that the material in Kahn's book had been prepared for him by the Soviet Foreign Office and was essentially a rewrite of the prosecution's case in the Moscow purge trials. Kahn was a specialist in hoaxes, and in his introduction to *False Witness,* he said: "I am completely convinced of the veracity of the revelations in this book."

The committee report on April 6, 1955, said that the publication of *False Witness* was part of an organized campaign by the Communists to demand new Smith Act trials. The evidence showed that *False Witness* contained numerous falsehoods and that Communist lawyers had manipulated Matusow to pervert the legal process, from the moment he was picked up destitute in Taos.[61]

As for Matusow's two affidavits, he got a split decision. In El Paso on March 15, 1955, Judge Robert Thomason heard Matusow's recantation, but he also had the tape in which Matusow told Kahn, "I knew Jencks was a party member and said so." Judge Thomason said in his charge: "Matusow alone or with others willfully and nefariously and for the purpose of defrauding this court . . . schemed and actually used this court of law as a forum for the purpose of calling attention to a book . . . entitled *False Witness.* . . . Officials of Mine, Mill . . . persuaded Matusow to lend himself to the perpetration of a fraud by means of his recanting his testimony. Matusow willfully lent himself to this evil scheme for money." The motion for a new trial for Jencks was denied.[62]

In New York on April 22, 1955, however, Judge Edward J. Dimock overturned the convictions of two of the thirteen Smith Act defendants, Alexander Trachtenberg and George Charney. Dimock ruled that Matusow's recantation was probably no more truthful than his original testimony, which only proved his complete lack of credibility.

In July 1955, a grand jury in New York indicted Harvey Matusow for scheming to obstruct justice. He was convicted and sentenced to five years, lost his appeal, and spent three and a half years in the federal prison in Lewisburg, Pennsylvania. Released in 1960, at the age of thirty-three, he moved to England and became a music impresario. Back in the States in 1973, he joined a Massachusetts commune, where he took the first name Job, sampled LSD, and flirted with Buddhism. In the eighties, he moved to Tucson, where he had a clown act on children's television, *The Magic Mouse Show.* In 1995 he joined a Mormon community in Glenwood, Utah. In 2001, he moved to Claremont, New Hampshire, where he worked in public access TV. On January 17, 2002, he died at home as the result of injuries suffered in a car accident.

After Matusow's SISS testimony in February 1955, John Steinbeck wrote in the April 2 issue of the *Saturday Review:* "I suspect that government informers, even if they had told the truth, can't survive Matusow's testimony. He has said that it was a good racket. It will never be so good again." Steinbeck was right. The Justice Department shut down its team of paid informants in 1955.[63]

As for the Jencks conviction, it was upheld on appeal by the Fifth Circuit Court in New Orleans in October 1955. Mine, Mill's compliance status with the Taft-Hartley Act was removed by the National Labor Relations Board. In 1956, Jencks was summoned to Denver by the Mine, Mill board and asked to resign from the union.[64]

On June 11, 1957, the Supreme Court reversed his conviction and ordered a new trial by a 7 to 1 majority. Justice William Brennan's opinion ruled that the defense had a right to look at Matusow's FBI reports, a blow to the restrictions that the FBI placed upon its information. The Justice Department decided to drop the case, not wanting to disclose the reports.[65]

—

On September 8, 1953, the sixty-three-year-old Kentucky-born Chief Justice, Fred Vinson, a three-pack-a-day smoker, died of a heart attack. Eisenhower named Earl Warren to replace him. Warren, the son of a railroad worker, had served three terms as governor of California, and in 1948 he was Dewey's running mate. In 1952, Warren, who was considered a middle-of-the-road Republican, campaigned for Ike in fourteen states. But he was not a legal scholar and had no prior experience on the bench.

To everyone's surprise, including the President's, Warren transformed the Supreme Court from a national security court into a civil liberties court. Three years later, Ike named William J. Brennan Jr., the son of Catholic Irish immigrants, a New Jersey judge, and a Democrat, to the court. By Ike's reckoning, Brennan was the second biggest mistake he made as President, Warren being the first. For both men joined the dissenters Hugo Black and William Douglas to form a liberal core that dominated the court for a decade and a half. Two other Eisenhower appointees were John Marshall Harlan, a Republican corporate lawyer and Rhodes scholar, in 1954, and Charles Evans Whittaker, a Kansas-born federal judge, in 1957. The holdovers were Felix Frankfurter, Tom Clark, and Harold Burton, onetime mayor of Cleveland.[66]

In case after case, the Warren court demolished the legal underpinnings that sustained McCarthyism. The court's first principle was that it must meet the changing needs of society. In upholding the Smith Act convictions of 1951, the Vinson court had invoked a clear and present danger, in the midst of the Korean War. But by the mid-fifties, with the war over, Stalin dead, Eisenhower at the helm, and McCarthy no longer a factor, the mood had changed. The curtailment of civil liberties in order to suppress the Communist Party was no longer necessary. The party was in crisis, having been crippled by the Vinson court, and by its slavish obedience to Moscow.

The removal of the Cold War judicial scaffolding began in earnest in 1956, with two decisions in swift succession in April. After serving as liaison with the San Francisco KGB in 1943, Steve Nelson was back in Pittsburgh in 1950. The *Pittsburgh Press* described him, not inaccurately, as "an inspector general for the Soviet underground." He was arrested under the Pennsylvania Sedition Act, which dated back to 1919, and went on trial in January 1951. Found guilty of sedition, he was sentenced to twenty years. He appealed, and in the meantime he was indicted by the federal government under the Smith Act. In 1952, the Pennsylvania Supreme Court reversed his 1951 conviction on the ground that the Smith Act indictment preempted state sedition laws. Saved from imprisonment by the state, Nelson went on trial in federal court in Pittsburgh and was found guilty in mid-August 1953. He was sentenced to five years and a $10,000 fine.

In November 1955, the Supreme Court heard arguments on Nelson's Pennsylvania case. Chief Justice Warren said in conference that it would be "no loss to the United States if these [state] acts are stricken." In April 1956, the court upheld the Pennsylvania Supreme Court's reversal in a 6 to 3 ruling. Warren wrote the decision. "Sedition against the United States is not a local offense," he wrote. "It is a crime against the Nation. As such, it should be prosecuted and punished in federal courts." The decision nullified the Pennsylvania Sedition Act of 1919, and, indirectly, those of thirty-two other states. All those state laws penalizing persons who refused to sign loyalty oaths or were charged with Communism were wiped from the books.

Nelson was off the hook on the twenty-year sentence, but still had the five-year Smith Act sentence to contend with. In October 1956, that conviction was also reversed in another 6 to 3 ruling, which threw out the Supreme Court verdict because the government had admitted that one of its key witnesses was a perjurer. Nelson was released.[67]

On the heels of the Pennsylvania case came another stunning decision on April 9, 1956, in *Slochower v. Board of Education.* Harry Slochower was a professor of philosophy and literature at Brooklyn College who appeared before the McCarthy Committee on Investigations in 1953. When asked about past membership in the Communist Party, he took the Fifth and lost his job. The 7 to 2 decision held that due process was required before the Board of Regents could fire Slochower, and that he should have been granted a hearing.

The ruling by Tom Clark, who had approved the Smith Act prosecutions as Truman's Attorney General, said: "At the outset, we must condemn the practice of imputing a sinister meaning to the exercise of a person's constitutional right under the 5th Amendment. . . . The privilege against self-incrimination would be reduced to a hollow mockery if its exercise could be taken as the equivalent either to a confession of guilt or a conclusive presumption of perjury. . . . A witness may have a reasonable fear of prosecution and yet be innocent of any wrongdoing."[68]

McCarthy, whom censure had not completely muzzled, took umbrage at the Nelson and Slochower decisions. "We made a mistake," he said, "in confirming as Chief Justice a man who had no judicial experience, who had practically no legal experience, except as a District Attorney, for a short time, and whose entire experience was as a politician."[69] Although discredited in the Senate, McCarthy found anti-Warren allies among Southern congressmen upset over the Supreme Court's civil rights decisions. As the Alabama Governor George Wallace put it: "Earl Warren does not have enough brains to try a chicken thief in my home county."

Undeterred, the Warren court on June 11, 1956, in *Cole v. Young,* made a ruling that limited the scope of the federal loyalty program. Kendrick M. Cole, a food and drug inspector employed in the Department of Health, Education, and Welfare, was charged with membership in Nature Friends of America, supposedly a hiking club, but in effect a full-service front group, with political lectures and classes, and a youth section for those under the age of twenty. Before the loyalty board, Cole refused to answer questions, saying it was an invasion of privacy. He was suspended in November 1953 and terminated soon after.

The argument was over whether loyalty programs should apply only to sensitive agencies and whether Health, Education, and Welfare was such an agency. The court ruled that it was not, and that the act was intended to dismiss only those in sensitive positions. Cole's termination was reversed. Tom Clark in his dissent said the ruling invalidated the President's executive order. The court struck down "the most effective weapon against subversive activity available to the government. . . . One never knows which job is sensitive. The janitor might be important, security-wise."[70]

One of the Southern senators who saw the Warren court as a menace to states' rights was James Eastland of Mississippi, the chairman of the Internal Security Subcommittee. On June 26, 1956, he invited McCarthy to testify in his capacity as an expert on Communism.

Eastland: "Is it the Communist line to say the Communist Party is just another party?"

McCarthy: "That is strictly the Communist line."

Eastland: "Is that not the line that the Chief Justice of the United States takes?"

McCarthy: "Unfortunately yes, Mr. Chairman. And I may say that I follow their line rather closely. And the Communist *Daily Worker* applauded this decision, the Nelson decision, and other decisions of the Supreme Court. In their book, Earl Warren is a hero."[71]

Warren, while outwardly maintaining his judicial impassiveness, was stung. In chambers he called McCarthy a "querulous, disreputable liar." Few went so far as to claim that he was a crypto-Communist, but many wondered over the change in Warren since he had joined the High Court. Was it the magnetic duo of Black and Douglas that had pulled him leftward? Or was it an affinity for the underdog that could be traced to his background? Raised in the parched, hardscrabble setting of Bakersfield, California, Warren was the son of a Norwegian-born foreman of the Southern Pacific Railroad who had prospered by fixing up shacks that he rented to itinerant laborers. At the age of seventeen, while still in high school, Earl Warren worked as a callboy, rounding up the crews to man the trains. He saw men laid off without notice, or mutilated in accidents, without compensation. His father had enough money to send him to college and law school, after which he made his name in public service, as district attorney, attorney general, and governor of California. Perhaps his ascent to the Supreme Court gave him the immunity and latitude to express a social conscience developed at an early age.

McCarthy died in May 1957, just as the Warren court struck again to disassemble the foundations of McCarthyism, in *Schware v. Bar Examiners.* Rudolph Schware wanted to take the bar exam in New Mexico, but the Board of Bar Examiners refused his application. In 1940, Schware had recruited volunteers to help refugees from Loyalist Spain. The New Mexico Supreme Court ruled that Schware was a Communist from 1932 to 1940 and that "one who had knowingly given his loyalty to such a program and belief for six to seven years . . . is a person of questionable character."

In a 5 to 4 decision, Justice Hugo Black found that the New Mexico court's "questionable character" ruling was "so dogmatic an inference as to be wholly unwarranted." Black noted that "many persons in this country actively supported the Spanish Loyalists" and that this alone did not indicate "moral turpitude." Schware in addition had used a false name as a labor organizer and had been arrested in the California strikes of the thirties. Black ruled that "the mere fact that a man was arrested has very little, if any, probative value in showing that he has engaged in any misconduct." In the 1934 strike in San Pedro, "great numbers of strikers were picked up by police in a series of arrests." Schware must be allowed to take the bar exam. Another precept of McCarthyism, "once a Commie always a Commie," went by the board.[72]

On June 11, 1957, came the decision reversing Clinton Jencks's conviction. Warren felt that Jencks and his lawyers had the right to see the FBI reports. Since he had been denied that right, his conviction could not stand. The decision triggered an uproar in Congress, where the anti-Warren coalition of Southern Democrats and conservative Republicans muttered that he had put the FBI "out of business."

Then, on June 17, 1957, came what became known as Red Monday, a cluster of three decisions, all striking at McCarthyism. In *Watkins v. United States,* the labor organizer John T. Watkins was cited for contempt when he appeared before HUAC in 1954 and agreed to discuss his own activities but not those of others.

In a 6 to 1 decision, the court reversed the contempt charge. Warren argued that HUAC had to show why Watkins's testimony was relevant to the proposal of further legislation. The purpose of congressional investigations was to write new laws. But too often committees exposed for the sake of exposing, or for headlines, or to sway an election. The legitimate need of Congress to pass new laws, Warren wrote, "cannot be inflated into a general power to expose where the predominant result can only be an invasion of the private rights of the individual."

Thus Warren limited the power of committees in two crucial ways: the questions they asked had to be pertinent to the development of new legislation; and there was to be no prying into the personal affairs of witnesses for the sake of prying.

The Watkins case placed strict limits on the obligation to name names and blunted the committees' routine use of contempt followed by jail, which it held over the heads of witnesses who refused to talk.[73]

In another Red Monday case, the court reinstated the China hand John Stewart Service. Investigated five times by the State Department loyalty board, Service was cleared four times. But on the fifth try, on December 13, 1951, the Loyalty Review Board found "a reasonable doubt as to his loyalty." Secretary of State Dean Acheson fired him. The Warren court ruled 8 to 0 on procedural grounds that Acheson had ignored his department's rules, but did not take up the security aspects of the case. Service was reinstated on July 3, 1957, and a position was created for him, that of special assistant to the deputy assistant secretary of operations. This lengthy title could be summed up in the one word *clerk*. Service's job was arranging for the shipment of the household and personal effects of Foreign Service employees to and from American missions abroad. Later, he was assigned to an obscure posting at the Liverpool consulate. He resigned in 1962 and died in 1999, after writing several books on China.[74]

In what was perhaps the most far-reaching of the Red Monday decisions, the court reversed a Smith Act conviction, that of fourteen California Communists who in August 1951 had been arrested, tried, and convicted. It was pure good luck that their appeal took two years to arrive before a completely different court than the one that had upheld the first Smith Act convictions. In October 1956, the Warren court agreed to hear the case of one of the fourteen, Oleta Yates. Unlike Vinson, Warren was critical of the government's case. At the October 12 conference, he argued that the only overt acts in the indictment were attendance at meetings. It had not been established "that the Communist Party is force and violence. The government has not made clear proof of the purpose of the party." Warren wanted to reverse, as did Bill Douglas and Hugo Black, who said the Yates trial "was a political trial—what the First Amendment was supposed to prevent."

Of the six remaining brethren, four wanted to affirm the convictions (Reed, Burton, Minton, and Clark), while two were undecided (Frankfurter and Harlan). Unsure of a majority, Warren set the case aside for a few weeks. When it was discussed again, Frankfurter and Harlan agreed to reverse on the narrow procedural ground that the instructions given to the jury were inadequate, and Warren mustered a majority of five.

Harlan, who wrote the majority opinion, had no intention of striking down the Smith Act on constitutional grounds. Instead, he stated that the government must provide a more precise definition of advocacy in trying Communists under the act. Released on June 17, 1957, Harlan's opinion ordered that five of the fourteen California Communists be acquitted, while the remaining nine should be given new trials. The Smith Act still stood, but very shakily, for the government had to prove more than vague advocacy. The government not only gave up on a retrial of the nine, but dropped all charges against other Smith Act defendants.[75]

In Congress, there was talk of impeaching Warren, and Representative Francis Walter of HUAC promised "to pass the type of legislation that even the Supreme Court will understand." The John Birch Society, which then claimed a membership of 100,000, took up the cause, complete with picket lines, leaflets, and radio programs clamoring that Warren should be hanged, not impeached. The clamor did not subside until the mid-sixties. Through it all, Warren kept his sense of humor. On the wall of his apartment he hung a *New Yorker* cartoon that showed Whistler's mother embroidering "Impeach Earl Warren" on a pillow cover.[76]

In a memo to the White House on June 26, 1957, J. Edgar Hoover said that "the Supreme Court decisions have been greeted with jubilation in all echelons of the Communist Party. Waning confidence of rank and file members in their leaders has been restored. . . . Unafraid of prosecution, Communist leaders have been stimulated to take a bold approach to building a stronger party."[77] In fact, the party was in disarray. The Smith Act convictions had done their work in dismantling the leadership and driving it underground, and the Warren court decisions did little to mend a party that was agonizing over the 1956 Khrushchev speech on Stalin's crimes and the Hungarian rebellion.

A more realistic appraisal was made by John Gates, a member of the national board, when he wrote in *Party Affairs,* the party's theoretical organ, in November 1956: "We have suffered great losses in membership and even more in influence. . . . Why . . . is our party at such a low point? . . . We are isolated almost entirely from the labor movement, the Negro people, and the farmers. . . . Even the confidence of our own members in the party and its leadership has been severely shaken. . . . We are still compelled to function largely as an illegal or semi-legal organization."

—

The fear of Communism in America went back to the Bolshevik Revolution, and expressed itself in various ways, from the deportation of aliens to the blacklisting of actors. But during those years, there was also a secret undermining of our institutions by the Soviets and their American surrogates, which was revealed to the public in bits and pieces, so that no one knew quite what to believe. It was in this climate of uncertainty that McCarthyism in all its forms thrived, as an exaggerated reaction to a real threat. By the time

McCarthy came on the scene in 1950, the threat was a mirage, but a mirage to be exploited, by the blacklist agencies for profit, by the Republicans in Congress for political gain, and by the self-appointed super-patriots to vent and focus their muddled rage.

McCarthyism was not an epidemic, but a series of scattered outbreaks. There was never a wholesale purge, either in universities or in the entertainment world. Instead of the "reign of terror" described by certain writers, there was a "reign of doubt," which demagogues like McCarthy took advantage of. His accusations, often but not always inaccurate, were believed precisely because the American party was an adjunct for espionage. McCarthy and the American party were mirror images, both employing falsehood and deceit, both using heated rhetoric and hidden informants, and both making unfounded charges against their government. They expressed two pathologies in a democratic society, one of the misguided or fanatical radical, the other of the anti-Red zealot. American institutions were tested and were not found wanting. The Senate *did* censure one of its own. The Warren court *did* reverse the decisions of its predecessor. Truman and Eisenhower *did* combat both Communism and McCarthyism.

Crippled by the measures of both administrations, the American party found in McCarthy an excuse to shout fascism. The treatment of the Hollywood Ten, those posturing beneficiaries of bourgeois entertainment, was called "Torture by Inquisition." There was a case of authentic torture by inquisition, in Moscow, not Hollywood. Vsevolod Meyerhold, one of the great innovators of the Russian theater, with his stylized and abstract productions, was accused of mysticism and neglect of socialist realism. In 1938, his theater was "liquidated" as "alien to Soviet art." On June 15, 1939, he was invited to criticize himself at a convention of theater directors presided over by the prosecutor of the purges, Andrei Vyshinsky. Meyerhold said: "The pitiful and wretched thing that pretends to the title of the theater of socialist realism has nothing in common with art. . . . Everything is gloomily well regulated . . . and murderous in its lack of talent. . . . You have done something monstrous. . . . In hunting down formalism, you have eliminated art!" Meyerhold, a man of sixty-five, was arrested and tortured. His interrogator, B. V. Rodus, broke his left arm and urinated in his mouth. Meyerhold wrote Vyshinsky that though one arm was broken, he could still use a pen with the other. On February 2, 1940, he was shot.[78]

EPILOGUE

Just as McCarthyism began long before McCarthy, it endured long after him. It metastasized to other sites in the body politic, one of which was the FBI. J. Edgar Hoover harbored a pathological conviction that Negroes were immoral animals with uncontrollable sexual appetites, which he expressed in his frenzied hounding of Martin Luther King Jr. Both of Hoover's parents came from long-established Washington families. His mother's family, the Scheitlins, had arrived before the Civil War. His great-grandfather, John Thomas Hoover, was a mason who worked on the Capitol, finished in 1865. His father and grandfather both worked for the government, as he did. The values of the Washington where Hoover was born in 1895 were Southern, white, and Christian. As head of the FBI, Hoover enforced the law against those elements that disrupted the social fabric, such as anarchist aliens, violence-prone Wobblies, Communists who threatened the American way of life, and all other criminals.[1] Part of that orderly social fabric was segregation, which made Hoover view black efforts at integration with misgivings. Eventually, with the Reverend King, the misgivings mutated into irrational loathing.

In his investigation of the Communist Party, Hoover established as early as 1946 that its policy was to infiltrate black organizations. On January 17, he alerted the Truman White House regarding the National Association for the Advancement of Colored People's meeting with the President on January 18 to discuss fair employment practices and recognition for Negro war veterans. "Information had been received," Hoover wrote, "that Communist elements are interested in attending the national meeting of the NAACP on Jan. 17 and 18 and desire to send a delegate to it."[2]

By repeatedly making a case that Communists had fastened on civil rights as an issue to divide the nation, Hoover cast a shadow of disloyalty over black advocates, even while acknowledging that the NAACP was outspokenly anti-Communist.

On January 16, 1956, Hoover informed the Eisenhower White House that the NAACP was planning a march on Washington on March 5 and 6 to promote civil rights. He said that the Communist Party had advanced a program for the conference that intended to embarrass the administration by forcing it to take a strong stand on civil rights. This would create a rift with the Dixiecrats, who were causing problems in an election year.[3]

While ostensibly impartial, Hoover's reports left the impression that the NAACP was vulnerable to Communist inroads. On March 9, he briefed the cabinet on "racial tension and civil rights." He said Communist operatives from New England were trying to infiltrate the NAACP in Alabama, Georgia, and Mississippi. They hoped to alienate the administration from its Southern supporters by forcing it to take "immediate action" to support the 1954 decision in *Brown v. Board of Education* that segregation in public schools was illegal. Hoover's briefing was said to have contributed to Eisenhower's inertness in passing civil rights legislation.[4]

——

In 1956, the Communist Party was in the doldrums, increasingly isolated, with a shriveling and aging membership. For a seasoned apparatchik like Steve Nelson, the 1956 Khrushchev speech and the invasion of Hungary took on malevolent overtones. He watched the faces of the men and women around him as they heard the news, and saw tears streaming down their faces, and these were people who had spent their entire lives in the party, who had been beaten up and jailed . . . It was like finding out that your dear old grandmother was an axe murderer, Nelson felt. All around him people were saying the party was finished. It was like devoting your life to promoting a miracle cure, which you discover is made from creosote. Nelson was one of the thousands who left the party in 1957.[5]

It was the twilight of the party. No longer was it used as a recruiting ground for Soviet espionage. No longer did it try to increase its membership through front groups. No organizations were added to the Attorney General's list after 1955.

FBI policy was to continue to treat the party as a threat, but it had to change its vocabulary. Instead of reporting on the party's growing strength, it said that it was "seeking to repair its losses." Instead of reporting Communist spies in government, it said the party was "hoping to move in," on movements with "laudable objectives," such as civil rights.[6]

After the 1957 Supreme Court decision reversing the Smith Act convictions, the FBI was forced to develop new tactics to effectively track down Communists, which led to the adoption of the Counter-Intelligence Program (COINTELPRO) in August 1956. William C. Sullivan, the wiry Irishman in charge of the Domestic Intelligence section, ran it as his own department of dirty tricks. Instead of making a case for prosecutors, COINTELPRO was meant "to divide, confuse, weaken . . . foster factionalism . . . cause confusion," as Sullivan testified in 1975 before the Select Committee to Study Governmental Operations with Respect to Intelligence Activities, chaired by Senator Frank Church of Idaho. It was a series of covert actions against the party, which were later extended to other troublesome groups. Under COINTELPRO, the bureau used anonymous letters and the so-called snitch-jacket technique, in which party officials were made to believe that one of their own was an FBI informant, thanks to planted material.[7]

In 1975, the Church Committee report said that with COINTELPRO "a government agency took the law into its own hands for the 'greater good' of the country." As Sullivan explained the FBI mentality in disregarding "the niceties of law," it began during the war. "We never freed ourselves from the psychology" of Pearl Harbor, that "it was just like a soldier on the battlefield. When he shot down an enemy, he did not ask himself is this legal, is it ethical? It was what he was expected to do as a soldier. It became part of our thinking, part of our personality."[8]

Hoover continued to keep a close watch on Communists and civil rights groups. Born in Atlanta in 1929, Martin Luther King came from a family steeped in the tradition of the Southern Negro ministry. His father and maternal grandfather were Baptist ministers, and he was the pastor of a church in Montgomery, Alabama. In 1956 he became the leader of a group formed to boycott the segregated transit system, the Montgomery Improvement Association. An inspiring leader with a doctrine previously untested in America, that of nonviolent resistance, King was in the spotlight. In February 1957, he launched the Southern Leadership Conference and announced that he would lead a pilgrimage to Washington if President Eisenhower maintained his silence on desegregation in the South.[9]

Hoover's first memo to the White House mentioning King reported on the march. He said that King and ninety-seven other Negro leaders from ten Southern states planned a "pilgrimage of prayer . . . unless president Eisenhower speaks out to the South on Segregation violence." Hoover noted the "action of the Communist Party in connection with [the infiltration of] this demonstration."

In an April memo, Hoover advised that Carl Winter, chairman of the Michigan party, said its number one project was the support of the "prayer crusade." Winter said that "all the machinery in the Communist Party was organized to make it click," though the party had no official connection and would remain in the background. Hoover said "that individuals associated with Rev. Martin Luther King and individuals affiliated with NAACP have orally and unofficially asked the Communist Party for support in this mobilization."[10]

The pilgrimage took place as planned on May 17, 1957. It ended in front of the Lincoln Memorial, with a smaller than expected crowd of about twenty thousand. King received an ovation when he said: "The executive branch of government is all too silent and apathetic. . . . Give us the ballot!" After this event, the black press began calling King "the number one black leader."

Also at this time came the first report of what was to become a recurring theme when a black newspaper, the *Pittsburgh Courier,* wrote that "a prominent minister in the Deep South who has been making headlines recently had better watch his step," for detectives hired by white segregationists had caught him in a hotel room in a Northern city with a woman other than his wife.[11]

King renamed his group the Southern Christian Leadership Conference. It was the first major civil rights organization to originate in the South. As King became a national figure, he drew Hoover's less than friendly attention.

Hoover diligently reported every move of the party in support of the civil rights movement. In the spring of 1959, when a Youth March for Integrated Schools was planned on Washington, Hoover explained in detail the Communist connection. One of the organizers in Washington, said Hoover, was Hunter Pitts O'Dell, the assistant head of Negro affairs for the party. He had official credentials from the NAACP. It was hoped, said Hoover, that the march "will result in the recruitment of young people into the Marxist-Leninist movement."[12]

The march took place on April 18, when a crowd of 26,000 gathered in front of the Washington Monument. King once again stressed the right to vote. Hoover reported that a delegation including O'Dell was received at the White House by presidential aide Gerald Morgan. Attending the march as observers were Ben Davis, a leading black Communist, James Jackson, head of the party's Negro affairs, Ted Bassett, a reporter for the *Daily Worker,* and about forty party members.

Hoover said that the march chairman, A. Philip Randolph, gave credit to Stanley D. Levison for helping set up "the mechanics" for the march. Hoover explained that Levison, a New York lawyer and businessman, "has been a substantial contributor to the Communist Party for a number of years. Recently, he has been closely associated personally and financially with Rev.

Martin Luther King Jr. It is apparent that while the Communist Party had no official connection with the planning of and execution of this march, it initiated a widespread program to stimulate Communist participation."[13]

A reasonable reaction would be "So what?" Were the civil rights leaders supposed to give up their struggle for integration because the party was acting as a spoiler? But the White House took Hoover's reports seriously, in part because King persistently nagged Eisenhower for being indifferent to civil rights.

———

Much of the information the FBI received on Communist efforts to infiltrate the civil rights movement came from two Soviet agents who had been turned by the bureau, the brothers Jack and Morris Childs (born Chilofsky). Jack had been a Moscow-trained Comintern agent in Nazi Germany in the thirties, while Morris was the leader of the Illinois party in 1944 and the editor of the *Daily Worker* in 1948. From 1945 to 1948, Jack served as the assistant to William Weiner, the party's financial secretary. He collected the cash from secret heavyweight contributors, which he placed in a safe deposit box in his name at a New York bank.[14]

When one of Jack's sons was blinded in one eye by cancer, the party ignored his plea for help in paying the medical bills. In 1948, both brothers became inactive in the party. In 1951, the FBI initiated a program called "cage rattling." FBI agents went up to known party members on the street and asked them if they wanted to talk. Most of the time, those approached fled, but not always. When agents ran down Jack Childs, he asked, "What took you so long?" Jack and Morris were recruited by the FBI, but by the time they began talking in 1952, they had been inactive for four years. The FBI, looking for a way to get them back inside the party, had a stroke of luck.[15]

Morris Childs had a heart condition and was living quietly in Chicago. In September 1952, he informed the FBI that William Weiner's assistant, Stanley Levison, had come to see him to ask why he had not kept up with the National Office.

Stanley Levison was a curious combination of Communist functionary and financial wizard. He and his twin brother, Roy, had a portfolio of companies whose intricate financial structure not even the FBI could figure out. They managed a couple of tool and die firms; they owned a Ford dealership in New Jersey; they dabbled in real estate and import and export—and they tithed to the party, sometimes as much as $50,000 a year.

After Levison's visit, Morris Childs went to New York, saw Weiner, and was rehabilitated. Jack Childs too came back into the fold after making a financial contribution, at a time when the party was starved for funds. Levison said that Morris "is a better Communist today than he ever was, and his best work is ahead of him." Indeed it was, for the information he provided to the FBI turned out to be a spectacular coup for the agency.[16]

When William Weiner died of liver cancer in February 1954, the Childs brothers were the first to place a wreath on his casket. Levison took over Weiner's duties. Informed of his rise to the top leadership, the FBI put a tap on his phone. In one of his conversations, Levison said that he was giving talks to get across the idea "that the Eisenhower administration is rapidly advancing toward fascism."[17]

Levison used the Childs brothers to channel the party's money pipeline to Moscow. In April 1958, Morris Childs conferred with Boris Ponomaref, head of the Central Committee's Interior Department, who offered $250,000 for the American party's 1959 budget. After that, Morris went to Moscow at least once a year with his shopping list. Back in New York, Jack Childs took delivery of the cash from KGB operatives and turned it over to the party. The Childs brothers routinely embezzled about 5 percent of the funds Jack collected and lived in style. This arrangement went on for more than twenty years, during which time the brothers provided the FBI with intelligence from the highest echelons of the party. Jack died in 1980, after making his last delivery, $255,437, and Morris and his wife retired to a condominium on the ocean, near Miami.[18]

In November 1954, when Levison had taken over the party's finances, he told Jack Childs that he was trying to rekindle major donors, or "angels," who could make large contributions. In 1955, however, Jack reported to the FBI that for some mysterious reason, Levison was "out of circulation." Did this mean that he had moved on to underground work? No one knew. On the basis of its wiretaps and FISUR (physical surveillance), the FBI remained convinced that Levison was still the leader of the party's financial apparat.

By March 1957, however, the FBI had dropped Levison from its list of "key" Communists. The Childs brothers reported that although Levison was still a party member, he no longer had any part in financial affairs.[19]

The event that removed Stanley Levison from party activities was his meeting with Martin Luther King. On December 28, 1956, King went to Baltimore to receive an award and make a speech. There to meet him at the airport was Bayard Rustin, a longtime civil rights activist who had become one of King's close allies and advisers. Rustin had gone to jail as a draft resister and had briefly belonged to the Young Communist League. He served as unofficial liaison between King and the white left-wingers who admired him. With Bayard Rustin at the airport was Stanley Levison, who had started raising money for

Southern activists that year. Levison seems to have made an immediate decision to devote himself wholeheartedly to King's cause, just as he was about to
organize the Southern Christian Leadership Conference, which would give
King a base of operations throughout the South.[20]

Levison quickly volunteered to help King prepare his voter registration
drive. Soon he was running SCLC's New York office, but did not ask to be paid.
He became the indispensable man, called upon for a variety of tasks, from
doing King's taxes to writing the occasional speech. In one sense, however,
Levison was a poisoned gift, for he was still under Communist discipline. In
1958, Jack Childs reported to the FBI a boast made by the prominent black
Communist James Jackson that "most secret and guarded people" were guiding the civil rights leader. One of those people, Childs said, was the secret
Communist Stanley Levison. In 1961, Levison hired as his assistant Hunter
Pitts O'Dell, a high-ranking black Communist who had served as district organizer in Louisiana. O'Dell's term for the American South was "the revolutionary front."[21]

O'Dell had a long history of party activities. In 1950, he helped organize a
longshoremen's strike in New Orleans. In 1954, he attended the party's
Southern Regional Convention in New York City. In his testimony before various congressional committees, he took the First, Fourth, and Fifth amendments to avoid admitting his party affiliation.

King knew that Levison and O'Dell were Communists, but they were also
extremely effective. Their fund-raising efforts in the New York office produced
a list of nine thousand contributors. As the SCLC expanded, King needed men
of their caliber more than ever. Their party training had prepared them for
the kind of work King was doing. In April 1962, O'Dell was named director
of voter registration and soon reported that a drive in Albany, Georgia, had
added 1,200 black voters in six weeks.

All proportions kept, King's use of Levison and O'Dell was not that different from General Leslie Groves's recruitment of Oppenheimer for Los Alamos despite his Communist affiliations, because he was a paragon among
physicists. There is no evidence that in working for King, Levison and
O'Dell followed the party line rather than the King line. In politics, however,
appearances count more than substance. King did not realize that Hoover
would use Levison and O'Dell to malign his movement to the Presidents he
served.

In the meantime, the FBI continued to provide the White House, in the
final years of the Eisenhower presidency, with information on Communist efforts in the field of civil rights. On March 1, 1960, a Hoover memo to President Eisenhower reported that a Communist group in Richmond, Virginia,

had instigated action on equal service for Negroes in restaurants. Students at three white colleges agreed to take part in the sit-ins. This was the first indication of Communist involvement in the sit-ins, said Hoover, who added that the party saw civil rights as its last chance to be relevant.[22]

———

In 1961, after the election of John F. Kennedy as President and the naming of Bobby Kennedy as Attorney General, Hoover started feeding the brothers reports on Communist efforts in civil rights. On January 8, 1962, he reported to Bobby Kennedy that one of King's most trusted advisers was the Communist Stanley Levison. According to Jack Childs, Levison had helped King write a major speech that he delivered to the AFL-CIO convention in Miami in December. In February, Hoover learned that O'Dell was working for Levison in the SCLC New York office. In spite of Hoover's admonitions that warning King about Levison would "definitely endanger our informant and the national security," Bobby Kennedy used back channels to alert him, but to no avail.[23] When stories about O'Dell's background appeared in a number of newspapers, King issued a statement that he had resigned, while in fact he remained in the SCLC New York office.

Hoover resumed surveillance of Levison in March 1962, though no evidence turned up that he was communicating with the party, except to contribute modest sums. Levison's sponsorship of O'Dell, however, convinced Hoover that both were still Communist agents.

In mid-May, when King presided over the spring board meeting of the SCLC in Chattanooga, Tennessee, it was O'Dell who explained the new voter registration program. On August 21, 1962, Levison advised King, who was familiar with O'Dell's background, that "as long as O'Dell does not have the title of executive director there will not be as much lightning flashing around him."[24]

On civil rights enforcement in the South, Hoover dragged his feet. In 1961, when the Freedom Riders were calling attention to racial discrimination in interstate travel, Hoover refused Bobby Kennedy's request to send agents to protect them, saying his was an investigative, not an enforcement, agency. Bobby Kennedy pressured him to hire black agents. Reluctantly, he hired ten, to join a force of more than five thousand.

After seeing FBI agents standing around and taking notes as peaceful demonstrators were arrested during a boycott in Albany, Georgia, King made his first frontal attack on Hoover in a speech on November 18, 1962, saying: "There is a considerable amount of distrust among Albany Negroes for local members of the FBI. . . . FBI men appear to Albany Negroes as vaguely interested observers of injustice, who diffidently write down complaints and do no more. . . . One of the great problems we face with the FBI in the South is that the agents are white Southerners who have been influenced by the mores of the community. To maintain their status, they have to be friendly with the local police and people who are promoting segregation."[25]

There was much truth in King's comments, but on the facts he was wrong, for in Albany, four out of the five agents were Northerners (though the fifth was a Southern segregationist). William Sullivan, in his testimony before the Church Committee in 1975, said that "Hoover was very upset" by King's criticism, "very distraught. . . . Behind it all was the racial bias, the dislike of Negroes. . . . I do not think he could rise above that."[26]

In January 1963, Hoover informed Bobby Kennedy that both Levison and O'Dell were still close aides to King. Kennedy wrote his assistant attorney general for civil rights, Burke Marshall: "Burke—this is not getting any better."

In March, however, the situation changed dramatically, for Jack Childs reported that Levison had severed his ties with the party. On March 19, Levison had lunch with Lem Harris, an affluent Communist whose father, a commodities trader, had founded a brokerage house. Harris was the party's expert on agriculture. He had gone to the Soviet Union with Hal Ware and had later led various front groups for farmers. At the lunch, Levison said he was through with the party. Harris wrote a memo on their conversation, which found its way to the FBI via Jack Childs. The memo said that "a whole group, formerly closely aligned to us . . . are now disenchanted," having decided that the party was "irrelevant and ineffective." This information was not relayed to Bobby Kennedy because it did not fit Hoover's thesis that King continued to be advised by Communists.[27]

In the spring of 1963, King asked O'Dell to describe his Communist affiliations in a letter. O'Dell wrote that while he had supported the Communist Party program, he no longer believed that the party was the solution for the South. Satisfied, King told O'Dell he could stay on.

As he traveled from flashpoint to flashpoint, King regularly consulted Levison by telephone on strategy. In May 1963, Levison said he should ask for a meeting with President Kennedy. If the meeting was granted, King could ask for more aggressive support of civil rights. If it was denied, he could ratchet up the pressure with more Birminghams, where that spring, the campaign to end segregation at lunch counters had drawn national attention when the police commissioner, Bull Connor, responded with snarling hounds and water hoses.

The Kennedy brothers, who were not told that Levison had broken with the party, were deeply troubled by Hoover's reports on King's continued Communist associations. As the result of their activism on civil rights, they were linked to King in the public mind. Any publicity regarding Levison and O'Dell was bound to splatter the White House and the Attorney General's office. The political fallout could be as damaging as Truman's failure to stop the confirmation of Harry Dexter White's appointment to the International Monetary Fund.

President Kennedy acknowledged the dilemma on May 20 when he said: "The trouble with King is everything he does, everybody says we stuck him in there." On May 30, King asked the White House for a conference. On May 31, Hoover filled Bobby Kennedy in on the King-Levison phone taps, showing that they were still in close touch. King was told that the President was too busy. He discussed the President's rebuff in two more conversations with Levison, who repeated that "the Birmingham pattern" could be used in other cities like Atlanta. King told Levison they should announce a march on Washington, "for the threat itself may so frighten the president that he would have to do something." King asked Levison if the time was right and he replied, "The time is now."[28]

Plans were made for a march in August 1963, down Pennsylvania Avenue to the Lincoln Memorial, with a target figure of 100,000. On June 11, Governor George Wallace barred the doors of the University of Alabama to two black students trying to enroll. President Kennedy federalized the Alabama National Guard, who returned the students to the university, and promised to send Congress a civil rights bill. On June 12, King told Levison: "He was really great."[29] Levison replied that the march must now be aimed at Congress, instead of the President. Kennedy's Civil Rights Act, which included provisions concerning access to public accommodations, the use of federal funds without discrimination, and equal employment opportunity, was finally signed into law in July 1964 by President Lyndon Johnson.

Concerned that King's march would hurt the chances of his civil rights legislation, President Kennedy called a meeting of black leaders, including King, to the White House on June 22, 1963. He told them that if the march took place, congressmen would say, "I'm damned if I will vote for it at the point of a gun." The bill wasn't even in committee yet. King argued that the march would dramatize the issue. After the meeting, Kennedy took King into the Rose Garden and told him he was concerned about Levison and O'Dell. Kennedy, who did not know that Levison had broken with the party, warned King: "I assume you know you're under very close surveillance." Kennedy said that if the King-Levison-O'Dell connection was made public, the presidency could be contaminated. "They're Communists," Kennedy said. "You've got to get rid of them." King agreed on O'Dell but said, "I know Stanley. . . . You will have to prove it." Kennedy said he would.[30] Even had he tried, the President could not have proven that Levison was still in the party. By providing slanted information to the Kennedy brothers and later to President Johnson, Hoover created a climate of suspicion in both presidencies that placed King under surveillance and cast a shadow over his movement. Perhaps no other single action of Hoover's during his long tenure had such an ill-starred bearing on the history of his time, for it gave King's bigoted enemies a rationale for their actions.

King fired O'Dell on July 3, 1963. After leaving the SCLC, O'Dell was involved with the magazine *Freedomways*, which received Soviet subsidies and covered black issues. Today, O'Dell is the foreign policy adviser for Jesse Jackson's Rainbow Coalition. King also broke with Levison, but maintained back channels.

In mid-July, at hearings before the Senate Commerce Committee, Governor Ross Barnett of Mississippi testified that the civil rights movement was a Communist conspiracy. Governor George Wallace of Alabama berated the Kennedy administration for "fawning and pawing over such people as Martin Luther King and his pro-Communist friends." Both of these Southern racists had evidently heard rumors about the Levison connection.[31]

But then, on August 23, a sixty-seven-page report from William Sullivan's Division of Domestic Intelligence that made light of the Communist–civil rights connection landed on Hoover's desk. It concluded that "there has been obvious failure of the Communist Party of the United States of America to appreciably infiltrate, influence, or control large numbers of American Negroes in this country."

This was not what Hoover wanted to hear, and he angrily returned the memo with a handwritten note across the bottom: "This memo reminds me vividly of those I received when Castro took over Cuba. You contended then that Castro and his cohorts were not Communists. Time alone proved you wrong. I for one cannot ignore the memos re [Levison and O'Dell] as having only an infinitesimal effect on the efforts to exploit the American Negro by the Communists."

Sullivan was in the doghouse. As he later told the Church Committee: "To be in trouble with Hoover was a serious matter. These men [including him] . . . lived in fear of getting transferred, losing money on their homes. . . . Their children in school." Sullivan had to play catch-up by catering to Hoover's prejudices, although the director was not mollified easily. When Sullivan reported that one hundred Communists were planning to join King's march on August 28, Hoover scrawled the sarcastic comment: "Just infinitesimal."[32]

At the massive August rally at the Lincoln Memorial, attended by 200,000, including an estimated two hundred Communists, Martin Luther King carried the crowd on the tide of his eloquence with his most famous speech. "I have a dream," he said, "that one day on the red hills of Georgia, the sons of former slaves and the sons of former slave owners will be able to sit down together at the table of brotherhood."

King's speech was a chance for Sullivan to show that he was back on Hoover's wavelength, and on August 30, 1963, he wrote: "In light of King's powerful demagogic speech . . . we must mark him now as the most dangerous Negro to the future of this nation from the standpoint of Communism. . . . The Communist Party of the United States of America does wield substantial influence over the Negroes, which one day could be decisive."

Sullivan testified in 1975: "Here again we had to engage in a lot of nonsense which we ourselves really did not believe in. We either had to do that or we would be finished."

When Sullivan reported that Communist Party officials were pleased with the march, Hoover noted, "I assume Communist Party claims are frivolous." On September 16, Sullivan proposed unleashing COINTELPRO on King. Hoover replied, "I can't understand how you can so agilely switch your thinking and evaluation." Sullivan had to kowtow one more time on September 25: "We are in complete agreement with the director that Communist influence is being exerted on Martin Luther King." Sullivan now led the campaign to discredit King, which would continue until his assassination in Memphis in 1968.[33]

On October 10, 1963, Bobby Kennedy approved taps on King's office and home in Atlanta. He felt that King had broken his promise by not getting rid of Levison, who had agreed to help King with the book he was writing on the Birmingham sit-ins. The tap on King's home was approved on a thirty-day trial basis, but on November 22 President Kennedy was killed and Bobby forgot about the thirty-day trial.[34] David J. Garrow, King's biographer, called Bobby Kennedy's authorization "one of the most ignominious acts in modern American history."

In December 1963, Bobby approved bugs in the hotel rooms where King stayed. From January 1964 to September 1966, bugs were placed in fifteen hotels, aside from other venues. Andrew Young, one of King's aides and later the first black congressman in Georgia since Reconstruction, recalled that "we found a bug in the pulpit of a church in Selma in 1965. . . . We took it out from under the pulpit and taped it on top of the pulpit. Rev. [Ralph] Abernathy called it 'this little do-hickey' and he said, 'I want you to tell Mr. Hoover, I don't want it under here where there is a whole lot of static. I want him to get it straight.'"[35]

In 1964, the COINTELPRO investigation intensified with the usual repertoire of dirty tricks. There was a "trash cover" of SCLC offices in Atlanta. The FBI sent letters on SCLC stationery with King's signature to SCLC donors, informing them that the IRS was checking SCLC tax returns. Letters were sent to universities and other groups planning to honor King, asking them to change their minds, in the light of his Communist connections.[36]

With the bugging of the hotel rooms, the thrust of the investigation shifted from Communist infiltration to King's personal conduct. A memo from Sullivan's office on January 28, 1964, explained that the bugs were intended to obtain information on "the private activities of Dr. King and his associates," so that King could be "completely discredited."[37]

The hotel bugs proved to the FBI that King associated not only with Communists, but also with women. The very first bug, at the Willard Hotel in Washington on January 4, 1964, produced a dozen reels on the festivities in King's room with two black women who worked at the Philadelphia Navy Yard. When he heard the tapes, Hoover exulted that they "will destroy the burrhead."[38]

At the Hyatt House in Los Angeles on February 22, 1964, the tapes found King in a jolly joke-telling mood, with a few of his friends and some girls. He conferred mock titles on his best-endowed friends, told Boccaccio-like tales that mixed sex and religion, and recounted a joke about the late President's sexual practices, the funeral, the coffin, and his wife, Jackie. The party was hilarious, but Bobby Kennedy was not amused. Hoover also gave copies to President Johnson, who appreciated them enormously.[39] In April in Las Vegas, the hotel room was not bugged but a local call girl complained of rough sex with King to the police. In several other cities, white call girls were brought to his room. Hoover said he wanted to "remove all doubts from the Attorney General's mind as to the type of person King is." Which was the same type of person that the late President Kennedy was, that is to say, a sex addict. Hoover knew quite a bit about Kennedy's escapades, for he had tapes going back to World War II of young Jack the Navy ensign in bed with the onetime Miss Denmark Inga Arvad, chirping away about military and government matters. He also had a dossier on Jack's liaison with Judith Campbell Exner, the mobster Sam Giancana's girlfriend. Not to mention a gaggle of other women, such as the Senate aide Pamela Turnure, the Washington party girl Ellen Rometsch, the actress Marilyn Monroe, the Boston madam Alicia Darr, various New York call girls, and naked parties in the White House swimming pool. As President Johnson's aide, Bobby Baker, told the author Seymour M. Hersh, Kennedy said: "I get a migraine headache if I don't get a strange piece of ass every day."[40] Martin Luther King, also under great stress, had the same predicament, telling a friend: "I'm away from home 25 to 27 days a month. Fucking's a form of anxiety reduction."[41]

Hoover had a low opinion of both Kennedys, one of whom played darts in his office in his shirtsleeves, while the other was a tomcat. But he did not call the President a "moral degenerate," which was what he called King. When *Time* magazine named King "Man of the Year" for 1963, Hoover said, "They had to dig deep in the garbage for this one." In another FBI memo, Hoover mentioned King's "obsessive degenerate sexual urges."[42]

———

On October 14, 1964, Martin Luther King became the youngest person ever to win the Nobel Peace Prize, at the age of thirty-five. As King's prestige mounted, so did Hoover's fury. He scrawled on one memo that King should have gotten the "top alley cat" prize. For Hoover, King seemed to embody all the uncontrollable social changes that were shaking up the country in the sixties.

Hoover's frustration came to a boil on November 18, when he held a press conference for twenty-two women reporters at the National Press Club. He was still fuming about King's charges that the FBI agents in the South were biased because they were Southerners, whereas in fact 70 percent were Northerners. He closed his remarks by calling King "the most notorious liar," and "one of the lowest characters in the country," which sent the ladies scurrying for the phones.[43]

King responded with a wire: "I was appalled and surprised at your reported statement maligning my integrity. What motivated such an irresponsible accusation is a mystery to me." King offered to meet with Hoover to discuss the bureau's "seeming inability to gain convictions in even the most heinous crimes perpetrated against civil rights workers." The FBI wiretaps caught King saying that Hoover was "too old and broken down" to continue as director.[44]

It was Stanley Levison who first proposed a meeting with Hoover, which took place in the director's Washington office on December 1, 1964. According to Andrew Young, who was present, Hoover turned on the charm and congratulated King on winning the Nobel. But Hoover claimed that "I never addressed him as Reverend or Doctor."

In one of his COINTELPRO stratagems, William Sullivan sent a composite tape of the hotel highlights to King on November 21 with a letter purporting to come from a Negro: "You are a complete fraud and a greater liability to all of us Negroes. . . . You are no clergyman. . . . You are done. . . . There is only one thing for you to do [commit suicide]. . . . You better take it before your filthy fraudulent self is bared to the nation."[45] The material on the tape was mostly dirty jokes and bawdy remarks made at the Willard Hotel, along with the grunts and groans of people having sex.

The package with the tape and the letter remained unopened at the SCLC headquarters in Atlanta, while King went to Oslo and Stockholm in December for the Peace Prize ceremonies. On this trip too there were wild incidents in hotel rooms, of which the FBI obtained a running account thanks to the tap on the talkative Bayard Rustin's phone.[46]

In early January 1965, Coretta King opened the box containing the reel of tape. When she played it, she recognized her husband's voice, but he was not delivering a sermon. King's shocked wife called her husband, who convened his close aides to listen to the tape. They realized that it came from the FBI, and that King's hotel rooms were being bugged. King finally stared into the depths of Hoover's hatred, and was too upset to sleep. He said in a tapped conversation, "They are out to get me, harass me, break my spirit." FBI memos regarding King continued to arrive on the desk of the new Attorney General, Nicholas de B. Katzenbach (Bobby Kennedy had resigned in September 1964 to run for the Senate in New York). One said: "King has recently become emotionally upset and once became extremely violent." Hoover was using the resources of the FBI to destroy a man he had come to loathe, a national figure of heroic stature.

Stanley Levison, who had relinquished his official connection with the SCLC after King's meeting with President Kennedy in June 1963, continued to act as King's chief strategist. Their frequent phone calls continued to be tapped. Levison was Martin Luther King's éminence grise, whispering in his ear as he flattered him. In January 1965, when King led the boycott in Selma, Alabama, Levison told him: "Selma and Montgomery made you one of the most powerful figures in the country—a leader now not merely of Negroes, but of millions of whites."[47]

Nineteen sixty-five was the year not only of Selma but of the buildup in Vietnam, matched by the buildup in the antiwar movement. It was Levison, in May in New York City, who told King in a bugged hotel room that he should speak out on Vietnam. This was party line united front thinking, but it was a tactical error, for King would lose the support of President Johnson, who had pushed for the most sweeping voting rights legislation of the century, the Voting Rights Act, which became law in the summer of 1965, after King's demonstration in Selma had dramatized the issue. To take on Vietnam would also dilute King's civil rights efforts. Vietnam was a foreign war, and King's expertise and leadership were at home.

King decided to speak out against the war because he saw it as a moral issue involving blacks, of whom a disproportionate number were serving in Vietnam. He saw himself as the anointed spokesman on moral questions of national importance and took a position that some would call courageous. Others would see it as creeping grandiosity.

In August 1965, he called for an end to the bombing of North Vietnam. On August 20, after the Watts riots in Los Angeles, which killed thirty-four and injured hundreds, he called President Johnson to warn him that a "full-scale race war can develop." Johnson rebuked King for opposing him on Vietnam. "I want peace as much as you do and more so," he said, "because I am the fellow that wakes up in the morning with a report that 50 of our boys have died."[48]

In a meeting with Levison and others, King said the press would call him "power drunk," and say the Nobel had gone to his head. Perhaps he should back off Vietnam. Levison agreed he could not fight on both fronts.

In September 1966, Hoover stopped bugging King's hotel rooms, fearing an upcoming congressional inquiry into wiretaps. But the SCLC phones in Atlanta were still tapped, as was Levison's phone. By now the FBI had a couple of informants inside the King organization.

King called Levison on February 18, 1967, with another change of heart. He said he was ready to break with Johnson over the war, even if it cost the SCLC financial support. Starting in 1966, there had been a decline in contributions. Levison said he should ally himself with Bobby Kennedy and CIO chief Walter Reuther instead of antiwar activists like Dr. Benjamin Spock. King said, "I see it as tying the peace movement to the civil rights movement," but Levison had doubts.

It was Levison, however, who wrote the antiwar speech that King delivered in Los Angeles on February 15, 1967, as the main speaker on a program with four antiwar senators. King said that Vietnam had led to America's "declining moral status in the world," and that Johnson's policies had exposed "our paranoid anti-communism." Vietnam now became a major concern, even though King knew that he would become alienated from Johnson.[49]

Hoover wrote Johnson: "Based on King's recent activities and public utterances, it is clear that he is an instrument in the hands of subversive forces seeking to undermine our nation."[50]

In the August 1967 Reader's Digest, the black columnist Carl Rowan wrote that King "has become persona non grata to Lyndon Johnson" and has "alienated many of the Negro's friends and armed the Negro's foes." King said the article was a "McCarthy-like response," and that Rowan "engaged in what McCarthy put us through."[51]

Levison, King's friend and familiar, saw him as essentially guilt-ridden. He did not feel he deserved the tribute he received. King lived at the heart of a contradiction. He was a man of the cloth, a family man, whose strength in the civil rights movement depended on taking the moral high ground. He preached that justice and fairness were words to live by. And yet in his private life he violated those standards. The SCLC culture was raunchy, with a permissive attitude toward sex that came from the top. King's closest associates knew he had two liaisons in Atlanta and kept an apartment where he could meet women. One of the SCLC leaders called King "a saint with clay feet." His example filtered through the rest of the SCLC hierarchy, and in the summer of 1967, a scandal had to be suppressed that involved a group party with a hired prostitute and the attempted rape of a seventeen-year-old secretary. Funds collected for the civil rights struggle were diverted to cover up scandals.[52]

On March 18, 1968, a strike of 1,300 mostly black sanitation workers in Memphis brought King there to speak to a large crowd. He promised to return later and lead a march on City Hall. When King led the march on March 28, a gang of young black radicals who called themselves "The Invaders" brought up the rear and began to break store windows and loot the stores. The police charged and the march turned into a riot. King fled the scene, jumping into a passing car and going to the Holiday Inn Rivermont, where he lay in bed under the covers, exhausted and disheartened. King had been outflanked by radical blacks. The march was a disaster, the antithesis of all he stood for. The FBI was quickly informed of the debacle by its informant in King's ranks, Jim Harrison. An FBI memo on March 29 stated: "King urged Negroes in Memphis to boycott white merchants and called for compliance with Negro demands in the sanitation workers' strike. Violence broke out in the march King led. King vanished on March 28. Instead of going to the first-class Negro Lorraine Motel, he hid out at the white-owned Holiday Inn Motel." This was proof of his hypocrisy, said the memo. He told Negroes to boycott white merchants but patronized a white motel. There was no boycott for King, said the memo, only for his followers.[53] This tendentious report was leaked to the Memphis papers. The *Memphis Commercial Appeal* wrote that King "wrecked his reputation" when "he took off at high speed when violence occurred, instead of using his persuasive prestige to stop it."

Depressed by the Memphis fiasco, King called Levison on March 29, and said he was thinking of calling off a proposed Poor People's March on Washington. "The Washington campaign is in trouble," King said. "It is going to be much harder to recruit people now because most of the people we recruit are not violent. . . . If they feel that a campaign is going to be taken over by violent elements . . . they will hold back. . . . This is a personal setback for me. Let's face it." Levison disagreed, but King predicted people would say, "Martin Luther King is dead. He's finished. His non-violence is nothing, no one is listening."

"I don't accept it," Levison said.

King decided to return to Memphis and hold another march on April 8,

1968. He arrived on April 3, staying this time in a second-floor room at the Lorraine, where he was served with a court order barring a mass protest. On April 4, around 6:00 P.M., he was dressing for a soul food dinner when he stepped out on the balcony of his room. Ralph Abernathy heard a sound like a car backfiring. He saw King slump to the ground. A sniper's bullet had hit him in the jaw, from which blood was gushing. King rolled over on his back and his eyes went blank.[54] That night, eighty riots broke out across the country, marking the end of nonviolence. When King died, nonviolence died with him, and the black radicals like Stokely Carmichael, H. Rap Brown, and the Panthers had a clear field.

Martin Luther King found, at the age of thirty-nine, the martyrdom he had so often alluded to and seemed to be wishing for. His name is written in stone as the inventive master of passive resistance in America. He was curiously indifferent to the methods the FBI used to hound him. After receiving the anonymous letter in 1964, he knew that his hotel rooms were bugged and his phones tapped, but he took no security measures. He depended on Levison so heavily that he could not cut him loose. Perhaps the key to King's temperament was that he had no interest in self-protection. He was out there on the front line, getting arrested, getting jailed, getting stabbed, and finally, getting killed.

Hoover's hounding of King was a textbook example of McCarthyism: the use of false information in the irrational pursuit of a fictitious enemy. In order to portray King as a crypto-Communist, Hoover withheld vital data provided by his own informants in his reports to two Presidents. He knew that Stanley Levison had broken with the party but continued to describe him as an active Communist agent. Nor did he pass on phone taps that showed King to be against Communism. In May 1965, when King was planning to make a public comment calling for unity with the more radical Student Non-Violent Coordinating Committee, King told Bayard Rustin in a tapped phone conversation: "There are things I wanted to say renouncing Communism in theory, but they [SNCC] would not go along with it. We wanted to say that it was an alien philosophy contrary to us, but they wouldn't go along with it."[55] Hoover kept this conversation to himself and succeeded in implanting in the minds of two Presidents the suspicion that King was too closely associated with the Communists to be trusted. In addition, Hoover did not tolerate the slightest dissent from his unwavering position that King was a crypto-Communist, as William Sullivan found out. The truth was that King's nonviolence movement developed strategies and goals that owed nothing to Communist doctrine. The struggle for racial equality became a massive grassroots movement with a scope and ideology of its own. Hoover exaggerated the presence of Levison and O'Dell in King's ranks out of all proportion. If anything, the two Communists became Kingsians rather than the other way around, just as the Czar's Secret Police had once reported that some of its spies in Lenin's movement had become Leninists.

What aberrant behavior there was came from the FBI. As Senator Walter Mondale put it after the Church Committee hearings revealed Hoover's role in tormenting King, "The way Martin Luther King was hounded and harassed is a disgrace to every American."[56] Hoover's vendetta would remain the most conspicuous blemish of his long tenure. After his death in 1972, the FBI dropped its surveillance of the civil rights organizations. In 1975, after the Church Committee hearings, the bureau returned to the restrictions it had been under in the Coolidge years—it could only investigate criminal violations or foreign intelligence threats.

———

By 1960, the FBI had been hunting Communists for more than forty years. The bureau and the party were partners in a marathon dance, wearily locked in each other's arms. The bureau had infiltrated the party from top to bottom, contributing to its downfall by providing informants in the Smith Act trials that locked up the party leadership. Having crippled the party, Hoover kept insisting that it remained a threat, for without it, he would lose much of his reason for being.

Although the party was in shambles, Gus Hall, who became the Secretary General in 1959, showed a remarkable ability for extracting funds from his Moscow bosses. Like the branch officer of a global corporation, he kept promising breakthroughs and bigger numbers. In 1959, he obtained $250,000, in 1962, $475,000, and in 1965, the first million-dollar subsidy.[57] The more insignificant the American party became, the more money Moscow poured into it. Thus, the party still tried to mount a few carefully chosen actions, such as its attempt to penetrate the civil rights movement.

Hoover felt comfortable denouncing Communists, telling Attorney General Robert Kennedy on January 19, 1961, that the party was a greater menace today than it had ever been.[58]

———

The rise of the first important New Left group, Students for a Democratic Society, emerged directly from the civil rights movement. It was the example of the Greensboro sit-ins that nudged the Michigan University undergraduate Tom Hayden into political activism. In the past, college students were birds of passage who spent four years on campus and then moved on to their new lives. The essential change in the turbulent sixties was that students by the thousands were ignited into activism in college and remained in the movement after graduation.[59]

In his senior year, 1960–61, Hayden was the editor-in-chief of the *Michigan Daily*, which gave him the credentials to poke around and interview people. He met Martin Luther King, who told him, "Ultimately, you have to take a stand in your life." He also came to the attention of the FBI, which reported on August 3, 1960, that he was "national coordinator of the non-violence movement in connection with Hiroshima and Nagasaki Day."[60]

When Hayden graduated, he was field secretary for the newly born Students for a Democratic Society. By 1962, SDS had about eight hundred members. A basic political document was needed, a declaration of intent, a call to arms. Sixty student leaders gathered in June 1962 at an AFL-CIO lakeside retreat in the village of Port Huron, north of Detroit, to draw up a manifesto.

Among the delegates were a small number of Red diaper babies, such as Steve Max, the son of a *Daily Worker* editor who had split from the party in 1958, and Dick Flacks, who had been a member of the party's Labor Youth League. They had inherited the activism gene, but not obedience to Moscow. It was Dick Flacks who drafted the passage in what became known as the Port Huron Statement that said, "We are in basic opposition to the Soviet Union. Communism as a system rests on the suppression of organized opposition. The Communist movement has failed in every sense."[61] Tom Hayden agreed. He felt that the Communist Party was totally irrelevant. It was no longer a political force (which Hoover also knew, but kept to himself). For Hayden, the Red and anti-Red debate was history. The Old Left might be hung up on the twilight of Socialism, but the New Left wanted to move on. As Hayden put it, "We are people of this generation. . . . If we wanted to change society, how would we do it?" The answer was "participatory democracy," a grab bag if ever there was one, but a useful slogan, on the order of "Ivory Soap is 99$^{44}/_{100}$s Pure." Twenty thousand copies of the Port Huron manifesto were sent out, putting the SDS on the map.

Hayden and his cohorts made the movement up as they went along, unburdened by Marxist-Leninist claptrap and using their own college dorm vocabulary, dividing issues into "bones," "widgets," and "gizmos." Hayden threw a few "gizmos" to the Red diaper contingent, critiquing "unreasoning anti-Communism," and wondering whether the Soviet Union was expansionist by nature or a victim of paranoia.[62]

The New Left was American-born, with Midwestern and West Coast roots, rather than immigrant-based. It was anti-authoritarian, rather than the servant of a rigidly structured party. It was action-oriented, rather than engaging in windy debates on the third period or infantile disorder. It was animated by a sense of outrage fed by events, not by a line dictated from abroad. Instead of the espionage and subversion of the Old Left, the New Left acted openly (some might say blatantly) with the ingenuous conviction that lying in front of a truck could change things. Out went the Old Left mothball culture of summer camps, hootenannies, and slogans like "All Out on May Day" or "United Front Against Fascism." In came new music, new amusements, and new threads, a comprehensive lifestyle.

Lurking behind Communist efforts to infiltrate the New Left was a deep antipathy for the young upstarts. The party tried to find points of convergence, in the antiwar movement, in civil rights, in sympathy for the Castro regime, but there could be no durable alliance. Steve Nelson's distaste for the New Left was based on the whole hippie trip. The Old Left worked in grease and dirt in factories, striking over a place to clean up, and prizing cleanliness, while the New Left tried to look as slovenly as possible, proud of being the Great Unwashed. Nelson was also shocked by the extremism of the New Left. The Communists were tame by comparison. Now, when there was an antiwar demonstration, the only ones who carried the Stars and Stripes were the veterans of the Spanish Civil War, most of them Communists.[63]

For Dorothy Healey, the "Red Queen" of Los Angeles, who in the early sixties was asked to host a fifteen-minute Sunday morning commentary on the radical radio station KPFA, it was the New Left's lack of seriousness. When the Black Panther leader Bobby Seale came to Los Angeles in 1966, Dorothy sat at his feet in admiration, but soon began to wonder as he explained his free grocery strategy in Oakland. She tactlessly asked, "How is the Black Panther party different from any soup kitchen?" "I'm afraid I can't explain it to you because you don't understand dialectical materialism," Seale said. To someone like Dorothy, who had been in the party since 1930, that was laughable. She soon saw through the Panthers' clownish bluster. Nor was she in favor of armed insurrection, though she saw quite clearly that the Panthers had outflanked the Communists, making them seem stodgy and démodé. Fed up with both Old and New Left, Healey left the Communist Party in 1968.[64] The Old Left sank as the New Left rose. Even John Abt, the party's steadfast lawyer, admitted that "by the sixties, exacerbated by its own internal problems and errors, the party had largely been crushed, reduced to . . . a few thousand members."[65]

———

In 1964, the SDS, now numbering in the thousands, with Tom Hayden as president, sent volunteers to poor communities in the North and South, while parents lamented that their sons and daughters were throwing their lives away. Even as King drew back from confrontation in the Selma-to-Montgomery march in March 1965, there came the contrapuntal devastation of Watts in August. Even as the big buildup came in Vietnam, so did the first big antiwar marches. Even as the SNCC hardened its black nationalism, its brutishness was exposed with Stokely Carmichael's pronouncement that "the only position for women in SNCC is prone." Even as North Vietnam was bombed in February 1965, the SDS made a sharp turn to the left. Its new president, Paul Potter, said at the march on Washington on April 17, "I would rather see Vietnam Communist than see it under . . . the ruin that American domination has brought." The Old Left wanted a Communist Vietnam in the Soviet orbit. The New Left wanted a Communist Vietnam because anything was better than American occupation, with the body count rising on both sides.

With violence in the ghettos and massive antiwar demonstrations, the FBI haltingly expanded its covert operations to New Left groups. It launched programs such as VIDEM (Vietnam Demonstrations) and STAG (Student Agitation). Since it had no files on student groups, the field offices were told to collect the names of the organizations and the identities of their leaders. A memo recommending COINTELPRO "disruption techniques" noted the New Left's "anarchistic tendencies" and its anti-bureau attitude: "The New Left has on many occasions viciously and scurrilously attacked the Director and the Bureau in an attempt to hamper our investigations and drive us off the college campuses."[66]

COINTELPRO seemed to be an effective tool to harass organizations against whom no legal action could be taken. On October 26, 1960, the Detroit field office made anonymous calls to the city desks of three newspapers advising them that a lecturer on the Wayne State campus was sponsored by a Communist front. In Buffalo, a letter signed "a black parent" was sent to the mayor, the superintendent of schools, and two newspapers, protesting that a Buffalo high school subscribed to a black power newspaper as part of its black history course. In El Paso, a teacher was targeted as being the faculty adviser to a radical campus group that was circulating a pamphlet entitled *The Student as Nigger*.[67]

The line in one of Bob Dylan's songs, "Something is happening here, but you don't know what it is," could have been dedicated to the FBI, which was slow to pick up on the New Left. The FBI was used to a rigidly organized party, whose membership lists it had been collecting since 1920, a party that took its orders from Moscow, which could be portrayed as the evil instrument of a foreign power, while the campus groups were grassroots and indigenous. Hoover still preferred to denounce Communists. He told Attorney General Kennedy on January 9, 1961, that the FBI had succeeded in preventing the party from taking control of the Chicago branch of the NAACP.[68]

The wake-up call for Hoover came on April 17, 1965, when the first national antiwar demonstration, the March on Washington, drew more than twenty thousand mostly young people. Hoover stated in a memo on April 28, 1965, that SDS was planning demonstrations in eighty-five cities and was "largely infiltrated by Communists and it has been woven into the civil rights situation, which we know has a large Communist influence." This was guesswork, since Hoover did not have the SDS membership lists. He admitted in-house that the FBI could not "technically state" that the SDS was "an actual Communist organization." President Johnson was concerned about the disturbances, Hoover said, and "what I want to get to the president is the background with the emphasis upon the Communist influence therein so that he will know exactly what the picture is." He wanted "a good strong memorandum" pinpointing that the demonstrations had been "largely participated in by Communists even though they may not have initiated them." Hoover was still stuck in the Old Left framework, with the knee-jerk reaction of blaming the Communists. It was the only way he had of understanding a phenomenon that eluded his grasp.[69]

COINTELPRO in the meantime continued to use McCarthyite tactics, with field offices competing to fabricate the most offensive anonymous letters. In 1966, in response to criticism that the FBI did nothing about Southern racists, the bureau launched an investigation of the Ku Klux Klan. On August 26, the Richmond field office sent an anonymous letter to the wife of a KKK Grand Dragon, supposedly from another Klanswoman, informing her that her husband had "taken the flesh of another woman unto himself." The woman, said the letter, was named Ruby, and had "lust-filled eyes and a smart-aleck figure."[70]

In 1967, the bureau began to get reports on a trend that had nothing to do with Communism—the rise of black power groups willing to take up arms. On March 8, a memo to William Sullivan reported that James Rollins of CORE (Congress of Racial Equality), which had taken part in Martin Luther King's nonviolent campaigns, was saying: "We have got to stop breaking into liquor stores and start breaking into gun stores to arm ourselves to stop these white honkie cops from killing us." Another report, on May 22, said twenty-two Black Panthers had invaded the California State Assembly in Sacramento while it was in session, armed with rifles and pistols. This was the first FBI mention of the Panthers, an organization founded in Oakland in 1966 by Huey Newton and Bobby Seale with a program of black liberation, and marking the rise of the hoodlum militant.

The FBI had to play catch-up. In October 1967, the bureau launched its "Ghetto Information Program," to recruit informants in black ghettos. A memo said that these informants might include "the proprietor of a candy store or barber shop." By 1969 the FBI claimed to have 4,067 ghetto informants, some of them members of black power groups.[71]

As Black Panther branches spread to a dozen cities, COINTELPRO was enlisted to harass them. Instructions went out in 1967 to develop "imaginative and hard-hitting counter-intelligence measures aimed at crippling the Black Panther party." Among the more imaginative measures was the one used against the Ku Klux Klan of sowing discord in marriages.

On February 14, 1969, the St. Louis field office sent a letter to the wife of a black power leader saying her husband had "been making it there" with other women in the group and "that he give us this jive about being better in bed than you."

In St. Louis, a married white woman belonged to a biracial group called ACTION, which was active in antiwar rallies and draft resistance. Her husband was not involved. Two FBI informants inside the group reported that the husband was making inquiries about his wife's relationship with some of the black males in ACTION. The St. Louis field office drafted an anonymous letter to the husband from "a soul sister," which Hoover authorized on February 17, 1970. The letter said: "Look man I guess your old lady doesn't get enough at home or she wouldn't be shucking and jiving with our black men in ACTION, you dig? Like all she wants to integrate is the bedroom . . . so lay it on her, man." On June 19, 1970, the St. Louis special agent in charge reported that the woman and her husband had separated, and that "this stress and strain should cause her to function much less effectively in ACTION."[72]

As the Church Committee report put it in 1975: "The image of an agent of the United States government scrawling a poison pen letter to someone's wife in language usually reserved for bathroom walls is not a happy one."

FBI policy was to prevent the alliance of militant black groups, which threatened to form "a real Mau Mau in America, the beginning of a true black revolution." When George C. Moore, the chief of the FBI's Racial Intelligence Section, testified before the Church Committee in 1975, he admitted that "in the black extremist movement . . . we got a late start . . . we had to play catch-up. . . . There were policemen killed. . . . There were bombs thrown. . . . There were establishments burned with Molotov cocktails. . . . All we know [is that] either through their own ineptitude, maybe through our counter-intelligence . . . maybe we gave [the fighting between the groups] a nudge."[73]

It could be argued that COINTELPRO gave them more than a nudge. On January 30, 1969, Hoover approved sending an anonymous letter to Jeff Fort, the leader of a black militant group in Chicago, the Blackstone Rangers, that was having a turf war with the Panthers. The letter would warn Fort that the Panthers had put out a contract on his life. The Chicago field office in its memo to Hoover asking for approval said: "It is believed that the above may intensify the degree of animosity between the two groups and occasion Fort to take retaliatory actions which could disrupt the Black Panther Party or lead to reprisals against his leadership. For the Rangers, violent type activity, shooting and the like are second nature." The letter to Fort was part of a COINTELPRO operation called HOODWINK.[74]

In San Diego, when five Black Panthers were arrested on February 11, 1969, by local police, four were released, but the leader was kept in custody. The FBI field office circulated a rumor that the detained Panther had struck a deal with the San Diego police. At the same time, he was informed that he had been arrested after a tip from a rival Panther leader. The San Diego Panther branch was so disrupted by the FBI's disinformation that it ceased to exist.[75]

As the number and ferocity of race riots and antiwar riots mounted each year, Hoover kept pushing the line that they were directed or abetted by Communists. He focused on rioters with Communist affiliations. During the Detroit riots in July 1967, Hoover wrote: "We had no information indicating that the Communists initiated the riots, but they, of course, joined in after they had once started." In focusing on the Communists, Hoover misled the President.[76] As Senator Church put it: "The FBI significantly impaired the democratic decision-making process by its distorted intelligence reporting on Communist infiltration of domestic political activity. In private remarks and public statements, the Bureau seriously exaggerated the extent of Communist influence in both the civil rights and the Vietnam War movement."

In the fall of 1967, Attorney General Ramsey Clark had to prod Hoover in a September 14 memo, urging him to find "sources or informants in black nationalist organizations." He went on to say that sources in SNCC, which in 1967 had expelled its white members and adopted a black power platform, "and other less publicized groups should be developed and expanded." On October 20, 1967, the FBI told field offices "to develop additional penetrative coverage of the militant black nationalist groups and the ghetto areas," and develop the ghetto informant program.[77]

Meanwhile, a coalition of New Left groups was planning a march on the Pentagon, as part of a trend toward more disruptive protests in an effort to dump Johnson. The SDS was now ready to tangle with the police. At the march on October 21, 1967, the boyish-looking SDS leader Rennie Davis, with tousled hair and horn-rimmed glasses, held up an American fragmentation bomb he had brought back from North Vietnam, where he had seen "rice-roots democracy."

The assassinations of Martin Luther King in April and Robert Kennedy in June punctuated the ugly mood of discontent pervading the American scene in 1968. The White House, expecting summer riots, and unable to rely on the FBI, brought in the Army to conduct its own intelligence study and rate the cities with black ghettos as to their "riot potential." The Army made contingency plans for troop movements, landing sites, and military facilities. A memo from the Army's general counsel to the Johnson White House on January 18, 1968, said that Attorney General Ramsey Clark had stressed "the difficulty of the intelligence effort," since there were "only 40 Negro FBI agents" out of a total of 6,300.[78]

Energized by the success of the Pentagon and Stop the Draft protests, the New Left had more ambitious plans than summer riots. Led by Tom Hayden and the SDS, the panoply of radical groups planned to disrupt the Democratic convention in Chicago that August. The Chicago convention protest was under the umbrella of the National Mobilization Committee to End the War in Vietnam, whose chairman was David Dellinger, one of the leaders of the march on the Pentagon, a pacifist and a Socialist.

Hayden and Rennie Davis went to Chicago in January 1968, set up offices at 407 South Dearborn Street, and named a Convention Committee, which included a small number of Communists. Among them was the femme fatale of the SDS, Bernardine Dohrn, who became a founder of the Weathermen and later approved of Charles Manson as "far out." Since she was a law student, she volunteered to serve on the team that would obtain bail for arrested demonstrators. Another was Michael Klonsky, an SDS national secretary, and a Red diaper baby who tried to lead the SDS into doctrinaire Marxism. Hayden described him as an arrogant troublemaker who derided the New Left "fallacy" and pushed the Marxist line. The Chicago protest was the Communist Party's last major attempt to play a role in the New Left, which it viewed as uncontrollable. The FBI, following the Communist thread, reported that a member of the party's National Committee had been named to act as liaison with the New Left in Chicago. The party helped finance Hayden's office, with full-time personnel to man it, the bureau reported.[79]

Hayden appealed to the Communist-controlled National Lawyers Guild for legal help. At a January 26 National Mobilization meeting at the NLG headquarters at 5 Beekman Street, which was monitored by the Chicago police subversive unit, he said: "There is an office in Chicago and the beginnings of a staff. . . . We are now in the initial stage. . . . The idea is to mobilize people. . . . The third stage would be the convention itself, in which we would have a pooling of 50,000 to 100,000 people. We don't want these people to be passive objects, but on the other hand we don't want chaos."

Ken Cloke, the executive secretary of the National Lawyers Guild, asked: "What do you think is going to be the dynamic? . . . Is there going to be mobile action?"

Hayden: ". . . We should have people organized who can fight the police, people who are willing to get arrested. No question that there will be lots of arrests."

Rennie Davis: "The biggest problem is going to be with Chicago lawyers. The real question for us is if 500 to 1,000 people are going to be in jail, who can go into court? The movement has not been successful with building up a large number of attorneys. . . . What we would like to do is call sometime in the early spring a conference of Chicago lawyers. . . . How do you get 20 full-time people?"

Dohrn: "What are the finances?"

Davis: "We need at least one person now."

Cloke: "Bernardine, I, Alicia Kaplow [of the NLG] and Dennis Roberts will be able to do approximately one month or more."

Davis: "Chicago operations should find the subsistence for 50 law students. . . . We see a major opportunity to organize a force that challenges the status quo. Clearly, Johnson and others are going to define us by whether we are violent or non-violent."

Cloke: "The whole question of jail or bail."

Davis: "All state misdemeanors start at $200 bail."

Eric Schmidt of SDS: "We have to have two hats—nice, and violent."[80]

At a February 11, 1968, meeting of the Convention Committee in Room 315 at 407 South Dearborn, the issue of violence was again discussed. Among those present were Rennie Davis, Dave Dellinger, the black activist Carlos Russell, Jack Spiegel, a member of the party who had run for office on the Communist ticket, and the Trotskyite Sidney Lens.

Carlos Russell: "Radical whites today are basically occupied with anti-war activity. Blacks are focusing on black liberation. There could be a parallel action based on racism and imperialism. Johnson per se is not the enemy. The enemy is racism and imperialism." (In fact, Johnson ceased being the enemy in March, when he decided not to run, which made Vice President Hubert Humphrey the probable candidate after Bobby Kennedy's assassination.)

Sid Lens: "It would not serve our purpose to disrupt the convention. We must expose it. . . . Americans must learn that the chairman of the Democratic Party is also the president of Con Edison."

Hayden: "We cannot call for violence, although violence is a major method of change in this society. We cannot mobilize thousands to fight a war."

Jack Spiegel: "We can't call 200,000 people to Chicago and then disassociate ourselves from violence. Disruptions and violence will occur."

Dagmar Wilson, of Women Strike for Peace: "At some point we've got to stop street-walking and go to war. But I don't want to go to war over nothing. It's too soon for war. I'm not sure about this event. I feel we need to do more to hack away at a dying system."

Corky Gonzalez, of the Crusade for Justice, a Mexican group: "We must support those who will put their bodies on the line."[81]

By March 1968, the FBI Chicago field office had located the National Mobilization office, which it sought to bug. But Attorney General Ramsey Clark turned down Hoover's request for wiretaps on May 12, saying there was not "an adequate demonstration of direct threat to our national security." Hoover fumed that Clark's refusal was "inexcusable."[82]

The FBI transition from the Old Left to New Left did not really get into gear until 1968, with the danger of disruptions at the Democratic convention. On May 14, Hoover expanded COINTELPRO to "disruption of the New Left," noting that "the anarchistic activities of a few could paralyze institutions of learning, induction centers, [and] cripple traffic. . . . The activist who spouts revolution . . . must not only be contained but must be neutralized."

A COINTELPRO directive to field offices on May 23, 1968, asked them to collect evidence on the "scurrilous and depraved nature of many of the characters, habits and living conditions representative of the New Left adherents. . . . Every avenue of possible embarrassment must be vigorously and enthusiastically exploited. . . . An imaginative approach is imperative to success." Among the "imaginative approaches," Hoover suggested anonymous letters to parents of student activists, with copies of articles from student newspapers regarding narcotics and free sex, and sending "concerned citizen" letters to foundations and government officials. Hoover asked field offices to concentrate on "the depraved nature and moral looseness of student radicals."[83]

The "imaginative approaches" in the field offices ranged from silly to alarming. The Newark field office sent a copy of *Screw* magazine to a New Jersey Senate committee, saying it was sold at Rutgers by hippies. The San Antonio field office sent letters to the University of Austin from "an irate parent," griping about extramarital co-habitation. In an effort to emulate New Left speech styles, the field offices came up with letters to parents that their children were prone "to dig the grass bit and ball them radical chicks . . . and go for grass and Jewish ass."[84] Here was the seventy-three-year-old Hoover, who had fought the good war against the comparatively sedate Communists all his adult life, now thrown into battle with hippies and flower children, and tackling a formless and, in his eyes, decadent movement that could nonetheless summon tens of thousands to a march or a rally.

Despite Johnson's departure, the protest was on, and all eyes were on Chicago. At a secret meeting on March 24, 1968, at a wooded YMCA camp outside Chicago with two hundred in attendance, a broad coalition was formed among Old Left, New Left, and black power, to coordinate the antiwar effort and disrupt the Democratic convention. Tom Hayden and Rennie Davis presented their program for an "Election Year Offensive." The degree of disruption was not spelled out, though the Cleveland SDS said in a circular: "We are going to Chicago to stop the Democratic Party convention from taking place. We want the delegates and the candidates to be forced out of the convention hall." On June 29, Dave Dellinger at a press conference promised "several days of escalating actions climaxed by a massive mobilization at the time of the nomination."[85] The demonstrators, having no fixed program, would be guided by events. If this was theater, it was improv.

The Yippies, led by Jerry Rubin and Abbie Hoffman, promised "a Festival of Fun," which would include spiking Chicago's water supply with LSD, faking delegate cards, releasing greased pigs in the park, painting cars to look like taxis, and walking the streets in Vietcong costumes.[86]

That June in Chicago, when Hayden and Rennie Davis tried to obtain permits for the demonstration, they hit a stone wall. Mayor Richard Daley had no intention of giving permits to outside agitators who planned to turn his city into a battleground. The public parks would not be turned into camp sites. There would be no march to the convention amphitheater.

On July 19, the SDS, which now claimed thirty thousand members and three hundred local chapters, met in Chicago to plan the convention protest. The leaders said, "If movement people are attacked by police our organizers won't be off in an office writing the 'History of the Tactical Failures of the Democratic Convention Protest.' " Mike Klonsky was assigned the key job of organizing the five SDS "movement centers" in Chicago. The SDS began issuing *New Left Notes*, its daily newspaper. SDS members were advised to "find out what your blood type is and carry an ID with that blood type on it."[87]

On August 4, Dellinger chaired a meeting of the National Mobilization Committee to discuss tactics and routes and break down tasks. Dellinger said that the presence of the military surrounding the amphitheater would lend political content to the protest. Two hundred SDS marshals trained in violent tactics would be under the command of John Froines, who would later be tried as one of the Chicago Eight, and who recalled Hayden saying that twenty to twenty-five demonstrators might be killed in the protest, and Vernon Gizzard, a Swarthmore student who had gone to Hanoi with Hayden. David Baker, an activist from Detroit, would lead the snake dance teams to break police lines. This was a method borrowed from Japanese students, which consisted of eight persons lined up and holding a pole, with locked arms, and hopping from foot to foot while shouting *Bo Shai*. Wolfe Lowenthal, a judo expert, demonstrated some defensive moves, such as how to stop a blow to the head, which was followed by a kick to the cop's groin. Other issues addressed were legal offices to handle bail, mobile medical teams plus four fixed first-aid stations, and cars for ambulances. The committee had detailed blueprints of buildings such as the Chicago Board of Trade.[88]

On August 15, Hoover sent out an advisory that "we are not going to get into anything political, but anything of extreme action or violence we would." From Chicago, Special Agent in Charge Marlin Johnson said things were tense and there would be trouble. Hoover told him to plug every possible hole for coverage.[89]

On August 16, Robert L. Pierson, an investigator for the Cook County State Attorney's Office, proposed a plan to infiltrate the demonstration and learn its strategies and goals. The plan was that Pierson, having let his hair and beard grow, would join a motorcycle gang called the Headhunters. On August 21, he bought a motorcycle and the proper attire and rode to the gang's headquarters at 147th and California, in the Chicago suburb of Posen. He expressed his desire to join to the president, Charles Lucas, known as "Gorilla." Gang members, he reported, carried a variety of weapons, such as switchblades, sunglasses with the stems filed down to points, and belt buckles leaded on the inside. They had stockpiled 2,500 sticks of dynamite in a garage at 10936 South Indiana, in preparation for the protest. Gorilla told Pierson: "We should blow up the fuckin' ball park to show the man we mean business and we would get a few of those shits while we are at it." Pierson was subjected to the Headhunters initiation, which consisted of passing the initiate through a car wash, while poking him with a cattle prod.[90]

In the meantime, Hayden's hopes for permits collapsed, with thousands of demonstrators about to arrive in Chicago to spend four or five days, and needing a park to unroll their sleeping bags in. By refusing the permits, Mayor Daley hoped to reduce their numbers. Hayden whipped himself up into a spirit of rebellion, and said at a meeting: "We have to fight just for the right to be here."[91]

The convention was to open on August 26, and the nomination was scheduled to take place on August 28. Hayden and the other protest leaders planned nonstop picketing, rallies, concerts, and marches from August 24 to 29. Demonstrators would be broken up into small units with high mobility, fifty to one hundred with a specific task such as picketing a draft board office.

The demonstrators were facing 11,000 Chicago police, 6,000 armed National Guard troops, and 7,500 Army troops, plus hundreds of FBI agents, many of them undercover. The Chicago police had infiltrated the National Mobilization Committee, and received a report a few days prior to the convention on protesters' plans to sabotage the National Guard Armory at Seneca and Chicago avenues. Thus, the police were on the alert for more drastic tactics than rallies and marches.[92]

On August 23, Rennie Davis and Dave Dellinger tried to get Mayor Daley to bend a little, but he refused to see them. Finally a permit was issued for the use of the Grant Park band shell, but the right to use Soldier Field or to assemble outside the convention amphitheater was denied. Dellinger said the mayor would be responsible for any bloodshed that took place.[93]

On August 23, Robert Pierson, now a member in good standing of the Headhunters, rode to Lincoln Park on his bike with two other gang members, known as "Banana" and "The Prospect." The oral contract between the gang and the protest leaders was that the bikers would provide muscle and the protesters would provide drugs. Pierson linked up with some pot-smoking Yippies, who were being given instructions by a marshal. The main thrust conveyed was "fuck the pigs." Pierson was assigned to protect the protest leaders Abbie Hoffman, Jerry Rubin, Wolfe Lowenthal, Tom Hayden, and the Black Panther leader Bobby Seale, who arrived from Oakland to make a cameo appearance. Pierson's job was to hold off the cops if they tried to arrest any of them.[94]

As convention delegates began arriving at their downtown hotels on August 25, thousands of the young and disruptive filled Lincoln Park to prepare for the inevitable confrontation with the Chicago police. They studied maps and took down the phone number for legal aid. A test march was held, without incident, from Lincoln Park to the Loop. Mayor Daley had ordered an 11:00 P.M. curfew at Lincoln Park, and when the park was not vacated, the police charged with clubs and tear gas. Many were arrested as the protesters ran for the exits, among them Tom Hayden and Wolfe Lowenthal, caught taking the air out of the tires of a police car.[95]

The convention opened, pitting Vice President Hubert Humphrey, Lyndon Johnson's designated successor, who championed the Vietnam War, against the Minnesota maverick Eugene McCarthy, who was running on the antiwar platform and whose daughter, Mary, was active in the antiwar movement at Radcliffe. In Lincoln Park, Robert Pierson was told that tonight they intended to hold the park and have a monster confrontation. His job was to guard Jerry Rubin and Abbie Hoffman.

When the police rearrested Tom Hayden and Wolfe Lowenthal for "soliciting mob action," Jerry Rubin cursed the cops and vowed to get even, saying they had to kill the candidates and promote the revolution. That night in Lincoln Park the police moved in with tear gas and Pierson was struck with a club while protecting Rubin. One Yippie leader shouted, "Pull fire alarms all over the Old Town area. Start some fires and fuck up this city real good."[96]

On August 28, at the convention amphitheater, surrounded by troops and coils of barbed wire, the peace plank was defeated and Humphrey was nominated. In the Loop, delegates wearing straw hats and festive buttons partied it up. In Lincoln Park, Bobby Seale, in beret and black leather jacket, addressed the crowd on the theme of "roasting pigs." As Peter, Paul, and Mary sang "This Land Is Your Land," there were chants of "Dump the Hump," but it was too late. The protesters had a permit to use the Grant Park band shell, where an estimated ten thousand had gathered. Between the band shell and the police line there was a flagpole, which a long-haired youth climbed, pulling down the flag.[97]

At the HUAC hearings on the riots in October 1968, the subcommittee chairman, Richard H. Ichord of Missouri, said that "one person who was present in Chicago has described to me incidents of the public collection of urine to throw on the police." Lieutenant Joseph J. Healy of the Chicago police responded that "I was in Grant Park on August 28 when the American flag was pulled down from the pole in the park. A number of policemen went over to make the arrest. The demonstrators began to throw rocks, bricks, stones, sticks, tiles [taken from public washrooms] and balloons filled with human waste."[98]

To which Tom Hayden replied, in his testimony: "Would you rather be hit by a bag of urine or by Mace?"[99]

Lieutenant Healy continued: "I myself was struck twice, once on the right leg and once on the left leg. . . . One policeman was hit in the face with a brick that had a steel rod sticking from it and was hospitalized for a week."[100]

At the band shell, Robert Pierson was playing his part, protecting Jerry Rubin, saying he would kill anyone who tried to touch Jerry. Pierson took part in the rock throwing once it began, to maintain his credibility, just as, when the Yippies passed out LSD-laced Oreos he took one but palmed it. But when the black power Blackstone Rangers, who knew Pierson as a state investigator, identified him, he had to leave in a hurry.[101]

There was no discounting the brutality of the police reaction at the band shell, just as there was no discounting the provocation of the protesters. In the subsequent march down Michigan Avenue to the Hilton, where convention delegates were whooping it up in the lounges, the marchers came nose-to-nose with a solid phalanx of police.

Connie Brown, a demure, diminutive Swarthmore undergraduate, managed to reach the Go-Go Lounge of the Palmer House and was arrested as she poured butyric acid, a chemical that smelled like rotten eggs, into a box of Kleenex in the ladies' room. The smell emanating from her purse betrayed her. Also found in her purse was the Chicago activist's shopping list: "Hunting slingshot, ball bearings—buy at sports shop. Jacks with points on all sides, cans of lighter fluid, cans of spray paint, pieces of garden hose, cherry bombs, firecrackers." Rennie Davis was leading the marshals in keeping their troops in position when the police line broke and they came after him. He fell and blows rained on his head, neck, and back. He crawled ten feet to a chain link fence and managed to climb over it into the park and saw that his shirt and tie were bloodstained. Then he passed out, awakening to see a man with a white coat bent over him, in a hospital.[102]

In the band shell and Hilton riots, seven hundred protesters were injured. The demonstrators did not achieve their objectives, though they did make their presence felt. In an interview on August 28 with Radio Havana, Mike Klonsky said: "We have been fighting in the streets for four days. Many of our people have been beaten up and many of them are in jail, but we are winning."[103]

—

The police estimated that eighty-two groups from all over the country had taken part in the Chicago protest. The 583 demonstrators arrested were charged with disorderly conduct and released by September 3, though eight leaders were later indicted for conspiring to incite riots. Of the 152 injured policemen, all but one were released from the hospital by September 3.[104]

On August 28, 1968, in a memo to the Chicago field office, Hoover urged that all the field offices who had sent informants to Chicago should be debriefed to show how demonstrators had started incidents that would lead the police to react with undue force. "Once again," Hoover wrote, "the liberals and the bleeding hearts and the forces of the left are taking advantage of the situation in Chicago to attack the police. . . . We must expose this activity and refute these allegations."[105] The Chicago riots were followed by an escalation in New Left violence. In a memo on October 24, 1968, Hoover summed up the situation: "Sabotage, arson, bombing, and a variety of destructive tactics have been openly advocated during the past year. In September 1968, within a five-day period, three ROTC establishments were sabotaged and a fourth was threatened. . . . A CIA recruitment office in Ann Arbor was bombed that month." Militant blacks were talking of dynamiting the Empire State Building, throwing dynamite on the floor of the New York Stock Exchange, and assassinating some white political candidates in retaliation for Martin Luther King. One militant black stated that if the right contact was made with White House staff, you could poison five hundred or six hundred people there.[106]

It was after the Chicago riots that Hoover realized he had been chasing the wrong horse. The New Left had left the Old Left in the dust. In a memo to the Albany field office on October 28, he wrote that the New Left was "a movement which is providing platforms alternate to those of Communist organizations . . . the so-called Old Left. . . . The New Left movement is a loosely-bound, free-wheeling, college-oriented movement spearheaded by the Students for a Democratic Society and includes the more militant anti–Vietnam war and anti-draft protest organizations. . . . There is a need to compile . . . a clear-cut picture of the entire New Left movement, which will identify the leaders, sources of funds and propaganda outlets and will show the extent to which the New Left has been influenced by domestic and foreign elements."[107] It had taken Hoover years to get there, but he was finally on the right page, though he still brought up Communist influence at appropriation time.

And so, in 1968, with Hoover's admission that the Old Left was no longer the main enemy, came the end of McCarthyism as an American response to Bolshevism. In a political variant of the Heisenberg indeterminacy principle, the American Communist Party ceased to matter once it was no longer observed. There were still a few thousand party members, but they drifted into insignificance. The phenomenon of McCarthyism, born as an immoderate reflex against the spread of Bolshevism, soon found other targets, as we will see.

—

Rennard Cordon Davis was another SDS leader formed in the trenches of the civil rights movement. As he testified before HUAC in October 1968, "My education came from having a cigarette ground out in the back of my neck when I was trying to get a hamburger with a black man. My education came from working with people from Alabama and South Carolina."[108]

His education continued, he said, when he went to North Vietnam and studied the cluster bombs that were killing civilians. "It sprayed pellets in every direction," he said, "splintering the bodies, splintering the bones, creating deep rips within the internal organs, and most people slowly bleed to death."

Davis initiated nonviolent support programs for young draftees, in the form of antiwar coffeehouses, "something to escape to other than whorehouses and saloons that make up these small towns like Waynesville [Missouri] or Queens, Texas." There were six such coffeehouses operating near military bases.

Frank Conley, subcommittee counsel: "You have posters that indicate that the war in Vietnam is immoral?"

Davis: "One poster in Mad Anthony's is a big kind of picture of a huge plane going off in the distance and it says, 'This summer spend your vacation in beautiful Vietnam.' That is a kind of anti-war poster I guess. . . . GI's really like it." But Mad Anthony's, near Fort Leonard Wood, had to be closed down, Davis said, due to harassment and broken windows.

For Davis, the coffeehouses were a way of reaching soldiers without haranguing them, with psychedelic paint on the windows, posters of rock stars, flashing colored lights, and a hi-fi playing Judy Collins or the Mothers of Invention; movement people and soldiers were the same age and listened to the same music.

"This doesn't involve urging anyone to oppose the war in Vietnam," Davis explained. "For us to ask soldiers to risk defection is, to put it kindly, arrogant." The immediate changes they could fight for "might include the removal of particularly sadistic NCO's from positions of authority, or doctors might demand a guaranteed eight hours sleep for trainees at a post where meningitis is endemic."[109]

———

The movement was widespread and ecumenical, instead of being sectarian and geriatric. Their agitprop was humorous rather than crafty, sardonic rather than dialectical. And then there was the music. The New Left had its bards, with Bob Dylan singing at voter registration rallies. Dylan's music came out of the "nothing artificial" topical song movement of the thirties founded by Woody Guthrie, who himself came out of the Oklahoma Dust Bowl and wrote the American anthem "This Land Is Your Land." But Dylan transcended the Old Left proletarian context to develop an allegorical style enigmatic enough to appeal to the disparate groups that made up the New left, black and white, college boys and hoodlums, misfits and idealists, outlaws and pastors, flower children and bomb-throwers. The Weathermen took their name from his innocuous line "You don't need a weatherman to know which way the wind blows," and those who adopted violence sang, "The pump don't work 'cause the vandals took the handles.' " "The Times They Are A-Changin' " became a blueprint for a generation, though the thought applied to every generation.

When Rennie Davis went to Hanoi and visited the English-language radio station, Voice of Vietnam, which was beamed to GIs, he realized they were a couple of generations behind, because they did not understand the music. They were playing Guy Lombardo records. Davis told them, "You are very out of touch with the mentality of the young people of America." He told them to play Judy Collins, play the Fugs, play Country Joe and the Fish: "One, two, three, What are we fighting for? Don't ask me, I don't give a damn. Next stop is Veeyetnam."[110]

What was true of the North Vietnamese was also true of the American Communists. The party survived, thanks to transfusions from Moscow, but it was like a mummy wrapped in bandages, deaf and blind to the rhythms and the pulse of American life. When a movement ceases to be a part of the culture of the nation, it expires. In America, music is the barometer of social and political change. Everything begins with a song and ends with a song. Like the Voice of Vietnam, the American Communists were frozen in time, singing folk songs, union songs, Spanish Civil War songs, and "The Internationale." When their music became outdated, they stopped being a relevant part of American political life. McCarthyism with its cheating heart continues to erupt in various guises, but Communism perished when they no longer sang the right songs.

—

A staple of anti-Communist rhetoric over the years was the comparison to contagious disease. The same comparison could be used to describe McCarthyism after Joe's death, when it spread viruslike into the FBI, and from the FBI into the White House.

Hoover had been conducting black bag jobs and wiretaps since the twenties, often at the request of successive Presidents, but in 1965 he had a scare. Senator Edward Long, a Missouri Democrat, chairman of the Judiciary Committee's Subcommittee on Administrative Practices and Procedures, launched an investigation of surveillance practices in agencies such as the Internal Revenue Service and the FBI. Long proposed to call FBI men, including Hoover, as witnesses, and to throw light on all questionable surveillance practices. Hoover mobilized friendly senators to neutralize Long, and asked Attorney General Nicholas Katzenbach to have a talk with him. Katzenbach stressed the national security aspects of surveillance techniques and Long refrained from calling any FBI witnesses.[111]

As a result of the Long hearings, Hoover decided to cut wiretaps by 50 percent and eliminated black bag jobs altogether, except for the installation of bugs. In a memo to his assistant Clyde Tolson on February 27, 1965, he wrote: "I don't see what all the excitement is about. I would have no hesitance in disconnecting all techniques—technical coverage [wiretapping], microphones, trash covers, mail covers, etc. While it might handicap us I doubt that they are as useful as some believe and none warrant FBI being used to justify them."[112]

On September 14, Hoover wrote Katzenbach, referring to the "recent atmosphere" of "Congressional public alarm and opposition to any activity which could in any way be termed invasion of privacy," that he was severely restricting his "sensitive" techniques. Bugs for internal security were reduced from fifty-nine in 1965 to four in 1966 and none in 1967; for criminal cases, from eighty-three in 1964 to forty-one in 1965 and none in 1966.[113]

The FBI's COINTELPRO activities under William Sullivan, however, continued unabated, and took in a staggering range of targets, from the Black Panthers to women's liberation groups. In 1969, the FBI monitored the Women's International Terrorist Conspiracy from Hell (WITCH), which disrupted the Miss America pageant in Atlantic City that year, invading the telecast to crown a live sheep, as they yodeled the Berber cry from the film *Battle of Algiers* and shuffled Bert Parks's cue cards.[114]

On a more serious note, the practice of infiltrating antiwar movements sometimes resulted in FBI informants acting as leaders and inciters. As Robert Hardy, an FBI informant in a New Jersey antiwar group that broke into the Camden Draft Board, recalled: "Everything they learned about breaking into a building or climbing a wall or cutting glass or destroying lockers, I taught them. And the FBI supplied me with the equipment I needed." By 1971, the FBI had 1,731 informants inside Old and New Left groups.[115]

Nor was Hoover averse to helping the White House carry out its political agenda. In a memo on May 18, 1970, he related that Vice President Spiro Agnew had called, concerned about "the inflammatory pronouncements of Ralph D. Abernathy [Martin Luther King's successor]. I commented that he is one of the worst. . . . I said [the media] emphasize all the things these jerks are doing. The Vice-President said he saw a picture of Negroes jumping out of store windows in Augusta with loot and booty [but] . . . the thrust of the article is that a bunch of police shot down six Negroes. . . . I said they were severely provoked. . . . The Vice-President said he thought he was going to have to start destroying Abernathy's credibility." Accordingly, on May 18, Hoover prepared a memo on Abernathy's support of the Black Panthers.[116]

Hoover also helped President Nixon in his efforts to purge liberal members of the Supreme Court. Abe Fortas resigned on May 15, 1969, after an article in *Life* magazine by William Lambert charged that he had received $20,000 from the Wolfson Foundation. Fortas had done legal work for Louis E. Wolfson, a millionaire businessman convicted of violating securities laws. Much of the material in the article was provided to Lambert by the FBI, and it was clear that Hoover had acted with Nixon's knowledge. Then, after two Southern conservatives that Nixon wanted to place on the bench, Clement Haynsworth and G. Harrold Carswell, were rejected by the Senate, the President mounted an attack to get rid of William O. Douglas. Gerald Ford, the House Minority Leader, led the charge, and on June 5, 1970, Nixon asked Hoover to provide Ford with derogatory information on Douglas, but the attempt to impeach him got nowhere.[117]

———

In 1969, his first year as President, Nixon became mired in the war he had inherited from his two predecessors. On the day of his inaugural, on January 20, as the parade moved slowly up Pennsylvania Avenue, with Nixon in the backseat of his car waving at the crowds, antiwar demonstrators threw smoke bombs at the cortege. Nixon ordered that they be arrested, and when they surged toward Lafayette Square, across the street from the White House, eighty-seven arrests were made. This was an inauguration that did not augur well.

Nixon's enemies were not the Communists, but mainstream America—the Democrats, the media, and the millions of antiwar protesters. He quickly developed a McCarthyite strain of paranoia. The White House was infected with a we-or-them, friend-or-foe team spirit. Nixon had aides drawing up enemies lists and monitoring the press. No incident was too trivial to be scrutinized and discussed—from political cartoons to Gina Lollobrigida asking for an autographed picture, to Director of Communications Herb Klein spending too much time with *New York Times* reporters, to Jack Paar's anti-administration bias (which a letter-writing campaign to the network would fix), to vetting the political background of a singer invited to perform after a White House dinner. The singer was Placido Domingo.[118]

Nixon, who had made his reputation in HUAC's anti-Communist probes, had been a friend and adviser to McCarthy. In the White House, he was surrounded with McCarthy admirers such as Pat Buchanan and Charles Colson. Nixon shared McCarthy's bias against the Eastern Establishment, Harvard, and think tanks like the Brookings Institution.

In 1969, the antiwar protests mounted as Nixon talked peace with Hanoi and announced that "we are on our way out of Vietnam," while at the same time he started bombing Cambodia in March.[119]

Nixon had brought into the White House a twenty-eight-year-old from Indiana, Thomas Charles Huston, to help with speechwriting. Huston had sound credentials as a campus conservative, and had served in Army Intelligence. He was a deeply committed right-wing ideologue who sometimes signed his memos "Cato the younger," after the Roman statesman with a reputation for incorruptibility who opposed Julius Caesar and ended up committing suicide after the defeat of Thapsus in 46 B.C.

Nixon soon moved Huston into political work on antiwar groups. In June, he was asked to prepare a report on the foreign funding of the movement and the tax-exempt status of some radical groups. Disappointed by lack of cooperation in the Internal Revenue Service, Huston told Chief of Staff Bob Haldeman that "making sensitive political inquiries at the IRS is about as safe as trusting a whore."[120]

On August 1, 1969, in a memo to Haldeman, Huston reported that according to an FBI informer, "there will be stepped-up campus disorder this fall, and the Communist party will be actively involved through its clandestine support of the SDS (Students for a Democratic Society). . . . I am going to state unequivocally that we will witness student disorders in the fall that will surpass anything we have seen before. Student militancy will sweep major campuses and flow into the streets of our major cities as the competing factions of the SDS strive to prove that each is more 'revolutionary' than the other and as antiwar protest organizations seek to escalate the fervor of opposition to the Vietnam War. You will see it most likely by Oct. 15, certainly by Nov. 15."[121]

Huston was right on target. On November 15, in the largest single protest in the nation's history, 750,000 demonstrators flowed through the streets of the capital to the Washington Monument. The police surrounded the White House with D.C. transit buses parked bumper to bumper. Nixon was inside, watching a Redskins game. Marchers in front of the Justice Department threw smoke bombs and were dispersed with tear gas. Attorney General John Mitchell said it looked like the Russian Revolution.

Huston was also right about the competing factions, for after November 15, extremist groups like the Weathermen began advocating violence with the slogan "Bring the War Back Home." Nixon became convinced that the antiwar movement controlled the media. Obsessed with leaks, he threatened to stop holding staff meetings. On February 3, 1970, a memo from Haldeman stated: "Up to now, the president has been sympathetic to the leak situation; no one has been fired." But now Nixon proposed to use leaks as the basis for eliminating meetings. "If anything leaks, there will be no more meetings." The President would make his decisions alone.[122]

On March 6, some Weathermen making pipe bombs in a New York City town house on 11th Street blew themselves up. Three bodies were found inside, as well as bombs studded with roofing nails, apparently intended for Columbia University. The war was indeed coming home, even as it spread abroad, for in March, Prince Norodom Sihanouk was overthrown in Cambodia, where the new government asked the United States for aid. On April 30, Nixon announced that he had ordered U.S. combat troops into Cambodia. On May 4, 1970, students at Kent State, a placid university in Ohio that had not been radicalized, rallied to protest the widening of the war and four fell dead, shot by National Guard troops, while nine others were wounded. Nixon called the demonstrators "bums." Some seven hundred colleges and universities closed down in sympathy, and an antiwar rally on May 9 brought close to 100,000 to Washington.

After Kent State, there was a phenomenal escalation of movement violence. Huston was getting reports of bombings in the thousands, of thirty-nine police officers killed by snipers, of six arsons a day committed in a two-week period in May against ROTC facilities. Something had to be done, at a time when seventy-five-year-old J. Edgar Hoover seemed fossilized and cranky. He was feuding with the CIA, with whom he had cut off all contacts, and refused to carry out bug-planting black bag jobs for the National Security Agency. Instead of responding to what Nixon thought of as an incipient insurrection, Hoover was sulking.[123]

Seeing himself faced with "domestic terrorism," Nixon felt an urgent need for improved intelligence. Were the antiwar groups subject to foreign influence? Did they receive funding from abroad? On June 5, he called a meeting of intelligence chiefs—Hoover of the FBI, Richard Helms of the CIA, Admiral Noel Gayler of the National Security Agency, and Donald V. Bennett of the Defense Intelligence Agency. He expressed his dissatisfaction with the intelligence he was getting on the antiwar movement. As General Bennett recalled, "the President chewed our butts." The goal was, as Nixon put it, "to curtail the illegal activities of those who are determined to destroy our society." Nixon asked the intelligence chiefs to set up an interagency committee that would come up with a plan. The plan would be submitted to his aide, Thomas Charles Huston, who would draw up a report.[124]

The term "interagency" was anathema to Hoover. He saw domestic intelligence as his bailiwick and did not want to be pulled into any clumsy alliances that would diminish his authority. When the intelligence chiefs and Huston met again three days later, Hoover professed to have understood that Nixon wanted a historical study of revolutionary violence. Not at all, Huston responded, the President was dissatisfied and wanted to know "what we can do to elevate the quality of our intelligence operations." Admiral Gayler said that was also his understanding. A furious Hoover turned beet red. He developed an intense dislike of Huston, whom he addressed as "Mr. Hoffman" and "Mr. Hutchinson," and whom he called "the hippie."

Working groups in each agency put together material from which Huston prepared his report. The amazing thing about what became known as "the Huston Plan" was that its author proclaimed its illegality. Its main features were:

- Intensified electronic surveillance of individuals and groups who pose a major threat to internal security. The existing coverage of New Left groups and of foreign embassies, Huston noted, was inadequate.
- Mail coverage should be resumed. Huston noted that "covert coverage is illegal and there are serious risks involved. However, the advantages outweigh the risks."
- Surreptitious entry (black bag jobs). "Use of this technique is clearly illegal. It amounts to burglary. . . . This technique could be particularly helpful if used against the Weathermen and the Black Panthers."
- Development of campus sources. The FBI, Huston said, does not currently recruit any campus sources among individuals below twenty-one years of age. "Mr. Hoover is afraid of a young student surfacing in the press as an FBI source . . . [but] the campus is a battleground." More sources were needed, regardless of age.
- A permanent committee should be named (presumably to be chaired by Huston, who would become a kind of intelligence czar) to coordinate the work of the intelligence agencies, "since Hoover is fearful of any mechanics that might jeopardize his autonomy."[125]

Not only did the Huston Plan recommend an increase in all the illegal surveillance methods that Hoover had curtailed, it was openly critical of the FBI chief. Thus, Huston sent the report to Helms, Bennett, and Gayler, but not to Hoover, for as he later explained, "It was felt that Hoover would refuse to go along with it" unless he was pressured by the others. But Huston was out of his league in going up against an old warrior with half a century of bureaucratic infighting behind him. When Hoover saw the draft signed by the others on June 23, he refused to sign it unless he could add footnotes objecting to all the recommendations.

Huston sent the footnoted report to the President with a cover letter to Haldeman that called Hoover "the only stumbling-block" and described his objections as "inconsistent and frivolous." Huston suggested that Nixon bring in Hoover for "a stroking session" and a photo op.

On July 14, Nixon approved the Huston Plan, but declined to sign a document that included illegal and unconstitutional instructions. Huston signed it and was left twisting in the wind. Hoover, whose agency would have to implement the illegal measures, went to Attorney General John Mitchell and made it clear that if he was to carry out the Huston Plan, the Attorney General or the President would have to sign off on it.[126]

This Nixon refused to do, for he realized that without Hoover's cooperation the plan was dead. On July 28, Nixon revoked his approval. As Howard Baker of Tennessee put it at the 1975 Church Committee hearings: "Hoover put the kibosh on the Huston Plan." At those same hearings, Huston testified that he resented the impression "that I created out of whole cloth an entire array of new techniques to exploit and infringe upon the civil liberties of the American people and that I forced it down [CIA director Richard] Helms's throat and that I blackjacked Admiral Gayler." All he had done was organize the recommendations of the working groups. His rationale was that "there was a serious crisis in 1970. I was not concerned with people who thought Nixon was a louse. We were talking about bombers. We were talking about assassins. We were talking about snipers." With his plan stillborn, Huston left the White House in June 1972 and went back to Indiana.[127]

As it turned out, Hoover's refusal to go along with the Huston Plan set off a chain reaction that destroyed the Nixon presidency. It's worth noting, in terms of the number of Nixon administration veterans who are today working for George W. Bush, that the word "plumber" was first used in a memo on May 29, 1970, from Nixon consigliere Murray Chotiner to Donald Rumsfeld, then director of the Office of Economic Opportunity. Concerned about leaks in Rumsfeld's office, Chotiner advised: "It will be appreciated if you can have someone call the plumber and plug the leak." Rumsfeld was then, as he is today, effective with the media. On October 17, 1969, Alexander P. Butterfield, the presidential aide who later revealed the Oval Office taping system, sent Nixon a media monitoring report that praised Rumsfeld's appearance on the CBS morning news: "Rummy was great and for six minutes went right down the line re our progress and current position on the Vietnam issue." Rumsfeld's advice was valued by the Nixon inner circle. On December 4, 1970, Haldeman told Nixon: "Rumsfeld has the feeling that Bob Dole may be losing some of his effectiveness because he is a knee-jerk defender of the Administration. . . . Another point that Rumsfeld makes quite effectively is that we are 'too busy selling something new each week.' What we have to do is to pound and pound on three or four major themes." Haldeman planned to create a "political control group" of Nixon loyalists, which would include John D. Ehrlichman, Colson, and Rumsfeld.[128]

Another loyalist, Pat Buchanan, recommended firing Hoover in a memo to Nixon on February 12, 1971, because he was drawing fire from the Democrats with a presidential election coming up. "He is going down steadily," Buchanan wrote. "Among young people, he is increasingly becoming a villain; and he is tied totally to us. McGovern is making him a focal point of attack.... Don't let him wind up his career a dead lion being chewed over by the jackals of the Left." It's ironic that Hoover, who had turned sour on illegal surveillance methods, was being portrayed as a villain. On April 5, the House Majority leader, Democrat Hale Boggs of Louisiana, called for his dismissal "for using the tactics of the Soviet Union and Hitler's Gestapo."[129]

Boggs's attack followed an unthinkable occurrence on March 8, a black bag job on the FBI office in Media, Pennsylvania. Eight hundred documents were stolen and released to the press, disclosing some of the COINTELPRO operations against the Black Panthers and campus protesters. Hoover was becoming a liability and there were discussions about him in the Oval Office.[130]

The more Nixon fretted over leaks, the worse the leaks seemed to get. On June 13, 1971, the *New York Times* began its publication of the *Pentagon Papers*, leaked by Daniel Ellsberg, who had been working in the Defense Department at the time when Secretary of Defense Robert McNamara commissioned the forty-seven-volume study of U.S. involvement in Vietnam, which a horrified Nixon called "the most massive leak of classified material in American history."[131]

That February, the tape recorders had been installed in the Oval Office. On June 17, while musing with Haldeman and Henry Kissinger over the leaks, Nixon asked: "Do you remember Huston's plan [for White House–sponsored break-ins as part of domestic counterintelligence operations]? Implement it."

Huston had told Haldeman that there were some classified Vietnam files at the Brookings Institution, a centrist think tank.

Kissinger: "Now Brookings has no right to have classified documents."

Nixon: "I want it implemented. . . . Goddamnit, get in and get those files. Blow the safe and get it."[132]

Nixon was convinced that the Ellsberg leak was part of a conspiracy, and as time passed, he came to the conclusion that Hoover was dragging his feet. So Nixon authorized a special White House investigative unit to "stop leaks and to investigate other sensitive security matters." It was headed by Egil "Bud" Krogh, a lawyer on the Domestic Council, and David Young, a lawyer on Kissinger's National Security Council staff. Their first job, as Charles Colson put it on July 1, was "to go down the line and nail the guy [Ellsberg] cold."[133]

Huston was gone, but on July 1, after the Supreme Court had ruled against the government's attempt to enjoin the publication of the *Pentagon Papers*, Nixon told Haldeman and Kissinger: "I've got to get somebody fast, either Huston or somebody like Huston. . . . I really need a son of a bitch like Huston who will work his butt off and do it dishonorably. . . . I can't have a high-minded lawyer. . . . I want somebody just as tough as I am for a change. . . . We are up against an enemy, a conspiracy. They're using any means. We are going to use any means. Is that clear?"

Later that morning, with Haldeman, Colson, and Ehrlichman, Nixon returned to his need for "a guy who's mean, tough, ruthless. He'll lie, he'll do anything.

"We want somebody to be a McCarthy," Nixon said. "Is there a senator?"

Haldeman: "There's no one."

Colson proposed Representative William Brock of Tennessee, but Nixon said: "No. Brock is not another McCarthy."

Here was the President holding up as the highest example of the dirty trickster, who would have been perfect to head the White House Plumbers unit, the censured and disgraced McCarthy, the man whose name was synonymous with false accusations and the entire arsenal of deceit. Unfortunately, McCarthy was no longer able to help, so the conversation drifted back to Huston.

"Huston knows more than anybody . . . about where stuff is and what there is," Nixon said.

The trouble with Huston, even if he were willing to return to the White House, was that he had antagonized the leaders of the various intelligence agencies with his brashness. As Nixon put it: "Well, [the FBI and the CIA] won't talk to him, probably Defense won't talk to him. There's your problem."

Nixon proposed the National Security Council aide Richard Allen. "What I'd really like," he said, "is Allen and Huston together . . . and let the two connive and screw around and just knock their brains out."

Colson had reservations about Huston, saying, "He picks the things that look good to him." Colson proposed Howard Hunt, who "just got out of the CIA, fifty. Kind of a tiger."

Haldeman agreed that Huston was "great on the stuff he wants to be great on."

"Arrogant little bastard," Nixon observed.[134]

The next day, Nixon complained to Haldeman and Colson that "Hoover is not going after this [Ellsberg] case as strong as I'd like. . . . There's something dragging him. . . . I don't know what it is."

Colson: "It's the fear of repression."

Nixon: "He's talking about Ellsberg and all of them are probably going to make a martyr out of him."

Haldeman agreed that the FBI was "slow as fish."[135]

By July 20, the Plumbers were operational, as Ehrlichman reported to Nixon.

"How does it presently stand?" Nixon asked.

Ehrlichman: "Well there're a lot of leaks. There are all kinds of leaks." Krogh and "his guys" were pulling together the evidence.[136]

In an "Eyes Only" memo to Colson on July 20, Ehrlichman explained that Krogh was trying to link Ellsberg "to a conspiracy that suggests treasonous conduct," in order to establish that there was a "counter government" undermining U.S. foreign policy. Krogh had "a good investigative mechanism," which at this point was doing research. Howard Hunt was going through the *Pentagon Papers* and the ex-FBI man G. Gordon Liddy had come on board. Describing Liddy, Haldeman said: "Apparently he's a little bit nuts. . . . Apparently, he's sort of a Tom Huston guy."[137]

On the night of September 3–4, 1971, a team of Plumbers led by Hunt and Liddy conducted their first break-in. They rifled the Los Angeles office of Ellsberg's psychiatrist, Dr. Lewis Fielding, but found nothing. To memorialize the event, Hunt and Liddy were photographed in mid-burglary. The break-in demonstrated that the White House had the ability to covertly penetrate a chosen target without the help of the FBI.

On September 8, Ehrlichman told Nixon: "We had one little operation . . . out in Los Angeles . . . which I think is better that you don't know about. But we've got some dirty tricks underway. It may pay off." Colson later explained to Nixon that "they weren't stealing anything. Really, they trespassed. They had broken and entered . . . with an intent to obtain information. . . . They were unarmed. They obtained no information."[138]

Later, after Watergate, Nixon was going over events with Attorney General Richard Kleindienst on April 25, 1973. "The initiative was undertaken at the White House," Nixon explained, "to see what the hell Ellsberg was leaking. That's what we call the plumber operation. Without any knowledge of anybody, these crazy fools went out and they went into the psychiatrist. They got nothing. It was a dry hole. . . . Shit, it's the dumbest Goddamn thing I've ever heard of. . . . These guys had the responsibility to conduct an investigation of the Ellsberg thing due to the fact that Hoover would not."[139]

Back in October 1971, a month after the black bag job on the psychiatrist, John Ehrlichman and others were urging Nixon to ask for Hoover's resignation. Ehrlichman thought he had become an embarrassment, he was like an old punch-drunk boxer, without judgment or vigor. Attorney General John Mitchell said he should be retired on January 1, 1972, his seventy-seventh birthday. Nixon summoned Hoover to a breakfast meeting but did not have the courage, or the heart, to demand his resignation. On May 1, 1972, the Hoover problem was solved when he went to bed and died in his sleep of a heart attack. He had been the director of the FBI for forty-eight years, under eight Presidents. After Hoover, the FBI became just another government department. It was no longer an independent fiefdom, ruled by a monarch.[140]

Hoover did not live to see the break-in on June 17, when five men carrying cameras and bugging equipment were arrested inside the Democratic Party headquarters in the Watergate complex. In August 1974, Richard Nixon became the first President to resign from office, as he faced impeachment on charges of abuse of power and obstruction of justice. The use of the Plumbers was at the heart of the abuse of power.

Nixon went beyond the excesses of McCarthy—the senator's attacks on George Marshall and Ralph Zwicker, the demand that government servants provide him with classified information, the doctored photographs and forged letters of the Army hearings. Nixon presided over a system of government by conniving, government by deceit, government by breaking laws. The original concept of the Huston Plan was that intelligence agencies should use illegal surveillance methods in the interest of national security. The Plumbers, on the other hand, were vigilantes operating for political purposes. To stifle dissent, in the Ellsberg case, and to gain political intelligence in an election year, in the Watergate break-in.

On May 16, 1973, when Nixon was facing impeachment and preparing his defense, his special counsel Fred Buzhardt expressed concern about the memos on the Huston Plan, which he considered "inflammatory" because they showed the President approving surreptitious entry, which would put Watergate in a new light. Nixon recalled the failure of the Huston Plan. "Huston got pissed off and left," he said. "Hoover wouldn't allow it. . . . I rescinded."

Nixon recalled that following the demise of the Huston Plan "we set up in the White House an independent group under Bud Krogh to cover the problems of the leaks involving the Goddamn Pentagon Papers. . . . I remember they called it the Plumbers operation."[141]

Nixon said the Plumbers were worse than the Huston Plan because the Plumbers "look like one of these Goddamn clowns hired a bunch of people here. But [in the Huston Plan] you've got the CIA, the DIA, the FBI, all working together. That's pretty Goddamn important isn't it?"

Buzhardt: "What I'm told is that Tolson found out about it and got to Hoover. . . . Clyde Tolson [Hoover's close friend and number two in the FBI] said this will ruin your image. Hoover then took his copy, footnoted it, screamed at Mitchell, got the issue raised. . . . And you suspended the operation."[142]

It was left to Haldeman on May 18 to link the Huston Plan with the Plumbers: "Of course," he said, "they make the case that [the Huston Plan] being turned off led to doing illicit things to accomplish the same thing . . . the Plumbers operation."[143]

———

Ronald Reagan's two terms, from 1980 to 1988, saw cataclysmic changes in the balance of power, from which America emerged as the only superpower. He practiced an aggressive anti-Communism at a time when many accepted mutual deterrence and the global position of the Soviet Union. Reagan initiated the policy of riposte, whether in Afghanistan, Nicaragua, or Poland, but he acted covertly through surrogates, so that during his presidency America was not at war, although U.S. troops were sent to Lebanon and to the tiny Caribbean island of Grenada, and U.S. planes bombed Libya.

It's still difficult to quantify the degree to which Reagan's policies contributed to the end result—the collapse of the Soviet empire, the liberation of the satellites, and the reunification of Germany. But the fact remains that this geopolitical rearrangement was incubated on his watch.

Reagan brought to Washington the values of conservative anti-Communism, which were sometimes tainted with McCarthyism. He expressed a qualified sympathy for McCarthy in a radio address in 1979. "The senator used a shotgun when a rifle was needed," he said, "injuring the innocent along with the guilty. Nevertheless, his broadsides should not be used today to infer that all who opposed Communist subversion were hysterical zealots."[144] Like McCarthy, he was capable of arguing that anyone who opposed him was being manipulated by the Communists. Thus, in the 1980 campaign against Jimmy Carter, he said that the Soviets wanted to see Carter elected and that they would "throw him a few bones in order to help him."[145] The Democratic congressman from Massachusetts, Edward J. Markey, said Reagan was guilty of "mud-slinging and McCarthy-like smear tactics."

Reagan shared McCarthy's distrust of the Eastern Establishment. In the 1978 Panama Canal debates, he echoed McCarthy's disparagement of the "striped-pants boys" when he said: "You know, giving up the Canal itself might be a better deal if we could throw in the State Department."[146]

In January 1983, Bob Mrazek of New York went to a reception at the White House and was invited by Ron and Nancy into the Red Room, where Attorney General Edwin Meese toasted McCarthy as "a truly great senator." Mrazek happened to be standing next to the President, who turned to him and said, "Isn't it a shame what happened to Joe and Roy?" Mrazek said, "I thought Senator McCarthy's wife's name was Abigail" (the wife of Senator Eugene McCarthy).[147]

But Reagan was no McCarthy. He was a marvel of affability with a sunny disposition, completely lacking in McCarthy's compulsive viciousness. Even when he called upon a group of church leaders on March 8, 1983, not to "ignore the facts of history and the aggressive impulses of an evil empire," he was genial and smiling. In the wake of Woodrow Wilson, he professed a foreign policy based on morality, a questionable premise. Nations follow their self-interest and cloak it in morality. Calling another nation evil is simplistic and nonspecific. Far better to show why their system is unworkable and doomed to failure, as the Soviet system was. Reagan ended up doing business with Mikhail Gorbachev, under a policy described as "trust, but verify," and in 1988 the Russians pulled out of Afghanistan. The only stumble that endangered his presidency was Iran-contra, which was called "Reagan's Watergate," although Reagan was not impeached and did not resign.

Iran-contra was a muddled, almost impenetrable affair, not a simple break-in like Watergate, that was over in minutes, but a labyrinthine plot that went on for years and involved dozens of agents, middlemen, and government officials. "It was so far-fetched," said Reagan's press aide, Lyn Nofziger, "that it doesn't even make good fiction."[148]

In the triangular deal, Reagan agreed to sell missiles to Iran, which was at war with Iraq. Reagan approved the deal at a meeting on August 6, 1985, over the objections of Secretary of State George Shultz and Secretary of Defense Caspar Weinberger. The first Tow missiles were shipped to Iran on August 19. In exchange, Iran's Ayatollah Khomeini would pressure the Hezbollah to release six American hostages they were holding in Lebanon. Finally, the profits from the sale would be diverted to the contras operating in Nicaragua, whose funding had been cut off by Congress. The operation was conducted covertly by officials of the National Security Council, principally John Poindexter, Robert C. McFarlane, and Oliver North. How much Reagan knew about it has remained uncertain. His rationale for freeing the hostages was "it's the same thing as if one of my children was kidnapped and there was a demand for ransom."[149]

The operation had inherent drawbacks, such as the greed of the middlemen, the inability to enforce the release of the hostages, and the risk of creating a fresh cycle of hostage-taking, in order to obtain more arms, which is what happened. Between 1984 and 1987, fourteen American hostages were kidnapped in Lebanon. One, the CIA head in Beirut, William Buckley, died as a result of torture in June 1985. Another, Peter Kilburn, the librarian at the American University in Beirut, was murdered in 1986 after the U.S. bombing of Libya. The other twelve were released between 1985 and 1991. As the saying goes, the road to hell is paved with good intentions. By November 1986, Reagan had to admit that arms were being shipped to Iran and that the funds were being diverted to the contras. After Iran-contra, the Teflon wore thin. Reagan was ridiculed for not knowing what was going on. He had Ollie North "running all over hell's half-acre," as Gerald Ford put it. There were too many competing agendas—some of the players did it for the money, others to bring Iran closer to the West, still others to help the contras, all under the guise of freeing the hostages. Oliver North was convicted of three felonies, but his conviction was reversed in 1990 by the U.S. Court of Appeals and in 1992 he ran for the Senate in Virginia. One of his backers was Dick Cheney.[150]

———

George W. Bush was elected president in November 2000, and less than a year later, the unthinkable happened. The American mainland was attacked, in its largest city and outside its capital, a deed that our enemies in two world wars had been unable to accomplish. The illusion of secure borders lay buried in the rubble of the World Trade Center.

The enemy, Islamic terrorism, was stateless. It had no longitude or latitude. It was not nation-based, but religion-based, much like the gang of medieval cutthroats who called themselves Hashishi (hashish-eaters), or Assassins, which thrived in twelfth-century Iran and Iraq. They believed that the murder of Christian crusaders was a religious duty.

The group that claimed responsibility for the 9/11 attack, Al Qaeda, had been given sanctuary in Afghanistan by the Taliban. A swift military operation ousted the Taliban and sent Al Qaeda scurrying to other locations, from which it continued to mount terrorist actions. Inside Afghanistan, small-scale combat disrupted nation-building, and much of the country remained under the control of warlords, who paid a surface obeisance to the central government. The President's repeated vow to capture the Al Qaeda leader, Osama bin Laden, dead or alive, had not been kept at the time of this writing, the summer of 2003.

The Cold War doctrine of containment, based on a system of alliances, was laid to rest after 9/11, for with stateless terrorism there were no borders to contain. The doctrine of preemption took hold, in the conviction that we could not sit back and wait for the next attack. As a precedent, it could be argued that had we known the Japanese fleet was heading toward Hawaii in December 1941, we could have sent it to the bottom of the Pacific.

In 2002, the President and his advisers began to promote preemption. At West Point on June 1, Mr. Bush said, "New threats . . . require new thinking. . . . We must take the battle to the enemy, . . . and confront the worst threats before they emerge. . . . The only path to safety is the path of action."[151]

On September 20, the doctrine was spelled out in the annual National Security Strategy document that the President submitted to Congress. The United States, it said, "will not hesitate to act alone," if necessary by "acting preemptively." This could happen in case of an immediate threat, such as the mobilization of a hostile army.[152]

The doctrine, however, was aimed at Iraq, which was seen as presenting a threat to the United States because of its arsenal of toxic weapons and its supposed attempts at a nuclear capability. Riding his post-9/11 popularity, the President identified Iraq as a terrorist regime with weapons of mass destruction and links to Al Qaeda. In fact, there was no similarity between the fanatical Islamists and the odious secular dictatorship of Saddam Hussein, who did not want to kill infidels but to grab land, as he had tried to do in Kuwait in 1990. During the Cold War, the United States had seen such dictators come and go, and of some we were quite fond, such as Mobutu Sese Seko in the Congo and Rafael Trujillo in the Dominican Republic. We had also helped Saddam in his war against Iran.

In the post-9/11 emergency, with America at war first in Afghanistan and then in Iraq, the McCarthyite strain in American political life reemerged with a vengeance—the politics of fear, the politics of insult, and the politics of deceit.

In the immediate aftermath of 9/11, the FBI rounded up 762 persons with Arab-sounding names, most of them illegal aliens. As in the Palmer raids of 1920, the emergency was real, but the methods trampled civil rights. In the Palmer raids, those held were denied lawyers and were unable to post high bail. In the Ashcroft raids, the detainees were not told the charges against them, which impaired their ability to get lawyers or bail hearings. When a detainee's family came looking for him, the staff at the detention centers claimed the detainee was not there. In some cases there were verbal taunts, such as "You're going to die here."[153]

Under the FBI policy of "hold until cleared," the 762 aliens in the Ashcroft raids were jailed for an average of eighty days, and 84 of them were subjected to twenty-three-hour lockdown. Not a single one was found to have any connection with terrorism. In June 2003, Glenn A. Fine, the Justice Department inspector general, issued a report that admitted "significant problems" with the roundup.[154]

With his new powers after the passage of the USA Patriot Act, Attorney General John Ashcroft could imprison suspects without due process before they were tried, bug mosques, and monitor jailhouse conversations between federal inmates and their lawyers. The opening of an FBI hot line was an invitation to all the vengeful losers in our society, from Arab-haters to unpaid creditors to disgruntled employees to angry one-time friends and spouses. Thousands of tips came in, many from settlers of scores. In Texas, a Moroccan student was held on a tip from his estranged wife. In Michigan, a Yemen-born trucker was jailed for seven days in December 2002 on a tip from a declared enemy. In Evansville, Illinois, nine men who had done nothing were jailed for a week and listed in a newly created National Crime Registry.[155]

Once again, those who disagreed with the emergency measures were branded as disloyal. At a Senate hearing in December 2001, Ashcroft said: "To those who scare peace-loving people with phantoms of lost liberties . . . your tactics aid terrorists."[156]

The wartime spirit fostered a revival of the politics of insult, pioneered by McCarthy when he called his fellow senator Ralph Flanders of Vermont "senile and vicious," and Senator Robert C. Hendrickson of New Jersey "a living miracle without brains or guts." Secretary of Defense Donald Rumsfeld dismissed France and Germany as "Old Europe," eclipsed by a serviceable "New Europe" consisting of former Soviet satellites. Before a House committee he lumped Germany with Libya and Cuba as three countries that "won't help in any respect" to deal with Iraq.[157]

Robert C. Byrd of West Virginia, at eighty-five the patriarch of the Senate, observed that "calling heads of state pygmies, labeling whole countries as evil, denigrating powerful European allies as irrelevant—these types of crude insensitivities can do our nation no good."[158]

The superpatriots on cable TV, clones of the pro-McCarthy media claque of the fifties, caught the drift, helping to create a climate reminiscent of the blacklist. The actor Sean Penn was accused of treason for writing an antiwar letter and visiting Baghdad. The quintessentially American Dixie Chicks, who sang the national anthem at the 2003 Super Bowl, were blacklisted on conservative radio stations. In Louisiana, their CDs and tapes were smashed under a 33,000-pound tractor. Their crime: In London, their Texas-born leader, Natalie Maines, told an audience, "Just so you know, we're ashamed the President of the United States is from Texas."[159]

There was a more sinister side to the politics of insult, which was to deny that there was such a thing as an adversary in good faith. This was McCarthy's approach when he said that everyone who opposed him, from the President on down, was doing the work of the Communist Party. And this was what the House Majority Leader, Tom DeLay, was prone to do. When Howard Dean, the former governor of Vermont and a Democratic candidate for President, accused Mr. Bush of waging a unilateral war, DeLay called his statement "outrageous" and said that the Democrats were fast becoming "the appeasement party."[160]

In the first week of April, another Democratic candidate, the decorated Vietnam veteran John Kerry, told an audience that "what we need now is not just a regime change in Saddam Hussein and Iraq, but we need a regime change in the United States." Kerry had won three Purple Hearts, a Bronze Star, and a Silver Star for his service in combat as commander of a gunboat on the Mekong Delta. DeLay, according to his House biography, never served in the military. He was, however, in the pest control business in Houston, and seems to have brought his DDT to Washington. When he called Kerry unpatriotic, Kerry fired back: "I'm not going to have my patriotism questioned by the likes of Tom DeLay."[161]

Joe McCarthy relied on the politics of deceit and the immunity he was granted on the Senate floor to make preposterous claims regarding Communists in government, slanderously identifying Owen Lattimore and others as Communist spies. There was massive evidence that the Bush administration used the politics of deceit to make the case for the war with Iraq, thanks to the fine work of a number of tenacious reporters and commentators, such as James Risen, Nicholas D. Kristof, and Paul Krugman of the *New York Times;* Seymour M. Hersh of *The New Yorker;* and John Judis and Spencer Ackerman of *The New Republic.*

After the war was over, American generals on the ground expressed their surprise that no chemical or biological weapons had been fired at their troops and that none had been found in the forward dispersal area. "We thought we understood what the regime was intending to do in its use of weapons," Lieutenant General James Conway, commander of the First Marine Expeditionary Force, said on May 31. "We were simply wrong."[162]

Whether or not the Iraqis had weapons of mass destruction at the time the United States invaded is the wrong question. There was plenty of evidence that they had those weapons in the past, that they used them, and that they might still have them. The correct question is what was the integrity and accuracy of the intelligence used by the administration to promote the war.

It soon became clear that to gain support for the war, the principal figures in the administration launched a propaganda campaign based on a pack of lies, which resulted in the deaths of hundreds of American soldiers. Deception on this scale on the part of the President, the Vice President, the national security adviser, the Secretaries of State and Defense, and their minions was unprecedented in American history. Never before had the United States declared war on another country for such specious reasons.

Efforts to brand Iraq as a rogue nation threatening American security began long before 9/11. In March 2001, five months before the terrorist attacks, Richard Perle, then the chairman of the Defense Policy Board, appeared before the Senate Foreign Relations Committee and made the case: "Does Saddam now have weapons of mass destruction? Sure he does. We know he has biological weapons. . . . How far he's gone on the nuclear side I don't think we really know. My guess is that it's further than we think." Perle resigned as chairman in April 2003 after Seymour Hersh exposed the deals he was cutting with defense-related companies as a lobbyist and consultant. He was, it turned out, a one-man military-industrial complex.[163]

On the weekend after 9/11, Paul D. Wolfowitz, the deputy secretary of defense and one of the most vocal proponents of a preemptive war, was at Camp David advancing the thesis that Iraq, which was on the State Department's list of terrorist-sponsoring states, should be held accountable at once.[164]

In February 2002, however, the *New York Times* reported that the CIA had found "no evidence that Iraq has engaged in terrorist operations against the United States in nearly a decade, and the agency is also convinced that President Saddam Hussein has not provided chemical or biological weapons to Al Qaeda or related terrorist groups." Nor did the CIA have any evidence that Iraq was updating its nuclear program.[165]

The CIA's findings did not conform to the administration line, as expressed by Vice President Richard Cheney in Nashville in August 2002. Cheney, the Secretary of Defense in the first Gulf War, had some unfinished business in Iraq. He asserted that Saddam, "armed with an arsenal of these weapons of terror," could "directly threaten America's friends through the region and subject the United States or any other nation to nuclear warfare."[166]

Such was not the assessment of the Pentagon's own Defense Intelligence Agency, in a report in September 2002 stating that "a substantial amount of Iraq's chemical warfare agents, precursors, munitions, and production equipment were destroyed between 1991 and 1998 as a result of Operation Desert Storm and United Nations Special Commission actions. There is no reliable information on whether Iraq is producing and stockpiling its chemical warfare agent production facilities."[167]

No wonder, in the light of these unalarming reports, that Secretary of Defense Donald Rumsfeld, another advocate of preemptive war, asked his undersecretary for policy, Douglas J. Feith, to set up a small intelligence shop of his own, the Office of Special Plans, which was essentially a second-guessing operation. The OSP took data provided by the CIA and DIA, ran it through its own computers, and provided its own analysis. Its mission seemed to be to present all the available evidence for going to war.[168]

According to some analysts, the Office of Special Plans highlighted information from Iraqi exiles under the control of Ahmed Chalabi of the Iraqi National Congress, which other agencies discarded. After the war, when special forces looked for weapons at the sites the OSP had pinpointed, they came up empty.[169] The use of defectors was like the use of professional witnesses in the Smith Act trials. Their livelihood depended on telling their employers what they wanted to hear. Nor were they above being coached, as Roy Cohn coached Harvey Matusow.

On the anniversary of 9/11 in 2002, the White House called for a congressional resolution endorsing a war. The administration's Anvil Chorus gave its full-throated approval. "Imagine a September 11 with weapons of mass destruction," said Rumsfeld. "It's not three thousand—it's tens of thousands of innocent men, women, and children." Or as Condoleezza Rice, the national security adviser, put it, "We don't want the smoking gun to be a mushroom cloud," as if it were a certainty that Saddam Hussein had a nuclear bomb. Practically the only naysayer at this point was Bob Graham, the Florida senator who was chairman of the Senate Intelligence Committee. He said on September 27, 2002, that he had seen nothing in the classified CIA reports that established a link between Saddam and Osama bin Laden.[170]

That was about to change, for certain pressures, whether from the White House, the Vice President's office, or the Office of Special Plans, were directed at George Tenet, the head of the CIA. In early October, a top-secret CIA National Intelligence Estimate, which drew on data from the entire intelligence community, gave the President the ammunition he needed. It concluded that Baghdad had chemical and biological weapons and was seeking to rebuild its nuclear program. It established a linkage between Iraq and Al Qaeda. And it stated that Iraq had obtained aluminum tubes that could be used as rotors for gas centrifuges that produced nuclear weapons material.[171]

On October 7, four days before the Senate vote on the war resolution, the President gave a speech at the Cincinnati Museum Center that was based on the CIA intelligence estimate. It was designed to scare the living daylights out of any sensible American. "We know," he said,

> that Iraq and the Al Qaeda have high-level contacts that go back a decade. We've learned that Iraq has trained Al Qaeda members in bomb-making and poisons and deadly gases. . . . [An] alliance with terrorists could allow the Iraqi regime to attack America without leaving fingerprints. . . . The evidence indicates that Iraq is reconstituting its nuclear weapons program. Saddam Hussein has held numerous meetings with Iraqi nuclear scientists, a group he calls his "nuclear mujahideen"—his nuclear holy warriors. . . . If the Iraqi regime is able to produce, buy, or steal an amount of highly enriched uranium a little larger than a softball, it could have a nuclear weapon in less than a year.

A number of detailed charges followed:

Iraq has attempted to purchase high-strength aluminum tubes and other equipment needed for gas centrifuges, which are used to enrich uranium for nuclear weapons. . . .

Iraq has a growing fleet of manned and unmanned aerial vehicles that could be used to disperse chemical or biological weapons across broad areas. We are concerned that Iraq is exploring ways of using these UAV's for missions targeting the United States.

More specifically, Mr. Bush said that Iraq

has produced more than 30,000 liters of anthrax and other deadly biological agents. This is a massive stockpile of biological weapons that has never been accounted for, and is capable of killing millions. . . .

Iraq could decide on any given day to provide biological or chemical weapons to a terrorist group or an individual.[172]

This shocking indictment went unchallenged at the time. It was only in the months that followed, when troubled intelligence analysts began leaking information to the press, that much of what Mr. Bush had said could be questioned.

On the linkage between Iraq and Al Qaeda: It was not until June 2003 that the *New York Times* was able to report that two captured Al Qaeda leaders independently confirmed that Osama bin Laden had rejected the idea of working with Saddam because he did not want to be obligated to him. One was Abu Zubaydah, captured in March 2002. The other was the Al Qaeda chief of operations, Khalid Shaikh Mohammed, caught in Pakistan in March 2003, who said there were no links between the two groups. Both were interrogated by the CIA.[173]

On the aluminum tubes, there were sharp differences among the different agencies. The CIA and the DIA saw them as components in a centrifuge project. But the State Department Bureau of Research and Intelligence and the Energy Department said the tubes' thick walls and anti-corrosion coating were not suited to uranium enrichment. The intelligence at the Department of Energy came from interviews with scientists at nuclear labs such as Oak Ridge who were experts in the techniques of nuclear enrichment. They said the tubes were probably for artillery rockets. But the analysis that survived in the National Intelligence Estimate, or at any rate the intelligence that the President adopted, was that the tubes were for nuclear use. Soon after that, analysts started warning of manipulation: "They kept telling us to go back and find the right answer."[174]

As for the massive stockpiling of biological weapons, this was based on information from General Hussein Kamel, the man in charge of Iraq's secret weapons program, who defected to Jordan in 1995 with crates of documents. He was interrogated by U.N. inspectors on August 22 of that year and said that the stockpiles had been destroyed in response to the ongoing U.N. inspections. He had ordered the destruction himself. "All weapons," he said, "biological, chemical, missiles, nuclear—were destroyed." In 1996 he was lured back to Iraq and murdered, but the stockpiles survived him in American intelligence estimates.[175]

As for Iraqi drones that might have targeted the United States, they had a range of three hundred miles. They could hit Florida if they took off from Cuba. Hans Blix, the chief U.N. weapons inspector in Iraq, who found a few, called them "pieces of junk."[176]

A statement from George Tenet after the Cincinnati speech showed that he was now on board. "There is no question," he said, "that the likelihood of Saddam Hussein using weapons of mass destruction against the United States or our allies . . . grows as his arsenal continues to build." On October 17, 2002, the Congress overwhelmingly voted for a resolution to allow war. Five of the nine Democrats on the Senate Intelligence Committee voted against the resolution.[177]

On January 28, 2003, when the President gave his State of the Union address, the use of forged documents by Woodrow Wilson came full circle. Wilson had wanted to believe the Sisson documents, which labeled the Bolshevik leaders as pliant tools of the Germans, in order to build a moral foundation for his invasion of Russia in 1919. He authorized their publication as a government pamphlet. In the same way, on January 28, an unquestioning President relied on forged documents because he wanted to believe that Iraq was buying uranium to make nuclear weapons.

Article II of the Constitution says that the President "shall from time to time give to the Congress Information of the State of the Union, and recommend to their Consideration such Measures as he shall judge necessary and expedient." Over the years, the message-giving authority was converted into a platform to focus congressional and public attention on the President's policies. The State of the Union address is a major event and easily commands prime-time and front-page coverage. It carries great weight and is assumed to reflect the best available intelligence.

Once again, the President was specific in his description of Saddam Hussein's arsenal, which contained thirty thousand warheads, five hundred tons of chemical weapons, twenty-five thousand liters of anthrax, thirty-eight thousand liters of botulinum toxin, and a secret program for nuclear weapons.

Once again, the President conflated Iraq and Al Qaeda: "Imagine those 19 hijackers with other weapons and other plans—this time armed by Saddam Hussein. It would take one vial, one canister, one crate slipped into this country to bring a day of horror like none we have ever known."[178]

One sentence in the speech stood out: "The British government has learned that Saddam Hussein recently sought significant quantities of uranium from Africa." It stood out first of all because the information came from the British, soon to be known as the purveyors of "dodgy dossiers."[179]

In his eagerness to be a loyal ally, and in his need to rally support for the war, Prime Minister Tony Blair had come up with actual evidence of toxic weapons that could pose a threat to other countries. In doing so, he was accused of corrupting the intelligence process with fraudulent data. The first dossier, in September 2002, included the dubious claim that Iraq could deploy its chemical and biological weapons in forty-five minutes. The second one, in February 2003, was entitled "Iraq: Its Infrastructure of Concealment, Deception, and Intimidation." It was found to be based in part on an article in *Jane's Intelligence Review* and in part on a graduate thesis by Ibrahim al-Marashi of the *Middle East Review*, which was downloaded from the Internet.[180]

These "dodgy dossiers" took on the drama of an Elizabethan tragedy when first exposed by Andrew Gilligan of the BBC, whose source was a British Deep Throat. The source told Gilligan that Blair's aides had doctored the dossier on Iraqi weapons to exaggerate the threat of Saddam and win backing for the war.

The source turned out to be fifty-nine-year-old Dr. David Kelly, Britain's most senior expert on Iraq's biological weapons programs, with years of experience in the field. As a top adviser to the Defence Ministry, he had worked closely on drawing up sections of the September dossier. He had the highest clearance for access to secret intelligence. He also knew quite a number of journalists, and spoke to two others besides Gilligan, who in his broadcasts and articles pointed the finger at Blair's spin doctor, the former tabloid journalist Alastair Campbell, in a government that has been described as "five parts spin to one part substance."

Campbell responded with what Clive Crook in the *National Journal* called "hysterical fury" and launched a campaign to discredit Gilligan and Kelly. When Kelly unwisely told the Ministry of Defence that he had talked to Gilligan, the ministry outed him by leaking clues about his identity to the press, then confirming it when asked, then denying the leaks.[181]

On July 15, Kelly was grilled by the members of the Foreign Affairs Select Committee. When I watched the hearing on C-SPAN, I was reminded of the Spanish Inquisition, as Kelly was bullied and badgered. It was clear from his evasive answers and melancholy mien that he was a broken man.

Three days later, Dr. Kelly was found dead near his home in Oxfordshire. He had taken painkillers, slashed his left wrist, and bled to death. With Dr. Kelly's corpse still warm in his grave, Mr. Blair's spokesman, Tom Kelly, made the outrageous comment that the scientist was a Walter Mitty figure who lived in a fantasy world, which further undercut confidence in the Prime Minister, since many saw Dr. Kelly as a patriotic Englishman who had exposed the flimflam tactics of the government. A judicial inquiry into the suicide was scheduled to open on August 11. Alastair Campbell was expected to resign once the inquiry was over. Tony Blair was expected to testify in public and his performance was viewed as vital to his political survival.

It also came out in the London press that, as part of the government's smear campaign against Dr. Kelly, Sir Kevin Tebbitt, a senior official at the Ministry of Defence, had told the BBC's diplomatic correspondent, James Robbins, that Dr. Kelly was "an eccentric" and that his department had deliberately outed him.[182]

Downing Street's messing about with the dossiers so embarrassed British intelligence analysts that Campbell apologized to the head of MI6, Sir Richard Dearlove. He promised that "far greater care" would be taken in the future in order not to discredit the Secret Intelligence Service.[183]

The fallout from the dodgy dossiers led to a crisis for Tony Blair and his Labour Party, which by August had dropped in the polls below the Conservatives. Blair was routinely called a liar in the British press and by prominent members of his own party. Two members of his cabinet had resigned. Robin Cook, who had quit as leader of the House of Commons, told the BBC that Blair had made a "monumental blunder" by sending British troops to Iraq. On June 17, in testimony before the House of Commons Foreign Affairs Committee, he called the February dossier "a shameful piece of work, a glorious and spectacular own goal" (in soccer, an own goal occurs when a player kicks the ball into his own team's net). Clare Short, who had quit as minister in charge of international development, said Blair had "duped" his colleagues and used fake intelligence to justify the war.[184]

The main exhibit in the fake intelligence department was the claim that Iraq had tried to buy significant quantities of uranium ore from an unnamed African country, which Blair made public in the September dossier. A headline in the London *Guardian* blared: AFRICAN GANGS OFFER ROUTE TO URANIUM.[185]

The forged documents supporting this claim had first turned up in West Africa at the end of 2001. They alleged that Iraq in the late 1990s had bought five hundred tons of "yellowcake" from the West African country of Niger, which had two mines that produced the ore. The Italian intelligence service (SISMI) obtained the documents and shared them with the British, who passed them on to Washington. Vice President Dick Cheney's office saw the report and asked the CIA about it. The CIA, looking for a veteran West Africa hand to check it out further, tapped the retired career Foreign Service officer Joseph C. Wilson IV. In a long career, Wilson had clocked fourteen years of service in Africa, with stints in Niger from 1976 to 1978, in Togo in 1978 and 1979, and in Congo-Brazzaville from 1986 to 1988. From 1988 to 1991 he served in Baghdad, and he was the last American diplomat to meet with Saddam Hussein before the launching of Operation Desert Storm. From 1992 to 1995 he was ambassador to Gabon.[186]

In late February 2002, Wilson arrived in Niamey, the capital of Niger, still a destination for camel caravans, and a river port whose banks are dotted with the rusted hulks of turn-of-the-century paddle wheelers. Winds off the Sahara blow up such clouds of dust there that the locals cover their faces with scarves, with slits for their eyes.[187]

The American ambassador, Barbro Owens-Kirkpatrick, told Wilson that she knew of the allegations and had discredited them in her reports to Washington. Wilson spent the following eight days drinking sweet mint tea with former and current government officials, including the President of Niger, and executives from the consortiums that run the two uranium mines, Somair and Cominak. Their production of yellowcake was earmarked for the countries that had an interest in the consortiums: France, Spain, Japan, Germany, and Nigeria.[188]

The government of Niger and the consortiums monitored one another. The government could not sell yellowcake to Iraq or anyone else without notifying the consortiums, which are strictly controlled by the International Atomic Energy Agency. Since the mines were also under close government oversight, any sale would require the consent of the President of Niger, its Prime Minister, and the minister of mines.[189]

Wilson did not have access to the forged documents, but Niger made a formal denial of the charges. In early March 2002, Wilson was back in Washington, briefing the CIA and the State Department African Affairs Bureau. In addition, Ambassador Owens-Kirkpatrick reported Wilson's findings to the State Department and the CIA wrote a report on his trip. The CIA also replied to the Cheney office request. But whether the reply was written or oral we do not yet know.[190]

Nonetheless, on September 24, 2002, prior to the vote on the war resolution, George Tenet and other CIA officials conducted a closed-door briefing before the Senate Intelligence Committee and mentioned the yellowcake allegations. Tenet said some questions had been raised regarding the evidence, but did not mention that an envoy had been sent to Niger and had concluded that the claims were false.[191] In December, the State Department published a fact sheet that mentioned the Niger case, and a month later the President, in his State of the Union address, cited the British dossier and repeated the charges. Around that time, Rumsfeld and Rice also mentioned the attempts to buy uranium. On February 20, 2003, the Voice of America broadcast a story saying that "U.S. officials tell VOA [that] Iraq and Niger signed an agreement in the summer of 2000 to resume shipments for an additional 500 tons of yellowcake," but there was no evidence the shipments took place. In March, Dick Cheney said on *Meet the Press* that Saddam Hussein was "trying once again to produce nuclear weapons." A senior intelligence official later said that the Wilson trip to Niger was a case of "extremely sloppy" handling.[192]

In the meantime, the International Atomic Energy Agency requested in December that the documents be turned over for examination by its Iraq Nuclear Verification Office. It was not until March 3, 2003, after a long delay, that Mohamed ElBaradei, the director general of the IAEA, told the Security Council that the documents, consisting of half a dozen letters and wires, were obvious forgeries. One letter dated October 10, 2000, was signed by Allele Habibou, Minister of Foreign Affairs; he had been out of office since 1989. Another letter, signed by the President of Niger, Tandja Mamadou, was found to be an obvious forgery (as Trotsky's signature was forged in the Sisson documents). The Niger dossier was a crude cut-and-paste job, with improper letterheads and signatures.[193]

Several commentators said the use of forged documents in a State of the Union address was a political scandal comparable to Watergate, which after all started as a banal bungled burglary on the Washington police blotter. Mr. Bush had blithely accepted this bum check from Niger and cashed it. It should, however, also be pointed out that his chief speechwriter, Mike Gerson, had prepared the address from a variety of sources, and that Stephen J. Hadley, the deputy national security adviser, took responsibility for the inclusion of the Niger sentence. Even so, as President Truman famously said, "The buck stops here."[194]

Prior to the war, the United Nations Security Council approved Resolution 1441, giving Saddam Hussein a "final opportunity" to disarm verifiably. In November 2002, the veteran U.N. inspector Hans Blix led a team into Iraq, and soon they were visiting sites in their white Jeeps. The Bush administration disparaged the work of the inspectors, particularly when Blix said "it will not take years, nor weeks, but months." By January 2003, U.S. troops were massing on Iraq's borders. On January 20, the French Foreign Minister, Dominique de Villepin, said that "nothing justifies envisaging military action."

On January 28, in his State of the Union address, Mr. Bush called the United Nations "an empty debating society."

On February 5, Secretary of State Colin Powell made a final attempt to bring the United Nations into the war. Prior to his presentation, he spent four days in a conference room at CIA headquarters in Langley, Virginia, with director George Tenet, his deputy John McLaughlin, and other officials, sifting through the intelligence. At one point, the irascible Powell flipped some pages in the air and exclaimed. "I'm not reading this. This is bullshit." He refused to say that the hijacker Mohammed Atta had met with an Iraqi official in Prague in 2001. The Czechs denied it, and evidence placed Atta in the United States at that time.[195]

What was most compelling about his presentation, however, was not what he left out, but what he included. Of course, he was trying to build a strong case so that the Security Council would vote to make the war a joint effort. So he spoke of liters of anthrax, tons of chemical weapons, and a possible nuclear program. He argued that the links between Saddam Hussein and Osama bin Laden presented an imminent threat to the world. He strongly suggested that the aluminum tubes were for nuclear bombs, even though the experts in the Department of Energy said they were for rocket launchers.[196]

"We know from sources," he said, "that a missile brigade outside Baghdad was dispersing rocket launchers and warheads containing biological warfare agents." CIA sources later said there was no evidence of this deployment or that any Iraqi units had been given the authority to deploy and use chemical weapons against advancing American troops.[197]

Powell showed the Security Council a photograph of a truck, which he said was a mobile factory for biological weapons. He said, "We have first-hand descriptions of biological weapons factories on wheels and on rails. . . . We know that Iraq has at least seven of these mobile biological agent factories . . . perhaps 18 trucks that we know of. . . . Just imagine trying to find 18 trucks among the thousands and thousands of trucks that travel the roads of Iraq every single day."[198]

Well, they did find a couple of trailers after the war, rusty from sitting in the rain. On May 28, a six-page paper entitled "Iraqi Mobile Biological Warfare Agent Production Plants" was declassified by the CIA. The paper said that two tractor-trailers similar to the one shown by Powell on February 5 had been found by Kurds in the northern city of Mosul in April and May. The material in the Powell presentation, said the paper, came from a chemical engineer who managed one of the mobile labs, and who had been provided by Ahmed Chalabi. This engineer said the program had been launched in the mid-1990s to evade U.N. inspections. The chemical agents were said to have been produced on Thursdays and Fridays, when the United Nations did not conduct inspections, in observance of the Muslim holy day.[199]

The self-contained system had a fermenter, water supply tanks, an air compressor, and a system for collecting exhaust gases. It was designed, said the CIA paper, to produce biological warfare agents in an unconcentrated liquid slurry.[200]

Other analysts expressed doubts, saying that a complete unit would consist of two or three trailers with equipment for growth media preparation, post-harvesting processing, mixing tanks, centrifuges, and spray dryers. The single trailer had no gear for steam sterilization, the lack of which would lead to contamination and worthless weapons. Nor did the single trailer have any equipment to remove the germ-laden liquid from the tank.[201]

Iraqi officials in Mosul, according to the CIA paper, said the trailers were for producing hydrogen for artillery weather balloons. This was a "plausible cover story," said the paper; "a gas collection system and the presence of caustic . . . are consistent with . . . hydrogen production." However, "compact, transportable hydrogen generation systems are commercially available, safe, and reliable." Why resort to trailers? On the other hand, no traces of biological warfare agents were found. The sludge inside the fermenter tested negative. The Iraqis may have decontaminated the vehicle. Each of the trailers found, said the paper, was one section of a three-trailer system needed to make weapons, but the other sections have not been found.[202] Thus, there was continued disagreement among intelligence analysts on the purpose of the trailers. A classified memo on June 2 from Mr. Powell's own shop, the State Department's Bureau of Research and Intelligence, said it was premature to conclude that the trailers were part of an Iraqi biological weapons program.[203]

It later came out that the DIA engineers who were examining the trailers in Iraq were furious that the May 28 CIA paper had been released before their work was completed. They saw the CIA paper as a rush to judgment while they were still doing their research. In a classified opinion reported by Douglas Jehl of the New York Times on August 9, a majority of the DIA engineers now disagreed that the trailers were intended to produce biological weapons. More likely, they said, they were an inefficient way of producing hydrogen for weather balloons used in artillery practice. The only source for the biological weapons allegation was a chemical engineer provided by Ahmed Chalabi. But a number of Iraqi officials questioned separately by American officers in Iraq gave a detailed description of the hydrogen-making capabilities, which the DIA engineers' own inspection confirmed, further discrediting Mr. Powell's February exposé.[204]

In his sessions at Langley, Mr. Powell, who was not an expert on chemical and biological weapons, was shown diagrams, charts, satellite photographs, and intercepts of conversations among Iraqi officials. His presentation to the Security Council ranked with the Cincinnati speech and the State of the Union address in the annals of distortion. He may be remembered as the most gullible Secretary of State since William Henry Seward failed to prevent the French invasion of Mexico. So extravagant was the administration's use of intelligence that disaffected analysts called it "RUMINT," intelligence based on rumors.

Mr. Powell's presentation failed to convince the Security Council that it should take part in the war. A "coalition" was quickly formed. The war itself was a swift and intimidating display of American might. The disparity in firepower made it seem more like war games with live ammunition that an actual war. Resistance quickly collapsed and the vaunted Iraqi Republican Guard vanished into the landscape, perhaps in some cases as the result of a covert defection program initiated by the CIA and U.S. military long before the war. In late 2002, Iraqi intermediaries persuaded Iraqi commanders to disband their units when hostilities broke out. Apparently a number of them did, which helps to explain the surprising absence of resistance, particularly in the Red Zone around Baghdad.[205]

But perhaps, in the war after the war, some of these same troops, who had been sent home with their weapons, returned to help launch the intifada against the occupation forces, who were easier to pick off in an urban setting, carrying out their occupation duties singly or in small groups, than they had been during "Shock and Awe." Even as the President stood on the deck of an aircraft carrier and proclaimed victory under a MISSION ACCOMPLISHED banner, the insurgency was breaking out and the body count was mounting. The war was a walkover, but the postwar fighting was drawn out, demoralizing, and politically perilous for the administration. Iraq was a classic occupation scenario, with one or more resistance movements relying on a frequently sympathetic population to plague and pester a deeply resented occupation army, which was seen as an invader rather than a savior. Young American soldiers, who thought they would be welcomed for having liberated the Iraqi people from a reviled dictator, found themselves in a hostile environment. Accidental alliances among former opponents, such as Saddam loyalists and Shiites, seemed now to be forming against the common enemy, under the banner GET OUT OF OUR COUNTRY. The American-trained police and army were hunted down as collaborators.

In the meantime, the Army's 75th Exploitation Task Force, which had led the search for illegal weapons, found nothing. In mid-June it was replaced by an Iraq Survey Group with a staff of fourteen hundred, including intelligence experts and dozens of former United Nations inspectors who had worked in Iraq. Major General Keith W. Dayton, in charge of the survey group, had high hopes that his experienced team would find stockpiles that would justify a preemptive war.[206]

Hans Blix, who retired on June 30, saw a headline in the *New York Times* on May 4 that said: "Bush Says It Will Take Time to Find Iraq's Banned Arms." The President, Blix reflected, had taken those words right out of his mouth.[207]

Joseph Wilson, the special envoy to Niamey, later observed:

If my information . . . was ignored because it did not fit certain preconceptions about Iraq, then a legitimate argument can be made that we went to war under false pretenses. . . .

. . . questioning the selective use of intelligence to justify the war in Iraq is neither idle sniping nor "revisionist history," as Mr. Bush has suggested. The act of war is the last option of a democracy, taken when there is a grave threat to our national security. More than 200 American soldiers have lost their lives in Iraq already. We have a duty to ensure that their sacrifice came for the right reasons.[208]

Wilson's op-ed piece in the *New York Times* on July 6 led to the first tear in the administration's curtain of denial. On July 7, the White House admitted that the President had used bogus intelligence in his State of the Union address. The White House admission created a split between Mr. Bush and the embattled Tony Blair, who insisted before Parliament on July 7 that he stood by his assessment, distancing himself from the President to save his political scalp.[209]

The British were asking themselves, "Why did we go to war? Where were the promised troves of anthrax and nerve gas?" Public support for the war fell from 64 percent in April to 45 percent in July. Sir Rodric Braithwaite, former chairman of the Joint Intelligence Committee, which reports directly to the Prime Minister, said that if no weapons were found it would "leave the government looking very tattered." At its best, he said, intelligence is "patchily reliable" and must be handled with care, to avoid accusations of "deliberate war-mongering."[210]

At home, Congress, which had voted the war resolution in the euphoria of fear, was becoming restive. The smell of doubt was in the air. With every new casualty, there was a mounting sense that the war had been foisted upon the American people with faulty data. A pattern of deceit was emerging like a skeleton on an X-ray, and it threatened to bring dishonor on the administration. When McCarthyite methods are used, the integrity of government is compromised and monumental mistakes are made.

As I finish this book in mid-August for publication in the fall, the president has released a twenty-four-page report on the first hundred days of the war, pointing to progress in water supplies, electricity, and schools.[211] After destroying Iraq's infrastructure, should we congratulate ourselves on almost bringing it back to prewar levels?

In any case, the situation on the ground was quite different. Just as the President's report was released, riots erupted in Basra, where mile-long lines snaked around gas stations and men waited twenty-four hours for gas in 120-degree heat. In their fury, they torched vehicles, threw rocks, and killed a Gurka security guard.[212]

Such was the reality: gas shortages in a country with the world's second-largest oil reserves, rolling blackouts, destroyed electric grids, sabotaged pipelines, and power failures at hospitals, while smugglers took fuel out of the country in tanker trucks and barges. An explosive device under a buried fuel pipe sets the desert aflame. An American civilian contractor is killed when his truck drives over an anti-tank mine. Iraq's Governing Council is mocked in Iraqi papers as an American puppet, while Arab satellite stations, watched by millions of Iraqis, show masked men who say their intention is to create a "graveyard for all the villain invaders."[213]

Far from tapering off, Iraqi resistance has escalated, from small-arms attacks to the use of rocket-propelled grenades, sixty-millimeter mortars, land mines, and car bombs detonated by remote control. The gunmen come from many sectors of Iraqi society—displaced Baathists, Saddam Fedayeen, Sunnis, Shiites, Wahhabis, Ansar al-Islam (Islamic Partisans), and the Badr Brigade, as well as new groups such as the Army of Mohammed.[214]

Enemies multiply in a population that has transferred its hatred from Saddam to the occupier, as edgy U.S. soldiers, under dozens of hit-and-run attacks daily, become trigger-happy. At the Baghdad morgue, more than three thousand civilians killed by gunshot wounds have been processed since May, with an estimated five hundred the victims of Coalition forces. Noble intentions, such as bringing democracy to Iraq, are buried under the incessant strife. Iraqis accumulate grievances. The hard core of resisters, intent on killing Americans, have no shortage of reasons, whether tribal or religious, or for personal revenge—homes destroyed, relatives killed, wives and mothers rudely searched. They also target Iraqi civilians who are helping Americans, such as translators, a dozen of whom were killed in July and August, according to the contractor that hired them, Titan Corporation. The message was clear: work for the Americans, even talk to them, and your name will appear on a list of collaborators marked for assassination.[215]

By mid-August, hundreds of Islamic militants were said to have slipped across porous borders from Syria and Iran into Iraq to carry out terrorist operations. Forged Italian passports have been found on captured terrorists. These fanatical Muslims from a dozen countries constitute a foreign legion whose aim is to kill Americans. Where else could they be killed so easily, with so many of them there? They also struck soft targets such as foreign embassies. Now the link between Saddam Hussein and Islamic radicals, fallaciously trumpeted by the administration before the war, became a reality. Every day, American soldiers were killed or wounded, making the President's "Bring 'em on" remark inanely callous. A bounty system was in place on both sides—$15 million for each of Saddam's sons, $5,000 for an American.

The invasion of Iraq has taken on some of the aspects of a colonial war. Out of this fractured third-world society, with its feudal tyranny, its endemic religious rivalries, its restive Kurdish minority, and its corrupt culture of favortism and the baksheesh, an incipient nationalism has arisen against the occupier. The Iraqis want to get rid of the Americans as they got rid of the British after 1920. We need Kipling, the bard of imperialism, to remind us that the invasion of Iraq may be remembered as an American tragedy—our first preemptive war, based on a fabricated threat, sending hundreds of Americans needlessly to their deaths. After Vietnam, to quote Kipling, "the burnt Fool's bandaged finger goes wabbling back to the Fire," and once again we have taken up "the White Man's burden" among "Your new-caught sullen peoples, Half devil and half child," with daily losses in the " 'Thin red line of 'eroes' when the drums begin to roll." Until the day comes when "The Captains and the Kings depart,—Still stands thine ancient sacrifice."

SOURCES

I: THE RUSSIAN REVOLUTION THROUGH AMERICAN EYES

1. John Keegan, *The First World War*, New York, 1999.
2. Ibid.
3. William L. Shirer, *The Collapse of the Third Republic*, New York, 1969.
4. *Source Records of the Great War*, editor-in-chief, Charles F. Horne, Chapter 11, "Dunajec: The Breaking of the Russian Front," New York, 1923.
5. Z. A. B. Zeman, *The Merchant of Revolution*, London, 1965.
6. Z. A. B. Zeman, *Germany and the Revolution in Russia*, London, 1958.
7. Ibid.
8. Zeman, *Merchant of Revolution*.
9. Zeman, *Germany and the Revolution*.
10. Ibid.
11. Ibid.
12. Ibid.
13. Ibid.
14. Huntington testimony, Vol. 3, Senate Judiciary Subcommittee on Brewing and Liquor Interests and German and Russian Bolshevik Propaganda, Feb. 1919. Hereinafter Overman Committee.
15. "Banality in the Face of Doom: Notes from the Czar's Last Days," *New York Times*, July 12, 1998.
16. Alexander Kerensky, *Russia and History's Turning Point*, New York, 1965.
17. D. F. Fleming, *The Cold War and Its Origins, 1917–1960*, Vol. 1, New York, 1961.
18. Kerensky, *Russia and History's Turning Point*.
19. David R. Francis papers, State Historical Society, Madison, Wisconsin; David R. Francis, *Russia from the American Embassy*, New York, 1921.
20. Francis, *Russia from the American Embassy*.
21. Francis papers.
22. David S. Foglesong, *America's Secret War Against Bolshevism: U.S. Intervention in the Russian Civil War, 1917–1920*, Chapel Hill, 1995. This is a groundbreaking book based on a great deal of primary research.
23. Ibid.
24. Zeman, *Germany and the Revolution*.
25. Ibid.
26. Michael Pearson, *The Sealed Train*, New York, 1975.
27. Zeman, *Germany and the Revolution*.

28. Huntington testimony, Overman Committee.
29. Williams testimony, Overman Committee.
30. Leonard testimony, Overman Committee.
31. *Source Records of the Great War.*
32. Kerensky, *Russia and History's Turning Point.*
33. Foglesong, *America's Secret War.*
34. Neil V. Salzman, *Reform and Revolution: The Life and Times of Raymond Robins,* Kent State, 1991.
35. Ibid.
36. Ibid.
37. George Creel, *Rebel at Large,* New York, 1947.
38. Salzman, *Reform and Revolution.*
39. Ibid.
40. Raymond Robins papers, State Historical Society, Madison, Wisconsin.
41. Salzman, *Reform and Revolution.*
42. Ibid.
43. Robins papers.
44. Ibid.
45. Ibid.
46. Salzman, *Reform and Revolution.*
47. Zeman, *Germany and the Revolution.*
48. Robins papers.
49. Salzman, *Reform and Revolution.*
50. John Reed, *Ten Days That Shook the World,* New York, 1935.
51. Ibid.
52. Robins papers.
53. Smith testimony, Overman Committee.
54. Saylor testimony, Overman Committee.
55. Keddie testimony, Overman Committee.
56. Williams testimony, Overman Committee.
57. Robins papers.
58. Hatzel testimony, Overman Committee.
59. Robins papers.
60. Salzman, *Reform and Revolution.*
61. Francis papers.
62. Salzman, *Reform and Revolution.*
63. Martin Gilbert, *Winston S. Churchill,* Vol. 4, Boston, 1975.
64. Salzman, *Reform and Revolution.*
65. Foglesong, *America's Secret War.*
66. Francis, *Russia from the American Embassy.*
67. Simons testimony, Overman Committee.
68. Ibid.
69. Foglesong, *America's Secret War.*
70. Ibid.
71. Ibid.; see also R. J. Maddox, *The Unknown War with Russia,* San Rafael, Calif., 1977.
72. Foglesong, *America's Secret War.*
73. Ibid.
74. Francis papers.

75. Foglesong, *America's Secret War.*
76. Ibid.
77. Ibid.
78. Ibid.
79. Edgar Sisson, *One Hundred Red Days*, New Haven, 1931.

II: THE FIRST AMERICAN ATTEMPT AT REGIME CHANGE

1. Edgar Sisson, *One Hundred Red Days*, New Haven, 1931.
2. Ibid.
3. Ibid.
4. Ibid.
5. Bertram D. Wolfe, *An Ideology in Power,* New York, 1969.
6. Huntington testimony, Overman Committee.
7. Sisson, *One Hundred Red Days.*
8. George Kennan, "The Sisson Documents," *Journal of Modern History,* Vol. 28, No. 2, June 1956.
9. Sisson, *One Hundred Red Days.*
10. Ibid.
11. Kennan, *Journal of Modern History.*
12. Francis papers.
13. David S. Foglesong, *America's Secret War Against Bolshevism: U.S. Intervention in the Russian Civil War, 1917–1920,* Chapel Hill, 1995.
14. Neil V. Salzman, *Reform and Revolution: The Life and Times of Raymond Robins,* Kent State, 1991.
15. Robins papers.
16. Salzman, *Reform and Revolution.*
17. Ibid.
18. Ibid.
19. Ibid.
20. George F. Kennan, *Soviet-American Relations, 1917–1920,* Vol. 1, *Russia Leaves the War,* Princeton, 1956; Vol. 2, *The Decision to Intervene,* Princeton, 1958.
21. Kennan, *The Decision to Intervene.*
22. Foglesong, *America's Secret War.*
23. Ibid.
24. Ibid.
25. Kennan, *The Decision to Intervene.*
26. J. A. White, *The Siberian Intervention,* Princeton, 1950; R. E. Dupuy, *Perish by the Sword,* Harrisburg, Pa., 1939; Betty M. Unterberger, *America's Siberian Intervention,* New York, 1956; and R. J. Maddox, *The Unknown War with Russia,* San Rafael, Calif., 1977.
27. Dupuy, *Perish by the Sword.*
28. White, *Siberian Intervention.*
29. Foglesong, *America's Secret War.*
30. Ibid.
31. Ibid.
32. Dennis Gordon, *Quartered in Hell,* Missoula, Mont., 1982; E. M. Halliday, *The Ignorant Armies,* New York, 1960.
33. Gordon, *Quartered in Hell.*
34. Ibid.

35. William S. Graves, *America's Siberian Adventure*, New York, 1971.
36. Ibid.
37. Ibid.
38. Ibid.
39. James R. Mock and Cedric Larson, *Words That Won the War*, Princeton, 1939.
40. Kennan, "The Sisson Documents," *Journal of Modern History*.
41. Ibid.
42. Ibid.
43. Sisson did not have access to the German Foreign Office documents quoted earlier in this chapter, which did not become available until they were captured by the Allies in 1945. They were published in 1958 by Z. A. B. Zeman in *Germany and the Revolution in Russia* (London), who mentioned in passing "the forged documents assembled by Edgar Sisson, a gullible American journalist in Russia: An incident which marred relations between Washington and the Soviets in their formative state."
44. Gordon, *Quartered in Hell*.
45. Foglesong, *America's Secret War*.
46. Gordon, *Quartered in Hell*.
47. Ibid.
48. Ibid.
49. Foglesong, *America's Secret War*.
50. Kennan, *The Decision to Intervene*.
51. Martin Gilbert, *Winston S. Churchill*, Vol. 4, Boston, 1975.
52. Gordon, *Quartered in Hell*.
53. Ibid.
54. Ibid.
55. Gilbert, *Winston S. Churchill*.
56. Graves, *America's Siberian Adventure*.
57. Gilbert, *Winston S. Churchill*.
58. Foglesong, *America's Secret War*.
59. Graves, *America's Siberian Adventure*.
60. Maddox, *Unknown War with Russia*; Kennan, *The Decision to Intervene*.
61. Graves, *America's Siberian Adventure*.
62. John Milton Cooper, *Breaking the Heart of the World: Woodrow Wilson and the Fight for the League of Nations*, New York, 2001.
63. Peter G. Filene, *Americans and the Soviet Experiment, 1917–1933*, Cambridge, Mass., 1967.
64. Ibid.
65. Phyllis Lee Levin, *Edith and Woodrow*, New York, 2001.
66. Cooper, *Breaking the Heart of the World*.
67. Graves, *America's Siberian Adventure*.
68. Ibid.; Kennan, *The Decision to Intervene*.
69. Maddox, *Unknown War with Russia*.

III: RED SCARE AND SCARY REDS

1. David Joseph Williams, "Without Understanding: The FBI and Political Surveillance, 1909–1941," Ph.D. thesis, University of New Hampshire, 1981.
2. Ibid.
3. Ibid.
4. Ibid.

5. Paul Avrich, *Sacco and Vanzetti: The Anarchist Background,* Princeton, 1991.

6. Robert K. Murray, *Red Scare,* New York, 1964.

7. A. Wesley Johns, *The Man Who Shot McKinley,* Cranbury, N.J., 1970.

8. Avrich, *Sacco and Vanzetti.*

9. Ibid.

10. Ibid.

11. Ibid.

12. Ibid.

13. Ibid.

14. Ibid.

15. Ibid.

16. Richard Gid Powers, *Secrecy and Power: The Life of J. Edgar Hoover,* New York, 1987.

17. Ibid.

18. William Lingaman, *1919: The Year Our World Began,* New York, 1987.

19. Murray, *Red Scare.*

20. Ibid.

21. David S. Foglesong, *America's Secret War Against Bolshevism: U.S. Intervention in the Russian Civil War, 1917–1920,* Chapel Hill, 1995.

22. Ibid.

23. Ibid.

24. Ibid.

25. Ibid.

26. Ibid.

27. Williams, "Without Understanding"; Murray, *Red Scare.*

28. Philip Louis Cantelon, "In Defense of America: Congressional Investigations of Communism in the United States, 1919–1935," Ph.D. thesis, Indiana University, 1971.

29. Ibid.

30. Overman committee.

31. Ibid.

32. Ibid.

33. Ibid.

34. Ibid.

35. Ibid.

36. Ibid.

37. Avrich, *Sacco and Vanzetti.*

38. Ibid.

39. Stanley Coben, *A. Mitchell Palmer: Politician,* New York, 1963.

40. Avrich, *Sacco and Vanzetti.*

41. Ibid.

42. New York State Legislature, Joint Legislative Committee to Investigate Seditious Activities, Hearings and Report, Albany, 1920. Hereinafter Lusk Committee.

43. Ibid.

44. Coben, *A. Mitchell Palmer.*

45. Ibid.

46. Ibid.

47. Ibid.

48. Max Lowenthal, *The Federal Bureau of Investigation,* New York, 1950.

49. Ibid.

50. Coben, *A. Mitchell Palmer.*
51. Powers, *Secrecy and Power.*
52. Ibid.
53. Ibid.
54. Lowenthal, *Federal Bureau of Investigation.*
55. Ibid.
56. Ibid.; Powers, *Secrecy and Power.*
57. Powers, *Secrecy and Power.*
58. Williams, "Without Understanding."
59. Benjamin Gitlow, *The Whole of Their Lives,* New York, 1948.
60. Cantelon, "In Defense of America."
61. Ibid.
62. Lowenthal, *Federal Bureau of Investigation.*
63. Cantelon, "In Defense of America."
64. Coben, *A. Mitchell Palmer.*
65. Williams, "Without Understanding."
66. Ibid.
67. Lowenthal, *Federal Bureau of Investigation.*
68. Louis F. Post, *Deportation Delirium,* New York, 1923.
69. Lowenthal, *Federal Bureau of Investigation.*
70. Post, *Deportation Delirium.*
71. Coben, *A. Mitchell Palmer.*
72. Lowenthal, *Federal Bureau of Investigation.*
73. Ibid.
74. Ibid.
75. Ibid.
76. Ibid.
77. Coben, *A. Mitchell Palmer.*
78. Lowenthal, *Federal Bureau of Investigation.*
79. Senate Committee on the Judiciary, Subcommittee on Charges of Illegal Practices of the Department of Justice, hearings January 19–March 3, 1921. Hereinafter Judiciary Committee.
80. Ibid.
81. Ibid.
82. Ibid.
83. Ibid.
84. Ibid.
85. Ibid.
86. Ibid.
87. Ibid.
88. Powers, *Secrecy and Power.*
89. Ibid.
90. Lovestone papers, Communist Party file, Hoover Institution for War, Revolution, and Peace.
91. Ibid.
92. C. Panunzio, *Immigration Crossroads,* New York, 1927.

IV: THE POLITICS OF FAMINE

1. George H. Nash, *The Life of Herbert Hoover: The Engineer, 1874–1914,* New York, 1983.

2. Herbert Hoover, *Memoirs*, Vol. 1, New York, 1952.
3. Nash, *Life of Herbert Hoover.*
4. Hoover, *Memoirs.*
5. Ibid.
6. George H. Nash, *The Life of Herbert Hoover: The Humanitarian, 1914–1917*, New York, 1990.
7. Hoover, *Memoirs.*
8. Herbert Hoover, *The Ordeal of Woodrow Wilson*, New York, 1958.
9. Richard Norton Smith, *An Uncommon Man*, New York, 1984.
10. David S. Foglesong, *America's Secret War Against Bolshevism: U.S. Intervention in the Russian Civil War, 1917–1920*, Chapel Hill, 1995.
11. Ibid.
12. Ibid.
13. Hoover, *Ordeal of Woodrow Wilson.*
14. Foglesong, *America's Secret War.*
15. Ibid.
16. Hoover, *Memoirs.*
17. Ibid.
18. Ibid.
19. Foglesong, *America's Secret War.*
20. Ibid.
21. Ibid.
22. Ibid.
23. Hoover, *Memoirs.*
24. Foglesong, *America's Secret War.*
25. W. Bruce Lincoln, *Red Victory*, New York, 1989.
26. Foglesong, *America's Secret War.*
27. Hoover, *Memoirs.*
28. Ibid.
29. Ibid.
30. Foglesong, *America's Secret War.*
31. Ibid.
32. Ibid.
33. Ibid.
34. Ibid.
35. Richard Luckett, *The White Generals*, New York, 1971.
36. Ibid.
37. Ibid.
38. Ibid.
39. Hoover, *Memoirs.*
40. H. H. Fisher, *The Famine in Soviet Russia*, New York, 1927.
41. Diane P. Koenker and Ronald D. Bachman, eds., *Revelations from the Russian Archives*, Washington, 1997.
42. Stephane Courtois, *The Black Book of Communism*, Cambridge, Mass., 1999.
43. Leonard Shapiro, *The Communist Party of the Soviet Union*, New York, 1959.
44. Benjamin M. Weissman, *Herbert Hoover and Famine Relief to Soviet Russia, 1921–1923*, Stanford, 1974.
45. Ibid.
46. Ibid.
47. Ibid.

48. Ibid.
49. Fisher, *Famine in Soviet Russia.*
50. Weissman, *Herbert Hoover and Famine Relief.*
51. Fisher, *Famine in Soviet Russia.*
52. Weissman, *Herbert Hoover and Famine Relief.*
53. Fisher, *Famine in Soviet Russia.*
54. Weissman, *Herbert Hoover and Famine Relief.*
55. *Revelations from the Russian Archives.*
56. Weissman, *Herbert Hoover and Famine Relief.*
57. Ibid.
58. Fisher, *Famine in Soviet Russia.*
59. Weissman, *Herbert Hoover and Famine Relief.*
60. Fisher, *Famine in Soviet Russia.*
61. Courtois, *Black Book of Communism.*
62. Fisher, *Famine in Soviet Russia.*
63. *Revelations from the Russian Archives.*
64. Weissman, *Herbert Hoover and Famine Relief.*
65. Ibid.
66. Ibid.
67. Ibid.
68. Ibid.

V: THE ROAD TO RECOGNITION

1. David Joseph Williams, "Without Understanding: The FBI and Political Surveillance, 1908–1941," Ph.D. thesis, University of New Hampshire, 1981.
2. William R. Hunt, *Front-Page Detective,* Bowling Green, 1990.
3. Richard Gid Powers, *Secrecy and Power,* New York, 1987.
4. Williams, "Without Understanding."
5. Powers, *Secrecy and Power.*
6. Max Lowenthal, *The Federal Bureau of Investigation,* New York, 1950.
7. Ibid.
8. Ibid.
9. Ibid.
10. Ibid.
11. Ibid.
12. Ibid.
13. Ibid.
14. Ibid.
15. House Un-American Activities Committee, hearings, Aug. 13, 1938.
16. Ibid.
17. James L. Giglio, *Harry M. Daugherty and the Politics of Expediency,* Kent State, 1978.
18. A. T. Mason, *Harlan Fiske Stone: Pillar of Law,* New York, 1956.
19. Ibid.
20. Powers, *Secrecy and Power.*
21. Lowenthal, *Federal Bureau of Investigation.*
22. Williams, "Without Understanding."
23. Ibid.
24. Harvey Klehr, John Earl Haynes, and Kyrill M. Anderson, *The Soviet World of American Communism,* New Haven, 1998.

25. Ibid.

26. House Un-American Activities Committee, hearings, May 21, 1940.

27. Ibid.

28. Ibid.

29. Ibid.

30. Ibid.

31. House Un-American Activities Committee, hearings regarding Communist espionage, Nov. 8, Dec. 2, 1949; Mar. 1, 1950.

32. House Un-American Activities Committee, hearings, Aug. 18, 1938.

33. Ibid.

34. Ibid.

35. Edward P. Johanningsmeier, *Forging American Communism: The Life of William Z. Foster*, Princeton, 1994.

36. House Un-American Activities Committee, hearings, Nov. 1938.

37. Ibid.

38. Ibid.

39. Ibid.

40. Ibid.

41. Ibid.

42. National Civic Federation papers, New York Public Library.

43. Neil V. Salzman, *Reform and Revolution*, Kent State, 1991.

44. Ibid.

45. Ibid.; Powers, *Secrecy and Power.*

46. Joseph P. Lash, *Eleanor and Franklin*, New York, 1971.

47. National Civic Federation papers.

48. Ibid.

49. Ibid.

50. Ibid.

51. Marguerite Green, *The National Civic Federation and the American Labor Movement*, Washington, 1956.

52. Williams, "Without Understanding."

53. Hamilton Fish, *Memoir of an American Patriot*, Washington, 1991.

54. Grover Whalen, *Mr. New York*, New York, 1955.

55. Ibid.

56. Ibid.

57. Cantelon, "In Defense of America," Ph.D. thesis, Indiana University, 1971.

58. Ibid.

59. John L. Spivak, *A Man in His Time*, New York, 1940.

60. Ibid.

61. Ibid.

62. Philip Louis Cantelon, "In Defense of America."

63. Ibid.

64. Ibid.

65. Ibid.

66. Ibid.

67. Special House Committee to Investigate Communist Activities in the United States. Hereinafter Fish Committee, July 22, 1938.

68. Fish Committee, July 15, 1938.

69. Fish Committee, Nov. 25, 1938.

70. Ibid.
71. Ibid.
72. Ibid.
73. Herbert Romerstein and Stanislas Levchenko, *The KGB Against the Main Enemy,* Lexington, Mass., 1989.
74. Cantelon, "In Defense of America."
75. Ibid.
76. Ibid.
77. Salzman, *Reform and Revolution.*
78. Ibid.
79. Ibid.
80. Ibid.
81. Ibid.
82. Ibid.
83. Ted Morgan, *FDR: A Biography,* New York, 1985.
84. Ibid.
85. Elliot A. Rosen, *Hoover, Roosevelt, and the Brain Trust,* New York, 1977.
86. Ibid.
87. Salzman, *Reform and Revolution.*
88. Stephane Courtois, *The Black Book of Communism,* Cambridge, Mass., 1999.
89. Ibid.
90. Diane P. Koenker and Ronald D. Bachman, eds., *Revelations from the Russian Archives,* Washington, 1997.
91. Courtois, *Black Book of Communism.*
92. *Revelations from the Russian Archives.*
93. Salzman, *Reform and Revolution.*
94. Morgenthau diaries, 1933, Roosevelt Library, Hyde Park, New York.
95. Ibid.
96. Ibid.
97. Orville H. Bullitt, *For the President, Personal and Secret,* Boston, 1972.
98. Ibid.
99. Ibid.
100. Morgenthau diaries, 1933.
101. Bullitt, *For the President.*
102. Cordell Hull, *Memoirs,* New York, 1948.
103. Morgan, *FDR.*
104. Bullitt, *For the President.*
105. Salzman, *Reform and Revolution.*
106. Ibid.
107. Bullitt, *For the President.*
108. Ibid.
109. Morgan, *FDR.*
110. Peter G. Filene, *Americans and the Soviet Experiment, 1917–1933,* Cambridge, Mass., 1967.
111. House Un-American Activities Committee, hearings, Sep. 19, 1939.
112. Raymond Robins papers, State Historical Society, Madison, Wisconsin.
113. Hull, *Memoirs.*
114. Bullitt, *For the President.*
115. HUAC, hearings, Sep. 19, 1939.

VI: WELCOME SOVIET SPIES!

1. Select Committee to Study Government Operations with Respect to Intelligence Activities, 1975, FBI Exhibits.
2. Richard Gid Powers, *Secrecy and Power*, New York, 1987.
3. Ibid.
4. Ted Morgan, *FDR: A Biography*, New York, 1985.
5. David Joseph Williams, "Without Understanding," Ph.D. thesis, University of New Hampshire, 1981.
6. Ibid.
7. Max Lowenthal, *The Federal Bureau of Investigation*, New York, 1950.
8. Powers, *Secrecy and Power.*
9. Peter H. Irons, *The New Deal Lawyers*, Princeton, 1982.
10. Allen Weinstein, *The Haunted Wood*, New York, 1999.
11. James G. Ryan, *Earl Browder*, Tuscaloosa, 1997.
12. Irwin F. Gellman, *Secret Affairs: Franklin Roosevelt, Cordell Hull, and Sumner Welles*, Baltimore, 1995.
13. Ibid.
14. Weinstein, *Haunted Wood.*
15. Subcommittee to Investigate the Administration of the Internal Security Act, Senate Committee on the Judiciary, Scope of Soviet Activity in the United States, Part 87, Apr. 26, 1957.
16. Weinstein, *Haunted Wood.*
17. Dorothy Waring, *American Defender*, New York, 1935.
18. Weinstein, *Haunted Wood.*
19. Earl Latham, *The Communist Conspiracy in Washington*, Cambridge, Mass., 1966.
20. Weinstein, *Haunted Wood.*
21. Ibid.
22. Ibid.
23. Christopher Andrew, *The Sword and the Shield*, New York, 1999.
24. Weinstein, *Haunted Wood.*
25. Ibid.
26. Williams, "Without Understanding."
27. Ibid.
28. Ibid.
29. Whittaker Chambers, *Witness*, New York, 1952.
30. Ibid.
31. Chambers testimony, HUAC executive session, Dec. 28, 1948.
32. Weinstein, *Haunted Wood.*
33. Ibid.
34. Ibid.
35. Chambers, *Witness.*
36. Ibid.
37. Ibid.
38. Irons, *New Deal Lawyers.*
39. Ibid.
40. Alger Hiss, *Recollections of a Life*, New York, 1988.
41. Chambers, *Witness.*
42. Ibid.
43. Ibid.

44. Hope Hale Davis, *Great Days Coming*, South Royalton, Vt., 1994.
45. Ibid.
46. Chambers, *Witness*.
47. Ibid.
48. Ibid.
49. Ibid.
50. Ibid.
51. Ibid.
52. Dorothy Gallagher, *All the Right Enemies*, New Brunswick, N.J., 1988.
53. Chambers, *Witness*.
54. Whittaker Chambers, "The Faking of Americans," in Herbert Solow papers, Hoover Institution on War, Revolution, and Peace.
55. Chambers, *Witness*.
56. Sam Tanenhaus, *Whittaker Chambers*, New York, 1997.
57. Weinstein, *Haunted Wood*.
58. Flora Lewis, *Red Pawn*, New York, 1965.
59. Weinstein, *Haunted Wood*.
60. Ibid.
61. Ibid.
62. Ibid.
63. Chambers, *Witness*.
64. Ibid.
65. Adolf A. Berle, *Navigating the Rapids*, New York, 1973.
66. Chambers, *Witness*.
67. Weinstein, *Haunted Wood*.
68. Ibid.
69. Ibid.
70. Tanenhaus, *Whittaker Chambers*.
71. Newspaper accounts.

VII: THE PINK DECADE

1. Harvey Klehr and John Earl Haynes, *The American Communist Movement*, New York, 1992.
2. Peter G. Filene, *Americans and the Soviet Experiment, 1917–1933*, Cambridge, Mass., 1967.
3. Robert E. Sherwood, *Roosevelt and Hopkins*, New York, 1948.
4. HUAC, Appendix, Part 9, Communist Front Organizations, 1944.
5. Frankwood E. Williams, *Russia, Youth, and the Present Day World*, New York, 1934.
6. D. F. Fleming, *The Cold War and Its Origins, 1917–1960*, Vol. 1, New York, 1961.
7. Eugene Lyons, *The Red Decade*, New York, 1941.
8. HUAC Investigation of Communist Activities in the San Francisco Area, Dec. 1, 1953.
9. Guenter Lewy, *The Cause That Failed*, New York, 1990.
10. HUAC, Appendix, Part 9, 1944.
11. Special House Committee for the Investigation of Un-American Activities. Hereinafter Dies Committee, hearings, Sep. 29, 1939.
12. Joseph P. Lash, *Dealers and Dreamers*, New York, 1988.
13. Ibid.

14. Ibid.
15. HUAC, Appendix, Part 9, 1944.
16. Ibid.
17. Ibid.
18. Lewy, *Cause That Failed.*
19. Ibid.
20. Ibid.
21. Ibid.
22. Bella Dodd, *School of Darkness*, New York, 1954.
23. HUAC, Hearings on Communist Methods of Infiltration (Education), Feb. 1953.
24. HUAC hearings on Education.
25. Ibid.
26. Ibid.
27. Harvey A. Levenstein, *Communism, Anti-Communism, and the CIO*, Westport, Conn., 1981.
28. Henry Kraus, *Heroes of Unwritten Story*, Urbana, Ill., 1993.
29. Gus Tyler, *Look for the Union Label*, Armonk, N.Y., 1995.
30. Levenstein, *Communism, Anti-Communism, and the CIO.*
31. Russian Center for Recent History, Moscow, Comintern files, 1938.
32. Paul H. Douglas, *In the Fullness of Time*, New York, 1971.
33. Dies Committee hearings, Aug. 17, 1938.
34. Ibid.
35. Ronald Radosh, Mary R. Habeck, and Grigory Sevostianov, eds., *Spain Betrayed*, New Haven, 2001.
36. Ibid.
37. Ibid.
38. Ibid.
39. Ibid.
40. Ibid.
41. Dies Committee hearings, Aug. 17, 1938.
42. Dies Committee hearings, Oct. 25, 1939.
43. Ibid.
44. Radosh et al., *Spain Betrayed.*
45. Ibid.
46. Ibid.
47. Ibid.
48. Dies Committee hearings, Mar. 25, 1940.
49. Ibid.
50. Harvey Klehr, John Earl Haynes, and Fridrikh Firsov, *The Secret World of American Communism*, New York, 1995.
51. Ibid.
52. Dies Committee hearings, Mar. 25, 1940.
53. Klehr et al., *Secret World of American Communism.*
54. Radosh et al., *Spain Betrayed.*
55. Ibid.

VIII: THE DIES COMMITTEE

1. Dennis Kay McDaniel, "Martin Dies of Un-American Activities: Life and Times," Ph.D. thesis, University of Houston, 1988.

2. Ibid.
3. Ibid.
4. Ibid.
5. Ibid.
6. Ibid.
7. Ted Morgan, *FDR: A Biography*, New York, 1985.
8. McDaniel, "Martin Dies."
9. Ibid.
10. Ibid.
11. Ibid.
12. Ibid.
13. Ibid.
14. Morgan, *FDR*.
15. McDaniel, "Martin Dies."
16. Ibid.
17. Ibid.
18. Ibid.
19. Jerrold S. Auerbach, *Labor and Liberty: The La Follette Committee and the New Deal*, New York, 1966.
20. 1939 report, Dies Committee papers, National Archives.
21. Investigators' files, Dies Committee papers, National Archives.
22. George Martin, *Madam Secretary: Frances Perkins*, New York, 1976.
23. Walter Goodman, *The Committee*, New York, 1955.
24. Auerbach, *Labor and Liberty*.
25. Dies Committee hearings, Aug. 13, 15, and 16, 1938.
26. Ibid.
27. McDaniel, "Martin Dies."
28. Auerbach, *Labor and Liberty*.
29. McDaniel, "Martin Dies."
30. Jerry Mangione, *The Dream and the Deal*, New York, 1972. According to a memo in the Dies Committee investigators' file, Mangione was a party member who helped place comrades on the Writers' Project. He was thought to have written for *New Masses* under the name Jerry Gerlando. Nonetheless, his book is an informative eyewitness account of the Writers' Project, once the navigational slant is corrected.
31. Dies Committee hearings, Aug. 19, 1938.
32. Ibid.
33. Ibid.
34. Ibid.
35. Ibid.
36. Dies Committee hearings, Aug. 20, 1938.
37. Ibid.
38. Sallie Saunders affidavit, investigators' files, Dies Committee papers, National Archives.
39. Dies Committee hearings, Aug. 20, 1938.
40. Ibid.
41. Ibid.
42. *The Secret Diary of Harold Ickes*, Vol. 2, *1936–1939*, New York, 1954.
43. Mangione, *Dream and the Deal*.

44. Ibid.
45. Dies Committee hearings, Sep. 15, 1938.
46. Ibid.
47. Ibid.
48. Ibid.
49. Dies Committee hearings, Nov. 16, 1938.
50. Mangione, *Dream and the Deal.*
51. Ibid.
52. McDaniel, "Martin Dies."
53. Dies Committee hearings, executive session, Nov. 19, 1938.
54. Mangione, *Dream and the Deal.*
55. Dies Committee hearings, Dec. 5, 1938.
56. Dies Committee hearings, Dec. 6, 1938.
57. Ibid.
58. Mangione, *Dream and the Deal.*
59. McDaniel, "Martin Dies."
60. Ibid.
61. Ibid.
62. Investigators' files, Dies Committee papers, National Archives.
63. Ibid.
64. Dies Committee Appendix, Part 9, 1944.
65. HUAC, Communist Activities in the San Francisco Area, Dec. 1, 1953.
66. HUAC, Communist Activities in the Los Angeles Area, March 1953.
67. Ibid.
68. Dies Committee hearings, Sep. 5, 1939.
69. Ibid.
70. Ibid.
71. Dies Committee Appendix, Part 9, 1944.
72. Investigators' files, Dies Committee papers, National Archives.
73. Ibid.
74. Dies Committee Appendix, Part 9, 1944.
75. Ickes, *Secret Diary.*
76. Dies Committee Appendix, Part 9, 1944.
77. Ibid.
78. Ibid.
79. Ibid.
80. Investigators' files, Dies Committee papers, National Archives.
81. Ibid.
82. Dies Committee hearings, executive session, Aug. 16, 1940.
83. Dies Committee hearings, executive session, Aug. 16 and 17, 1940.
84. Dies Committee hearings, executive session, Aug. 17, 1940.
85. Ibid.
86. Dies Committee hearings, executive session, Aug. 26, 1940.
87. Investigators' files, Dies Committee papers, National Archives.
88. Ibid.
89. Ickes, *Secret Diary.*
90. Dies Committee papers, Dies correspondence, National Archives.
91. Ibid.
92. Ibid.

93. Morgan, *FDR*.
94. McDaniel, "Martin Dies."
95. Ibid.
96. Ibid.
97. Ibid.
98. Ibid.
99. Ibid.
100. John Earl Haynes and Harvey Klehr, *Venona: Decoding Soviet Espionage in America*, New Haven, 1999.
101. Dies Committee papers, Dies correspondence, National Archives.
102. McDaniel, "Martin Dies."
103. Francis Biddle, *In Brief Authority*, New York, 1962.
104. McDaniel, "Martin Dies."
105. Cuneo to author.
106. Dies Committee papers, Dies correspondence, National Archives.
107. McDaniel, "Martin Dies."
108. Ibid.
109. Ibid.
110. Ibid.
111. Ibid.

IX: WORLD WAR II AND THE SOVIET INVASION OF AMERICA

1. Robert E. Sherwood, *Roosevelt and Hopkins*, New York, 1948.
2. Richard Overy, *Why the Allies Won*, New York, 1995.
3. Diane P. Koenker and Ronald D. Bachman, eds., *Revelations from the Russian Archives*, Washington, 1997.
4. Alexander Feklisov, *The Man Behind the Rosenbergs*, New York, 2001.
5. Overy, *Why the Allies Won*.
6. Venona transcripts, second series.
7. Venona, second series, March 27, 1946.
8. *Introductory History of Venona and Guide to the Translations*, National Security Agency, 1994; John Earl Haynes and Harvey Klehr, *Venona*, New Haven, 1999; Herbert L. Romerstein, *The Venona Secrets*, Washington, 2000.
9. *Introductory History of Venona*.
10. Ibid.
11. David Martin, "The Code War," *Washington Post*, May 10, 1998.
12. Michael Dobbs, "The Man Who Picked the Lock," *Washington Post*, May 10, 1998.
13. Ibid.
14. Robert Louis Benson, Venona Historical Monograph No. 3, *The 1944–45 New York and Washington–Moscow KGB Messages*, NSA, 1994.
15. Dobbs, "Man Who Picked the Lock."
16. Venona, second series.
17. Ibid.
18. Ibid.
19. Ibid.
20. Ibid.
21. Ibid.
22. Ibid.

23. Ibid.
24. Ibid.
25. Ibid.
26. Ibid.
27. Victor Kravchenko, *I Chose Freedom*, New York, 1946.
28. George McJimsey, *Harry Hopkins*, Cambridge, Mass., 1987.
29. Venona, third series.
30. Ibid.
31. Ibid.
32. Ibid.
33. Ibid.
34. Ibid.
35. Ibid.
36. Romerstein, *Venona Secrets*.
37. Allen Weinstein, *The Haunted Wood*, New York, 1999.
38. Hoover to White House, Mar. 18, 1946, Truman Library.
39. Ibid.
40. Hoover to White House, Feb. 17, 1947, Truman Library.
41. Ibid.
42. Gregg Herken, *Brotherhood of the Bomb*, New York, 2002.
43. Ibid.
44. Ibid.
45. Hoover to White House, Feb. 17, 1947, Truman Library.
46. Haynes and Klehr, *Venona*.
47. Herken, *Brotherhood of the Bomb*.
48. Ibid.
49. Ibid.
50. Hoover to White House, Feb. 17, 1947, Truman Library.
51. Hoover to White House, Feb. 17, 1947, Truman Library.
52. Herken, *Brotherhood of the Bomb*.
53. Ibid.
54. Ibid.
55. Ibid.
56. Haynes and Klehr, *Venona*.
57. Romerstein, *Venona Secrets*.
58. Pavel Sudoplatov, *Special Tasks*, New York, 1994.
59. Romerstein, *Venona Secrets*.
60. Christopher Andrew, *The Sword and the Shield*, New York, 1999.
61. Haynes and Klehr, *Venona*.
62. Gary May, *Un-American Activities: The Trials of William Remington*, New York, 1994.
63. Elizabeth Bentley, *Out of Bondage*, New York, 1957.
64. Weinstein, *Haunted Wood*.
65. Bentley, *Out of Bondage*.
66. Weinstein, *Haunted Wood*.
67. Venona, second series.
68. Ibid.
69. Don S. Kirschner, *Cold War Exile: The Unclosed Case of Maurice Halperin*, Columbia, Mo., 1995.

70. Ibid.
71. Venona, second series.
72. Weinstein, *Haunted Wood.*
73. Senate Committee on Expenditures in the Executive Department, Subcommittee on Investigations, July 30, 1948.
74. Ibid.
75. HUAC hearings, Regarding Communist Espionage in the United States Government, Aug. 4, 1948.
76. Ibid.
77. Ibid.
78. Weinstein, *Haunted Wood.*
79. Senate Internal Security Subcommittee (SISS) hearings, Apr. 6, 1954.
80. Ibid.
81. Weinstein, *Haunted Wood.*
82. Venona, third series.
83. Weinstein, *Haunted Wood.*
84. Venona, third series.
85. Bentley, *Out of Bondage.*
86. Weinstein, *Haunted Wood.*
87. Ibid.
88. Ibid.
89. Bentley, *Out of Bondage.*
90. Ibid.
91. May, *Un-American Activities.*
92. Hoover memo, Truman Library.
93. Weinstein, *Haunted Wood.*
94. May, *Un-American Activities.*
95. HUAC hearings, Aug. 10, 1948.
96. HUAC hearings, Aug. 9, 1948.
97. HUAC hearings, Aug. 4, 1948.
98. HUAC hearings, Aug. 10, 1948.
99. May, *Un-American Activities.*
100. Ibid.
101. Morgenthau diaries, FDR Library.
102. Venona, third series.
103. Ibid.
104. HUAC hearings, Aug. 13, 1948.
105. Morgenthau diaries.
106. David Rees, *Harry Dexter White,* New York, 1973.
107. Venona, third series.
108. Ibid.
109. Rees, *Harry Dexter White.*
110. Ibid.
111. Venona, second series.
112. Ted Morgan, *FDR: A Biography,* New York, 1985.
113. Venona, third series.
114. Morgenthau diaries.
115. Senate Committee on Government Operations, Subcommittee on Investigations, Transfer of Occupation Currency Plates Espionage Phase, report, Dec. 15, 1953.

116. Hoover memo, Truman Library.
117. Hoover memo, Truman Library.
118. Ibid.
119. HUAC hearings, Aug. 13, 1948.
120. Rees, *Harry Dexter White.*
121. Hoover memo, Sep. 12, 1945, Truman Library.
122. Hoover memo, Sep. 18, 1945, Truman Library.
123. Hoover memo, Oct. 16, 1945, Truman Library.
124. Robert Bothwell, ed., *The Gouzenko Transcripts*, Ottawa, 1981.
125. Venona, first series.
126. Paul Boyer, *By the Bomb's Early Light*, New York, 1958.
127. Hoover to White House, Nov. 15, 1945, Truman Library.
128. Hoover to White House, Feb. 17, 1947, Truman Library.
129. Hoover to White House, March 18, 1946, Truman Library.
130. Ibid.
131. Hoover to White House, Feb. 17, 1947, Truman Library.
132. Herken, *Brotherhood of the Bomb.*
133. Ibid.
134. Alger Hiss, *Recollections of a Life*, New York, 1988.
135. SISS hearings, Mar. 24, 1954.
136. Weinstein, *Haunted Wood.*
137. Ibid.
138. Venona, first series.
139. Andrew, *Sword and the Shield.*
140. SISS hearings, Mar. 24, 1954.
141. Ibid.
142. Hiss, *Recollections.*
143. Ibid.
144. Ibid.
145. Jason Roberts, "New Evidence in the Hiss Case," *American Communist History*, December 2002.
146. HUAC hearings, Aug. 25, 1948.
147. Hiss, *Recollections.*
148. Harvey Klehr and Ronald Radosh, *The Amerasia Case*, Chapel Hill, 1996.
149. Ibid.
150. Ibid.
151. Ibid.
152. Ibid.
153. Ibid.
154. Hoover memo, Aug. 10, 1945, Truman Library.
155. Robert Chadwell Williams, *Klaus Fuchs*, Cambridge, Mass., 1987.
156. Feklisov, *Man Behind the Rosenbergs.*
157. Venona, first series.
158. Feklisov, *Man Behind the Rosenbergs.*
159. Venona, first series.
160. SISS hearings, Apr. 26, 1956, Harry Gold testimony.
161. David Holloway, *Stalin and the Bomb*, New Haven, 1994.
162. Feklisov, *Man Behind the Rosenbergs.*
163. Holloway, *Stalin and the Bomb.*

164. Williams, *Klaus Fuchs.*
165. Ibid.
166. Feklisov, *Man Behind the Rosenbergs.*
167. Robert J. Lamphere and Tom Shactman, *The FBI-KGB War*, New York, 1996.
168. Hoover memo, Sep. 20, 1949, Truman Library.
169. Williams, *Klaus Fuchs.*
170. Ibid.
171. Lamphere and Shactman, *FBI-KGB War.*
172. SISS hearings, Apr. 26, 1953, Harry Gold testimony.
173. Williams, *Klaus Fuchs.*
174. Lamphere and Shactman, *FBI-KGB War.*
175. Venona, first series.
176. Ibid.
177. Romerstein, *Venona Secrets.*
178. Venona, first series.
179. Haynes and Klehr, *Venona.*
180. Venona, first series.
181. Ibid.
182. Ibid.
183. Ronald Radosh and Joyce Milton, *The Rosenberg File*, New York, 1983.
184. SISS hearings, Apr. and May 1956, Greenglass testimony.
185. Venona, first series.
186. Venona, introduction.
187. Venona, first series.
188. Feklisov, *Man Behind the Rosenbergs.*
189. Venona, first series.
190. Feklisov, *Man Behind the Rosenbergs.*
191. SISS hearings, Apr. and May 1956, Greenglass testimony.
192. Radosh and Milton, *Rosenberg File.*
193. Ibid.
194. Ibid.
195. Dwight D. Eisenhower to John Eisenhower, June 16, 1953, Eisenhower Library.
196. David Martin, "Code War."
197. Haynes and Klehr, *Venona.*
198. Romerstein to author.
199. One example of a dupe is Tony Hiss, who has made a career out of filial piety and continues to proclaim the innocence of his father in the face of irrefutable evidence. A prime example of an opportunist is Victor Navasky of *The Nation*, the only magazine editor in America ever to be called "a chiseler" by the United States Supreme Court (for his theft of the Gerald Ford memoirs). He also wrote in *The Nation* that the Venona transcripts were forgeries. One of his friends described him as being "frozen into false positions."
200. Feklisov, *Man Behind the Rosenbergs.*

X: TRUMAN TAKES CHARGE
1. Venona transcripts, New York to Moscow, May 26, 1945.
2. Venona transcripts, San Francisco to Moscow, June 14, 1945.
3. David Holloway, *Stalin and the Bomb*, New Haven, 1994.
4. Ibid.

5. Truman Library, internal security file.
6. Truman to Cates, Truman Library, Jan. 12, 1953.
7. Vladislav Zubok and Constantine Pleshakov, *Inside the Kremlin's Cold War*, Cambridge, Mass., 1996.
8. Ibid.
9. Hoover to Vaughan, Truman Library.
10. Hoover to Attorney General, memo on Redin, Apr. 1, 1946, Truman Library.
11. Hoover to George E. Allen, Mar. 18, 1946, Truman Library.
12. Hoover to Vaughan, May 31, 1956, Truman Library.
13. Ibid.
14. Ibid.
15. James G. Ryan, *Earl Browder*, Tuscaloosa, 1997.
16. Ted Morgan, *A Covert Life*, New York, 1999.
17. Ryan, *Earl Browder.*
18. HUAC, Investigation of Communist Activities in the Los Angeles Area, June 2, 1951.
19. HUAC, Los Angeles hearings, Apr. 13, 1951.
20. Hoover to Allen, Sep. 25, 1946, Truman Library.
21. David McCullough, *Truman*, New York, 1992.
22. Michael Paul Poder, "The Senatorial Career of William J. Jenner," Ph.D. thesis, University of Notre Dame, 1976.
23. *The Journals of David E. Lilienthal*, Vol. 2, New York, 1964.
24. Ibid.
25. Ibid.
26. Hoover to Vaughan, Feb. 17, 1947, Truman Library.
27. Lilienthal, *Journals.* Mar. 28, 1947.
28. Truman to Earle, Feb. 28, 1947, Truman Library.
29. Clifford memo, Mar. 23, 1947, Truman Library.
30. Bontecou papers, Truman Library.
31. Eleanor Bontecou, *The Federal Loyalty Security Program*, Ithaca, 1953.
32. Ibid.
33. Walter Gelhorn, *Security, Loyalty, and Science*, Ithaca, 1950.
34. McCullough, *Truman.*
35. Allen Weinstein, *The Haunted Wood*, New York, 1999.
36. Henry A. Wallace, *The Price of Vision*, Boston, 1993.
37. Weinstein, *Haunted Wood.*
38. Harry Truman, *Off the Record*, New York, 1980.
39. Hoover to Vaughan, Apr. 3, 1947, Truman Library.
40. Hoover to Vaughan, June 17, 1947, Truman Library.
41. Hoover to Vaughan, Jan. 15, 1948, Truman Library.
42. Ibid.
43. Irwin Ross, *The Loneliest Campaign*, New York, 1968.
44. Harvey A. Levenstein, *Communism, Anti-Communism, and the CIO*, Westport, Conn., 1981.
45. William O'Neill, *A Better World*, New York, 1982.
46. Excerpts from press conferences, Truman Library.
47. Letters to Truman, Truman Library.
48. Elsey memo, Aug. 16, 1948, Truman Library.
49. Excerpts from press conference, Truman Library.

50. Lovestone papers, CIO file, Hoover Institution.
51. Senate Committee on Labor and Public Welfare, Subcommittee on Labor and Management Relations, report on Communist Domination of Certain Unions, Oct. 19, 1951.
52. Michael R. Belknap, *Cold War Political Justice*, Westport, Conn., 1977.
53. Ibid.
54. Athan G. Theoharis and John Stuart Cox, *The Boss: J. Edgar Hoover and the Great American Inquisition*, Philadelphia, 1988.
55. Belknap, *Cold War Political Justice*.
56. Ibid.
57. Hawthorne Daniel, *Judge Medina*, New York, 1952.
58. Ibid.
59. Ibid.
60. Ibid.
61. Belknap, *Cold War Political Justice*.
62. Howard Ball and Phillip J. Cooper, *Of Power and Right*, New York, 1992.
63. Ibid.
64. Ibid.
65. Ibid.
66. Ibid.
67. Ibid.
68. Gil Green, *Cold War Fugitive*, New York, 1984.
69. Ibid.
70. HUAC hearings on Communism in Northern California, May 13, 1960.
71. HUAC hearings on Communism in the Detroit Area, Feb. 1952.
72. HUAC hearings on Communist Activities in the Pacific Northwest, June 1954.
73. Clifford memo, April 29, 1949, Truman Library.
74. Truman Library, national security file.
75. Forrest C. Pogue, *George C. Marshall, Statesman, 1945–1959*, New York, 1987.
76. Melvyn P. Leffler, *A Preponderance of Power*, Stanford, 1992.
77. Theoharis and Cox, *The Boss*.
78. Ibid.
79. Lowenthal to Truman, June 10, 1949, Truman Library.
80. Lowenthal to Truman, June 16, 1949, Truman Library.
81. Lowenthal file, Nichols to Hoover, June 12, 1950, Truman Library.
82. Lowenthal file, Truman to Lowenthal, July 25, 1950, Truman Library.
83. Lowenthal file, Truman to Lowenthal, Sep. 8, 1950, Truman Library.

XI: JUDGE JOE

1. Michael O'Brien, *McCarthy and McCarthyism in Wisconsin*, Columbia, Mo., 1980.
2. Ibid.
3. Ibid.
4. McCarthy to Holt, McCarthy Papers, Marquette University archives.
5. Ibid.
6. Ibid.
7. O'Brien, *McCarthy and McCarthyism*.
8. Marquette archives.
9. O'Brien, *McCarthy and McCarthyism*.

10. Ibid.
11. Ibid.
12. Ibid.
13. Marquette archives.
14. Ibid.
15. Ibid.
16. Ibid.
17. Ibid.
18. Ibid.
19. Ibid.
20. Ibid.
21. Ibid.
22. Ibid.
23. Ibid.
24. Ibid.
25. Ibid.
26. Ibid.
27. Ibid.
28. Ibid.
29. Ibid.
30. Ibid.
31. Ibid.
32. Ibid.
33. Ibid.
34. Thomas Reeves, *The Life and Times of Joe McCarthy*, New York, 1982.
35. O'Brien, *McCarthy and McCarthyism.*
36. Marquette archives.
37. Ibid.
38. Ibid.
39. Ibid.
40. McCarthy citations, internal security file, Truman Library.
41. Ibid.
42. Reeves, *Life and Times of Joe McCarthy.*
43. Evjue papers, Wisconsin Historical Society.
44. O'Brien, *McCarthy and McCarthyism.*
45. Ibid.
46. Marquette archives.
47. Ibid.
48. Ibid.
49. Ibid.
50. Ibid.
51. O'Brien, *McCarthy and McCarthyism.*
52. Marquette archives.
53. O'Brien, *McCarthy and McCarthyism.*
54. Marquette archives.
55. Ibid.
56. Ibid.
57. Ibid.
58. Ibid.

59. O'Brien, *McCarthy and McCarthyism.*
60. Marquette archives.
61. O'Brien, *McCarthy and McCarthyism.*
62. Ibid.
63. Marquette archives.
64. Ibid.
65. Ibid.
66. Ibid.
67. O'Brien, *McCarthy and McCarthyism.*
68. Ibid.

XII: SENATOR JOE

1. Harold F. Gosnell, *Truman's Crises,* Westport, Conn., 1980.
2. Thomas Reeves, *The Life and Times of Joe McCarthy,* New York, 1982.
3. Michael O'Brien, *McCarthy and McCarthyism in Wisconsin,* Columbia, Mo., 1980.
4. James T. Patterson, *Mr. Republican,* Boston, 1972.
5. Reeves, *Life and Times of Joe McCarthy.*
6. Memo on housing, Apr. 24, 1954, William A. Roberts papers, Wisconsin State Historical Society.
7. Testimony of Robert C. Byers, Aug. 1, 1951, U.S. District Court, Bankruptcy Division, in Roberts papers.
8. Byers affidavit, Fleming papers, State Historical Society, Madison, Wisconsin.
9. Fleming papers.
10. "The House of Tomorrow," *New York Times,* Aug. 1, 2001.
11. Roberts papers and Fleming papers.
12. Gosnell, *Truman's Crises.*
13. Reeves, *Life and Times of Joe McCarthy.*
14. William L. Shirer, *The Rise and Fall of the Third Reich,* New York, 1960.
15. Ibid.
16. James L. Weingarten, *Malmédy,* Berkeley, 1979.
17. Hearings of the Subcommittee of the Committee on Armed Services, U.S. Senate, Malmédy Massacre Investigation, April, May, June 1949.
18. Weingarten, *Malmédy.*
19. Jean Edward Smith, *Lucius D. Clay: An American Life,* New York, 1990.
20. Malmédy hearings.
21. Ibid.
22. Ibid.
23. Smith, *Lucius D. Clay.*
24. Malmédy hearings.
25. Ibid.
26. Ibid.
27. Ibid.
28. Ibid.
29. Ibid.
30. Ibid.
31. Malmédy hearings, appendix.
32. Malmédy hearings.
33. Ibid.

34. Marquette archives.
35. Ibid.
36. O'Brien, *McCarthy and McCarthyism.*
37. Ibid.
38. Marquette archives.
39. O'Brien, *McCarthy and McCarthyism.*
40. Evjue papers, Wisconsin State Historical Society.
41. Malmédy hearings.
42. Ibid.
43. Ibid.
44. Ibid.
45. Ibid.
46. Ibid.
47. Ibid.
48. Ibid.
49. Ibid.
50. Malmédy hearings, appendix.
51. Ibid.
52. Ibid.
53. Macdonald to Freda Kirchwey, Feb. 15, 1950.
54. Roberts papers.
55. O'Brien, *McCarthy and McCarthyism.*

XIII: RED-HUNTER JOE

1. Allen Weinstein, *The Haunted Wood,* New York, 1999.
2. Ibid.
3. Ibid.
4. Ibid.
5. James G. Ryan, *Earl Browder,* Tuscaloosa, 1997.
6. Spingarn to Truman, May 4, 1950, internal security file, Truman Library.
7. Richard Gid Powers, *Secrecy and Power,* New York, 1987.
8. Spingarn memo, June 28, 1950, internal security file, Truman Library.
9. Senate Committee to Investigate Foreign Affairs, Subcommittee to Investigate Disloyal Employees, hearings, July 1950. Hereinafter Tydings Committee.
10. James F. Byrnes, *Speaking Frankly,* New York, 1969.
11. Mark Riebling, *Wedge,* New York, 1994.
12. Ibid.
13. Dean Acheson, *Present at the Creation,* New York, 1969.
14. Murphy to Panuch, June 13, 1946, internal security file, Truman Library.
15. Panuch to Russell, Nov. 14, 1945, internal security file, Truman Library.
16. *New York Times,* March 15, 1946.
17. *New York Times,* March 20, 1946.
18. Acheson, *Present at the Creation.*
19. Report, Senate Appropriations Committee, July 1947.
20. Harold F. Gosnell, *Truman's Crises,* Westport, Conn., 1980.
21. House Appropriations Committee, Subcommittee on the Appropriations Bill for Fiscal Year, 1949. Hereinafter Stefan Committee.
22. Stefan Committee hearings, Jan. 26, 1948.
23. Ibid.

24. Stefan Committee hearings, Feb. 27, 1948.
25. House Committee on Expenditures in the Executive Departments, hearings on the State Department Office of Controls. Hereinafter the Chenoweth Committee.
26. Chenoweth Committee hearings, Mar. 10, 1948.
27. John Earl Haynes and Harvey Klehr, *Venona*, New Haven, 1999.
28. Ibid.
29. Chenoweth Committee hearings, Mar. 12, 1948.
30. *Congressional Record*, Mar. 12, 1948.
31. Gosnell, *Truman's Crises.*
32. Michael O'Brien, *McCarthy and McCarthyism in Wisconsin*, Columbia, Mo., 1980.
33. Thomas Reeves, *The Life and Times of Joe McCarthy*, New York, 1982.
34. Roberts papers, Wisconsin Historical Society.
35. Reeves, *Life and Times of Joe McCarthy.*
36. McCarthy telegram, Feb. 11, 1950, Truman Library.
37. Draft of Truman reply, Feb. 15, 1950, Truman Library.
38. M. Stanton Evans to author.
39. *Major Speeches and Debates of Senator Joe McCarthy, Delivered in the United States Senate 1950–51*, U.S. Government Printing Office, undated.
40. Ibid.
41. Lee list, Tydings Committee hearings.
42. Ibid.
43. Haynes and Klehr, *Venona.*
44. Esther Brunauer, State Department Loyalty Board report, Case No. 325, HUAC files, Walter correspondence, National Archives.
45. Ibid.
46. Humelsine to Tydings, undated Benton papers, Wisconsin Historical Society.
47. Lorwin Civil Service Commission hearings, Bontecou papers, Truman Library.
48. Lorwin loyalty board hearings, Bontecou papers, Truman Library.
49. Brownell to Langer, July 7, 1954, courtesy of Morris Weisz.
50. Ibid.
51. Ibid.
52. Ibid.
53. Lorwin statement, Bontecou papers, Truman Library.
54. Evjue papers, State Historical Society, Madison, Wisconsin.
55. Sidney Hyman, *The Lives of William Benton*, Chicago, 1969.
56. Gregory Peter Gallant, "Margaret Chase Smith," Ph.D. thesis, University of Maine, 1992.
57. Ibid.
58. *Major Speeches and Debates.*
59. Tydings Committee hearings, Mar. 8, 1950.
60. Tydings Committee hearings, Mar. 27, 1950.
61. Robert P. Newman, *Owen Lattimore and the Loss of China*, Berkeley, 1992.
62. Tydings Committee hearings, Mar. 21, 1950.
63. *Major Speeches and Debates*, Mar. 30, 1950.
64. Newman, *Owen Lattimore.*
65. Institute of Pacific Relations hearings, Subcommittee of Senate Committee on the Judiciary, 1951–52.

66. Ibid.
67. Ibid.
68. Newman, *Owen Lattimore.*
69. Henry A. Wallace, *The Price of Vision,* Boston, 1973.
70. Ibid.
71. Robert Conquest, *The Great Terror,* New York, 1990.
72. IPR hearings.
73. Newman, *Owen Lattimore.*
74. Louis Budenz, *Men Without Faces,* New York, 1950.
75. FBI memo, Hoover to McGrath, Apr. 21, 1950, Truman Library.
76. Tydings Committee hearings, Mar. 1950.
77. Edwin R. Bayley, *Joe McCarthy and the Press,* Madison, Wis., 1981.
78. Dawson memo, Mar. 16, 1950, Truman Library.
79. *Truman in the White House: The Diary of Eben A. Ayers,* Robert H. Ferrell, ed., Columbia, Mo., 1991.
80. M. Stanton Evans, "Joe McCarthy and the Historians," *Human Events,* Jan. 1. 1999.
81. Robert Griffith, *The Politics of Fear,* Amherst, 1987.
82. Ayers, *Diary.*
83. Tydings Committee, June 1950.
84. Tydings Committee report, July 20, 1950.
85. Evans, "Joe McCarthy and the Historians."
86. Reeves, *Life and Times of Joe McCarthy.*
87. IPR hearings.
88. Newman, *Owen Lattimore.*
89. Reeves, *Life and Times of Joe McCarthy.*
90. McCarthy to Truman, July 12, 1950, Truman Library.
91. McCarthy to Coleman, July 26, 1950, Coleman papers, State Historical Society, Madison, Wisconsin.
92. Griffith, *Politics of Fear.*
93. Committee on Rules and Administration, Subcommittee on Privileges and Elections, hearings on the Maryland senatorial election of 1950, Feb., Mar., and Apr.
94. Ibid.
95. Ibid.
96. Reeves, *Life and Times of Joe McCarthy.*
97. Report on Rosenberg confirmation, Roberts papers.
98. Ibid.
99. Ibid.
100. Ibid.
101. Bayley, *Joe McCarthy and the Press.*
102. Jack Anderson, *Confessions of a Muckraker,* New York, 1979.
103. Roberts papers.
104. Ibid.
105. *McCarthy, Major Speeches.*
106. Roberts papers, McCarthy deposition.
107. *McCarthy, Major Speeches.*
108. Ibid.
109. Forrest C. Pogue, *George C. Marshall, Statesman, 1945–1959,* New York, 1987.

110. James T. Patterson, *Mr. Republican*, Boston, 1972.
111. Hyman, *Lives of William Benton*.
112. Ibid.
113. *McCarthy, Major Speeches*.
114. Elsey to Murphy, Aug. 14, 1951, Truman Library.
115. Reeves, *Life and Times of Joe McCarthy*.
116. Gallant, "Margaret Chase Smith."
117. Hyman, *Lives of William Benton*.
118. Griffith, *Politics of Fear*.
119. Ibid.
120. Benton papers, State Historical Society, Madison, Wisconsin.
121. Griffith, *Politics of Fear*.
122. Benton papers.
123. Ibid.
124. Reeves, *Life and Times of Joe McCarthy*.
125. Van Susteren oral history, State Historical Society, Madison, Wisconsin.
126. Benton papers.
127. Jeff Broadwater, *Eisenhower and the Anti-Communist Crusade*, Chapel Hill, 1992.
128. Fleming papers, State Historical Society, Madison, Wisconsin.
129. FBI memo, V. F. Keay to A. H. Belmont, July 17, 1952, Truman Library.
130. FBI memo, Papich to Hoover, Aug. 3, 1953, Truman Library.
131. Smith deposition, Sep. 30, 1952, Benton papers.
132. Smith to Truman, Oct. 2, 1952, Truman Library.
133. Smith testimony before HUAC, Oct. 13, 1952, Truman Library.
134. FBI memo, V. F. Keay to A. H. Belmont, Oct. 8, 1952, Truman Library.
135. O'Brien, *McCarthy and McCarthyism*.
136. Benton papers.

XIV: DECLINE AND FALL

1. Stephen E. Ambrose, *Eisenhower the President*, New York, 1984.
2. James T. Patterson, *Mr. Republican*, Boston, 1972.
3. McCarthy to Eisenhower, Feb. 3, 1953, Eisenhower Library.
4. Dulles to Adams, Mar. 13, 1953, phone transcripts, Eisenhower Library.
5. Dulles to Taft and Bohlen, Mar. 16, 1953, phone transcripts, Eisenhower Library.
6. Dulles memo, March 18, 1953, Eisenhower Library.
7. Dulles to Adams, Mar. 19, 1953, phone transcripts, Eisenhower Library.
8. Dulles to Adams, Mar. 20, 1953, phone transcripts, Eisenhower Library.
9. Thayer security report, courtesy of M. Stanton Evans.
10. Ambrose, *Eisenhower the President*.
11. Thomas Reeves, *The Life and Times of Joe McCarthy*, New York, 1982.
12. Nicholas Von Hoffman, *Citizen Cohn*, New York, 1988.
13. Executive Sessions of the Senate Permanent Subcommittee on Investigations of the Committee on Government Operations, Donald A. Ritchie, ed., Preface, p. xi, U.S. Government Printing Office. Hereinafter McCarthy closed hearings.
14. Robert F. Kennedy, *The Enemy Within*, New York, 1960.
15. McCarthy closed hearings, Preface, p. xi.
16. Ibid.
17. Ibid.

18. Michael O'Brien, *McCarthy and McCarthyism in Wisconsin,* Columbia, Mo., 1980.
19. McCarthy closed hearings, Vol. 1, p. 1.
20. Ibid., p. 33.
21. Ibid., p. 1.
22. Ibid., p. 97.
23. McCarthy to Dulles, Jan. 28, 1953, phone transcripts, Eisenhower Library.
24. McCarthy closed hearings, Vol. 1, p. 207.
25. Ibid., p. 143.
26. Ibid., p. 177.
27. Ibid., p. 283.
28. Senate Committee on Government Operations, Subcommittee on Investigations, State Department File Survey, Feb. 4, 5, and 6, May–June, 1953.
29. McCarthy closed hearings, Vol. 1, p. 411.
30. Ibid.
31. Ibid., p. 457.
32. Ibid.
33. Martin Merson, *The Private Diary of a Public Servant,* New York, 1955.
34. McCarthy closed hearings, Vol. 1, p. 457.
35. Ibid.
36. Ibid., p. 499.
37. Ibid., p. 577.
38. Reeves, *Life and Times of Joe McCarthy.*
39. Ibid.
40. McCarthy closed hearings, Vol. 1, p. 615.
41. Ibid.
42. Ibid.
43. Senate Committee on Government Operations, Subcommittee on Investigations, State Department Information Program Hearings, Feb. 1953. Hereinafter VOA hearings.
44. McCarthy closed hearings, Vol. 1, p. 795.
45. Ibid.
46. Ibid.
47. Ibid.
48. VOA hearings, Mar. 24, 1953.
49. Ibid.
50. Ibid., Mar. 25, 1953.
51. Ibid., Mar. 26, 1953.
52. Ibid., Mar. 27, 1953.
53. C. L. Sulzberger, *A Long Row of Candles,* New York, 1969.
54. Von Hoffman, *Citizen Cohn.*
55. Kai Bird, *The Chairman,* New York, 1992.
56. Merson, *Private Diary of a Public Servant.*
57. McCarthy closed hearings, Vol. 2, p. 1073.
58. VOA hearings, Apr. 29, 1953.
59. James Aronson, *The Press and the Cold War,* New York, 1990.
60. John Earl Haynes and Harvey Klehr, *Venona,* New Haven, 1999.
61. McCarthy closed hearings, Vol. 2, p. 1135.
62. Cedric Belfrage, *The American Inquisition, 1945–1960,* Indianapolis, 1973.

63. McCarthy closed hearings, Vol. 2, p. 1267.
64. Ibid., p. 1367.
65. Ibid., p. 1117.
66. Ibid., p. 1349.
67. Ibid., p. 1367.
68. Haynes and Klehr, *Venona.*
69. Emmet John Hughes, *The Ordeal of Power,* New York, 1963.
70. Ibid.
71. Bernard Shanley diaries, Eisenhower Library.
72. Reeves, *Life and Times of Joe McCarthy.*
73. McCarthy closed hearings, Vol. 2, p. 1399.
74. Ibid.
75. Ibid.
76. Ibid.
77. Ibid.
78. Dulles to Dulles, July 10, 1953, phone transcripts, Eisenhower Library.
79. Ambrose, *Eisenhower the President;* Reeves, *Life and Times of Joe McCarthy.*
80. Senate Committee on Government Operations, Subcommittee on Investigations, hearings on the Government Printing Office, Aug. 1953.
81. Ibid.
82. Reeves, *Life and Times of Joe McCarthy.*
83. Papich to Hoover, Aug. 5, 1953, FBI files, Eisenhower Library.
84. Reeves, *Life and Times of Joe McCarthy.*
85. O'Brien, *McCarthy and McCarthyism in Wisconsin.*
86. Evjue to Pearson, June 12, 1953, Evjue papers, State Historical Society, Madison, Wisconsin.
87. Benton papers, State Historical Society, Madison, Wisconsin.
88. McCarthy closed hearings, Vol. 2, p. 1625.
89. Ibid.
90. Ibid., p. 1651.
91. Ibid.
92. Ibid., p. 1695.
93. Ibid., p. 1745.
94. Drew Pearson, *Diaries, 1949–1959,* New York, 1974.
95. Seaton papers, Eisenhower Library.
96. Ibid.
97. Ibid.
98. Senate Committee on Government Operations, Subcommittee on Investigations, hearings on Communist Infiltration among Army civilian workers, Sep. 1953. Hereinafter Army civilian hearings.
99. Stevens to Lawton, Oct. 2, 1953, Seaton papers, Eisenhower Library.
100. McCarthy closed hearings, Vol. 3, p. 2275.
101. Ibid., p. 2389.
102. Ibid., p. 2563.
103. Ibid., p. 2389.
104. Ibid., p. 2563.
105. Ibid., p. 2625.
106. Stevens to Hoover, Oct. 19, 1953, Seaton papers, Eisenhower Library.
107. Schine to Stevens, Oct. 21, 1953, Seaton papers, Eisenhower Library.

108. John G. Adams, *Without Precedent,* New York, 1983.
109. Cohn to Stevens, Oct. 27, 1953, Seaton papers, Eisenhower Library.
110. Seaton to Stevens, Oct. 28, 1953, Seaton papers, Eisenhower Library.
111. Adams, *Without Precedent.*
112. McCarthy closed hearings, Vol. 4, p. 2953.
113. Ibid.
114. Adams, *Without Precedent.*
115. Adams to Stevens, Nov. 25, 1953, Seaton papers.
116. McCarthy closed hearings, Vol. 4, p. 3639.
117. Ryan to Adams, Dec. 8, 1953, Seaton papers.
118. Flanders papers, State Historical Society, Madison, Wisconsin.
119. Undated, unsigned, handwritten memo labeled "Office of the Assistant Secretary of Defense," Seaton papers, Eisenhower Library.
120. Adams, *Without Precedent.*
121. McCarthy closed hearings, Vol. 5, p. 31.
122. Ibid.
123. Adams, *Without Precedent.*
124. Ibid.
125. Ibid.
126. Reeves, *Life and Times of Joe McCarthy.*
127. Army civilian hearings, Feb. 18.
128. McCarthy closed hearings, Vol. 5, p. 33.
129. Army civilian hearings, Feb. 18.
130. Reeves, *Life and Times of Joe McCarthy.*
131. Stevens to Zwicker, Feb. 19, 1954, Seaton papers, Eisenhower Library.
132. Stevens to McCarthy, Feb. 20, 1954, Seaton papers, Eisenhower Library.
133. Hagerty diary, Eisenhower Library.
134. Shanley diary, Eisenhower Library.
135. Lodge to Stevens, Feb. 24, 1954, Seaton papers, Eisenhower Library.
136. Hagerty diary, Eisenhower Library.
137. McCarthy closed hearings, Vol. 5, p. 165.
138. Adams, *Without Precedent.*
139. Charles E. Potter, *Days of Shame,* New York, 1955.
140. Robert Griffith, *The Politics of Fear,* Amherst, 1987.
141. A. M. Sperber, *Murrow: His Life and Times,* New York, 1986.
142. Potter, *Days of Shame.*
143. Hagerty diary, Eisenhower Library.
144. Jeff Broadwater, *Eisenhower and the Anti-Communist Crusade,* Chapel Hill, 1992.
145. Hagerty diary, Eisenhower Library.
146. Gregg Herken, *Brotherhood of the Bomb,* New York, 2002.
147. Ibid.
148. Hoover memo, Mar. 26, 1952, Eisenhower Library.
149. Herken, *Brotherhood of the Bomb.*
150. Broadwater, *Eisenhower and the Anti-Communist Crusade.*
151. Herken, *Brotherhood of the Bomb.*
152. Richard Pfau, *No Sacrifice Too Great,* Charlottesville, 1984.
153. *The Eisenhower Diaries,* Robert H. Ferrell, ed., New York, 1981.
154. Broadwater, *Eisenhower and the Anti-Communist Crusade.*
155. *Eisenhower Diaries.*

156. Pfau, *No Sacrifice Too Great.*
157. Herken, *Brotherhood of the Bomb.*
158. Ibid.
159. Ibid.
160. Ibid.
161. Ibid.
162. *The Journals of David E. Lilienthal,* Vol. 3, New York, 1966.
163. Herken, *Brotherhood of the Bomb.*
164. Pfau, *No Sacrifice Too Great.*
165. Broadwater, *Eisenhower and the Anti-Communist Crusade.*
166. Lilienthal, *Journals.*
167. McCloy to Eisenhower, Apr. 16, 1954, Eisenhower Library.
168. Senate Committee on Government Operations, Subcommittee on Investigations, hearings on charges and countercharges involving: Sec. of the Army Robert T. Stevens, John G. Adams, H. Struve Hensel, and Sen. Joseph McCarthy, Roy M. Cohn, and Francis P. Carr. Hereinafter Army-McCarthy hearings.
169. Ibid.
170. Ibid.
171. Bird, *The Chairman.*
172. Army-McCarthy hearings.
173. McCarthy closed hearings, Vol. 5, p. 213.
174. Ibid.
175. Ibid., p. 223.
176. Ibid.
177. Army-McCarthy hearings.
178. Ibid.
179. Potter, *Days of Shame.*
180. McCarthy closed hearings, Vol. 5, p. 241.
181. Hagerty diary, Eisenhower Library.
182. Army-McCarthy hearings.
183. Ibid.
184. Ibid.
185. Ibid.
186. Ibid.
187. Potter, *Days of Shame.*
188. O'Brien, *McCarthy and McCarthyism in Wisconsin.*
189. Griffith, *Politics of Fear.*
190. Army-McCarthy hearings.
191. Ibid.
192. Sidney Zion, *The Autobiography of Roy Cohn,* Secaucus, N.J., 1988.
193. Army-McCarthy hearings.
194. Notes on Censure, Flanders papers, State Historical Society, Madison, Wisconsin.
195. Arthur V. Watkins, *Enough Rope,* Salt Lake City, 1969.
196. Ibid.
197. Ibid.
198. Ibid.
199. Ibid.
200. Ibid.
201. Barry M. Goldwater, *With No Apologies,* New York, 1979.

202. Watkins, *Enough Rope.*
203. Ibid.
204. Benton papers, State Historical Society, Madison, Wisconsin.
205. Bobby Baker, *Wheeling and Dealing,* New York, 1978.
206. Eisenhower to Roberts, Dec. 7, 1954, Eisenhower Library.
207. Watkins, *Enough Rope.*
208. Flanders papers, State Historical Society, Madison, Wisconsin.
209. Hagerty diary, Eisenhower Library.
210. Watkins, *Enough Rope.*
211. Minnich papers, Eisenhower Library.
212. Griffith, *Politics of Fear.*
213. Von Hoffman, *Citizen Cohn.*
214. Knowland to Dulles, Aug. 1, 1955, phone transcripts, Eisenhower Library.
215. McCarthy to Eisenhower, Sep. 21, 1955, Eisenhower Library.
216. McCarthy to Eisenhower, Feb. 16, 1956, Eisenhower Library.
217. O'Brien, *McCarthy and McCarthyism in Wisconsin.*
218. Brownell to Eisenhower, Oct. 8, 1956, Eisenhower Library.
219. Van Susteren papers, State Historical Society, Madison, Wisconsin.
220. O'Konski to May, May papers, State Historical Society, Madison, Wisconsin.
221. Griffith, *Politics of Fear.*
222. Reeves, *Life and Times of Joe McCarthy.*
223. Evjue papers, State Historical Society, Madison, Wisconsin.
224. Senate memorial service, Aug. 14, 1957.
225. Coleman papers, State Historical Society, Madison, Wisconsin.
226. Ibid.
227. Flanders papers, State Historical Society, Madison, Wisconsin.
228. Von Hoffman, *Citizen Cohn.*

XV: McCARTHYISM

1. Ronald Wayne Johnson, "The Communist Issue in Missouri: 1946–1956," Ph.D. thesis, University of Missouri, 1973.
2. James Truett Selcraig, "The Red Scare in the Midwest," Ph.D. thesis, University of Illinois, 1981.
3. Jane Sanders, *Cold War on Campus,* Seattle, 1979.
4. Ibid.
5. Selcraig, "Red Scare in the Midwest."
6. Sigmund Diamond, *Compromised Campus,* New York, 1992.
7. Don Edwards Carlton, "A Crisis of Rapid Change: The Red Scare in Houston, 1945–1955," Ph.D. thesis, University of Houston, 1978.
8. Patrick McGilligan and Paul Buhle, *Tender Comrades: A Back Story of the Hollywood Blacklist,* New York, 1997.
9. House Un-American Activities Committee, hearings regarding Communist Activities in the Los Angeles Area, Nathan Benoff testimony, 1953.
10. HUAC in Los Angeles, Bart Lytton testimony, Mar. 25, 1953.
11. Ibid.
12. HUAC in Los Angeles, Bernice Fleury testimony, Mar. 25, 1953.
13. House Un-American Activities Committee, hearings regarding the Communist Infiltration of the Motion Picture Industry, Oct. 20, 1947.
14. Trumbo papers, State Historical Society, Madison, Wisconsin.

15. HUAC in Los Angeles, Dmytryk testimony, Apr. 25, 1951.
16. Robert Kenny papers, State Historical Society, Madison, Wisconsin.
17. McGilligan and Buhle, *Tender Comrades.*
18. HUAC, 1947 Hollywood hearings.
19. Margolis to Kenny, Dec. 8, 1947, Kenny papers.
20. Trumbo papers.
21. Ibid.
22. HUAC in Los Angeles, Frank Tuttle testimony, May 24, 1951.
23. HUAC in New York, Jerome Robbins testimony, May 10, 1953.
24. HUAC in Hollywood, Sterling Hayden testimony, Apr. 10, 1952.
25. Elia Kazan, *A Life,* New York, 1988.
26. Ibid.
27. HUAC hearings, Elia Kazan testimony, Apr. 10, 1952.
28. Kazan, *A Life.*
29. McGilligan and Buhle, *Tender Comrades.*
30. HUAC hearings, Apr. 8, 1953.
31. Carlton, "A Crisis of Rapid Change."
32. A. M. Sperber, *Murrow,* New York, 1986.
33. Howard Suber, "The Anti-Communist Blacklist in the Hollywood Motion Picture Industry," Ph.D. thesis, University of California, 1968.
34. Robert Lichtman and Ronald D. Cohen, "Harvey Matusow, the FBI, and the Justice Department: Becoming a Government Informer-Witness in the McCarthy Era," *American Communist History,* Vol. 1, No. 1, 2002.
35. HUAC hearings on Communist Activities in New England, Penha and Garczynski, Mar. 19, 1958.
36. HUAC hearings on Communist Activities in Cleveland, Ohio, area, June 1962, Brown testimony.
37. HUAC hearings, Communist Activities in the defense area of Baltimore, June, July 1951, Marcy Stalcup Markward testimony.
38. Senate Internal Security Subcommittee, Strategy and Tactics of World Communism, the Significance of the Matusow Case, Feb.–June 1955.
39. HUAC hearings, Communist Activities Among Youth Groups.
40. Matusow case hearings.
41. Mine, Mill, and Smelter papers, SISS files, National Archives.
42. Ibid.
43. Matusow case hearings.
44. Ibid.
45. Ibid.
46. Ibid.
47. Ibid.
48. Lichtman and Cohen, "Harvey Matusow."
49. Matusow case hearings.
50. Ibid.
51. Harvey Matusow, *False Witness,* New York, 1955.
52. Matusow case hearings.
53. Ibid.
54. Ibid.
55. Ibid.
56. Ibid.

57. Ibid.
58. Ibid.
59. Mine, Mill papers.
60. Matusow case hearings.
61. Ibid.
62. SISS report on Matusow case.
63. Lichtman and Cohen, "Harvey Matusow."
64. Mine, Mill papers.
65. Ed Cray, *Chief Justice*, New York, 1997.
66. Ibid.
67. Steve Nelson, *American Radical*, Pittsburgh, 1981.
68. Howard Ball and Phillip J. Cooper, *Of Power and Right: Hugo Black, William O. Douglas, and America's Constitutional Revolution*, New York, 1992.
69. Cray, *Chief Justice*.
70. Ball and Cooper, *Of Power and Right*.
71. Cray, *Chief Justice*.
72. Ball and Cooper, *Of Power and Right*.
73. Ibid.
74. SISS files, Assistant Secretary of State William B. Macomber Jr. to Senator James Eastland, Nov. 18, 1957, National Archives.
75. Ball and Cooper, *Of Power and Right*.
76. Cray, *Chief Justice*.
77. Hoover memo, June 26, 1957, Eisenhower Library.
78. Robert Conquest, *The Great Terror*, New York, 1990.

EPILOGUE

1. Richard Gid Powers, *Secrecy and Power: The Life of J. Edgar Hoover*, New York, 1987.
2. Hoover to Vaughan, Jan. 17, 1946, Truman Library.
3. Hoover to Cutler, Jan. 16, 1956, Eisenhower Library.
4. Hoover briefing, Mar. 9, 1956, Eisenhower Library.
5. Steve Nelson, *American Radical*, Pittsburgh, 1981.
6. Sullivan testimony, Select Committee to Study Governmental Operations with Respect to Intelligence Activities, Book 1, U.S. Senate, 1975. Hereinafter Church Committee.
7. Sullivan and Moore testimony, Church Committee.
8. Sullivan testimony, Church Committee.
9. David J. Garrow, *Bearing the Cross*, New York, 1986.
10. Hoover to Cutler, May 15, 1957, Eisenhower Library.
11. Garrow, *Bearing the Cross*.
12. Ibid.
13. Ibid.
14. David J. Garrow, "The FBI and Martin Luther King," *The Atlantic Monthly*, July/August 2002.
15. Ibid.
16. Ibid.
17. Ibid.
18. Harvey Klehr, John Earl Haynes, and Kyrill M. Anderson, *The Soviet World of American Communism*, New Haven, 1998.

19. Garrow, "FBI and Martin Luther King."
20. Garrow, *Bearing the Cross.*
21. Ibid.
22. Hoover to Cutler, Mar. 1, 1960, Eisenhower Library.
23. Powers, *Secrecy and Power.*
24. Garrow, "FBI and Martin Luther King."
25. Garrow, *Bearing the Cross.*
26. Sullivan testimony, Church Committee.
27. Garrow, "FBI and Martin Luther King."
28. Garrow, *Bearing the Cross.*
29. Garrow, "FBI and Martin Luther King."
30. Ibid.
31. Powers, *Secrecy and Power.*
32. Church Committee.
33. Ibid.
34. Garrow, "FBI and Martin Luther King."
35. Garrow, *Bearing the Cross.*
36. Church Committee.
37. Garrow, *Bearing the Cross.*
38. Ibid.
39. Ibid.
40. Seymour M. Hersh, *The Dark Side of Camelot,* New York, 1997.
41. Garrow, *Bearing the Cross.*
42. Garrow, "FBI and Martin Luther King."
43. Ibid.
44. Ibid.
45. Church Committee, FBI Exhibits.
46. Garrow, "FBI and Martin Luther King."
47. Ibid.
48. Telephone records, Aug. 20, 1956, Lyndon Baines Johnson Library, Austin, Texas.
49. Garrow, "FBI and Martin Luther King."
50. Ibid.
51. Ibid.
52. Ibid.
53. Church Committee, FBI Exhibits.
54. Garrow, "FBI and Martin Luther King."
55. Ibid.
56. Church Committee report.
57. Klehr et al., *Soviet World of American Communism.*
58. Church Committee report.
59. Tom Hayden, *Reunion,* New York, 1988.
60. Ibid.
61. Ibid.
62. Ibid.
63. Nelson, *American Radical.*
64. Dorothy Healey, *Dorothy Healey Remembers,* New York, 1990.
65. John Abt, *Advocate and Activist,* Urbana, Ill., 1993.
66. Church Committee, FBI Exhibits.

67. Ibid.
68. Ibid.
69. Ibid.
70. Ibid.
71. Ibid.
72. Ibid.
73. Church Committee, Moore testimony.
74. Church Committee, FBI Exhibits.
75. Powers, *Secrecy and Power.*
76. Church Committee, FBI Exhibits.
77. Ibid.
78. Ibid.
79. Ibid.
80. House Un-American Activities Committee, Subcommittee on Subversive Involvement in Disruption of 1968 Democratic Party Convention, Oct. 1968, testimony of James L. Gallagher, HUAC investigator. Hereinafter HUAC hearings.
81. Ibid.
82. HUAC hearings.
83. Ibid.
84. Church Committee, Hardy testimony.
85. HUAC hearings.
86. Ibid.
87. Ibid.
88. Ibid.
89. Church Committee, FBI Exhibits.
90. HUAC hearings, Pierson testimony.
91. Hayden, *Reunion.*
92. HUAC hearings, Gallagher testimony.
93. Hayden, *Reunion.*
94. HUAC hearings, Pierson testimony.
95. Hayden, *Reunion.*
96. HUAC hearings, Pierson testimony.
97. Todd Gitlin, *The Sixties,* New York, 1987.
98. HUAC hearings, Healy testimony.
99. HUAC hearings, Hayden testimony.
100. HUAC hearings, Healy testimony.
101. HUAC hearings, Pierson testimony.
102. Hayden, *Reunion.*
103. HUAC hearings, Gallagher testimony.
104. HUAC hearings, subcommittee report.
105. Church Committee, FBI Exhibits.
106. Ibid.
107. Ibid.
108. HUAC hearings, Davis testimony.
109. Ibid.
110. Ibid.
111. Athan G. Theoharis and John Stuart Cox, *The Boss: J. Edgar Hoover and the Great American Inquisition,* Philadelphia, 1988.
112. Church Committee, FBI Exhibits.

113. Ibid.
114. Ibid.
115. Ibid.
116. Ibid.
117. Theoharis and Cox, *The Boss.*
118. Bruce Oudes, ed., *From the President: Richard Nixon's Secret Files*, New York, 1989.
119. Gitlin, *The Sixties.*
120. Oudes, *From the President.*
121. Ibid.
122. Ibid.
123. Church Committee, Huston testimony.
124. Powers, *Secrecy and Power.*
125. Ibid.
126. Church Committee, FBI Exhibits.
127. Church Committee, Huston testimony.
128. Oudes, *From the President.*
129. Ibid.
130. Theoharis and Cox, *The Boss.*
131. Oudes, *From the President.*
132. Stanley I. Kutler, *Abuse of Power: The New Nixon Tapes*, New York, 1997.
133. Ibid.
134. Ibid.
135. Ibid.
136. Ibid.
137. Ibid.
138. Ibid.
139. Ibid.
140. Ibid.
141. Ibid.
142. Ibid.
143. Ibid.
144. Ronnie Dugger, *On Reagan: The Man and His Presidency*, New York, 1983.
145. Ibid.
146. Ibid.
147. Ibid.
148. Deborah Hart Strober and Gerald S. Strober, *Reagan: The Man and His Presidency*, New York, 1998.
149. Ibid.
150. Ibid.
151. Clyde Prestowitz, *Rogue Nation*, New York, 2003.
152. Ibid.
153. *New York Times*, June 2, 2003.
154. Ibid.
155. Ibid.
156. *New York Times*, Dec. 12, 2001.
157. *New York Times*, Feb. 20, 2003.
158. *New York Times*, Feb. 22, 2003.
159. *New York Times*, Mar. 10, 2003, and July 8, 2003.

160. *New York Times,* Apr. 16, 2003.
161. *New York Times,* Apr. 23, 2003.
162. *New York Times,* May 31, 2003.
163. *New Yorker,* Mar. 17, 2003.
164. Prestowitz, *Rogue Nation.*
165. *New York Times,* Feb. 20, 2002.
166. Prestowitz, *Rogue Nation.*
167. *New Republic,* June 24, 2003.
168. *New York Times,* June 4, 2003.
169. *New Yorker,* Apr. 7, 2003.
170. *New York Times,* Sep. 28, 2002.
171. *New York Times,* June 3, 2003.
172. *New York Times,* Oct. 8, 2002.
173. *New York Times,* June 8, 2003.
174. *New Republic,* June 24, 2003.
175. Ibid.
176. *New York Press,* July 8, 2003.
177. *New Republic,* June 24, 2003.
178. *New York Times,* Jan. 29, 2003.
179. Ibid.
180. UPI, May 29, 2003; *New York Times,* June 4, 2003.
181. *National Journal,* Aug. 6, 2003.
182. *Financial Times,* Aug. 9, 2003, and Aug. 11, 2003.
183. *New York Times,* June 8, 2003.
184. Netscape News, June 1, 2003; *New York Times,* June 17, 2003.
185. *New Yorker,* June 30, 2003.
186. *New York Times,* July 6, 2003.
187. Ibid.
188. Ibid.
189. Ibid.
190. Ibid.
191. Knight-Ridder Washington Bureau, June 12, 2003.
192. *New York Times,* July 6, 2003; *Washington Post,* June 12, 2003.
193. *New York Times,* May 6, 2003.
194. In the *New York Times* on June 3, 2003, Paul Krugman wrote that if the claim that Saddam was an imminent threat proved to be fraudulent, "the selling of the war is arguably the worst scandal in American political history—worse than Watergate, worse than Iran-contra." If Bush is not found out, "our political system has become utterly, and perhaps irrevocably, corrupted."
195. *U.S. News & World Report,* June 9, 2003.
196. *New York Times,* Feb. 5, 2003.
197. Ibid.
198. Ibid.
199. "Iraqi Mobile Biological Warfare Agent Production Plants," CIA.gov website.
200. Ibid.
201. *New York Times,* June 9, 2003.
202. "Iraqi Mobile Biological Warfare Agent Production Plants."
203. *New York Times,* June 25, 2003.
204. *New York Times,* Aug. 9, 2003.

205. *New York Times,* Aug. 10, 2003.
206. Reuters, June 9, 2003.
207. *New York Press,* July 8, 2003.
208. *New York Times,* July 8, 2003.
209. *New York Times,* July 8, 2003; London *Times,* July 8, 2003.
210. *Financial Times,* July 6, 2003.
211. *New York Times,* Aug. 9, 2003.
212. Ibid.
213. *Economist,* Aug. 15, 2003.
214. *Time,* Aug. 18, 2003.
215. *Newsweek,* Aug. 18, 2003.
216. *New York Times,* Aug. 10, 2003, and Aug. 13, 2003.

INDEX

129, 131, 136, 172–73, 203–4, 214*n*,
218, 223, 257, 264, 268, 280, 298,
321, 398, 400
death of, 426, 505
Hopkins's meeting with, 293
Katyn Forest massacre ordered by, 240
League of Nations and, 167–68
1932 famine and, 131–33
postwar foreign policy of, 296–97
at Potsdam Conference, 295
purges and, 147–48, 157–60, 162
Spanish Civil War and, 175–77, 182–83
Stanarm, Hans, 227
Stander, Lionel, 171, 212
Starnes, Joe, 187, 191, 194, 197–99, 205,
207
Starr, George J., 410–11
Stassen, Harold, 419
Stassenman (atomic scientist), 227
State Department, U.S., 13, 14, 23, 26, 28,
34, 43, 46, 49, 50, 63, 78, 94, 103,
121, 133, 143, 144, 149, 160, 173,
181, 243, 256, 260, 297, 299, 423,
603, 607, 610
Amerasia case and, 274–77
Chenoweth hearings on, 381–83
EUR/X office of, 378
file handling issue and, 432–35
homosexual issue and, 432–35
libraries issue and, 441–47
loyalty files of, 380, 402–3
as McCarthy's target, 374, 377, 379,
384–89, 415, 432–40
OSS transferred to, 377–78
Soviet agents in, 145, 151, 152, 156–57,
160–64, 267–70, 271, 291, 374, 375,
382–83, 388–91
Stefan Subcommittee investigation of,
379–81
Tydings Committee hearings on, 395–97,
400–405
Voice of America hearings and, 435–40,
444, 447
wartime agencies transferred to, 377–79
Wilson mission and, 607–8
Stearns, Perry, 347
Steedman, James, 213
Stefan, Karl, 379, 381
Stefan Subcommittee, 379–81, 404
Steffens, Lincoln, 120, 150
Steinbeck, John, 540
Steinberg, William, 312
Steinman, Louise Tinsley, 411–12
Stennis, John, 500, 503
Sterling, Thomas, 64
Stern, Bernard J., 442
Stern, Moishe, 117, 177
Sterngluss, Jacob, 139
Stettinius, E. R., 267, 268, 269

Stevens, Robert Ten Broeck, 456, 473, 476,
477, 485, 490, 495, 498, 499
Army-McCarthy hearings testimony of,
486–87, 489, 491
Lodge's phone conversation with, 474–75
McCarthy's Army hearings and, 459–66
Schine affair and, 467–68, 469
Stevenson, Adlai, 420, 422–24, 428, 448,
508
Stevenson, Archibald, 65, 71
Stevenson, Suzanne Silvercruys, 516
Stevenson, William, 445
Stewart, George Evan, 41, 48
Stimson, Henry, 114, 162, 233, 257, 295
Stokes, Richard L., 199
Stone, Harlan Fiske, 73, 113–14, 120, 140,
142
Stone, I. F., 232–33, 262
Stone, William T., 246
Storey, Charles M., 74
Strand, Paul, 171
Strandlund, Carl G., 355–56
Strauss, Lewis, 480
Stripling, Robert E., 188, 201, 211, 213, 520
Strong, Anna Louise, 103
Strong, George V., 246
Strout, Richard L., 401
Student as Nigger, The, 569
Student Non-Violent Coordinating
Committee, 566, 570, 573
Students for a Democratic Society, 567, 568,
569–70, 571, 573, 574, 577–78, 582,
587
Sudoplatov, Pavel, 240
Sullivan, Edward E., 203
Sullivan, William C., 551, 557, 559–62, 567,
571, 585
Sulloway, Frank J., 497
Sulzberger, Cy, 443
Summers, Maddin, 27, 28, 35–36
Sunday Worker, 529
Supreme Court, New Mexico, 544
Supreme Court, Pennsylvania, 541
Supreme Court, U.S., 73, 417
Bridges deportation decision of, 203
Eisenhower appointments to, 540–41
FDR's court-packing scheme for, 186–87
Hollywood Ten case and, 520
Jencks conviction ruling of, 540
Malmédy verdict and, 361
Nixon and, 585–86
Pennsylvania Sedition Act in, 541–42
Pentagon Papers ruling of, 591
Red Monday of, 544–45
Smith Act rulings of, 317–18, 375,
545–46
wiretap evidence ruling of, 277
Supreme War Council, Allied, 38
Surine, Don, 410, 475

ABOUT THE AUTHOR

TED MORGAN is the author of *FDR; Churchill*, a finalist for the Pulitzer Prize; *Somerset Maugham*, a finalist for the National Book Award; and two epic narrative histories of America, *Wilderness at Dawn: The Settling of the North American Continent* and *A Shovel of Stars: The Making of the American West—1800 to the Present*. He lives in New York.

ABOUT THE TYPE

This book was set in Photina, a typeface designed by José Mendoza in 1971. It is a very elegant design with high legibility, and its close character fit has made it a popular choice for use in quality magazines and art gallery publications.